W9-CDV-420

Pacific Northwest

© Robert Holmes

"Doubling cape after cape, passing uncounted islands,
new combinations break on the view in endless variety,
sufficient to satisfy the lover of wild beauty
through a whole life."

John Muir on the Puget Sound in 1915, *Travels in Alaska*

Travel Publications

Michelin North America
One Parkway South, Greenville SC 29615, USA
Tel. 1-800-423-0485
www.michelin-travel.com

Manufacture Française des Pneumatiques Michelin
Société en commandite par actions au capital de 2 000 000 000 de francs
Place des Carmes-Déchaux – 63000 Clermont-Ferrand (France)
R.C.S. Clermont-Fd B 855 200 507

Michelin et Cie, Propriétaires-éditeurs, 2000
Dépôt légal avril 2000 – ISBN 2-06-158401-2 – ISSN 0763-1383

No part of this publication may be reproduced in any from
without prior permission of the publisher.

Printed in the EU 03-00/1/1

Compogravure : NORD COMPO, Villeneuve d'Ascq
Impression et brochage : I.M.E. Baume-les-Dames

THE GREEN GUIDE:
The Spirit of Discovery

*The exhilaration of new horizons,
the fun of seeing the world,
the excitement of discovery:
this is what we seek to share with you.
To help you make the most
of your travel experience,
we offer first-hand knowledge
and turn a discerning eye
on places to visit.
This wealth of information
gives you the expertise to plan
your own enriching adventure.
With THE GREEN GUIDE
showing you the way,
you can explore new destinations
with confidence or rediscover old ones.
Leisure time spent with THE GREEN
GUIDE is also a time for refreshing
your spirit, enjoying yourself,
and taking advantage of our selection
of fine restaurants, hotels
and other places for relaxing.
So turn the page and open a window
on the world. Join THE GREEN GUIDE
in the spirit of discovery.*

Contents

Dear Reader

Introduction

Oregon

Portland Building, Portland,
Oregon

Old Man and the Sea Mural, Newport,
Oregon

Father Pandosy
Mission

The Prospector

5

Maps and Plans

COMPANION UBLICATIONS

Map 493 Western USA and Western Canada

Large-format map providing detailed road systems; includes driving distances, interstate rest stops, border crossings and interchanges.

– Comprehensive city and town index
– Scale 1:2,400,000 (1 inch = approx. 38 miles

Map 930 USA Road Map

Covers principal US road network while also presenting shaded relief detail of overall physiography of the land.

– State flags with statistical data and state tourism office telephone numbers
– Scale: 1:3,450,000

Map 933 USA Recreational

Descriptive section with color photos and profiles of 51 national parks complements a fold-out map of the US designating 500 parks, monuments, historic sites, scenic rivers and other recreational points of interest.

Bird's-eye View of Seattle, WA (1878)

Historic Urban Plans

6

LIST OF MAPS AND PLANS

Using this guide

- The guide is organized by state, each with its own introduction. Within each state, the text is organized into geographic regions. Each Entry Heading is followed by a map reference; tourist information phone number and web site when available; and population figure (where applicable).

- Following the names of sights mentioned in this guide you will find useful information in *italics*: sight location addresses, recommended visiting times, opening hours, admission charges, telephone numbers and web addresses. Symbols used in sight, hotel and restaurant descriptions include ♿ wheelchair access, ✗ on-site eating facilities, 🅿 on-site parking and 🄺🄸🄳 sights of special interest to children.

- Many entries contain digressions, entertaining breaks from sightseeing, that are marked by a purple bar. Those digressions that appear on a map within the guide are indicated by a black dot ❶ with the number identifying it on the corresponding map.

- Sections with a blue background offer practical information, such as available transportation, contact information for visitors bureaus recreation opportunities for a city or region, as well as hotel and restaurant recommendations.

- Cross-references to destinations described elsewhere in the text appear in SMALL CAPITALS; consult the **Index** at the back of the guide for the appropriate page number.
We welcome corrections and suggestions that may assist us in preparing the next edition. Please send your comments to Michelin Travel Publications, Editorial Department, P. O. Box 19001, Greenville, SC 29602-9001 or to our web site: www.michelin-travel.com.

© Dianne Dietrich Leis

Legend

★★★ **Worth the trip**
★★ **Worth a detour**
★ **Interesting**

Sight Symbols

⇒ ◉ ▬▬▬	Recommended itineraries with departure point	
▲ ⚲ Church, chapel	▬	Building described
○ Town described	▬	Other building
AZ B Map co-ordinates locating sights	■	Small building, statue
■ ▲ Other points of interest	◎ ⁂	Fountain – Ruins
⤫ Mine	🛈	Visitor information
⚓ Windmill – Lighthouse	⊜ ⚓	Ship – Shipwreck
☆ ⌒ Fort – Cave	⁑ ♈	Panorama – View

Other Symbols

🛡 Interstate highway (USA)	🛡 US highway	⑱⓪ Other route
🍁 Trans-Canada highway	🛡 Canadian highway	

Highway, bridge		Major city thoroughfare	
Toll highway, interchange		City street with median	
Divided highway		One-way street	
Major, minor route		Pedestrian Street	
15 (21) Distance in miles (kilometers)		⇥⇤ Tunnel	
2149/655 Pass, elevation *(feet/meters)*		Steps – Gate	
△6288(1917) Mtn. peak, elevation *(feet/meters)*		△ ♖ Drawbridge - Water tower	
✈ ✦ Airport – Airfield		🅿 ✉ Parking – Main post office	
⛴ Ferry: Cars and passengers		▣ University	
⛵ Ferry: Passengers only		🚆 🚌 Train station – Bus station	
↞↤⊏ Waterfall – Lock – Dam		● ⓜ Subway station	
— ·· — ·· — International boundary		❶ Digressions	
— — — — — State boundary		✝ ≈ Cemetery – Swamp	

Recreation

■-○-○-○-■ Gondola, chairlift	❀ ▬ ▤	Park, garden – Wooded area
🚂 Tourist or steam railway	❺	Wildlife reserve
⚓ ⚓ Harbor, lake cruise – Marina	❺ ⚐	Wildlife/Safari park, zoo
⛷ ⚑ Ski area – Golf course	— — — —	Walking path, trail
⊂⃝ Stadium	⚲	Hiking trail
🎠	Sight of special interest for children	

Abbreviations and special symbols

NP	National Park	NMem	National Memorial	SP	State Park
NM	National Monument	NHS	National Historic Site	SF	State Forest
NWR	National Wildlife Refuge	NHP	National Historical Park	SR	State Reserve
	NF	National Forest		NVM	National Volcanic Monument

🛡	National Park	▲	National Forest
🛡	State Park	△	State Forest

All maps are oriented north, unless otherwise indicated by a directional arrow.

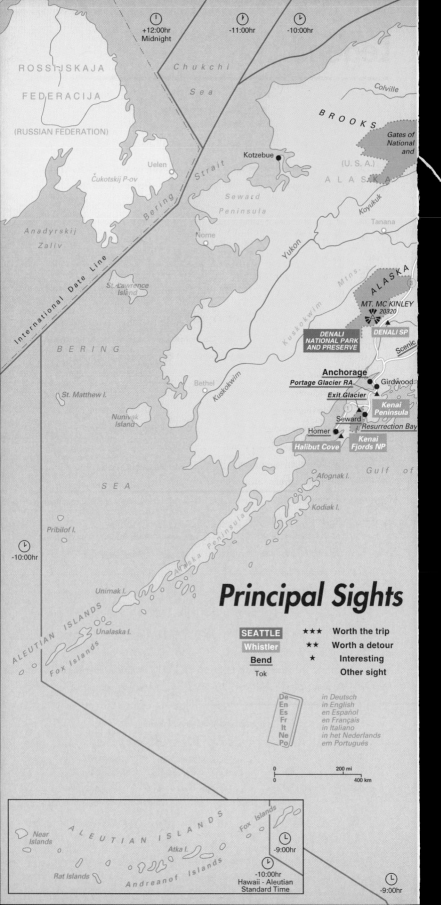

ROSSIJSKAJA

FEDERACIJA

(RUSSIAN FEDERATION)

Čukotskij P-ov

Anadyrskij
Zaliv

Uelen

Chukchi
Sea

Kotzebue

Seward
Peninsula

Nome

B R O O K S

Colville

Gates of
National
and

(U. S. A.)

A L A S K A

Koyukuk

Tanana

Yukon

St. Lawrence
Island

B E R I N G

St. Matthew I.

Bethel

Kuskokwim

Nunivak
Island

S E A

Pribilof I.

Unimak I.

Unalaska I.

Fox Islands

ALASKA

MT. MC KINLEY
20320

DENALI SP

DENALI NATIONAL PARK
AND PRESERVE

Scenic

Anchorage

Portage Glacier RA   Girdwood

Exit Glacier

Seward   *Kenai*
Peninsula

Homer   *Resurrection Bay*

Halibut Cove   *Kenai*
Fjords NP

Gulf of

Afognak I.

Kodiak I.

Alaska Peninsula

Principal Sights

SEATTLE   ★★★   Worth the trip
Whistler   ★★   Worth a detour
Bend   ★   Interesting
Tok   Other sight

De — *in Deutsch*
En — *in English*
Es — *en Español*
Fr — *en Français*
It — *in Italiano*
Ne — *in het Nederlands*
Po — *em Português*

0   200 mi
0   400 km

Near
Islands

A L E U T I A N   I S L A N D S

Atka I.

Fox Islands

Rat Islands   Andreanof Islands

-10:00hr
Hawaii - Aleutian
Standard Time

-9:00hr

-9:00hr

+12:00hr
Midnight

-11:00hr

-10:00hr

-10:00hr

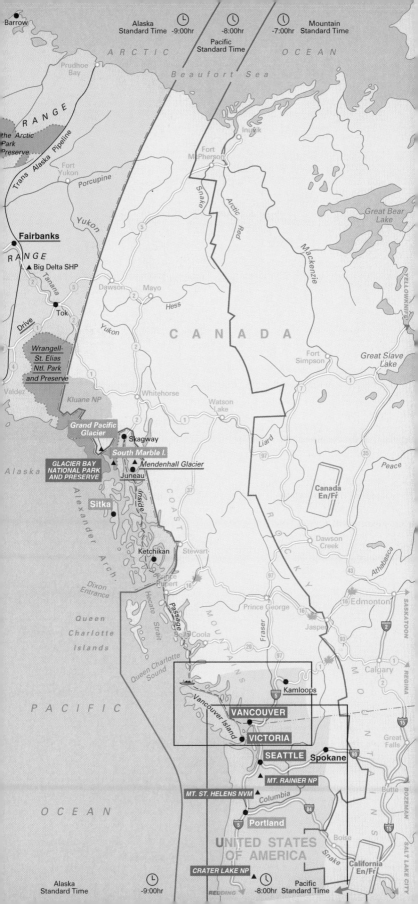

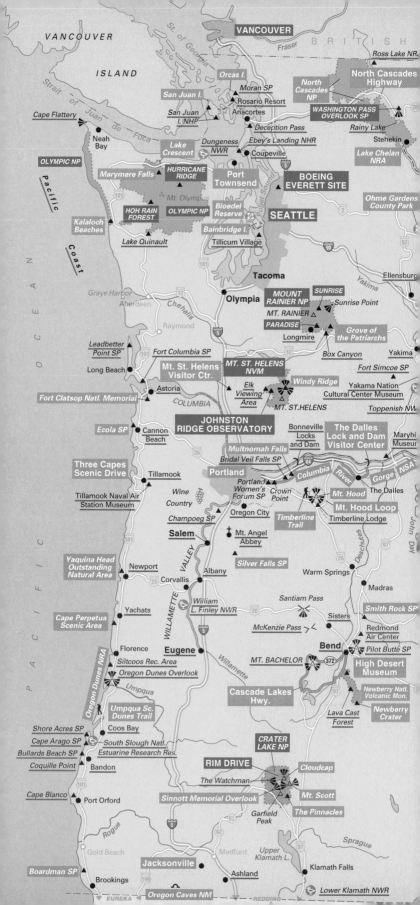

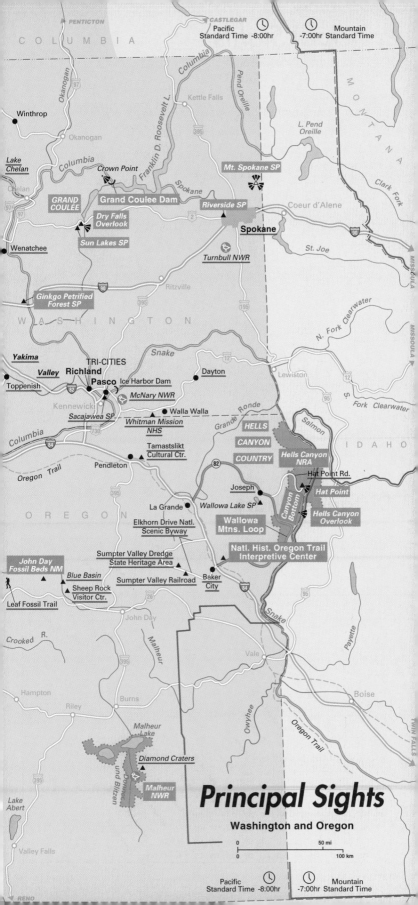

Principal Sights

Washington and Oregon

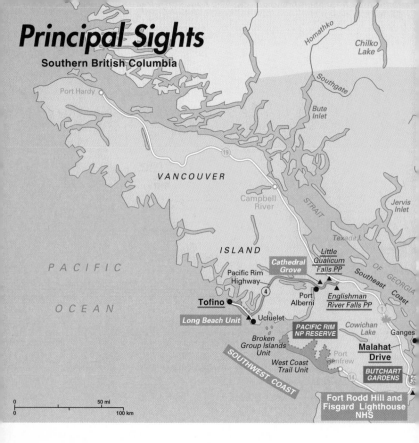

Principal Sights

Southern British Columbia

Port Hardy

VANCOUVER

Homathko

Chilko Lake

Southgate

Bute Inlet

Campbell River

STRAIT

Jervis Inlet

Texada I.

ISLAND

PACIFIC

OCEAN

Pacific Rim Highway

Cathedral Grove

Little Qualicum Falls PP

Southeast Coast

Tofino

Port Alberni

Englishman River Falls PP

OF GEORGIA

Ucluelet

Ganges

Long Beach Unit

PACIFIC RIM NP RESERVE

Cowichan Lake

Malahat Drive

Broken Group Islands Unit

Port Renfrew

West Coast Trail Unit

BUTCHART GARDENS

SOUTHWEST COAST

Fort Rodd Hill and Fisgard Lighthouse NHS

0   50 mi
0   100 km

Distance Chart

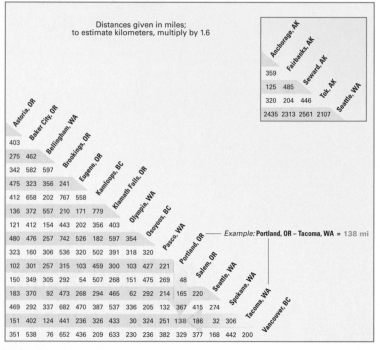

Distances given in miles;
to estimate kilometers, multiply by 1.6

	Anchorage, AK	Fairbanks, AK	Seward, AK	Tok, AK
Fairbanks, AK	359			
Seward, AK	125	485		
Tok, AK	320	204	446	
Seattle, WA	2435	2313	2561	2107

Example: Portland, OR – Tacoma, WA = 138 mi

	Astoria, OR	Baker City, OR	Bellingham, WA	Brookings, OR	Eugene, OR	Kamloops, BC	Klamath Falls, OR	Olympia, WA	Osoyoos, BC	Pasco, WA	Portland, OR	Salem, OR	Seattle, WA	Spokane, WA	Tacoma, WA
Baker City, OR	403														
Bellingham, WA	275	462													
Brookings, OR	342	582	597												
Eugene, OR	475	323	356	241											
Kamloops, BC	412	658	202	767	558										
Klamath Falls, OR	136	372	557	210	171	779									
Olympia, WA	121	412	154	443	202	356	403								
Osoyoos, BC	480	476	257	742	526	182	597	354							
Pasco, WA	323	160	306	536	320	502	391	318	320						
Portland, OR	102	301	257	315	103	459	300	103	427	221					
Salem, OR	150	349	305	292	54	507	268	151	475	269	48				
Seattle, WA	183	370	92	473	268	294	465	62	292	214	165	220			
Spokane, WA	469	292	337	682	470	387	537	336	205	132	367	415	274		
Tacoma, WA	151	402	124	441	236	326	433	30	324	251	138	186	32	306	
Vancouver, BC	351	538	76	652	436	209	633	230	236	382	329	377	168	442	200

WILLIAMS LAKE

Hat Creek Ranch
Cache Creek
Kamloops
Adams Lake
Lake Revelstoke
Shuswap Lake
Wildlife Preserve
Salmon Arm
CALGARY

Lillooet
Thompson Canyon
Nicola Valley Loop
Kamloops Wildlife Park
O'Keefe Ranch

Whistler Mountain Gondola
Lytton
Quilchena Hotel
Douglas Lake Ranch
Vernon
Kalamalka Lake
Westside Road

Whistler
Sea to Sky Highway
Fintry PP
Okanagan Valley

Squamish
Garibaldi PP
Fraser Canyon Country
Nicola Valley
Kelowna

West Coast Railway Heritage Park
Hell's Gate Airtram
Okanagan L.

Shannon Falls
Hell's Gate
Kettle Valley Railway

BC Museum of Mining
Alexandra Bridge
Penticton

VANCOUVER
New Westminster
Hope
Coquihalla Canyon PP
Keremeos Grist Mill
Skaha Lake

Fort Langley NHS
Hope Slide
Keremeos
Vaseux Lake

Rhododendron Flats
Manning PP
Cathedral PP
Anarchist Mtn.

George C. Reifel Bird Sanctuary
Cascade Lookout

Sidney
Osoyoos

San Juan Islands
WASHINGTON

VICTORIA
SEATTLE
WENATCHEE

Columbia

LETHBRIDGE

Regional Maps

- **A** Interior Alaska
- **B** Central Plateau
- **C** Columbia River Gorge
- **D** Eastern Oregon
- **E** Eastern Washington
- **F** Kenai Peninsula
- **G** North Cascades
- **H** North Coast
- **I** Olympic Peninsula
- **J** San Juan Islands
- **K** Sea to Sky Highway
- **L** Seattle
- **M** South Cascades
- **N** South Coast
- **O** Southeast Coast
- **P** Southern British Columbia
- **Q** Southern Highlands
- **R** Vancouver Island
- **S** Willamette Valley
- **T** Yakima Valley

Arctic Circle
Great Bear Lake
Yukon
Fairbanks
YUKON TERRITORY
Mackenzie
NORTHWEST TERRITORIES
A
Tanana
(U.S.A.)
ALASKA
Yukon
CANADA
Anchorage
F
Gulf of Alaska
Peace
O
BRITISH
AB
PACIFIC
COLUMBIA
Fraser
Columbia
K P
Vancouver
R
J L G WA
I Seattle
E
M T
H Portland
C D ID
S
N B
OR
Snake
Q
U.S.A.
CA
NV
OCEAN

Sunset at Devil's Elbow, Oregon

© Dianne Dietrich Leis

Pacific Northwest

Landscapes

Comprised of Alaska, a portion of Canada's British Columbia, and the states of Washington and Oregon, the Pacific Northwest is more vast than any other North American region. Together, the landmass of these three US states and the section of British Columbia covers roughly 1,029,000sq mi, exceeding the combined areas of Sweden, Norway, France, Germany, Austria, Italy, Portugal and Spain.

The only boundaries of this great territory not subject to debate are its saltwater shorelines, which run from northern Alaska's Arctic Ocean beaches down the forested Pacific Ocean coast of British Columbia and along the wave-battered beaches of Washington and Oregon to California. Its eastern boundaries are indistinct, fingerlike extensions of typically Northwestern climatic zones and terrain poking here and there into Idaho and Montana. Generally, however, the Rocky Mountains, which trend southeast from southern Alaska through northern British Columbia, Idaho and Montana, are accepted as the Pacific Northwest's easternmost fringe. The astonishing diversity of topography, vegetation and geology that combine to create the Pacific Northwest's distinctive landscapes, however, respects no political boundaries.

Geologic Past

Past is present along the leading edge of North America, the continent's most geologically restless region, where sleeping volcanoes occasionally awake in a fury, as Washington's Mt. St. Helens did in 1980. And the earth occasionally convulses, as it did in the vicinity of Anchorage in 1964, dropping some coastal plains by as much as eight feet. The Pacific Northwest is a textbook example of the visible results of plate tectonics—the collisions, grinding sideswipes and pileups of the massive moving slabs of continental crust floating atop the earth's depths.

Origins – About 100 million years ago, the primordial Pacific Northwest coast ran approximately from what is now eastern California up through central Oregon and Idaho, across eastern Washington and British Columbia. The **North American Plate** crunched west, colliding with the eastward-moving **Pacific Plate**, then overriding it amidst a fiery volcanic landscape, and commencing the formation of the region's great mountain ranges.

Far to the west and out at sea, smaller fragments known as "microcontinents" were next carried eastward atop the Pacific Plate. Eventually they collided and fused with the Pacific Northwest coast to form the bulk of northwestern Oregon, Washington, western British Columbia and Alaska. Some 50 million years after that another colossal landmass, the Cascade microcontinent—stretching from Washington's Puget Sound to Alaska—arrived from the Pacific and welded itself to the North American coast.

About 10 million years into the Tertiary Period (which began with the disappearance of dinosaurs 65 million years ago) a **volcanic age** ensued, building up many of the Pacific Northwest's most significant mountain ranges, notably Oregon's Coast and Cascade systems, the inland Blue Mountains and the Olympics of Washington's Olympic Peninsula. This volcanism subsided about 25 million years ago. Some 14 million years back, a great rupture in the earth's crust opened along what is now Idaho's western border, initiating a single seven-day event that produced an estimated 170cu mi of new rock and released tidal waves of molten basalt some geologists believe might have reached heights of 100ft. These searing juggernauts flooded over 15,000sq mi of Oregon and Washington's Columbia River Plateau and parts of Idaho as well, layering it with lava plains ranging from 2,000ft to a mile thick, and extending as far west as the Cascades. Lava flows from thousands of volcanic vents surged west along what is now the Columbia River gorge and poured out onto the seafloor.

Then, roughly six million years ago, massive uplifts formed the great coastal mountains of British Columbia and southeastern Alaska. Less dramatic uplifts continued the formation of Washington's and Oregon's **Cascades**, where volcanoes subsequently did most of the mountain-building by spewing out layers of lava and ash. One of the greatest of these eruptions occurred about 7,000 years ago in southern Oregon's Cascades, where 12,000ft Mt. Mazama exploded, blasting more than 12cu mi of its bulk over much of the Northwest before collapsing into its emptied magma cavity, today's CRATER LAKE.

The final shaping of the Pacific Northwest, however, was not by fire but by ice. With the advent of the Pleistocene Epoch about three million years ago, the Northern Hemisphere's weather turned cool for reasons still not understood. Winters lengthened and snowfalls became heavier. Cooler summers failed to completely melt the winter accumulation of ice, and within a few eons the Pacific Northwest, including its tallest peaks, was buried beneath vast fields of ice. From Alaska to Montana, **glaciers** formed, advanced, retreated and advanced again. Some, like the Cordilleran Ice Sheet that slid down from Canada into Washington, were so vast, heavy and powerful that they broke up mountains and plowed deep troughs—future fjords—as they pushed into the sea.

At the close of the Pleistocene Era some 10,000 years ago, the Ice Age had been in retreat for about 5,000 years. As it melted northward, the Cordilleran, a conveyor belt of broken rock, dumped its mammoth cargo, creating many of the rolling hills rumpling the Puget Sound's southern terminus in the Seattle-Tacoma area.

The Pacific Northwest Today – In British Columbia's Coast Mountains, and in Alaska's Chugach, Wrangell, St. Elias and Fairweather mountain systems, North America's biggest glaciers still audibly grind their way down between the peaks that guide them to the sea, or to melting places in gravel-strewn valleys. The glaciers' Northwest handiwork is distinctive: deep U-shaped valleys in south-central Alaska, **fjords** like those found on western Vancouver Island and Puget Sound, the sharp and broken ridges found atop mountain ranges from Alaska to southern Oregon, and everywhere above the timber line, bare peaks ground into roughly pyramidal shapes, with burnished stone flanks glinting in the sun like steel plate.

Volcanoes remain active throughout the Pacific Northwest: From northern California to Alaska a **Ring of Fire** marks the relentless shoving match between underlying tectonic plates. In Oregon, glacier-mantled 11,235ft Mt. Hood broods just east of Portland. To the north, across the Columbia River, Mt. St. Helens (8,365ft) sputters and fumes. Seattleites prize their view of nearby **Mount Rainier**, a 14,410ft behemoth whose snow-topped sloped shoulders at sunset take on the hue of peach ice cream. Yet some geologists worry about its historically mercurial personality and its sleeping geologic siblings in the Cascades, seven of which reach 10,000ft. Alaska alone contains over 100 volcanoes and volcanic fields, 40 of them active since written histories commenced, and accounting for about 80 percent of all active volcanoes in the US. In 1992 three eruptions of Mt. Spurr's Crater Peak showered Anchorage and surrounding communities with ash, closing airports and impeding travel as far south as Juneau in the Alaskan Panhandle. Hardly a year goes by without a major eruption from a volcano in the Aleutian Arc.

Regional Landscapes

The unique character of the lower Pacific Northwest, which runs from Alaska's Panhandle into California, is created by three major landform systems. The westernmost, the **Cascade-Coast Mountain Province** includes systems roughly paralleling the orientation of the Pacific coastline. British Columbia's **Fraser Plateau Province**, a region of rolling upland country, lies between the foothills of the coastal mountains that rumple Canada's western edge and the western slope of the Canadian Rockies. Surprising to many newcomers is the aridity and tawny desert appearance of the **Columbia Basin Province**, which includes most of eastern Washington and the lofty lava plains and Blue Mountains of eastern Oregon. The province's western boundary is the Cascade Range, while the Rockies form its northern and eastern borders; its southern boundary is less distinct-where it extends into southern Idaho subtle landform changes mark its handshake with the Great Basin.

The most significant physical feature is the nearly continuous system of coastal mountain ranges. In Oregon and Washington these are the **Coast and Cascade ranges** (parallel systems some 700mi in length and, although separate, often treated as a single double-spined coastal mountain system). In British Columbia these converge into the 1,000mi **Coast Range** (reaching widths of 200mi), which links up with Alaska's **Fairweather** and **St. Elias ranges** to form one of the earth's lengthiest mountain systems. Between northern British Columbia and southern Oregon, they create a nearly continuous barrier limiting the amount of moisture that reaches inland while simultaneously shielding coastal regions from colder inland weather systems. Thus they divide the Pacific Northwest into two profoundly different climates and natural environments, one characterized by moisture, the other by thirst.

Coastal Country – To the west of the Cascade-Coast Range system are the well-watered landscapes for which the region is widely known: densely timbered evergreen forests, deep valleys and fjords, and lofty peaks. A moist and temperate arc, where damp maritime breezes and ocean fogs reign, this wet zone curves from southwestern Alaska down through British Columbia to well south of the Oregon border.

The **coastal zone** holds many **rain forests**, notably those in British Columbia's lonely Queen Charlotte Islands, southwestern Vancouver Island, and on the seaward slope of Washington's Olympic Peninsula. In their mossy, fern-choked grottoes, Sitka spruce (Alaska's state tree) and western hemlock dominate. Along the Washington and Oregon coast, fingers of evergreen forest reach across tawny grasslands to precipitous headlands dropping to driftwood-strewn beaches known for powerful gusts and pounding surf.

The coastal zone's most temperate rain shadow is **Oregon's Willamette River Valley**, a fecund farming plain between the Oregon Coast Range and the Cascades—the promised land for thousands of 19C settlers arriving via the Oregon Trail. Here, in the lee of the Coast Range's half-mile-high ridges, fertile alluvial soils and warm, relatively dry summers produce a remarkably productive growing season hospitable to an extraordinary variety of crops.

Oregon's "Desert Country" – East of Oregon's Cascades, an immense rain shadow perpetuates a **high desert steppe** of sagebrush and greasewood, juniper and grassland that runs into Idaho. Its elevations generally range between 2,500ft and 5,000ft, creating a desert, where more have perished from freezing than from thirst. There are, however, pockets of extreme aridity and heat such as the powdery white **Alvord Desert**

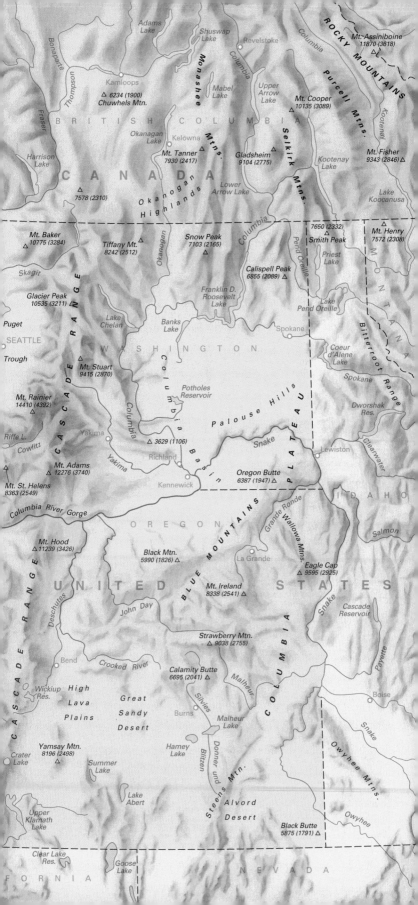

adjoining the basin-and-range fault-block mountains of the Steens and Hart ranges in Oregon's extreme southeast corner. In some parts of this region, rainfall and snowmelt do not flow into the **Columbia River System** (which drains about 250,000sq mi of the basin) but into great depressions, forming reedy wetlands like the birding paradise of **Malheur Lake** near Burns. Volcanism left striking features on these landscapes, including the odd shapes of Fort Rock and Smith Rock in the **High Lava Plains** near Bend and the Columbia River basalt flows that solidified into the cliffs over which Multnomah and other waterfalls flow into the **Columbia River Gorge**.

Washington Landscapes – The Coast and Cascade ranges run the length of the Evergreen State's western region, beginning in the southwest in parks known as the **Willapa Hills** (the lowest stretch of the Pacific Coast mountains, reaching a height of about 3,110ft) and rising as they run north to join the perennially snow-capped **Olympics**, some of the handsomest in the Pacific mountain system, peaking at 7,965ft **Mount Olympus**. Between the Olympics and the Cascades, cradling the Seattle-Tacoma metropolis, is the **Puget Trough**, a generally flat lowland basin running the length of the state. About half of it is submerged by Puget Sound.

The southeastern part of the state is dominated by the **Columbia Plateau**, a vast basaltic basin created by ancient lava flows and deeply trenched by the Columbia and Snake rivers. The **Okanogan Highlands** form the plateau's northern boundary, and its north-eastern corner is rimmed with peaks in the **Rocky Mountain** system, several rising above 7,000ft. To the south stand the Basin's gently rolling **Palouse Hills**, great deposits of windblown fertile dust that produce most of eastern Washington's huge wheat harvests. In the extreme southeast are the low-lying, semiarid **Blue Mountains**, which run from Oregon's northern Cascades into Idaho.

Farther North – Alaska's great size and extreme northern latitudes set the 49th state apart from the lower Pacific Northwest. Measured from south to north, it stands 1,400mi tall and tops out at the United States' northernmost reach at Barrow, a town of 4,000 on the Chukchi Sea, 330mi above the **Arctic Circle**. Alaska's **Pacific Mountain** system is a complex region of high mountains, broad valleys and numerous islands. The Coast Range looms over southeastern Alaska's 500mi-long **Panhandle**, and a portion of it enters the sea and submerges just off the southeast coast, its exposed summits appearing as more than 1,000 islands known as the **Alexander Archipelago**. The principal landform of south-central Alaska, the **Alaska Range** is a great arc of stupendous peaks including **Mount McKinley**. Southwestern Alaska—the **Alaska Peninsula**, Aleutian Islands, Kodiak Island, the Shumagins and other isles—is less accessible, but of great interest to geologists, as the Peninsula and the Aleutians hold the volcanically active **Aleutian Range**. The Interior lies between the Alaska Range and the **Brooks Range**, whose highest peaks top out at over 9,000ft. This central portion is a wild and lonely country of mountains and often boggy lowlands, particularly along the Yukon River and near the Bering Sea. The **Arctic Coastal Plain** or North Slope gradually inclines northward from the Brooks Range to the Arctic Ocean. Beneath its bleak **tundra** lies permafrost, and far below that the petroleum and natural gas that underlie Alaska's economy.

Alsek Lake, Glacier Bay National Park

RGK Photography/Tony Stone Images

Climate

By the 1850s, the reputation of the Pacific Northwest for rain had Californians, used to milder seasons, referring to those living to the north as "webfeet." The novelist Bernard Malamud called Oregon's coastal rains "ubiquitous, continuous, monotonous [and] formless." While it is true that many areas are subject to extended periods of drizzly wetness—and rainfall is in some places nothing short of phenomenal—the Pacific Northwest's sheer size and diverse topography produce a variety of climes determined by latitude, altitude, proximity to the sea, and position relative to the mountain ranges that determine precipitation patterns. A reliable rule of thumb is that weather becomes generally wetter and colder as you move north, and drier and warmer further inland. The four seasons assert themselves in varying strengths throughout the Pacific Northwest, although as the latitudes grow higher, summer is squeezed between prolonged, wet and chilly springs and early-arriving winters.

The warm **North Pacific Current**, which flows in a great arc down from the Gulf of Alaska, acts as a moderating influence on coastal weather, making freezes rare and limiting average coastal temperature swings to roughly half the range of inland highs and lows. Consequently, west of the Cascades and Coast ranges, winters, though wet and occasionally stormy, are generally warmer than those inland, while coastal summers are typically cooler than those east of the mountains. The net effect is that travelers often encounter much milder weather than the region's reputation would imply.

The west-to-east pattern is apparent in the differences of seasonal temperatures in Seattle, on Puget Sound, and those in Spokane, 275mi due east in the Palouse region. In Seattle, July high temperatures average a comfortably humid 75°F, whereas a dry 84°F warms up the wheat-country capital. In January, Seattle temperatures average about 40°F, while Spokane's hover around a chilly 25°F.

Willamette National Forest, Oregon

Coast Ranges – The south-to-north trends are characterized by increasing precipitation levels. Southwestern Oregon records about 70in of rain per year, most of it falling between October and May. A day's drive north, Washington's Olympic Peninsula receives an annual rainfall of about 130in. On the Peninsula's western slopes—the wettest region in the 48 coterminous states—the total often exceeds 200in. This phenomenon of extreme precipitation, which occurs in many places along the forested coasts of Oregon, Washington and British Columbia, takes place where relatively warm moisture-laden maritime westerlies—the Pacific Northwest's weather engine—are ramped rapidly upward, producing a sudden cooling. In the Olympics and in the western ramparts of British Columbia's Coast Range, the effect includes annual snow levels exceeding 400in.

By the time these eastward-moving air masses vault the coastal ranges, however, they are so depleted of water vapor that regions to the east are typically much drier. The Olympic Peninsula's lowlands on Puget Sound, for example, rarely receive more than 20in of rain in a year. Nowhere is this **rain shadow** phenomenon more pronounced than east of the Cascades in Oregon and Washington; while their western slopes can receive 160in annually, average yearly rainfall east of the peaks drops in some places to 6in. The relentless flow of wet air from the Gulf of Alaska produces frequent cloud cover, fogs and long-lasting drizzles that increase in frequency and duration as you travel north. Though southern British Columbia may seem a kind of Canadian California to the rest of the province, Vancouver annually averages 45 days of fog, 168 days of rain and 80 days without measurable sunshine. Indeed, between October and March from Alaska's western coast to Oregon's southern coast, weeks may pass without a completely clear sky. Known for wet gray skies, Seattle, lying in the rain shadow of the Olympics, in fact records only about 38in of rain per year, and only about 3in of that falls between June and August. Also on the plus side, the Pacific Northwest's persistent cloud covers tend to exempt coastal zones from the inland's hot summer weather. The overcast also captures daytime radiant heat and holds it, moderating nighttime lows. British Columbia's coastal zone, for example, records longer frost-free periods than any place in Canada.

Water Resources

Abundance is the rule throughout the Pacific Northwest, a colossal water engine fueled by some of the earth's heaviest rain and snowfalls which in turn supply its great rivers—most notably Alaska's Yukon, British Columbia's Fraser and Thompson, Washington's Columbia, Yakima and Wenatchee, and Oregon's Willamette, which receives more runoff per square mile of drainage area than any other major river in the US. Estimates that Alaska's snowfields, glaciers and three million lakes hold perhaps 40 percent of the nation's freshwater have engendered talk of someday supplying the increasingly thirsty lower 48 states via a water conduit like the Alaska Pipeline.

British Columbia, like Oregon, is laced with about 7,000sq mi of rivers, lakes and streams—more than enough to supply its burgeoning urban populations and increasing agricultural acreage. Supplied by rain and snowmelt, the province is the source of the Columbia River. Its mightiest stream, the **Fraser River** flows in a great inverted V from the Canadian Rockies, cutting a spectacularly rugged canyon before emptying into the Strait of Georgia near Vancouver.

Washington's main freshwater artery is the **Columbia River**, which loops some 1,450mi from Lake Columbia in British Columbia to the Pacific. Many smaller rivers flow west from the Cascade and Coast Ranges. Supplied mainly by the Snake, Spokane, Wenatchee, and Yakima Rivers, the Columbia's great flow and many plunges generate an extraordinary amount of hydroelectric power. Water from the Columbia, the Wenatchee and the Yakima supplies the Yakima Valley's extensive system of irrigation canals, a project that transformed the arid but fertile sagebrush basin into the state's most productive agricultural basin. Washington's most economically significant body of water is **Puget Sound**, about one-fifth the size of Lake Erie, which serves as a highway of commerce, a vast recreational area and a valuable fishing ground.

Oregon is etched by about 112,000mi of rivers and streams (notably the Willamette, Deschutes, John Day, Klamath, Owyhee, Rogue and Umpqua systems) that capture runoff from winter rains and snow packs to annually supply more than 6,000 lakes and reservoirs with over 66 million acre-feet—enough to cover the entire state under a foot of water. Even so, many areas including some west of the Cascades suffer chronic shortages during Oregon's typically dry summers, when stream flows are lowest but demand from agriculture and cities peaks. Geologists, concerned over rising populations in the Willamette Valley and Central Oregon, are surveying groundwater resources in the Deschutes and Willamette Basins.

Flora

The Pacific Northwest's plant productivity rivals that of equatorial South America. Indeed, from July through September, coastal zone biomasses may be ten times those found in southern hemispheric rain forests.

A Congress of Conifers – Conifers (evergreens yielding seed-bearing cones) dominate the region. **Sitka spruce** (Alaska's state tree) and western hemlock reign in coastal forests from Oregon to south-central Alaska, sharing higher elevations with Douglas fir and western red cedar. North of Sitka, spruce-hemlock forests command Alaska's timberlands. Inland forests from lower British Columbia through southern Oregon are characterized by drought-resistant species including Ponderosa pine and Engelmann spruce. These intertwined coastal forest systems span 20 degrees of latitude from California to south-central Alaska, extending inland over the Cascade and Coast ranges. Of the three species of **spruce** (Picea) native to the Pacific Northwest, the shaggy Sitka (Picea sitchensis) predominates, darkly fringing coastlines from northern California to southern Alaska, where "fog drip" from spreading boughs supplements rainfall by as much as 30 percent. Where trees lose limbs to Pacific gales, headland forests take on a "pruned" appearance. Still young at 100, a well-watered Sitka can live eight centuries, achieve diameters of 12ft, and rise to 250ft.

Another long-lived behemoth is the **Douglas fir** (Pseudotsuga), which endures 700 years to reach heights of 260ft. Of six species native to North America, only one (Pseudotsuga menziesii, Oregon's state tree) is exclusively Pacific Northwestern. Its vast coverage of coastal plains and slopes from California to Alaska makes it the leading member of the Douglas fir family. Pyramidal and symmetrical, with arching, wide-reaching soft-needled branches, it is a favorite holiday tree, as are the fragrant grand fir and the cone-like noble fir, sturdy conifers able to bear the heavy snowfalls of the Coast, Cascade and Rocky Mountain high country.

Though **cedars** are popularly regarded as a trademark of the Pacific Northwest, none of the region's four trees commonly identified as such are true cedars, which are native only to the Mediterranean and Himalayas. No regional evergreen can match the cultural significance of **western red cedar** (Thuja plicata). It was the tree most useful to coastal tribes, who shaped them into seagoing canoes, totem poles and planks for building shelters and furniture. Limbs were carved into implements, and its sap and woody parts were rendered into tonics and medicines. The tree's reddish-brown and stringy bark was fashioned into serving plates and combed into fibers for weaving fabric; its roots were plaited to create baskets.

A Plethora of Pines – Fully eight are associated primarily with the Pacific Northwest, leading 19C Scottish botanist David Douglas (who classified four) to caution patrons at the Royal Horticulture Society of England against suspecting that "I manufacture pines at my pleasure." He identified the lodgepole, the ponderosa, the sugar and the western white. Others, also relying mainly on differences in their needle patterns, distinguished the Jeffrey, knobcone, limber and whitebark. Unlike the region's heavily shaded, sword and deer fern-choked rain forests, the sun-loving pine creates open, airy glades whose needle-strewn floors are dappled with light. Many consider these the Pacific Northwest's most inviting forests, where wind through boughs of bundled needles resembling whisk brooms generates a soothing whisper.

© Dianne Dietrich Leis

Rhododendrons

Oregon's Unofficial State Tree – Though neither native nor plentiful, no tree is more cherished in the Pacific Northwest than the California laurel *(Umbellularia california)*. Indeed, above the California border, its admirers insist on calling it the **Oregon myrtle**. A broad-leaf evergreen with a gumdrop profile rising to 80ft, it is related to the camphor, cinnamon and sassafras trees. The aromatic oil in its dark green leaves (used regionally in cooking as a substitute for bay leaf) scents perfumes, incense and candles.

The tree's primary allure, however, derives from its dense hardwood, which comes in golden tans, muted reds, yellow greens, soft grays, ash blonds and seal browns, sometimes patterned with streaks of black. Able to hold a gleaming polish, it is put to myriad uses, from boxes and bowls to acoustic guitars, by a thriving cottage industry of Oregon craftspeople. You're more likely to see it in finished forms than in the wild, however, for it grows only in scattered groves tucked into shaded canyons along southwestern Oregon's rivers.

Beyond The Big Trees – The moist climate of the Pacific Northwest also supports myriad flowers that color the landscape, beginning with the bright patches of **wildflowers**-lupine, paintbrush, asters, monkeyflowers-that appear in the high-country meadows in spring. In the coastal rain forests, epiphytes cling to the trees and some 90 species of velvety mosses, ferns and lichens carpet the forest floor. Thickets of native **Pacific rhododendron** thrive in the acid soils of the upland woods along the coast. Washington's Skagit Valley is known as a **tulip bulb** cultivation area. In this flat swath of fertile land that parallels the Skagit River west from the North Cascades, spring is heralded by a dazzling spectacle as thousands of acres of tulips burst into bloom.

■ Tundra

Tundra vegetation carpets about half of Alaska, including most of the west and virtually all the land above the Arctic Circle. A treeless plain found in arctic and subarctic regions, tundra comprises a surface layer of black, mucky soil underlain by permanently frozen subsoil. For many the term, which derives from the language of Laplanders, connotes a barren landscape, but in fact tundra includes a hardy mix of verdant lichens and mosses, flowering ground cover and grasses, and low brush.

Fauna

The Pacific Northwest possesses a diversity and abundance of wildlife surpassing any other North American region, much of it easily observed from roadside vantage points.

Myriad Mammals – Summer visitors to Alaska's coastal areas often glimpse the **Alaskan brown bear** *(Ursus arctos)*, the largest of the brown bear family, weighing up to 1,400 pounds and, when reared up on its hind legs, standing 9ft tall. Biologists estimate Alaska's

© Lynn M. Stone

Grizzly Bear

number at 30,000—over 98 percent of America's count. In salmon– and berry-rich south-eastern coastal areas, their density reaches one per square mile.

A photographer's favorite because of their white coats and sharply curved horns, **Dall sheep** *(Ovis dalli)* inhabit Alaska's mountain ranges, escaping predators by retreating to precipitous perches. Plentiful on mountainsides near Anchorage, when absorbed in their habit of chewing dirt (to ingest minerals from naturally-occurring formations called "licks"), they seem unconcerned by the approach of humans.

From Alaska to Oregon, the **beaver** *(Castor canadensis)* is forever building dams. The beady-eyed rodent, North America's largest, lives a dozen years, reaching 3-4ft tall and fattening up on a diet of bark, roots and underwater grasses to a top weight of 70 pounds. Needing at least 3ft of water to elude wolves, lynx and bears, beavers construct dams and lodges of sticks, mud and rocks where natural watercourses are too shallow to provide refuge. The resulting backwaters serve as protective moats surrounding their scruffy dome-shaped bastions. Examples of beaver ingenuity include canals for floating gnawed-down timber to construction sites, and lodges with underwater exits for unfettered passage when ponds freeze.

A perennial poster child of wildlife advocates, nearly made extinct by trappers, the delightfully watchable **sea otter** *(Enhydra lutris)* congregates in shallows off the Alaskan coast, with smaller populations off Vancouver Island, Washington and Oregon. The only marine mammal known to use a tool, they subsist on clams, mussels, urchins, crabs and abalone by placing a rock on their chest as they float belly-up, holding the shell in their forepaws and striking it against the rock until it breaks open. Their industry is essential, for despite having the densest fur of any mammal—over a million hairs per square inch of skin—unlike other marine mammals they have no blubber layer to insulate them against chilly ocean water, relying instead on a racing metabolism demanding a daily food intake equivalent to one-third of their body weight.

Denizens of the Deep – One of the most compelling reasons for a Northwest vacation are the spring and autumn coastal gatherings and boat trips to observe the migration of **humpback whales** *(Megaptera novaeangliae)* between North Pacific summer feeding grounds and winter breeding areas in warm southern waters. The humpback's scientific name means "large-winged," referring to its long white flippers, which flash in contrast to its dark chest and belly. Despite lengths of 45-52ft and weights of 35-40 tons, the humpback is an agile acrobat, often breaking the surface in a high-jump motion known as breaching. What appears to be playful exuberance, biologists say, may actually be a form of communication, the loud splashes audible underwater over great distances. The humpbacks' haunting vocalizations may last up to 20min. The singers are males, possessing a repertoire of oft-repeated songs spanning many octaves and including frequencies beyond the threshold of human hearing. Some experts believe their atonal chirps, squeals and groans may relate to dominance, aggression and mate attraction.

Mindful that whaling reduced the humpback population to a tenth of its original size, wildlife watchers now fear similar harm to the Pacific Northwest's dwindling schools of **salmon**, mysterious fish with life cycles still not wholly documented, and which until recently symbolized what many considered an inexhaustible resource. Long a demigod of Native art and legend, once the mainstay of the region's fishing industry, genus Oncorhynchus invites mythical treatment. Born in streams and lakes from Alaska to Oregon, an estimated 10 billion salmon smolts migrate annually to the sea. There they mature, out of sight for years, before the 50 percent who survive return to their natal waters.

History

Prehistoric And Native Peoples

Prehistoric peoples inhabited the Pacific Northwest at least 15,000 years ago, having migrated from what is now Siberia. By eight thousand years ago, they had advanced south far enough to witness the eruption of Mt. Mazama in the Oregon Cascades. When the first Europeans arrived, the area was populated by some 125 different tribes speaking more than 50 languages. Some of the place names they gave to their homelands, like Neakhanie, Snoqualmie and Skamokawa, have survived the centuries. All of the tribes developed rich oral traditions, featuring tales of such godlike creatures as Coyote, Beaver, Raven, Otter and Blue Jay, less symbols of morality or justice than metaphorical attempts to clarify humankind's relationship to the natural world.

Some early inhabitants lived along the coast, among them the **Tlingit**, **Haida** and **Kwakiutl**. With abundant natural resources at hand, there was no need to cultivate crops. They fished for salmon and halibut, gathered shellfish, berries and roots, and became expert whalers. Alaska's Inuits hunted bears, seals, waterfowl and walruses. Cedar trees—fragrant, rot-resistant and plentiful—were made into houses, dugout canoes, elaborately carved chests, cooking containers, dance masks, totem poles, and even bark clothing. Many tribes alternated between summer and winter dwellings. Warfare was relatively rare, but captives were sometimes taken as slaves. Accumulated wealth gave rise to the potlatch *(p 35)*, a ritual practiced widely throughout the region.

Other tribes, such as the **Nez Percé**, **Cayuse**, **Modoc** and **Yakama**, lived on high plateaus east of the Cascade Mountains, fishing steel-

Chief Joseph, Nez Percé (1903)

Special Collections/University of Washington Libraries, Neg.NA124

head, salmon and eel from the Columbia River; hunting elk, deer and sheep; and foraging bulbs and berries. Dressed in fringed and beaded buckskins, Alaska's nomadic **Athabaskans** hunted moose and caribou. By the early 1700s, some inland tribes had acquired horses (from tribes that had gotten them, in turn, from the Spanish). Horses, plus river access, allowed them to travel great distances. Thus, many of these inland tribes (Washington's Yakima especially) became great traders between their coastal neighbors to the west and the buffalo-hunting Plains Indians to the east. In the process, they adopted such innovations as skin tepees and, for special festivities, feathered headdresses.

Because of its distance from "the civilized world," its uncharted landscape and treacherous coastline, the Pacific Northwest was one of the last parts of the globe to be exploited for economic gain. Exactly how large the indigenous population was prior to European arrival is unknown. By the early 1800s, however, it had been reduced to a pitiful fraction of its original size by epidemics of measles, smallpox, influenza and syphilis introduced by the newcomers. What remained of their traditional cultures was further eroded by the introduction of liquor and firearms.

First Contact

The first Europeans to arrive were probably the crew of Spanish explorer **Juan Rodriguez Cabrillo**, whose ship reached the mouth of Oregon's Rogue River in 1543. In 1580 **Francis Drake**, the notorious English pirate, stumbled onto the region while attempting to escape from the Spanish, whose South American ships he'd plundered. Drake sailed north to what is now the Oregon coast where, from the deck of the *Golden Hind*, he observed "unnatural congealed and frozen" rain and the "most vile, thicke and stinking fogges," the earliest surviving complaint about Northwest weather. On his return voyage, Drake stopped long enough to dub the West Coast "New Albion" in defiance of Spain's prior claims to the area.

Meanwhile, to the north, Russian fur hunters were making forays in search of sable and sea otter pelts, but it wasn't until 1726 that they established a base, at Okhotsk, Alaska. In 1728, Czar Peter the Great commissioned **Vitus Bering**, a Dane, to explore Siberia's parameters. Twelve years later, Bering charted Alaska's Aleutian Peninsula (the Bering Strait). Rumors of Russian activity prompted the Spanish to establish a string of Jesuit missions and fortified settlements along California's coast.

It was believed then that a sea route must exist along North America's "northern" coast, linking the Atlantic and Pacific Oceans and offering a shortcut to the Orient. Discovering the fabled Northwest Passage, as it was called, became the goal of every major power. In 1776, when Britain's government offered a £20,000 reward, **Capt. James Cook** took up the challenge. He didn't find the coveted passage, but on a subsequent voyage Cook explored the coasts of Oregon, Washington and British Columbia. On board was midshipman **George Vancouver**, who in 1792 would become the first to circumnavigate Vancouver Island. Later, with Second Lt. **Peter Puget**, he explored what became Puget Sound, establishing a strong British claim to the area.

In 1790, the Nuu-chah-nulth Convention temporarily settled the competing claims of Britain, Spain and Russia for sovereignty over the region's coastline. Not represented at the discussions were the thousands of indigenous people who had inhabited the region for centuries and whose future was about to change, violently and inexorably.

The Fur Trade

By the late 1700s, during the reign of Empress Catherine the Great, Russia's Alaskan adventures had developed into the richest fur enterprise in the world. Establishing Sitka as their center of operations, Russian traders commandeered local Aleuts to hunt down **sea otters** in kayak flotillas, often holding the hunters' families hostage to ensure cooperation. Meanwhile, in the name of the British crown, fur trader Alexander Mackenzie traversed the width of Canada, becoming the first European ever to do so. Also willing to "risk his skin for a skin," as the popular saying went, was American Capt. Robert Gray, who managed to locate the mouth of one of the largest rivers in the US, which he named after his ship, the Columbia. In 1811, Yankee trader John Jacob Astor chose this sight for **Fort Astoria**, the first coastal fur-trading post.

During James Cook's 1778 voyage, he had traded with Native Americans along the Pacific Northwest coast, exchanging trinkets and iron bars for sea otter pelts which sold for exorbitantly high prices in China—a single skin could fetch three times what a man earned in a year. It was the start of a trade triangle that would dominate US and British economic interests in this part of the world for a generation. In China, the pelts (sometimes referred to as "soft gold") were traded for tea, silk, porcelain and other luxuries that found their way to London and Boston.

As early as 1807, Britain's **Hudson's Bay Company** had established a series of trading posts in Washington and Idaho as barriers against American fur traders. Traders induced local Indians to trap otters, foxes, wolves and beavers (whose fur came into vogue as a covering for men's stovepipe hats) in exchange for blankets, beads and whiskey. When the Americans finally did arrive, the widespread presence of so many Hudson's Bay Company flags waving at so many locations led to the joke that the firm's initials stood for "Here Before Christ." The company's economic clout and geographic reach were such that it ruled western Canada and the Pacific Northwest until the mid-19C, discouraging immigration in order to protect its assets.

Pioneer Years

In 1803 President Thomas Jefferson commissioned 29-year-old **Meriwether Lewis** (his former private secretary) and Lewis' good friend **William Clark**, an experienced frontiersman, to explore the Louisiana Purchase, newly acquired from France. In 1804, Jefferson obtained funding from Congress and called on the pair to find a waterway to the Pacific. He believed that the Rocky Mountains formed a natural westernmost boundary for the country, but he did not like the fact that the British seemed intent on securing a position on the North American continent, and he hoped to redirect the fur trade south into the US. That May, the Corps of Discovery left St. Louis, Missouri, with a company of 40. During their 4,000mi journey west, they documented plant and animal life and in November of 1805, 27 years after James Cook, they reached the Oregon coast.

The published journals of Lewis and Clark spurred the imaginations of many would-be pioneers, including a Boston textile-mill owner named Hall Jackson Kelly. In 1829, newly bankrupt, he founded the American Society for Encouraging Settlement of the Oregon Territory, published pamphlets proclaiming Oregon the "New Eden" (though he'd never been there), and claimed that God was beseeching him to spread Christianity among the region's heathen tribes. A bigger spur to America's burgeoning evangelism was the 1832 visit of four Nez Percé Indians to St. Louis. They came to confer with William Clark, who, during his famous Pacific expedition, had spoken to them of a "Book of Heaven" which described how best to reach the happy hunting grounds. Disappointed to learn that the "Good Book" was an enigmatic tome, rather than a practical road map, the Nez Percé headed home, but their visit sparked the ambitions of Methodist ministers who soon found their way to Oregon. Met with apathy from the local Calapooia Indians, they removed native children from their families and placed them in missionary schools. Presbyterians, Baptists, Lutherans and Latter-Day Saints would soon follow, along with several utopian colonies.

In the mid-19C an expansionist ideal stirred the country with the premise that it was America's destiny to rule from sea to sea. Between 1843 and 1860 Manifest Destiny inspired some 53,000 settlers to head west in ox-drawn wagon trains hoping for a new life. During what came to be known as the **Great Migration**, they traveled the 2,000mi-long **Oregon Trail** hazarding an arduous six-month journey that began, appropriately, in Independence, Missouri, and ended in Oregon City, the first American town to be incorporated (1844) west of the Rockies. Meanwhile, the spreading of religious faith was taking place to the north, in Russian Alaska. One of the first men of God to arrive was young **Father Ivan Veniaminov**, who would spend 44 years spreading Russian Orthodoxy to the Aleuts. Unlike many of the missionaries who would follow, Veniaminov respected native culture. A gifted scholar and linguist, he preached in Aleut, prepared an Aleut dictionary, and wrote a primer in the language as a bridge to native literacy. So successful was he in gaining the Tlingit's trust that, in 1836, they allowed him to inoculate them against smallpox.

Other missionaries, though well-meaning, were less successful. **Dr. Marcus Whitman** had settled near Walla Walla, Washington, with his family when, in 1847, a measles epidemic hit the area, brought in by traders and settlers. Though he'd been warned about the dangers of doing so, Whitman insisted on administering medicine to the local Cayuse Indians. Nearly half the tribe succumbed, their children being especially vulnerable, but few of the settlers fell ill. The Cayuse became convinced that Whitman had intentionally mistreated them, saving his good medicine for his own people. Nor did it help that Whitman's wife, Narcissa, accused the Cayuse of being "proud, haughty and insolent." In retaliation, the Indians murdered the Whitmans and nine others, and took some 50 women and children captive. The **Whitman Massacre** was later cited as justification for usurping Indian land, forbidding traditional potlatches and incarcerating Indians on reservations where they depended on federal largesse.

Of Whales and Walruses – As during the fur trading years, Aleuts were in demand in the mid-19C for their skill at hunting whales. Despite the efforts of people like Veniaminov to protect his flock from exploitation, commercial interests usually won out over humanitarian sentiments. At that time the world prized whale oil, rendered from blubber, as lamp fuel. Baleen, a horny substance attached in two plates to the upper jaws of baleen whales as an evolutionary aid to feeding on plankton, was made into everything from corsets and collar stays to buggy whips and umbrella ribbing. There were fortunes to be made, often by merchant princes in faraway New England. Square-rigger whaling reached its heyday in the 1840s. As the Atlantic's right whale population declined, hunters sought out the Pacific Northwest's plentiful bowhead whales. By the 1860s, with the advent of harpoon guns and steam-powered whaling ships, the stronger, faster humpback whales became vulnerable prey.

When whales couldn't be found, walruses were slaughtered as a source of both oil and tusk ivory. In 1859 the discovery of petroleum in Pennsylvania helped save the whales by sending the lamp-oil market into a free-fall. Baleen and ivory, however, remained in demand, and over the next two decades an estimated 200,000 walruses were taken.

Gold Fever

In 1848, following the news of gold strikes in California's Sierra Nevada foothills, two-thirds of Oregon's male population rushed south. The fevered exodus of men, many of whom abandoned mercantile and laboring jobs, proved a windfall to Oregon's economy, as the vast army of fortune-seekers created a ready market for its agricultural products and lumber. In fact, the majority of gold rush fortunes were made by merchants who charged premium—sometimes exorbitant—prices for essentials like boots, shovels and gold pans. Within a year, gold dust was pouring into Oregon banks, and in 1850 gold was discovered in Oregon. To encourage orderly development of the state's arable lands, the **Donation Land Claim Act** was established, offering each settler 320 acres, plus an additional 320 in his wife's name. Gold fever gripped Washington in 1855 with strikes along the upper Columbia River. Dismayed at seeing their traditional lands invaded and dug up by prospectors who paid them no respect, the Spokane, Yakama, Coeur d'Alene and Palouse tribes banded together to resist the encroachment. The US Army retaliated with its new long-range rifles, slaughtering 700 Yakima horses and hanging 24 tribal chiefs in what came to be known as the Yakama War.

Racism – Native people weren't the only target of pioneer prejudice. Blacks, Japanese, Chinese and Hawaiians who came to the region to work in the railroad and lumber industries were denied civil rights and often treated with disdain. During the fur

Special Collections/University of Washington Libraries, Wilse Neg. NA245

The *Cleveland* Leaving Seattle (c.1897)

trading era, marriage between Scottish and French-Canadian men, primarily, and Native American and Hawaiian women was fairly common. But by the 1860s, Washington and Oregon and Idaho had passed legislation prohibiting the practice.

In Tacoma, sinophobes tried to deport the city's Asians to Portland by train, and several hundred Chinese in Seattle—informed that they lived in buildings that had been condemned—were escorted to the waterfront for shipment to San Francisco. In 1922 Oregon's Klu Klux Klan was at its height, with 25,000 active members dedicated to the persecution of religious minorities they considered undeserving of respect. A vestige of this sentiment arose in 1942 in the wake of the Japanese Navy's attack on Pearl Harbor, when 10,000 residents of Japanese origin, most of them American citizens, were forcibly relocated to internment camps for "protective custody."

■ Reminders of the Past

Historic Homes

Pioneer Days

The 20th Century

Determined to win over some of the markets fueling Seattle's thriving mercantilism and shipping industry, Portland hosted a World's Fair in 1905. The fete marked the 100th anniversary of Lewis and Clark's arrival at the nearby mouth of the Columbia, a theme that captured the attention of a nation caught up in a resurgence of pride over its economic expansion and growing international clout. Four years later, Seattle reciprocated with the Alaska-Yukon-Pacific Exposition, which helped shape the Puget Sound city's reputation as a portal to Pacific Rim and Canadian markets. In 1906 Juneau replaced Sitka as Alaska's capital, evidence of the commercial triumph of gold over furs. Alaska's now-endangered fur seals, once numbering in the tens of thousands, gained protection under international agreement in 1911. The following year, Alaska became a US territory, assembled its own legislature and granted female residents the right to vote—eight years before the 20th Amendment gave suffrage to women in the rest of the country.

The **Boeing Airplane Company**, founded in Seattle in 1916, created regional employment for some 50,000 during World War II. Oregon remained the nation's leading timber-producing state until the mid-1950s, when over-supply and competition from eastern forests forced many sawmills to close. During the 1960s, Native Americans began increasingly to assert their rights, which came to include licenses to operate gambling casinos; these created thousands of jobs and, for many, a measure of economic self-sufficiency. In the 1970s, the public became more aware of environmental issues and began to demand protective legislation for the region's rivers, old-growth forests, wildlife and farmlands.

The 1980s saw a huge influx of newcomers (including many so-called "lifestyle refugees" from California). Owing to their traditions of progressive politics, Oregon and Washington became the focus of a sentimental "back to the land" movement that attracted predominately young urbanites. Among them were some 4,000 red-clad disciples of Bhagwan Shree Rajneesh *(p 96)*, who established a controversial 64,000-acre commune in Oregon's rural Wasco County, for a time taking over the farming community of Antelope. Starting in the 1980s, Microsoft's dominance of America's software markets almost single-handedly established the region as a high-tech center. Today, the entire Pacific Northwest struggles to find a balance between its economically advantageous self-promotion as a region of exceptional lifestyle attributes and diverse commercial opportunities, and the resulting rapid growth that threatens to diminish the qualities that make it so attractive as a tourist destination.

■ Out and About ...

Aquariums and Zoos

Woodland Park Zoological Gardens★★ *p 193*
Oregon Coast Aquarium★★ Newport (OR) *p 122*
Oregon Zoo★ Portland (OR) *p 77*
Oregon Coast Aquarium★★ Newport (OR) *p 122*
Seattle Aquarium★ Seattle (WA) *p 178*
Vancouver Aquarium★★ Vancouver (BC) *p 297*
Greater Vancouver Zoo Vancouver (BC) *p 307*
Whale Park Sitka (AK) *p 376*
Alaska Zoo Anchorage (AK) *p 384*
Alaska SeaLife Center★★ Seward (AK) *p 388*

Something Different

Windsurfing the Gorge *p 83*
Rockhounding *p 97*
Pendleton Round-up *p 111*
Thar She Blows Oregon Coast (OR) *p 120*
Riding the Rogue (OR) *p 141*
Okanagan Wineries (BC) *p 342*
Ports of Call (AK) *p 376*
The Iditarod (AK) *p 383*

Time Line

24,000 BC	Estimated earliest human crossings of the land bridge across the Bering Strait from Mongolia to present-day Alaska.
7,300 BC	"Kennewick Man" dies along the Columbia River; his skeleton will survive as one of the most complete of an ancient North American yet found.
1543	Seafaring Spanish explorer Juan Rodriguez Cabrillo skirts the Oregon Coast and sights the mouth of the Rogue River.
1580	English privateer Francis Drake, sailing north, finds the Oregon coast inhospitable and unpromising.
1741	Vitus Bering sets out to explore the perimeters of Siberia and sights Alaska's Aleutian Islands.
1765	"Ouragon", first known use of Oregon, appears in a proposal by military surveyor Robert Rogers.
1774	Spanish ships reach British Columbia's Queen Charlotte Islands and claim the Pacific Northwest coast for Madrid.
1775	Bruno Heceta and Juan Francisco de Bodega y Quadra land on Washington's coast, becoming the first known Europeans to set foot on its soil.
1778	Capt. James Cook explores the coasts of Oregon, Washington and British Columbia.
1788	Capt. Robert Gray is the first American known to set foot in Oregon, arriving by sea at Tillamook.
1790	The Nuu-chah-nulth Convention temporarily settles competing claims of Spain, Britain and Russia for sovereignty over the Pacific Northwest coastline.
1792	Spain relinquishes its claim to the Northwest coast to Britain. Robert Gray discovers the mouth of the Columbia River.
1793	Fur trader Alexander Mackenzie becomes the first European to cross Canada, giving Great Britain its second claim to the area.
1804-1806	Meriwether Lewis and William Clark explore the Pacific Northwest for President Thomas Jefferson.
early 1800s	Epidemics of influenza, smallpox and measles decimate the Nez Percé in Oregon's Willamette Valley.
1807	Working for Britain's Hudson's Bay Company, David Thompson establishes a series of trading posts.
1808	Sitka, Alaska, becomes center of Russian operations in America.
1811	The Pacific Fur Company, financed by John Jacob Astor, establishes Fort Astoria at the mouth of the Columbia River.
1818	Britain and the US agree to joint occupancy of the region, but each continues to strive for complete domination.
1819	Treaties push Spanish land claims to below the latitude of 42 degrees.
1820	Sea otters near extinction along the Pacific coast, victims of the lucrative fur trade.
1821	The Hudson's Bay Company expands, monopolizing trade in western Canada and the Pacific Northwest until the mid-19C.
1824	Father Ivan Veniaminov arrives in the Aleutian Islands from Russia to spend the next 44 years spreading Christianity among Native Americans.
1828	Russian land claims are established north of latitudes lines 54-40.

William Clark (c.1810)
by Charles Willson Peale

Independence National Historical Park

Meriwether Lewis (c.1807)
by Charles Willson Peale

Independence National Historical Park

1829	Oregon City becomes the first town in the Pacific Northwest to be incorporated.
1830-1831	A mysterious fever kills 90 percent of the population of the Chinook tribes living along the Columbia River, littering riverbanks with unburied dead.
1832	Four Nez Percé Indians travel to St. Louis to consult with explorer William Clark about the "Good Book", a visit that inspires evangelists to head west.
1834	New England Methodists establish a mission in Oregon, hoping to convert local Indians.
1840s	Whalers invade Alaskan waters, introducing firearms, liquor, foreign diseases and a cash economy.
1843	The greatest migration in US history commences when 900 American settlers traverse the Oregon Trail to the Willamette Valley; over the next 17 years, approximately 53,000 people make the 2,000mi-long trek.
1844	The US Presidential campaign slogan, "54/40 or Fight", urges the nation to occupy Washington, British Columbia and all of the Northwest up to the present-day Alaska border.
1845	Portland is laid out as a trading post.
1846	Pioneer Sam Barlow opens a land route into the Willamette Valley. It proves to be the most grueling part of the Oregon Trail. Great Britain cedes all land south of the 49th parallel, including the coveted natural harbor of Puget Sound, to the US.
1847	Cayuse Indians murder missionary Dr. Marcus Whitman as well as his wife and nine others. The Oregon Territory is established.
1848	Congress launches an ambitious program to build lighthouses along the Pacific coast. Abraham Lincoln is offered the governorship of the just-organized Oregon Territory.
1850	Gold discovered in Oregon. The Donation Land Claim Act gives each male settler 320 acres. Oregon's population of non-Indians passes 13,000.
1851	The port city of Seattle is founded.
1852	President Millard Fillmore signs a bill creating the Territory of Washington.
1855-1979	The majority of the region's Native Americans are forcibly relocated to reservations.
1858	Gold is discovered in British Columbia.
1859	Oregon becomes the 33rd US state.
1867	Russia sells Alaska to US for $7.2 million.
1869	Alaska's first river steamboat, the Yukon, is launched.
1870	With sea otters unavailable, hunters in Alaska switch to harvesting fur seals.
1879	Fascinated by glaciers, Scottish naturalist John Muir travels to Alaska. Reports of his 800mi canoe trip inaugurate Alaska tourism.
1880	Joe Juneau's discovery of gold ushers in Alaska's gold-rush era. Thousands of fortune-seekers arrive.
1884	Potlatch is outlawed in Canada.
1885	Lt. Henry Allen reaches the headwaters of Alaska's Copper River.
1886	The first train runs from Montreal to Vancouver, opening the West to ready settlement.
1887	The Dawes Severalty Act requires Native Americans to select 160-acre reservation landholdings while some two-thirds of their land is turned over to settlers.
1889	Washington achieves statehood.
1896	The first of several gold discoveries is made in the Yukon.
1900	One of the earth's richest copper reserves is discovered along Alaska's Chitina River.
1902	Gold is discovered in Fairbanks, Alaska.
1905	Portland hosts a World's Fair, marking the 100th anniversary of Lewis & Clark's expedition.
1906	Juneau replaces Sitka as Alaska's capital.
1909	Seattle hosts the Alaska-Yukon-Pacific Exposition.
1911	Endangered northern fur seals gain protection under international agreement.

1912	Alaska becomes a US territory.
1914	Seattle's 42-story Smith Tower is completed, the tallest building west of the Mississippi River.
1916	The Boeing Airplane Company is founded in Seattle.
1919	Seattle becomes the site of the nation's first general strike when 60,000 "Wobblies" walk off the job.
1923	Congress grants citizenship to Native Americans. The 400mi Alaska Railroad is completed.
1925	Alaska's Glacier Bay is designated a national park.
1930s	Poverty-weary citizens in Oregon tear up their backyards to find thousands of dollars in gold from old mining claims.
1942	Washington and Oregon are designated military areas; 10,000 residents of Japanese ancestry are relocated to government internment camps. The 1,400mi Alaska Highway is built.
1943	The Battle of Attu (the first battle fought on American soil since the Civil War) results in 3,829 Japanese and American casualties.
1959	Alaska becomes the 49th US state.
1962	Seattle World's Fair creates the city's monorail and its futuristic Space Needle.
1968	Huge reserves of petroleum and natural gas are discovered in Alaska's Arctic coastal plain.
1977	The $7.7 billion Trans-Alaska Pipeline begins to transport crude oil from Prudhoe Bay to the port of Valdez, 800mi south.
1979	Many of the region's sawmills close, laying off some 20,000 employees. But the lumber industry is soon revived by the export log market. Software entrepreneurs Bill Gates and Paul Allen move their Microsoft Corp. from Albuquerque, New Mexico to Bellevue, Washington.
1980s	A huge influx of newcomers flocks to the region, an average of 220 a day in Oregon alone.
1980	Mount St. Helens erupts in southwestern Washington, devastating 200sq mi of forestland.
1981	Indian guru Bhagwan Shree Rajneesh establishes a controversial 64,000-acre commune in Oregon with 4,000 disciples.
1988	Indian Gaming Regulation Act allows Native Americans to operate gambling casinos.
1989	Exxon Valdez spills 11 million gallons of crude oil into Prince William Sound.
1989-1990	The spotted owl controversy in Oregon pits environmentalists against logging interests in a landmark battle over wildlife habitats; environmentalists claim victory when the federal government declares the bird a threatened species.
1994	Oregon enacts the nation's first state law allowing terminally ill adults to obtain a prescription for lethal drugs.
1995	Microsoft, demonstrating its domination of the software industry, delays licensing of a new computer operating system to IBM. IBM sues Microsoft, alleging the tactic nearly drove the company out of business.
1996	Alaska's North Slope Milne Field achieves production of 65,000 barrels of oil per day, placing it among the top 10 producing fields in the US.
1998	Forbes ranks Microsoft co-founder Bill Gates the world's richest individual with an estimated worth of $51 billion.
1998-99	Winter snowfall on Mount Baker sets a world's record of 96.6ft.
1999	Makah Indians kill a gray whale off coast of Washington in a controversial hunt.

■ Potlatch

Held for centuries throughout the Pacific Northwest by a dozen different Native American groups, potlatches were a way of publicly acknowledging and validating events before witnesses. While smaller potlatches served to repay debts or to celebrate births, marriages or a young girl's coming of age, the most elaborate were eight-day-long memorials to honor a deceased high-ranking chief and to name his successor. Hundreds of guests, many of whom might have traveled great distances to attend, were treated to a series of parties, followed by the more serious rituals of mourning songs and the recitation of the host clan's history, lineage and property. Storytellers recited the feats of Raven, a capricious near-deity believed to have created humans and given them light, fire and water. Next came the distribution of gifts, which might include blankets, jewelry, carved boxes, copper shields and large woven baskets. The quality of gifts given was a direct reflection of a host's status, and guests were expected to reciprocate at future potlatches—a distribution of wealth that kept goods circulating and encouraged the arts. Then came a great feast, after which guests entertained their host with songs and dancing.

By the mid-19C, the burgeoning fur trade meant increasingly wealthy chiefs, resulting in the prestige potlatch—gift giving (and sometimes gift burning) on a lavish scale. Unfettered generosity raised a host's social status and political power, as well as the status of his children. Some chiefs impoverished themselves trying to emulate the largesse of their more affluent neighbors.

By the early 20C, missionary influence and government laws had suppressed potlatches, but during the 1960s, public interest in Native American cultures led to a revival. Today the ceremony lasts one to two days and is usually held to celebrate a totem pole raising or a memorial of some kind. Non-natives are often invited to attend. Though potlatches no longer exert their former social, political and economic influence, they still serve to connect native Pacific Northwestern peoples to their cultural heritage.

Economy

Abundant natural resources—particularly the bounty of its seas and forests—were the original pillars of the Pacific Northwest's wealth and continue to play a significant role in the economic well-being of its communities. Immediately after its purchase from Russia in 1867, Alaska began to pay off with a series of gold strikes that eventually eclipsed trading in seal hides and otter fur as the territory's leading industries. British Columbia's economic saga is similar: Timber and sea otters were initially its prime commodities. Early mining and agriculture followed, making modest contributions— only four percent of the province is arable—while fishing, the primary survival skill of its native people, slowly expanded. Washington and Oregon were first exploited by British and Russian fur traders and a few solitary American trappers. Settlers' timber cutting set the stage for ever-expanding 19C harvests that, once railroads arrived, established the region as America's richest potential source of commercial woods, and spun off a vigorous shipbuilding trade that relied particularly on the Northwest's forests of red and white cedar. By the turn of the century, commercial agriculture flourished in British Columbia's Fraser Valley and in Oregon's vast Willamette River basin. With the arrival of World War II, south-central Washington's arid Yakima Valley, irrigated with water diverted from the Yakima River by a spiderweb of government-financed canals, was on its way to becoming the Northwest's most productive agricultural cornucopia. Meanwhile, Michigan-born **William Boeing**, a dropout of Yale's engineering college, had built his Seattle-based Boeing Airplane Company into one of the nation's top suppliers of combat aircraft. Another boost to the regional economy came from the growth of the Japanese paper industry, a huge new market for wood chips that were once considered worthless by-products of lumber production.

In 1977 the $7.7 billion **Alaska Pipeline** began to tap the state's colossal Prudhoe Bay oil and gas reserve—a reservoir estimated to be twice as big as any other North American oil field. In the 1970s Seattle and Portland began to appear regularly on lists of American cities with exceptional qualities and promise. In 1979 Seattle natives Bill Gates and Paul Allen came home, bringing their fledgling Albuquerque firm with them and thus establishing the Northwest's first computer software company, Microsoft.

Industry – A generally well-educated populace, relatively low living costs and a good transportation network (including modern seaports) make the Pacific Northwest attractive to high-tech and export-oriented manufacturers.

Oregon's economy continues to depend heavily on **lumber** and **agriculture**. Portland's seaport leads the West in grain exports and is one of the top five entry points for autos imported into the US, ranking third in overall tonnage behind Los Angeles and San Diego. A newer industry, **electronics** has developed and is significantly broadening the state's economic base. Electronics manufacturers regard the Pacific Northwest's urban centers as desirable locations, since the industry is not dependent upon raw materials or close proximity to markets but does require a skilled labor force. Particularly along its I-5 corridor between Portland and Eugene, Oregon has recently experienced steady job growth in high technology. Some 500 high-tech firms do business out of Portland, and statewide their vitality has been exceptional. Other thriving industries include makers of forest products, metal products, and a wide range of transportation equipment. In both Washington and Oregon, high-yielding agricultural and **fishing** activity supplies a thriving food processing industry producing canned and frozen vegetables and fruits, bread products, fresh and frozen fish, packaged meats, milk and cheese, nuts, wine, beer and soft drinks, among many other products. In Washington, manufacturing currently generates nearly one-sixth of the annual gross state product; goods include transportation equipment (especially aircraft and aerospace hardware), lumber and wood products, paper, food products and industrial machinery. Most of this enterprise is found along Puget Sound between Olympia and Bellingham. Government-built dams like the much-photographed Grand Coulee on the mighty Columbia have long supplied the Northwest with inexpensive hydroelectric power, encouraging the growth of aluminum refineries, steel mills and metal fabricators.

In British Columbia, two long-established industries—**lumber manufacturing** and **paper milling**—lead in terms of dollar volume. Newcomers showing strength include textile makers and fabricators of sports and leisure equipment targeted to the region's outdoor-oriented populace. Canada's only large-scale marine outlet to Pacific Rim markets, Vancouver traffics in lumber, wheat and minerals; it now outranks New York as North America's largest port, handling more dry tonnage than Seattle, Tacoma, Portland, San Francisco and San Diego combined. Alaskan industry remains relatively limited because of the state's remote location and long dark winters, impediments to shipping raw materials in and finished products out. Maintenance and distribution take precedence over manufacturing endeavors, which are generally more economically feasible in the lower 48.

Natural Resources – One of the Northwest's first and still important industries is **commercial fishing**; Oregon, for example, typically lands over half a billion pounds and generates personal income of $139 million for coastal communities. Chinook and Coho have historically made up the bulk of the salmon catch, most taken by ocean trollers and

Columbia River gill-netters. In 1994, however, catches dwindled to virtually nothing—the seas off Oregon were depleted from overfishing and the destruction of spawning streams ashore by logging and development. Catches are slowly rebounding, but the Oregon coastal Coho salmon is now listed under the federal Endangered Species Act. Commercial fishing accounts for less than one percent of Washington's gross state product. Ports on Puget Sound and the Pacific Ocean handle virtually all the landings—less than 1 percent comes from fresh water—with salmon accounting for about a third of the catch in dollar value, followed by oysters, crab, shrimp, and other shellfish.

Timber rules from Oregon to Alaska. Harvesting of Douglas fir and western hemlock is a major industry in Washington in particular. A bit over 40 percent becomes lumber, about 40 percent is left as roundwood for export, and the rest, usually of inferior grade, ends up at pulp and plywood mills.

Fisherman Hauling in Nets, Kodiak Island, Alaska

Jim Nilsen/Tony Stone Images

British Columbia's abundance of softwood—nearly half of the province is timbered with commercial-grade fir, spruce, pine and hemlock—supplies about half of Canada's needs and is the province's single most important source of income. The provincial government owns 94 percent of the forests.

North Slope **oil and natural gas** production contributes most to the North Star state's treasury. Despite sitting atop recoverable reserves double those of any other known American field, Alaska must ride the yo-yo of world oil prices, deprived, some estimate, of about $150 million in annual income for every dollar drop in the price of a barrel of crude. Yet in boom times and bad, Alaska supplies a significant percentage of the nation's oil, funding the state's treasury mainly with related taxes and royalties. Though dwarfed in value by the oil business, long-standing traditional industries such as forestry and fishing, along with tourism, play especially important roles in sustaining the economies of outlying communities unable to benefit from the petroleum trade.

Agriculture – Among the Pacific Northwest's political divisions, Washington is the agricultural star, in recent years consistently ringing up well over $5.5 billion in annual sales. East of the Cascades, long warm growing seasons (with about two hours more summer sunlight than California's prime growing regions), fertile soils rich in volcanic ash (which retains moisture), and abundant water from the Columbia, Snake, Yakima and lesser river systems are key reasons the state leads the nation in the production of apples, pears, sweet cherries, Concord grapes, wrinkled seed peas and dry edible peas, hop flowers, lentils, asparagus, and red raspberries. Washington's fall potato production is surpassed only by Idaho, and its harvest of wheat (the state's leading field crop) typically places it third to fifth nationwide behind perennial front-runner Kansas.

Long a producer of fruit and berry wines, Oregon has made its mark in recent years in the premium **wine trade**, at the start of 1999 inventorying over one million cases in its cellars. Reviews of its Pinot Noirs, Merlots, white Rieslings and Chardonnays are typically positive, crediting long hours of summer sunshine and cool marine breezes that ripen wine grapes gradually. Like their Washington counterparts, Oregon's vintners market their wines as regional products to be appreciated for their unique merits rather than for their similarities to California or French wines.

ROYAL RIVIERA
BRAND
PEARS
THE WORLD'S
FINEST AND RAREST
DIRECT FROM
TREE TO YOU
BEAR CREEK ORCHARDS
ROSENBERG BROS.
MEDFORD, OREGON, U.S.A.

© Dianne Dietrich Leis

Harry & David Fruit Packing Label (1939)

British Columbia's mountainous character precludes widespread agriculture. Less than five percent of the province is suitable for farming, and agronomists rate only slightly more than one percent of it as prime growing land. Moreover, they note, the best land is usually found in narrow valley bottoms, where agriculture must compete with other high-priority uses including housing, industry, transportation, recreation and wildlife habitat. Though Alaska has farms scattered throughout, agriculture accounts for a mere .2 percent of the state's land. Much of the industry revolves around **aquaculture**, followed by greenhouse and nursery crops, and potatoes and barley. Reindeer ranches dot the Seward Peninsula, and arguably the loneliest beef cattle in America graze out on the windswept Aleutian Islands.

Tourism – Scenery and outdoor recreation are what most people seek when they come to the Pacific Northwest. Although possessed of sophisticated urban attributes and lauded for the quality of life they offer, Portland, Seattle, Vancouver, Victoria and Anchorage alone are not what draw most out-of-state visitors.

Tourism now injects nearly $5 billion into Oregon's economy—a 42 percent increase since 1991 that boosted industry employment to over 70,000 and did much to replace jobs lost in the coast's lumbering and fishing industries during the 1970s and 1980s. Only recently perceived here as an industry, tourism is now the state's third-largest source of revenue. To the delight of the Pacific Northwest's battle-scarred environmentalists, a growing general awareness that pristine natural landscapes are the strongest tourist draw is enlisting supporters for stronger environmental policies among those who once considered them politically unattractive or financially unfeasible. The 1962 World's Fair made Seattle's Space Needle and downtown monorail system its trademarks, and, some say, seeded the Northwest's nationwide reputation for high-quality urban living in close proximity to wilderness. That reputation, say Washington officials, is a primary reason that each year several million tourists contribute some $4.8 billion to the state's economy, most of them coming to tour national parks, forests and recreation areas.

The value of tourism to British Columbia, which annually welcomes over 21 million overnight visitors, is immense; annual revenues now exceed $5.8 billion US, and over 235,000 British Columbians (nearly six percent of the population) pursue tourism-related work. Tourism enterprises make up one of the fastest growing sectors of the provincial economy and are regarded as its second-largest export industry after forestry. The trend has been bolstered by an international boom in so-called adventure tourism, which often requires extensive outfitting, professional guides and a challenging wilderness, all of which British Columbia offers in convenient proximity. No newcomer to adventure travel, Alaska also offers an abundance of outdoor pursuits. Few roads penetrate interior wilds; most visitors are seasoned outdoor enthusiasts or determined anglers, flown into and out of the backcountry by professional outfitters.

Economic Forecast – Once solely dependent upon the exploitation of natural resources, the Pacific Northwest is turning to longer-range management strategies intended to ensure sustainable yields from its timber, wildlife and fisheries. In British Columbia and Alaska, where in the past environmentalism has found less support than in Oregon and Washington, there is growing sentiment in favor of resource protection and preservation, based less on emotion than a realization that sound policies will benefit local and regional economies. In Washington and British Columbia and especially in Oregon, the loss of agricultural land to development is a major concern. Meanwhile, rising land prices and production costs make private agriculture more difficult, if not impossible, for a new generation of family farmers.

Despite the chronic swings in the fishing and forest-products industries, many believe that improved methods of reforestation and acquaculture, along with wiser policies, will eventually restore both to a point where sustainable yields can support a considerable work force. In Oregon, minerals are projected as a source of new wealth well into the 21C. Petroleum engineers are optimistic that new technologies for extracting oil and natural gas from aging fields (where depleted underground pressure often leaves some 60 percent of the known reserves unrecoverable) will extend the life of the region's petroleum reserves through the next century, a boon to Alaska especially, and an inducement to exploration and the revival of old fields.

Economic activity from ever-increasing tourism and outdoor recreation is expected to strengthen all of the region's economies. In Oregon, wildlife viewing and photography, a relatively new and rapidly expanding activity, already contributes $400 million to the state's economy, and is making a similar impact all the way to Alaska. One result is widespread construction and upgrading of public viewing facilities, as well as increased legislative support for increasing the number and size of state and federal parks and preserves. Since the passage of the 1988 National Indian Gaming Regulatory Act, all nine of Oregon's Indian tribes have opened gaming centers on their reservations (now called trust lands). Besides providing employment for tribal members and citizens of nearby communities, these federally approved enterprises provide revenues that are earmarked for health clinics, education scholarships, housing and other tribal services.

One telling indicator of tourism's remarkable impact is found in Alaska, whose livelihood once depended exclusively upon military patronage, fishing, logging and oil. The state now officially lists tourism as an integral part of its economy.

The Arts

The Pacific Northwest is rich in tribal art, the living expression of cultures that pre-date written histories. Because of a revived interest in the region's cultural heritage during the 1960s, many traditional crafts that often had only a few remaining and usually elderly practitioners have been saved from extinction.

The 1930s saw the widespread growth of art departments in local colleges and universities, as well as the establishment of the Portland and Seattle Art Museums. The latter continue their original mandate to showcase regional artists. Visiting WPA (Works Progress Administration) project artists also gave a great boost to this relatively isolated area, so far from the influences of New York and Europe. Thirty years later, the 1962 Seattle World's Fair caught the nation's attention once more, and introduced thousands of people to Seattle's unsung performing arts troupes. What the Royal Philharmonic Orchestra's eminent conductor Sir Thomas Beecham once dismissed as a "cultural wasteland" is now alive with a vast array of artists, concerts and exhibitions.

Native American Art – Among the region's ancient artifacts are pottery, ornamental baskets, beadwork, ivory pipes, arrowheads, wood carvings, rattles, dance masks, dugout canoes, and ceremonial blankets, many of which were created for tribal pot-latches *(p 35)*. Elegant cribbage boards carved onto walrus tusks, the work of Inuit engravers, made their appearance in the early 20C. The Museum at Warm Springs *(p 96)* near Bend, Oregon, built at a cost of over $7.5 million, is said to have one of the most complete collections of Indian heirlooms, trade items, gifts and historic photographs owned by an Indian tribe.

Among other ancient artifacts are petroglyphs, pictures chipped or carved into cliffs and boulders. Most were created facing the Pacific Ocean or overlooking rivers or waterways. Their makers and their meanings remain unknown; anthropologists speculate that they might include messages, boundary markers, homages to deities—and mere doodles. Alaska's **Petroglyph Beach** *(80mi northwest of Ketchikan)* features over three dozen large stones. The Nanaimo area of Vancouver Island is another good place to view etchings of wolves, birds, humans and supernatural creatures.

The Pacific Northwest's best-known art form, and one uniquely its own in all the world, is the **totem pole**—enormous red cedar tree trunks that have been carved and sometimes painted. Popular totemic designs included eagles, bears, beavers, wolves, frogs and killer whales. Different tribal groups had different pole-raising ceremonies, and each pole was given a name. Historically, most were commissioned by wealthy preliterate chiefs as public records of their lineage, exploits and achievements. They served other functions as well. Welcome poles, placed just outside a village, featured a larger-than-life human figure with outstretched arms to receive visitors to local feasts and potlatches. House posts supported the roof beams inside the homes of high-ranking chiefs and sported family crests and pictorial histories, while house front poles stood outside. Memorial poles were created to honor a deceased chief, and mortuary poles held a chief's ashes in a specially carved cavity. There were even shame poles, commissioned by chiefs who wished to ridicule someone who had broken a trust or accrued a long-standing unpaid debt. The pole, depicting the errant in an unflattering attitude for all to see, would stand until the issue was resolved.

Today, most totem poles are seen out of context—placed in parks, along highways, outside of hotels or schools. Some depict famous Northwest native legends, such as "How Raven Stole the Sun" or "Nanasimget and the Whale." Others are commercial totems, commissioned by governments, corporations or institutions. In ancient times, one totem pole reached the extraordinary height of 60ft, but modern pole-raising equipment led to the creation of a spectacular 173ft-tall pole at Alert Bay on Vancouver Island. Totem Heritage Center in Ketchikan, Alaska, features mostly 50-year-old replicas of older designs; poles can also be seen at Sitka National Historical Park, Thunderbird Park in Victoria, and Stanley Park in Vancouver. Etiquette dictates that the poles never be climbed or leaned against.

Native Structures – Some Inuit groups spent the freezing winter months in **sod houses**, semi-subterranean shelters with long, downward-sloping tunnel entrances and raised sleeping decks—a design that took maximum advantage of both human body heat and oil-burning soapstone lamps (kuliq). Others built circular, domed snow houses known as **igloos** or igluvigak that sometimes featured a windowpane of freshwater ice or seal intestine. Yet another winter house was the **quarmang**, its stone foundation supporting whalebone frames covered with animal skins. These dwellings were exchanged in summer for **tupik**, tents pitched near rivers or the ocean, where their owners fished, berried, hunted and embarked on whaling expeditions.

The Tlingit tribe built massive gable-roofed winter houses with sculpted cedar posts, cedar plank exteriors and polished wood floors to shelter their extended families. For ceremonial occasions, these were decorated with elaborate carved and painted screens. Sometimes 500ft in length, the cedar longhouses of the Salish of Washington and Oregon were often home to entire tribes. High-ranking chiefs had their own handsome cedarwood dwellings.

Chief Weah's House, Massett, BC (c.1850)

Oregon Historical Society, ORHI5651

Pioneer Architecture – Early prospectors often braved the winters in one-room shacks built around potbellied stoves, later followed by homesteaders' log cabins with newspaper-lined walls. With the economic boom in the late 19C came pragmatic brick mercantile buildings, cobblestone streets and, for the wealthy, elaborate Victorian mansions, many of which have been restored and are still in use. PORT TOWNSEND, Washington, is particularly blessed with the latter. For the citizen of average means, bungalows were an affordable alternative to standard middle-class dwellings. By 1910 these small, single-story houses with verandahs and fireplaces were much in evidence, particularly in Vancouver.

Discovery of gold in the Sierras brought about the urgent need for lighthouses along the Pacific's rocky, irregular coastline, with its heavy fog and fierce winter storms. By the 1850s, over a dozen had been built, some graced with octagonal freestanding towers. Many remain in use today.

Visual Arts – The first to provide visual records of the area's landscape and peoples were maritime artists who accompanied coastal expeditions. The most famous of these was Londoner **John Webber** (1751-1793), who sailed with Capt. James Cook. Though professionals were usually chosen for the task, ships occasionally took on talented amateurs like Jose Cardero, a cabin boy on a Spanish voyage to Alaska and Vancouver in 1791. Next came itinerant painter-signmakers and a few hardy photographers who set up shop in gold and timber boom towns.

Twentieth-century painters of repute include **Mark Tobey** (1890-1976), who was influenced by Asian calligraphy; Oregon-born octogenarian **Morris Graves**, known for emotional depictions of Northwest subjects; Washington native and landscape painter **Richard Gilkey** (1926-1997); and **Edward Kienholz** (1927-1994), also Washington-born, who earned international recognition with his mixed-media constructions. The **Pilchuck Glass School**, established outside Seattle in 1971, has led to the region's reputation as the "Venice of contemporary blown glass." **Dale Chihuly** (p 204), one of the school's founders, has been honored with a retrospective of his work at the Louvre in Paris.

Alaska's spectacular topography began attracting painters in the 19C, and by the early 20C several had taken up residence. Chief among them was Brooklyn-born **Sydney Laurence** (1865-1940), whose large-scale romantic landscapes are prominently displayed in Alaskan museums. Inuit artists,

Chihuly Glass Art, Union Station, Tacoma, WA

© Robert Holmes

whose images ranged from realism to native mythology, began gaining prominence between the two world wars. The work of Florence Nupok Malewotkuk and George Aden Ahgupuk, among others, adorns everything from paper to sealskin, reindeer and moose hides.

Performing Arts – During the 1990s, Seattle garnered considerable attention as the birthplace of the so-called **grunge movement**, exemplified by the success of the phenomenally popular rock group Nirvana, formed in 1986 by Washington native Kurt Cobain. Other musical offerings include the opera houses, symphony orchestras and ballet companies found in the major cities. Among popular annual events are the **Mount Hood Jazz Festival** in Gresham near Portland, which attracts top-billed stars every August; Sitka, Alaska's, **Summer Music Festival**, a series of chamber music performances in June; and Portland's **Waterfront Blues Festival** on the July 4th weekend. British Columbia is home to ethnic music from around the world at the **Vancouver Folk Music Festival** and Victoria's TerrifVic Jazz Party, featuring top Dixieland bands. For decades, people have flocked to the Pacific Northwest for Ashland, Oregon's internationally acclaimed **Shakespeare Festival** *(p 133)*, a program of both classic and contemporary plays that runs mid-February through early November and draws more than 100,000 attendees each year.

Film and Television – Despite the Pacific Northwest's photogenic appeal, moviemakers were slow to take advantage of it as a backdrop. Two of the earliest films shot here, both in the 1920s, were *The Alaskan* (in British Columbia) and Buster Keaton's comedy classic *The General* (in Oregon). Ironically, the latter was set in Civil War-ravaged Georgia. In the 1950s, Oregon provided scenery for two Jimmy Stewart Westerns, *Bend in the River* and *The Far Country*. In the 1970s, director Bob Rafelson's cult favorite *Five Easy Pieces* made use of Washington's San Juan Islands; Milos Forman chose the Oregon State Hospital for *One Flew Over the Cuckoo's Nest*; and Michael Cimino flew Robert De Niro to Washington's Cascades for part of his Vietnam-era epic *The Deer Hunter*. *An Officer and a Gentleman* was shot in Port Townsend in the 1980s. More recently, David Lynch used Washington's logging towns and snow-capped peaks as a setting for his *Twin Peaks* TV series (1989-91).

Portland is a favorite locale for director Gus Van Sant (who was born there), though his explicit portrayals of drug addicts, hustlers and homosexuals in films such as *Drugstore Cowboy* (1989) and *My Private Idaho* (1991) made local tourism officials cringe. Bits of Seattle can be seen in *Sleepless in Seattle* (1993) and *Disclosure* (1994). Vancouver, however, wins hands down as the region's film location of choice *(p 283)*. The current popularity of "Hollywood North" can be traced back to the 1930s, when local Leon Shelly took control of Vancouver Motion Pictures and assembled a talented pool of camera operators, technical wizards, writers and directors and set a precedent for independent productions. Momentum gathered with the making of Robert Altman's *McCabe and Mrs. Miller* and Mike Nichols' *Carnal Knowledge* in the early 1970s. Popular TV series *The X-Files* was filmed in Vancouver from 1993-98. Current film and television production budgets in British Columbia bring the province hundreds of millions of dollars and generate hundreds of jobs. The Vancouver International Film Festival attracts top directors and films every October, as do the Portland International Film Festival (February through March) and the Seattle International Film Festival in May.

Literature – The region's rich oral tradition can be traced back at least 1,000 years. Many of the local Native American legends and folk tales feature the mischievous exploits of semi-deities like Raven and Coyote the Trickster. Among the earliest published writings about the Pacific Northwest were the exploration journals of Capt. Meriwether Lewis and his fellow officer William Clark. Joaquin Miller recorded his early 20C impressions of the region in drawings, diaries and poetry, while John Muir's *Travels in Alaska* (1915) brought the frozen hinterlands to the attention of outsiders. Novelist Jack London wrote about the Klondike Gold Rush of the 1890s and about the north country's rugged life in *The Call of the Wild* (1903) and *White Fang* (1906), and Ernest Haycox achieved a national following for his cowboy Westerns, many of which were first serialized in the pulp magazines of the 1920s and 30s.

If there is a recurring theme in the area's literature, it is the influence of the Pacific Coast's rugged and varied landscape, so different from the Eastern Seaboard or from Europe. This influence is evident, in varying degrees, in the work of contemporary novelists Ken Kesey (*Sometimes a Great Notion*, 1964), Margaret Craven (*I Heard the Owl Call My Name*, 1974), Tom Robbins (*Even Cowgirls Get the Blues*, 1976), Tobias Wolff (*This Boy's Life*, 1989), David Guterson (*Snow Falling on Cedars*, 1995), a few of Raymond Carver's short stories and in the work of poets Theodore Roethke, Richard Hugo, David Wagoner and William Stafford.

*Consult Michelin map **493 Western USA/ Western Canada** for sights mentioned in this guide.*

People

From the first unrecorded trek of early humans across the Siberia-Alaska land bridge to America's 19C western movement, from the gold rushes that opened remote places to America's postwar population shift west, migration has been a recurrent theme in the region's saga. In recent decades newcomers have been drawn by the Pacific Northwest's promise of escape from many urban ills amidst landscapes of exceptional beauty. People also keep coming for economic gain and for the chance to work and recreate in a region known for practical liberalism and populist sentiment, and they share with established residents a determination not to repeat the mistakes of other places.

Rancher, Fraser River Valley, BC

© Robert Holmes

But migration itself often works against those good intentions. Oregon and Washington expect at least another two million people to arrive by 2015—a 22 percent increase over present numbers. And old-timers in the Seattle-Tacoma and Portland-Willamette Valley areas have watched in dismay as housing prices have ratcheted up, driven by cash-rich newcomers from financially inflated out-of-state metropolitan areas. British Columbia is experiencing influxes for the same reasons; many Canadians perceive their part of the Pacific Northwest as offering a new beginning in a familiar cultural setting—and a temperate and scenic one as well. Population increase rates in Vancouver (currently running about 1.5 percent annually) roughly match those of Seattle and Portland, with all three cities reporting significantly increased competition for jobs. Alaska, as with most everything, marches to its own and very different demographic drummer. During the 1970s and 80s its population, recently estimated at about 614,000, increased by more than 36 percent—nearly four times the national growth rate. Still, Alaska boasts the country's lowest human density, counting about one resident per square mile; Oregon claims 32 and Washington 82.

Race and Ethnicity – The higher the latitude, the more one encounters multiculturalism. Below the Canadian border Caucasians dominate the population, though much more so in Oregon than in Washington. Oregon has nine federally recognized tribes and a Native American populace of about 39,000 enrolled tribal members—less than 1.2 percent of its citizens. Roughly 9 of every 10 are urban dwellers, and relatively few live on tribally-owned trust lands. Seattle's emergence as a major American "window city" to Pacific Rim commerce and tourism accounts for the Puget Sound area's burgeoning Asian population. Over 81,000 Washingtonians consider themselves Native Americans, most of them members of the Yakama, Pend d'Oreille, Spokane or Makah tribes. As in Oregon, the majority live outside tribal lands.

British Columbia has always stood apart demographically from Canada as a whole, in which about 22 percent of people claim French origins. In British Columbia they account for a mere 1.3 percent of the populace. The province also, unlike the rest of Canada, has fewer Catholics than Protestants. These, however, are nearly invisible differences. Much more evident are the province's generally well-assimilated Italian, German, Polish, Spanish, Portuguese, Punjabi, Ukrainian and Dutch communities, where homeland ties and heritage are cherished. In recent years, an unprecedented immigration of people from Hong Kong and China has so dramatically expanded existing Chinese communities in Vancouver (and to a lesser extent Victoria) that over 250,000 of British Columbia's nearly 300,000 residents of Chinese descent cite Chinese as their first language. The influx has been remarkably frictionless, mainly because many of the émigrés brought capital, professional training, business acumen and English language skills.

Not ignored, but certainly not in so bright a spotlight, are the province's aboriginal people, about 83 percent of whom reside in outlying rural areas. In Canada's 1986 census, 61,125 British Columbians claimed Native roots. In the 1991 count,

74,420 responded in kind-and in 1996 the total grew to 139,665, leading authorities to conclude that increased pride, not natural increase, was primarily responsible for the otherwise inexplicable rise. Still, that same year only 1,330 respondents claimed Cree as a mother tongue, while a scant 45 cited Inuktitut or Inuit, a curiously low number in a region where maps bear hundreds of ancient place names and native arts are a pervasive motif, and also a source of worry to those who fear an eventual fading away of the region's oldest cultural heritage.

Alaska's 86,000 aboriginal people are even less integrated into the urban mainstream; many live in isolated tribal communities and support themselves in part by catching fish and sea mammals and by herding reindeer. Alaska's principal American Indian groups are the Athabascan-speaking Indians of the interior, and the Haida, Tlingit and Tsimshian of the southeast. The **Aleut**, who are closely related to the **Inuit**, live on the Alaska Peninsula and on the Aleutian and Shumagin islands. Native cultural ties, however, extend much further. Prior to statehood in 1959, representatives of Alaska's tribes—facing difficult negotiations with federal agencies—sought advice from Washington's Yakama, whose aggressive assertion (usually in state and federal courts) of property, mineral and fishing rights under their hard-won 19C treaty gained them the respect of tribes throughout the Pacific Northwest, and turned their spokespeople into skilled negotiators.

Recreation

The Pacific Northwest's natural places—its mountain ranges, beaches, rain forests, rivers and interior deserts—are the region's top draws. Oregon and Washington hold four national parks, Alaska eight, including Wrangell-St. Elias, the nation's biggest (six times the area of Yellowstone). Of British Columbia's six national parks, two are in the southwest: Vancouver Island's Pacific Rim, with old-growth rain forest and significant archaeological sites, and verdant Gwaii Haanas in the Queen Charlottes, a World Heritage Site including A 138-island seabird sanctuary abounding with wildlife and steeped in Haida Indian heritage.

For decades, sightseeing and taking photographs from an automobile window or the deck of a ferry were the main activities of most visitors to the far North. On the shores of Washington and Oregon, locals and tourists alike enjoyed beachcombing, surf fishing and camping. Inland, the most active pursuits were fly-casting, hunting and dude ranching. Today, wildlife-watching, wilderness hiking and camping, mountain bicycling, kayaking, mountain climbing and white-water rafting are common pursuits, widely offered by licensed outfitters who provide all required equipment. Strong prevailing breezes and sheltered water make for reliable windsurfing on the Columbia River Gorge and Puget Sound inlets like Hood Canal.

Across the River – Rough-and-tumble terrain and plenty of water provide Oregon, Washington and British Columbia with nearly a dozen streams where **rafters** and skilled **kayakers** can brave white water. In Oregon, most guides prefer the dorylike Mackenzie River boat for negotiating the Deschutes River, which threads a remote canyon through desert and Warm Springs Indian lands to the Columbia, and for zigzagging down the boulder-strewn Rogue, which spills out into the Pacific at Gold Beach. Washington's most interesting and challenging waters are found in Olympic National Park, where the rapids of the Elwha, the Hoh and the Queets corkscrew through rain forests. Inland, the Skagit thrashes through verdant coastal country; farther east beyond the Cascades, the Wenatchee, Skagit and Yakima are gentle enough to permit kayakers of intermediate levels to get downstream without undue mishap. Vancouver is the jumping-off place for rafting the Fraser, whose steep canyon once stymied railroad builders, and also for convenient day-long guided floats down segments of the Chilliwack, the Lillooet and the Thompson. Alaska's Kenai Peninsula offers river-running options just south of Anchorage.

Into the Trees – The Pacific Northwest is etched with thousands of miles of well-maintained hiking trails. The best-known is the **Pacific Crest Trail**, a 2,638mi path from Mexico to Canada that closely follows the ridgelines of the Cascade Range through Oregon and Washington to British Columbia at an average elevation of 5,000ft. The Oregon-Washington segment takes about two months; most hikers, however, access the route from trailheads in state and national park campgrounds and walk a stretch of it for its lofty panoramas and solitude. Oregon's **Coast Trail** system explores the state's Pacific shore. The **Timberline Trail** (p 90) circling Mt. Hood features A 40mi-long spectrum of alpine terrain, including glaciers, and shares a segment with the Pacific Crest Trail. Washington's hikers rate Olympic National Park's **Hoh River Trail**'s route through rain forest, and the glaciated segments of Mt. Rainier National Park's 93mi **Wonderland Trail** loop, among the state's finest. Trails radiate from Vancouver's fringe into terrain of varying difficulty and unvarying beauty. On Vancouver Island, the premiere footpath is Pacific Rim National Park's 48mi **Coast Trail**, which wanders along an utterly wild ocean beach. Much of Alaska, including renowned Denali National Park, remains wilderness, open for exploration by only the most intrepid hikers.

Sea Kayaking in the San Juan Islands

Into the Sea – Chilly currents and high surf year-round discourage ocean swimming—even in late June, water temperatures off the Oregon coast and in the Gulf of Alaska hover around 45°F, with the warmest readings (in the high 50s) found off British Columbia and Washington. Still, pellucid waters and pristine shorelines from Washington's Olympic National Park coastal strip and the San Juan Islands to Alaska's Panhandle make for some of North America's finest sea-kayaking and cold-water scuba diving. Sheltered inlets in Puget Sound and off Victoria and Vancouver and the Inside Passage make for usually placid sailing.

Onto the Slopes – The undisputed queen of Pacific Northwest ski areas is British Columbia's WHISTLER—a 2010 Winter Olympics host candidate—with runs and facilities consistently topping ski magazine reader polls. Good late spring snow conditions draw huge crowds to Oregon's Mt. Hood and its five resorts, where snowboarding schools often stay open into the summer. Washington's Snowqualmie Pass ski bowl profits from proximity to Seattle, while Mt. Baker, shouldered up against the vast Yakama Indian Nation, retains an off-the-beaten-path ambience. The region's abundant snowfall and myriad network of logging and forest service roads make for some of the most convenient cross-country skiing in America.

Spectator Sports – Football and basketball draw the biggest crowds between Portland and Vancouver. Among football teams, Seattle's Seahawks and the Canadian Football League's B.C. Lions enjoy loyal followings, as do the University of Washington Huskies and the University of Oregon Ducks. The region holds three National Basketball Association teams—the Portland Trail Blazers, the Seattle SuperSonics and the Vancouver Grizzlies. During the hockey season *(Oct–Apr)*, the region's strongest team is usually the National Hockey League's Vancouver Canucks; Portland's Winter Hawks and the Seattle Thunderbirds are known for scrappy play in the American Hockey League.

The Seattle Mariners are the Pacific Northwest's only Major League baseball club, but Vancouver's Canadians and Tacoma's Rainiers provide top-tier AAA Minor League action. Top-drawer soccer has arrived; the Portland Pride, Vancouver 86ers and Seattle Sounders compete under the American Professional Soccer League banner, and rising attendance suggests that the sport is capturing a new generation of fans.

Addresses, telephone numbers, opening hours and prices published in this guide are accurate at press time. We apologize for any inconvenience resulting from outdated information. Please send us your comments:

Michelin Travel Publications
Editorial Department
P. O. Box 19001
Greenville, SC 29602-9001

Cuisine

Pacific Northwest cooking reflects the region's heritage—a lively mix of Native Americans, French settlers, New Englanders, Scandinavians, Germans, Italians and Asians. Thanks to a diverse topography and climate, almost everything short of citrus grows here, and fine dining has a long tradition. A century ago, locals were feasting on everything from curries, blueberry catsup, alder-smoked salmon and asparagus to roast elk, venison stew, pear butter and bear steak with chanterelles.

The region is known for its abundant berries—cranberries, strawberries, raspberries, boysenberries, loganberries, huckleberries and marionberries. Berries in pies and cobblers are a traditional favorite. Here too is the continent's major source of apples (Granny Smith, Macintosh, Newton Pippins, Red and Golden Delicious) and pears (Bartlett, Red Bartlett, Bosc, Seckel, Anjou, Comice, and Eldorado). Washington's Yakima Valley boasts more fruit trees (including plums, peaches, quince, apricots and at least eight kinds of cherries) than any other place in the US. The forests and meadows are abundant with some 50 different edible wild mushrooms, including shitakes, morels, chanterelles, snowy matsutakes and boletes, and these turn up in a variety of sauces, gravies, soups and pastas.

Chinook salmon, **Dungeness crab** and **Alaskan King crab** are three of the region's more famous seafood specialties. Other fare includes albacore tuna, lingcod, clams, scallops, shrimp and mussels (grown suspended beneath rafts in Puget Sound). **Oysters** are a $20-million-a-year industry that began in the mid-1800s. Native Olympia oysters, once close to extinction from over-harvesting and pollution, have made a modest comeback; the larger Pacific oysters, originally imported from Japan, are very popular. Unique to the area is the **geoduck** (GOO-ee-duck), the world's largest clam, which averages two to three pounds but has been known to reach thirteen. A regional cookbook published in 1914 suggests the following tools for harvesting geoducks: "a pair of gum boots, a gunny sack and a spade," then adds, "They bite best when the tide is low."

Fish Vendors, Pike Place Market, Seattle, WA

Connie Coleman/Tony Stone Images

Also particular to the Pacific Northwest are sweet **Walla Walla onions**, which many insist can only be appreciated raw. **Hazelnuts** are an important commercial crop here, as are peppermint and spearmint—used for everything from foods to toothpastes, mouthwashes and medicines. Cow and goat milk cheeses are plentiful, including Oregon's distinctive **Oregon Blue** and famed **Tillamook cheddar**.

Although the region's wine industry is only about three decades old, the vineyards of Oregon, Washington and British Columbia are garnering both national and international recognition. Prior to the 1980s, the Pacific Northwest was believed by many to

© Dianne Dietrich Leis

Wine Tasting, Willamette Valley, OR

be too damp and cold to produce Vitis vinifera grapes, the source of the world's great wines. But eventually it was discovered that the area's many microclimates could produce world-class whites and reds, particularly **Pinot Noirs**; they tend to be more acidic than California wines, and the locals like them that way. During the last decade or two, microbreweries have gained in popularity. They produce a fascinating selection of beers and ales, some of which incorporate such untraditional ingredients as wheat, blueberries, apricots or pumpkin.

■ Further Reading

Glory Days of Logging/ Action in the Big Woods, British Columbia to California by Ralph W. Andrews 1994

Northwest Passages: A Literary Anthology of the Pacific Northwest from Coyote Tales to Roadside Attractions edited by Bruce Barcott 1994

Iditarod Country: Exploring the Route of The Last Great Race by Tricia Brown 1998

Encyclopedia of Northwest Music by James Bush 1999

Gold Rush Gateway: Skagway and Dyea, Alaska by Stan Cohen 1986

Experiences in a Promised Land: Essays in Pacific Northwest History by G. Thomas Edwards 1986

Gone Whaling: A Search for Orcas in Northwest Waters by Douglas Hand 1996

The Dust of Everyday Life: An Epic Poem of the Pacific Northwest by Jana Harris 1997

Astorian Adventure: The Journal of Alfred Seton 1811-1815 edited by Robert F. Jones 1993

The Gale Encyclopedia of Native American Tribes, Volume IV edited by Sharon Malinowski 1998

Deep Down Things: Poems of the Inland Pacific Northwest edited by Ron McFarland 1991

One Woman's West: Recollections of the Oregon Trail and Settling of the Northwest Country by Martha Gay Masterson 1990

Skid Road: An Informal Portrait of Seattle by Murray Morgan 1982

The Interwoven Lives of George Vancouver, Archibald Menzies, Joseph Whidbey and Peter Puget: Exploring the Pacific Northwest by John Michael Naish 1996

Geology of the Pacific Northwest by Elizabeth L. Orr 1996

Connoisseur's Handbook of the Wines of California and the Pacific Northwest by Charles E. Olken and Norman S. Roby 1998

Alaska's History: The People, Land and Events of the North Country by Harry Ritter 1993

Seattle Past to Present by Roger Sale 1976

Totem Poles by Pat Kramer 1998

Looking at Totem Poles by Hilary Stewart 1993

Looking at Indian Art of the Northwest Coast by Hilary Stewart 1979

Field Guide to the Pacific Salmon by Robert Steelquist 1992

Cannon Beach

© Dianne Dietrich Leis

Oregon

Introduction to Oregon

Canadian Tourism Commission, Paris

Once upon a time, "Oregon Country" referred to virtually the whole of northwestern America, from the Rocky Mountains to the ocean. If the state that now bears the name is much reduced in size, it is little reduced in spirit. It still embodies the West of wide-open dreams, sweeping ranchlands, sky-piercing mountains and a deeply cherished independence.

Bounded by Washington and the mighty Columbia— "River of the West"—on its northern border, by the twisting Snake along much of its eastern border with Idaho, and by California and Nevada to the south, the rectangle of the Beaver State stretches across 97,073sq mi, making it the 10th largest state in the US, but its 3.3 million residents rank it only 29th in population. Its spectacular, 362mi-long Pacific coastline is peppered with quaint villages and fine beaches, though its major port, Portland, lies inland on the Willamette. The majority of Oregon's residents live along the lush western lands that end in the towering front of the Cascade Range. Beyond the Cascades, eastern Oregon is still an untrammeled world where animals are almost as plentiful as people, and nature—with help from farmers and ranchers—rules.

Oregon State Facts

Capital: Salem

Land Area: 96,000 square miles

Population: 3,281,974

Nickname: Beaver State

Motto: *Alis volat Propriis* ("She Flies With Her Own Wings")

State Flower: Oregon grape

Geographical Notes

Geologic Past – Some 30 million years ago, much of present-day Oregon lay beneath a vast sea that covered large parts of the Pacific Northwest. Below the sea, however, the tectonic plates on which the landmasses float were caught in a dynamic struggle, as the North American landmass shoved west into ocean plates, causing them to subduct, or plow under it. Forced down toward the earth's internal furnace, the subducting plates melted and their molten rock bubbled upward through volcanic vents. About 15 to 20 million years ago, this molten rock began to feed the peaks that would become the Cascade Range, now spining the interior of the state from north to south. As the process of subduction and volcanism continued (and continues today), the basin and range complex in the east began to push west about five million years ago, inching the Klamath Mountains and the Coast Range farther west. Through these processes basaltic lavas spread and thickened across the land to form the Columbia River Plateau. Also sculpting the land were recurring ice ages. With the peaking of the most recent ice age, some 18,000 years ago, glaciers blanketed much of present-day Oregon, incising the mountains and churning out vast cavities in the landscape. About 12,000 years ago, the glaciers began to leave the lowland, and the valleys, ravines and holes they had gouged slowly filled with lakes, bays and sounds. They still claimed the high peaks, however, and their icy remnants can be seen there even today. Though the age of the glaciers gradually ended, the drama of land building and blasting did not. About 6,600 years ago, a huge volcanic explosion on Mount Mazama left behind a tremendous crater that eventually filled to become CRATER LAKE. To this day, western Oregon remains tectonically active, part of the volatile Pacific Ring of Fire that is plagued by volcanism, earthquakes and other cataclysms caused by earth's ever-shifting forces.

Regional Landscapes – Oregon's terrain is characteristic of the Pacific Northwest: a lush western coastal area that is separated from the drier eastern expanse of the state by a backbone of high mountains that cuts the land from north to south. Extending 30mi to 50mi inland and north to south along the arcing Pacific shoreline, the **Coastal Region** is furrowed by the low, forested **Coast Ranges**, whose deep ravines and valleys make for a dramatic landscape. To the south the range merges with the somewhat higher **Klamath Mountains**. Spurs from these ranges create towering coastal headlands that frame sandy pocket beaches pounded by Pacific surf.

Flowing into the Pacific and forming the northern boundary of the state, the **Columbia River** has cut a spectacular gorge that extends far inland. Bounded by the Coast Range and the Cascades, the verdant **Willamette Valley** stretches more than 100mi south to north across some 30mi of level ground, watered by the Willamette River and its tributaries, the Yamhill and Tualatin rivers. Its east side is guarded by the **Cascade Range**, which forms a north-south spine running through the interior of the state and north into Washington. Oregon's somewhat lower Cascade peaks still reach heights of 10,000ft, topping off at 11,235ft **Mount Hood** in the north.

East of the Cascades, the high **Central Plateau** blankets more than half the state, with the north-flowing Deschutes River draining its north-central section. The wedge of the **Wallowa-Umatilla** and **Blue Mountains**, whose elevations range from 2,000ft to 10,000ft, separates the northeastern **Columbia Plateau** from the southeastern plateau regions. Along the state's northeastern edge, the **Snake River**, the Columbia's largest tributary, forms the boundary with neighboring Idaho. The high, **Great Sandy Desert** and **Harney**

Basin on the southeast are chopped by faulted mountains, escarpments and truncated rivers. Geologically, they are part of the Great Basin that extends east to Wyoming and south to California.

Climate – Though temperatures along the 300mi length of the state do vary somewhat from north to south, the more radical climatic differentiation occurs from west to east. The marine climate along the coast, on the west side of the Cascades, is temperate (January temperatures of about 45°F, and July temperatures in the 70s), but rainy and often stormy weather prevails from late November through March. Annual precipitation in the coastal region averages about 70in, while the Willamette and Rogue valleys receive about 6in a month in the rainy season and very little in the dry summers. Oregon's abundant western precipitation occurs because, as the saturated ocean air climbs up and over the Cascade Range, it dumps its precipitation on the western slopes. While snowfall at higher elevations can be significant, scant snow falls along the coast. The eastern side of the range, which lies in the so-called rain shadow, experiences much drier weather but greater temperature fluctuations and serious snowfall accumulations. Lying against the east side of the Cascades, central Oregon receives heavy summer rains and winter snows in the mountains and near their bases; nighttime temperatures dip to the teens, while summer temperatures can climb into the 80s. Eastern Oregon's high desert has a much more severe climate. Here, winter temperatures can plummet to far below freezing, and summer thermometer readings easily soar to 90°F.

Historical Notes

The First Immigrants – The earliest signs of humans in this area are slim but ancient—a 13,000-year-old pair of sandals found in a cave in central Oregon. Anthropological finds indicate that the eastern part of the state and attendant stretches of the Columbia were settled first, before early hunters and gatherers crossed the Cascades to the western side of the state. Over eons, various Native American groups filtered in from surrounding areas: Shoshone speakers (Paiute) from northern California and Athabascan and Coast Salish speakers from the north and west. By the time Europeans began making their first tentative contacts with the area, the great Northwest Indian tribes—the Cayuse, Nez Percé, Klamaths, Modocs and others-had long been flourishing off the bounty of this land.

Spanish navigators sailing up from Mexico in the mid-16C were probably the first Europeans to lay eyes on what is now Oregon, but it wasn't until the 1770s that serious exploration of the area began. In 1775 Spanish navigator, **Bruno Heceta**, sighted a large river flowing into the Pacific, but the daunting sandbar at its entrance prohibited him from exploring it. Nonetheless, he claimed the area for Spain. Soon thereafter, in 1778-80, Britain's Capt. James Cook reconnoitered along the Oregon coast, and one of his captains, **George Vancouver**, came again in 1792, making a detailed exploration of the Pacific coast.

Ultimately, it was an American, Capt. **Robert Gray**, who sailed into the elusive and legendary "River of the West" in 1792. An industrious Boston trader involved in the silk trade with China, Gray had heard of the river, particularly from Vancouver, who had spotted it but taken little interest. Gray was more curious, sailing into its mouth and naming the great river Columbia, for his ship, the *Columbia Rediviva*. To the Indians it had long been the Ouragon (a native word whose exact meaning is now lost). While Gray rechristened the river, the name Oregon came to encompass a broad territory that extended from the Rocky Mountains to the Pacific.

Into these rich lands came explorers **Meriwether Lewis** and **William Clark** in 1805. Dispatched by President Thomas Jefferson to explore the newly acquired Louisiana Purchase lands and to hunt for a river route that would link the continent from coast to coast, the Lewis and Clark Expedition had crossed America overland, mapping, exploring and observing the Native American tribes as it went. Near present-day Astoria, the group reached the endpoint of their journey and established a rustic camp, Fort Clatsop *(p 117)*, where they spent a "wet, cold, and disagreeable" winter. Despite the weather, Clark described parts of the Pacific coastline as "the grandest and most pleasing prospects which my eyes ever surveyed."

The Fight for the Oregon Country – Other Europeans following in Lewis and Clark's footsteps agreed. Fur traders were the first to arrive, and by 1810 the Canadian North West Company had set up a post. A year later American John Jacob Astor's Pacific Fur Company had established Fort Astoria at the mouth of the Columbia. Predictably, dispute quickly arose between Britain and the US over claims to the lucrative fur trade, and, during the War of 1812, the Astorians, threatened by increased tension with Britain, sold their fort to the North West Company. In 1818, with the war over, the two countries reached a precarious agreement to exploit the fur trade jointly. But Britain's Hudson's Bay Company, which had joined with the North West Company, soon emerged as the strongest non-native presence in the area, with the closest ties to Indian traders. From its Fort Vancouver headquarters, at the mouth of the Willamette River, the company and its powerful chief agent, Dr. John McLoughlin, acted as the unofficial law in the Oregon Country.

That remained the case until the mid-1830s, when American missionaries, fur traders and settlers began slowly filtering in, many settling in the fertile Willamette Valley, bringing with them such diseases as measles and smallpox that decimated the native population. By the 1840s, a steady stream of hopeful pioneers were trudging west on the Oregon Trail to what seemed like a promised land. With tensions again growing between American and British claims to the region, the presidential election of 1844 focused on the "Oregon question," and victorious candidate James K. Polk took as his slogan, "Fifty-four forty or fight"—a reference to the boundary parallel Americans insisted the British observe. In 1846, a treaty established America's right to the territory south of the 49th parallel. But such diplomatic niceties were never brought to bear on Native American rights to their traditional lands. European diseases had already reduced Indian populations, and settler encroachment continually forced them into smaller areas, even as erstwhile promises made to protect their rights were broken.

In 1847 a group of Cayuse massacred prominent missionary Dr. Marcus Whitman, his wife and other settlers in Walla Walla, an action that captured the attention of the US Congress. As early as 1838 American settlers had petitioned Congress to admit Oregon to the Union, in order to provide residents with the protection of government. In the wake of the massacre, Congress complied and in 1848 the vast Oregon country became a US territory.

From Territory to State – The Oregon Territory's population quickly increased. Settlers streamed in, drawn by the Donation Land Claim Act of 1850, which guaranteed new arrivals large, free parcels of land (320 acres before 1852, 160 acres from 1852-55). At the same time, the native peoples were forced off their lands and made to resettle east of the Cascades.

Though two-thirds of Oregon's male population raced to California after the discovery of gold in 1849, the Oregon farmers who stayed behind found a rising market for their produce. In the 1850s Oregonians experienced their own brief gold rush in the Rogue Valley, but more important to the economy were the discoveries made in nearby Washington, Montana and Idaho. As the goldfields flourished, so did Oregon, with Portland becoming a major supply center. Though its fortunes continued to rise, the size of the territory did not. In 1853 the vast lands north of the Columbia separated to form Washington Territory. Nonetheless, in 1859, the now reduced Oregon Territory became the 33rd state admitted to the Union.

Oregon remained geographically isolated until 1883, when the Northern Pacific Railroad at last linked the state to the rest of the continent. With the coming of the railroads, Oregonians turned from strictly farming to lumbering, and by the turn of the century, the state was third in timber production. During World War I, Oregon spruce became a prized commodity in the manufacture of aircraft, and shipbuilding also flourished. Ranching, too, became a big business on the vast grasslands of eastern Oregon, while apple and pear orchards blossomed profusely in the Hood River Valley. In this land of abundance, even the waterways yielded up bountiful harvests of salmon, and canneries lined the lower Columbia.

With so much natural bounty, Oregonians weathered the Depression of the 1930s better than the industrialized states of the Northeast and Midwest. The federal government also helped to mitigate the tough economic times, providing public works projects jobs, particularly in building dams along the Columbia.

As the nation entered World War II, a shipbuilding boom jerked Oregon back into prosperity. The call for Oregon lumber lasted long after the war, making the state the nation's largest producer by mid-century. But the war also brought disgrace, as Oregon's many Japanese-American families, along with others in the nation, were forced from their homes and into internment camps for the duration of the war.

Throughout the 20C, Oregon has been at the forefront of social reform. As early as 1915, the state enacted workmen's compensation laws, women's suffrage and laws to protect working mothers. In the 1990s, it led the way in pioneering health reform laws. But it has been unable satisfactorily to resolve the controversy between late 20C environmental awareness and the traditional pioneer spirit of independence and resource exploitation. The "spotted owl" controversy that raged in the late 1980s, in which the logging of a forest was prohibited to protect the habitat of the endangered bird, was emblematic of Oregon's woes. In a state blessed with such enormous natural beauty, all citizens have an opinion on how best to appreciate their land.

Economy

Since mid-century, when it ranked as the nation's largest timber producer, the state has been gradually diversifying its economy. With the recession of the early 1980s and the resulting downturn in timber sales, the push to diversify intensified, and now the state's economy is fueled by many factors. While traditional farming, logging and fishing are still pursued, other industrial interests have made inroads into the Oregon workplace. Despite these low-key pockets of industrialization, the state still feels largely rural, particularly on the dry eastern side of the Cascades.

Natural Resources – Though timber is no longer king here, forest resources, including lumber, paper and other wood products, account for five percent or more of the state economy. Until 10 years ago, Oregon was the nation's largest producer of plywood, but it no longer holds that ranking. Fishing, too, another traditional mainstay in the economy, has suffered in recent years, owing to declining salmon harvests caused by environmental factors and more protective legislation. However, small sole proprietors as well as larger commercial vessels still ply Oregon's coastal waters for bottom dwellers like halibut and rockfish.

Industry – As with much of the West Coast, Oregon has benefited greatly from the high-tech industry. Intel's main plant for designing and producing the Pentium chip is located in the Portland suburb of Hillsboro. Other manufacturing companies produce semiconductor chips, calculators and such computer peripherals as printers.

In addition, metal processing for steel and aluminum thrives in Oregon because the state's navigable waterways allow easy, relatively inexpensive transport of raw materials by water. Also fueling the industry is the abundance of inexpensive energy from hydroelectric dams along the Columbia and from imported Canadian natural gas. In recent years, the metal-processing industry has suffered a downturn, owing to the availability of cheaper metals in Japan and Russia. Oregon is also a significant producer of transportation equipment, such as motor coaches and industrial rail cars. In the service industries, **tourism** contributes a healthy 2.5 to 3 percent of the total economy, as visitors come to partake of the state's renowned dramatic beaches, snow-capped peaks, myriad lakes and sylvan gorges.

Agriculture – Though the Beaver State was founded by farmers and ranchers, those traditional businesses now account for less than five percent of the total state economy. But cattle and calf ranching still goes on east of the Cascades, wheat fields still blanket stretches of the northeast and field crops and dairy products are produced throughout the state. In April and May apple and pear trees put on a flowery show in the Willamette Valley. But new agricultural products have replaced traditional ones. On the wet side of the state west of the Cascades, nurseries flourish, growing ornamentals and garden plants. In addition to these nurseries, Oregon's tree farms contribute the nation's largest harvest of Christmas trees, and its seed producers are major suppliers of grass seeds for lawns and golf courses throughout the nation. In recent decades, Oregon vineyards have also earned a respected place among national wine producers.

The State Today

Though the urban culture of the late 20C has strongly impacted Oregon's neighbors to the north and south (Washington and California), Oregonians have proudly nurtured and maintained the more independent, pioneering spirit of their forbears, and even major urban hubs like Portland have a friendly, unpretentious atmosphere. The state has also remained surprisingly homogeneous; almost 93 percent of its **population** is Caucasian, some 4 percent Hispanic, about 2.8 percent Asian and less than 2 percent either Native American or black.

The stunning natural beauty of much of the state has become both Oregon's blessing and its curse. Traditional ranching and timbering interests are anxious to curb what they see as overweening interference from the federal government and from environmental groups-interference they believe will severely restrict personal freedoms, particularly regarding how one administers one's own lands. This anxiety has spawned an active militia movement in some parts of the state. Visitors to Oregon, on the other hand, may enjoy the results of such land protection, as it has preserved such natural spectacles as the towering Oregon Dunes along the coast, the pristine wildness of Crater Lake, the twisted landforms of Newberry National Volcanic Monument and the rich wetlands of the Malheur National Wildlife Refuge. In fact, three of this state's four borders are at least partially defined by corridors of natural beauty: the Pacific coast in the west, the raging Snake River and Hell's Canyon along much of the border with Idaho, and the renowned Columbia River and its gorge on the northern border. Aside from the state's natural beauty, ASHLAND's annual Shakespeare Festival draws audiences from across the country and PENDLETON's famous rodeo offers visitors a chance to revisit the traditions of the West.

Sights described in this guide are rated:

★★★	*Worth the trip*
★★	*Worth a detour*
★	*Interesting*

Portland Area

Portland Skyline with Mount Hood/©Dianne Dietrich Leis

Spread over a verdant landscape of fields, rolling hills and forested basaltic ridges in the northern Willamette (Wil-LAM-ette) Valley, Portland and its neighboring counties lie between the majestic Cascade Mountains and the Coast Range. The Willamette River flows north through the valley and joins the Columbia, America's second-largest river, at the northern edge of the city. Vancouver, Washington, on the river's north bank, is also considered part of the greater Portland metropolitan area. The region's mild (if frequently wet) climate is strongly influenced by the Pacific Ocean 78mi to the west.

Snow-capped Mt. Hood, the tallest mountain (11,245ft) in the state, is the area's most famous topographical icon. Surrounded by the 1.1-million-acre Mt. Hood National Forest, this glacier-sculpted Cascade peak located some 60mi east of the city is a year-round playground. The Mt. Hood Loop *(p 90)* climbs up the mountain's western slope, providing access to ski areas, hiking trails and alpine resorts. Only 16mi east of downtown Portland lie the thundering waterfalls, fir-clad cliffs and towering rock formations of the Columbia River Gorge. In 1805 Lewis and Clark passed through the gorge on a trail-blazing journey that was instrumental in opening the Oregon Territory to American settlers.

The first part of Oregon to be settled, the lush Willamette Valley remains the region's economic and political power base. Wheat, fruits, vegetables and nuts are grown in the rich farmlands surrounding Portland, as are the garden plants, bulbs, and nursery stock that now rank as Oregon's number-one commodity. Several dozen wineries *(p 146)* producing award-winning Pinot Noirs are located in the hills of the Willamette Valley just southwest of the city. In recent years Portland's suburbs have also seen an influx of high-tech and supporting industries—so many, in fact, that the valley is sometimes referred to as "Silicon Forest."

Although the region as a whole is growing at a dizzying pace, visitors to the Portland area—home to 44 percent of the state's population—can enjoy the comforts and cultural benefits of a thriving, forward-looking city that recognizes the importance of nature in everyday life. Forests, mountains, streams and the two mighty rivers remain essential components of an urban landscape that remains wild around the edges.

54

PORTLAND★★

Michelin map 493 B 4 and map p 72-73
Population 503,891
Tourist Information ☏ 877-678-5263 or www.travelportland.com

Oregon's largest city sits at the north end of the Willamette Valley, straddling the Willamette River near its confluence with the Columbia. Spanned by a dozen distinctive bridges, the Willamette is deep enough to make Portland one of the West Coast's largest inland ports and a gateway to the Pacific Rim. The river also acts as a natural dividing line between the city's east side and its hilly, forested west side.

The natural beauty of its surroundings enhances Portland's urban vitality. Mt. Hood and the Cascades form a magisterial backdrop to a city filled with some 200 parks, gardens and wild areas. In the handsome downtown core and lively neighborhoods on both sides of the river visitors will find museums and cultural attractions, sophisticated restaurants, excellent shopping and a wealth of noteworthy historic and contemporary architecture. Smaller and less showy than Seattle, Portland downplays ostentation of any kind. Much of the city's charm lies in its relaxed atmosphere and the beauty of its setting.

Historical Notes

A Coin Toss – The site of present-day Portland was originally a small clearing in the woods on the west side of the Willamette River. It was used by Chinook Indian tribes, including the Multnomahs and the Clackamas, and French-Canadian fur traders traveling between Oregon City and Fort Vancouver, the Hudson's Bay trading headquarters on the Columbia River. Lewis and Clark camped along the Columbia Slough in what is now North Portland in 1805.

Even before the opening of the Oregon Trail in the early 1840s, trappers and homesteaders had been settling around the confluence of the two rivers. In 1843 Asa Lovejoy, a lawyer from Massachusetts, and William Overton, a drifter from Tennessee, filed a joint land claim for the riverside clearing. Overton, who lacked the 25-cent filing fee, later sold his portion to merchant and developer Francis W. Pettygrove, who wanted the new townsite to be called Portland, after his hometown in Maine. Lovejoy wanted to name it Boston. In 1845 the two New Englanders flipped a coin and the site—today's downtown—became Portland.

Territorial disputes between the US and Britain ended in 1846 when the Oregon Country was divided along the 49th parallel, the present-day northern border with Washington state. Congress established the Territorial Government of Oregon in 1848 and nearby Oregon City became its capital the following year. Under the Donation Land Claim Act, males arriving in the Oregon Territory by December 1, 1850 could claim 320 acres (twice that amount for married couples) if they agreed to cultivate the land. As a result, land-hungry pioneers—about a quarter of them from New England and New York—poured into the Willamette Valley. In 1848, when Lovejoy and Pettygrove platted the first streets, Portland had a population of about 80. Two years later, a census counted just over 800 people.

Stumps of fir trees cut down for the newly laid-out streets gave rise to the city's first nickname: Stumptown. Puddletown, another nickname, referred to the rain-filled tracks and ruts. The first plank road (part of today's Canyon Road) was laid in 1851, the same year the city was officially incorporated, providing a trade route between Portland and the farmlands of the Tualatin Valley to the southwest.

River City – Until the arrival of the transcontinental railroads in the 1880s the Willamette and Columbia rivers served as the region's main highways. Situated at the head of navigation on the Willamette, Portland quickly emerged as the region's best site for the development of a shipping port and trade center. Masted schooners and steam-driven sternwheelers crowded the waterfront. Passengers and cargo from the East Coast came in ships sailing around Cape Horn, and trade soon extended across the Pacific to China. Like other port cities during this rough, raucous era, Portland had its share of waterfront saloons, opium dens and bordellos.

The California gold rush and the rapid growth of San Francisco fueled the city's river-trade economy. Hawaiians were brought to Portland to help build ships. For area farmers, Portland was the most accessible port for shipping wheat. The region's vast conifer forests provided lumber for ships and for the new towns springing up throughout the West.

The city's progress was shared with other nearby towns on the Willamette River. In 1864 transcontinental telegraph lines reached Oregon. The West Coast's first paper mill was constructed in Oregon City in 1866, and the first iron foundry in the Pacific Northwest was established a few miles south of Portland, in 1867.

New Immigrants – A second wave of immigration, this time from Ireland, Germany, China, Japan, England, Scandinavia and Canada, started to arrive in 1860. The flatlands closest to the river were the first areas to be settled, while the main business district stood on the west side, clustered around the waterfront. East Portland, where most of the city's newly arrived foreigners and transient workers lived, was laid out in 1850-51 and incorporated in 1870; it remained a separate town until it was annexed by the City of Portland in 1891. Ferries shuttled people, livestock and goods back and forth across the Willamette.

Disastrous fires in 1872 and 1873 destroyed all of Portland's early wood-framed waterfront buildings and led to the construction of brick buildings with cast-iron facades and structural supports. A significant number of late-19C cast-iron commercial buildings still remain in the Yamhill and Skidmore/Old Town districts along First, Second and Third Avenues.

Arrival of the Railroads – Major expansion continued from 1880 until the end of the century as immigrants from around the world arrived, hoping to make their fortunes in shipping, farming, lumber and gold. By 1900, when the population had swelled to over 90,000, some 58 percent of Portland residents had either been born outside the US or were children of immigrants.

With the arrival in 1883 of the first transcontinental railroad and the completion four years later of the Portland-San Francisco line, the city's reliance on the river began to diminish. East and West Portland were joined by the Morrison Bridge, the first span across the Willamette, in 1887. By 1889 downtown streets were illuminated by electric street lamps fueled by hydropower from Willamette Falls.

The business center gradually shifted to the west, away from the waterfront, as fashionable new buildings and public institutions began to rise on downtown's Morrison Street in the 1890s. One of the city's grandest buildings, the Portland Hotel (1890), was designed by the famous New York firm of McKim, Mead & White. Demolished in the 1950s, it occupied the site of today's Pioneer Courthouse Square.

The 20th Century – Portland's population doubled between 1900 and 1910, the growth due, in large part, to the Lewis and Clark Exposition of 1905, a well-planned exercise in boosterism that introduced tens of thousands of visitors to the city. In 1903, to help prepare for the event, noted Boston landscape architect John Olmsted (stepson of Frederick Law Olmsted, who designed New York's Central Park) was hired to design a site plan for the exposition and to develop a citywide park plan. Some of Olmsted's recommendations, including the acquisition of land for Mt. Tabor Park, Laurelhurst Park, and Peninsula Park *(N. Portland Blvd. and Albina St.)*, were implemented a few years later.

Early land claims were soon being subdivided as the city experienced two major real-estate booms, one from 1905-13 and another from 1922-28. Electric trolleys carried people throughout the downtown area and to new east-side flatland neighborhoods such as Sellwood, Ladd's Addition and Irvington. Portland's first "streetcar suburbs," these east-side neighborhoods were built on streets that generally follow a straight north/south and east/west grid. Many of the new homes were modest wood-framed bungalows with open front porches and overhanging eaves, a Craftsman-derived style now known as "Old Portland."

More affluent Portlanders built homes in the "highlands" of southwest and northwest Portland on streets that curve around and rise in sharp switchbacks up the hills. Settled between 1920 and 1940, desirable areas such as Portland Heights, Willamette Heights, Arlington Heights and Council Crest (at 1,040ft the highest point in the city) boasted wonderful views of Portland, the river and the Cascade Mountains. The hill homes were often built to resemble alpine chalets, Mediterranean villas or English cottages with half-timbered facades.

The Lewis and Clark Exposition also served to stimulate rapid development of the present downtown. Tall commercial buildings with steel frames and distinctive white terra-cotta façades were constructed along the major downtown streetcar lines. Today these buildings form the Glazed Terra-Cotta Historic District.

The St. John's Bridge about 6.5mi west of downtown was one of the few structures built during the Great Depression of the 1930s, when construction in Portland came to a virtual standstill. The designer of this graceful, Gothic-inspired span dedicated in 1931 was D.B. Steinman, who also designed San Francisco's Golden Gate Bridge.

War Boom – The demand for workers in Portland's shipyards created a phenomenal wartime boom. Men and women were brought in by chartered trains from the East Coast and employed by the Kaiser shipbuilding yards in Vancouver, Washington, and Portland's shipyards. At the peak of

International Rose Test Garden

© Dianne Dietrich Leis

wartime production in 1943-44, metropolitan Portland counted some 140,000 defense workers. The city's population leapt from 501,000 to 661,000. A significant number of these workers were African-Americans who settled in North and Northeast Portland. In the 1950s and 1960s, as streetcars vanished and a car culture took over, many of Portland's oldest buildings and west-side neighborhoods were demolished to make way for highways and parking lots. Only in the late 1960s and early 1970s did the city's first high-rise towers appear on the downtown skyline.

Urban Planning – Portland's reputation as one of the country's best-planned cities dates back to 1972 when the Downtown Plan was approved by the city council. This detailed agenda, which set forth new strategies for land use, commercial development, architecture and public transportation, resulted in a series of urban renewal projects that effectively reclaimed the downtown area for pedestrians. In the following years a new light-rail system was built; a transit mall lined with trees, sculptures and fountains was constructed; a parking lot in the center of the downtown was re-fashioned into a public piazza; and the highway that ran along the downtown waterfront was replaced by Waterfront Park. Historic structures were preserved, with ordinances limiting the height of new buildings and thus protecting views of the mountains. Neil Goldschmidt, mayor from 1973-79 (Governor of Oregon 1987-91) was a vigorous proponent of the Downtown Plan and pushed additional citywide goals for neighborhood revitalization and regional planning as part of an overall growth strategy. As a result of these planning efforts, Portland's downtown has remained a vital retail, office, housing, government and entertainment center and has attracted more than $3 billion in new private investment since 1970.

Portland's Urban Growth Boundary, adopted in 1980, was designed to preserve neighboring farmlands and open spaces from unchecked commercial development. Roughly 200mi in circumference, it set aside enough land for 20 years of growth and promoted urban density over suburban sprawl. Its impact on the city has been considerable: Older neighborhoods have been rejuvenated, new neighborhoods are being created and multi-unit housing rather than single-family homes is now standard inner-city construction. Yet the greater Portland metropolitan area, with a population of about 1.8 million (503,000 within the Portland city limits), is growing so quickly—at a pace twice the national average—that the old growth boundary is no longer sufficient and new areas for development are being studied.

Keeping developers on their toes, Portland has over the years seen its share of natural disasters. From the city's founding until the construction of the seawall on the Willamette River in 1929, floods were a regular occurrence in downtown Portland. In 1948 a catastrophic flood completely destroyed Vanport, a suburban Portland city built to house 17,500 wartime workers. When Mt. St. Helens erupted in 1980 the city was coated with volcanic ash but spared major damage. On March 25, 1993, soon after a geologic study verified the existence of two earthquake faults under the city, a quake measuring 5.6 on the Richter scale rocked the entire region. Its epicenter was located about 30mi south of Portland. Since that time city seismic codes have been updated to make buildings more earthquake-resistant. Another flood in 1996 caused considerable damage in low-lying areas north and south of downtown. That same year, rapid snowmelt and above-average rainfall, combined with tree-cutting and erosion, resulted in mudslides and property damage in residential sections of the West Hills. Mudslides remain an ongoing problem.

Built around a manufacturing base, the city's diversified economy has been greatly bolstered by high-tech companies; plant expansions in the semi-conductor industry in the greater metropolitan area have totaled about $13 billion since 1995. Retail, financial, construction and service sectors continue to expand. Other industries include aerospace, transportation, medical research and health care, metals, sportswear, wood products, printing and publishing, food processing, and advertising. Portland also remains one of the Pacific Northwest's most important trade and transportation centers. It is the largest grain port in the nation, exporting one-third of all US wheat through the Port of Portland. More than $14 billion of cargo moves through the ports of the Lower Columbia each year. Tourism, another growing industry, added $1.9 billion to Portland's economy in 1998. Visitors to Portland will find a clean, green, undeniably attractive city where urban pleasures of all kinds abound but proximity to nature remains a top priority.

Admission prices and hours published in this guide are accurate at press time. We apologize for any inconvenience resulting from outdated information.

Getting There

By Air – Portland International Airport (PDX) 12mi from downtown: serviced by major international and domestic airlines. Information: ☎ 877-739-4636. Transportation to downtown via shuttle service, hotel courtesy shuttles and taxis. **GrayLine** offers bus service to certain hotels as well as to bus and train depots *(departs every 30min; 5am–midnight; $8.50 one-way; ☎ 246-3301)*. Public transit available to downtown via Tri-Met's 12-Sandy Boulevard bus line *($1.05)*. Rental car agencies *(p 405)* are located inside terminal.

By Train and Bus – Amtrak **train** station: Union Station at 800 N.W. 6th Ave.; reservations ☎ 800-872-7245. Greyhound/Trailways **bus** station: 550 N.W. 6th Ave.; Information ☎ 243-2316; reservations ☎ 800-231-2222.

Getting Around

By Public Transportation – The **Tri-Met** bus system works in conjunction with light-rail service using interchangeable tickets and the same fare rates *($1.05-$1.35)*. **MAX** (Metropolitan Area Express) light rail *(5:30am–1am; unlimited all-day pass $3.60; ☎ 228-7246; www.tri-met.org)* operates on a 15mi course from downtown and accesses Lloyd Center, Convention Center and Rose Quarter. Tickets & information for bus and rail: Tri-Met Customer Service Office at Pioneer Courthouse Square *(open Mon–Fri 9am–5pm; ☎ 238-7433)*. No fare is charged for Tri-Met or MAX within the 300-block downtown area known as "Fareless Square." **Vintage Trolleys** *(depart every 30min; May–Dec, Mon–Fri 9:30am–3pm, weekends 10am–6pm; Mar & Apr weekends 10am–6pm only)* provides free round-trip service from downtown to Lloyd Center.

By Car – Interstate highway I-5 runs north-south from Canada to Portland and beyond. I-84 is the major east-west thoroughfare to Boise ID. I-405 circles downtown and connects with Rte. 26. Most downtown streets are one-way. Downtown metered **parking**: 25¢ for 15min; check posted rush-hour regulations. Parking lots and garages in downtown average $3/hr or up to $12/day.

By Taxi – Portland Taxi Co. ☎ 256-5400; Broadway Cab ☎ 227-1234; Radio Cab ☎ 227-1212.

General Information

Visitor Information – For information and brochures on points of interest, seasonal events, accommodations, shopping, entertainment, recreation and tour operators, contact the **Portland Oregon Visitors Association**, 26 S.W. Salmon St., Portland OR 97204; ☎ 275-9750 or 877-678-5263, www.travelportland.com. Or stop by the **Downtown Visitor Information Center**, 2 World Trade Center, 26 S.W. Salmon St. *(open Memorial Day-Labor Day daily 9am–5pm; rest of the year Mon–Fri 9am–5pm, Sat 10am–2pm; closed major holidays)*.

Accommodations – Area visitors' guide including lodging directory available *(free)* from Portland Visitors Assoc. *(above)*. Hotels, motels and bed-and-breakfast inns range from modest to luxurious. There is a 11.5% hotel tax in Portland. **Reservation service:** Downtown Visitor Information Center ☎ 877-678-5263; Northwest Bed and Breakfast Reservation Service ☎ 243-7616. **Youth Hostel:** Hostelling International, 3031 Hawthorne Blvd., ☎ 236-3380; Northwest Portland, 1818 NW Glisan St., ☎ 241-2783. **RV sites:** Jantzen Beach RV Park ☎ 289-7626.

Local Press – Daily news: *The Oregonian (morning & afternoon)*. Weekly periodicals distributed free: *Our Town* and *Willamette Week*.

Foreign Exchange Office – Thomas Cook Foreign Exchange, 701 S.W. 6ᵗʰ St., ☎ 222-2665; Travelex America, Airport lower level *(daily 5:30am–5pm)* ☎ 281-3045.

Sports and Leisure

Sightseeing – For self-guided walking tours of public art in Portland, visitors can obtain the pamphlet *Public Art: Walking Tour ($2)* from the Visitor Information Center. Peter Chausse's Walking Tours *(2 hrs 30min; $10; schedules & reservations: ☎ 665-2558)*; E & E Specialty Tours *(1/2 day; $20; ☎ 655-3251)*. The *Portland Spirit* offers narrated sightseeing **cruises** on the Willamette River *(p 69 schedules & reservations ☎ 503-224-3900)*. Sightseeing cruises also given by Great Rivers Cruises & Tours *(year-round daily; 6 hrs round-trip; $27; ☎ 228-6228)*. The sternwheeler *Columbia Gorge* cruises Portland's

© Dianne Dietrich Leis

harbor *(Oct–Jun daily; 2 hrs; $12.95;)*; excursion cruises on the Columbia River Gorge and the Willamette River *(mid-Jun–Sept; daily; fall & spring schedules vary; $12.95)*; dinner/dance cruises run on Friday *($37.95)*; weekend brunch and dinner cruises *($25-35)*; for schedules & reservations: Sternwheeler Columbia Gorge & Marine Park Co. ☎ 223-3928. The historic Mount Hood Railroad offers excursions *($22.95)* through the Hood River Valley: dinner train *($67.50)* and brunch train *($55)*; schedules & reservations: ☎ 541-386-3556.

Entertainment – Consult the arts and entertainment section of local newspapers *(Friday)* for schedules of cultural events and addresses of theaters and concert halls, or call the Events Infoline *(☎ 796-9293)*. To purchase tickets, contact the box office, Ticketmaster *(☎ 224-4400)*, or Fastixx *(☎ 224-8499)*.

Venue	Performances	☎
Civic Auditorium	Portland Opera; Broadway Musicals	241-1802
Arlene Schnitzer Concert Hall	Oregon Symphony Orchestra	228-1353
Portland Center for the Performing Arts	Oregon Ballet Theater	222-5538
	Portland Center Stage, Newmark Theatre	274-6588
The Reiersgaard Theatre	Artists Repertory Theatre	241-1278

Spectator Sports – The Trail Blazers, Portland's NBA basketball team *(☎ 231-8000)*, and the WHL Winterhawks *(☎ 238-6366)* both play at the Rose Garden. The Portland Rockies play baseball *(☎ 223-2837)* at Portland Civic Stadium. Live *(Oct–Apr)* and simulcast horse racing at Portland Meadows *(☎ 285-9144)*. Dog racing at Multnomah Greyhound Park *(information & schedules: ☎ 667-7700)*. Order tickets from Ticketmaster *(☎ 224-4400)*.

Shopping – The open-air Saturday Market *(open Mar–late Dec; weekends; ☎ 222-6072)* in the Old Town District features craft and food vendors. Old Sellwood Antique Row in East Portland comprises a variety of antique shops and malls. Pioneer Place includes upscale retail and specialty shops.

Recreation – Biking enthusiasts can rent bikes from Bike Central *(☎ 227-4439)*; procure trail maps of selected parks from the Portland Park Bureau *(☎ 823-5132)*. Fat Tire Farm Mountain Bike Company *(☎ 222-3276)* offers rentals for rougher terrain in the Forest Park area.
Prefer paddling to pedaling? Tour the Willamette River by sea kayak or canoe. Alder Creek Kayak & Canoe rents canoes and kayaks *($12/2 hrs or $65/day full gear & canoe/kayak; ☎ 285-0464; www.aldercreek.com)*. Ebb & Flow Canoe & Kayak offers half-day rental with full gear and single or double kayak *($20; ☎ 245-1756)* or take a guided tour with Portland River Company *(2 hrs 30min; $35; ☎ 229-0551)*.
During warmer months, golfers can play at one of several public golf courses including Heron Lakes *(☎ 289-1818)* and Pumpkin Ridge *(☎ 647-4747)*.

Winter Activities: The slopes of Mt. Hood Skibowl *(52mi east of Portland; winter season: mid-Nov–mid-Apr daily; hours vary; ☎ 272-3206 or www.skibowl.com)*, include 65 day runs, cross-country trails and a snowboard park. Mt. Hood Meadows offers 87 ski trails over 2,150 acres *(67mi. east of Portland; ☎ 287-5438; www.skihood.com)*.

Useful Numbers ....

24-hour pharmacy:Rite-Aid, 5431 SW Beaverton-Hillsdale Hwy.	245-7231
Chamber of Commerce	228-9411
Dentist Referral	223-4731
Doctor Referral	222-0156
Weather	275-9792

ADDRESS BOOK

Staying in Portland

Lodgings in Portland range from beautifully restored early 1900s hotels to homey neighborhood inns scattered about the city. The finer hotels are concentrated downtown, some featuring jazz clubs, health facilities and top-ranked restaurants. Reserve well in advance for summer travel.

The accommodations listed below have been chosen for their location, character or value for money. All venues are in Portland, unless otherwise specified. Rates are for a standard room, double occupancy in high season; some hotels offer lower weekend rates.

$$$$	over $250
$$$	$175-$250
$$	$100-$175
$	under $100

The Benson – *309 S.W. Broadway Ave. at Oak St.* 🍴 ♿ 🅿 ☎ *503-228-2000 or 800-426-0670. Fax* ☎ *503-226-4603. www.citysearch.com/pdx/Benson hotel.* **$$$** A dramatic wood-paneled lobby anchors this grand 1912 hotel, which hosts divas and presidents. 286 rooms.

Embassy Suites – *319 S.W. Pine St.* 🍴 ♿ 🅿 ☎ *503-279-9000; reservations 800-Embassy. Fax* ☎ *503-497-9051. www.embassy-suites.com.* **$$$** Newly restored 1912 hotel with indoor pool and fitness center; complimentary cooked-to-order breakfast served in elegant lobby. 276 rooms.

Fifth Avenue Suites Hotel – *506 S.W. Washington St. at 5th Ave.* 🍴 🅿 ☎ *503-222-0001 or 800-711-2971. Fax* ☎ *503-222-0004. www.5thavenuesuites.com.* **$$$** Elegant boutique hotel in remodeled 1912 department store; complimentary evening wine and continental breakfast. 221 rooms.

The Governor Hotel – *611 S.W. 10th Ave. at Alder St.* 🍴 ♿ 🅿 ☎ *503-224-3400 or 800-554-3456. Fax* ☎ *503-224-9426. www.govhotel.com.* **$$$** Beautifully restored 1909 Craftsman-style landmark with striking lobby mural of Lewis and Clark's expedition; attentive service. 100 rooms.

The Heathman Hotel – *1001 S.W. Broadway Ave. at Salmon St.* 🍴 ♿ 🅿 ☎ *503-241-4100; reservations 800-551-0011. Fax* ☎ *503-790-7110.* **$$$** Classy 1920s boutique hotel known for first-class service, top restaurant, jazz nightly in historic Tea Court. 150 rooms.

Hotel Vintage Plaza – *422 S.W. Broadway Ave. at Washington St.* 🍴 ♿ 🅿 ☎ *503-228-1212; reservations* ☎ *800-243-0555 or 888-454-8403 direct to hotel. www.Vintageplaza.com.* **$$$** Stylish 107-room boutique hotel accessible to theater, shopping, public transit; noted for Pazzo, a popular Italian restaurant.

RiverPlace Hotel – *1510 S.W. Harbor Way.* ♿ 🅿 ☎ *503-228-3233 or 800-227-1333. Fax* ☎ *503-295-6190. www.RiverPlaceHotel.com.* **$$$** Spectacular Mt. Hood views from riverfront location, plus top-notch service; complimentary use of the city's best health club nearby. 150 rooms.

The Heathman Lodge – *7801 Greenwood Dr. near I-205 and Rte. 200, Vancouver, WA.* 🍴 ♿ 🅿 ☎ *360-254-3100; reservations* ☎ *888-475-3100. Fax* ☎ *360-254-6100.* **$$** New chalet-style lodge with spacious rooms; 15min from Portland International Airport and 25min from downtown Portland. 143 rooms.

The Lion and the Rose – *1810 N.E. 15th Ave., just north of N.E. Broadway.* ☎ *503-287-9245 or 800-955-1647. Fax* ☎ *503-287-9247. www.LionRose.com.* **$$** Richly restored 1906 Queen Anne B&B in historic neighborhood near public transit and downtown; complimentary tea in the afternoon. 7 rooms.

MacMaster House – *1041 S.W. Vista Ave., 2 blocks south of W. Burnside Rd., near Washington Park. Phone & fax:* ☎ *503-223-7362 or 800-774-9523. www.macmaster.com.* **$** Antique-filled c.1895 B&B a short walk from lively shopping on N.W. 23rd Ave. 8 rooms.

Mallory Hotel – *729 S.W. 15th Ave. at Yamhill St.* ✗ ♿ 🅿 ☎ *503-223-6311 or 800-228-8657. Fax* ☎ *503-223-0522. www.MalloryHotel.com.* **$** Good value in a pleasantly renovated 1912 building convenient to downtown; breakfasts here are a longtime local favorite. 143 rooms.

Dining in Portland

Portland's dining scene emphasizes fresh seafood and game, as well as locally-grown mushrooms and other produce, served in a variety of styles with local wines and brews often appearing on the menu; even the trendiest restaurants maintain an informal atmosphere. Ethnic influences include Thai, Japanese, French and Indian. Most restaurants are concentrated downtown and in the fashionable Nob Hill district.

The list below represents a sample of some of the city's more popular establishments. Prices indicate the average cost of an entree, an appetizer or dessert, and a beverage for one person (not including tax and tip, or alcoholic beverages). Reservations are highly recommended for $$$ and $$$$ restaurants.

$$$$ = deluxe (over $50)

$$$ = expensive ($30-$50)

$$ = moderate ($15-$30)

$ = inexpensive (under $15)

Genoa – *2832 S.E. Belmont.* ☎ *503-238-1464.* **$$$$ Northern Italian**. Four– and seven-course prix-fixe menus of exquisite seasonal dishes; exemplary service and wine list. No lunch. Closed Sun.

Cafe Azul – *112 N.W. 9th Ave.* ♿ ☎ *503-525-4422.* **$$$ Mexican**. Authentic, rarely seen Oaxacan cuisine featuring complex moles, fire-roasted chiles, hand-made tamales. Some diners make a meal of appetizers like the savory salsas and chips and the selection of tacos. No lunch. Closed Sun & Mon.

Caprial's Bistro – *7015 S.E. Milwaukie Blvd.* ♿ ☎ *503-236-6457. caprial @caprial.com.* **$$$ New American**. Celebrity chef and cookbook author Caprial Pence presides over this busy restaurant melding Northwest, Asian and Italian influences. Inexpensive lunch menu lists dishes similar to dinner menu. 15min drive from downtown Portland. Closed Sun & Mon.

The Heathman – *1001 S.W. Broadway Ave.* ☎ *503-241-4100.* **$$$ French**. Classical French technique meets some of America's best food products in this quiet, elegant dining room. Breakfast, lunch and dinner daily.

Higgins – *1239 S.W. Broadway Ave.* ♿ 🅿 ☎ *503-222-9070.* **$$$ Pacific Northwest**. Innovative restaurant noted for seafood and vegetarian specialties in light, spacious room; bar menu features hamburgers and other bistro fare. Huge beer selection complements wide-ranging wine list. No lunch Sat & Sun.

Jake's Famous Crawfish – *401 S.W. 12th Ave.* ♿ ☎ *503-226-1419.* **$$$ Seafood**. Bustling century-old eatery known for impeccably fresh Pacific Northwest fish and shellfish, simply prepared. No lunch Sat & Sun.

Paley's Place – *1204 N.W. 21st Ave.* 🅿 ☎ *503-243-2403. www.Paleys Place. CitySearch.com.* **$$$ New American**. Intimate bistro combines top-notch regional produce with French inspiration in sophisticated combinations. Dinner only.

Wildwood – *1221 N.W. 21st Ave.* ♿ 🅿 ☎ *503-248-9663. www.Wildwood. CitySearch.com.* **$$$ Pacific Northwest**. Intensely flavorful, hearty American cuisine showcasing Northwest meats, seafood and produce. Outstanding wine list features Oregon and Washington wines. Popular Sunday brunch.

Southpark – *901 S.W. Salmon St.* ♿ 🅿 ☎ *503-326-1300.* **$$ Mediterranean Seafood**. The bar is a downtown hot spot, and dishes like bourride (Provençal fish soup), paella and house-smoked seafood showcase fine fresh fish.

Typhoon! – *2 locations: 400 S.W. Broadway Ave.,* ♿ 🅿 ☎ *503-224-8285; and 2310 N.W. Everett St.* ♿ 🅿 *503-243-7557. www.Typhoon.Citysearch.com.* **$$ Thai**. Traditional Thai dishes invigorated with quality ingredients, a light hand with salt and gooey sauces. The Broadway location is quieter and more comfortable than the spot in Northwest Portland. Wide-ranging wine list, and over 50 teas on the "tea list." No lunch Sun.

Zefiro – *500 N.W. 21st Ave.* ♿ 🅿 ☎ *503-226-3394.* **$$ New American**. See-and-be-seen corner in hip Northwest Portland attracts stylish crowd for creative seasonal fare with Asian, Latin American and Mediterranean accents. No lunch Sat. Closed Sun.

Bijou Cafe – *132 S.W. 3rd Ave.* ♿ ☎ *503-222-3187. www.BijouCafe.com.* **$ New American**. At breakfast and lunch, Bijou is an inexpensive, diner-style spot that's a favorite of downtown business types; at dinner, the cafe becomes a casual eatery with well prepared, dressed-up dishes. Breakfast and lunch daily.

PORTLAND

Northrup • St. • 19th • 17th • 15th • 13th • 12th
Lovejoy • St. • Lovejoy
405
Irving • St. • Ave. • 10th
Blue Sky Gallery
Hoyt • Pulliam/Deffenbaugh Gallery • A. Duckler Gallery
COUCH PARK • Glisan • St.
PEARL DISTRICT
19th • 17th • 15th • 12th • 13th • NORTHWEST
Everett • ❹
Davis • St. • Ave.
Couch • St.
Burnside • St. • ❸
Alder • L. Washington
Federal Reserve Bank Bldg.
Morrison • St.
Yamhill • Princeton Bldg.
Taylor • Charles F. Berg
Multnomah County Public Library • Weather Machine
Salmon • PIONEER COURTHOUSE SQUARE • Jackson Tower
DOWNTOWN
Portland Center for the Performing Arts
Main • B
Columbia • A • T
PORTLAND ART MUSEUM • R • F
St. • Jefferson • OREGON HISTORY CENTER
Old Church
Clay • Sixth Church of Christ Scientist
Market • Oregonian Bldg.
SOUTH PARK BLOCKS
P • Portland • P • P
State • P
University • Harrison
405 • Jackson • St.

0 ___ 1/4 mi
0 ___ 250 m

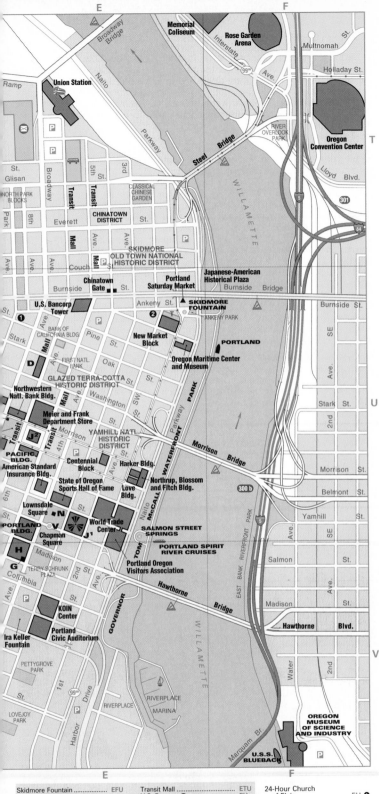

★DOWNTOWN *1 day. Map pp 62-63*

Thanks to farsighted planning efforts, Portland's attractive downtown area has become a model for cities around the country. Compact, clean and pedestrian-friendly, with short, 200ft square blocks and three historic districts, the city's core is a destination and gathering spot for residents and workers from all over the city. Parks, fountains, public artworks and a rich texture of building and street materials add to its appeal. Brick-paved **Transit Malls** (one-way streets reserved for buses) completed in 1978 along Southwest Fifth and Sixth Avenues bisect the main retail and business district.

The central downtown area is bounded by the Willamette River on the east and by the curve of I-405 on the other sides. Clustered along the south end are the buildings of **Portland State University** *(defined by I-405, S.W. Market St., S.W. 12th Ave. and S.W. 5th Ave.)*. Rising at the north end is the sleek, rhomboid-shaped 1985 **U.S. Bancorp Tower** *(111 S.W. 5th Ave.)*, known locally as "Big Pink." Oregon's tallest building (43 stories), it has a reflective orange-pink façade that plays off the changing light. Atwaters bar and restaurant *(☎ 503-275-3600)* on the 30th floor provides outstanding views of the city, the mountains and the river. Other downtown high-rise landmarks include Skidmore, Owings and Merrill's 1970 **American Standard Insurance Building** *(bounded by S.W. 4th & 5th Aves. and S.W. Salmon & Taylor Sts.)*, a 30-story tower of white quartz and bronze tinted glass; and the 1984 **KOIN Center** *(S.W. Columbia St. and S.W. 3rd Ave.)*, a 29-story office-residential tower with a blue pyramidal roof.

Scattered throughout downtown are dozens of distinctive cast-bronze "four-bubbler" drinking fountains installed in 1912-13. They were a gift from Simon Benson, a teetotaling lumber baron who believed a supply of fresh, cool water would help distract imbibers from the lure of the saloons. Portland's drinking water comes from Bull Run, a watershed on the northwest slope of Mt. Hood.

Portland Oregon Visitors Association – *26 S.W. Salmon St.* ☎ *877-678-5263 or www.travelportland.com.* Housed on the ground floor of **The World Trade Center**, an elegant complex of buildings faced with silvery-gray Italian granite and connected by white skyways, the Visitors Association provides a full range of literature and detailed information about sights and activities in Portland and throughout Oregon.

★**Pioneer Courthouse Square** – *Bounded by S.W. Broadway & 6th Ave. and S.W. Morrison & Yamhill Sts.* Dedicated in 1984, this open, brick-paved public piazza in the heart of downtown sits on land formerly occupied by Portland's first public schoolhouse (1858) and the Portland Hotel (1890), demolished for a parking lot in 1952. It's a favorite lunchtime gathering spot for office workers and the scene of city-wide political rallies and special events. Lined with 12 monumental terra-cotta-faced columns with rose capitals, the plaza has a limestone-faced fountain

Pioneer Courthouse Square

© Dianne Dietrich Leis

projecting from its west end and a curving amphitheater on its south side. Every day at noon a fanfare plays and a weather symbol appears from the sphere atop the 25ft **Weather Machine**—on clear days a sun, on stormy days a dragon, and on Portland's frequent gray days, a blue heron. Wrought-iron gates from the Portland Hotel stand in their original location on Sixth Avenue.

The octagonal cupola of the Classic Revival **Pioneer Courthouse** *(701 S.W. 6th Ave.)* at the east end of the square has been a Portland landmark since it was completed in 1873. The first federal building constructed in the Pacific Northwest, the court-house was designed by Alfred Mullet, who also designed the San Francisco Mint, and is faced with blue freestone. The two large wings on its west façade were added in 1903.

★**Glazed Terra-Cotta Historic District** – *Bounded by S.W. 5th and 10th Aves. and S.W. Oak and Yamhill Sts.* A handful of architects with formal training in classical architecture designed most of the distinctive white buildings surrounding Pioneer Courthouse Square. Development of the area—originally centered around McKim, Mead & White's famous Portland Hotel—was spurred on by the Lewis and Clark Exposition of 1905. By that time, steel framing had replaced cast-iron, allowing new buildings to be considerably taller than earlier structures. Facades were dec-orated with glazed terra-cotta tiles, a hard-baked clay shaped by hand into hollow blocks and pressed into plaster molds. Their terra-cotta faces give these buildings a soft white glow even on overcast days.

Albert E. Doyle (1877-1928), who opened an office in 1907 with William Patterson, eventually had the largest and most prestigious architectural practice in Portland. His first major commission, the 15-story **Meier and Frank Department Store** *(bounded by S.W. 5th & 6th Aves. and S.W. Morrison & Alder Sts.)* on the north side of Pioneer Courthouse, was the first Portland building sheathed entirely in white terra-cotta. Dating from 1926, Doyle's elegant **Pacific Building**★ *(520 S.W. Yamhill)*, modeled after an Italian Renaissance palazzo, faces the south side of the court-house. It has a glazed terra-cotta cornice and a three-story rusticated terra-cotta base. His **Northwestern National Bank Building** (1913, remodeled 1936-37), facing Pioneer Courthouse Square on the north, has an off-white glazed terra-cotta base and upper floors ornamented with classical details, griffins and eagles. Doyle also designed the Multnomah County Public Library *(p 67)* and the cast-bronze drinking fountains found on so many downtown streets.

Jackson Tower *(southeast corner of Broadway and Yamhill St.)*, a glazed terra-cotta and brick building with a freestanding tower illuminated at night, served as the offices for the Oregon Journal from 1912 until 1948. **Charles F. Berg** *(615 Broadway between Morrison and Alder)*, a former ladies' apparel store, is the only example of Art Deco-style glazed terra-cotta in Portland. The black terra-cotta façade, tex-tured with 18-carat gold and ornamental details of rain clouds, sunbursts, spirals and peacocks, was a 1930 remodel by Grand Rapids Design Service of a building constructed in 1902.

Portland architects Houghtaling and Dougan adapted their design for the 1920 **Princeton Building** *(614 S.W. 11th Ave.)* from the Farnese Palace in Rome. Originally built as an Elks Temple, its pink-tinged terra-cotta façade features a rich variety of plant and animal forms, including lions' heads in the sheet-metal cornice, and Doric columns supporting a sculptured frieze.

Portland Center for the Performing Arts – *S.W. Broadway Ave. and S.W. Main St. Events Information ☎ 503-796-9293.* Three downtown buildings collectively known as the Portland Center for the Performing Arts are dedicated to music, theater and dance. In 1987 the Italian Renaissance-style Paramount Theater, a former vaudeville and movie palace built in 1927, was completely restored and renamed the **Arlene Schnitzer Concert Hall**. Home of the Oregon Symphony, "the Schnitz" has a 2,800-seat auditorium. Directly across the street stands the **New Theatre Building**, where Portland Center Stage performs in the 950-seat Newmark Theatre and other theater troupes in the 450-seat Winningstad Theater. Shimmering above the cherry-paneled lobby shared by both theaters are the vari-colored glass panels of James Carpenter's **Spectral Light Done** (1987). The Civic Auditorium, several blocks southeast of here, is also part of the Portland Center for the Performing Arts.

★**South Park Blocks** – *Park & 9th Aves. between Salmon St. & I-405.* In 1848, when Portland was still a raw pioneer settlement, Daniel Lownsdale, a prosperous tannery owner, set aside the strip of land which eventually became the South Park Blocks, a leafy 12-block greenbelt that runs north-south through downtown. At its north end stand the city's four major cultural institutions: the Portland Art Museum, the Oregon History Center, the Arlene Schnitzer Concert Hall and the New Theatre Building; at its south end, the elm-shaded promenade becomes the urban campus of Portland State University. The oldest landmark on the park blocks is the 1895 **First Congregational Church** *(1126 S.W. Park)* with its elaborate 175ft Venetian Gothic-inspired tower designed by Swiss architect Henry J. Hefty.

■ **Pietro Belluschi: Maestro of Modernism**

Portland claims an important place in the annals of modern architecture because of the early work of Pietro Belluschi (1899-1994), one of the seminal thinkers of Modernism. Born in Ancona, Italy, and trained as a civil engineer, Belluschi came to America in 1923 and began his architectural career in 1925 in the office of A.E. Doyle, the most prominent Portland architect of his day. Belluschi's first important commission was for the **Portland Art Museum** *(below)*, completed in 1932. Stylistically, he moved away from the prevailing Beaux-Arts historicism and created a Northwest regional modernism in a series of houses and churches noted for their simple, elegant forms, spare details, clearly delineated surfaces and use of native materials. The 1950 **Zion Lutheran Church★** *(1015 S.W. 18th Ave.)*, one of his most celebrated churches, is a finely detailed brick and wood structure with a generously overhanging roof and a Scandinavian-looking bell tower. Built in 1949, the **Federal Reserve Bank Building** *(915 S.W. Stark St.)*, a simple rectangular form, is distinguished by a sleek white marble skin set with square repeating windows, while the 1948 **Oregonian Building** *(1320 S.W. Broadway Ave.)* follows the same design concept but with more complexity; it was built to house the printing presses of a large newspaper.

Belluschi skyrocketed to fame with the elegant 1948 **Equitable Building★** *(421 S.W. 6th Ave.; now called the Commonwealth Building)*, the first curtain-wall *(a grid of metal supporting glass and opaque panels)* and aluminum office tower ever built. Recognized throughout the world, it established Belluschi as one of the preeminent modern architects in the US. He left Portland in 1950, served as Dean of Architecture and Planning at MIT in Boston from 1951-65, and in 1972 was awarded the American Institute of Architects Gold Medal, the highest honor in the profession. During Belluschi's 69-year career he designed or consulted on the design of more than 1,000 buildings, including the Pan Am Building in Manhattan. Belluschi returned to Portland in 1973 and lived in West Hills until his death in 1994. His last work in Portland, completed in 1986, was the **University of Portland Chapel** *(5000 N. Willamette Blvd.)*.

Sixth Church of Christ Scientist *(corner of S.W. Park and Columbia)*, completed in 1932, is a striking example of Art Deco Byzantine with beautiful sculptured brickwork and a central octagonal dome. Most of the sculptures found along the park blocks are contemporary pieces; older works include an equestrian bronze **Theodore Roosevelt, Rough Rider** (1922) by Phiminster Proctor and a 1926 bronze of **Abraham Lincoln** by George Waters *(between Main and Madison Sts.)*.

★**Oregon History Center** – *1200 S.W. Park Ave. Galleries accessed from the ticket and information desk, located one level down from the entrance doors. Open year-round Tue-Sat 10am–5pm (Thu 8pm), Sun noon–5pm. Closed major holidays. $6.* ♿ ☏ *503-222-1741. www.ohs.org.* Eight-story-high trompe-l'œil murals of Lewis and Clark and the Oregon Trail rise beside the entrance plaza of this important repository of historical artifacts and documents. Plan to devote the majority of your time to the permanent installation called "**Portland!**"★ To reach it, pass through the small gallery containing a colorful collection of 19C and early-20C quilts and a second gallery with changing exhibits of **folk art**. Here, a stairway leads to "Portland!" one floor up. The "copper" used in the famous coin toss that decided Portland's name is displayed at the entrance. Filled with interactive displays and snippets of period music, the self-guided exhibition begins with the 1840s when the first settlers arrived. The city's growth is then traced chronologically. Special points of interest include the 1905 Lewis and Clark Exposition; World War II, which saw the influx of some 160,000 people who came to work in the shipyards and war-related industries; and the rise of the car culture in the 1950s. A worthwhile cyber walk through Portland's neighborhoods is offered at two computer terminals.

In the small **Hayes Maritime Gallery**, beside the ticket desk, you'll find models of ships used by 18C explorers of the Pacific Northwest. The Center's renowned **Photographic Archives**, containing over two million images, is housed in the third-floor Research Library; the collection is not on view but it is accessible to visitors.

★**Portland Art Museum** – *1219 S.W. Park Ave. Open year-round Tue–Sun 10am–5pm (1st Thu of month until 9pm). $7.50.* ✗ ♿ 🅿 ☏ *503-226-2811. www.pam.org.* A low brick building with travertine trim, the Portland Art Museum was the first building by architect Pietro Belluschi to achieve national recognition. The complex comprises three wings: the Ayer Wing (1932), on the north; the Hirsch Wing (1939), with a sculpture court; and the Hoffman Wing, completed in

1970. In the past, only a small fraction of the museum's holdings—some 32,000 objects spanning 35 centuries—could be exhibited. A $30 million expansion program, scheduled for completion in the summer of 2000, will substantially increase exhibition space for traveling shows and provide permanent galleries for the museum's outstanding collections of Pacific Northwest Native American art and Northwest art. The museum, founded in 1892, is the oldest art museum in the Pacific Northwest.

Standing near the entrance lobby is a large bronze sculpture, Venus Victorieuse, by Auguste Renoir. The **East Asian Galleries★** to the left of the sculpture court contain a small but choice collection of sculpture, ceramics, furniture, textiles and woodblock prints from China, Korea and Japan. The earliest piece, a carved wooden horse from China, dates from the 3C BC. On the second floor, the museum's permanent collection of **French Impressionists★** includes works by Monet, Corot, Cézanne, Morisot, Pissarro, Rodin (*Young Girls Reading*, 1891), Manet, Toulouse-Lautrec, and Maurice Utrillo. The **Gilkey Center for Graphic Arts** on the basement level contains over 22,000 prints, drawings and photographs, a portion of which are exhibited on a rotating basis.

Multnomah County Public Library – *801 S.W. 10th Ave. Open year-round Mon–Thu 9am–9pm, Fri & Sat 9am–6pm, Sun 1pm–5pm. Closed major holidays.* ♿ ☏ *503-248-5402. www.multnomah.lib.or.us/lib.* A.E. Doyle, who designed several of the glazed terra-cotta buildings around Pioneer Courthouse Square, used brick, limestone and Wilkinson sandstone for the façade of this dignified Georgian Revival-style library. Completed in 1913, and considered a landmark of early Portland architecture, the library recently underwent a major structural and interior renovation, reopening in 1998 with a Starbucks coffee bar.

Old Church – *1422 S.W. 11th Ave. Open year-round Mon–Fri 11am–3pm.* ☏ *503-222-2031.* "Carpenter Gothic" is the term used to describe the ornate Gothic Revival wooden church designed by Portland architect Warren Heywood Williams and completed in 1883. One of the finer late-Victorian churches in the state, the building features a tall belfry tower, slender pointed arches and ornate tracery windows. The interior is a mixture of Victorian Gothic, Renaissance and Baroque styles. Lunchtime concerts are held on Wednesdays *(year-round at noon)*.

Ira Keller Fountain – *S.W. 3rd Ave. between Clay and Market Sts.* Inspired by the rivers and waterfalls of the Pacific Northwest, a giant, rugged-looking fountain occupies a full city block directly opposite the Civic Auditorium. Water flowing down through a grassy park planted with pine trees cascades over a series of 18ft multilevel concrete cliffs. Square, irregularly placed platforms over the pool act as stepping stones, allowing visitors to get close to the waterfall and even duck behind it. Angela Danadjieva designed the fountain for Lawrence Halprin Associates.

Across the street, the **Portland Civic Auditorium** *(222 S.W. Clay St.)*, part of the Portland Center for the Performing Arts, was built in 1917 and given a facelift in 1968. Portland Opera *(p 59)* and Oregon Ballet Theater *(p 59)* use the 3,000-seat hall as their home base.

Chapman and Lownsdale Squares – *Bounded by S.W. Madison and Salmon Sts. and S.W. 3rd and 4th Aves.* Set aside as public parks in 1852, these two adjacent blocks planted with elms, pines, cedars and gingko trees form the green heart of Portland's government quarter. They were the scene of anti-Chinese riots in the 1880s and in the 1920s were sexually segregated to protect women from unwanted advances. Chapman Square (between Madison and Main), the women's park, was named for Judge William Chapman, a founder of the Oregonian newspaper. Men were confined to Lownsdale Square (between Main and Salmon), named for Daniel Lownsdale, a 19C Oregon legislator who was also responsible for building the city's first plank road in 1851. After considerable controversy, a bronze sculpture called **Promised Land** (1993) by David Manuel was placed here in 1999; its detractors maintain that the figures of the settlers are insensitive to Oregon's Native American past. Between the two squares, in the center of Main Street, is the arresting **Thompson Elk Fountain★** (1900). Roland Perry's life-size bronze statue of an elk—an animal that reputedly grazed here in the early 1850s—tops a pedestal with four granite horse troughs at its base.

Portland City Hall – *1221 S.W. 4th Ave. Open year-round Mon–Fri 7am–7pm. Closed major holidays.* ⚹ ♿ ☏ *503-823-4000.* William Whidden, a prominent architect in late-19C and early 20C Portland, designed this robust four-story building, modeled on an Italian palazzo and completed in 1895. Faced with Wyoming sandstone, it features an entrance loggia upheld by pink scagliola columns and urns (replicas of the original limestone) atop a balustraded roof. A two-year, $29 million renovation completed in 1998 restored many of the interior's original details, including light courts; open, steel elevator shafts with wrought-iron stair rails; and marble-tile floors. A bronze replica of the **Liberty Bell**, cast in 1964, sits outside at the southeast corner of the building.

Mark O. Hatfield U.S. Courthouse – *1000 S.W. 3rd Ave. Open year-round Mon–Fri 7:30am–5:30pm. Closed major holidays.* ⅙ ☏ *503-326-8000.* Designed by Kohn Pedersen Fox and completed in 1997, this stylish tower on the east side of Lownsdale Square boasts a façade of Indiana limestone juxtaposed against a vast glass wall with strong horizontal fenestration. Visitors are free to enter but must first go through a security check (cameras are not allowed inside the building). The marble—clad lobby is graced by two water sculptures—**Passage of Time** and **Ocean of Thought**—by Eric Orr. An outdoor sculpture garden on the 9th floor is more notable for its wonderful **views**★ of downtown and the river than for its oddly cartoonlike bronze sculptures.

★**Portland Building** – *1120 S.W. 5th Ave.* ☏ *503-823-5111.* The first major post-modern building in the US, the Portland Building designed by New Jersey architect Michael Graves has aroused strong local feelings since it was completed in 1982.

The buff-colored building—basically a box with small windows and a recessed ground-level arcade—is over-laid with a pastiche of flat, ornamental motifs above a blue-tile base. Brown pilasters are capped by quasi-Egypt-ian capitals, while rib-bon-like metallic swags decorate the upper sto-ries and lend the whole a playful, Art Deco feel that softens the build-ing's 15-story height. The 36ft hammered-copper sculpture of a muscular giantess named **Portlandia**★ (1984) crouches on the second-floor balcony with a trident in her left hand. The artist, Ray-mond Kaskey, based his design on Lady Commerce, the sym-bolic figure of agricul-ture and industry on Portland's city seal.

Portlandia (1984) by Raymond Kaskey

State of Oregon Sports Hall of Fame – ⃞Kids *321 S.W. Salmon St. Open year-round Tue–Sun 10am–6pm. $6.* ⅙ ☏ *503-227-7466.* Distance runner Steve Prefontaine, basketball star Bill Walton of the Portland Trail Blazers, Atlanta Braves center fielder Dale Murphy, and Terry Baker, who won the Heisman Trophy in 1962 as the great-est college football player in the nation, are among the famous Oregon athletes whose stories and memorabilia are found in this museum. The Oregon Sports Time-line chronicles the major events in the state's sporting history and a Wall of Fame lists the accomplishments of individual athletes. One interactive virtual-reality dis-play allows visitors to experience what it feels like to catch a fast ball thrown at 90mph. The museum also hosts frequent sports-related traveling exhibits.

★**Governor Tom McCall Waterfront Park** – *Bordering S.W. Naito Pkwy. and the Willamette River between the Marquam Bridge and the Steel Bridge.* The grassy 23-acre park that now stretches for about 1.5mi along the Willamette River was once Portland's raucous river port. A waterfront esplanade used by strollers, joggers, bicyclists and in-line skaters reaches almost the entire length of the park, from Riverplace, an upscale retail, hotel and condominium development, up to the Steel Bridge. In 1929 the old downtown wharves were demolished and the first seawall erected; from the 1940s until the 1970s a major east-west highway plowed through the area. As part of its downtown urban renewal scheme, the city reclaimed the land and named the new park after Tom McCall (1913-83), an early proponent of land-use planning who served as governor from 1967-75.

The park is frequently the venue for summertime concerts and festivals, the most famous being the **Rose Festival** in June, when a fleet of Coast Guard ships docks alongside the seawall. **Salmon Street Springs**★, a 100-jet fountain is located next to an early modernist pavilion (now McCall's Waterfront Restaurant) designed in 1949 by John Yeon, one of Portland's most prominent mid-20C architects, and formerly used as the city's visitor information center.

Eight Portland bridges can be seen by strolling the length of the park. The most notable are the buff-colored **Hawthorne Bridge** (1910), the oldest operating vertical-lift bridge in the world; the **Morrison Bridge**, which opened in 1887 as a wooden toll bridge—the first span across the Willamette—and was replaced in 1905 and 1958; and the **Steel Bridge** (1912), the world's only telescoping double-deck vertical-lift bridge. Its bottom deck (for trains only) can lift up into the top deck like a slide trombone to allow ships to pass underneath; for really big ships, both decks can move up together in about 90 seconds.

© Dianne Dietrich Leis

Paddle Boat on the Willamette River

★**Portland Spirit River Cruises** – *Depart from Salmon Street Springs in Tom McCall Waterfront Park year-round daily. Sightseeing cruise ($14), lunch cruise ($26), dinner cruise ($49) and Sunday Champagne Brunch cruise ($36). Commentary.* ✗ ⊡ *For departure times & reservations call Portland Spirit River Cruises ☎ 503-224-3900 or 800-224-3901. www.portlandspirit.com.* From its dock near Salmon Street Springs, the Portland Spirit excursion boat heads out along the Willamette River for 2 hr lunch, Sunday brunch, and sightseeing cruises and 2 1/2 hr dinner cruises. The main cabin is reserved for dining; sightseers can view the scenery from the open upper deck or bar/lounge area. As the sleek, 150ft-long boat heads upstream, it passes Ross Island, home of nesting bald eagles, great blue herons and ospreys, and secluded riverside estates on the east and west banks.

★**Yamhill National Historic District** – *Bounded by S.W. Front Ave. (Naito Pkwy.), Morrison St., Taylor St. and 3rd Ave.* This compact, six-block area known for its fine examples of late-19C cast-iron architecture, marked the southern end of the city's first, waterfront-based commercial core. By the 1880s—spurred by the opening of the Morrison Street Bridge—a number of Victorian Italianate structures were built. Later remodeling hid much of the ornamental cast-iron work on their facades. In the 1950s, when many buildings in the area were demolished for parking lots and to facilitate construction of the present Morrison Street Bridge, the area became isolated from its contemporaneous extension to the north, the area now known as the Skidmore/Old Town Historic District. Restoration and renovation of the remaining buildings began in the 1970s. Italianate buildings erected between 1878-1887 define the character of the district but there are also examples of later commercial structures built in the Second Empire and Colonial Revival styles.

The district's most historically important structure is the 1858 **Northrup, Blossom and Fitch Building** *(731-737 S.W. Naito Pkwy.)*, the only commercial building still standing from the period before the Great Fire of 1873. Originally two separate one-story brick buildings, it was joined at the third floor sometime prior to 1894. The Italianate **Centennial Block** *(210-218 S.W. Morrison St.)* was completed in 1876 and named for the American Centennial, celebrated that year. Three separate commercial structures built in 1878 at the corner of Southwest Yamhill Street and First Avenue—the **Harker Building** *(728 S.W. 1st Ave.)*, the **Love Building** *(730-732 S.W. 1st Ave.)* and the **Van Rensselaer Building** *(65-73 S.W. Yamhill St.)*—form a unified ensemble with identical second-floor windows and cast-iron columns ornamented with cartouches.

① 24-Hour Church of Elvis

Map p 62-63. 720 S.W. Ankeny St. (between S.W. Broadway and Park Aves.). ☎ 503-226-3671. www.churchofelvis.com.
If you only want to buy an official Church of Elvis T-shirt, say so when you enter, otherwise stay for the hilarious 20min "tour" led by Stephanie G. Pierce, "Artist to the Stars." The wacky 24-Hour Church of Elvis began in 1989 as a storefront installation with a coin-operated shrine offering around-the-clock weddings, psychic readings and a photo opportunity with the King. It's now housed in a second-floor gallery cluttered with a mind-boggling assortment of Elvis icons, toys, weird machines and kitschy paraphernalia. The tour is really a piece of interactive performance art that pokes fun at celebrity. In her role as ordained Minister, Pierce invites visitors to kneel at the Altar of the Church of Elvis, shows them the Miracle of the Tortilla (a tortilla chip with a face of Elvis on it), and, with help from volunteers, hosts a dramatic reenactment of Let's Make a Deal.

Additional Sight *Map p 72.*

Children's Museum – [Kids] *3037 S.W. 2nd Ave. (just off S.W. Barbur Blvd., 1mi south of downtown). Open year-round Tue–Sun 9am–5pm. $4.* ▣ ☎ 503-823-2227. www.parks.ci.port-land.or.us. Children must be accompanied by care-givers.* A unique museum in the Lair Hill neighborhood offers three floors of play areas where young children can have fun while exercising their imaginations. The rooms are set up with different kinds of child-sized environments, some from the real world (a grocery store for pretend shopping, a restaurant for pretend cooking), others from the world of fantasy (a Peter Rabbit area). There is a clay workshop in the basement and a playground outdoors. By 2001 the museum hopes to be in its new Washington Park location.

*SKIDMORE/OLD TOWN NATIONAL HISTORIC DISTRICT

1/2 day. Map pp 62-63.

Running parallel to the Willamette River, this area *(bounded by S.W. Naito Pkwy., S.W. Oak St., 3rd Ave. and N.W. Davis St.)* along with the Yamhill Historic District to the south, was part of the 1843 land claim that led to the establishment of Portland. From the mid– to late-19C it served as the city's main riverfront business and entertainment district. The area began to decline in the 1890s when the logging boom ended and railroads decreased the city's reliance on river trade. Dating from 1896, **Union Station** *(800 N.W. 6th Ave. near the Broadway Bridge)* with its 150ft tower is a prominent landmark from the railroad era and one of the oldest continuously operating passenger train stations in the nation. The red-brick building, by the Boston/Missouri firm of Vant Brunt & Howe, is somewhat Richardsonian in style. As the city center shifted west toward higher ground, Old Town gradually became a neglected skid row and many of the district's brick and cast-iron "commercial palaces" were demolished, leaving gaping holes. Since its designation in 1975 as a National Historic Landmark District, most of the late-19C buildings have been restored. Still seedy in places, the area has a thriving nightlife and is home to many restaurants, art galleries and nightclubs.

*Skidmore Fountain – *S.W. Ankeny St. at S.W. 1st Ave.* A graceful fountain, with caryatids holding aloft a bronze basin in the center of an octagonal granite pool, with the inscription "Good citizens are the riches of a city," acts as the centerpiece of the Skidmore/Old Town Historic District. Designed by Olin Warner, a prominent New York sculptor, the fountain was built in 1888 in a bid to attract more business to the area. It was named for Stephen Skidmore, a city councilman who partially funded its construction. Cast-iron artifacts from demolished 19C Portland buildings are set into a brick wall and covered arcade in Ankeny Park, a small plaza on the east side of the fountain.

New Market Block – *Bounded by Ankeny & Ash Sts., and 1st & 2nd Aves.* Captain Alexander P. Ankeny, financier, banker, steamboat owner and mine operator, developed this ensemble of Italianate buildings on the west side of Skidmore Fountain in the 1870s. The New Market Theater *(50 S.W. 2nd Ave.),* built on the site of Portland's first cemetery in 1872, has a 200ft-long interior that was originally lined with produce stalls; the second floor was a lavish, gas-lit theater where the Portland (now Oregon) Symphony began in 1882. Later used as a parking lot, the building was restored in 1984. Cast-iron pilasters with grape, leaf and scroll motifs in their capitals adorn the adjacent 1872 New Market Block South Wing *(29 S.W. 1st Ave.).* The Ankeny Block Colonnade, defining the street edge across from Skidmore Fountain, is all that remains from the New Market Block North Wing, demolished in 1956.

Portland Saturday Market – *Beneath west end of Burnside Bridge, from S.W. Naito Pkwy. to Ankeny Sq. Open Mar-Christmas Eve Sat 10am–5pm, Sun 11am–4:30pm.* ✗ ♿ ☎ *503-222-6072. www.saturdaymarket.org.* Old Town is liveliest on weekends from March to December when hundreds of people descend on the Portland Saturday Market, billing itself the largest outdoor crafts market in the US. The market began in 1974 with 30 vendors; today there are about 275 stalls and booths selling everything from pottery, baskets, candles and tie-dyed T-shirts to herbs, walking sticks, music boxes and exotic foods. Bands and entertainers add to the festive atmosphere.

Oregon Maritime Center and Museum – [Kids] *113 S.W. Naito Pkwy. Open year-round Fri–Sun 11am–4pm. Closed major holidays. $4.* ♿ ☎ *503-224-7724. www.teleport.com/~omcm/.* A handsome brick Italianate building dating from 1872 houses this compact, informative museum devoted to the maritime history of Portland. On display are historic photographs, nautical memorabilia and meticulously crafted models of the various ships that have sailed up and down the Willamette and Columbia rivers from the mid-19C to the present. The museum's largest exhibit, the **Portland★**, is docked in the Willamette River across the street. Built in 1947 and in use until 1981, it is the last operational steam-powered sternwheeler tugboat in the

② Dan & Louis Oyster Bar Restaurant

Map p 62-63. 208 S.W. Ankeny (between S.W. 2nd Ave. and 3rd Aves.). ☎ *503-227-5906.* Founded by Louis C. Wachsmuth, who grew up in Oysterville, Washington, Dan & Louis began in 1907 as a wholesale and retail seafood store serving oyster cocktails. The lobby of this resolutely untrendy restaurant in Old Town dates from 1915; the two dining rooms, built to look like the wood-paneled interior of a sailing ship covered with nautical memorabilia, haven't changed since they were added in 1937 and 1940. For more than 80 years the restaurant has been famous for its oysters from Yaquina Bay on the Oregon coast. The bivalves are served up fresh on the half-shell, in rich oyster stew or pan-fried. The simple cuisine at this Portland institution is a pleasant reminder of days gone by, when a sack full of fresh oysters cost 50 cents.

country. On self-guided tours visitors can see the engine room, pilot's and captain's cabins and the pilothouse. In 1993 the ship was given a temporary Victorian makeover and used in the movie *Maverick*.

Japanese-American Historical Plaza – *In Tom McCall Waterfront Park between W. Burnside and N.W. Couch Sts.* Three large stones mark the entrance to this paved riverside plaza commemorating a tragic episode in American history. The Japanese pioneers who arrived in Portland between 1880-1924 lived in Nihonmachi (Japan Town), a neighborhood located a few blocks north of here. In 1942, victims of wartime hysteria, they and all Japanese-Americans on the West Coast were ordered to leave their homes; over 110,000 Japanese-Americans (2,617 from the Portland area) spent the next three years in internment camps. Short, poignant poems relating to their experiences in the camps are engraved on stones in a raised earthen bank planted with cherry trees.

NORTHWEST *1/2 day*

West Burnside Street is the dividing line between Southwest and Northwest Portland, but both areas share the same topographical features, rising gradually from the flatlands along the Willamette River to the high ridge that runs parallel to it. Portland's small Chinatown District lies closest to downtown. Farther west, in the Pearl District and the Nob Hill neighborhood around Northwest 23rd Avenue, you'll find art galleries, upscale boutiques, coffeehouses, restaurants and stately Victorian homes. Forest Park covers much of the north slope of the ridge and extends southwest to Washington Park *(p 76)*.

Chinatown – *Between N.W. 2nd & 5th Aves., W. Burnside & N.W. Glisan Sts.* Two carved lions stand in front of the colorful **Chinatown Gate** *(N.W. 4th Ave. and W. Burnside St.)*, erected in 1986 to commemorate 135 years of Chinese contributions to the city of Portland and the state of Oregon. The five-tiered gate marks the official entrance to Portland's low-key Chinatown district, home to several Chinese restaurants and grocery stores. A new Classical Chinese Garden, scheduled to open in the year 2000, will cover the block between Northwest Second and Third Avenues and Northwest Glisan and Flanders Streets. A joint project between the City of Portland and its sister-city of Suzhou, it will feature serpentine walkways, ponds, bridges and a landscape of rocks, trees, shrubs, screens and pavilions.

★**Pearl District** – *Bounded by W. Burnside St., N.W. Lovejoy St., N.W. 8th Ave., and N.W. 15th Ave. The trendy Pearl District extends west from the North Park Blocks (N.W. 8th and Park Aves. between W. Burnside and N.W. Glisan Sts.) to I-405.* Over the last decade, this former industrial area, with its renovated buildings and new housing developments, has been transformed into the art and design

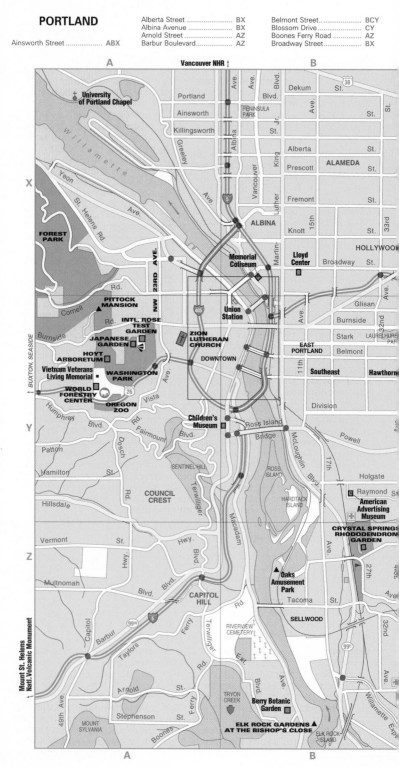

72

center of Portland. Warehouses, manufacturing plants and garages have been converted into upscale lofts, galleries, furniture showrooms, restaurants and small shops. Loading docks and cobbled streets with old train tracks running through them add to the character of the district, giving it a hip urban ambience found nowhere else in Portland. On **First Thursday**, a popular evening social event held on

③ Powell's City of Books

Map pp 62-63. 1005 W. Burnside St. ☎ 503-228-4651. www.powells.com. Claiming title of the largest bookstore in the world, with an on-hand inventory of a million volumes, Powell's City of Books is a book-lover's dream and a tourist attraction in its own right. Over 3,000 visitors a day make the pilgrimage to this Portland institution, which opened its doors in 1971 and hasn't closed them since (it's open 365 days a year). The store is so large, it covers an entire city block and has 122 major book sections and 4,000 subsections. Each of its six rooms is the size of a large bookstore, and there are plans for expansion across the street. Color-coded maps are provided as a navigational aid, but getting lost in Powell's is a pleasure. Unlike superstore book chains, 70 percent of Powell's stock is comprised of used, hard-to-find and rare books. Hardcovers and paperbacks share the same shelves. There is also an enormous selection of sale books in every subject area. In the Anne Hughes Coffee Room you can sip coffee while you read. Author appearances and readings are regular evening events.

the first Thursday of every month, the art galleries here (and throughout the city) preview their new shows. **Alysia Duckler Gallery** *(512 N.W. 9th Ave.; ☎ 503-223-7595)*, **Blue Sky Gallery** *(1231 N.W. Hoyt St.; ☎ 503-225-0210)*, and **Pulliam/Deffenbaugh Gallery** *(522 N.W. 12th Ave.; ☎ 503-228-6665)* are among the contemporary exhibit spaces found in the Pearl District.

★ **Northwest 23rd Avenue** – Small in scale and long on charm, Northwest 23rd has become the focal point of one of the most attractive neighborhoods in Portland. The busy blocks between West Burnside and Northwest Lovejoy Streets now comprise a hot "destination street," known for its shopping, sidewalk cafes, variety of restaurants and good people watching. The upscale commercial aspect of Northwest 23rd is a fairly recent phenomenon. Two decades ago it was a quiet residential street, a bit shabby around the edges, with little more than a drugstore, a bank and a couple of stores to serve the needs of the neighborhood. Gradually, old houses were turned into small shops, existing structures were renovated, and new coffeehouses, boutiques and restaurants moved in.

The Nob Hill neighborhood around Northwest 23rd Avenue became fashionable in the prosperous 1880s and there are still many fine Victorian homes to be seen on the streets between Northwest 17th and 25th Avenues and Northwest Everett to Thurman Streets. These homes remain private residences, or have been converted into offices, and are not open to the public, but you can spend a fun hour or so strolling the area, perhaps working off calories from a lunch at Zefiro, Wildwood or one of the other trendy area restaurants. Among the houses worth taking a look at: The 1892 **Pettygrove House** *(2287 N.W. Pettygrove St.)*, is a modest, late Victorian wood-frame house with gingerbread trim. Six blocks south, there are three notable Victorian homes on Johnson Street between 23rd and 22nd Avenues: the Italianate **Sprague-Marshall-Bowie House** *(no. 2234)* dates from 1882; the Stick-style **Albert Tanner House** *(no. 2248)*, completed in 1883, has a wraparound porch and richly decorated front gables; and the **Mary Smith House** *(no. 2256)*, its verandah graced by a central bowed portico supported by Ionic columns, was completed in 1906 and is a variant of the Colonial Revival style.

★★ **Pittock Mansion** – *3229 N.W. Pittock Dr. (head west on W. Burnside St., turn right on N.W. Barnes Rd. and follow signs). Open Feb–Dec daily 11am–4pm. Closed major holidays. $4.50. ✗ ▣ ☎ 503-823-3624.* The largest and most opulent home in Portland perches on a 940ft crest in Imperial Heights, looking east over the city, the river and the major peaks of the Cascade Mountains. Built for Henry Pittock (1835-1919), who came west on the Oregon Trail in 1853 and eventually amassed a fortune as the publisher of the *Oregonian*, the mansion was designed by San Francisco architect Edward T. Foulkes and completed in 1914. Stylistically the structure is a French Renaissance Revival chateau with exterior walls of Tenino sandstone from Washington State.

Visit – *1hr.* Visitors may wander through on their own or join a guided tour (45min) to learn more about the mansion's history and details of its design. The fine period furnishings and Oriental rugs are not original to the house but amply convey the luxurious lifestyle of this prominent Portland family.

Nearly one-third of the mansion is taken up by a magnificent marble **staircase** and hallway constructed of Italian and domestic marbles with bronze grillwork and a handrail of eucalyptus gumwood. Interconnecting rooms are entered from the hallway. The elliptical **Drawing Room**, with its elaborate plaster moldings and cornices, commands a 180-degree vista of the city and Mt. Hood. Superlative plasterwork and marquetry floors are found in the small, circular **Turkish Smoking Room★**. Honduran mahogany was used for the wainscoting and ceiling beams in the Edwardian-style **Dining Room**. On the second floor, a four-room **Master Suite** used by Pittock and his wife, Georgiana, is buffered by two smaller suites once occupied by the couple's daughters and their husbands.

Gate Lodge (☎ 503-823-3627), the former grounds keeper's house, is now a restaurant serving lunch and afternoon tea. The landscaped grounds of Pittock mansion adjoin Forest Park, with trailheads at the west end of the parking lot and beyond Gate Lodge.

★Forest Park – [Kids] *Take N.W. Lovejoy St. west to where it becomes N.W. Cornell Rd. and follow to the park.* On a 1903 visit to Portland, landscape designer John Olmsted drew up a city park plan calling for "a succession of ravines and spurs

④ Cafe Torrefazione Italia
Map pp 62-63. 1140 N.W. Everett St. ☎ *503-224-9896.* This spacious cafe in the Pearl District opened in 1999 and makes for a good place to relax with a cup of what is arguably the best non-flavored, full-bodied and highly aromatic coffee in super-caffeinated Portland. Pastries and Italian-style *panini* (sandwiches) are also on the menu. The cafe occupies a large corner building and has been outfitted like a sophisticated Italian coffee shop. The interior boasts slate floors, a long, curving marble-topped wooden bar, and wood tables inset with Deruta ceramic tiles. The work of local artists hangs on the walls.

covered with remarkably beautiful woods." His recommendation led to the establishment of 5,000-acre Forest Park in 1948. The largest urban park in North America, this forest is part of a 9,000-acre park system that forms a wildlife corridor to the Coast Range dividing the Willamette Valley from the Pacific Ocean. This lovely preserve is home to more than 50 species of mammals—including rarely seen deer and bobcats—and about 150 species of birds. Some 50mi of interconnected hiking trails wind up and down the slopes of Forest Park, where a canopy of towering Douglas firs rises above an understory of alders, aspens, hemlock, native holly, and maidenhair and sword ferns. White trilliums glow along the paths in the spring. The 33mi-long **Wildwood Trail** connects Forest Park to Washington Park and to the Hoyt Arboretum *(p 77)*.

■ Portland's Brew Pubs

With more breweries and brew pubs per capita than any other city in the nation, Portland has become known as the "Microbrew Capital of the World." Since the early 1980s microbreweries have proliferated almost as fast as coffee bars. The total now stands at over 40 in the metropolitan area, each dispensing its own handcrafted beers brewed on the premises. Two-row barley (starchier and more expensive), 14 varieties of hops, and pure glacier water from Mt. Hood are among the local ingredients brewmeisters use to create their carefully blended and richly textured brews, which range from pale ales and bitters to dark, creamy English-style stouts, hearty bocks and seasonal brews flavored with raspberries. Like English pubs and German beer halls, Portland's brew pubs are popular, informal gathering spots where pub food is served along with the beer.

Portland's better-known brew pubs include:

Bridgeport Brew Pub *(1313 N.W. Marshall St.* ☎ *503-241-7179)*

Brewhouse Tap Room and Grill *(2730 N.W. 31st Ave.* ☎ *503-228-5269)*

Widmer Brewing and Gasthaus *(929 N. Russell St.* ☎ *503-281-3333)*

Ringlers *(1332 W. Burnside St.* ☎ *503-225-0543)*

Hair of the Dog Brewing Company *(4509 S.E. 23rd Ave.* ☎ *503-232-6585)*

Lucky Labrador Brewing Company *(915 S.E. Hawthorne Blvd.* ☎ *503-236-3555)*

On Saturday afternoons the Portland **BrewBus** *(reservations* ☎ *503-647-0021 or 888-244-2739)* offers a four-hour, behind-the-scenes brewery tour which includes sampling 15 to 20 different brews. At the Oregon Brewers Festival—the largest event of its kind in the country—held in Tom McCall Waterfront Park in late July, enthusiasts can sample some 70 different beers produced by local, national and international breweries.

★★WASHINGTON PARK *1 day. Map pp 72-73.*

Entrances south of W. Burnside Rd. and west of S.W. Vista Ave. Open year-round daily dawn-dusk. ☎ *503-823-7529.* The city bought the land for Washington Park, located in Portland's southwest hills, in 1871. Unlike Forest Park, most of Washington Park has been landscaped to serve as a setting for its acclaimed gardens, zoo and nature-related attractions. Surrounded at its north end by the exclusive Portland Heights neighborhood, the park winds south along the ridge that stretches along the entire west side of the city. Southwest Kingston Avenue connects the Rose Garden and the Japanese Garden to Hoyt Arboretum, the World Forestry Center and the Oregon Zoo. The new extension of the city's light-rail system includes a stop at Washington Park, providing easy access from downtown; in the summer a narrow-gauge excursion train runs from the Rose Garden to the zoo. A new Children's Museum is scheduled to open next to the World Forestry Center in the former Oregon Museum of Science and Industry (OMSI) building in fall 2000.

★★ **International Rose Test Garden** – *400 S.W. Kingston Ave. Open year-round daily dawn-dusk.* ☎ *503-823-3636.* Established in 1917, the oldest public rose test garden in the nation offers a dazzling display of Portland's favorite flower. About 8,000 roses representing 525 species grow in formal terraces overlooking downtown Portland and Mt. Hood. Since 1940 the Rose Gardens in Washington Park have been one of 24 official testing gardens for the All-American Rose Selections and one of five test gardens for miniature roses.

The city's fondness for the genus Rosa dates back to 1887 and the founding of the Portland Rose Society, the oldest such group in the country. In 1907 rose-loving citizens began a campaign to nickname Portland the "City of Roses," which it has been called ever since. The Rose Festival, held every June, coincides with the flowers' peak blooming period and is one of the largest floral-themed extravaganzas in the country.

From the parking lot, steps descend to an information kiosk surrounded by elevated beds of miniature roses. Extending east, and covering two broad terraces, spreads the **All-American Rose Test Garden**. The roses tested here are given a code number rather than a name; four plants of each variety are evaluated for two years by an official judge using 13 different criteria, including bloom quality, how prolific they are, shape, color and vigor. The City of Portland annually awards the best-performing roses with a gold or silver medal. Winners are then given fanciful names such as Fragrant Cloud or Audrey Hepburn and moved to the Gold Award Garden, located on the terraces below the Beach Memorial Fountain, a walk-through stainless-steel sculpture named for Frank E. Beach, who spearheaded efforts to nickname Portland the "City of Roses."

Queens' Walk, on the lowest promenade, is inset with bronze markers for every Rose Festival queen since 1907. Annual and perennial flowers named in Shakespeare's plays are planted in the Shakespeare Garden, in the lower southeast corner.

★★ **Japanese Garden** – *611 S.W. Kingston Ave. Open Apr–Sept daily 10am–7pm. Rest of the year daily 10am–4pm. Closed Jan 1, Thanksgiving Day, Dec 25. $6.* ▣ ☎ *503-223-1321.* One of the most authentic Japanese gardens outside of Japan occupies a 5.5-acre site directly above the rose gardens. Designed by Professor Takuma Tono, a Japanese landscape master from Tokyo, the garden took four years to complete and was opened to the public in 1967. The immaculately tended grounds contain superb examples of ancient Japanese gardening styles influenced by Shinto, Buddhist and Taoist philosophies. Plants, stones and water are employed to create areas of serene and contemplative beauty. From April to October an open-sided bus is available to take visitors from the parking lot up to the entrance. More scenic is the graveled **foot path** which begins at the lovely Antique Gate, constructed of wood, stone, and clay tiles, and climbs up through the forest to the entrance. Inside the main gate, the path to your right passes through a wisteria arbor framing an antique five-tiered stone pagoda lantern and leads down a gentle incline to the **Strolling Pond Garden**, the largest garden on the site. The picturesque Moon Bridge crosses the north end of the Upper Pond. In the **Tea Garden** at the northwest corner of this area there is a ceremonial teahouse constructed in Japan and reassembled here in 1968. The traditional four-and-a-half-mat room is used for the study and practice of the tea ceremony; each mat is named and has a special use—entrance mat, utensil mat, principal guest mat, hostess mat and hearth mat (the half mat). Farther south, at the Lower Pond, giant koi slowly navigate below a waterfall.

A path from the south hillside leads to an abstract, Zen-inspired **Sand and Stone Garden** with weathered stones rising from a bed of gravel raked in undulating lines to suggest the sea. The large wooden pavilion behind the Flat Garden is used for special events and provides a majestic **view★** of Portland and Mt. Hood from its eastern terrace.

Japanese Garden, Washington Park

Hoyt Arboretum – *Visitor center located at 4033 S.W. Fairview Blvd. (from the south, take Zoo-Forestry Center exit off Rte. 26). Open year-round daily dawn-dusk. Closed Dec 25.* 🚻 🅿 ☎ *503-228-8733.* Over 900 species of trees, some indigenous to the Pacific Northwest, others imported from around the world, are found in the hills and meadows of the 175-acre arboretum at the south end of Washington Park. Trails wind through well-established stands of magnolias, maples, oaks, hawthorns, cherries and the most extensive conifer collection in the US. The short **Overlook Trail** just south of the Washington Park light-rail station leads to the visitor center (you can also drive there) where you'll find maps and booklets for self-guided tours. **Bristlecone Pine Trail** off Fischer Lane is a 1mi paved trail with handicapped access parking.

The **Vietnam Veterans Living Memorial**, dedicated in 1987, lies at the southwest corner of the arboretum, just above the World Forestry Center. From a central bowl-shaped area an ascending walkway spirals up to six black Indian granite markers inscribed with the names of Oregonians reported as dead or missing from 1959-1976. In the middle of the garden a granite plaque reads, "So long as we are not forgotten we do not die. And thus this garden is a place of life."

★**World Forestry Center** – 🧒 *4033 S.W. Canyon Rd. Open Memorial Day-Labor Day daily 9am–5pm. Rest of the year daily 10am–5pm. Closed Dec 25.* 🚻 🅿 ☎ *503-228-1367. www.worldforest.org.* Housed in an octagonal, cedar-clad building with a tentlike roof, this museum just west of the zoo is a storehouse of information about the world's forests. Most of the wood used in the building, both inside and out, is splendid old-growth vertical grain cedar and fir. In the center of a soaring central exhibition space supported by eight octagonal fir columns, the multilingual **Talking Tree** greets visitors and explains how a tree grows. Petrified wood is displayed around the tree, and a slide show *(18min)* in the adjacent theater provides an to the world's forests. **Memorial Hall** looks out on a rocky, naturalistic water fountain and contains a beautiful Arts and Crafts myrtlewood table built for the 1905 Lewis & Clark Exposition.

A grand staircase leads up to two timely and thought-provoking exhibits on the second floor: "Old Growth Forests: Treasure in Transition" and "Tropical Rainforests: a Disappearing Treasure." Both rely heavily on panels of text but are enlivened by photographs, videos, dioramas and multimedia displays. Visitors can easily combine a visit to the Forestry Center with a walk in Hoyt Arboretum, which extends north, east and west of the building.

★**Oregon Zoo** – 🧒 *4001 S.W. Canyon Rd. (Zoo-Forestry Center exit off Rte. 26 west, from downtown). Open Apr–Sept daily 9am–6pm. Rest of the year daily 9am–4pm. Closed Dec 25. $5.50, children $3.50.* 🍴 🚻 🅿 ☎ *503-226-1561. www.oregonzoo.org.* The state's most visited attraction, the Oregon Zoo is home to over 1,000 animals representing 200 species of birds, mammals reptiles and amphibians, including 54 that are threatened or endangered. Its outdoor habitats and modern indoor pavilions are spread over 64 forested acres. When they are completed in 2001, five new exhibits collectively called The Great Northwest will introduce visitors to the animals found in habitats ranging from the Cascade Mountains to the rocky shores of the Pacific Ocean. Cascade Crest, with mountain goats clambering over craggy outcroppings, is the only one finished to date.

The zoo is famous for its Asian **elephants★**, one of the largest breeding herds in the world. Since 1962, 28 calves have been born in the zoo; currently three males and three females live here. The four-acre Africa Plains exhibit replicates the dry, open bush country of East Africa and features rare black rhinos, Nile hippos, giraffes and **naked mole-rats★**. Housed in their own building, these tiny African animals with permanently closed eyes inhabit a warren of underground tunnels with glass-sided viewing areas. The impressive **Alaska Tundra★** exhibit re-creates the harsh environment of Alaska's North Slope. Musk ox, wolves and brown bears inhabit a natural setting of forests, caves and rushing streams. The popular indoor **Penguinarium** is home to a colony of endangered Peruvian Humboldt penguins and a flock of Inca terns.

EAST PORTLAND *1/2 day*

East Portland, divided by East Burnside Street into Northeast and Southeast sections, has dozens of small, pleasant neighborhoods but far fewer tourist attractions than the Westside. When it opened in 1960, **Lloyd Center** *(N.E. Multnomah St. at N.E. 9th Ave.)* was one of the first covered shopping malls in the country. **Memorial Coliseum** *(1 Center Ct.)*, designed by Skidmore, Owings and Merrill and completed the same year, serves as a venue for sports events, concerts and trade shows. The completion of the east-west light-rail system in 1987 brought the two sides of the city closer together and was instrumental in the development of the 1990 **Oregon Convention Center** *(777 N.E. Martin Luther King Blvd.)*, with its tapered twin glass spires, and the giant, oyster-shaped **Rose Garden Arena**, built for the Portland Trail Blazers.

★★**Oregon Museum of Science and Industry** – Kids *1945 S.E. Water St. (south of the Morrison Bridge). Open mid-Jun–Labor Day daily 9:30am–7pm. Rest of the year Tue–Sun 9:30am–5:30pm. Closed major holidays. $6.50.* ✗ ♿ ▣ ☎ *503-797-4000. www.omsi.edu.* The Eastside's major attraction is housed in a 1992 brick-and-glass building beside the Willamette River on the site of a former power plant. OMSI features an outstanding array of hands-on exhibits, an Omnimax Theater, a planetarium and a submarine.

Visit – *2 hrs galleries; allot extra time for Omnimax, planetarium and submarine.* On the first floor, to the left of the glass-towered entrance lobby, the five-story **Omnimax Theater** shows three different films daily (each film lasts about 50min) on its enormous super-70mm screen. Here, too, there is a Changing Exhibit Hall, a well-stocked science store and a cafe. To the right of the lobby, the **Murdock Planetarium** boasts a 52ft-high dome onto which multimedia astronomy and laser-light shows *(45min)* are projected, featuring state-of-the-art visual and sound systems. The adjacent **Physical Science Turbine Hall** occupies the former power plant and is loaded with hands-on activities that allow kids to build bridges, launch boats and design and test aircraft. Just beyond, Busytown is a new creative play area for younger children. On the second floor there are three interconnected gallery areas with a dizzying assortment of activities. Start your explorations in the Life Sciences Hall, where the highlight is an exhibit on reproduction and childbirth called **Beginning the Journey★**. It features a collection of human embryos and fetuses in various stages of development from 28 days to 32 weeks. Other exhibits deal with the human body, body structure, growth and development. "Climate and El Niño" is the focus of interactive displays in the Earth Sciences Hall, devoted to the interrelationships between all of Earth's elements. In the **Earthquake Room★** visitors can experience the jolting effects of a major quake. A host of computer-oriented exhibits in the High Tech Hall highlight recent advances in sending, storing and receiving information and explain the basics of electronic technology.

Moored in the river behind the museum is the **U.S.S. Blueback**, the nation's last diesel-electric submarine, built in 1959 and decommissioned in 1994. Guided tours *(40min)* lead visitors through the cramped quarters of this sub, which was featured in the 1990 movie *The Hunt For Red October*.

Southeast Hawthorne Boulevard – The Eastside's answer to Northwest 23rd Avenue, Southeast Hawthorne Boulevard is a lively neighborhood and citywide destination known for its eclectic mix of restaurants, juice bars, bakeries, music stores, bookshops, theaters and coffeehouses. The boulevard extends all the way from the Hawthorne Bridge to Mount Tabor Park, but the "happening" section lies between 30th and 42nd Avenues.

Mount Tabor Park – *S.E. 60th Ave. and Salmon St.* Portland is the only major city in the continental US that has an extinct volcano within its borders. Mt. Tabor, one of the few "highland" areas in East Portland, ranks as the youngest of the hundreds of volcanoes that erupted in the foothills of Mt. Hood eons ago. Southeast Salmon Street leads up through a residential section to the large forested park that crowns the summit of the ancient cinder cone. From the reservoir on the west slope, visitors obtain expansive **views**★ of downtown Portland and the West Hills; walking paths and a series of stairways ascend to a grassy area on top where the jagged buttes and mounded hills formed by earlier volcanic activity can be seen to the east.

American Advertising Museum – *5035 S.E. 24th Ave. at Raymond St. Call for hours. $3.* 🅿 ☎ *503-226-0000. www.admuseum.org.* Small, informative and fun, the Advertising Museum traces the development of advertising in America from the first ad placed in a newspaper *(Boston News-Letter, 1704)* to the slick, multimillion-dollar ad campaigns of today. Print ads span a 100-year period, from 19C Coca-Cola to contemporary Nike, and are supplemented by displays of product-related icons (Michelin Tire Man, Campbell Soup Kids, Pillsbury Doughboy). Vintage radios play ads from the 1940s; famous TV ads from the 1950s through the 1970s are screened in a separate room.

★**Crystal Springs Rhododendron Garden** – *S.E. 28th Ave., 1 block north of Woodstock Blvd. Open year-round daily dawn-dusk. $3.* ♿ 🅿 ☎ *503-777-8386.* Lovely year-round, this seven-acre garden in the Eastmoreland neighborhood turns spectacular from April through June when 600 varieties of rhododendrons and azaleas burst into bloom. The Portland chapter of the American Rhododendron Society began planting the prize collection of rhododendrons in 1950. From the gatehouse, visitors cross a bridge overlooking a small waterfall and follow paths through the shade-loving "rhodies" to Crystal Springs Lake, created in 1917 by damming 13 area springs. Congregated near the shoreline and bobbing on the water are coots, widgeons, wood ducks, mallards and Canada geese. Paddison Fountain shoots a geyser of water into the lake's South Lagoon.

Oaks Amusement Park – 🈂 *S.E. Spokane St. (just east of Sellwood Bridge). Open Jun–Sept Tue–Thu noon–9pm, Fri & Sat noon–10pm, Sun noon–7pm. Rest of the year weekends noon–5pm. Call ahead for holiday hours.* 🍴 ♿ 🅿 ☎ *503-233-5777.* One of the nation's oldest continuously operating amusement parks, Oaks Park opened in 1905 to compete with the Lewis and Clark Exposition. The attractions here are family oriented and decidedly old-fashioned-a roller rink with a Wurlitzer organ, a dance pavilion, a carousel, non-tech game arcades, and 28 rides. The **Ladybug Theater** *(☎ 503-232-2346)* on the grounds presents plays for children. In season, "Samtrak," an electric open-air excursion train, runs between the Oregon Museum of Science and Industry and Oaks Park. A footpath provides access to the marshes of the Oaks Bottom Wildlife Refuge on the east.

Additional Sights

The Grotto – *8840 N.E. Skidmore St. (at the Sanctuary of Our Sorrowful Mother, N.E. Sandy Blvd. and N.E. 85th Ave.). Open Jun–Labor Day daily 9am–8pm. Rest of the year daily 9am–5:30pm. Closed Dec. 25.* 🍴 ♿ 🅿 ☎ *503-254-7371. www.thegrotto.org.* Woodland gardens with spring-blooming rhododendrons and azaleas cover the 62-acre grounds of this outdoor Catholic shrine established in 1924. On the lower level a reproduction of Michaelangelo's *Pietà* is set within a grotto carved into a 110ft-high basalt cliff. An elevator takes visitors to the top of the bluff for panoramic views of the Cascade Mountains and Columbia River Valley. Perched on the edge of the cliff, the Meditation Chapel is a granite-clad structure with a triangular floor plan and immense structural glass windows looking north to Mt. St. Helens.

★**Leach Botanical Garden** – *6704 S.E. 122nd Ave. (just south of S.E. Foster Rd.). Open year-round Tue–Sat 9am–4pm, Sun 1pm–4pm. Closed major holidays.* 🅿 ☎ *503-761-9503.* Botanists Lilla and John Leach started this natural garden beside Johnson Creek in the 1930s. Lilla Leach became world-famous as the discoverer of a small rhododendron-type plant named Kalmiopsis leachiana in her honor. The cottage-style Manor House, now a visitor center, provides a self-guided map of the nine-acre site. Surrounding the house, 1.5mi of mostly woodland trails lace through rock gardens, bog displays, Pacific Northwest woodland gardens and displays of southeastern US azaleas. Camellias, viburnums, wildflowers, ferns, bamboo and Lilla Leach's discoveries are among 1,500 different species and cultivars found here. A footbridge (open summers only) spans Johnson Creek and leads to a charming stone cottage.

EXCURSIONS

★★**Elk Rock Gardens at the Bishop's Close** – *1 hr. 6mi south of downtown Portland. Take S.W. Macadam Ave. south from downtown toward Lake Oswego, turn left on S.W. Military Rd., then take an immediate right on S.W. Military Lane. Open year-round daily 8am–5pm. Closed major holidays.* ☎ *503-636-5613.* Located on a high bluff overlooking Elk Rock Island, the Willamette River and Mt. Hood, this exceptionally beautiful estate garden designed by John Olmsted has had several

■ Antiquing

Antiques stores are scattered throughout Portland, but the **Sellwood** neighborhood just east of the Sellwood Bridge is the best place for concentrated shopping. Named for the Rev. James Sellwood, who settled in this area in 1856, Sellwood became an incorporated town in 1887 and was annexed by the City of Portland in 1891. One of the first "streetcar suburbs," it has a number of modest Victorian homes-trolley-car drivers lived in many of them-and the quiet, unassuming ambience of a small town. Antique Row, on 13th Avenue between Southeast Malden and Clatsop Streets, holds the largest concentration of antiques and collectible stores in the state. Victorian, Mission and Arts and Crafts furniture; linens; glassware; and paintings are among the items you'll find here. **Sellwood Antique Mall** (7875 S.E. 13th Ave.; ☎ 503-232-3755); the **Sellwood Antique Collective** (8027 S.E. 13th Ave.; ☎ 503-736-1399); and **Stars Antique Mall** (7027 S.E. Milwaukie Blvd.; ☎ 503-239-0346) are multi-dealer emporiums good for all-purpose treasure-hunting. The **1874 House** (8070 S.E. 13th Ave.; ☎ 503-233-1874) deals in antique hardware for buildings and architectural fragments. **Rara Avis** (8121 S.E. 13th Ave.; ☎ 503-232-5311) specializes in European furniture, mirrors, lighting and art. **The Handwerk Shop** (8317 S.E. 13th Ave.; ☎ 503-236-7870) is oriented towards fine, handcrafted Arts and Crafts and Mission oak furniture, metalwork and pottery.

The best place to look for antique Japanese and Chinese furniture and accessories is **Shogun's Gallery** in northwest Portland (206 N.W. 23rd Ave.; ☎ 503-224-0328). Located in the Pearl District, **Portland Antique Company** (1211 N.W. Glisan St.; ☎ 503-223-0999) harbors the city's largest selection of European antiques.

decades to establish itself and is now considered one of the great gardens of the Pacific Northwest. Peter Kerr, the owner of the estate, was a Scotsman who came to Portland in 1888 and prospered as a grain merchant. The 1916 house (not open to the public) that acts as the focal pivot of the gardens was built to resemble a Scottish manor. During the 1920s, using Olmsted's basic plan, Kerr created an English landscape garden around it, continually adding plants obtained during his world travels. Both house and gardens now belong to the Episcopal Diocese of Oregon. Graveled paths and rock steps meander up and down the cliffside gardens, one of the first in the Northwest to use native trees and plants-madrones, Douglas firs, western dogwoods and Oregon grape-in a cultivated landscape. Interspersed with the native flora are imported exotics such as weeping Atlas cedars, Japanese snowball trees, Dawn redwoods, witch hazels and numerous magnolias.

Berry Botanic Garden – *25min. 6.5mi south of downtown Portland. Take Macadam Ave. south from downtown and turn right on S.W. Military Rd., then right again on S.W. Summerville Ave. to no. 11505. Open year-round daily dawn-dusk. $5.* 🅿 ☎ *503-636-4112. www.berrybot.org.* Noted for its rare and endangered Northwest natives-alpines, primroses and rhododendrons and lilies-this species garden was started in the 1940s by Rae Selling Berry, an internationally known gardener who worked here for over 40 years. The six-acre site, located near the Willamette River on a ridge just north of Lake Oswego, has a variety of informal microhabitats springs, creeks, a meadow and a marsh. Mrs. Berry's house is now a visitor center, where you'll find maps and information about the plants. To the east and north of the house lies a rhododendron forest, planted 60 years ago from seeds obtained on expeditions in China.

Bybee-Howell House – *45min. 12.5mi northwest of Portland in Bybee-Howell Territorial Park on Sauvie Island. Take US-30 northwest to Sauvie Island exit, then east over the bridge. Turn left off the bridge and follow signs. Visit by guided tour (30min) only, Jun–Labor Day weekends noon–5pm. $3.* 🅿 ☎ *503-306-5221. www.osh.org.* Built in 1858, the Bybee-Howell House is a rare example of the Classical Revival style. The nine-room, two-story residence was built for James Bybee, who came to Oregon in 1847 and established a 642-acre land claim on Sauvie Island. In 1873 the house was sold to Joseph and John Howell; it is now owned and maintained by the Metro Regional Parks & Greenspaces. The wood-frame façade features symmetrically placed chimneys, double-hung sash windows and pedimented gables. Behind the house stands an Agricultural Museum displaying 19C farming equipment, and the Pioneer Orchard with many varieties of apple trees brought here by pioneers. Bucolic Sauvie Island is peppered with fruit and vegetable stands, a wildlife refuge and sandy beaches on the Columbia River.

★**Vancouver National Historic Reserve** – *3 hrs. 8mi north of Portland in Vancouver, WA. Take I-5 north to Mill Plain Blvd. and follow signs to various sites within the Reserve). Open Mar–Oct daily 9am–5pm. Rest of the year daily 9am–4pm. Closed*

Thanksgiving Day, Dec 24-25. ♿ 🅿 ☎ *360-992-1820.* Established by Congress in 1996, the Reserve contains several historically important sites located along and adjacent to the Columbia River in Vancouver, Washington. Start your tour in the **O.O. Howard House Visitor Center★** *(750 Anderson St.)* located in a restored 1878 Victorian house. A self-guided exhibit provides a broad historical overview of early British and American exploration of the Pacific Northwest, Native American cultures, the establishment of Fort Vancouver (1825) and Vancouver Barracks (1849). Just north of the visitor center is **Officers Row★**, 22 impressive 19C and early 20C houses constructed for US Army officers stationed at Vancouver Barracks. The 1886 **Marshall House★** *(no. 1301; open year-round Mon–Fri 9am–5pm, weekends 11am–6pm; closed Thanksgiving Day, Dec 25;* ♿ 🅿 ☎ *360-693-3103)* is a turreted Queen Anne Victorian named for Gen. George C. Marshall, who served as commander of Vancouver Barracks from 1936 to 1938. A 20min video here provides details about Officers Row. The rooms on view, with the exception of Gen. Marshall's office, are furnished in the Victorian style and feature lavish wood ornamentation. The **Grant House Folk Art Center** *(no. 1101; open year-round Tue–Sat 11am–3pm; closed Thanksgiving Day, Dec 24-25;* ✗ ♿ 🅿 ☎ *360-694-5252)* was first built in 1849 as a log cabin. Named for Gen. Ulysses S. Grant, who lived on post prior to the Civil War, it now houses a gallery and restaurant.

Fort Vancouver (1848) by Capt. Henry J. Warre

Oregon Historical Society, ORHI83437

★Fort Vancouver National Historic Site – 🆔 *Open Mar–Oct daily 9am–5pm. Rest of the year daily 9am–4pm. Closed Jan 1, Thanksgiving Day, Dec 24-25. $2.* ♿ 🅿 ☎ *360-696-7655. www.nps.gov/fova.* Located just south of Officers Row alongside the Columbia River, the fort functioned as the main supply depot for the Columbia Department of the British-controlled Hudson's Bay Company from 1825 until 1849, when the area came under American rule. With territory extending for some 400,000sq mi, it became the fur-trade capital of the Pacific Coast. Archaeologists began a systematic excavation of the site in 1948 and recovered more than one million objects. From the visitor center, which provides a useful introduction, drive just south for a guided walking tour *(1 hr)* of the reconstructed fort with its simple, rough-hewn buildings: A carpenter's shop, fur warehouse and a bakehouse stand along the peripheries of a tall wooden stockade. The white-frame **Chief Factor's Residence** is the most "civilized" of the fort's buildings. If your time is limited, you can wander through the grounds and visit the Blacksmith's Shop without joining a tour.

Pearson Air Museum – 🆔 *1105 E. 5th St; Open year-round Tue–Sun 10am–5pm. Closed Jan 1, Thanksgiving Day, Dec 25. $4.* ♿ 🅿 ☎ *360-694-7026. www.pearsonairmuseum.org.* Adjacent to Fort Vancouver, this museum is situated on the grounds of Pearson Airfield, in use since 1905 and one of the oldest operating airfields in the US. An impressive collection of vintage aircraft, including a replica of the first biplane to fly from Portland to Pearson Airfield in 1911, is on display in the main hangar. One curiosity, a lounge seat from the Hindenburg, is the only remaining piece of the famous German dirigible that exploded in 1937. Video clips; short films about early aviation, modern warplanes and air races; and interactive computer displays and exhibits pertaining to the mechanics of flight are featured in the museum.

★★★Mt. St. Helens National Volcanic Monument – *Visitor center located 65mi north of Portland, 5mi east of I-5 Exit 49, on Rte. 504. Description p. 266*

COLUMBIA RIVER GORGE NATIONAL SCENIC AREA★★

Michelin map 493 B, C 4 and map pp 86-87
Tourist Information ☎ 800-984-6743

Portland's playground, the 295,000-acre Columbia River Gorge National Scenic Area stretches about 80mi from Troutdale east to the Deschutes River, encompassing seven major waterfalls, nine state parks, and dramatic 700ft-high, cliff-edge vistas. Here the Columbia River creates fjord-like grandeur as it slices through a volcanic basalt gorge, its towering banks spiked with Douglas firs. The gorge, claimed by Oregon on the south shore and Washington on the north, begins 17mi east of downtown Portland and continues east for about 67mi to the town of The Dalles. Almost three million visitors come here year-round to admire the falls, photograph the views (especially at sunrise or sunset), hike, fish, mountain bike and windsurf.

Native Americans at Celilo Falls, Columbia River (c.1899) by Benjamin Gifford

Oregon Historical Society, ORH189622

Historical Notes

Between 12 and 17 million years ago, a series of volcanic eruptions blanketed most of present-day Washington and Oregon with black basaltic lava and altered the course of the Columbia many times. During the last ice age, about 15,000 years ago, a 2,500ft-high lobe of ice dammed the waters of Montana's Clark Fork River to the northeast. As the dam's ice periodically melted and refroze, nearly 90 catastrophic floods—now known as the Bretz Floods—unleashed 500 cubic miles of water across eastern Washington. Carrying ice and massive boulders in their wake, these floodwaters scoured out the Columbia River Gorge, further molding the canyon we know today. The rapid erosion caused by the floods cut off many of the Columbia's cliffside tributaries, forming a series of "hanging valleys" which now hold more than 35 waterfalls-some more than 100ft high—and provide dramatic scenery for hikers in the gorge.

Starting about 10,000 years ago, Indians began occupying the Columbia Gorge, living on big game, fish, and such plants as camas and yampah. The gorge was not only an important fishing site but also a gathering spot for Indians trading up and down the river, which they called *Nchi-a-wah-na*, or "Big River." It was renamed in 1792, when Boston trader Captain Robert Gray briefly stumbled upon the waterway, christening it "Columbia," after his ship, *Columbia Rediviva*.

Encouraged by the reports of Lewis and Clark and other early 1800s explorers, settlers began streaming through the gorge to a place called The Dalles, which signified the official end of the Oregon Trail, though not the end of the pioneers' road. Their ultimate destination, the temperate Willamette Valley, lay another 90mi away, over some of the worst terrain they had yet encountered. At The Dalles settlers faced the difficult choice of riding the dangerous rapids of the Columbia or ascending a precipitous, unstable wagon trail over the south side of Mt. Hood. Some, daunted by their harsh options, simply chose to go no farther.

It was not long before these first settlers discovered the bounty of the river; by 1,876 450,000 cases of canned salmon had been shipped out of the area to destinations back east. Highly efficient fish wheels were scooping up hundreds of fish at a time, so many that the devices were banned by 1934. Towering ponderosa pines and

Douglas firs on both sides of the river provided another economic resource. Loggers felled trees with two-man saws, built flumes and railroad spurs to pull the timber off the hills, created logging mills, and built paper mills farther west up the river.

The course of the river was altered again in 1937 with the construction of Bonneville Dam; The Dalles Dam followed twenty years later. In addition to destroying the Indians' fishing grounds, construction of The Dalles Dam nearly submerged forever a group of Indian petroglyphs and pictographs. Recovered at the last minute, these ancient rock artworks are now displayed at the dam's facility *(p 88)*. Other vestiges of early native life survive all along the gorge. One of the most famous petroglyphs—the haunting, large-eyed spirit Tsagaglalal, "She Who Watches"—is carved into cliffs now contained in **Horsethief Lake State Park** in Wishram, Washington *(off Rte. 14;* ☏ *509-767-1159)*. Although the logging and fishing industries built the first towns on the Columbia, as early as 1910 committees were being established to regulate these industries before they depleted the area's once-abundant resources. As the logging and fishing waned, the towns' futures hung in the balance while the area slowly switched from a timber-based economy to tourism as recently as the mid 1980s. Ironically, it was the people of Portland who pushed to preserve the gorge; residents of the small struggling gorge towns of Stevenson, White Salmon and Hood River did not want to be limited in the type of economic development they could pursue. Following a bitter political battle, the Portlanders won out: On November 17, 1986, President Ronald Reagan signed into law the Columbia River Gorge National Scenic Area Act to preserve the existing 264,000 acres of rural and scenic areas and to encourage economic growth within the designated 28,500 acres of urban areas. The US Forest Service currently maintains the federal public lands within the gorge. Today the timber and fishing industries of old have yielded to more modern occupations: Hydropower plants at Bonneville and The Dalles fuel aluminum and other manufacturing facilities along the gorge; farmers cultivate fruit orchards in Hood River Valley; and sailboarders ride the river's famed winds.

■ Windsurfing the Gorge

Skipping across the waves like colorful flying fish, sailboarders have found a paradise near the town of Hood River, where steady currents from the east meet strong winds tunneled from the west. With the area's summer winds averaging 20-25mph, windsurfing enthusiasts had discovered the gorge by the mid 1980s. After a short period of adjustment, the small town recognized the sport's importance to the local economy by developing Columbia Gorge Sailpark at the marina, with a beach, jogging trails and picnic benches. Though competitive windsurfing has died down somewhat, Hood River's streets are still packed in July with shiny new sports-utility vehicles driven by neoprene-clad wind worshippers. The most dedicated sign up for paging systems that beep when the wind is right for a "nuclear" day. So favorable are Hood River's sailboarding conditions that the US Windsurfing Association, the national organizing authority for the sport, has chosen the town as its home, along with more than three dozen sailboard retailers, distributors, and custom board and accessory manufacturers.

Windsurfing on the Hood River

© Dianne Dietrich Leis

★★HISTORIC COLUMBIA RIVER HIGHWAY *1 day*

Skirting the steep cliffs above the Columbia River, this historic highway recalls the days when early motorists ventured out for a Sunday drive in their Model Ts. The route—designed to frame stunning views along the way—abounds with breathtaking glimpses of the gorge and detours to glistening waterfalls. It now provides a more leisurely and scenic alternative to Interstate-84.

Wealthy local landowner Sam Hill *(p 88)* was one of the first to envision a road through the gorge, a task once considered impossible. Dreaming of a European-style highway by which to access the area's scenery, Hill enlisted the help of his friend, renowned Tennessee engineer Samuel Lancaster. Together they convinced the Oregon Legislature in 1913 to create a highway from Troutdale to The Dalles. Since Lancaster intended for the road to "provide maximum scenic opportunities, yet do as little damage as possible to the environment," he and Hill drove the mountain roads of Europe to get ideas for the highway's design. A Portland journalist at the time wrote that to Lancaster "the highway is a religion, a work of art to be given the devotion of a life-time." Workers soon began blasting the road out of the basalt cliffs along the river and stonemasons fashioned the arched guardrails to complement the natural rock in the gorge. The highway was completed in 1915.

Today, owing to deterioration of the road since the construction of I-84 in the mid 1950s, the historic highway is only driveable in two distinct sections linked by the interstate: the first from Troutdale to Ainsworth State Park *(22mi)*; the second from Mosier to The Dalles *(16mi)*. Even so, the winding highway remains "a poem in stone."

Sights

From Portland take I-84 east, then Exit 17 in Troutdale. Follow signs for the Historic Columbia River Highway (US 30) which continues east 22mi to Ainsworth State Park (just beyond Oneonta Gorge) located at I-84, Exit 35. At this point you must get on I-84 East. The historic highway begins again in Mosier (I-84, Exit 69), 35mi east, and ends 16mi later in The Dalles. Sights below are described from west to east.

Park passes (which must be displayed in your car) are required at some trailheads in Oregon and Washington; this includes the parking lots at all of the waterfalls except Multnomah; day passes ($3) or annual passes ($25) are available through the Columbia River Gorge National Scenic Area, US Forest Service, Hood River, OR 97031; ☎ 541-386-2333.

Portland Women's Forum State Park– *Mile 10.* One of the best **views★** of the gorge happens to be the first. At this small park donated by the group that led the "Save the Gorge" movement in the 1950s, you can see the broad river and east past Crown Point up the serene neck of the gorge.

View from Crown Point, Columbia River

Vista House at Crown Point – *Mile 11, Historic Columbia River Hwy. Open mid-Apr–mid-Oct daily 8:30am–6pm.* 🅿 ☎ *503-695-2230. www.vistahouse.com.* A popular viewpoint, this octagonal gray sandstone structure (1918, Edgar M. Lazarus), with its distinctive copper roof, perches 733ft above the Columbia River. When historic highway engineer Samuel Lancaster scouted out the overlook he claimed it to be one of the world's most spectacular vistas and suggested building an observatory here, where "the Columbia could be viewed in silent communion with the infinite." On May 5, 1918 the Vista House opened as a rest area, an observatory, and a memorial to Oregon's pioneers. Its dome contains eight panels, each inscribed with settlers' names. Today, the modest visitor's center, in need of some repair, includes a small gift shop and restrooms. To get the best **views★★**, climb the narrow staircase to the observatory deck.

★**Bridal Veil Falls State Park** – *Mile 16. Open year-round dawn-dusk. Day use only.* ♿ 🅿 ☎ *800-551-6949.* Though the falls themselves are not showstoppers and you must take a steep .75mi round-trip trail to see them, this park still makes for a historically interesting stop. Early settlers with an eye on the timber decided this was a natural place for a lumber mill. Water-filled flumes were constructed to carry logs down from Palmer Logging Camp (built 1886), just 2mi upstream from Bridal Veil Falls, to the Bridal Veil Lumber Company at the base of the falls. The first commercial logging and planing mill at the western end of the gorge, Bridal Veil Lumber Company made boxes for apples, ammunition (during World War II) and cheese (when under the ownership of Kraft Cheese Company). The mill stayed in operation until the early 1980s. An easier .25mi loop leads to stunning **views★** over the cliffs.

★★**Multnomah Falls** – *Mile 19, or Exit 31 from I-84.* ☎ *503-695-2376.* "There are higher waterfalls and falls of greater volume, but there are none more beautiful than Multnomah," highway engineer Samuel Lancaster once enthused. Collecting the waters of Larch Mountain and spilling them from a 620ft cliff, these breathtaking falls draw 2.5 million annual visitors, making them one of Oregon's top attractions. A well-trodden trail *(.5mi)* leads to the 1916 Benson Bridge and provides views of the upper and lower plunge pools. Or you can just stand in awe at the base of the falls and watch the cascade and its shimmering spray. A newly repaired trail leads to the upper falls. Just off the road stands the stone-faced **Multnomah Falls Lodge** (1925), which houses a Columbia River Gorge National Scenic Area information center, a gift shop and a casual restaurant.

Oneonta Gorge – *Mile 22.* A cool, wet canyon draped with moss and other vegetation features walls hundreds of feet high that function like an open book of the geologic history of the region. Adventurers hike straight up the gorge, right through the stream that waters it. Others opt for the trail from Horsetail Falls *(2.7mi round-trip)*, a half-mile west, which takes them to the south end of Oneonta Gorge.

© Dick Dietrich

Columbia Gorge Hotel

I-84, Exit 64; 4000 Westcliff Dr., Hood River, OR 97031. ☎ *541-386-5566 or 800-345-1921.*

www.gorge.net/lodging/cghotel. Recognizing the lack of amenities for travelers on the highway, lumber baron Simon Benson built the stately hotel in 1921 on the site of a previous hostelry. Visited by presidents and movie stars in its heyday, this luxury property closed during the Depression, serving as a retirement home until 1977 when it was purchased and restored to its present-day splendor. The grand yellow stucco building with its terra-cotta roof has now reclaimed its original elegance, and is surrounded by rock gardens, water fountains, arched bridges, swinging chairs in romantic nooks, and cliff-edge views over Wah Gwin Gwin Falls and the gorge. The five-course breakfasts here challenge even the most voracious appetite.

★ **Bonneville Locks and Dam** – *I-84, Exit 40. Open year-round daily 9am–5pm. Closed Jan 1, Thanksgiving Day, Dec 25.* & 🅿 ☎ *541-374-8820. www.nwp.usace.army.mil/op/b.* The growing need for electricity, the frequency of floods, and the necessity for jobs during the Depression convinced Franklin D. Roosevelt to allocate Federal money for the construction of a dam at Cascade Rapids (the first of six on the Columbia). Started in 1933, the Bonneville Dam provided jobs for 3,000 workers and took four years to complete. Its massive spillway and twin powerhouses make it one of the state's most awesome works of engineering. The five-story **Bradford Island Visitor Center** *(same hours as above)* offers a brief history of the gorge and exhibits about the purpose and building of the dam. A theater screens continuous films on the Columbia, fish migration, and current US Army Corps of Engineers projects. On the ground floor an underwater window provides views of a fish ladder that allows salmon and other fish to bypass the dam in their seasonal migrations. Go inside the powerhouse to view generators and learn about the path of electricity from turbine to transformers, or walk outside to watch such regional cargo as wheat, corn and fertilizer barge through the westernmost lock in a 465mi waterway running from the Pacific Ocean to Lewiston, Idaho.

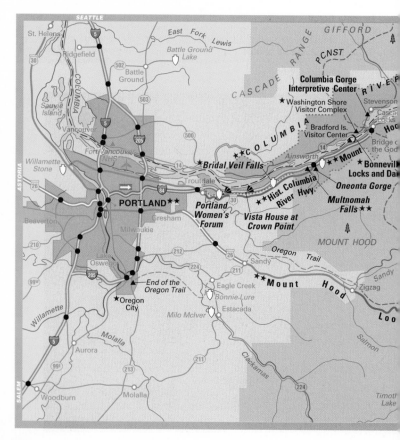

A more up-close look at the inside of a generator can be had inside powerhouse two at the Bonneville Dam's **Washington Shore Visitor Complex★** *(I-84, Exit 44 at Cascade Locks; cross over at Bridge of the Gods and go 2mi west on Rte. 14; same hours as above).*

Columbia Gorge Interpretive Center – *I-84, Exit 44, across the Bridge of the Gods and east 2mi, then left to 990 S.W. Rock Creek Dr., Stevenson, WA. Open year-round daily 10am–5pm. Closed Jan 1, Thanksgiving Day, Dec 25. $6.* & 🄿 ☏ *509-427-8211 or 800-991-2338.* Boasting 23,000sq ft of state-of-the-art display space, this impressive museum does a fine job interpreting the cultural and natural history of the gorge. Just past the entrance on the main floor, pictographs (paintings on rock), petroglyphs (carvings on rock), and root-and-berry gathering baskets vie for attention with a 37ft fish wheel replica, native dip nets, and exhibits on fur trappers. A 12min slide presentation describes the volcanic activity, ice dams, and floods that created the gorge. Community memorabilia on the third floor includes a small area devoted to the Japanese laborer-an acknowledgment of the common man who built the railways, roads and tunnels.

The hairpin turns, cliffhanger views and picturesque white wooden guardrails of the Historic Columbia River Highway begin again in the little town of Mosier, just 5mi east of Hood River. Be sure to stop at **Rowena Crest Viewpoint★★** *(9mi east of Mosier),* where a grand Columbia River vista is complemented by a vast array of wildflowers found in the adjacent 230-acre Tom McCall Preserve.

The Dalles – *Exit 84 off I-84.* About 7mi farther east along the highway, this Western-style town sits on a bend in the river where rapids once forced travelers to take a break in their journeys. Indians had long used the area as a center of trade and fishing. They would stand out on platforms along the basalt cliffs, dip their hemp-woven nets into the river, and pull out fish after fish. In 1850 Col. William Loring established an army post here to protect wayfarers on the Oregon Trail, and the following year the town was founded and named by French-Canadian trappers for the gutter-like stone formations *(les dalles)* east of town. Some of the original fort structures still stand, but even more impressive are the examples of Italianate, Colonial Revival and Queen Anne-style architecture that remain from the town's early days. Most of the buildings are private residences; The Dalles Chamber of Commerce *(404 W. 2nd St. ☏ 541-296-2231)* provides a good walking-tour map.

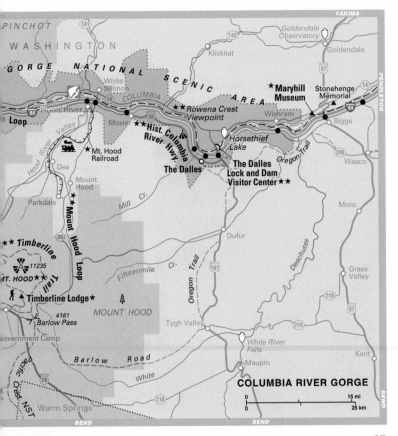

★★**Columbia Gorge Discovery Center & Wasco County Historical Museum** – *5000 Discovery Dr., The Dalles, OR. Open year-round daily 10am–6pm.Closed Jan 1, Thanksgiving Day, Dec 25. $6.50.* ✗ ᕮ 🄿 ☏ *541-296-8600. www.gorgediscovery.org.* This museum serves as an excellent showcase for the geographical history of the gorge. Walk past simulated basalt cliffs, through a forest thunderstorm, and under a waterfall. Learn about Native American culture, their tools, fishing equipment, and baskets. And check out the hauntingly realistic diorama of a pioneer family aboard a wagon on a log raft crossing the Columbia. Several short but excellent films describe the five main industries in the region: timber, orchards, fishing, electricity and tourism. The historical museum allows you to travel back in time to the early 19C where you can board a sternwheeler, visit a cannery or pump a railroad handcar.

★**The Dalles Lock and Dam Visitor Center** – *On N.E. Frontage Rd., off US-197: Exit 87 off I-84. Open mid-Jun–early Sept daily 9am–6pm. Rest of the year Wed–Sun 10am–5pm.* ᕮ 🄿 ☏ *541-298-7650. www.nwp.usace.army.mil/op/d/tdjdwc.htm.* Harnessing the once raging waters of Celilo Falls, a fortress-like concrete wall and its connected powerhouse and navigation lock extend 1.5mi across the Columbia. In 1915 the US Army Corps of Engineers dug an 8.5mi-long canal which skirted the hazardous falls, and in 1957 completion of The Dalles Dam flooded the falls area to provide hydropower and a safe route around. From the visitor center, a small train takes you to guided tours of the fish ladder and powerhouse.

EXCURSION

★**Maryhill Museum** – *24mi east of The Dalles. I-84, Exit 104 to Sam Hill Bridge; north to Rte. 14, then west 2.7mi to 35 Maryhill Museum Dr., Goldendale, WA 98620. Open mid-Mar–mid-Nov daily 9am–5pm. $6.50.*✗ᕮ 🄿 ☏ *509-773-3733. www.maryhillmuseum.org.* Dubbed "the loneliest museum in the world" by *Time* magazine when it opened in 1940, Maryhill overlooks the river from a remote bluff 100mi east of Portland. Seattle lawyer and millionaire Samuel Hill purchased 7,000 acres of land along the arid slopes of the Columbia River in 1907 with the dream of establishing an agricultural colony for a Quaker sect here. He named the settlement Maryhill, after his wife and daughter. Construction of the poured concrete and steel chateau (no structural wood was used) began in 1914. The design, conceived by the Washington, DC firm of Hornblower & Marshall, recalls Marie Antoinette's Petit Trianon at Versailles outside Paris. What Hill referred to as his "ranch house" mushroomed into a monumental three-story manse with 3ft-thick concrete walls-where Sam and his family never lived. Unfortunately, Maryhill never got off the ground as a Quaker community.

After his interest in Maryhill waned, Hill was convinced to convert the mansion into an art museum by his friend, famed Folies-Bergère dancer Loie Fuller of Chicago. In 1926 **Queen Marie of Romania** (1875-1938), granddaughter of Queen Victoria of England and Czar Alexander II of Russia (whom Hill had met during his extensive travels to Europe), made a special trip to the US to dedicate Maryhill

Jerry Taylor/Courtesy Maryhill Museum of Art

Christ as Pantocrator (17C)

Museum. Upon her arrival, however, she found the museum unfinished. Queen Marie gave an inspirational speech regardless, spurring a flurry of acquisitions that included many furnishings and paintings from her own collection, footage of Loie Fuller's avant-garde performances, and over 75 sculptures and sketches by Auguste Rodin (a close friend of Loie Fuller). Despite Queen Marie's 1926 dedication, the museum did not open to the public until 14 years later. Today Maryhill draws over 85,000 visitors a year.

Visit – *2 hrs.* The largest gallery of the entry level is devoted to **Queen Marie's collection** of decorative arts and costumes—including her coronation crown.

Smaller galleries on this level contain 19C Russian religious icons and exhibits on the history of Maryhill and its founder. Upstairs you'll find the charming **Théâtre de la Mode**, a series of small-scale stage sets with mid-20C costumes designed by French couturiers. The Théâtre was conceived as a means of raising funds for war relief during World War II. Also upstairs are American classical realism paintings. Hill's collection of sculptures and watercolors by **Auguste Rodin** is the highlight of the basement level. This intimate cluster of plaster models and bronze casts, arranged in a graceful circular gallery, once served as Rodin's studio reference works. Also on this floor is a gallery containing a noteworthy group of Native American baskets, implements and jewelry, plus an extensive collection of historical chess sets.

A pacifist, Sam Hill also built a memorial for the soldiers from Klickitat County who died in World War I. The monument *(4.4mi east of Maryhill off Rte. 14)*, located on the original Maryhill townsite, consists of a full-scale concrete replica of England's **Stonehenge**. Hill's grave is just south of the memorial.

MOUNT HOOD★★

Michelin map 493 B 4 and map pp 86-87
Tourist Information ☎ 888-622-4822 or www.mthood.org

Piercing the sky 50mi east of Portland, the familiar snow-clad cone of Mt. Hood rises to 11,235ft, making it the state's highest peak. Exerting an irresistible pull on Oregon's center of population, the mountain stays busy all year with visitors who come to explore its forested trails, alpine glaciers, challenging ski areas, scenic roads and rustic lodges.

Historical Notes

According to an American Indian legend, the two brothers in charge of the Columbia River began fighting over the same lovely maiden. Wy'East, who controlled the south side of the river, and Klickitat, who guarded the north, started heaving rocks and lava at each other. Angered by the battle, the Great Spirit turned them into basalt— Klickitat became Mt. Adams and Wy'East became Mt. Hood. Although quiet of late, Wy'East did erupt several times in the 19C, but never with the power of the 1980 Mt. St. Helens explosion *(p 266)*.

The volcanic mountain's present name stems from British explorer Lt. William Broughton, who spotted the peak from the confluence of the Columbia and Willamette Rivers in 1792; he named it after a member of the illustrious Hood family, several of whom were high-ranking English naval officers. In 1805 Meriwether Lewis and William Clark became perhaps the first American expeditioners to lay eyes on Mt. Hood, arriving from the opposite direction—down the Columbia to the Pacific.

The sight of snow-capped Mt. Hood would soon become a beacon of road's end to the thousands of weary travelers who journeyed over the Oregon Trail in the 1800s. In the early 1840s, the first years of the Trail, emigrants had no choice but to continue along the treacherous Columbia River, many losing their possessions and lives in the rapids. The fee was high too—$50 a wagon and $10 per person, paid for the services of the Hudson's Bay Company. But in 1846, a second choice opened up. For $5 a wagon, travelers could head south around Mt. Hood on a new toll road cleared by Samuel Barlow and other pioneers.

Operated until 1919, the **Barlow Road** quickly became the favored alternative to the promised land. But it was really the lesser of two evils. Many emigrants considered the road over the Cascades the toughest trial of their six-month, 2,000mi ordeal. Described as "terrible" and "intolerable," the road bumped over logs and rocks, slogged down in creek beds, and was closed in by thick forest that offered no forage for livestock. Once over **Barlow Pass**, travelers faced the worst pitch of all—the infamous Laurel Hill. The road was so steep here that 40ft-long trees had to be tied to the rear axles of wagons to slow them down; or, failing that, wagons were lowered by ropes. Such heavy use gouged sections of road into long narrow chutes up to seven feet deep. Little wonder that wagon ruts still remain—most prominently along a 1mi trail between the Pioneer Woman's Grave and Barlow Pass, off Route 26. Beyond the toll road, travelers journeyed another 10 days to reach the fertile Willamette Valley, but the worst was over. The US Forest Service maintains a 23mi segment of the old Barlow Road (Route 3530), a rugged unpaved road with historical markers accessible in several places from Route 48.

Many of today's visitors take on the extra challenge of climbing Mt. Hood. Since the first ascent in 1857, thousands have successfully made the summit. More than 10,000 now set out for the top every year between late April and mid-July, making it one of the most climbed glaciated peaks in the country. Usually taking a full day, hikers rely on fixed ropes, ice axes and crampons, and must contend with steep glaciers, avalanches, sudden storms and a 5,000ft vertical ascent from Timberline Lodge. Among the lives Mt. Hood has claimed were eight high school climbers during a whiteout in 1986. Many hikers content themselves with the terrific views afforded by other, lower trails, including the popular Timberline Trail. Five ski areas and one Nordic center keep the mountain busy in winter with snowboarders and downhill and cross-country skiers; one area even offers year-round skiing. Close to Portland's maritime climate, slopes are often wet and slushy, but the 21ft annual snowfall proves a strong magnet for some two million people a year.

SIGHTS *2 days*

★ **Timberline Lodge** – *Off US-26, 6mi north of Government Camp. ☎ 503-272-3311. www.timberlinelodge.com.* Situated at the 6,000ft timberline, this impressive hostelry acts as a living showcase of American arts and crafts of the 1930s. More than 500 Oregon artisans, employed by the WPA, built Timberline in 1936-37, using native stone and local fir and pine. Handmade appointments include fine examples of stained glass, mosaic, inlaid marquetry, carved wood, wrought iron, weaving, applique, and painting. The spacious hexagonal lobby has oak floors with wooden pegs, six corner columns hand-hewn from 36ft-long sections of Douglas fir, and a massive stone chimney rising 92ft. Everywhere you look are detailed touches that show the care and artistry that went into the creation of this sturdy National Historic Landmark that harmonizes well with its surroundings. Many visitors will remember the lodge, shrouded in snow, as the setting for Stanley Kubrick's film *The Shining* (1980).

★★ **Timberline Trail** – *Accessible on the south side from Timberline, and on the north from Cloud Cap. For information, call the Hood River Ranger District ☎ 541-352-6002.* One of the state's premier hiking circuits, this 40mi trail loops Mt. Hood and provides spectacular **views**★★★ of the Cascades, Willamette Valley, wildflower meadows and sparkling waterfalls. Whether walking the whole trail or just a part of it, you will behold a changing panorama of scenic wonders spread like a full table before you. August and September offer the best trail conditions.

★★ **Mount Hood Loop** – *160mi. Drive east from Portland on I-84 or US-30; at Hood River turn south on Rte. 35. To return to Portland, go west on US-26. Mount Hood Information Center open Apr–Nov daily 8am–6pm. Rest of the year daily 8am–4:30pm. Closed Thanksgiving Day, Dec 25. ☎ 888-622-4822.* This full day's drive begins in Portland, heads out through the picturesque Columbia River Gorge, turns up through the farm and orchard country of the Hood River Valley, then crosses the Cascades at 4,157ft Barlow Pass—from which a section of historic Barlow Road (on the old Oregon Trail) is accessible—before returning to Portland. Allow time to stop at scenic pull-overs, U-pick fruit farms, and to walk through hemlock and spruce forests. Dating from 1906, the **Mount Hood Railroad**★ *(110 Railroad Ave., Hood River.; operates Apr–Dec Tue–Sun daily 10am, weekends 3pm; $22.95; special excursions and brunch & dinner trains; call for schedules & reservations ☎ 541-386-3556 or 800-872-4661),* formerly instrumental in transporting apples and pears from area orchards, offers 4 hr excursions through the Hood River Valley to the quaint town of Parkdale.

Mount Hood

Central Oregon

Newberry National Volcanic Monument © Dianne Dietrich Leis

Oregon's central plateau was born of volcanic cataclysm. The legacy is scrawled across the modern landscape as if the last eruption had occurred only yesterday. Rivers of ancient lava cloak the flanks of the Cascade Range's majestic, solitary, snow-covered domes on the region's western border. Lava tubes and fields of obsidian mark Newberry National Volcanic Monument to the south, its mountain walls enclosing not one, but two deep-blue crater lakes. Outcroppings of solidified magma, eroded by eons of wind and water, created Smith Rock State Park, renowned the world over for its challenging rock climbing.

Some 12 to 14 million years ago, an upwelling of lava through a long fissure gave rise to the Three Sisters, Mount Bachelor and other peaks south of modern McKenzie Pass. Where ancient rivers were blocked by lava flows, huge basins filled with water, evolving into the myriad lakes seen today along the Cascade Lakes Highway. The Deschutes River flows northward along the east side of this mountain front, continuing some 200mi to the Columbia River. In the rain shadow of the Cascades, the high-desert plateau (2,200-4,000ft) averages only 12in of precipitation a year, compared with 42in in the Willamette Valley.

First settled after the Civil War, Central Oregon was sparsely populated for a century, until a tourist economy took root in outdoor recreation in the 1960s and 70s. Fishing and hunting had long been popular here, but with the emergence of sports such as skiing, mountain biking and white-water rafting, the area began to attract permanent residents seeking a laid-back lifestyle.

Bend is the region's hub and largest city. Although Bend's US-97 highway corridor is a victim of commercial sprawl, the early-20C downtown has kept charming restaurants and galleries, and numerous recreational outfitters line the byways heading toward the mountains. The city's High Desert Museum is considered one of Oregon's finest manmade sights.

Within an hour's drive north of Bend are three other important towns: Redmond with its smoke-jumping center, Sisters with its 1880s frontier facade, and Madras with its geological heritage. Nearby Warm Springs Indian Reservation is the home of an acclaimed tribal museum. For most visitors, however, Central Oregon's communities are merely places to base themselves while exploring the region's beautiful mountains and lakes.

BEND★

Michelin map 493 B 5 and map p 95
Population 34,321
Tourist Information ☎ 541-382-3221 or 800-905-2363
www.bendchamber.org

Central Oregon's tourism and recreation capital, Bend boasts a glorious location on the banks of the Deschutes River, framed to the west by the Three Sisters mountains and other perpetually snow-capped Cascade peaks. Although wood products provide an economic foundation, the growth of active sports is guiding the city's path into the 21C. Bend was founded in 1900 at a wide spot on the Deschutes River, near John Todd's Farewell Bend Ranch. Alexander Drake, who had emigrated from Michigan, built an irrigation system and platted a townsite, and in 1904 Bend was incorporated. A dam was built on the Deschutes in 1910; rail service arrived a year later; and in 1915 two major lumber mills were constructed on opposite sides of the river—giving rise to the community's leading industry. Population growth was steady but slow until the early 1960s, when the Mount Bachelor Ski Resort, 22mi west of Bend, established itself as the premier winter-sports area in Oregon and Washington. Much of Bend's subsequent growth has shifted away from downtown to adjacent resort developments.

SIGHTS *1 day*

Downtown Historic District – *Wall and Bond Sts. between Greenwood and Franklin Aves.* Early 20C buildings line several square blocks of central Bend, with many original businesses replaced by tourist-oriented restaurants and coffee houses, art galleries and antique stores. Of particular note are the **Bean Building** *(855 N.W. Wall St.)*, built of locally fired brick and volcanic tuff in 1919, and the adjoining white-stucco **Liberty Theater** *(849-851 N.W. Wall St.)*, erected in Mission style in 1917.

Drake Park – *Riverside Blvd., west end of Franklin Ave.* Eleven acres of grassy lawn and trees flanking both banks of the Deschutes River on the west side of downtown, the park is well known for the swans, geese and ducks that congregate on placid Mirror Pond. A 1908 Craftsman-style bungalow, the **H.E. Allen House** *(910 N.W. Brooks St.)*, on the east side of the park, has recently been converted into a community arts center. Look riverside for the **Frank T. Johns Landmark**: Johns, a US presidential candidate, was delivering a campaign speech in Drake Park in 1928 when he dove into the river in a doomed attempt to rescue a 10-year-old boy swept away by the current. Both drowned.

Deschutes Historical Museum – *129 N.W. Idaho Ave. Open year-round Tue–Sat 10am–4:30pm. $2.50.* ⬜ ☎ *541-389-1813.* The three-story Reid School was considered "a marvel of masonry" when it was built of locally quarried volcanic tuff in 1914. The interesting collection now contained here includes an original classroom restored to its early-20C condition. Also exhibited are a re-created 1898 kitchen; household items including a 1903 Voss washing machine; a two-cylinder,

Cabin Interior, High Desert Museum

© Dianne Dietrich Leis

1907 Holsman motor buggy; early logging items; US Forest Service field equipment; and pioneer history archives. Ask for a self-guided tour booklet to 45 Bend historic sites.

★**Pilot Butte State Park** – *Summit Dr., .8mi east of US-97 on Greenwood Ave. (US-20). Park is open daily year-round. Road to the summit closed in winter due to snow.* 🅿 ☎ *541-388-6055. www.prd.state.or.us.* a 1.1mi scenic drive in the park spirals to the top of 4,138ft Pilot Butte, a cinder cone rising more than 500ft above the surrounding city. The **view★** from the summit extends from Mount Hood *(90mi north)* to Mount Scott *(overlooking Crater Lake 70mi south)* and takes in the entire breadth of Oregon's solitary, snow-covered Cascade crests: from north to south, Mounts Hood and Jefferson, Three-Fingered Jack and Mount Washington; the North, Middle and South Sisters; Broken Top and Mount Bachelor. Two 1mi trails, one of them gentle and paved, the other one steeper and unpaved, ascend the butte from the trailhead parking area *(.5mi east of Summit Dr. on US-20).*

★★**High Desert Museum** – Kids *59800 S. US-97. Open year-round daily 9am–5pm. Closed Jan 1, Thanksgiving Day, Dec. 25. $7.75.* ✗ ♿ 🅿 ☎ *541-382-4754. www.highdesert.org.* Nestled in a pine forest 3.5mi south of Bend's city limits, this facility is a unique blend of a small-scale zoo and a museum of regional history, culture and art. Open since 1982, the museum continues to grow—new additions include a wing devoted to Plateau Indians and a center for birds of prey (set for the year 2000).

Visit – *1/2 day.* Among exhibits of history and culture are works of frontier artists interspersed in thought-provoking fashion with relics of the eras they depicted; two Charles Russell paintings and lithographs by John J. Audubon and Thomas Moran; and local art, sculpture and photography. The highlight of the Chiles Center is the **Hall of Exploration and Settlement★**, a series of life-size dioramas that depict the region's historical evolution, complete with sound. Visitors see an 18C Northern Paiute rock shelter, a Hudson's Bay Company fur traders' camp, an emigrant family crossing the desert, and a late-19C high-desert settlement. A walk-through, hard-rock silver mine features heavily laden carts and the clink of background hammers. Organized by high-plateau ecosystems, the indoor **Desertarium** features a simulated trout stream and pool, a lizard habitat, desert and sagebrush aviaries and ranch sheds with pallid bats and a barn owl.

A half-mile ponderosa-forest trail winds through an **Outdoor Exhibit Area★**, where North American river otters frolic in the "Life in the Stream" display. A historic section re-creates a c.1850 pioneer log cabin and a c.1910 sawmill (still used for museum construction projects); nearby stands an exhibit on forest ecology and biodiversity.

★★CASCADE LAKES HIGHWAY

94mi. 1/2 day. Start in west Bend at the intersection of Galveston and 14th Sts. Follow Rte. 372 (Century Dr.) and Forest Rd. 46 west and south of Bend. ☎ *541-388-5664. This route follows a widely used and rewarding version of the drive; several alternate routes also exist.*

A delightful day's excursion that can easily be made to fill a long weekend, a 94mi loop through Deschutes National Forest skirts tree-fringed lakes, mountain trailheads and rustic fishing camps, liberally peppered with sightings of deer, marmots and other wildlife. Heading south on 14th Street in Bend, the road soon becomes **Century Drive**—the name most locals assign to this entire route since, historically, the loop measured 100mi. The road eventually swings west, climbing steadily to a scenic **viewpoint** overlooking a vast lava flow that extends southeast across the Deschutes River to **Newberry National Volcanic Monument**. Interpretive displays describe how the river's course was altered by the ancient lava flow.

The enormous cone of 9,065ft **Mount Bachelor★** dominates the northern portion of the Cascade Lakes Highway. Considered one of the nation's top destinations for skiers and snowboarders, the resort mountain *(☎ 541-382-2442 or 800-829-2442; www.mtbachelor.com)*, located 22mi west of Bend, has 11 lifts that serve 3,365 vertical feet of descents, beginning in November and often extending through June. In summer the Summit Express lift ferries sightseers and mountain bikers to the mountain's crest for 360-degree **views★★★** extending 400mi from Washington's Mt. Rainier to California's Mt. Shasta. Cross-country skiers in Dutchman Flat, a pumice desert at the base of Bachelor, may recognize an alpine panorama featured in such movies as *How the West Was Won* (1963) and *Homeward Bound, The Incredible Journey* (1993). Although there are six day-lodges at Bachelor, none serve overnight guests, who instead stay in Bend or nearby communities.

Past Mount Bachelor, lakes are strung like pearls beneath the Cascade crest. Wedged between Bachelor and 9,152ft Broken Top is small, picturesque **Todd Lake**. Dominating a large meadow, **Sparks Lake★** reflects nearby peaks within its marshy fringes. Resembling the surface of the moon, the lava landscape of **Devils Garden★**

was an astronaut training site for lunar missions in the mid-1960s. Delicate wild-flowers enclose **Devils Lake**, whose clear, shallow waters appear turquoise over a white pumice floor.

The road then bends south to **Elk Lake**, which draws windsurfers in summer and snowmobilers in winter. Although there's no road access during the snow, the lodge remains open year-round. Neighboring **Hosmer Lake**, a favorite of fly fish-ermen, is the only lake in the western US stocked with Atlantic salmon. A short distance away lies pretty **Lava Lake**, with a small resort. **Cultus Lake**—nestled among conifers representing both the wet and dry sides of the mountains—has a marina and resort center, a rare sandy beach and an enormous lake trout. **Crane Prairie Reservoir★**, created in 1929 to impound waters for farm irrigation, has become a breeding ground for osprey. Between May and October, the handsome hawks—known for their rocket-like behavior in diving for fish—can be spotted from an observation area on the west side of the reservoir.

At the "T" intersection with Forest Rd. 42 (50.5mi from Bend), the street sign indicates that Cascade Lakes Hwy. continues south. That road goes 21mi, passing **Davis Lake**, *a large, shallow lake seasonally popular with duck hunters, and ends at Rte. 58.*

South Century Drive, the road popularly known as the Cascade Lakes Highway, continues east on Forest Road 42, and joins US-97 back to Bend. Five miles along Forest Road 42 is the turnoff to **Twin Lakes**, a pair of symmetrical crater lakes about 60ft deep but without defined inlets or outlets. South Twin, where former President Herbert Hoover stayed on a fishing trip in 1940, has a small resort. The same turnoff leads to adjacent **Wickiup Reservoir**, a large body of water created for irrigation in 1949 that gets its name from the *wickiup* (hut) poles left by nomadic Indian tribes.

Continue 5mi past the Twin Lakes turnoff to the intersection with Forest Rd. 43.

This road branches southeast 4mi to lovely **Pringle Falls** and runs another 7mi more to US-97, just north of **La Pine**. The main route follows Forest Road 42, angling northeast along the Fall River—and past the **Fall River Fish Hatchery**, which produces 140,000 rainbow trout fingerlings annually—for 13.5mi until it crosses the Deschutes River.

At the stop sign, turn north, staying on South Century Dr. Continue just over a mile to Vendevert Rd. Turn east on Vendevert and go one mile to US-97, then take the highway north 16mi back to Bend.

Sunriver Nature Center and Observatory – 🄺🄸🄳🅂 *1 hr. 15mi south of Bend via US-97, then 2mi west to 17620 River Rd., Sunriver. Open Jun–Sept daily 9am–5pm. Rest of the year Tue–Sat 10am–4pm. Closed Jan 1, Labor Day, Thanksgiving Day. $2.* ♿ 🄿 ☎ *541-593-4442. www.sunrivernaturecenter.org.* This Nature Center is geared to a younger audience with its collection of "Creepy Crawlies"—reptiles, amphibians and insects—and other natural-history exhibits. A short trail skirts a carefully plotted botanical garden outside, while the observatory *(open sea-sonally; ☎ 541-593-4442)*, with its 20in reflecting telescope, features a spring, summer and fall astronomy program for families.

MADRAS-WARM SPRINGS AREA

Michelin map 493 B 5 and map p 95
Tourist Information ☎ 503-986-0000

Situated on a wide, arid upland with mountains and lakes on the west, prairie grasslands and rich mineral deposits on the east, and lush fields of peppermint in the middle, the Madras area would appear to have the best of several worlds. And just out its back door, barely 15mi away, lies another whole world: the Warm Springs Indian Reservation, largest of eight Oregon reservations.

Created by the Treaty of 1855 from 10 million acres of Wasco and Sahapto tribal land, the reservation now encompasses about five percent of the Indians' original territory. Madras was homesteaded as early as 1888 but remained unincorporated until 1910, less than a year before the railroad arrived. Today the small town is an agricultural trade crossroads and recreational center.

SIGHTS *1 day*

Jefferson County Historical Society & Museum – *34 S.E. D St., Madras. Open June–Sept Tue–Fri 1pm–5pm. Rest of the year by appointment.* 🄿 ☎ *541-475-3808.* Housed in Madras' 1917 city hall building, the museum showcases photos and artifacts preserving the region's colorful history. Exhibits include pioneer arti-facts packed across the Oregon Trail, a restored Victorian bedroom (with late-19C plumbing and early-20C wedding gowns), a replica of an optometrist's office, farm implements and hand tools.

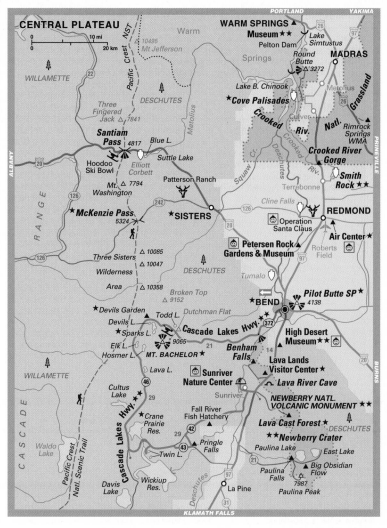

Crooked River National Grassland – *Headquarters: 813 S.W. US-97, Madras. Open year-round Mon–Fri 7:30am–noon & 1pm–4:30pm.* △ 🅿 ☎ *541-416-6640.* Managed by the US Forest Service for multiple uses, this rolling juniper-and-sage-brush steppe sprawls across 112,000 acres south and east of Madras and provides habitat for deer, pronghorn and other upland game animals. The best observation point is at the **Rimrock Springs Wildlife Management Area** on US-26, 10mi south of Madras. A 1.5mi trail leads to a pair of viewing decks on a wetland dotted with ponds and springs and continues around a hilltop for views of the Cascade Mountains. *Trails & viewing decks open year-round.*

★**Cove Palisades State Park** – *7300 Jordan Rd., Culver. From Madras, take Culver Hwy. southwest 6.5mi through Metolius; turn west 1.3mi on Gem Lane, and go south. 2mi on Frazier Dr. to Peck Rd. Park entrance is .5mi down Peck Rd. Open year-round daily. $3/car.* △ ♿ 🅿 ☎ *541-546-3412.* One of Oregon's most striking state parks, Cove Palisades surrounds **Lake Billy Chinook**, created in 1964 by the construction of Round Butte Dam just above the confluence of the Deschutes, Crooked and Metolius Rivers. Billy Chinook's 200ft-deep waters backed 7-10mi up the stark river canyons, their near-vertical basalt cliffs—marked by column-like palisades in the rimrocks—towering 700ft above the lake. Two marinas and several campgrounds have made the 3,900-acre park a popular place for trout and bass fishing, hiking and even houseboating. Homesteaded in the 19C, the area has significant evidence of earlier habitation, including an indecipherable set of petroglyph symbols on a huge boulder near the group camp.

In the northern portion of the park, fine views overlook **Round Butte Dam** from a road atop 3,272ft **Round Butte**. An observatory at the dam offers exhibits on geology, natural history and archaeology. Above the dam, **Lake Simtustus** extends another 7.5mi to **Pelton Dam**, notable for the world's longest fish ladder.

★★The Museum at Warm Springs – 🅺🅸🅳🆂 *2189 US-26, Warm Springs. Open year-round daily 10am–5pm. Closed Jan 1, Thanksgiving Day, Dec 25. $6.* ♿ 🄿 ☎ *541-553-3331. www.tmas.org.* This modern 25,000sq ft museum boasts a collection as stunning as its architecture. Built of native stone, heavy timber and brick to resemble a traditional encampment beside Shitike Creek, the museum's design features water symbolically flowing through volcanic basalt at its entrance.

Rajneeshpuram

Muddy Rd., 21mi southeast of Antelope off Rte. 218 and Cold Camp Rd. A Christian youth retreat now occupies the isolated sheep ranch that Indian guru **Bhagwan Shree Rajneesh** turned into his personal utopia between 1981 and 1986. The silent but extravagant holy man—bedecked in diamonds, he owned dozens of Rolls Royces—lured thousands of red-clad disciples to his communal ranch, where he preached a doctrine of meditation, celebration and sexual freedom. Charges of corruption and criminal activity led to the commune's closure in 1986.

Exhibits leave visitors wondering how three tribes of such diverse language and culture—the Wasco, Northern Paiute and Warm Springs (Sahapto)—have found common ground as the Confederated Tribes. After viewing a stirring 8min introductory film, visitors pass a wall of petroglyphs and enter a video theater, where tribal members illustrate traditional song and dance. Corridors then open into the main exhibit space, one of the largest collections of tribal heirlooms and photographs in the US. In addition to beadwork, basketry and ceramics, displays depict traditional plants used for food; hunting and fishing practices; and ritual ceremonies. A village of domicile models, from teepee to wickiup, is followed by a historic timeline of US-Indian relations. Highlighted are the Treaty of 1855 that established this reservation; the Indian Reorganization Act of 1934 that restored partial tribal autonomy; and modern challenges, including management of the timber and hydroelectric industries.

NEWBERRY NATIONAL VOLCANIC MONUMENT★★

Michelin map 493 B 5 and map p 95
Tourist Information ☎ 541-593-2421

Extending south of Bend from the Deschutes River to 7,987ft Paulina Peak, this US Forest Service-administered preserve embraces lava caves and tubes, pumice and cinder cones, fields of obsidian (black volcanic glass), ancient archeological sites, hiking trails, waterfalls, a forest of "stone trees" and two crater lakes of remarkable scenic beauty.

Established within Deschutes National Forest in 1990, the 55,500-acre national monument comprises the massive Newberry Volcano and lava flows to its northwest. Its most recent eruption occurring 1,300 years ago, this 500sq mi shield volcano (a rounded volcano built up from successive lava flows) is considered dormant, though hot springs still bubble beneath the waters of its lakes. Seven thousand years have passed since the last major activity created Lava Butte and, to the south, divided the crater lakes. Yet even as surface flows crusted over, subterranean "rivers" of molten lava formed unusual caverns in the volcanic plateau's armor.

VISIT *2 days*

Open Apr–Oct daily, snow conditions permitting. Entrance fee $3/car. Recreation passes ($3) are valid for two days. There are four main access points to the monument off US-97 south of Bend. All roads closed in winter.

★Lava Lands Visitor Center – *US-97, 11mi south of Bend. Open Memorial Day-Labor Day daily 9:30am–5pm.* ♿ 🄿 ☎ *541-593-2421.* Interpretive exhibits on regional geology, archaeology, natural history and forest ecology provide an overall introduction to Newberry National Volcanic Monument, which encompasses the lava lands. Dioramas and slide shows bring ancient volcanic activity to life. A 1.75mi road provides the only access to the summit of Lava Butte, which rises 500ft above the visitor center. From mid–May to Labor Day visitors can reach the summit by walking or via shuttle bus *(10am–4:30pm; $2.50).* From early April until mid–May and from Labor Day until late October, motorists can drive up in their own vehicles. At the summit, visitors can take a .25mi interpretive trail around the cinder cone, peruse exhibits in the working forest-fire lookout, and take in the panoramic views. Two trails leave from the visitor center: a .3mi path through the pine forest and a .75mi trail through the lava beds at the base of the butte.

Benham Falls – *4mi west of Lava Lands Visitor Center on Forest Rd.* More a spectacular set of untamed rapids, Benham Falls was created by an ancient lava flow that extended into the Deschutes River. Only expert whitewater veterans challenge these Class V rapids. To see the falls, take the trail *(.75mi one-way)* from the parking area across the footbridge over the Deschutes River, and then follow the trail along the river's western bank.

Lava River Cave – *US-97, 1mi south of Lava Lands Visitor Center. Open mid-May–mid-Oct. $3. Lantern rental $2.* 🅿. This clean, dry .9mi passage, the longest known uncollapsed lava tube in Oregon, requires about an hour to explore. Hikers are advised to wear comfortable walking shoes and dress warmly, as the temperature within the cavern is a constant 42°F.

★ **Lava Cast Forest** – *3.5mi south of Lava Lands Visitor Center on US-97 at Sunriver junction.* ♿ 🅿. A 1mi paved interpretive trail loops through this "forest" of molds left 6,000 to 7,000 years ago when molten lava flowed through a stand of ponderosa pine, coating tree trunks, cooling to rock and remaining as casts after the trees themselves had burned away. Considered one of the finest of these rare stands in the Western Hemisphere, the lava casts now share their rocky soil with re-established ponderosas and a variety of wildflowers.

★★ **Newberry Crater** – *Rte. 21 (Newberry Crater Rd.), intersects US-97 12mi south of Lava Lands Visitor Center. Go 13mi east on Rte. 21 to crater. In winter Rte. 21 closes at Sno-park (permits required) 10mi from US-97.* The monument's centerpiece is this 18sq mi caldera, within whose forested floor snuggle deep-blue Paulina and East lakes, a massive obsidian flow and numerous archeological sites.

Beginning about a million years ago, the first of hundreds of volcanic eruptions created concentric fractures that, by 200,000 years ago, had collapsed to form the 5mi-wide caldera. A single large lake—much like Oregon's Crater Lake—filled the basin. Ten thousand years ago, even before smaller eruptions and lava flows had divided the lake in two, Native Americans were maintaining Stone Age camps in the crater. They quarried obsidian, the black volcanic glass used in making tools and weapons. Signposts mark several camps and quarries.

Fur trapper Peter Skene Ogden apparently was the first visitor of European ancestry when he stumbled upon the lakes in 1826. The crater was named for Dr. John Newberry, A 19C railroad surveyor and scientist; Paulina Lake was named for a Paiute chief who made the caldera his hunting ground.

Paulina and East Lakes – Renowned for their trout fishing, the lakes were devoid of fish prior to being stocked by the US Forest Service. Their underwater hot springs have been found to produce such a variety of vegetative nutrients that fingerlings grow at a phenomenal rate. Paulina Lake is slightly larger (1,531 acres) and deeper (240ft) than East Lake, which is the higher (6,371ft) of the two by about 40ft. Both are famous throughout the fishing world for their record-breaking German brown trout, rainbow trout and Eastern brook trout. East Lake has no surface inlet or outlet. Paulina Lake, also spring-fed, empties at its west end through Paulina Creek. A quarter-mile west of the lake lodge, **Paulina Falls** drops 80ft off the outer crater face, the only break in the precipitous walls of the caldera.

During the summer, naturalist-led walks depart from the **Paulina Visitor Center** *(open Apr–Sept Wed–Sun 9:30am–5pm;* ♿ 🅿*)* at Paulina Lake. Demonstrations of arrowhead making and campfire programs are presented at a nearby outdoor amphitheater.

Big Obsidian Flow – The youngest dated volcanic feature in central Oregon is the legacy of a c.680 eruption, which spewed enough black lava to pave 70,000mi of road-three times the circumference of the Earth. Trails south of Paulina Lake access the flow on three sides.

Paulina Peak – At 7,987ft the highest elevation in the national monument, this summit can be reached by strenuous trail or winding gravel road *(not suitable for trailers or motor homes).* A 360-degree panoramic view rewards visitors at the top.

■ Rockhounding

Amateur geologists who love nothing better than scrounging and digging for minerals and semi-precious stones have a paradise in the Prineville and Madras areas. The rimrocks surrounding the towns boast extensive agate beds, often containing quartz-filled thunder eggs as well as moss and rainbow agates, jasper and malachite.

There are public and private dig sites throughout the region. Perhaps the best set-up for rockhounds is at **Richardson's Recreational Ranch** *(Gateway Rte., 14 mi northeast of Madras; open year-round daily 7am–5pm;* ☎ *541-475-2680),* east of US-97 at Milepost 81. Visitors can rent or buy picks and other tools to attack the Priday Agate Beds, and leave their finds for sanding and polishing at the lapidary shop.

Central Oregon rock has been dated to the Eocene era, 40 million years ago. The John Day area, just to the east, reveals Oligocene (30 million years ago) fossils. Many of today's richest deposits are in Miocene (10 million years ago) lake basins created by Columbia basalts.

Redmond and Sisters are the northern gateways to Bend's metropolis. Redmond, a town of about 7,000 on US-97, 16mi north of Bend, is home to the regional airport and a center for outdoor recreation, only three hours from Portland. On US-20, Sisters, to the east of Santiam and McKenzie passes, counts fewer than 1,000 citizens, but its false-front late-19C buildings never fail to charm travelers. Scenic attractions like Smith Rock State Park and the Three Sisters Wilderness make this area a destination in its own right.

Though founded as a ranching and lumber town in 1904, Redmond did not achieve importance until the Redmond Army Air Base was constructed during World War II. When ownership of the base was transferred to the city after the war ended, Redmond found its niche as a regional trading center. Sisters, named for the trio of volcanic peaks that loom over the community on the southwest, has had a post office since the 1880s. Sawmills and ranching sustained the town until the late-20C tourism boom that made this a center for the ranching of exotic pack animals, especially llamas.

REDMOND *2 days*

A three-hour drive southeast of Portland via US-26 west and US-97 south, downtown Redmond features several fine examples of Art Deco architecture from the late 1930s and 40s. Foremost is the 1937 **Milton Odem House**, *(623 S.W. 12th St; not open to public)*, considered Oregon's best example of residential Streamline Moderne architecture.

★**Redmond Air Center** – [Kids] *1740 S.E. Ochoco Way. From downtown Redmond, take Rte. 126 1mi east and turn south on S.E. 10th St. After .5mi, turn east on S.E. US Forest Service Dr. Visit by guided tour (30min) only, year-round Mon–Fri, call ahead for schedule. Closed major holidays.* & 🅿 ☎ *541-548-5071.* The primary base for US Forest Service firefighters in the Pacific Northwest, this facility employs 100 people during the summer fire season but trains 3,600 firefighters annually from Oregon and Washington. Tours include the **Smoke Jumper Base**, where visitors see a video on the dangers of the profession, learn about the intensive four-week training program, and see the "Paraloft" where parachutes are rigged, hung and repaired. Unless chemical retardants are being loaded, visitors may board an air tanker at adjacent Roberts Field, then wander through the Fire Support Cache, where supplies for the entire Northwest region are stored. Best visiting times are May or early June, when smoke-jumpers have arrived but the main fire season has yet to strike.

Petersen Rock Gardens & Museum – [Kids] *7930 S.W. 77th St. 2.5mi west of US-97 off S. Canal Blvd. (Old Redmond-Bend Hwy.). Gardens open May–Sept daily 9am–9pm; rest of the year 9am–dusk. Museum open May–Sept daily 9am–5pm; rest of the year daily 9am–4:pm. $3.* 🅿 ☎ *541-382-5574.* The zeal of an immigrant farmer is highlighted in four acres of castles, churches, ponds and bridges made of lava and other volcanic rocks. Rasmus Petersen (1883-1952), a Dane, began his unique landscaping project in 1935; he expertly recreated many famous European buildings, as well as America's Independence Hall, from agate, jasper, obsidian, malachite, petrified wood and geode-like thunder eggs. Petersen's descendants have opened a rock and gem museum here that features a fluorescent display.

© Dianne Dietrich Leis

Climber at Smith Rock State Park

★★**Smith Rock State Park** – *N.E. Crooked River Dr., Terrebonne. From downtown Redmond, go 5mi north on US-97, east on Smith Rock Way and follow signs 3.5mi to park. Open year-round daily dawn-dusk. $3/car, day use only.* ⚠ 🅿 ☎ *541-548-7501.* Internationally renowned for its challenging rock climbing, this spectacular set of multicolored cliffs framing the Crooked River Canyon is equally stirring for sightseers, especially during the early morning and pre-sunset hours. Miles of hiking trails weave along the river banks and to the top of Misery Ridge. Igneous spires with names like Morning Glory Wall and the Christian Brothers tower more than 550ft above the river. Millions of years ago lava flows caused the ancestral river to seek a new channel. Ensuing erosion exposed the interior of the vent and its "welded tuff"—volcanic ash expulsed under extreme heat and pressure.

Crooked River Gorge – *8.5mi north of Redmond on US-97*. Three bridges, including a 1911 rail bridge, cross this dramatic canyon, which gouges a 403ft-deep trough through lava rock. The 1926 steel automobile bridge was once the highest single-arch span in the country. A new **Crooked River Gorge Bridge** is now under construction 300ft upstream for a cost of $18.3 million. The **Peter Skene Ogden Scenic Wayside**, on the south side of the US-97 bridge, has a viewing and interpretive area.

★SISTERS *1 day*

Like an Old West movie set, the bewitching town of Sisters offers block after block of 1880s-style storefronts and wooden sidewalks along Cascade Avenue (US-20) and flanking Main and Hood Avenues. Galleries and gift shops as well as banks, pharmacies, the library and fire station have adopted the pioneer look since the early 1970s. Not all facades are false, however. The **Hotel Sisters★** *(190 E. Cascade Ave., ☎ 541-549-7427)* offered hot– and cold-running water as early as 1912, and still has a fine-dining restaurant. The 1908 **Hardy Allen House** *(401 E. Main Ave.)* is an even earlier reminder of Sisters' authentic past.

★**McKenzie Pass** – *Rte. 242, 14mi west of Sisters*. This 5,324ft Cascade Pass is closed in winter, but the winding highway (following an 1860s wagon route) is well worth a drive during the snowless months. A 65sq mi lava flow surrounds the **Dee Wright Memorial Observatory**, above the summit parking area; the view extends across six Cascade peaks and numerous smaller volcanic cones and craters. The .5mi **Lava River Trail** is a self-guided interpretive walk through lava gutters and crevasses.

The **Pacific Crest National Scenic Trail**, linking Canada with Mexico down the Cascade-Sierra crest, crosses McKenzie Pass and offers the most direct hiking access to the **Three Sisters Wilderness**, immediately south. Nine sizable glaciers and numerous small lakes cloak the heights of these volcanic cones-the North (10,085ft), Middle (10,047ft) and South (10,358ft) Sisters.

Santiam Pass – *US-20, 21mi west of Sisters*. The principal highway crossing of Oregon's central Cascades, the 4,817ft pass affords an impressive **view★** *(turnout is located below east side of pass)* of sharp-peaked 7,794ft **Mount Washington** and deep (314ft) **Blue Lake**, filling an ancient crater; 2mi farther downhill lies green glacial **Suttle Lake**. **Hoodoo Ski Bowl** *(US-20; ☎ 541-822-3799; www.hoodoo.com)*, a medium-size, family-oriented winter resort, is adjacent to the summit.

■ A Breed Apart

If you expect horses, sheep and cattle to dominate the ranchland of Central Oregon, you may be in for a surprise. The Redmond-Sisters area, in particular, is home to perhaps the weirdest collection of livestock in the lower 48 states. Llamas and reindeer, emus and ostriches, elk and bison are among the more exotic creatures you'll find here, along with various obscure strains of horses and donkeys.

Most accessible to visitors is **Operation Santa Claus** Kids *(4355 W. Rte. 126, Redmond; open year-round daily dawn-dusk; ☐ ☎ 541-548-8910)*, which claims to be the world's largest commercial reindeer ranch. More than 100 domesticated reindeer are bred primarily to pull the sleighs of masquerading Santas nationwide during the Christmas season.

The **Patterson Ranch** *(McKenzie Pass Hwy., .5mi west of Sisters; not open to the public)*, established in the early 1970s, is the largest breeding ranch in the world for llamas, natives of South America's Andes. There's good roadside viewing of the ranch's Rocky Mountain elk and Polish Arabian horses, as well as 500 llamas.

Emus and ostriches, large flightless birds from Australia and Africa, respectively, have found their way onto restaurant menus as high-protein, low-cholesterol meats. Leather and feathers are used by the fashion industry, and the oil makes a fine moisturizer. Both are ranched in small numbers at various locations in the Redmond-Sisters region, including along Smith Rock Way northeast of Redmond. American bison, better known as buffalo, are also raised in this area for their lean meat.

Friesian, Icelandic, Peruvian Paso and Rocky Mountain horses are among the lesser-known equine breeds raised by private ranchers in the Redmond-Sisters area, along with miniature donkeys. Keep your eyes open as you pass the long ranch fences, and you may see some surprising creatures.

Eastern Oregon

Painted Hills, John Day Fossil Beds National Monument / © Dianne Dietrich Leis

Oregon divides dramatically along the spine of the Cascade Mountains. While the west side is a green land of rain forest, volcanic peaks and shoreline, the east side is higher, drier, more open and less populated. Here, broad grassy valleys, timbered mountains, deep canyons, badlands and high desert prevail. Uplifted by tectonic forces, piled still higher with deposits of lava and volcanic ash, the region was shaped by a combination of erosion and aridity, its climate dictated primarily by the Cascades, which intercept Pacific moisture.

She northeast is dominated by two mountain ranges, the Blues and the Wallowas, and by the deepest gorge in North America, Hells Canyon. A tangle of complicated country surrounds these features: Smaller ranges run helter-skelter; rivers make sharp, unexpected turns; and highways twist their way over numerous passes. While valleys are often treeless, dense forest covers the higher mountains. Southeast Oregon is drier yet, with part of the region lying within the Great Basin, a landscape characterized by isolated mountain ranges rising above a wide-open sea of sagebrush.

Long the home of the Nez Percé, Umatilla and Cayuse, eastern Oregon was passed up by the first immigrants on the Oregon Trail, most of them farmers who were eager to stake claims in the rich soil of the Willamette Valley. Only when most of the choice farmland was taken did some settlers turn back to the lands they had rolled through so hurriedly. They found the valleys excellent for ranching and the mountains covered with timber and full of precious minerals.

The eastern Oregon economy today continues to rely on natural resources and industries such as ranching and logging. As it has always been, ranching is hard work for low pay; mining has nearly dried up; and the timber industry is fading. Politics here, often in direct opposition to the other side of the state, are staunchly Republican; a local joke claims that in eastern Oregon, cougars outnumber Democrats. But the residents of eastern Oregon welcome travelers with true country hospitality, a blessing to visitors who seek simple pleasures in a strikingly beautiful landscape.

BAKER CITY★

Michelin map 493 D 5 and map p 103
Population 9,765
Tourist Information ☎ 541-523-3356

Shadowed by the Elkhorn Range of the Blue Mountains, Baker City sits at the east end of a broad prairie once called the Lone Pine Valley. The name refers to a giant solitary tree that once stood in the middle of the plain. Immigrants on the Oregon Trail could see the tree as they topped the ridge near Flagstaff Hill. For them, it marked an important stage of their long journey. Having survived the arduous pull across southern Idaho's desert, they crossed the Snake River, dragged their loads up the rugged valley of the Powder River, and stood on the threshold of their destination. The Blue Mountains were the last range standing between them and the fabled Columbia River. Nowadays, I-84 zips right by on its way west, but visitors who linger here will find Baker City a perfect staging point for explorations of the Blue Mountains (west), the Wallowas (east), and the courageous history of the Oregon Trail pioneers. The first non-Indian settlers in the valley were farmers who sold hay to feed the livestock of passing immigrants. Few thought of settling here until 1861, when Henry Griffin discovered gold in the foothills of the Blues. Word spread, and the next summer saw a rush of prospectors to the area. The town of Auburn burst into existence, but soon lost prominence to Baker City. The region got a major boost in 1883 with the arrival of transcontinental rails. Easy transport gave incentive to developers including lumberman David Eccles, who built a narrow-gauge branch line to carry logs out of the timber-rich Elkhorn Range. This in turn helped miners in isolated mountain towns like Sumpter, who previously had been unable to haul in heavy machinery. With new equipment, the mines boomed. Well-supplied with logs, sawmills proliferated.

Baker City prospered despite fires that periodically destroyed wooden buildings in the city center. Over time, the original buildings were replaced by less flammable structures of red brick and the area's distinctive volcanic tuff, which today form the core of the historic district, centered on Main Street. Its anchor is the 1889 **Geiser Grand Hotel**, newly restored and still operating. Other historically significant buildings downtown within easy walking distance of each other include **St. Francis Cathedral**, **Palmer Brothers Jewelry Block**, and the **Ison House**.

Oregon Trail

"Eastward I go only by force but westward I go free."
Oregon Trail immigrant

Stretching nearly 2,000mi from its official starting point at Independence, Missouri, to Oregon City on the Columbia River, the Oregon Trail was not just one trail but various branches, all of them difficult. There were no roads, and in the early years, no improvements, even in the roughest stretches. Several trading posts along the way provided repairs, fresh livestock and other supplies to those who could afford them. Yet for the most part, travelers had to be self-sufficient from their first day on the trail.

It was the biggest peacetime migration in American history. Between 1840 and 1869 more than 350,000 made the journey. Or attempted to. The trail took a terrible toll: Some years, one person in ten died along the way. Among the hazards and difficulties were flash floods, storms, hail and rain, wind and driven sleet; mosquitoes, flies, rattlesnakes and cholera; choking dust and parching heat; and rocky ground that could tear up animal hooves and shatter wagon wheels.

The journey typically took about six months. To avoid the chance of October snow, it was best to start in early spring. First came the great plains, rising gradually to the Rocky Mountains. By July, immigrants hoped to be rolling across the Continental Divide in Wyoming, which then was the border of the vast Oregon Territory. Ahead lay the awful traverse of the "wormwood barrens," as they called the volcanic desert of the Snake River Plain; then the rugged country of eastern Oregon where snowstorms in the Blue Mountains caught many stragglers. And transferring their wagons to log rafts, settlers often faced dangerous rapids on the great Columbia River.

The decision to go to Oregon was a momentous one. It meant leaving behind family, friends, and all but the most essential possessions. Immigrants could take only what fit in their wagons, and eventually not even that. As they fought their way across ever more rugged terrain with animals growing progressively weaker, travelers were forced to jettison much of their cargo. The trail was lined with abandoned tools, furniture, prized heirlooms, entire wagons and, most sadly, bodies of family members and friends who died along the way. There was little time for grieving. Survivors prayed beside hastily dug graves and moved on.

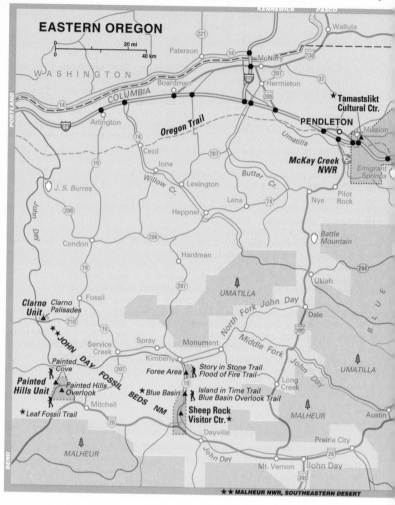

SIGHTS *1 day*

★★ **National Historic Oregon Trail Interpretive Center** – *Flagstaff Hill, Rte. 86 (5mi east of I-84). Open Apr–Oct daily 9am–6pm. Rest of the year daily 9am–4pm. Closed Jan 1, Dec 25. $5.* ♿ 🅿 ☎ *541-523-1843. www.or.blm.gov/NHOTIC.* Perched atop Flagstaff Hill, the museum overlooks the ruts of the Oregon Trail where immigrants made their way through a gap in the ridge. Before them lay the flat valley of the Powder River, and the imposing wall of the Blue Mountains. Having come so far, they still faced dangerous hazards, but knew they were close to their goal. The journey and the spirit of the people who made it come to life in this excellent museum. Displays begin with a full-scale wagon train. Visitors walk through this life-size diorama to the sounds of laboring animals, creaking wheels, and voices of both immigrants and the Indians who watched them pass. The people are covered with dust, their clothes ragged, their faces travel-worn and weary. Further exhibits outline the long journey, starting with the loading of wagons and moving through important landmarks along the way. Because the artifacts are replicas, visitors are permitted to handle some of them, adding to the experience. The hands-on journey is enriched by detailed and literate quotes from travelers' diaries. Outside the museum, paths lead downhill to the old ruts and several interpretive viewpoints.

U.S. National Bank – *2000 Main St. Open year-round Mon–Thu 10am–5pm, Fri til 6pm. Closed major holidays.* ♿ 🅿 ☎ *541-523-7791.* Across the street from the Geiser Grand Hotel, the lobby of the US Bank offers a display of gold as it is found in nature—nuggets, flakes, leaf, and feathery crystallized forms. The 80.4oz Armstrong nugget is the centerpiece; it is said to be one of the purest gold nuggets ever found.

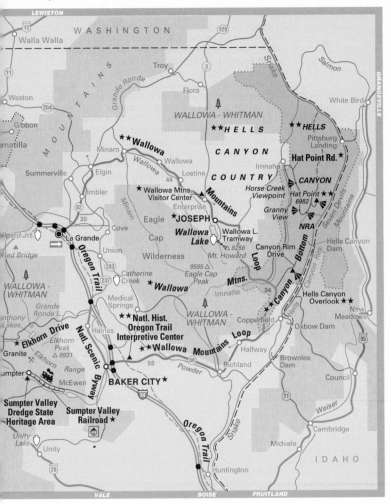

★**Oregon Trail Regional Museum** – *2480 Grove St. Open late Mar–Oct daily 9am–5pm. $2.50.* ♿ 🅿 ☎ *541-523-9308.* In the city's old brick natatorium, this 32,000sq ft museum houses an extensive collection of pioneer memorabilia reflecting the history of the surrounding region. Items include mining equipment, horse-drawn vehicles, furniture, an outstanding mineral and rock collection and more than 2,000 cabochons—gems, which, when polished, look like landscapes.

EXCURSIONS

★**Elkhorn Drive National Scenic Byway** – *1/2 day. Loop beginning in Baker City, on Rte. 7 south, 30mi to Sumpter. From here take Forest Rte. 51 15mi west to Granite, then 9mi north to Forest Rte. 73. Head east 35mi to US 30, then south 17mi back to Baker City.* Circling the Elkhorn Range of the Blue Mountains in a clockwise direction, this 106mi drive takes in pioneer mining towns, alpine forest, splendid views of the Elkhorn Range, and several scenic lakes. The first leg leads to **Sumpter**, where a restored railroad, gold dredge and historic buildings hark back to the mining boom. Next stop, over Blue Springs Summit (5,864ft) is **Granite** (via Forest Route 51), site of an 1862 gold discovery, now a ghost town of crumbling buildings and a handful of year-round residents. The rickety one-room town hall still serves its original purpose.

From there, Forest Route 73 climbs through woods and meadows to 7,392ft **Elkhorn Mountain Summit**. On the downhill side, Anthony Lakes and Grande Ronde Lake are popular recreation areas. The loop continues to Haines, then returns on US-30 to Baker City.

★**Sumpter Valley Railroad** – [Kids] *3 hrs. 22mi west of Baker City via Rte. 7, in McEwen Station. Trains run Memorial Day–Sept weekends & holidays 10am, noon & 3pm. Round-trip 1 hr 30min. $9.* ☎ *541-894-2268.* Chugging along 5mi of track between Sumpter and McEwen, this historic narrow-gauge train commemorates the Stump Dodger, a railroad founded in 1890 to haul timber out of the mountains to Baker City. As the railroad grew, it carried passengers and other cargo to a network of communities as far away as Prairie City in the John Day Valley. Unable to compete with highway traffic for passengers and freight, it ceased operating in 1947. The restoration is an ongoing project, done mainly by volunteers who have re-laid rails and collected rolling stock from other restoration projects in Colorado and Alaska. Tracks run on the tailings of the Sumpter Valley Dredge, which literally upended the valley floor. The mess has never been cleaned up, but not all is devastation. Narrow sloughs between rows of piled gravel provide habitat for waterbirds, beavers and other animals. Nature trails varying from less than a mile to several miles start at the depot and lead through this odd but rewarding wildlife sanctuary.

★**Sumpter Valley Dredge State Heritage Area** – *1 hr. 30mi west of Baker City off Rte. 7, on the outskirts of Sumpter. Open mid–May-mid–Sept daily 9am–4pm. Rest of the year open weather permitting.* & ⌨ ☎ *541-894-2486.* Here, where it was retired from service in 1954, rests the wood and steel monster that chewed up and disgorged 6mi of the valley floor, sifting through vast quantities of gravel and dirt for gold. It cost $350,000 to build in 1935 and, over the next 19 years, removed about nine tons of gold, or approximately one cubic yard. At then-existing prices of $35 an ounce, that amounted to some $4.5 million worth. Powered by electricity, the dredge floated in a pond of its own making. A chain of buckets brought a steady load of rocks and soil to the surface. Everything larger than three-quarters of an inch was dumped out the back end; the smaller material was run through sluice boxes that trapped the gold. Ironically, a big nugget like the five-pound Armstrong would have passed right through, undetected.

HELLS CANYON COUNTRY★★

Michelin map 493 D 4, 5 and map p 102-103
Tourist Information ☎ 541-426-5546

Tucked into the northeast corner of Oregon between the Wallowa Mountains and the deepest gorge on the continent, the Hells Canyon area remains one of the wildest places in America, isolated from development and overlooked by the casual traveler— all the better for those willing to do a little exploring. The dramatic landscape resulted from a combination of geologic events, the most important being the vast outpouring of volcanic basalt that began around 17 million years ago, covering much of eastern Oregon and Washington and building the broad Columbia Plateau. Both the Blue and Wallowa mountains, made of granite, were here before the basalt flows and stood high enough not to be buried. A relatively recent creation, Hells Canyon was carved through the basalt over the last two million years by the Snake River, which during the ice ages was a much more powerful stream than we see today.

People who know this place grow fiercely attached to it. The first and most famous were the Nez Percé tribe, who cherished the grassy hills and high forests as their ancestral homeland, but were forced to abandon it in 1877 when white settlers demanded their eviction. It was in the Wallowa Valley that **Chief Joseph** and his people began their tragic retreat toward Canada. In their wake, miners, loggers, farmers and ranchers moved in to find a land rich in timber and precious minerals, with good range for cattle and sheep. Today much of the Hells Canyon area remains pristine. Touring it requires some determination, but the rewards are proportional.

★★HELLS CANYON NATIONAL RECREATION AREA

Hells Canyon is a vertical landscape whose dark cliffs and sleek grassy foothills tumble headlong for thousands of feet to the swiftly moving river at its heart. Covering 652,000 acres, including 214,000 acres of designated and exceedingly rugged wilderness, the recreation area sprawls across both sides of the canyon and the adjacent high rim country. Elevations range from under 1,000ft at river level to 6,982ft at Hat Point on the Oregon side, and to 9,393ft in the Seven Devils Mountains on the Idaho side. Combined with the neighboring lands of three national forests, the national recreation area makes up the core of a huge natural area with very few roads or other developments. Even foot travel is limited by the difficult geography. At the bottom of the gorge, the Snake, a designated Wild and Scenic River, tumbles over frothing rapids.

People have lived in the canyon area for at least 8,000 years, from prehistoric hunters to ranch families residing along the river today. In 1975 the national recreation area was established and is today administered by the Forest Service. Many people would now like to see the canyon become a national park, citing its readily observable international significance: scenery on a grand scale, diverse wildlife, a

Getting There – The main north-south route through the region is I-84. Route 82 runs east from La Grande to Joseph. The southern entrance to Hells Canyon National Recreation Area is reached from Baker City traveling east on Rte. 86 to Oxbow. Wallowa Mountain Road (Forest Rd. 39) provides access to Hells Canyon Overlook; Snake River Road between Oxbow Crossing and Hells Canyon Dam travels deep into the canyon. Most forest roads are narrow, steep and paved with gravel. Check road conditions with the Forest Service before traveling. Summer temperatures range from 90°F to 40°F. Carry insect repellent and layers of clothing for sudden weather changes.

Closest airport: **Eastern Oregon Regional Airport** (☎ *276-7754*) in Pendleton is served by Horizon Air (☎ *800-547-9308*). Greyhound **bus** service stops in La Grande and Baker City (☎ *800-231-2222*). Wallowa Valley Stage Line (☎ *963-5165*) operates buses between La Grande and Joseph *(Mon–Sat year-round)*.

Visitor Information – The **Wallowa Mountains Visitor Center** distributes information and maps on **Hells Canyon National Recreation Area**, 88401 Hwy. 82, Enterprise OR 97828, ☎ 426-5546, www.fs.fed.us/r6lw.w *(open Memorial Day–Labor Day Mon–Sat 8am–5pm, Sun noon–5pm; rest of the year Mon–Fri 8am–5pm)*. Contact the **Baker County Visitor & Convention Bureau** *(490 Campbell St., Baker City OR 97814; ☎ 523-3356 or 800-523-1235; www.neoregon.com/visitBaker.html)* for information, maps and brochures on points of interest, accommodations, sightseeing, outfitters and seasonal events. For additional information: **La Grande-Union County Visitors & Convention Bureau**, 1912 4th St., #200, La Grande OR 97850; ☎ 963-8588 or 800-848-9969; www.ucinet.com/~lagrande; **Wallowa County Chamber of Commerce**, P.O. Box 427, Enterprise OR 97828 , ☎ 426-4622 or www.enoi.com/~wallowa/.

Accommodations – Area visitors' guides including lodging directories are available *(free)* from regional tourism agencies *(above)*. Accommodations operate year-round and include motels, bed-and-breakfast inns, lodges and cabins. Campgrounds and RV camping facilities are available in the area (some are open in the winter). Numerous **campgrounds** in the Hells Canyon National Recreation Area and Wallowa-Whitman National Forest offer mostly primitive facilities; bring your own drinking water. All are available on a first-come, first-served basis; some require a fee *($4-$12/night)*. For further information and camping restrictions: ☎ 426-5546.

Recreation and Sightseeing – The area offers year-round recreational opportunities that include boating, float trips, backpacking, llama trekking and horseback riding. **Hiking** trails are usually open year-round. Trail Park Passes *($3/day)* are required for some trails; available from Wallowa Mountains Visitor Center *(above)*. Wilderness permits, available *(free)* at the trailhead, are mandatory and limited to 12 people in Eagle Cap Wilderness. Wallowa Llamas offers guided llama pack trips into Hells Canyon and the Wallowa Mountains for the whole family *(all-inclusive 3-7 days; reservations: ☎ 742-2961)*. Rentals of paddleboats, motorboats and canoes *(hourly & daily)* available at **Wallowa Lake Marina** (☎ 432-9115). **White-water rafting**, and jet-boat trips through Hells Canyon on the Snake River led by: Steens Wilderness Adventures, Oxbow OR (☎ 432-5315); and Hells Canyon Adventures, Oxbow OR ☎ 785-3352 or 800-422-3568, www.hellscanyonadventures.com. For a list of local outfitters, contact the supervisor at Hells Canyon National Recreation Area or the Wallowa Mountains Visitor Center *(above)*. **Fishing** and **hunting** are allowed with an appropriate license *(available at Hells Canyon Outdoor Supply at Pine Creek, and Oxbow, OR ☎ 800-785-3358)*. Guided fishing trips into Hells Canyon and Eagle Cap Wilderness are organized by Eagle Cap Fishing Guides, Enterprise OR *(reservations: ☎ 426-3493)*.

Winter activities include skiing, cross-country skiing, snow boarding and snowmobiling in the Wallowa Mountains region.

varied and largely unspoiled landscape. They also point to the economic benefits that would come with national park status, precisely what opponents object to. The canyon is fine the way it is, they claim. And while they recognize the wild attractions, they fear that a national park will only bring crowds, new development, new regulations, and an increased, unwanted federal presence. Meanwhile, visitors who take the time to probe this convoluted landscape find the effort well justified. Services are few but natural splendor abounds. Practically anywhere you stand provides a vista of sweeping grandeur. In lower reaches, the predominantly volcanic rocks, craggy and dark, are softened by the velvety sheen of grass that covers the open slopes. Although dense forest covers the high country, trees survive at lower elevations only in ravines and on sheltered north-facing slopes; you'll also find prickly pear cactus and dryland wildflowers.

Often compared with Arizona's Grand Canyon, Hells Canyon is similarly huge but has significant differences. While the Grand Canyon's walls are stepped and made of brightly colored sedimentary rock, those of Hells Canyon are sloped, and carved through dark volcanics. The Grand Canyon rims are flat, those of Hells Canyon mountainous and broken. Though not as long as the Grand, Hells Canyon is deeper, yet it seems more like a steep mountain valley than a huge canyon. But both are vast and intimidatingly rugged. Gazing into the blue-shadowed depths of Hells, it is hard to imagine traveling without the help of roads and trails. In fact, it's not wise to deviate from main routes without careful preparation and awareness of such hazards as rattlesnakes, poison ivy, loose rock, withering summer heat and ferociously cold winters.

Sights *2 days*

★★Wallowa Mountains Loop – *208mi from La Grande, northeast on Rte. 82 through Joseph to Rte. 350, then south on Rte. 39; go west on Rte. 86 through Halfway to Baker City. Allow at least 5 hrs. For information ☎ 541-426-5546.* Circling the range from Baker City to La Grande, this glorious and demanding drive features nearly the entire sweep of Hells Canyon. Short side trips take in visits to both the rim of Hells Canyon and its bottom. The loop consists of the two official **Hells Canyon Scenic Byways**, one leading 70mi from Baker City to the town of Copperfield (near Oxbow Dam) on the Snake River, the other encompassing the 71mi from La Grande to Joseph. The two can be connected from late May to late October by paved but narrow Route 39 (32mi) on the east end of the Wallowas. Beginning in La Grande, Route 82 passes through Elgin before approaching the Wallowas. At the town of Lostine, a Forest Route ascends the Lostine River into the heart of the range. The byway continues to the head of the valley at Wallowa Lake near the arts town of Joseph. From Joseph, Route 350 leads 8mi to Route 39, which heads south over the east end of the Wallowas through rugged forested country past occasional mountain views, frequent alpine streams, and numerous side roads. One side-trip should not be missed: Paved Route 3965 (16mi north of Rte. 86) leads shortly to **Hells Canyon Overlook★★**, a terrific vista of the south end of the big canyon. Beyond the overlook, the unpaved **Canyon Rim Drive** winds 7mi north along the rim, past numerous viewpoints beneath the tall pines.

★Hat Point Road – *23mi from Imnaha southeast to Hat Point on Forest Rte. 4240; allow a full day.* At 7,000ft, Hat Point offers a long-distance view of the Snake River more than a vertical mile below, and the Seven Devils Mountains on the other side of the canyon. Getting to the point is no trivial matter. The 23mi dirt road begins a steep climb at Imnaha, and the first 5mi are no place for those with a fear of heights. Although the road is maintained for passenger cars, no guardrails or wide shoulders stand between vehicles and dizzying drops, and severe weather

© Dianne Dietrich Leis

Highview Ranch, Wallowa Mountains Region

can make it impassable. However, the grade eases and the views get bigger the farther you go. From **Horse Creek Viewpoint** *(11mi)* and **Granny View** *(17mi)* you look west into the Imnaha Canyon. From Saddle Creek *(19mi)* the **view** eastward into Hells Canyon stays with you all the way to **Hat Point★★**, where you'll find rest rooms, interpretive exhibits, a lookout tower and a small campground-but no drinking water. The two-wheel-drive road continues 4mi to Warnock Corrals. From here, the Western Rim National Recreation Trail leads along the rim, then drops several thousand feet to the river and a road access point at Nez Percé Crossing, a distance of 33mi.

★★ **The Canyon Bottom** – Route 86 winds down to the Snake River and crosses to the Idaho side at the upper (south) end of Hells Canyon Reservoir, a sinuous lake north of Oxbow Dam hemmed in by high volcanic walls. The road follows the lakeshore over rocky points, and past numerous stopping places and undeveloped campsites about 30mi to Hells Canyon Dam. At the foot of the reservoir, it crosses the Hells Canyon Dam, drops to river level, and ends at a boat launch beside a small visitor center. From here, the only way to proceed is by boat or on foot. In pioneer days, the section of the canyon below the dam was considered unnavigable. Today, with inflatable rafts and jet boats, traveling the river has become routine. Rafts pull out after 33mi at Pittsburg Landing, or run the full 100mi to near Lewiston, Idaho. For those who prefer foot travel, a short hike along the riverbank conveys a sense of what lies ahead; A 1mi trail starts at the boat launch. Among noteworthy wildlife are bighorn sheep, mountain goats, elk, deer, black bears, cougar, eagles, osprey and 29 species of fish including some of America's last giant white sturgeon.

Even so, the canyon is an incomplete wilderness. Once present in great numbers, salmon have all but disappeared from the Snake River system. In the past, some 40 percent of the Columbia River Basin's Chinook came from the Snake; now they are endangered. Manmade dams are not the first to block the salmon runs. Ten to fifteen thousand years ago, a giant landslide at Rush Creek, well downstream from the end of the road, created a natural dam 400ft high. It must have had a devastating impact on river life for many years, until the Snake hacked it apart.

Excursion

★ **Wallowa Mountains** – *1/2 day. 20mi west of Hells Canyon via Rtes. 39 & 82. For information, contact Wallowa-Whitman National Forest, 1550 Dewey Ave., Baker City, OR 97814. ☎ 541-523-6391 or www.fs.fed.us/r6/w-w.* Running southeast to northwest for approximately 40mi, the Wallowa Mountains create an imposing line of snow-covered granite summits rising through a dense blanket of forest. Elevations range from near 10,000ft on the high peaks to around 5,000ft in valley bottoms. The core of the range is included in 359,000-acre Eagle Cap Wilderness, the largest designated wilderness in Oregon. Start your visit at the **Wallowa Mountains Visitor Center★** *(Rte. 82 just outside Enterprise; p 105)*.

A good choice for auto-touring or short hikes, the Lostine River Road begins at the town of Lostine and climbs 18mi south up a scenic glacier-carved canyon. Deeply forested, and in places just a narrow gorge, the canyon eventually opens out in meadows where the river forks. From these meadows there are good views up East Lostine River to the best-known summit in the range, 9,595ft Eagle Cap Peak, standing above Lake Basin. Close to timberline, the basin's rolling bedrock floor is strewn with lakes, streams, wildflowers and scattered groves of conifers, making it a popular, sometimes crowded destination for hikers and horseback riders. Campsites and opportunities for hiking and fishing are scattered along the road. *Wallowa-Whitman National Forest requires a fee for parking at most trailheads; passes cost $3/day or $25/year, and must be purchased in advance at ranger stations or other designated outlets.*

★JOSEPH

Although named for the renowned Nez Percé leader, the town was never seen by Chief Joseph. He and his people were ordered out of their beloved Wallowas to make room for settlers. Their eviction, and their long, tragic attempt to reach freedom in Canada, makes for one of the West's bravest epic stories. It is not hard to see why the Nez Percé wanted to stay here. Surrounded by rich grassland, the old brick and wood storefronts of Main Street look straight up at the high and shining Wallowas. Lately, increasing popularity among artists and urban refugees, along with outstanding recreational attractions, have made it a regional focal point. The town is a widely recognized center for bronze sculpture, which often includes heroic representations of Nez Percé warriors; several foundries offer tours that walk you through the ancient art of lost-wax bronze casting. Joseph also serves as a gateway to nearby Wallowa Lake and Hells Canyon.

© Dianne Dietrich Leis

Joseph

Sights *1/2 day*

Valley Bronze of Oregon – *18 Main St. Open year-round daily.* ☎ *541-432-7445.* The Main Street gallery displays bronze sculpture, photographs, paintings and other artwork by a variety of artists. Highly detailed, patinated bronzes are currently in fashion; other more impressionistic works are also on display. Tours of the foundry are offered daily.

★**Manuel Museum** – *400 N. Main St. Open May–Sept Mon–Sat 9am–5pm, Sun 10am–5pm. Rest of the year Mon–Sat 10am–4pm. Closed Jan 1, Thanksgiving Day, Dec 25. $6.* ⚒ 🅿 ☎ *541-432-7235.* Displaying the personal collection of sculptor David Manuel, this fine museum devotes itself primarily to the history of the Nez Percé as seen through historic artifacts, many of which serve as research material for Manuel's detailed bronze work. In addition to headdresses, beadwork, baskets and ceremonial clothing are hundreds of stone arrowheads and spear points, several pioneer wagons and buggies, war memorabilia and Manuel's sculpture. One-hour foundry tours are offered twice a day.

★**Wallowa Lake** – *South of town off Wallowa Lake Hwy. For information, contact Wallowa Lake Lodge, 60060 Wallowa Lake Hwy., Joseph, OR 97846.* ⚒ ☎ *541-432-9821 or www.wallowalakelodge.com.* A long clear-water lake confined on three sides by glacial moraines, and by the mountains at its head, Wallowa Lake has been a resort area for over 100 years. In the early days visitors reached the end of the lake on excursion boats, and enjoyed an amusement park. Today a road running 4mi on the east side to the end of the lake provides access, and though the amusement park is gone there are still plenty of things to do. On the southern end of the lake, **Wallowa Lake State Park** *(open May–Sept daily 6am–11pm; rest of the year daily 8am–4:30pm;* ⛺ ♿ 🅿 ☎ *541-432-4185)* offers campsites, boat launching and picnicking under the huge pines. The rustic log **Wallowa Lake Lodge** is worth a visit; built in the 1920s and being gradually restored, it still provides meals and accommodations. Big-sky vistas can be had from the top of the **Wallowa Lake Tramway**, whose four-passenger gondolas rise to the 8,256ft summit of Mount Howard in 15min *(operates Memorial Day–Sept daily 10am–5pm; 2 weeks in Dec; round–trip $14.95;* ⚒ 🅿 ☎ *541-432-5331).* The road ends at a popular trailhead for the Eagle Cap Wilderness.

When planning your trip, consult the Practical Information section for travel tips, useful addresses and phone numbers, and information on sports and recreation, and annual events.

JOHN DAY FOSSIL BEDS NATIONAL MONUMENT★★

Michelin map 493 C 5 and map p 102
Tourist Information ☎ 541-987-2333 or www.nps.gov/joda

If you were to write a wildlife guide to eastern Oregon as it was, say, 30 million years ago, you'd have to describe bear-dogs, entelodonts, saber-toothed cats, rhinoceros and many other strange creatures. In fact, the book exists, in the form of fossil beds that cover some 10,000sq mi (including more than 670 identified sites) of north central Oregon. Named for a major river that flows through the region, which in turn was named after an obscure fur trapper who passed through Oregon around 1811, the national monument protects a few of the better pages of that great book. Together they tell the story of ancient plants, animals, climate, and the grand workings of geology.

What makes these fossil beds significant is that they preserve not just one era but a nearly continuous fossil record from 54 million years ago to about 6 million years ago. During that time, the Cascade Mountains came into being. As they rose, they created a barrier that cut off ocean moisture from the interior, gradually transforming what had been a warm semi-tropical forest soaked by about 100in of rain per year, to the near-desert that exists today. As the climate changed, resident plants and animals also changed, through evolution and migration. Meanwhile the volcanic Cascades belched periodic waves of airborne ash which buried and preserved the various organic remains of that changing scene. In some cases, specimens were washed into ash-filled ponds and streambeds, creating deposits that would one day provide rich ground for paleontologists and a wealth of sites for visitors to explore.

VISIT *1 day*

The monument has three units: Sheep Rock, the largest unit, holds the visitor center; Painted Hills; and Clarno.

★**Sheep Rock Visitor Center** – *40mi west of John Day on Rte. 19, 2mi north of US-26. Open Memorial Day-Labor Day daily 9am–6pm. Labor Day–Thanksgiving & Mar–Memorial Day daily 9-5. Thanksgiving–Feb Mon–Fri 9am–5pm.* ♿ 🅿 ☎ *541-987-2333.* Begin your visit at the visitor center, which occupies a 12-room ranch house. This is the place to get an overall picture of the fossil beds and the cycles of deposition and climate change that created them. A 15min video shows the geologic history of the region. Actual fossils display the concrete results of paleontology, including a rhinoceros skull, the shell of a land tortoise, and delicate leaves, seed pods, and fish from the bottoms of ancient ponds. From these beautiful and instructive artifacts stories emerge. The rhino skull, 30 million years old, shows tooth-marks of an ancient scavenger—perhaps a dog-like animal. Among other animals of the time was the bear-dog, a predator the size of a black bear with bear-like feet but rounded chest and the legs and muzzle of a dog. Another was the entelodont, a bison-sized, omnivorous pig-like animal with a head more than 3ft long.

The John Day Formation's light-colored beds show up clearly on **Sheep Rock**, a dramatic pinnacle that rises across the river from the visitor center. Drive .5mi south on Route 19 for a scenic but distant look at it from an interpretive pullout. A closer experience can be had a few miles north along Route 19, where two trails lead to **Blue Basin★**—a natural amphitheater of badlands loaded with fossils. Everything here, even the stream that drains the basin, is colored by blue-green sediments. The 3mi **Blue Basin Overlook Trail** follows a rugged route on the hills circling the basin. The easier **Island in Time Trail** *(.6mi)* climbs gradually up the floor of the basin to its head. Along the way, several fossils (replicas of originals discovered nearby) lie beneath protective plastic bubbles with interpretive remarks. At one stop is the carapace of a land tortoise. Farther on, an oreodont lies curled in the rock. A leaf-eating creature the size of a sheep, this one is missing a forequarter and a hindquarter. Nearby is a cat-like animal called a nimravid, its skull and long stabbing teeth exposed to view.

North along the highway another few miles is the **Foree Area**, another exposure of the blueish John Day formation. The paved **Story in Stone Trail** leads 1,000ft into the colored layers, and the **Flood of Fire Trail** *(.25mi)* ends at a good view of the valley from the edge of claystone cliffs.

Painted Hills Unit – *9mi northwest of Mitchell off US-26.* Some 40mi west of the Foree Area, near Mitchell, Painted Hills has a different character. Here, the lower John Day Formation is shaped into soft domes streaked red and tan and black. Stop at the **Painted Hills Overlook** for a good general view of the area. The half-mile trail that starts here goes close to the colored domes. A short distance west on the unpaved monument road at **Painted Cove**, a .25mi nature trail circles a hill of bright red sediment. Although not rich in fossils, the geology is interesting and well-explained by brochures available on site.

Nearby, **Leaf Fossil Trail★** tells a fascinating story of conditions 33-34 million years ago. The .25mi loop circles a seemingly insignificant beige-colored hill. Yet this hill has yielded a rich trove of fossils, starting in 1923, when paleontologist Ralph Chaney began work here. In a mere 98 cubic feet of shale he found more than 20,000 plant and animal specimens. Chaney speculated that these deposits were in a lake within a warm forest 30 million years ago. More recent work has shown that this hill records a more complicated process of change beginning with temperate hardwood forest, transforming to savannah, then to a series of swamps and lakes, and finally another forest that was obliterated by a volcanic eruption. A big story for a little hill.

Clarno Unit – *On Rte. 218, 18mi west of Fossil.* The main feature of this unit is the **Clarno Palisades**, a dramatic cluster of pinnacles rich in plant fossils. Two .25mi trails lead into the palisades for close-up observation of fossils.

EXCURSION

★**Kam Wah Chung & Company Museum** – *1/2 hr. 38mi east of Sheep Rock Unit, just north of US-26, adjacent to City Park in town of John Day. Open May–Oct Mon–Thu 9am–noon & 1pm–5pm, weekends 1pm–5pm. Closed Jul 4, Labor Day. $3.* & ⊡ ☎ *541-575-0028.* The city of John Day was named for a trapper who came through Oregon with the Astorian fur-trapping brigades in the early 1800s. A pleasant ranch-based community, it grew up following the 1862 gold discovery along nearby Canyon Creek. After the mines played out, repeated fires and natural disasters took their toll, so that few relics of mining days survived. One that did is the Kam Wah Chung & Company building, now a museum.

The company was started by two young Chinese immigrants, Lung On, a businessman with various real-estate interests, and Ing Hay, an herbalist renowned for his ability to diagnose illnesses by reading a patient's pulse. In 1887 the partners bought a 20-year-old trading post on The Dalles Military Road, the main highway of the time. They sold groceries, dry goods and other supplies to miners, the majority of whom were Chinese immigrants themselves, working in the gold fields of eastern Oregon. The store became more than a supply source; it was also a social club, doctor's office and religious temple. Both men lived in the store until the 1940s. After they died, the building was given to the city, which left it alone from 1948 to 1968 when it was discovered to be a small historic treasure. The objects inside reflect the lives and times of Chinese immigrants. Noteworthy artifacts include Doc Hay's pharmacopoeia of some 1,000 medicinal herbs, a religious shrine redolent from decades of devotions and incense-burning, and the personal objects and furniture in the men's living quarters.

PENDLETON

Michelin map 493 C 4 and map p 102
Population 16,060
Tourist Information ☎ 541-276-7411

Bucking broncos and wool shirts come to mind first when you think of Pendleton. The annual Round-Up ranks as one of the country's biggest rodeos, while Pendleton Woolen Mills is an equally famous outgrowth of the region's ranching economy. Tucked beneath high bluffs on the sheltered banks of the Umatilla River off I-84, this small city stays true to its cowboy roots—friendly, practical, sometimes exuberant, never rich but never poor.

A walk through the compact business district tells just about the whole story, with history tangible in the old Victorian homes north of the river, in the antique shops along Court Avenue, and in businesses like Hamley & Co., which for nearly a century has been making and repairing custom saddles from the hide up. While many of the original 19C facades have been altered, some including the Masonic Hall have been nicely restored. Others have survived simply by neglect—because the Empire Block, for example, was off Main Street, rent was low and owners had no incentive to remodel. The tower in front of the courthouse features a glass-enclosed Seth Thomas clock bought by the city in 1889. When the old courthouse was demolished in 1954, the 57ft clock was saved and now stands in a new tower.

SIGHTS *1 day*

★**Pendleton Underground Tours** – *37 S.W. Emigrant Ave. Open Mar–Nov Mon–Sat & holidays 9:30am–5pm, Sun (mid–Jun–Aug) 11am–1pm. Rest of the year Mon,Fri–Sat 10am–3pm. Closed Jan 1, Thanksgiving Day, Dec 25. $10.* ☎ *541-276-0730 or 800-226-6398.* Beneath the pavement of Pendleton lies a shadow city, an underground network used from the 1880s to 1950s. Back then, the town was a rambunctious place with as many as 32 saloons and 18 brothels. Although law enforcement was often lax, there were times when clients of those establishments needed to make a fast exit. On such occasions they could dive through hidden doorways into a warren of basements and passageways. During prohibition, entire saloons and gambling parlors went underground. These spaces also provided living quarters and some freedom of movement for Chinese laborers before the turn of the century, when racist curfews forbade them from being out after dark. No one knows how extensive the tunnels were, but one reportedly ran 5mi to the town of Rieth. The 90min guided tour leads through subterranean saloons, gambling parlors, living quarters, a jail, and an aboveground brothel. Most of the spaces are set up to look as they might have when in use.

⋆**Pendleton Woolen Mills** – *1307 S.E. Court Pl. Visit by guided tour (20min) only, year-round Mon–Fri 9am, 11am, 1:30pm & 3pm. Closed major holidays, 2 weeks in Aug & Dec.*   🕭 🖪 ☎ *541-276-6911. www.pendleton-usa.com.* Built in 1909 to take advantage of wool from ranches in the region, the mill grew famous as a producer of trade blankets and durable clothing. A guided tour takes visitors through the whole process of turning wool into blankets, from carding and spinning to weaving. Although some of the machines are now controlled by computers, they are originals made of heavy steel. It's a delight to watch them thunder away as they make soft, beautiful fabric. The attached retail store sells Pendleton products, including bargains on seconds and discontinued items.

■ Pendleton Round-Up

Since it started in 1910, the Pendleton Round-Up has been one of the most spirited celebrations in the west. In the second full week of September, after the grain harvest and the late summer check-up of livestock, Pendleton becomes 100 percent cow town, fully decked out in spur-jangling, skirt-twirling regalia. An old-fashioned parade with no motors allowed—only buggies, wagons and stagecoaches—kicks off a week of rodeo and pageant and city-wide partying that attracts more than 50,000 people. The rodeo itself is the last of the "Big 4," a grueling series of back-to-back rodeos in Walla Walla; Ellensburg; Lewiston, Idaho; and finally Pendleton. Some contestants do all four, vying for the bonus payment that goes to the top point winner. But Pendleton is the big show. Each afternoon for four days, spectators jam the stands to see who is best at bronc riding, bull riding, steer wrestling, and roping. The competition grows more heated as elimination rounds narrow the field.

In the evenings, the **Happy Canyon Pageant** historical drama rates as a historic artifact in its own right. First performed in 1915, the show hasn't changed significantly since. Performed in partnership with Native Americans throughout the region, it still begins with a portrayal of their traditional lives; then come the settlers; confrontation leads to conflict, which ends in peaceful resolution. The pageant continues with dancing, gambling and partying into the wee hours.

Jess Stahl on *Grave Digger*, Pendleton Round-Up (c.1916)

Oregon Historical Society, ORHI12526

★**Round-Up Hall of Fame** – *On the Round-Up Grounds (Exit 207 off I-84). Open May–Oct Mon–Sat 10am–5pm.* ♿ 🅿 ☎ *541-278-0815. www.roundup.com.* Tucked beneath the south stands of the Round-Up stadium, the Hall of Fame commemorates the annual rodeo and its participants. The largest display is the famous bucking bronc, War Paint, mounted and kicking, while engraved on plaques are the names of rodeo winners and other inductees, including Jackson Sundown, a famous Indian champion who took the bronc-riding title when he was 50 years old. Photos, paintings, saddles, bridles and other paraphernalia celebrate what sportswriter Red Smith called the American Cowboy: "Athletes and competitors and one thing more—they ride the last frontier of rugged individualism, paying their own dusty way earning only what they are good enough to win."

EXCURSIONS

McKay Creek National Wildlife Refuge – *1 hr. North entrance located 6mi south of Pendleton off US-395. Open Mar–Sept daily 5am–dusk.* 🅿 ☎ *541-922-3232.* A haven for wintering waterfowl, the 1,836-acre refuge provides habitat for wildlife all year long. Willows and cottonwoods crowd the marshy bottomland along McKay Creek, offering good bird-watching. Most of the terrain is covered by the reservoir, and is best seen from a road that parallels the west shore.

© Dianne Dietrich Leis

Bead Work, Tamastslikt Cultural Center

★**Tamastslikt Cultural Center** – *2 hrs. 7mi east of Pendleton, north of I-84, Exit 216 on Rte. 331. Open year-round daily 9am–5pm. Closed Jan 1, Thanksgiving Day, Dec 25. $6.* ⚠ ✗ ♿ 🅿 ☎ *541-966-9748.* This superb new museum on the Umatilla Reservation tells the story of the Cayuse, Umatilla and Walla Walla tribes. Organized in a circle, the exhibit hall begins with pre-Columbian times and moves to the present. Three divisions—Who We Were, Who We Are, and Who We Will Be—tell the story of the tribes. Exhibits begin with natural sounds and the artifacts of indigenous life: Coyotes call, elk bugle, geese fly overhead, owls hoot as you walk through displays of fishing, hunting and gathering. The artifacts show fine craftsmanship and include baskets, bows, nets, root diggers, arrows and storage containers. In a replica longhouse, native voices recount adventures of Coyote the trickster and other tales.

The acquisition of Spanish horses around 1730 marked the beginning of affluence for some families, represented with displays of elaborate regalia: saddles with high-beaded cantles and pommels, beaded saddle blankets, braided reins, and beaded collars and stirrups. Prosperity ended with the arrival of immigrants, missionaries, miners and soldiers. The tribes lost the bulk of their land, and even most of their treasured horses—a tragic tale, but as the museum eloquently points out, an unfinished one. Displays end with confident statements about the growing role of native people in regional politics, especially relating to environmental issues.

■ Southeastern Desert

One of the least known and least traveled corners of America, the southeastern corner of Oregon belongs geographically to Nevada's Great Basin, and like that vast congregation of mountains and dusty valleys, it is a high desert marked by extreme temperatures, oceanic expanses of sagebrush, shimmering alkali playas, and strange formations of basalt. Towns are few, and often little more than a gas station and cafe. Ranches are huge—it takes many acres to support a single cow. Some travelers want only to speed through on their way to somewhere more interesting, but to anyone who likes open spaces and can stand a little rough travel, the area offers many hidden pleasures and surprises. Be aware that summers are hot, winters cold, and services are scattered. While back roads are the most interesting, safety requires preparation and knowledge of local conditions. If in doubt, stick to main routes.

As some geologists tell it, a large meteorite struck this corner of the state 17 million years ago, punching a hole in the earth's crust and triggering vast geologic events including the eruption of basalts that built the Columbia Plateau. According to that theory, southeast Oregon was periodically a great lake of molten lava that overflowed toward the north. It also set in motion the faulting that created the Great Basin, where rivers and streams have no outlet to the sea. Trapped water collects in huge shallow lakes where it evaporates, leaving behind alkali flats that shimmer in the summer heat. Or, if there is enough water, it supports marshes where the shimmering is done by bird wings.

Malheur National Wildlife Refuge★★, 6mi east of Route 205, is such a place *(open year-round dawn-dusk; visitor center open year-round Mon–Thu 7am–4:30pm, Fri 7am–3:30pm, weekends & holidays 8am–4pm; closed weekends & holidays in winter △ ⅙ ₽ ☎ 541-493-2612; www.r1.fws.gov/malheur)*. Located 32mi south of Burns, the refuge comprises 187,000 acres of marsh around lakes Harney and Malheur. Each spring and fall, thousands of birds migrating along the Pacific Flyway stop here, to the delight of bird-watchers. Among the 320 bird species sojourning at Malheur are sandhill cranes, white-faced ibis, white pelicans, long-billed curlews, snowy egrets, trumpeter swans, avocets and snow geese. Check out the refuge visitor center for information on the 42mi self-guided auto tour through Blitzen Valley. An alternate route leads to **Diamond Craters★** *(18mi southwest of New Princeton)*, site of a recent lava eruption (within the last 25,000 years), complete with spatter cones, lava tubes, craters and cinder fields.

One river does flow out of the desert. The **Owyhee River** curves along the Idaho border east of Steens Mountain, slices a deep, spectacular canyon, and eventually joins the Snake. A Wild and Scenic River, it is virtually inaccessible except to white-water boaters who treasure it as a seasonal paradise. Only in spring is there enough water to float beneath the 1,200ft basalt walls. From Three Forks to Rome, rapids with such names as Widowmaker present a serious challenge; the tame stretch from Rome to the Owyhee Reservoir is popular with families.

We welcome corrections and suggestions that may assist us in preparing the next edition. Please send us your comments:

Michelin Travel Publications
Editorial Department
P. O. Box 19001
Greenville, SC 29602-9001

Oregon Coast

Natural Bridge, Boardman State Park / © Dianne Dietrich Leis

A blend of wave-swept rocks and sandy beaches, the 362mi of the Oregon coastline are mostly scenic and wild. Here, where the hand of civilization falls lightly, the largest town, Coos Bay, holds only 15,520 people, and travelers can find beaches that are occupied only by gulls and sea stars—even on a summer weekend. Homes and businesses may border the shore, but they cannot own it. In 1967 the state legislature passed the landmark Oregon Beach Bill, which decrees that all Oregon beaches are open to the public.

The forest, a mossy mix of Sitka spruce, western red cedar, and other conifers, is an integral part of the complex coastal ecosystem. Unfortunately, the forest has not received the same level of protection as the beaches; the vast majority of the old growth has been cut. Fortunately, the stretches of forest right on the shoreline have generally fared better than those farther inland.

This lush landscape has attracted human settlement for thousands of years. Fish, mussels, berries, crabs, elk—the bounty of the sea and forest—plus a mild climate enabled coastal tribes to thrive and establish permanent villages, unlike many inland tribes who led more difficult nomadic lives. European explorers sailed along the Oregon shores as early as 1543, but there was little interest in the region until the end of the 18C, when the Northwest's resources—especially sea otter and beaver pelts—attracted attention. Small and isolated, early coastal towns weren't fully connected to the outside world until the coast highway (Highway 101) was completed in the early 1930s.

Thanks to its remoteness, the Oregon coast has remained largely unspoiled. As close as 90min from the urban center of Portland, the coast is known for the simpler pleasures of nature. Though few restaurants and inns carry the cosmopolitan fanfare of Portland, they do offer a delightful mix of locally grown produce and fresh-caught seafood—salmon, clam chowder, mussels, shrimp and succulent Dungeness crab. And while few people actually take to the cold ocean waters, visitors continue to flock to this rugged, windy place where birds nest in cliffholds and ancient trees lean far leeward, where a wave-whipped sea pierced by huge seastacks is all you need for a fine day on the beach.

PRACTICAL INFORMATION

When to Go

Summer temperatures along the 400mi-long coast range from 60°F to 75°F. Winters are mild and temperatures rarely dip below freezing. Fog, drizzle and rain showers are frequent in spring and winter. A windbreaker comes in handy for walks on the beach in any season.

Getting There – The region is best explored by car. The main north-south route along the coast is US-101. Access to the region is from I-5, which runs parallel to the coastal highway. US-30 runs west from Portland to Astoria in the north; US-20 connects Albany and Newport. Route 126 travels west from Eugene to Florence and Rte. 42 connects Roseburg with the coast south of Coos Bay. International and domestic flights service **Portland International Airport** (PDX) (☎ *503-335-1234*). Rogue International Airport in Medford (☎ *541-772-8068*) and Eugene Regional Airport (☎ *541-687-5430*) are serviced by United Airlines/United Express (☎ *800-241-6522*) and Horizon Air (☎ *800-547-9308*). Closest **Amtrak** stations are in Albany, Eugene and Medford (☎ *800-872-7245*). Greyhound **bus** serves Astoria, Coos Bay, Newport and Florence; check for stops at other coastal cities (☎ *800-231-2222*).

General Information

Visitor Information – Contact the **Oregon Coast Visitors Association, Inc.** *(P.O. Box 74, Newport OR 97365; ☎ 541-574-2679 or 888-628-2101; www.oregoncoast.org)* for information and brochures on points of interest, accommodations, sightseeing, recreation and seasonal events. For additional information, contact: **Astoria-Warrenton Area Chamber of Commerce**, 111 W. Marine Dr., Astoria OR 97103, ☎ 503-325-6311 or 800-523-1235; **Greater Newport Chamber of Commerce**, 555 SW Coast Hwy, Newport OR 97365, ☎ 541-265-8801 or 800-262-7844; **Florence Chamber of Commerce**, 270 Hwy. 101, Florence OR 97439, ☎ 541-997-3128; **Bay Area Chamber of Commerce**, P.O. Box 210, Coos Bay OR 97420, ☎ 541-269-0215 or 800-824-8486; **Brookings-Harbor Chamber of Commerce**, 16330 Lower Harbor Rd., Brookings OR 97415, ☎ 541-469-3181 or 800-535-9469.

Accommodations – Area visitors' guides including lodging directories are available *(free)* from regional tourism agencies *(above)*. A wide range of accommodations can be found throughout the area year-round, including hotels and motels, seaside cottages, bed-and-breakfast inns and resorts. Make reservations well in advance; many facilities fill up quickly in the summer as well as on holidays and winter weekends. **Youth hostel:** Sea Star, 375 Second St., Bandon OR 97411, ☎ 541-347-9632; Seaside, 930 N. Holladay Dr., Seaside OR 97238, ☎ 503-738-7911.

Camping – Campgrounds and **RV parks** are spread throughout the region. Most are open year-round; reservations in summer are strongly recommended. State Park campgrounds accept reservations up to 11 months in advance; yurts-domed tents with plywood floors—are available for rent *($25/night)*. Additional information on camping is available by calling ☎ 800-452-5687 or www.oregoncoast.com/camping.htm, or through area tourist offices *(above)*.

Salmon Fishing on the Rogue River

© Dianne Dietrich Leis

Sports and Leisure

Historic homes, museums, area aquariums, local art galleries and antique shops as well as art and music festivals provide visitors with myriad activities. Seaside communities offer a wide choice of water sports including sailing, windsurfing, water-skiing, canoeing and kayaking. Miles of public beaches invite travelers to relax, beachcomb or enjoy a horseback ride.

Boating and Rafting – Whale-watching excursions *(best viewing from mid-Mar–mid-Apr)* and nature sightseeing tours depart from most harbor towns. Chartered fishing excursions leave from many area marinas. River **rafting** trips, jet boat tours or **fishing trips** on the Rogue River depart from Gold Beach year-round *(schedules and reservations: Rogue River Reservations, Inc., ☎ 541-247-6022 or 800-525-2161; or Rogue River Mail Boat Trips ☎ 541-247-7033)*. The angler will find fishing for salmon and steelhead in nearby rivers enticing.

Other Outdoor Activities – An exciting way to explore the region is to **bike** along the **Oregon Coast Bike Route**. The trip is best planned from north to south to take advantage of prevailing winds *(367mi/587km from Astoria to Brookings)*. For maps and additional information, call **Bicycle Hotline**, ☎ 503-986-3556. The area's many parks and national forests abound with recreational activities for the whole family. Oregon Dunes National Recreation Area is the perfect spot for **hiking**, camping, **bird-watching** and dune-riding. The **golf** enthusiast will find windy seaside courses a challenge.

NORTH COAST★★

Michelin map 493 A, B 4 and map p 118
Tourist Information ☎ 541-574-2679 or www.oregon-coast.org

The northern half of the Oregon coast runs from Astoria, at the mouth of the Columbia, 115mi south to Newport. It is more historic and more civilized than its southern counterpart. Arguably, the north coast's head start on development can be traced back to 1792, when the first American explorer in this region, Robert Gray, sailed up the Columbia, setting the stage for US claims to the Northwest. The trend continued in 1805, when Lewis and Clark ended their westward trek at the mouth of the Columbia, and in 1811, when fur traders working for John Jacob Astor founded Fort Astoria, the oldest town on the Oregon coast. Development of the north coast was probably assured during the 1840s and 1850s, when tens of thousands of pioneers trekked the Oregon Trail and settled in the Willamette Valley, just across the Coast Range from the northern shore. All this at a time when no appreciable European-American settlement of the south coast had yet occurred.

Today, as in the 19C, the vast majority of Oregon's population resides in the northern part of the state. It's no coincidence that places like the posh little resort village of Cannon Beach and the major coastal tourist town of Newport are located within a couple of hours' drive of Portland and the Willamette Valley. Though influenced by the proximity of the inland population centers, the north coast remains lightly developed by most standards; instead, it is known for its small towns and uncrowded beaches, deep forests and rocky headlands. The smattering of museums, cafes, hotels, galleries, monuments and other trappings of civilization have intrinsic merit, but much of their appeal stems from their scenic settings.

★ASTORIA   *1 day*

Founded as a fur trading post in 1811, just five years after Lewis and Clark left the area, Astoria is the first permanent American settlement in the Oregon Territory. The fur trade soon faded but fishing and logging rose to prominence. By the 1850s Astoria was a thriving port, largely due to its location at the mouth of the Columbia River. Around 1880 the town's economy further boomed when business turned to the millions of salmon that migrated up the Columbia; soon salmon canneries thronged the waterfront. By this time the population exceeded 7,000, not far from today's figure of roughly 10,000. Overfishing led to the crash of the salmon industry several decades ago, but Astoria continues as a busy port for oceangoing vessels and commercial fishermen. Several museums and a great many preserved and restored historic buildings keep history fresh in Astoria. A 1.4mi **walking tour★** that runs from Flavel House to the Columbia River Maritime Museum features no fewer than 67 sites. Get the walking-tour guide at Flavel House *(441 8th St.)*.

★**Astoria Column** – [Kids] *1mi south of US-30 in downtown; head uphill on 16th St. and follow signs. Open year-round daily 7am–dusk.* ⬛ ☎ *503-325-2963*. Dedicated in 1926 and restored in the mid-1990s, the Astoria Column gives visitors a glimpse of both the area's past and present. Using a bas-relief technique called sgraffito (skrah-FEE-toe), Italian artist Attilio Pusterla created a spiraling depiction of Northwest history that starts with the pre-European Indians, moves through the Lewis and Clark expedition and the fur-trading era, and ends with the coming of the railroad in 1893. The best way to view this artist's version of a historical timeline is to walk counter-clockwise around the column, beginning at the base with the earliest events and tracking the spiral upwards. Binoculars help with the higher scenes. To view present-day Astoria and the lower Columbia region, take those binoculars up the 164 steps to the top of the 125ft column, which stands on 600ft Coxcomb Hill. From here, you can see freighters heading up the Columbia to Portland under the 4mi Astoria-Megler Bridge that spans the mouth of the Columbia,

© Dianne Dietrich Leis

Astoria Column

tugboats hauling barges heaped with logs, and thousands of square miles of forests, mountains and ocean.

Heritage Museum – *1618 Exchange St. Open May–Sept daily 10am–5pm. Rest of the year daily 11am–4pm. Closed Jan 1, Thanksgiving Day, Dec 24-25. $5.* & ⓟ ☎ *503-325-2203.* Visitors will find a little bit of everything pertaining to local history in this sprawling 1905 Neoclassical building, formerly Astoria's city hall. Displays detail the lives of the local Clatsop tribe, the journey of Lewis and Clark, pioneer days and the early years of development. Unusual exhibits include a Tong Altar, which hearkens back to the time when thousands of Chinese immigrants came to Astoria to work in the salmon canneries, and photos and artifacts about the dark days in the 1910s and 1920s when the Ku Klux Klan controlled much of Astoria's political and social life.

★**Columbia River Maritime Museum** – *On the waterfront, corner of US-30 (Marine Dr.) and 17th St., 1792 Marine Dr. Open year-round daily 9:30am–5pm. Closed Thanksgiving Day & Dec 25. $5.* & ⓟ ☎ *503-325-2323. www.crmm.org.* In 24,000sq ft of well-designed exhibit space, the maritime museum captures the long and proud seafaring heritage of Astoria and the lower Columbia region. Historic boats dot the Great Hall, including a 36ft motor lifeboat built in 1943 and a 1950s-vintage fishing boat. At the north wall, visitors will peer through the periscope of a World War II submarine and watch river traffic outside the museum. The galleries east of the Great Hall cover many themes, including early exploration, whaling and navigation. Among the thousands of artifacts are examples of scrimshaw carved from sperm-whale teeth, Bowie knives made to fit 1861 naval rifles, 1920s photos of horses hauling fishing nets through shallow water, and a fid (a pointy tool for separating rope strands while splicing). Much of the museum is given to naval history; in fact, the museum was literally built around the 13-ton bridge of the USS *Knapp*, a 1943 destroyer that saw action in World War II and the Korean War. Outside at the pier, visitors can board the *Columbia*, a floating lighthouse that until 1979 was stationed at the treacherous mouth of the Columbia River, the "Graveyard of the Pacific."

★★**Fort Clatsop National Memorial** – *1 hr. 6mi southwest of Astoria. Cross Youngs Bay on Hwy. 101 bridge and head southeast on Business 101 to Fort Clatsop Rd. following signs. Open mid-Jun–Labor Day daily 8am–5pm. Rest of the year daily 8am–6pm. Closed Dec 25. $2.* ⓟ ☎ *503-861-2471. www.nps.gov/focl.* The Meriwether Lewis and William Clark expedition wintered here from December 7, 1805 to March 23, 1806 in a stockade they named Fort Clatsop, after the local Indians. Exhibits in the visitor center cover the entire expedition and the events that led up to it. Some of the artifacts, such as a 1795 musket and a bear-hide quiver, merit more

117

than a glance, as do the journal entries that have been reproduced. Following an encounter with a grizzly, which was still charging after being shot eight times, one explorer wrote, "These bears…rather intimidate us all." The visitor center shows a 32min video detailing the entire expedition, a 17min slide show on the winter at Fort Clatsop, and shorter laser disk programs on subjects from canoe building to elk hunting. Outside, visitors can wander through a full-size replica of Fort Clatsop and imagine how life must have been that winter. All 33 members of the expedition stayed in this crude fort, which is little bigger than a typical house, and endured an infestation of fleas, a spotty diet, and rain on 94 of the 106 days they stayed here.

Fort Stevens State Park – *1 1/2 hrs. 10mi west of Astoria in Hammond, OR. Cross Youngs Bay on Hwy. 101 bridge and go west on Harbor Dr. Follow signs north on Fort Stevens Hwy. Open May–Sept daily 10am–6pm. Rest of the year Wed–Sun 10am–4pm. Closed Dec 25. $3/day. △ ▣ ☏ 503-861-2000.* During the Civil War, Union soldiers brought their cannons to this site above the mouth of the Columbia to guard the entrance to the mighty river. The increasingly modern artillery remained on sentry duty at Fort Stevens until shortly after World War II. A small museum tells of those many years of being on alert, with a special emphasis on the fort's one moment of action—the night of June 21, 1942, when a Japanese submarine fired 17 rounds onto the fort's grounds, causing tremendous excitement but no harm. Visitors may wander through the old concrete bunkers on the bluff.

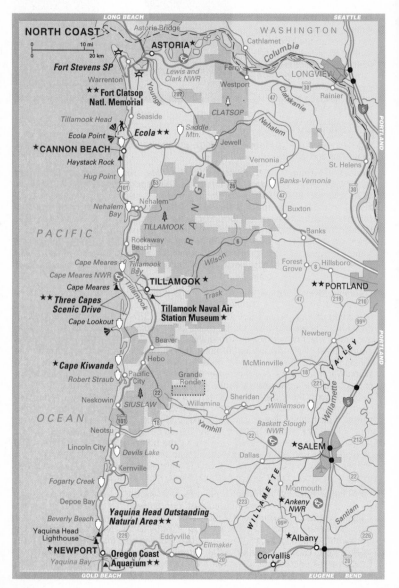

★CANNON BEACH   *1/2 day*

This beach-hugging village of 1,400 caters to artistic-minded residents and well-heeled travelers. The town got its name in 1846 when a cannon from a ship-wrecked schooner washed up on a nearby beach. Almost all traces of its pioneer days having vanished, Cannon Beach today displays an architecturally coherent blend of handsome weathered-cedar houses and commercial buildings. Strict codes and a .5mi separation from Highway 101 have prevented unsightly strip development.

A long, lovely curve of sandy **beach**★ gives the town its charm and character. Rising 235ft into the sky at water's edge is the beach's centerpiece, **Haystack Rock**, one of the world's tallest coastal monoliths. Beachgoers can skirt some of the base at low tide, exploring the tide pools and examining the starfish and anemones that cling to the dark rock. Resist the temptation to climb this sanctuary for area seabirds. Many people have fallen and many have been stranded after the incoming tide has turned the rock into an island.

★**Hemlock Street** – Dozens of galleries, shops and eateries, nearly all of them distinctive and worth exploring, line both sides of this half-mile heart of Cannon Beach *(between 1st and 3rd Sts.)*. Strolling is *de rigueur*, as cars jam Hemlock Street during summer and on off-season weekends. Among the best galleries for fine art is Ballantyne & Douglass *(no. 123)*. For elegant arts and crafts browse the Purple Pelican, across the street, or White Bird *(no. 251)*. Perhaps the most striking art in town is on display at Valley Bronze *(Sandpiper Sq., no. 172)*, an outlet for a famed eastern Oregon bronze factory. And if you just want to picnic on the beach, you'll find ample supplies at the Cannon Beach Bakery *(no. 144)* and Osburn's Ice Creamery & Deli *(no. 240)*. *Information and maps are available from Cannon Beach Information Center, 2nd and Spruce Sts., open year-round Mon–Sat 10am–5pm, Sun 11am–4pm;* ☎ *503-436-2623.*

★★**Ecola State Park** – *2mi north of town via Ecola Park Rd. Open year-round daily 6am–10pm. $3/car.* ⚐ 🅿 ☎ *503-436-2844.* Measuring 9mi long and on average about .5mi wide, the 1,303-acre park encompasses a lush belt of old-growth rain forest and one of the most storied sections of Oregon coastline. Tales of its beauty go back to the winter of 1806, when William Clark, Sacajawea and other members of the Lewis and Clark expedition hiked through what is now the park in search of whale blubber—they were desperate to add anything to their monotonous diet. After gazing out at the sea from a 1,000ft cliff above Tillamook Head, Clark wrote in his journal: "I beheld the grandest and most pleasing prospect which my eyes ever surveyed." Visitors can see what elicited such superlatives by driving to Indian Beach, at the end of the park road *(5mi north of entrance)*, and hiking north on the 6mi **Tillamook Head Trail**. In addition to providing spectacular coastal **views**★, the trail winds through vaulting groves of massive Sitka spruce draped with moss and ferns. Only slightly less dramatic views can be savored at **Ecola Point**, 2mi north of the park entrance. Here, a .25mi trail from the parking lot leads out to the end of the headland.

★TILLAMOOK   *1 day*

In the local Indian language "Tillamook" means "land of many waters," a fitting name for a town set on the flat, fertile bottomlands at the confluence of the Tillamook, Trask, Wilson, Kilchis and Miami rivers. Located a couple of miles from Tillamook Bay and 10mi from the open ocean, Tillamook is more inland farming community than coastal town. The dairy industry, particularly cheesemaking, is one of Tillamook's economic mainstays; motorists pass acre after acre of verdant pasture filled with grazing black-and-white Holsteins. Its pastoral nature notwithstanding, Tillamook does serve as the gateway to some of the most scenic stretches of the Oregon coast, including the justly celebrated Three Capes scenic drive.

Tillamook County Pioneer Museum – *2106 2nd St. (2nd and Pacific Aves.), east of Hwy. 101. Open year-round Mon–Sat 8am–5pm, Sun 11am–5pm. Closed Thanksgiving Day, Dec 25. $2.* ☎ *503-842-4553.* The Tillamook County Pioneer Association has stuffed artifacts into every inch of this 1905-vintage building, formerly the courthouse. Visitors wade through butter churns, stagecoaches, muskets and pump organs. Close scrutiny yields little treasures, such as the photo of Leonard Wallulis shaving his face with an ax at a 1938 timber carnival. Note the replica of the hollow spruce stump in which the area's first settler lived for a year.

★**Tillamook County Creamery Association** – *North edge of town, 4175 Hwy. 101. Open mid-Jun–mid-Sept daily 8am–8pm. Rest of the year daily 8am–6pm. Closed Thankgiving Day, Dec 25.* ✗ ⚐ 🅿 ☎ *503-815-1300. www.tillamookcheese.com.* In this sprawling factory, workers annually convert the milk from Tillamook county's 40,000 dairy cows into roughly 61 million pounds of cheese. Exceptionally accommodating to visitors, the facility boasts huge windows in a spacious second-floor gallery that provide views of the state-of-the-art equipment and the workers who produce and package the cheese. Each station in the gallery has a video presentation that explains the part of the process that visitors are looking at in the factory below. On the main floor, museum-like displays tell the 150-year history of the county dairy industry and provide "Udderly Amazing Cow Facts": Did you know that an average dairy cow eats 32,850 pounds of food a year and produces 10,000 gallons of milk in its lifetime? Around the corner from the displays visitors can sample Tillamook's famous cheddar and other cheeses.

★**Tillamook Naval Air Station Museum** – *2mi south of Tillamook, east of Hwy. 101 via Long Prairie Rd. to 6030 Hangar Rd. Open Memorial Day–Labor Day daily 9am–6pm. Rest of the year daily 10am–5pm. Closed Thanksgiving Day, Dec 25. $8.* ╳ ⴺ ▯ ☎ *503-842-1130. www.tillamookair.com.* The former blimp hangar at the naval air station houses a big and varied collection of vintage airplanes, but visitors first should admire the hangar itself. The world's largest building of its type, it measures 192ft high, 300ft wide, and 1,072ft long. Mostly military, the aircraft include such models as a P-51 Mustang and a World War I Spad, as well as oddities, such as a J2F-6 Duck, one of the US Navy's earliest floatplanes. A wealth of interpretive information breathes life into the history of military aviation.

Excursion

★★**Three Capes Scenic Drive** – *2 hrs. 40mi route beginning in downtown Tillamook at Hwy. 101 and 3rd St.; head west on 3rd St. and follow the signs.* This delightful drive takes in dairy farms, bays alive with diving pelicans, coastal forests, tiny hidden towns, sand dunes, sea lion haul-outs and long vistas of the open Pacific. To fully appreciate the drive, you must get out of your car, especially at the three capes themselves. The northernmost, **Cape Meares**, has an 1890 lighthouse, a gigantic, candelabra-shaped Sitka spruce nicknamed the Octopus Tree, offshore rocks seasonally packed with nesting seabirds, and a .25mi interpretive trail along the edge of the headland. Midway along the drive, **Cape Lookout State Park** shelters lush old-growth rainforest, miles of driftwood-dotted sandy beach, and spectacular **views**★★ from the cliff at the end of the cape. The main entrance, about 10mi south of Cape Meares, provides access to the beach and the forest. A 2.5mi trail winds up through moss-draped Sitka spruce and western hemlock to the trailhead for an easy 2.5mi hike out to the end of the cape. You can also drive to the cape trailhead, 2mi south of the main entrance along the scenic route. Near the end of the drive stands **Cape Kiwanda**★, a massive sandstone cliff that has been sculpted by the sea. Walk a few hundred yards north along the beach and up the sand dune to stand atop the cape. The beach by the parking lot also happens to be the launch site for the area's renowned dory fleet. Early in the morning fishermen tow these small, flat-bottomed boats (originally designed for river fishing) to the water's edge, then motor straight out through the surf-a dicey procedure compared with the usual practice of putting out to sea from a harbor. In the afternoon the fishermen return and run their boats through the breakers and up onto the beach as close to their trailers as possible.

■ Thar She Blows

Every spring and winter gray whales migrate along the Oregon coast, often passing within easy viewing distance. Though whalers nearly harpooned them to extinction, these 50ft, 30-ton leviathans recovered following government protection. Now more than 20,000 gray whales ply the 6,000mi route between the Bering Sea and Mexico, the longest known migration of any mammal. Southbound whales pass the Oregon coast from early December to early February, peaking at about 30 whales per hour in the last half of December. Northbound whales are less concentrated, passing from March through June and peaking around late March. Several hundred gray whales live along the Oregon coast throughout the year.

Some tips for whale-watchers: Station yourself on high ground, preferably on a headland that juts into the sea. Go on a calm day, if possible, as it's easier to spot the "blow" (the steamy exhalation whales make when they surface); scan for the 12ft-high blow with the naked eye, then zoom in with binoculars. Mornings are best, when the sun is at your back.

During Christmas break and spring break *(late March)*, whale-watching becomes a public passion in Oregon. Tens of thousands of visitors throng the best vantage points, particularly the 30 sites staffed by trained volunteers brimming with whale knowledge. Between 10am and 1pm look for someone wearing a cap, shirt or jacket emblazoned with the phrase "Whale Watching Spoken Here." You also may want to try watching whales from a boat; most larger coastal towns have tour operators who run whale-watching trips-a good bet are cruises from Depoe Bay. *For more information, call Oregon State Park and ask about the "Whale Watching Spoken Here" Volunteer Program;* ☎ *541-563-2002 or www.hmsc.orst.edu/education/whalewatch.*

Fishing Fleet, Newport Harbor

© Dianne Dietrich Leis

★NEWPORT *2 days*

Like most towns on the Oregon Coast, Newport enjoys a rich history of occupation by pioneers engaged in agriculture, logging and fishing. Unlike most towns on the Oregon Coast, Newport also has a century-long history of industrial-strength tourism, which has both positive and negative ramifications for present-day visitors. On the down side, cookie-cutter motels, souvenir shops and fast-food joints litter the Highway 101 corridor through town. On the up side, many notable attractions have developed here, particularly those dedicated to marine and coastal science. And, of course, the area still prides itself on the beaches and bay that spurred tourism here in the first place.

The central business district of Newport until Highway 101 bypassed it in the 1930s, the **Bayfront** *(north side of Yaquina Bay about .5mi southeast of Hwy. 101)* comprises a lively jumble of commercial fishing boats, art galleries, T-shirt shops, seafood canneries, knickknack stores, restaurants and contrived tourist attractions. The latter range from the reasonably educational **Undersea Gardens** *(250 S.W. Bay Blvd.;* ☎ *541-265-2206)* to the tacky wax museum. Dozens of raucous sea lions often congregate on floating docks next door to Undersea Gardens.

Yaquina Bay State Park – *Just west of Hwy. 101 at the north end of Yaquina Bay Bridge. Open mid-May–Sept daily 11am–5pm. Rest of the year daily noon–4pm. Closed Jan 1, Thanksgiving Day, Dec 25.* ▣ ☎ *541-265-5679.* Focal point of the park, the 42ft Yaquina Bay Lighthouse first cast its light to sea in 1871. The light went dark only three years later, however, when the more powerful beam of the nearby Yaquina Head Lighthouse came on line, but it was relit in 1996 as an official aid to navigation. Visitors can tour the historic keeper's house, which serves as a small museum. From the park's cliff-edge viewpoint, across the parking lot from the lighthouse, you can gaze at Yaquina Bay and read the many interpretive signs.

Oregon Coast History Center – *One block east of Hwy. 101 between Fall and Alder Sts. at 545 S.W. 9th St. Open Jun–Sept Tue–Sun 10am–5pm. Rest of the year Tue–Sun 11am–4pm. Closed major holidays.* ♿ ▣ ☎ *541-265-7509. http://newportnet.com/coasthistory.* Start at the Burrows House, a restored 1895 Queen Anne Victorian, erected by local contractor and builder John Burrows, that houses period artifacts, rotating exhibits on local history and a worthy photo collection. (Look for the early 20C surfers whose surfboards appear to be pointed wooden planks.) The house now functions as the home of the Lincoln County Historical Society. Just south, the Log Cabin Museum contains pioneer and Indian artifacts.

Newport Visual Arts Center – *West of Hwy. 101 via 3rd St. to 777 N.W. Beach Dr. Open Apr–Sept Tue–Sun noon–4pm. Rest of the year Tue–Sun 11am–3pm. Closed major holidays.* ♿ ▣ ☎ *541-265-6540. www.newportnet.com/occa/vac.*

The arts center displays both local and outside work of considerable repute, most of which is for sale, and the building itself makes its own strong visual statement with its airy, multilevel spaces and its setting on the bluff above Nye Beach.

★★**Oregon Coast Aquarium** – 🚼 *2820 S.E. Ferry Slip Rd., 1/4mi east of Hwy. 101 on the south shore of Yaquina Bay, just across the 101 bridge. Open Memorial Day–Labor Day daily 9am–6pm. Rest of the year daily 10am–5pm. Closed Dec 25. $8.75.* ✗ ⅙ 🅿 ☎ *541-867-3474. www.aquarium.org.* One of the nation's leading aquariums, the Oregon Coast Aquarium combines five major indoor galleries with six acres of outdoor exhibits—and it is engaged in an ambitious expansion program (a salmon exhibit opened in the summer of 1999 and the elaborate Open Ocean is slated for summer 2000). With minor exceptions, the nearly 200 species exhibited are native to the coastal waters of Oregon. The aquarium complements its exhibits with many well-informed docents, a hands-on lab, an estuary trail, a theater and other interpretive efforts. Until September 1998, the aquarium was famous as the home of Keiko, star of the movie *Free Willy* (1993), who was relocated to a bay pen in his home waters off Iceland in 1998.

Visit – *1/2 day.* To begin the recommended tour, head south out of the lobby past the gift shop to view the introductory video. Just beyond the video area lies the first major stop, **Sandy Shores**, whose central exhibit is a 9,000gal tank depicting life under a pier. You'll immediately spot the leopard sharks and the twinkling squadron of anchovies, but look closer to find helmet crabs, tubesnouts and other animals lurking in crevices. Next comes **Rocky Shores**★, where small tanks harbor wolf eels, neon-colored sea slugs, abalones and other rock-loving sea creatures. At the big touch tank visitors can get a feel for tide-pool life by gently handling sea stars (starfish), anemones and chitons. In the adjacent **Coastal Waters**★★ exhibit, dozens of plate-size moon jellies drift hypnotically in an upright, cylindrical glass tank, their

© Dianne Dietrich Leis

Sea Otter at Oregon Coast Aquarium

white, translucent bodies slowly pulsing as they gracefully propel themselves. A nearby panel explains that jellies are not properly called jellyfish—95 percent water and salts, they lack spine, brain, bones and heart, and are thus not true fish. Exit Coastal Waters and head outside, where you will find the **Aviary**★★. Beneath the towering screen enclosure tufted puffins scoot comically across a long pond, flapping furiously as if about to take off; oystercatchers scream in territorial dispute; murres cruise underwater, stroking with their wings— you can watch them through the underwater viewing windows. The birds' neighbors, the **sea otters**★★, **sea lions**, and **seals**, are equally active, shooting past underwater windows with speed and agility you'd never imagine when watching them laboring along on rocks.

★**Hatfield Marine Science Center** – 🚼 *25mi north of the Oregon Coast Aquarium, 2030 S. Marine Science Dr. Open Jun–Sept daily 10am–5pm. Rest of the year Thu–Mon 10am–4pm. Closed Thanksgiving Day, Dec 25. Donation requested.* ⅙ 🅿 ☎ *541-867-0100. www.hmsc.orst.edu.* Hatfield is the headquarters for Oregon State University's highly esteemed marine research program, an affiliation that explains the authoritative and richly detailed marine science exhibits in the large, newly expanded public wing. Interactive computer games, videos, a microscope lab and many other exhibits teach visitors about such matters as whale calls, the prediction of tsunamis (tidal waves), and the connections between the learning processes of sea slugs and those of humans. Many of the exhibits reflect the latest research being conducted by Hatfield scientists. Though important scientific concepts are examined, they are presented in clear, entertaining ways for a lay audience; numerous exhibits are geared for children.

★★**Yaquina Head Outstanding Natural Area** – *4mi north of Newport on Hwy. 101 and .5mi west on N.W. Lighthouse Dr. Open daily year-round. $5/car.* ⅙ 🅿 ☎ *541-574-3100.* A 100-acre finger of old lava that extends a mile into the Pacific, Yaquina Head offers both human and natural history. Through high-quality exhibits and numerous videos, the Yaquina Head Interpretive Center (opened in 1997) provides an overview of the headland, from the seabirds that flock there every spring to the Indians who lived there 4,000 years ago. Just south of the interpretive center lies the Quarry Cove Intertidal Area, billed as the world's only wheelchair-accessible tide-pool site. At the tip of the headland stands **Yaquina Head Lighthouse** (1873), its 93ft height making it the tallest lighthouse in Oregon *(visit by guided tour only, Jul–mid-Sept daily 10am–4pm; rest of the year daily noon–4pm weather permitting).* From platforms near the lighthouse visitors can look down on Colony Rock, a mere 100 yards away. From April through June thousands of common murres, cormorants, seagulls and other nesting seabirds turn Colony Rock into a preening, squabbling, feeding, flapping riot. In contrast, the marine gardens below the lighthouse parking lot, at Cobble Beach, remain quiet and tranquil, except for the rumble of the surf and the wind-chime tinkling the cobbles make when pushed around by the waves. Look for the Bureau of Land Management naturalists, who will tell you about the sunflower stars, gumboot chitons, kelp crabs and other denizens of these tide pools—and teach you how to explore the rocky intertidal zone without harming yourself or the plants and animals that live there.

SOUTH COAST★★

Michelin map 493 a 5, 6 and map p 125
Tourist Information ☎ 541-574-2679 or www.oregon-coast.org

Heading south from the town of Yachats, the wildness that characterizes the South Coast reveals itself almost immediately. Here Highway 101 begins ascending, hugging the burly cliffs above the ocean and snaking through undergrowth-choked rain forest. Within a few miles you pass white-laced breakers thundering into defiant basalt headlands; tide pools thick with hermit crabs, sea stars and anemones; and broad sandy beaches that have never felt the tread of a crowd—unless you count shorebirds. On the inland side of the highway lie some of the largest tracts of old-growth coastal forest left in the Northwest, home to 9ft-diameter Sitka spruce that rise 200ft above a luxuriant understory of sword ferns, rhododendrons and golden-fruited salmonberries. Elk, black bear and deer wander the 2,000ft ridges, while fish and salamanders swim in shady creeks.

This mosaic of beach, rocky shore and conifer forest continues all the way to California, though the forest is second-growth in many places and the Oregon Dunes alter the formula for some 40mi. The wildlife list grows as you encounter offshore rocks that provide safe nesting for murres, puffins and cormorants, as well as resting spots for harbor seals, sea lions, and an occasional elephant seal. The outposts of civilization are few and far between and, except for Coos Bay, they blend well enough into the landscape. The towns here face the sea, in fact and in spirit, and in most of them life revolves around the harbor. And when you leave these towns you'll quickly return to unsettled shore and forest.

★YACHATS *1/2 day*

The seaside village of Yachats (YA-hots) rests on a flat bit of marine terrace embraced by towering hills and husky headlands. Views of the coast and access to tide pools are available right in town at **Yachats State Park** *(3 blocks west of Hwy. 101 via Ocean View Dr.; open year-round dawn–dusk)*. Access to beaches and to the mouth of the Yachats River, on the south side of town, can be found at **Yachats Ocean Wayside** *(west on Yachats Ocean Rd. from Hwy. 101, just south of the bridge)*. Up on dry land in this small town of 635 people, visitors find a quiet community with a low-key artistic flavor. Yachat's history comes to light at **The Little Log Church and Museum** *(3rd and Pontiac Sts., one block west of Hwy. 101; open year-round Mon–Wed, Fri noon–3pm; weekends 10am–4pm; ♿ ☎ 541-547-3976)*.

★★**Cape Perpetua Scenic Area** – *3mi south of Yachats on Hwy. 101. Open Memorial Day–Labor Day daily 9am–5pm. Rest of the year weekends 10am–4pm. ⚠ ♿ 🅿 ☎ 541-547-3289. www.orcoast.* In its 2,700 acres, the Cape Perpetua Scenic Area combines some of the finest coastal forest and most striking rocky shoreline in the Northwest. Start at the interpretive center, which features well-presented exhibits on coastal ecology, the rain forest and the coastal Indians. Several easy hiking trails fan out from the center, leading both to the shore and into the forest. The Giant Spruce Trail is a 1mi path along Cape Creek that ends at a monumental Sitka spruce tree; pick up one of the interpretive brochures that will guide you through this old-growth ecosystem. The **Captain Cook Trail**★ wends half a mile down to a dramatic section of wave-blasted basalt. Check out **Cook's Chasm** at the south end, a narrow channel that froths madly when waves shoulder their way up its length and explode from the blowhole called Spouting Horn. A steep trail labors up to the 800ft top of Cape Perpetua, one of the highest **viewpoints**★ on the Oregon coast—or you can drive to the top. Ambitious hikers can trek a 10mi loop that passes through the superb old growth of the Cummins Creek Wilderness.

★★OREGON DUNES NATIONAL RECREATION AREA
2 days

Forty miles of sand dunes arching as high as 200ft arguably make Oregon Dunes the most impressive coastal dune system in the US. This stretch of central Oregon coast has all the ingredients for dune formation: a coast range of easily eroded sedimentary rock, plenty of rain and rivers to erode the rock and carry the sand to the sea, strong winds to blow the sand inland, and a low topographical profile that allows the sand to move inland a significant distance. (Most of the Northwest coast features steep headlands that keep blowing sand on the shore.) Unfortunately, invasive European beach grass has overgrown the fore dunes in the recreation area, permitting them to build up much higher than they did before this type of beach grass was introduced in the 1940s. These unnaturally tall fore dunes function like headlands, preventing sand from blowing inland. Without a supply of new sand to replenish them, the dunes are succumbing to the encroachment of the surrounding coastal forest. In 50 years the open dunes may be gone. In the meantime, visitors can explore this fascinating ecosystem of sand, tree islands, wetlands, estuaries and beaches via numerous trails, viewpoints and roads. *Open daily year-round. $3/car. ⚠ ⬥ ▣ ☎ 541-271-3611; www.fs.fed.us/r6/siuslaw/odnra/htm. Hikers should be aware that some trails, especially in the south part of the recreation area, are designated for off-road vehicle use; these trails can be noisy and hazardous.*

Oregon Dunes National Recreation Area

Florence – *On Hwy. 101 at north end of dunes area.* Most of Florence is anonymous highway sprawl, but tucked along the Siuslaw River under the north end of the Highway 101 bridge lies an appealing historic area called **Old Town**. In addition to harboring the sizeable commercial fishing fleet, Old Town is home to numerous galleries (the Blue Heron, at Bay and Maple Sts., stands out), shops (such as Incredible & Edible Oregon on Bay between Maple and Laurel Sts.), and restaurants. From some tables at the International C-food Market, at Bay and Nopal, you can watch fishermen off-loading their latest catch while you dine handsomely on their previous catch. Five miles north of Florence on 101, signs direct you just east of the highway to **Darlingtonia Botanical Wayside**, home to thousands of robust specimens of *Darlingtonia californica*, the cobra lily. From the parking lot a 100-yard trail leads to a bog bristling with these carnivorous plants. Follow Highway 101 6mi farther north to **Sea Lion Caves** *(91560 Hwy.101; open Jul–Aug daily 8am–dusk; rest of the year 9am–dusk; $6.50; ▣ ☎ 541-547-3111; www.sealioncaves.com)*, a privately owned attraction that provides access to grand overlooks of sea lion colonies and, via a 208ft elevator ride, to a huge cavern seasonally occupied by these bellowing marine mammals.

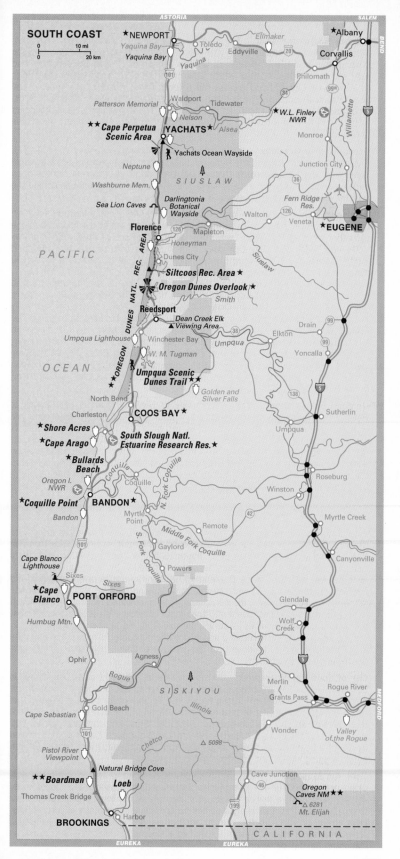

SOUTH COAST

★ NEWPORT

0 — 10 mi
0 — 20 km

Yaquina Bay
Yaquina Bay

Toledo
Eddyville
Ellmaker

ASTORIA
SALEM

★ Albany
Corvallis
Philomath

99w

Patterson Memorial
Waldport
Tidewater
Alsea

Nelson
★ YACHATS ★

★★ *Cape Perpetua*
Scenic Area

Yachats Ocean Wayside

★ W.L. Finley
NWR

Monroe

Neptune

SIUSLAW

Washburne Mem.

Junction City

36

Darlingtonia
Botanical
Wayside

Walton

Veneta

Fern Ridge
Res.

Sea Lion Caves

PACIFIC

Florence
126
Mapleton
Honeyman

★ EUGENE

Dunes City

Siltcoos Rec. Area ★

Oregon Dunes Overlook ★

Smith

Reedsport

Siuslaw

Dean Creek Elk
▲ *Viewing Area*

38

Drain
99

Umpqua Lighthouse
Winchester Bay
W. M. Tugman

Umpqua
Elkton
99

Yoncalla

OCEAN

Umpqua Scenic
Dunes Trail ★★

OREGON DUNES NATL. REC. AREA

Golden and
Silver Falls

138

North Bend

Charleston

★ *Shore Acres*

★ *Cape Arago*

COOS BAY ★

South Slough Natl.
Estuarine Research Res. ★

Sutherlin

Umpqua

★ *Bullards*
Beach

Oregon I.
NWR

Coquille

N. Fork Coquille

Roseburg

★ *Coquille Point*

BANDON ★

Bandon

Myrtle
Point

Winston

Myrtle Creek

101

S. Fork Coquille

Middle Fork Coquille

Remote

42

Canyonville

Cape Blanco
Lighthouse

Gaylord

Sixes

Powers

Glendale

★ *Cape*
Blanco

PORT ORFORD

Sixes

Wolf
Creek

Humbug Mtn.

Ophir

Agness

5

Merlin

Rogue River

MEDFORD

SISKIYOU

Illinois

Grants Pass

BEND

Willamette

34

Yaquina

20

101

Cape Sebastian
Gold Beach

Pistol River
Viewpoint

▲ *Natural Bridge Cove*

★★ *Boardman*
Loeb

Thomas Creek Bridge

BROOKINGS

Harbor

Chetco

△ 5098

Wonder

Valley
of the Rogue

Cave Junction

46

Oregon
Caves NM ★★

⌂ △ 6281
Mt. Elijah

199

EUREKA
EUREKA

CALIFORNIA

PACIFIC

OCEAN

125

★Siltcoos Recreation Area – *7mi south of Florence, turn west off Hwy. 101 onto Siltcoos Beach Rd. Open daily year-round. Restricted access of Siltcoos River nesting area mid-Mar–mid-Sept.* △ ⊞. This section of Oregon Dunes offers two easy and lovely hikes, both of which leave from the beach road where the bridge to Waxmyrtle Campground crosses the Siltcoos River. North of the road, a 1mi boardwalk trail loops along a winding lagoon, its dark, still water alive with frogs, wood ducks and newts. South of the road, the 1.5mi Waxmyrtle Trail meanders along the bird-filled estuary to the beach; look for osprey, shorebirds, great blue heron and deer.

★Oregon Dunes Overlook – *About 10mi south of Florence on Hwy. 101.* ⊞ *($1).* Three raised platforms just off Highway 101 provide fines views of some sizeable dunes and interpretive boards that explain their origin. A 1mi trail crosses open dunes, passes tree islands, slogs through the moisture-loving vegetation behind the fore dune and ends at the beach.

Reedsport – *21mi south of Florence on Hwy. 101.* An unassuming port town on the Umpqua River a few miles from the sea, Reedsport sits at the midpoint of the recreation area. At the **Oregon Dunes Visitor Center** *(north end of town, 855 Highway 101; open Memorial Day–Oct daily 8am–4:30pm; rest of the year Mon–Fri 8am–4:30pm, Sat 10am–4pm; closed major holidays;* ⊞ ☏ *541-271-3611)* you can pick up maps and brochures.

Across 101 from the visitor center, take Route 38 (Umpqua Avenue) about a mile east and turn north on Water Avenue to the banks of the Umpqua River, where you'll find the **Umpqua Discovery Center** *(409 Riverfront Way.; open Jun–Sept daily 9am–5pm; rest of the year daily 10am–4pm; closed Jan 1, Thanksgiving Day, Dec 25; $3;* ♿ ⊞ ☏ *541-271-4816; www.coos.or.us/~discover).* Here displays and interactive exhibits teach visitors about the natural and human history of the river, the coast and the forest. About 4mi east of Reedsport on Route 38 lies the **Dean Creek Elk Viewing Area** *(*☏ *541-756-0100),* home to a herd of 60 to 100 Roosevelt elk. At least some of the elk are in view much of the year as they rest and feed in the bottomlands of the Umpqua.

★★Umpqua Scenic Dunes Trail – *West side of Hwy. 101 about 11mi south of Reedsport.* Visitors walk through half a mile of coastal forest, then ascend the highest unvegetated dunes in the whole recreation area. You can follow posts across the sand 2mi to the beach, but most people shed their shoes and frolic on the curvaceous dunes, laboring up and bounding down the soft, fine-grained flanks. Some people even bring snow sleds and slide down the steeper slopes. From the tops of the highest dunes you obtain a panoramic view of the dune system, the Coast Range and the ocean.

★COOS BAY   *1 day*

Coos Bay and the neighboring towns of North Bend and Charleston constitute Oregon's Bay Area, where life revolves around the largest natural harbor between Puget Sound and San Francisco Bay. Thousands of members of the Coos tribe were living in this area when European explorers first sailed by, starting, some historians believe, with Sir Francis Drake in 1579. Significant European settlement did not occur until the 1850s, when people came looking for gold and stayed for the farmland, the coal deposits, the vast coastal forests, and the fine harbor from which to ship their commodities. Eventually the timber industry and the shipping of forest products became preeminent—during the mid-20C, 71 lumber mills operated in the Bay Area—but overharvesting and environmental concerns have led to a decline in the timber and fishing industries. The area's economy is diversifying, with particular emphasis on tourism.

City of Coos Bay Boardwalk – *On the bay side of Hwy. 101 at Anderson Ave. in downtown Coos Bay.* Wooden walkways and covered decks along the waterfront offer museum-like exhibits on the area's history and present-day economy. One series of signs, for example, tells of the pre-World War I transportation network that revolved around the bay and its tributaries. Small launches and ferries, collectively called the Mosquito Fleet, served residents as buses. Even religion traveled by water; a boat called *Lifeline* carried the Word from the American Baptist Church out to logging camps and isolated farm communities.

Coos Art Museum – *Two blocks west of the boardwalk, at 235 Anderson Ave. Open year-round Tue–Fri 10am–4pm, Sat 1pm–4pm. Closed major holidays.* ♿ ☏ *541-267-3901. www.coos.or.us/cam.* Serving as the town's main post office from 1935-85, this federal-style edifice houses changing exhibits of local artists' work, most of which is for sale. In addition to seeing the expected paintings, sculptures and pottery, visitors sometimes encounter offbeat offerings, such as elaborate, handmade wooden canoes.

The Oregon Connection (House of Myrtlewood) – *Off Hwy. 101 at 1125 S. 1st St. Open Jun–Sept daily 8:30am–6pm. Rest of the year Mon–Sat 9am–5pm, Sun 11am–4pm. Closed major holidays.* ♿ ⚑ ☎ *541-267-7804 or 800-255-5318.* A combination store and factory produces and sells products made from the Oregon myrtle, *Umbellularia californica*, which actually belongs in the laurel family. Whatever their taxonomy, these trees native to southern Oregon and northern California produce easily worked wood of varied grains that polish like marble. The store is chockablock with bowls, tables, golf clubs and other myrtlewood products. Visitors can watch a video that shows how these items are made and then take a short, self-guided tour through the low-tech factory, where artisans carve the supple wood.

Excursions

★**Shore Acres State Park** – *1/2 hr. 13mi southwest of Coos Bay via Cape Arago Hwy. Open year-round daily 8am–dusk.* △ ♿ ⚑ ☎ *541-888-3778 or 800-551-6949. www.prd.state.or.us.* Set on a craggy bluff above the Pacific Ocean, Shore Acres is a public park born from a private estate. In the early 1900s, lumber magnate and shipbuilder Louis Simpson built a mansion and elaborate gardens on the site. A devastating fire and the Great Depression eventually forced him to sell. The state bought the property and restored the gardens. Walkways lead visitors through a formal garden of rhododendrons, azaleas, dahlias and other flowering plants. Bordering the formal garden are a sizeable rose garden and a Japanese-style garden fashioned around a 100ft-long lily pond.

© Dianne Dietrich Leis

Shore Acres State Park

★**Cape Arago State Park** – *1 hr. 14.5mi southwest of Coos Bay at the end of Cape Arago Hwy. Open year-round daily 8am–dusk.* ⚑ ☎ *541-888-3778 or 800-551-6949. www.prd.state.or.us.* Serving as a window to the sea, Cape Arago harbors 150ft bluffs from which visitors can look west to the horizon and many miles north and south along the coast, where whales are often sighted. Just a few hundred yards northwest lie Simpson Reef and Shell Island, refuges for elephant seals, Steller's sea lions, harbor seals and California sea lions. California sea lions are the loud ones, barking and gurgling in an almost ceaseless social frenzy; as many as 2,000 haul out at Cape Arago during the late summer and fall.

★**South Slough National Estuarine Research Reserve** – *1 hr. 14mi southwest of Coos Bay. Take Cape Arago Hwy. to Charleston; then take Seven Devils Rd. 4mi south. Trails open year-round dawn–dusk. Interpretive Center open Memorial Day–Labor Day daily 8am–4:30pm. Rest of the year Mon–Fri 8am–4:30pm. Closed major holidays.* ♿ ⚑ ☎ *541-888-5558. www.southsloughestuary.com.* Nearly all American estuaries have been seriously degraded by development, but South Slough's 4,500 acres of open water, marsh, mudflats and upland forest remain remarkably unspoiled. (A slough is a quiet arm of an estuary—an area near the mouth of a river where sea water mixes with freshwater.) These highly productive habitats teem with life, from clams and eelgrass to eagles and bears. Stop at the interpretive center to see the displays and to get maps showing hiking and canoe trails. If time permits only one hike, take the **Estuary Study Trail**, a 3mi series of loops that begins behind the center.

★BANDON *1 day*

Though only 2,760 people live in Bandon, it has a surprisingly diverse economy, anchored by timber, fishing, agriculture and tourism. Much of Bandon's appeal for travelers stems from its industries; many people tour the cheese factory, the cranberry bogs, or simply sit on the waterfront and watch the fishing boats come in. The town's other great attraction is its location, partly on the Coquille River estuary, partly on the seaside cliffs just south of the mouth of the Coquille.

★**Old Town** – *Located between Hwy. 101 and the Coquille River; take Chicago, 2nd, or Delaware Sts. off Hwy. 101.* Though nearly 150 years have passed since pioneers settled here, Old Town remains the heart of Bandon. The district serves both residents and tourists, mixing galleries, shops and restaurants with a fish-processing plant, law offices and a lumber mill. Several Old Town galleries surpass souvenir-shop status, and one, **Second Street Gallery**★ *(corner of 2nd St. and Baltimore Ave.)*, offers genuinely fine art in an elegant, expansive space. **Cranberry Sweets** *(corner of 1st St. and Chicago Ave.)* overwhelms the senses with candies, particularly local products made of cranberries and other fruits. There are samples of everything, including cheddar cheese fudge, a dubious concoction created in honor of the nearby cheese factory.

Bandon Historical Society Museum – *Eastern edge of Old Town at Hwy. 101 and Fillmore Ave. Open Jun–Sept Mon–Sat 10am–4pm, Sun noon–3pm. Rest of the year Mon–Sat 10am–4pm. Closed during January. $2.* 🅿 ☎ *541-347-2164.* This hodgepodge of artifacts is complemented by many evocative historical photos, such as shots of the local lifesaving crews carrying out perilous ocean rescues. Don't miss the extensive display on the fire of 1936, which burned all but a handful of the town's 500 buildings.

Bandon Cheese Factory – *On Hwy. 101 about a half-block east of the historical museum. Open year-round Mon–Sat 8:30am–5:30pm, Sun 9am–5pm.* 🅿 ☎ *541-347-2456 or 800-548-8961.* Visitors are confined to the retail shop, but big windows allow them to watch the cheesemakers at work—usually every other morning. There is also a 10min video that follows the creation of Bandon cheddar cheese from cow to table. Be sure to graze the sampling bins, filled with redolent cubes of jalapeño, garlic, onion and other flavors of Bandon cheddar.

★**Coquille Point** – *On ocean bluffs at west end of 11th St., off Beach Loop Dr.* ♿ 🅿 ☎ *541-867-4550.* Paved pathways and well-sited benches entice visitors to linger and savor the fine views of Bandon Beach, the open ocean, and a sculpture garden of massive seastacks. Those seastacks—and the point itself—are part of Oregon Islands National Wildlife Refuge. Train your binoculars on the offshore rocks and surrounding waters and you may spot puffins, harbor seals, pelicans, cormorants and many other animals. Memorably informative interpretive panels along the trail describe these creatures as well as local Indian and pioneer history.

★**Bullards Beach State Park** – *2mi north of Bandon via Hwy. 101. Open daily year-round.* ⛺ ♿ 🅿 ☎ *541-347-2209.* A 3mi road runs from Highway 101 through the coastal forest, along the north bank of the Coquille estuary, and out to the Coquille River Lighthouse. About half a mile from the road, travelers can look across the Coquille at the 800 acres of salt marsh that are protected as Bandon Marsh National Wildlife Refuge. During spring and fall migrations you may spot sun-blocking flights of waterfowl and shorebirds. Another mile brings you to a parking lot; hike 100 yards over the grass-covered sand dune to discover several miles of sandy beach. At the end of the road another parking lot provides additional access to the beach and brings you to the lighthouse, a squat 1896 structure at the mouth of the Coquille, a long stone's throw across the river from Bandon's Old Town.

PORT ORFORD

A workaday burg with a population of 1,050, Port Orford is anchored by its port and its fishing fleet. In the town's lack of glitzy tourist attractions lies its appeal, along with its clifftop setting on the rough-hewn southern Oregon coast. Views of that coastline can be enjoyed from numerous vantage points, including **Battle Rock Park** *(south end of town)*, named for an 1851 battle between the local Tututni Indians and the area's first band of settlers, who used the rock outcropping on the beach as a fort. Just over the bluff to the north lies the **Port of Port Orford**, home to several dozen commercial and recreational fishing boats. Visitors can stroll amid the nets and crab pots and chat with locals, who may talk about some of the unusual ocean harvests for which the port is known, notably sea urchins. In the processing plant on the dock, roe is removed from the urchins, packed and air freighted posthaste to the sushi bars of Tokyo. The center of port activity is the hoist: Because the harbor is relatively unprotected, most boats are lifted onto the dock instead of moored in the water.

Excursion

★**Cape Blanco State Park** – *3 hrs. 9mi northwest of Port Orford. Take Hwy. 101 4mi north and go west on Cape Blanco Hwy. Open year-round daily dawn-dusk.* ⚠ ⚹ ▣ ☎ *541-332-6774. www.prd.state.or.us.* Cape Blanco combines history with ample natural attributes. Halfway along the Cape Blanco Highway take a right to the **Hughes House** *(visit by 30min guided tour only, Apr–Oct Thu–Mon 10am–3:30pm; donation requested; ☎ 541-332-0248)*, a freshly restored 1898 Eastlake Victorian open for tours from spring to fall. The family patriarch, an Irishman named Patrick Hughes, came to Cape Blanco just before the Civil War; it took him nearly four decades to amass the wealth to build the 11-room, cedar mansion overlooking the Sixes River. The 2,000-acre ranch he developed was occupied by the Hughes family for 111 years, until it became Cape Blanco State Park. At the end of the highway towers the 1870 **Cape Blanco Lighthouse** *(Apr–Oct Thu–Mon 10am–3:30pm; donation requested)*, the oldest continuously operating lighthouse in Oregon, the most westerly lighthouse, and the highest above the sea (245ft). The headland offers sweeping views of the sea, and trails lead down to tide pools and a driftwood-littered beach.

BROOKINGS *1 day*

Located just 5mi north of California, this town of 5,400 lies at the center of Oregon's "banana belt." Though bananas are not actually grown here, a weather phenomenon known as the Brookings Effect does produce the warmest coastal weather in the Pacific Northwest—even winter temperatures often reach into the 60s and 70s. Small wonder the area produces as much as 90 percent of the nation's Easter lilies and many other winter flowers. The fine weather also enhances the pleasant **harbor area**—a working port and marina bordered by a boardwalk and dozens of restaurants and shops.

Azalea Park – *.25mi north of Hwy. 101 via Park Rd.; just west of the Chetco River bridge.* This popular local park offers an elaborate playground, spacious lawns, paths that wind among ancient conifers, and a diversity of flowers that assures blooms of some sort no matter the season. But the park's pièce de résistance is its display of 1,000 10ft-high azalea plants, whose radiant blossoms peak in April and May.

■ War and Peace

On September 9, 1942, a Japanese submarine surfaced off the coast of Oregon. A small plane was assembled and launched from the sub's deck and flew over the dense forests just east of Brookings, where the pilot dropped an incendiary bomb on the slopes of Mt. Emily hoping to start a major forest fire. The bomb did start a fire, but wet conditions helped firefighters easily control the small blaze that ensued. This attack remains the only bombing of the mainland US by enemy aircraft. An 18mi drive and A 1mi hike will take you to the site of the bombing, which lies in an old-growth forest reserve *(bomb-site brochure available from Brookings-Harbor Chamber of Commerce, Port of Brookings-Harbor. ☎ 541-469-3181 or 800-535-9469)*.

The pilot of that plane, Nobuo Fujita, returned to Brookings in 1962 on a different mission. In a traditional Japanese gesture of peace, he presented the city with a samurai sword that had been in his family for 400 years. The sword remains on display in the Chetco Community Library *(420 Alder St., Brookings)*. In 1992, on the 50th anniversary of the bombing, Fujita returned to Brookings to plant a redwood tree to honor the peace between Japan and the United States. Fujita died in 1997 and the following year, as he had requested, some of his ashes were scattered over the bomb site.

★★ **Boardman State Park** – *Southern boundary lies about 4mi north of downtown Brookings via Hwy. 101. Open year-round dawn–dusk.* 🅿 ☏ *541-469-3181.* A long, slender park encompasses this ruggedly handsome stretch of Oregon coastline—the first dozen miles of what is known as the "fabulous fifty miles." Lush stands of Sitka spruce and Douglas fir spill down mountainsides to the rims of shoreline cliffs. About a dozen named viewpoints provide easy access to this dramatic salutation of land and sea. Perhaps the most scenic is **Natural Bridge Cove**, about 2mi south of the park's northern boundary. A minute's stroll down the trail that leads south from the parking lot sits a viewing platform that hangs over this azure cove and the eponymous rock bridge. When a mist slides through the tall conifers that jut from the cliffs and offshore monoliths you feel as if you've stepped into a traditional Japanese landscape painting. Visitors who enjoy vertiginous views should also stop about a mile south of Natural Bridge Cove and walk out onto the Thomas Creek Bridge—at 345ft, the highest in Oregon. The Oregon Coast Trail connects Boardman's viewpoints, allowing hikes of many different lengths and levels of difficulty.

Excursion

Loeb State Park – *8mi northeast of Brookings via North Bank Chetco River Rd. Open daily year-round.* ⛺ ♿ 🅿 ☏ *541-469-2021.* Established in 1948, the 320-acre park protects a large grove of myrtlewoods (Oregon myrtles), those trees prized by woodworkers and found only in southern Oregon and Northern California. A trail leads through this grove and along the scenic Chetco River—note the camphor aroma of the trees, especially if you crush a leaf. The eastern end of the 1mi trail connects to the Redwood Nature Trail in Siskiyou National Forest, a 1mi loop through the northernmost natural stand of the world's tallest tree species.

■ **Gardens of the Pacific Northwest**

The moist climate of the Pacific Northwest supports myriad trees and flowersand no stay in the Pacific Northwest would be complete without a visit to one or more of the great gardens or arboretums. A listing of some of those described follows:

Southern Oregon Highlands

The Phantom Ship, Crater Lake / © Dianne Dietrich Leis

Stretching 130mi along the California border—from the Rogue River whitewaters to the Klamath Basin wheatfields—Oregon's southern highlands present a microcosm of the Pacific Northwest's landscapes and people. This remote region encompasses three major climate zones and two distinct mountain ranges with dormant volcanoes, abundant forests, alpine lakes and rugged canyons. Passions run deep here for natural resources, and where there is passion there is usually conflict. Cattle ranchers and bird-watchers contend for the marshlands; fishermen and whitewater rafters pursue the rivers; environmentalists and loggers stake claims on the Douglas fir; and private citizens and public officials tap into the region's geothermal heat.

Even before 1846 when Jesse and Lindsay Applegate led the first group of pioneers on the Oregon Trail's alternate route around the Cascades, this land was not without strife. For over 11,000 years, well before the eruption of 12,000ft Mt. Mazama and the creation of Crater Lake in its caldera, the Klamath and Modoc Indians fought each other here. In 1869 the Klamath and Modoc tribes were forced to share a reservation north of Klamath Falls. Four years later, when the Modocs attempted to return to Tule Lake, they, too, were banished from their Oregon homelands—to a reservation in Oklahoma.

During the mid-19C, gold seekers from California headed north when they heard word of a strike in Jacksonville, Oregon. The strike was short-lived, and most discouraged gold diggers returned south. Those who stayed found the valleys suitable for farms, orchards and vineyards, and the mountains rich in timber.

Today, timber sales are down, but the little town of Ashland is now host to one of the country's finest Shakespeare festivals. And those who come to watch a play in the open-air amphitheater, also come to play in the outdoors, for recreation—white-water rafting, steelhead fishing, hiking, cross-country skiing, snowmobiling and bird-watching—draws more and more people to this relatively undiscovered corner of Oregon, a four-hour drive south of Portland.

ASHLAND★

Michelin map 493 A 6 and map p 137
Population 18,095
Tourist Information ☏ 541-482-3486

Attractive, temperate Ashland, surrounded by orchards, vineyards and Arabian horse farms, looks like it belongs more to Northern California (just 15mi south) than to the rugged Pacific Northwest. This former timber country on the eastern flanks of the Siskiyou Mountains has been slowly gentrified into one of the premier cultural centers of the Pacific Northwest, if not the country.

Centuries ago, Ashland was no more than a trading post for flour and lumber. In the early 19C a water-powered saw– and flour mill flanked the banks of Ashland Creek. Gold seekers flocked here in the mid-19C for a short-lived gold rush, but the farmers reaped the biggest rewards—hops, apples and pears grew extremely well in this "Italy of Oregon." When water rich in lithium was discovered a few miles outside of town in the early 20C, locals dreamed of turning Ashland into a world-class spa, but that, like the gold, never quite panned out. Instead, Ashland struck it rich in a very different way—thanks to an idea from a professor at Southern Oregon Normal School (now Southern Oregon University). In 1935, Angus Bowmer suggested turning a dilapidated building site in Lithia Park into an outdoor Shakespearean theater. Today, the thriving **Oregon Shakespeare Festival** attracts directors, actors and audiences from all over the world.

Like most places in the Northwest, the outdoors also rates as a big part of life, and Ashland offers many opportunities for swimming, fishing, hiking and skiing. The region also touts seven wineries, two of which are in Ashland: **Ashland Winery** *(2775 E Main St.; ☏ 541-488-0088)* and **Weisinger's Winery** *(3150 Siskiyou Blvd.; ☏ 541-488-5989)*.

SIGHTS *2 days.*

★**Festival Exhibit Center** – *E. Main and Pioneer Sts. Open mid-Feb–Oct Tue–Sun 10:30am–1:30pm. $3.* ☏ *541-482-4331.* The official hands-on museum of the **Oregon Shakespeare Festival★★★** *(p 133),* this yellow brick building should not be missed. Main-floor exhibits outline past shows with costumes, photographs, programs and props. Upstairs visitors can turn on music from past performances and try on a roomful of hats and costumes. Learn the intricacies of costume-making and compare costumes and interpretations used in different productions of the same play. An interesting 15min video explains how sets are changed.

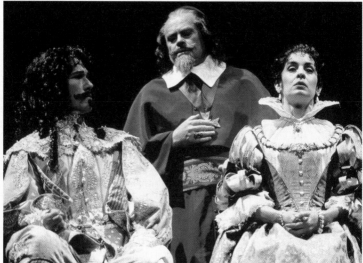

The Three Musketeers, Oregon Shakespeare Festival 1999 Production

Lithia Plaza – *Siskiyou Blvd. and Main St.* A little triangular fountained plaza of shops, galleries, restaurants and the visitor booth *(open Memorial Day-Labor Day Mon–Sat 10am–6pm, Sun 11am–5pm),* Lithia bustles just before and after show time. Eight porcelain drinking fountains bubble with the sulfur-smelling mineral waters around which Ashlanders once hoped to build a world-class health resort. Lithium springs, with the world's second-highest natural concentration of lithium, are located 3mi east of the city.

■ Oregon Shakespeare Festival

15 South Pioneer St., Box 158, Ashland, OR 97520. Box office, located at Pioneer and E. Main Sts., open daily mid-Feb–Oct. ♿ 🅿 ☎ *541-482-4331; www.orshakes.org.* When mild-mannered drama professor Angus Bowmer put together the first Oregon Shakespeare Festival in 1935, he could not have guessed how well his brainchild would grow. Converting A 42-year-old dilapidated Chautauqua performance site into an amphitheater, the original festival staged three performances of *Twelfth Night* and *The Merchant of Venice*, selling a total of 500 tickets. These days, some 70 actors put on 762 performances of 11 plays in three different theaters from February to October. Number of tickets sold? More than 350,000. Such phenomenal success attests not only to the enduring popularity of the Bard but to the undeniable appeal of rural yet sophisticated Ashland as a setting for outdoor drama. Many of the spectators come down from Portland, where event organizers and promoters over the years have wisely touted Ashland's appeal. Having staged the entire Shakespeare canon three times over, the festival is poised to continue its firmly entrenched tradition.

The open-air **Elizabethan Theater** opened in 1935 on the site of the Chautauqua building. A new stage modeled after London's Fortune Theatre opened in 1959. The intimate **Angus Bowmer Theater**, noted for its acoustics, shows a diverse mix of Shakespeare, O'Neill, Chekhov, and others ranging from Richard Brinsley Sheridan to Steven Dietz. The 140-seat **Black Swan** also presents classical and contemporary works.

The energetic, information-packed **backstage tour**★★ reveals the behind-the-scenes intricacies of creating such a high-caliber festival *(by 1 hr 30min guided tour only; mid-Feb–Oct Tue–Sun 10am; $11; reservations required;* ☎ *541-482-4331).* First stop on the tour is the three-sided stage in the Black Swan Theater, where a witty actor details the festival's history. Next, the guide points out the scene shop (a former ice skating rink), the production facility, costume storage and the great hall for rehearsals. Standing in the loft-like display room, tourists are awed by the time, labor and creativity that go into each production: An army of volunteers spend hours painting portraits, marbleizing floors, texturing columns and creating costumes. In the Elizabethan Theater, visitors take in such architectural highlights as the trap room, the musician gallery, and the heavens from which trumpets announce show time.

EXCURSIONS

Rogue River National Forest – *1 day. Southwest of Ashland. Main Office, 333 W. 8th St., Medford. Open year-round Mon–Fri 7:45am–4:30pm. Closed major holidays.* ⚠ ♿ 🅿 ☎ *541-858-2200. www.fs.fed.us/r6/rogue.* Established in 1908, the 630,000-acre Rogue River National Forest encompasses two very different territories. Southwest of I-5, the 7,533ft Mt. Ashland towers above narrow canyons, high ridges, dense conifer forests and the Applegate River in the ancient Siskiyou Mountains. Northeast of the highway, the turbulent waters of the upper Rogue River cut through Shasta red fir and mountain hemlock forests on the younger, volcanic slopes of the Cascade range where Mt. McLoughlin (9,495ft) stands as one of the major volcanic cones in Oregon. Locally known as the Upper Rogue, this section embraces myriad alpine lakes in glacial basins, huckleberry slopes, wild mushrooms and old-growth forests. On A 3.5mi trail to Natural Bridge *(1mi west of Union Creek)*, the raging river suddenly disappears into an underground maze of lava tubes, then blasts out 200ft later to surge through the narrow chasms of Takelma Gorge.

★★ **Jacksonville** – *1/2 day. 14mi northwest of Ashland via Rtes. 99 and 238. Visitor Information Center open May–Sept Mon–Fri 10am–5pm, Sat 11am–5pm, Sun noon–4pm. Rest of the year Tue–Fri 10am–4pm, Sat noon–4pm.* ♿ ☎ *541-899-8118. www.jacksonvilleoregon.org.* Surrounded by verdant rolling hills and world-famous pear and apple orchards, the Old West community of Jacksonville is one of only eight towns nationwide to be entirely designated a National Historic Landmark. This once-forgotten gold-rush-era town with some 84 brick and wooden buildings dating from the 1850s now thrives because of its well-preserved history.

The village boomed to life after the 1851 discovery of gold in Rich Gulch Creek. When the gold ran out in about 1856, a dwindling population turned to farming the fertile valley; nearby Medford eventually usurped the commerce and the county seat. A revival of the town began in the 1950s when the former county courthouse opened as the Jacksonville Museum. Launched in 1963 on the erstwhile estate of photographer Peter Britt (1819-1905), the annual **Britt Festival★★** *(evening concerts Jun–Sept; ✗ ⚲ call for schedule ☎ 541-779-0847 or 800-882-7488; www.brittfest.org)*, an outdoor summer music series, attracts some 60,000 listeners to concerts of classical, blues, jazz, country, folk and rock music. Many of Jacksonville's historic homes now operate as B&Bs or restaurants. The Jacksonville Visitor Information Center at the old railway depot *(Oregon and C Sts.)* offers walking-tour maps.

Jacksonville Museum of Southern Oregon History *– 5th and C Sts. Open Memorial Day–Labor Day daily 10am–5pm. Rest of the year Wed–Sat 10am–5pm, Sun noon–5pm. $2.* 🖪 ☎ *541-773-6536. www.sohs.org.* Housed in the massive gray stone building that served as the county courthouse from 1883 to 1927, this repository of regional history holds exhibits on the gold rush, the railroad, flooding and a local measles epidemic. A 20min video depicts the daily life of the Takelmas, the native people of the Rogue Valley, well before the discovery of gold. Kids can pan for gold, bunk in a miner's cabin, and hand-turn laundry through a washbin in a replica gold town.

Next door to the main museum in the former jail, the **Children's Museum** 🄺🄸🄳🅂 *(5th and D Sts.; same hours as above)* features an exhibit on Jacksonville's favorite resident, Vance "Pinto" Colvig—illustrator for Disney who provided the voice for Goofy and for the first Bozo the Clown. A Takelma house and a pioneer home and wagon encourage improvisational play, and a miniature train toots through replica valley towns.

Michelin Green Guides available in English
for North America include:

California
Canada
Chicago
Florida
Mexico
New England
New York City
New York, New Jersey, Pennsylvania
Quebec
San Francisco
Washington DC

CRATER LAKE NATIONAL PARK★★★

Michelin map 493 B 5 and map pp 136-137
Tourist Information ☎ 541-594-2211
or www.nps.gov/crla/home.htm

The deepest lake in the United States at 1,932ft, and the seventh-deepest in the world, rests in the caldera of a collapsed volcano called Mount Mazama. Spectacularly ringed by mountains that stay snow-covered most of the year, this crystal-clear sapphire lake, 6mi in diameter, forms the centerpiece of Oregon's only national park, attracting hikers, geologists, naturalists and those who are simply compelled by the mysterious presence of an immense bowl of blue water.

Historical Notes

Glaciated Mount Mazama formed half a million years ago, possibly a contemporary of better-known Cascade volcanoes such as Mount Shasta or Mount Rainier, when a group of overlapping volcanoes began blistering up from the earth's surface. Likely the mountain grew as high as 12,000ft before its cataclysmic eruption just 7,700 years ago. More than 18 cubic miles of pumice and ash were hurled into the air, covering the surrounding valleys. The rest of the mountain then collapsed, creating a bowl-shaped caldera, 4,000ft deep and 6mi wide. Several more eruptions filled in part of the caldera with lava. Within 400 years the lake had filled with rain water, and with no inlets in the lake, precipitation and evaporation keep it at a constant level. The water is so clear that on some days objects are visible down to 115ft.

Local Native Americans may have witnessed the collapse of Mount Mazama, as their stories closely parallel what geologists understand today. They later revered the lake as a sacred place. Not until 1853 did a party of three gold prospectors happen upon the lake, which they hastily named Deep Blue Lake. Peter Britt, a photographer from Jacksonville, took the earliest known photograph of it in 1874.

Inspired by a story he read in a newspaper as a boy, Kansan **William Gladstone Steel** journeyed to Crater Lake in 1885 and was so taken with its beauty that he decided to push for its preservation as a national park. The campaign would become his life's work. Over the next decade Steel wrote newspaper and magazine articles, took soundings of the lake with Clarence Dutton of the US Geological Survey, wrote a thousand letters appealing for support, and even authored a book that he sent to the President and Congress. Though sheep ranchers and land speculators lobbied against bills for a national park, Steel never gave up. He finally hit the jackpot when President Theodore Roosevelt proclaimed Crater Lake the fifth national park in 1902. Steel continued petitioning Congress and private developers for money, which led to the completion of the Rim Drive and the establishment of Crater Lake Lodge Company. Few parks owe their existence so entirely to one man.

Practical Information ....Area Code: 541

Getting There – The southern and western entrances to Crater Lake National Park are both located off Rte. 62 *(55mi north of Klamath Falls via US-97 & Rte. 62; or 75mi northwest of Medford via Rte. 62)*. From the north the park is reached via Rte. 138 *(80mi from Roseburg)*. The access road leading to Rim Village remains open daily in the winter, weather permitting. Rim Drive and the road to North Entrance Station are closed from October to early July because of snow. Gasoline is available at Mazama Village from early June to mid-October only. Closest Amtrak **train** station is in Klamath Falls (☎ 800-872-7245). Greyhound **bus** service stops in Klamath Falls and Medford (☎ 800-231-2222). There is no public transportation to the park. The closest airport, **Medford/Rogue Valley International Airport** in Medford (☎ 772-8068), is serviced by United Airlines/United Express (☎ 800-241-6522) and Horizon Air (☎ 800-547-9308).

Visitor Information – The park is open year-round. $10/car, $5/bicycle or on foot (valid for 7 days) ⚠✗⊟. For information and brochures on points of interest, recreation and seasonal activities, contact: **Superintendent Crater Lake National Park** *(P.O. Box 7, Crater Lake OR 97604,* ☎ *594-2211, ext. 402, www.nps.gov/crla/dir.htm)*; **Steel Information Center** *(p 136)*; **Rim Village Visitor Center** *(open late Jun – Labor Day daily 8:30am–6pm; early Jun & Sept daily 9:30am–5pm)*. Visitor centers offer exhibits, ranger-guided walks, summer campfire and children's programs, backcountry permits, maps and the park newspaper *Crater Lake Reflections*, all available free. Narrated boat tours run from late June to mid-September. Facilities at **Rim Village** include a restaurant, cafeteria, gift shop, post office and Crater Lake Lodge. For additional information on the area, contact **Medford Convention & Visitors Bureau**, 101 E. 8th St., Medford OR 97501 ☎ 779-4847; or **Klamath County Department of Tourism**, P.O. Box 1867, Klamath Falls OR 97601 ☎ 884-0666.

Accommodations – Facilities within the park are open from late May to mid-October: Crater Lake Lodge *($111-$200)* and Mazama Village Motor Inn *($85)*. Reservations should be made well in advance by contacting Crater Lake Lodge Inc., P.O. Box 2704, White City OR 97503, ☎ 830-8700. Visitors can choose among lodges, motels and small inns in the surrounding communities of Chiloquin, Diamond Lake, Fort Klamath and Prospect.

There are two **campgrounds** *($10-$16/night)* located within park boundaries, both available on a first-come, first-served basis; both offer drinking water and toilets. Mazama Campground offers 217 full-service campsites, Lost Creek Campground has 16 tent sites only. Both campgrounds open when snow melts and close in late September. Camping outside of designated campgrounds requires a wilderness permit *(free)*, available from visitor centers. For campsites and **RV parks** outside the park, check with local visitors' bureaus.

Recreation – There are 90mi of maintained **hiking** trails to explore ranging from A 30min stroll to Sun Notch viewpoint to a strenuous 3 hr hike to Mt. Scott, the highest peak in the park. The nearby Rogue River National Forest offers fishing, hunting and rafting.

Winter is the longest season in this area *(Oct–Jun)*. **Cross-country skiing** is popular throughout the park. Snow **walks** led by park rangers leave from Rim Village Information Desk *(Thanksgiving Day–Mar, Sat & Sun 1pm; ☎ 594-2211, ext. 402)*; snowshoes are provided free. Popular **ski trails** for the beginner are Wizard Island Overlook *(2mi)* and Mazama Village Loop *(1mi)*; the advanced skier will enjoy Raven Trail *(2mi)* and Dutton Creek Trail *(9mi)*. Skiing around Crater Lake requires careful planning and should only be undertaken by experienced skiers. There are no shelters along the 30mi route, so snow camping is necessary *(permit required, free)*. **Snowmobiles** are permitted only on the north entrance road.

★★★RIM DRIVE *1 day*

The 33mi rim road around the edge of the immense caldera could be done in two hours, but it's best to allow a little more time to absorb the richness of the area, hike the trails, and enjoy the wildflowers and the solace of the surroundings. Sights below are organized starting at the Steel Information Center *(south side of the lake)*, 4mi north of Route 62, which provides access to the park from the south and west. The route continues clockwise around the lake. *The road is open early July to mid-Oct, weather permitting.*

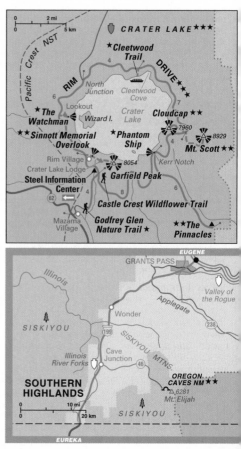

Steel Information Center – *3mi south of Crater Lake. Open year-round daily 9am–5pm; closed Dec 25.* 🅿 ☎ *541-594-2211 ext. 402.* The year-round park headquarters and administrative hub offers a small exhibit on flora and fauna found in the park, a photo montage about snow removal, and an 18min video on the people, history and geology of Crater Lake.

Castle Crest Wild-flower Trail – *Across street from Steel Information Center.* One of the park's best displays of wildflowers *(July–August)* is available along an easy .4mi stroll through a Shasta red fir and mountain hemlock forest. The trail passes wild raspberries, pioneer violets, shooting stars and a boulder-strewn meadow of trickling waterfalls.

Continue 3mi north to Rim Village Visitor Center for the first view of the lake.

★★**Sinnott Memorial Overlook** – *In Rim Village on south side of lake. Exhibit building open summers only; ranger-led talks held here in summer.* Most visitors get their first glimpse of the lake at Rim Village, but A 100ft stroll down a paved path here leads to an unobstructed, spectacular view of the entire caldera and the symmetrical cinder cone of **Wizard Island**, which formed after the initial collapse of Mount Mazama.

Garfield Peak – *3.4 mi round-trip trail begins just west of Crater Lake Lodge.* This strenuous hike from the rim (1,000ft elevation gain) is rewarded by a breathtaking panoramic **view**★★★ from the top of Garfield Peak, 1,900ft above the lake's surface and 8,054ft above sea level. Those who don't make it to the top will still find many marvelous views along the way. Ranger-led walks are held several times a week.

Continue 3mi west (clockwise) from Rim Village around the lake.

★**The Watchman** – *1.4mi round-trip hike from parking area.* Site of a historic fire tower, this vantage point provides one of the most exquisite **views**★★ on the drive, and the closest look at Wizard Island. An equally impressive view, without the hike, is available from the Watchman Overlook.

Continue 8mi, passing North Junction (park entrance from the north), to Cleetwood Cove.

★**Cleetwood Trail** – *2mi round-trip hike.* With 700-1,000ft walls rising nearly sheer from the lake to the rim, access points to the water's edge are hard to find. This very steep descent of 720 vertical feet takes you down to the lake and to the *Cleetwood* dock. Named for the 26ft boat used by Steel and Dutton in their 1886 surveys, the modern vessel offers 2 hr **boat tours** with a park naturalist to Wizard Island, where a tough 1mi trail leads to a cinder cone crater 760ft above the lake's

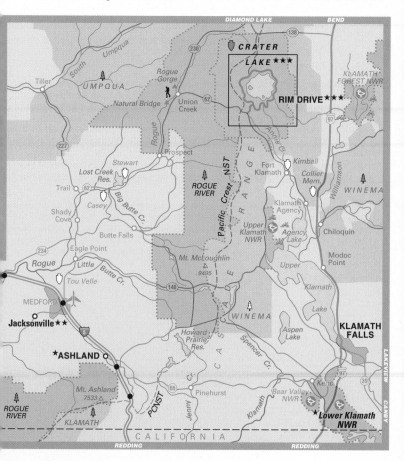

■ **Underneath Crater Lake**

In the summers of 1988 and 1989, the National Park Service, National Geographic Society, and the US Geological Survey sent a one-man submersible, Deep Rover, to study the bottom of the lake. Wizard Island served as a base for supplies and equipment. It took the sub 30min just to reach the lake floor. One of the most interesting discoveries was of hydrothermal activity in two regions of the crater, with mineral waters averaging up to 28 degrees warmer than surrounding waters. An 18min video of the project can be viewed upon request at the Steel Information Center *(p 136)*.

---

surface. *Depart from Cleetwood Cove Jul–mid-Sept daily 10am–430pm; round-trip 2 hrs. Commentary. $12.50. Reservations required ☎ 541-830-8700. Bring sturdy shoes for the 1mi hike to the dock and a jacket for the boat ride.*

Continue 5mi.

★★ **Mount Scott** – *5mi round-trip hike begins near the Whitebark Pine picnic area on Rim Dr.* From the highest peak in the park (8,929ft) it is easy to imagine the vanished summit of Mount Mazama. A strenuous hike with about a 1,500ft elevation gain offers wide, wonderful views. On clear days 14,162ft Mount Shasta, 100mi south in California, may be visible. Watch for spring and summer migrations of eagles, falcons and hawks.

Continue .2mi to Cloudcap spur road and turn right.

★★ **Cloudcap** – *1mi spur road west of Rim Dr.* An elevation of 7,960ft makes Cloudcap the highest point accessible by car on the Rim Drive. Up here beyond the wind-twisted whitebark pines you have an excellent 360-degree panorama of continuous forests to the north, the arid Klamath Basin with its shallow lake to the south, the highest peak in the park (Mount Scott) to the east, and an almost aerial view of Crater Lake to the west.

Continue 3mi to Kerr Notch.

★ **Phantom Ship** – *View from Kerr Notch (intersection of Pinnacles Rd. and Rim Dr.).* A 300ft-long island that rises a jagged 160ft from the lake's surface resembles a tall ship lost at sea. In fact, it's the exposed section of a subsurface andesite ridge, or lava dike. Drivers view it from Kerr Notch, but hikers can get a closer look via a .5mi round-trip trail to Sun Notch.

Turn east on spur road from Kerr Notch.

★★ **The Pinnacles** – *7mi spur road east of Rim Dr. at Kerr Notch.* Hundreds of hollow sand-colored spires up to 80ft tall, called fossil fumaroles, show a piece of Mount Mazama's geologic past turned inside out. The eruption laid thick layers of pumice and gray andesite scoria (ash) over the ground. Years later, gases and water were released through fumerole vents. The heat cemented the pumice and ash to the fumerole walls; erosion removed the loose sediment and left these unusual pumice pipes.

Return 7mi to Rim Dr. Turn left on Rim Dr. and continue 7mi to junction of Munson Valley Rd. at park headquarters. Turn left on Munson Valley Rd. and continue 2mi.

★ **Godfrey Glen Nature Trail** – *2mi south of Steel Information Center on Munson Valley Rd.* Another opportunity to view spiny fossil fumeroles, this easy trail *(1mi round-trip)* through dense mountain hemlock and Shasta red fir looks 200ft down into the Munson Creek canyon. The spires (not quite as needlelike as The Pinnacles) spike out of Godfrey Glen meadow at the confluence of Annie and Munson creeks.

Addresses, telephone numbers, opening hours and prices published in this guide are accurate at press time. We apologize for any inconvenience resulting from outdated information. Please send us your comments:

Michelin Travel Publications
Editorial Department
P. O. Box 19001
Greenville, SC 29602-9001

KLAMATH FALLS

Michelin map 493 B 6 and map p 137
Tourist Information ☎ 541-884-0666
or www.klamathcountytourism.com

A sun-drenched farming community, isolated and irrigated Klamath Falls sits in the middle of what was once a huge Pleistocene lake but is now a mosaic of smaller, shallow lakes, marsh, and farmland. Located on an active fault line between Crater Lake and Lassen Peak (in northern California), the town taps into over 500 geothermal wells to heat some 750 homes and government buildings, as well as the entire campus of the Oregon Institute of Technology. Building murals and a summer trolley brighten up a downtown that is undergoing much new construction.

Klamath, Yahooskin and Modoc Indians dwelled in this wide, flat, river basin for over 11,000 years. Spring, summer and fall they would stock up on salmon, bird eggs, camas plants and the crunchy bran-like seeds of the wocus lily. An abundance of deer and elk living in the valley's uplands provided further sustenance. The ancient lava flows that covered most of Oregon were a major source of obsidian used for arrowheads. Thus happily ensconced the Indians were little pleased when pioneers on the Applegate Trail chose to stay and farm this fertile valley. For one moment in time, the three tribes put aside their bitter disputes with each other and launched raids against the settlers. In 1863 the government authorized protection of the pioneers with a new military outpost, Fort Klamath, 42mi north of today's Klamath Falls. By 1869 about 1,000 Indians reluctantly agreed to live on a reservation near Klamath Lake. The Modocs, who did not relish reservation life, returned to their Tule Lake homelands during the winter of 1872-73. When troops from Fort Klamath were dispatched to take them back to the reservation, the Modocs fled into the labyrinth of lava beds near Tule Lake, now called Captain Jack's Stronghold. The Modoc War had begun. Led by chief Kientpoos (Captain Jack), a mere 60 Modocs, intimately familiar with this rugged cave country, were able to fend off 1,200 US soldiers for nearly six months. In June 1873 the Modocs surrendered. The leaders were hanged at Fort Klamath, the remaining tribe exiled to a reservation in Oklahoma. By the 1950s, Klamath Indians were left landless when the US government purchased reservation lands after the termination of the Klamath tribes. The tribes were reinstated in 1986 and are working to revive their culture.

SIGHTS *1/2 day*

Favell Museum of Western Art and Indian Artifacts – *125 W. Main St. Open year-round Mon–Sat 9:30am–5:30pm. Closed Jan 1, Thanksgiving Day, Dec 25. $4.* ♿ 🅿 ☎ *541-882-9996.* A hexagonal rock building at the edge of the Link River displays 60,000 arrowheads primarily from the Northwest, along with more than 800 original Western works by 300 artists from British Columbia to Mexico. An odd mix of cowboy art and Indian artifacts, the collection began when young Eugene Favell found his first arrowhead; as his archaeological skills grew, he could at times unearth more than 200 obsidian arrowheads in a matter of hours. The walk-in vault in the middle of the building safeguards an extraordinary collection of 135 **miniature working guns**, from one-third-size Gatlings to inch-long Colt 45s that actually fire.

Klamath County Museum – *1451 Main St. Open Jun–Sept Mon–Sat 9am–5:30pm. Rest of the year Mon–Sat 8am–4:30pm. $2.* ♿ 🅿 ☎ *541-883-4208.* Housed in a geothermally heated building, this compendium of community history contains World War II regalia. A 7,700-year-old tree stump entombed by the eruption of Mount Mazama, a diorama of the 1872-73 Modoc War, and an explanation for those who wonder where the town's falls are—after the town changed its name from "Linkville" to "Klamath Falls" in 1893, the 150ft-wide falls in the Link River were ironically submerged by A 1921 dam. In the summer the museum also offers guided tours of the nostalgic four-story 1906 **Baldwin Hotel** *(31 Main St.; open Jun–Sept Tue–Sat 10am–4pm; visit of some rooms by guided tour only; $3;* 🅿 ☎ *541-883-4208),* which boasts original furniture.

EXCURSION

★**Lower Klamath National Wildlife Refuge** – *1 hr. 20mi south of Klamath Falls on Rte. 161, east of US-97. Open year-round daily dawn-dusk. $3/car.* ♿ 🅿 ☎ *530-667-2231. www.klamathnwr.org.* The first wildlife refuge for waterfowl in this country, Lower Klamath, located in both Oregon and California, was established by Teddy Roosevelt in 1908 to preserve a two-million-year-old nesting and feeding ground for migratory birds that was nearly destroyed in the early 1900s by irrigation and hunting. At 53,600 acres, this marshy refuge is the largest of six in the Klamath Basin and provides resting and brood-rearing habitat for tens of thousands of snow geese and other waterfowl. Nine years after it was made a refuge, the lake turned into a dry alkaline dust bowl when railroad construction blocked its main water source. A tunnel dug in 1942 from Tule Lake to Lower Klamath revived the lake. A 15mi driving-tour route traverses the dikes and marshlands and offers bird-watching opportunities.

OREGON CAVES NATIONAL MONUMENT★★

Michelin map 493 A 6 and map p 136
Tourist Information ☎ 541-592-2100
or www.nps.gov/orca/index.html

In the southwest corner of the state 20mi east of Cave Junction lies a web of marble chambers bejeweled with stalactites, stalagmites and other wondrous calcite formations. Situated underneath 6,281ft Mount Elijah, the Oregon Caves attract more than 75,000 visitors each year.

When the continental plates collided millions of years ago, the impact cooked up molten rock which pushed away the Pacific Ocean, created the Siskiyou Mountains and cooled into limestone and marble. Acidic water trickled through the mountain's faults, dissolved the marble and eventually carved out what is now a national monument with 3mi of known passageways. Recent fossil and footprint discoveries have revealed the presence of grizzlies, jaguars and bats in the caves during the last ice age; currently 10 species of bats use the caves.

No evidence exists of any Native American use of the cave system. The discovery of the caves did not occur until A 25-year-old hunter named Elijah Davidson chased his dog, who was pursuing a bear, into the mountainside in 1874. Davidson found his way out of the darkness by following a creek and returned three years later with his brother and a friend to explore deeper into the subterranean chambers. On the next trip he brought a teacher who wrote a letter to the editor of the *Oregonian* about the discovery. Elijah and his comrades agreed that "it would be a shame to desecrate or deface anything so beautiful." But after the letter appeared, numerous less-considerate adventurers made the trek up to Josephine County's underground world. In the summer of 1885, two miners who had laid claim to the surrounding 160 acres opened "The Limestone Caves" as a tourist attraction. Its remote location quickly proved the attraction an unprofitable venture. The caves, too difficult for the general public to navigate, were left to local explorers until July 12, 1909 when President William Howard Taft established the Oregon Caves National Monument. Official cave guide, ranger Dick Rowley, spearheaded a movement to make the caves more accessible to the public, with projects that included building a road, blasting "wriggle holes" into comfortable walkways, and mapping the caves. A 470ft exit tunnel from the Ghost Room was drilled in 1933 to avoid retracing steps. Since 1985, under the direction of the National Park Service, the caves have been undergoing restoration, with such projects as removal of rubble, restoration of broken formations, and the addition of new lighting that reduces evaporation caused by heat.

Visit *1 1/2 hrs.*

Open daily year-round. Caves can be visited by guided tour (1 hr15min) only. Hours vary: Jun–Aug daily 9am–7pm on the half hour. May & Sept–Oct daily 9am–5pm on the hour. Mar–Apr & Nov daily 10am, 11:30am, 1pm, 2:30pm & 4pm. Closed Dec–Feb. $7. ✗ ▣ ☎ 541-592-2100. Wear warm clothes (cave temperatures average 41°F) and good walking shoes.

Stalagmites, Oregon Caves National Monument

Nieland/Oregon Caves National Monument

Cave tours begin at the original entrance which Elijah Davidson crawled into in 1874, then continue in Watson's Grotto with commentary on how water seeped through marble to form the cavern. After the grotto, prepare to climb 500 stairs and navigate a number of low-ceilinged passages in the next half-mile stretch. The tour then passes by the River Styx, and pauses for close examination of such remarkable features as A 60ft-deep Douglas fir root, moonmilk (tiny calcite crystals that look like cottage cheese), and peculiar formations like cave pearls, cave bacon and rimstone dams.

Among the popular chambers are **Niagara Falls**—a calcite formation inscribed with signatures from the late 1800s; **Joaquin Miller's Chapel**, a stunning cathedral-like room filled with numerous formations; and the immense 40ft-high by 250ft-long **Ghost Room**, so-called for the ghostly shadows created by the chamber's original lighting. From here, the tour ascends a long tunnel to the exit.

■ Riding The Rogue

A fervently revered and protected waterway, this federally designated Wild and Scenic River tumbles 200mi down the western slopes of the Cascades and chisels its way through the coast mountains to the Pacific Ocean at Gold Beach. Many famous people including Gary Cooper, John Wayne and writer Zane Grey regarded the river as one of the world's finest steelhead, salmon and trout fishing streams. *The River Wild* (1994) with Meryl Streep was filmed here, where tumultuous rapids attain as high as Class V in difficulty.

Today 40mi of the Rogue (from just west of Grants Pass to just east of Gold Beach) is protected within the Siskiyou National Forest. The only access is by foot (along the river's north bank) or by raft. Jet-boat excursions *(only permitted part of the way into the Wild and Scenic area)* depart from Gold Beach or Grants Pass and vary from 2 hr, 36mi jaunts to 8 hr, 104mi trips. A number of outfitters offer quieter two– and three-day rafting excursions with camping or backcountry lodging options. On day and overnight trips, otter, beaver, blue herons, bald eagles and deer are often sighted along the way.

Those interested in unsupervised white-water trips should sign up for a permit by February for the following summer. *Maps and permit information are available through the Siskiyou National Forest Service office in Grants Pass (☎ 541-471-6500). Call Rogue River Reservations (☎ 541-247-6504 or 800-525-2161) to book a trip with any of the local boat operators (May–Oct).*

Rafting the Rogue River

© Dianne Dietrich Leis/Adventure Center Ashland OR

Willamette Valley

The Willamette Valley is the heart of Oregon today just as it has been since the pioneers first headed west in their covered wagons 150 years ago. When promoters extolled the glories of the Oregon Country, telling of the rich soil, mild climate, plentiful water and beautiful scenery, it was the valley defined by the Willamette River to which they referred. This area runs roughly 110mi north-to-south between Portland and Eugene and 30-40mi east-to-west between the Cascades and the Coast Range. This was the promised land that motivated settlers to forsake their homes and brave the rigors of the 2,000mi journey.

Before the pioneers arrived, Kalapuyan Indians lived off this generous land, fishing and hunting abundant game. Settlers began trickling into the Willamette in the 1830s, and arrived in large numbers starting in the 1840s with the opening of the Oregon Trail. It was here at the end of the trail that the state's first town, Oregon City, was founded. It was also here, at a place called Champoeg (pronounced sham-POO-ee), that American settlers wrested the Oregon Country away from Great Britain. And the first center of higher learning in the west, Willamette University in Salem, was founded in the valley in 1842 by Methodist missionaries.

Today the valley ranks as Oregon's most populated region by far, home to the state's one large city, PORTLAND, and its two medium-sized cities, Eugene and Salem. The valley also contains most of Oregon's industry, especially its swelling high-tech businesses, all its major centers of higher education, and the vast majority of the state's cultural institutions. Yet the valley remains more rural than urban, its handful of cities surrounded by small towns and farms. Wandering visitors will encounter few sprawling suburbs and brimming metropolitan areas; instead they will find vineyards, sheep ranches, iris and tulip fields, hazelnut orchards, covered bridges and towns whose entire population could fit into a high-school gym. The valley has been able to retain much of its pastoral character because Oregon remains relatively lightly populated and its land-use laws have prevented sprawl.

On a map of Oregon, more place names crowd the northern half of the Willamette Valley—which stretches from Oregon City to Salem—than any other part of the state, many of them marking towns that were founded by Oregon Trail pioneers. After coming to the end of the trail, in Oregon City, many early settlers occupied the closest desirable land. Often they carved out their farms and villages along the Willamette River because it was the main transportation corridor. During the California gold rush, which began in 1849, huge amounts of produce were shipped down the Willamette to Portland and on to San Francisco. Indeed, the insatiable appetites of the '49ers led to the establishment of many a farm along the river. That early development has left numerous historic sites in the northern valley. Most towns harbor at least a few well-preserved 19C buildings, several of which are open to the public.

The northern valley's head start spurred population growth unmatched elsewhere in the state. Today the area includes Oregon City, within the embrace of Portland, and Salem, Oregon's capital and third-largest city. Travelers are a bit more likely to come across a fine restaurant or a posh bed and breakfast in this thoroughly civilized, 2,000sq mi chunk of Oregon than in its other regions. And yet, though urbane, the northern valley for the most part is not urban. Farms and ranches still cover the majority of its land and many of the little towns favor Formica-table cafes to Starbucks. One special feature of the northern valley, the **wine country** *(p 146)*, blends the bucolic with the sophisticated—thousands of acres of neatly tended grapevines on dozens of wineries add an elegant, orderly touch to the rolling hills.

★OREGON CITY *1 day*

Today a modest town of 20,000 overshadowed by the adjacent Portland metropolitan area, Oregon City was once the hub of a vast realm that stretched from southern Alaska to northern California—the area known as the Oregon Country. During the early years of the 19C, when the US and Great Britain shared a claim to the region, Oregon City was the seat of American power. Sitting atop the bluffs above the Willamette River at the northern end of the Willamette Valley, the town marked the end of the Oregon Trail. In 1844 Oregon City became the first incorporated municipality west of the Rockies. Though its prominence has faded, the town's many museums and historic buildings still evoke its glory years.

★**End of the Oregon Trail Interpretive Center** – *1726 Washington St. Visit by guided tour (1 hr) only, year-round Mon–Sat 9am–5pm, Sun 10am–5pm. Closed Jan 1, Thanksgiving Day, Dec 25. $5.50.* ♿ 🅿 ☎ *503-657-9336. www.endoftheoregontrail.org.* Sprawling across 8.5 acres of Abernathy Green, the historic main arrival area for Oregon Trail travelers, the Interpretive Center comprises three 50ft-high buildings shaped like covered wagons. The interior of the first building mimics a mid-19C store, such as those located at the beginning of the Oregon Trail in Independence, Missouri, where Oregon-bound travelers bought their provisions. Dressed in pioneer garb, guides recount the travails of a journey on the trail, from the preparations made by those embarking to the joy and relief they experienced when they finally reached Oregon City. The guides spice their narrative with fascinating details, describing, for example,

Gary Polish / ZUMA

Tour Guide at End of the Oregon Trail Interpretive Center

143

Practical Information

Getting There – The main north-south route through the valley is I-5. Route 99W runs parallel to the Interstate offering a more scenic drive. To reach Willamette National Forest from Salem, take Rte. 22 east, then head west on US-20 to form a loop through Linn County arriving in Albany. Route 126 runs east from Eugene to the Willamette National Forest; going west from town the road heads toward Siuslaw National Forest and the coast.

International and domestic flights service **Portland International Airport** (☎ 503-335-1234). Horizon Air (☎ 800-547-9308) and United Express (☎ 800-241-6522) fly into Eugene Regional Airport (☎ 541-687-5430). Amtrak **train** stations are located in Salem, Albany and Eugene (☎ 800-872-7245). Greyhound **bus** serves Eugene, Salem and stops at many cities in the region (☎ 800-231-2222).

Visitor Information – For information on points of interest, accommodations, sightseeing, recreation and seasonal events for the region, contact **Willamette Valley Visitors Assoc.**, P.O. Box 965, Albany OR 97321, ☎ 541-928-0911 or 800-526-2256. For additional information: **Salem Convention & Visitors Assoc.**, 1313 Mill St. SE, Salem OR 97301, ☎ 503-581-4325 or 800-874-7012, www.scva.org; **Convention & Visitors Assoc. of Lane County**, 115 W. 8th Ave., Ste. 190, Eugene OR 974010, ☎ 541-484-5307 or 800-547-5445, www.cvalco.org; **Clackamas County Tourism Development Council**, 621 High St., Oregon City OR 97045, ☎ 503-655-5511 or 800-647-3843, www.clackamas-oregon.com.

Accommodations – Area visitors' guides including lodging directories are available *(free)* from regional tourism agencies *(above)*. A wide range of accommodations can be found throughout the area year-round, including hotels and motels, bed-and-breakfast inns, historic inns, resorts and rustic guest ranches. **Youth hostels**: 351 N.W. Jackson Ave., Corvallis, OR, ☎ 541-753-9036; Lost Valley Hostel, Dexter, OR, ☎ 541-937-3351. Campgrounds and RV camping facilities are plentiful near towns and in area state parks.

Recreation and Sightseeing – The region's rolling hills make **bicycling** a favorite pastime. The brochure, *Willamette Valley Scenic Loop*, including maps detailing A 195mi bicycling tour, is available from the Willamette Valley Visitors Assoc. *(above)*. Bicycle rentals available from: Peak Sports (☎ 541-754-6444) in Corvallis; and High Street Bicycles (☎ 541-687-1775) in Eugene. Silver Falls State Park abounds with recreational opportunities from biking and **hiking** to **horseback riding** and camping. Mountain biking and hiking are popular activities in Willamette National Forest. The Willamette, Santiam and McKenzie rivers are ideal for rafting and kayaking expeditions for both experienced and inexperienced paddlers *(May–Oct; half– to 2-day trips; all inclusive; $45-$165/person)*; for schedules & reservations, contact Oregon Whitewater Adventures; ☎ 541-746-5422 or 800-820-7238, www.oregonwhitewater.com. Fern Ridge Reservoir is a favorite **fishing** spot for large-mouth bass, white crappie and blue gill. Enthusiasts enjoy **sailing** and windsurfing on the area's rivers and lakes. Many of the region's **golf** courses allow non-residents to play.

Brochures outlining self-guided **driving and walking tours** that highlight historic sights, covered bridges and local farmers' markets are available from visitor centers in most towns. Stop at one of the many nurseries that grow irises and tulips and sell bulbs *(gardens open May–early June daily 8am–sunset)*.

Shopping: Lafayette Schoolhouse Antique Mall (over 100 dealers) near McMinnville *(open year-round daily 10am–5pm; ☎ 503-864-2720)*. Produce stands along rural roads offer locally grown fruits and vegetables; area farmers' markets also sell arts and crafts. Vineyards *(p 146)* along Highway 99W welcome visitors with free wine tastings.

Winter activities include cross-country skiing and snowshoeing. Downhill skiing and snowboarding are accessible within an hour's drive at Willamette Pass and Hoodoo Ski Bowl in the Cascade Range.

how pioneers made butter by putting churns in their wagons and letting the bumpy ride do the churning.

In the second building is a theater where visitors can watch A 20min mixed-media show called *The Spirit Lives On!*, in which a taped narration weaves together the stories of three pioneers. Though fictional composites, the tales are based on the diaries of actual settlers. A gift shop and offices occupy the third building.

McLoughlin House – *713 Center St. Open Feb–Dec Tue–Sat 10am–4pm, Sun 1pm–4pm. Closed major holidays. $4.* 🅿 ☎ *503-656-5146. www.mcloughlin-house.org.* This 1845 clapboard house was built by Dr. John McLoughlin, the man often referred to as the "Father of Oregon." Though considered a mansion in its time, the two-story edifice is not particularly grand, nor are the period furnishings especially memorable. But listen to the docents and you'll hear the unforgettable story of how McLoughlin, a British citizen, helped bring the Oregon Territory into the United States. Though he was the territorial head of Britain's powerful Hudson's Bay Company, McLoughlin's humanitarian impulses compelled him to repeatedly assist American pioneers in distress. His efforts led to a rising population of Americans in Oregon City and the Willamette Valley, and the influence of their numbers eventually solidified America's claim to the Northwest. When the region became part of the United States, McLoughlin stayed on, becoming an American citizen.

Clackamas County Historical Society Museum – *211 Tumwater Dr. Open year-round Mon–Fri 10am–4pm, weekends 1pm–5pm. Closed Jan 1, Easter, July 4th, Thanksgiving Day, Dec 25. $4. ⴴ P ☎ 503-655-5574. www.orcity.com/museum.* A handsome modern building houses artifacts and interpretive displays that describe Oregon City's past, from pre-settlement days up to the last few decades. Before going inside, look down from the 90ft bluff at roaring Willamette Falls, a short but broad cascade that stretches across most of the Willamette River. Inside, the exhibits include needlework genealogy charts, ancient Indian petroglyphs and class photos from historic one-room schoolhouses.

John Inskeep Environmental Learning Center – *19600 S. Molalla Ave., on the campus of Clackamas Community College. For schedules of guided walks, call ☎ 503-657-6958, ext. 2351.* Reclaimed from a former industrial site, this 15-acre oasis of nature provides visitors with pleasant walking paths, an inside look at wildlife rehabilitation and an opportunity to gaze at the stars from the small observatory. Especially notable is **Hawk Haven**, the rehab area for birds of prey, and a native flora and wetlands nursery.

NEWBERG *1 hr*

Lying in the heart of the upper Willamette Valley, Newberg claims a location that accounts in part for its considerable pioneer history and for its current status as a hub of the scenic agricultural region that lies beyond the Portland metropolitan area. Though the town's charm is tainted by strip development along much of Highway 99W, you can still find some fine historic houses in the neighborhoods off the highway.

Hoover-Minthorn House – *115 S. River St. Open Mar–Nov Wed–Sun 1pm–4pm. Feb & Dec open weekends 1pm–4pm. Closed major holidays. $2. ☎ 503-538-6629.* A plain but substantial dwelling built in 1881 by Jesse Edwards, the Quaker who founded Newberg, is the oldest house still standing in town. Dr. Henry Minthorn bought the house in 1885, and that same year he invited his orphaned, 11-year-old nephew, **Herbert Hoover** (1874-1964), to leave Iowa and live with the Minthorn family in Newberg. Young "Bertie" came and stayed until 1889, when the family moved to Salem. Bertie went on to become the 31st president of the US (1929-33), and the house is maintained as a museum to him; original furnishings, photographs and Hoover memorabilia are displayed.

Excursions

★**Champoeg State Park** – *2 hrs. 7mi southeast of Newberg. Take Rte. 219 about 5mi south to Champoeg Rd. (just south of Willamette River bridge) and drive 2mi east to the park. Open year–round daily dawn-dusk. $3/car. △ P ☎ 503-678-1251.* Champoeg's 615 acres of oak and conifer woodlands along the Willamette River harbor shady picnic areas and 10mi of appealing trails, but the park's main claim to fame harks back to 1843. Americans and a few others who wanted to form a provisional government, with an eye to eventually joining the United States, called all male Willamette Valley settlers—which included British subjects and French-Canadians—to Champoeg for a May 2, 1843 meeting. By A 51-50 vote, they decided to create a democratic government, an act that eventually led to the creation of Oregon as a US territory in 1849. This turning point in Oregon's history is chronicled at the park's museum, housed in the visitor center.

★**Old Aurora Colony Museum** – *1 hr. 19mi southeast of Newberg in Aurora. Take Rte. 219 5mi south to Champoeg Rd.; pass Champoeg State Park and continue east 1mi, and turn south on Case Rd. Continue 1mi and turn east on Yergen Rd. (which turns into Ehlen Rd.); go 1mi to downtown Aurora; museum is at 2nd and Liberty Sts. Open Mar–mid-Apr & mid-Oct–Dec Fri–Sat 10am–4pm, Sun noon–4pm. Mid-Apr–mid-Oct Tue–Sat 10am–4pm, Sun noon–4pm. $3.50. P ☎ 503-678-5754.* In the midst of this tiny (population 675) town's many antique stores and old houses lies the museum compound, which tells the story of the Germanic Christians who founded Aurora as their commune in 1856 and thrived here for 26 years. They believed in living simply, pacifistically and non-politically, but they did not isolate themselves from mainstream society as rigidly as some sects did. In the museum—housed in a converted 1862 ox barn—visitors may observe photos of the highly regarded hotel the Aurorans ran and the musical instruments that the colony band played at events around the region. Guides crank up an old phonograph that plays a scratchy but lusty recording made by the band.

■ Willamette Valley Wine Country

Oregon's premier wine-producing region, the Willamette Valley has recently developed into one of the finest wine regions in the world. A large majority of the state's 134 wineries and 9,500 acres of vineyards green the rolling hills of the valley, especially the northwest section between Salem and Portland and west of Interstate 5. The town of **McMinnville** acts as a hub for the wine region; the **Greater McMinnville Chamber of Commerce** offers tour information and bed-and-breakfast listings *(417 N.W. Adams St.; ☎ 503-472-6196)*. For detailed wine country information and area maps, contact the **Oregon Wine Advisory Board** *(☎ 503-228-8336)* or the **Yamhill County Wineries Association** *(☎ 503-646-2985)*.

Pioneers planted wine grapes as long ago as the mid-19C, but the modern Oregon wine industry began during the 1960s with the establishment of a few small family wineries, such as Eyrie Vineyards, near the little town of **Dundee**. For about 20 years little expansion took place in the industry. Then, in a French-sponsored tasting in 1979, a Pinot Noir from Eyrie Vineyards bested several esteemed French Burgundies. Chagrined French vintners wondered how a wine from Oregon, which barely existed on the wine world's map, could beat vintages from one of the world's most hallowed wine-producing regions.

The answer lies in the favorable soils, climate and latitude that suit certain varieties of grapes—notably **Pinot Noir**: wet winters; warm, dry summers; and long, cool fall days create excellent growing conditions in this part of Oregon. Following that shocking 1979 tasting, winegrowers began migrating to the Willamette Valley, planting neat rows of grape vines amid the oaks and grassy meadows. The region got a second big boost when Joseph Drouhin, a major producer based in Burgundy, opened Domaine Drouhin Oregon in the north Willamette Valley. By the early 1990s dozens of wineries flourished where once only a handful had existed.

Willamette Valley vineyards produce some good Chardonnay, Pinot Gris, Riesling, and other varietals, but Pinot Noir is the region's mainstay and outstanding performer. That has proved both a blessing and a curse. Widely considered the world's most temperamental wine grape, Pinot Noir requires gentle handling, particular weather and sophisticated wine-making savvy. But the great Pinot Noirs that result when everything falls into place rank among the top wines of the world.

To some extent the ascendance of Pinot Noir has shaped the Willamette Valley wine industry. Because this fickle grape demands so much of the wine-maker, Pinot Noirs generally fall into the category of costly premium wines—a specialty taken on by smaller vintners. Thus, the Oregon wine country remains low-key and informal. Even in the heart of the state's wine-producing region—the northwestern part of the Willamette Valley—visitors won't encounter the traffic jams and crowded tasting rooms that characterize California's Napa Valley during summer and fall.

Thanks to Oregon's farsighted land-use laws, which have largely prevented urban sprawl from overrunning the countryside, the area remains agricultural. But vineyards don't dominate the landscape here; most of it is devoted to pasture or crops other than grapes. Hazelnut orchards dot much of the land—95 percent of the nation's hazelnuts are grown in Oregon. Bucolic scenes abound, from the traditional sights of cows, sheep and horses grazing the lush grass of this rainy valley to the smattering of llama and alpaca ranches that add an exotic note.

The rest of the compound includes an 1877 log cabin used by one of the Auroran families, a heritage herb garden and a typical two-story frame house (1864) containing a spinning wheel, pump organ and other original colony furnishings.

★SALEM *1 1/2 days*

The capital of Oregon and one of the state's oldest cities, Salem provides visitors with a close look at Oregon politics and history. The city traces its founding to 1840, when Jason Lee moved the headquarters of his Methodist Mission to this mid-valley location. It was designated the capital of the Oregon Territory in 1851. As the seat of state government and the hub of the area's commerce, Salem is now the third largest city in Oregon, with a population of 126,702.

Visiting the Wine Country – *The following wineries are arranged in a clockwise loop south of Portland. Along Rtes. 99 and 47, blue highway signs guide visitors to the many wineries that welcome the public.* Visitors driving southwest from Portland can track down wineries just minutes beyond the metropolitan boundaries. The closest is one of Oregon's landmark operations, **Ponzi Vineyards★** *(from Rte. 217, head west about 4.5mi on Rte. 210; then south on Vandermost Rd. about .75mi; ☎ 503-628-1227).* An aerospace engineer, Dick Ponzi left his job designing rides for Disney in 1969 to come north and start this small, family-owned affair, one of Oregon's first wineries. Ponzi went on to produce numerous award-winning wines. The *Wine Spectator* has listed Ponzi vintages among its top 100 wines twice in the past five years, and *Wine Advocate* called Ponzi one of the top 15 wine-makers in the world. Don't leave without trying the Pinot Noir.

Taste buds are primed by the pleasant surroundings at **Rex Hill Vineyards★** *(2mi east of Newberg at 30835 N. Hwy. 99W; ☎ 503-538-0666).* Outside on the lush grounds, a terraced picnic area offers shady respite for sipping wine during hot summers. Inside, visitors sample the vineyard's wares in a spacious tasting room anchored by a massive fireplace. Rows of oak casks line a long, narrow passageway; in summer the facility is open for tours.

In little Dundee, stop at the **Argyle Winery** *(691 Hwy. 99W at corner of 7th St.; ☎ 503-538-8520).* The tasting room occupies the first floor of a restored Victorian farmhouse and the winery is around back in a re-tooled filbert processing plant. Argyle produces a wide range of wines, but it specializes in sparkling varieties. Call ahead and they'll be happy to arrange a tour. Across the highway in the incongruous Tuscan-style building is the **Ponzi Wine Bar and Tasting Room** *(☎ 503-554-1500).* The shop not only offers a wide array of choices from Ponzi but carries products from other vineyards.

Views compete with wines at the hilltop **Sokol Blosser Winery★** *(3mi west of Dundee on Hwy. 99W; ☎ 503-864-2282 or 800-582-6668).* Take your glass out to the deck and enjoy the scenery while you sip. After you sample the wines, stroll through the adjacent Showcase Vineyard, where you'll learn some basics about grape varieties and the grape-growing process.

In the tiny town of Carlton, a visit to **The Tasting Room★**, located in the old Carlton Bank *(105 W. Main St. in Carlton; 4mi south of Yamhill off Rte. 47 CK; ☎ 503-852-6733),* offers an opportunity to sample wines from some highly esteemed wineries that are generally closed to the public, such as Domaine Drouhin, Hamacher and Beaux Frères.

Visitors seeking a classic wine estate need look no farther than **Montinore Vineyards★** *(3663 S.W. Dilley Rd., 2.5mi south of Forest Grove on Rte. 47, then .5mi west on Dudney Ave.; ☎ 503-359-5012).* The hillside tasting room and the neighboring elegant historic mansion give the vineyard a venerable air. The 585-acre estate was a filbert and walnut ranch until 1980, when Mount St. Helens dumped ash on the fields and destroyed the crops.

For a change of pace, drop by the **Momokawa Sake Brewery** *(1mi south of Forest Grove, take cutoff from Rte. 47 .8mi northeast toward Rte. 8; go south on Elm St. .2mi to 820 Elm St.; ☎ 503-357-7056 or 800-550-7253).* America's first premium sake brewery is allied with Japan's Momokawa Brewing, Inc., which has been making fine rice wine since 1856. The chilled, flavorful beverages available in the tasting room will surprise visitors who think of sake as a warm, rather flat drink.

★**State Capitol** – *Bounded by Court, Capitol, State and Cottage Sts., 900 Court St., N.E. Open year-round Mon–Fri 7:30am–5:30pm, Sat 9am–4pm, Sun noon–4pm. Closed major holidays. ╳ ⅙ ▣ ☎ 503-986-1388.* The third of Oregon's three capitol buildings (fire claimed the first two) this 1938 **Greek Revival** edifice, designed by New York architect Francis Keally, houses the Legislature, the Governor, the Secretary of State and the State Treasurer. A 23ft bronze and gold-leaf statue of a pioneer stands atop the capitol. Other artworks scattered about the building also recall the state's history, including the massive Vermont marble sculptures of a covered wagon and of Lewis and Clark being guided by Sacajawea that flank the main entrance. Stand near the large replica of the Oregon state seal in the center of the rotunda and you can look up 106ft to the ceiling of the capitol dome, painted with murals.

Oregon State Capitol

★**Willamette University** – *900 State St., just south of the capitol.* ☎ *503-370-6300. Campus maps available at Putnam University Center on Mill St. Campus tours (1 hr) year-round by reservation 1 week in advance.* ☎ *503-370-6303. www.willamette.edu.* Founded in 1842 as the first institution of higher learning in the West, Willamette has become a well-regarded university with an enrollment of about 2,400. The 61-acre campus harbors many attractions, from the old brick buildings (including 1867 Waller Hall) to the botanical garden, which includes an alpine rock garden, a butterfly garden and a native plant garden. A recent addition to the campus, opened in 1998, the spacious **Hallie Ford Museum of Art**★ *(700 State St.; open year-round Tue–Sat noon–5pm; closed major holidays; $3;* ᵫ ☎ *503-370-6855)* displays a wide range of art, from the work of university professors to internationally known figures, with emphasis on Pacific Northwest artists.

★★**Mission Mill Museum** – *1313 Mill St. S.E. Open Jun–Sept Tue–Sat 10am–4:30pm,Sun 1pm–4:30pm. Rest of the year Tue–Sat 10am–4pm. Closed Jan 1, Dec 25. $4.* ✗ ᵫ ▯ ☎ *503-585-7012.* This worthy five-acre historical park holds two main attractions: the buildings of early Salem missionaries and the Thomas Kay Woolen Mill. Visitors are issued tape recorders and earphones and sent off on one-hour self-guided tours of each section. The mission area features the 1841 home of Jason Lee, the Methodist missionary who played the prominent role in the founding of Salem, and several other buildings from the city's earliest years that were moved here. The woolen mill dates back to 1889 and consists of one cavernous building and several adjacent structures. In the machine shop you'll see the "mouse feeding station": a bottle-cap dish and tiny table at which mice conditioned to appear at the blast of the lunch whistle came for crumbs provided by the millwright.

★**Historic Deepwood Estate** – *Northeast corner of Bush's Pasture Park, 12th St. and Mission St. S.E. Open May–Sept Sun–Fri noon–5pm. Rest of the year Tue–Sat noon–5pm. $4.* ▯ ☎ *503-363-1825. www.oregonlink.com/deepwood.* Since its completion in 1894, the ornate, immaculately maintained Queen Anne mansion has drawn envious looks, with its multi-gabled roofline and decorative details. The warm interior features golden oak woodwork and stained-glass windows. In the 1930s a pair of women architects from Salem, Lord and Schryver (who went on to achieve national fame) designed a formal English garden to complement the house. Visitors may stroll the brick-lined walks, past spreading oaks and fragrant magnolias, accented by sundials and birdbaths.

★**Bush House** – *Northwest corner of Bush's Pasture Park, Mission and High Sts., parking off High St. Visit by guided tour (40min) only. May–Sept Tue–Sun noon–5pm. Rest of the year Tue–Sun 2pm–5pm. Closed major holidays. $3.* ᵫ ▯ ☎ *503-363-4714. www.oregon/link.com/bush-house.* These two Salem landmarks sit in the 100-acre park that formerly was the gentleman's estate of Asahel Bush II, one of the city's and Oregon's most prominent 19C citizens. Bush started Salem's leading newspaper, helped author the Oregon constitution and founded Salem's first bank. He settled into the Bush House after its completion in 1878. In addition to the elegant features one might expect—10 Italian marble fireplaces and an estimable collection of fine art—the house was a high-tech marvel in its time, with gaslights, hot-and cold-running water and central heating. More than half the furnishings are original. Amid the gardens that surround the house stands an 1882 conservatory devoted to period plants. Next door in the converted estate barn is the **Bush Barn Art Center** *(open year-round Tue–Fri 10am–5pm, weekends 1pm–5pm; closed major holidays;* ☐ ☎ *503-581-2228)*, whose two galleries display the work of local, regional and national artists.

★**A.C. Gilbert's Discovery Village** – **Kids** *116 Marion St. N.E. Open Feb–Sept Mon–Sat 10am–5pm (late Jun–Aug Wed–Fri til 8pm), Sun noon–5. Rest of the year Tue–Sat 10am–5pm, Sun noon–5. Closed major holidays. $4.* ☐ ☎ *503-371-3631. www.acgilbert.org.* Set on the bank of the Willamette River, this sprawling wonderland of puzzles, imagination-stirring activities and scientific exploration invites children to use their hands and minds together. The museum reflects the fun-loving genius of Salem resident A.C. Gilbert—Olympic athlete, world-class magician and renowned inventor of toys, including the Erector Set. Roaming the many rooms of several historic houses, kids can operate recycling cranes, imprint their silhouettes on the shadow wall and create the illusion of flying in a room of mirrors. Outside they can hammer on the oversized xylophones, dig for mammoth bones or wander through the Erector Set tower and maze.

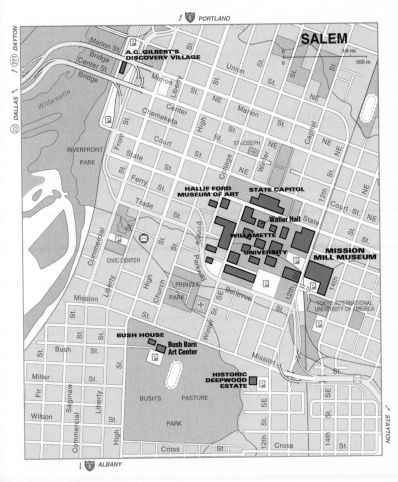

Excursions

Wheatland Ferry – *10min. 9mi north of Salem via Wheatland Rd., at Willamette Mission State Park. Runs continuously year-round daily 6am–9:45pm. 5min one-way. Does not operate Thanksgiving Day & Dec 25. $1/car, $2/vehicle & trailer, pedestrians & bicycles free.* ♿ ☎ *503-588-7979.* This six-car ferry crosses the

Willamette River at the tiny community of Wheatland. Vineyards on the western side give way to hop fields to the east. Lines from the ferry attach to a high cable that spans the river just upstream, so the boat can motor across without drifting with the current. The ferry service has been crossing here at river mile 72 since 1844, upgrading several times to more modern boats. Call ahead during winter, when high water sometimes shuts the operation down.

★**Mount Angel Abbey** – *1 hr. 15mi northeast of Salem via Rte. 213 east to Silverton and Rte. 214 north to the town of Mount Angel, then east on Church and College Sts. to the abbey.* ♿ 🅿 ☎ *503-845-3030.* Founded in 1882, this Benedictine monastery and seminary perch on A 300ft bluff, yielding heavenly views of the Willamette Valley and surrounding mountains. Visitors are welcome to explore most of the complex, including the high-ceilinged church; the monastery museum; the **Russian museum** *(open Mon–Fri 10am–11:30am & 1pm–5pm)*, which contains artifacts related to old believers driven from the Soviet Union in the 17C; and the **library**, a striking piece of modern architecture designed by the highly esteemed Finnish architect Alvar Aalto and completed in 1970. A highlight in the library is the **rare book collection**.

★★**Silver Falls State Park** – *1 day. 26mi east of Salem via Rtes. 22 and 214. Open May–Sept daily 6am–9pm. Rest of the year daily 8am–5pm. $3/car.* ⚠ ✗ 🅿 ☎ *503-873-8681. www.prd.stat.or.us.* The largest state park in Oregon at 8,700 acres, Silver Falls offers a variety of features, including a swimming area, equestrian trails, a historic lodge that doubles as an interpretive center, bike paths, picnic grounds and campsites. But, as the name of the park suggests, the waterfalls occupy center stage. The **Trail of Ten Falls★★**, A 7mi loop along Silver Creek, takes hikers through deep forest to all ten falls, which range in height from 27ft to 178ft. The trail even passes behind some of the falls, where softer material behind the basaltic lip of the cascades has eroded away. Some of the falls can be seen from viewpoints along the highway.

SOUTHERN WILLAMETTE VALLEY

Michelin map 493 B 4, 5 and map p 152
Tourist Information ☎ 541-484-5307 or www.cvalco.org

As visitors head south from Salem into the southern portion of the Willamette Valley, which spreads down to Eugene, the human influence lightens. Civilization hardly vanishes—scarcely any of the valley has been left in its natural state—but the towns grow smaller and farther apart, fewer roads cut through the farm fields and pastures, wineries become less common and traffic diminishes. With a population of 128,240, Eugene is the area's largest city, yet despite its major university and considerable cultural offerings it remains a small town at heart.

As in the northern valley, Kalapuyans lived here in the south before settlers and their foreign diseases drove them out in the middle of the 19C. Soon after pioneers began arriving in the northern valley, some filtered down to the south, finding the same fertile land and mild climate. Little towns such as Brownsville and Albany harbor many well-preserved homes and public and commercial buildings from that early era.

Farming, which brought the first settlers to the southern Willamette Valley, remains a pillar of the local economy; the local agricultural bounty includes grass seed, strawberries, hazelnuts and Christmas trees. The timber industry came shortly after farming had taken root and played a major role in the southern valley's development. Although trees were logged in the forests of the Coast Range and the Cascades, the lumber mills and allied enterprises were in valley towns such as Springfield, Albany and Philomath. Decades of over-cutting caused timber to slip in recent years, but high-tech companies have filled the gap, with plants such as the 5,000-person Hewlett-Packard operation in Corvallis.

CORVALLIS *1/2 day*

Known as a great place to live but not a particularly exciting place to visit, this quintessential college town may lack classic tourist attractions but it appeals to those looking for that mythical, pleasant all-American city. Settlers who founded the town in the mid-1840s gave it the Latin name Corvallis for its location in "the heart of the valley." Visitors can experience its livability simply by strolling through the verdant campus of Oregon State University or the thriving downtown, which nestles against the Willamette River. And the city's flavor can be sampled at myriad coffeehouses, bookstores and galleries.

Oregon State University – *The main campus is bordered by 35th St. on the west, 14th St. on the east, Monroe St. on the north and Washington Way on the south. Guided tours of the campus are given during the school year Mon–Fri.* 🔗 🖸 *Call for schedule* ☎ *541-737-0123.* Founded as a small, private college in 1856 and evolving into a public, land-grant college by 1868, Oregon State still boasts a strong agriculture department, though nowadays other programs, such as forestry and engineering, also command respect. Today the university enrolls more than 15,000 students. Outlying tracts of the university include an experimental forest and the sheep barn, where visitors can watch lambs being born in the spring. The campus core consists of stately early-20C brick buildings, notably the Italian Renaissance **Women's Building** (1926), just west of the Quad.

Excursions

★**Albany** – *4 hrs. 11mi northeast of Corvallis via US-20.* The old parts of this river-front town, just south of the Route 20 bridge over the Willamette River, brim with mid– to late–19C buildings—more than 700 representing many architectural styles, including Italianate, French Second Empire and Queen Anne. The **Albany Convention & Visitors Association** *(300 2nd Ave.; open year-round Mon–Fri 10am–5pm, Sat 10am–2pm;* ☎ *541-928-0911)* offers detailed driving-tour brochures to the area's many historic homes and covered bridges. An appropriate place to start a tour is the Federal-style **Monteith House**★ *(518 2nd Ave.; open mid-Jun–Sept Wed–Sat noon–4pm; $2;* 🖸 ☎ *541-928-0911),* Albany's first frame home, completed in 1849 by the town's founders, Walter and Thomas Monteith. The local historical society has meticulously restored the simple, two-story building to accurately reflect those early days; there's even a replica store in one of the first-floor rooms stocked with candles, powderhorns, and other pioneer goods. The Monteith brothers came to Oregon with the intention of building a store, but when they heard that rivals were also planning to open a store in the area, they immediately started a business in their home.

★**William L. Finley National Wildlife Refuge** – *4 hrs. 12mi south of Corvallis via Hwy. 99W and Finley Refuge Rd. For hours, call* ☎ *541-757-7236.* One of the valley's few and best natural remnants, Finley encompasses 5,325 acres of oak savanna, bottomland ash forest, wetlands, old-growth big-leaf maple, prairie and scattered fields planted with crops favored by wildlife. The refuge's native wet prairie is the largest such tract left in the valley. Created largely to protect water-fowl, the refuge attracts ducks, geese and swans by the thousands, especially during the winter. The refuge also shelters deer, frogs, bald eagles, elk, newts, hawks and hundreds of other species. Several roads and trails provide easy access, though some parts of the refuge are closed seasonally to protect wildlife.

© Dianne Dietrich Leis

Schreiner's Iris Farm, Salem

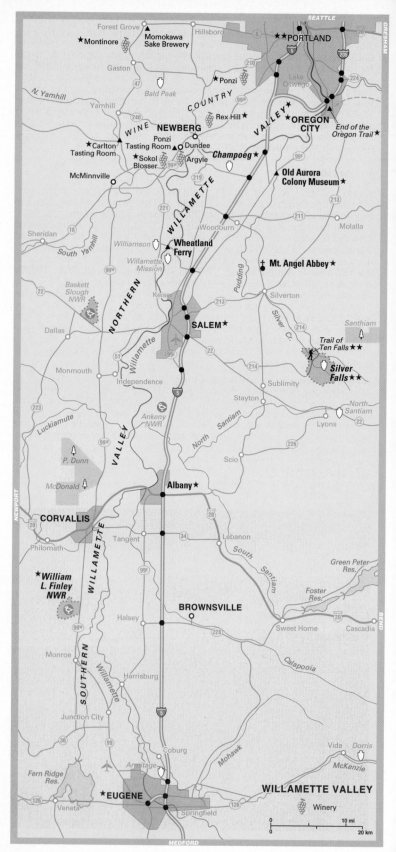

BROWNSVILLE *2 hrs*

Founded in 1846, this small town was one of the earliest settlements in the Willamette Valley and to this day it retains much of that 19C flavor, notably in the historic buildings that dot the three or four blocks of downtown.

Linn County Historical Museum – *101 Park Ave. Open year-round Mon–Sat 11am–4pm, Sun 1pm–5pm. Closed Jan 1, Easter Sunday, Thanksgiving Day, Dec 25. $2.* & ☎ *541-466-3390.* Located in the historic railroad depot and including several railroad cars, the museum dedicates most of its space to the pioneer and early 20C heritage of Linn County, with a bit on the Kalapuya Indians, who preceded the settlers. The highlight of the pioneer artifacts is the **Drinkard covered wagon**, one of only three remaining wagons that crossed the Oregon Trail. Also part of the museum, the **Moyer House**, an 1881 Italianate mansion, lies a block south on Main Street *(visit by guided tour only, Sat 11am–4pm, Sun 1pm–5pm).*

Living Rock Studios – [Kids] *911 W. Bishop Way. Open year-round Tue–Sat 10am–5pm. Closed major holidays. Donation requested.* & 🅿 ☎ *541-466-5814.* A classic roadside attraction off Route 228, Living Rock Studios is a fascinating monument to one family's passion for their Christian faith, their pioneer roots and their rocks. For some 10 years back in the 1970s and 80s the Taylor family labored to build a broad, round, two-story stone tower, its interior walls studded with agates, crystals, scoria (pumice-like volcanic rock), obsidian and Indian and pioneer artifacts. The pièce de résistance is the series of seven "Living Rock Pictures," each about the size of a small desktop. Patriarch Howard Taylor, the driving force behind this enterprise, painstakingly created Biblical scenes from thinly sliced bits of translucent rock, which are backlighted to illuminate the radiant, natural colors. Typically, one of the Taylor daughters conducts the tour.

★EUGENE *1 1/2 days*

Greater Eugene and the adjacent town of Springfield shelter about a quarter of a million people, making this Oregon's second-largest metropolitan area, yet Eugene's scenic setting, abundant open space and quiet neighborhoods retain the atmosphere of a small town—and a handsome one, at that. Founded in the 1840s by pioneers seeking farmland and timber, Eugene still has ties to both agriculture and the forest industry, but these influences have been overshadowed by the University of Oregon. Now matriculating about 17,200 students, the university opened its doors in 1876 and has shaped the community ever since. The presence of the university largely accounts for the city's thriving counterculture, evident in the casual dress, the many health-food stores, and a plethora of environmental organizations.

Skinner Butte Park – *2nd Ave. and High St. Open year-round daily 7am–11pm.* ☎ *541-682-4800.* Part of the original claim of Eugene Skinner, who Butte occupies a central position along the Willamette River. Visitors can drive to the top of the butte for expansive views of Eugene and the Willamette Valley all the way east to the Cascades and west to the Coast Range. On the south slope of Skinner Butte sits the Queen Anne-style **Shelton-McMurphey-Johnson House** *(303 Willamette St.),* built in 1888.

★**Owen Rose Garden** – *N. Jefferson St. at the Willamette River, just northwest of Skinner Butte. Open year-round daily 7am–11pm.* ☎ *541-682-4800.* At this 8.5-acre riverfront park more than 4,500 roses representing some 300 varieties bloom along curving paths. Visitors can savor the sights and smells of both old-fashioned and modern roses with such evocative names as Rio Samba, Patrician and Pleasure. The roses usually peak in mid–June; many varieties bloom throughout the summer and early fall.

Fifth Street Public Market – *Corner of 5th Ave. and High St. Open year-round daily 10am–6pm. Closed Easter Sunday, Thanksgiving Day, Dec 25.* ✗ & 🅿 ☎ *541-484-0383.* Locals and visitors alike meet at this former feed mill to lunch, people-watch and just hang out. The market's labyrinth of galleries, specialty shops and cafes are anchored by an open-air atrium and central courtyard. Musicians, artists and acrobats are among the street performers who provide a bazaar-like atmosphere, while a wide range of tenants includes a scent shop, travel store, massage therapist, bookstore and 10 eateries that tend toward the exotic—from Thai to health food.

★★**Hult Center for the Performing Arts** – *7th Ave. and Willamette St. Open year-round Tue–Fri 11am–5pm, Sat 11am–3pm. The Center is open one hour before all performances. Closed major holidays.* & 🅿 ☎ *541-682-5087. Ticket office,* ☎ *541-682-5000. www.hultcenter.org.* The dramatic, multi-peaked Hult Center (1982) stands out as a performance venue, civic space and major work of architecture, designed by New York architect Norman Pfeiffer and the local firm of Lutes Amundson. Critics have called the Hult "unquestionably one of the two or three finest performing-arts complexes in the world." For the full effect, attend a performance: the incredibly busy center hosts hundreds of events annually. In addition to the work of eight resident groups, such as the Eugene Symphony Orchestra and the Eugene Ballet, the Hult Center stages Broadway shows and events from Riverdance and Mikhail Baryshnikov to Itzhak Perlman and Bobby McFerrin. Guided tours start in the soaring lobby, where a peaked ceiling mirrors the Cascade Mountains and enormous timber pillars evoke Oregon's forests. Next is the versatile 500-seat Soreng Theater and the 2,500-seat Silva Concert Hall, renowned for its bold design and superb acoustics. Note the basket-weave ceiling and the light, curved wood that roofs the mezzanine. Don't overlook the idiosyncratic art that crops up throughout the complex, such as the Anita Fisk bronze of a push-broom leaning against a wall.

★**University of Oregon** – *Bounded by Franklin Blvd., 18th Ave., Agate St. and Alder St. Campus maps available in Oregon Hall. For general information ☎ 541-346-3201 or www.uoregon.edu.* Graced by more than 400 species of trees, the largest university in the state maintains a peaceful central campus, with limited car traffic; bicycle and foot travel are the rule here. **Deady Hall** (1876), the university's first building, still stands; its builders proclaimed the Second Empire-style edifice would last 1,000 years.

★★**Museum of Art** – *near Kincaid St., on Memorial Quadrangle next to library. Open year-round Wed noon–8pm, Thu–Sun noon–5pm. Closed major holidays.* ⑤ ☎ *541-346-3027.* Another architectural masterpiece on campus, the museum of art (1932) is a fantasy of intricate brickwork listed on the National Register of Historic Places. Worthy of such a striking building, the art objects inside number more than 8,000. Most impressive is the **Asian collection**, which includes Samurai armor, ancient Buddhist sculptures and many items from royal Chinese tombs. One room is dominated by a dazzlingly elaborate, 10ft-high 18C Chinese pagoda fashioned from jade, teak and bronze. The museum also contains a fine collection of **Northwest art**. Visitors weary of walking may seek respite in the interior courtyard, a quiet sanctuary of fountains, flowers and colonnades.

★**Museum of Natural History** – *1680 E. 15th Ave. Open year-round Tue–Sun noon–5pm. Closed major holidays.* ⑤ 🅿 ☎ *541-346-3024.* Most of the exhibit space here is devoted to indigenous peoples. Exhibits on Northwest Indians include local Kalapuya artifacts, such as projectile points, and items from ancient regional residents that include pairs of 9,000-year-old sagebrush sandals. The museum also includes displays on the cultures of Africa and Australia, as well as exhibits on local birds and Oregon geology.

★**Alton Baker Park** – *Along the northeast bank of the Willamette River, across from downtown. Open year-round daily 7am–11pm.* ☎ *541-682-4800.* Largest and wildest of the many parks that provide verdant oases in Eugene's urban core, the 143-acre haven offers a natural blend of riverfront lined with cottonwoods and willows, grassy meadows favored by meadowlarks and butterflies, and woods of incense cedars, Douglas firs and white oaks. Several ponds and other wetlands abound with ducks, frogs, great blue herons, dragonflies and busy but seldom-seen beavers. Developed sections include a rock garden, playground and community garden.

★**Willamette Science and Technology Center** – 🄺🄸🄳🅂 *2300 Leo Harris Pkwy., on the northwest border of Alton Baker Park. Open year-round Wed–Fri noon–5pm; weekends 11am–5pm. Closed major holidays. $4.* ⑤ 🅿 ☎ *541-682-7888. www.wistec.org.* Known to locals and visitors alike as "Wistec," this science center has been stimulating the imaginations of children (and adults) since 1961. The small facility changes its theme every few months, covering subjects from forests to atomic particles to bridges. Displays, many of them interactive, manage to be both whimsical and educational; an exhibition on vision includes a microscope through which you can view a fly's eye, and a color vision test that allows visitors to compare human color vision with that of dogs and shrimp. Next door, the **Lane ESD Planetarium** *(shows Fri & Sat 9:30pm, 10:30pm & midnight; $6; recorded show schedule ☎ 541-687-7827; for all other information ☎ 541-461-8227)* ranks as one of the largest in the Pacific Northwest.

Consult the practical information section at the end of the guide
for travel tips, useful addresses and phone numbers, and
a wealth of details on shopping, recreation, entertainment
and annual events.

■ National Lands

The Pacific Northwest is especially rich in national parks and wildlife reserves. Here is a listing of some of the national lands described in this guide:

Columbia River Gorge National Scenic Area★★ (OR) *p 82*

Newberry National Volcanic Monument★★ (OR) *p 96*

Elkhorn Drive National Scenic Byway★ (OR) *p 103*

Hells Canyon National Recreational Area★★ (OR) *p 104*

John Day Fossil Beds National Monument★★ (OR) *p 109*

McKay Creek National Wildlife Refuge (OR) *p 112*

Malheur National Wildlife Refuge★★ (OR) *p 113*

Oregon Dunes National Recreation Area★★ (OR) *p 124*

South Slough National Estuarine Research Reserve★ (OR) *p 127*

Rogue River National Forest (OR) *p 133*

Crater Lake National Park★★★ (OR) *p 135*

Lower Klamath National Wildlife Refuge★ (OR) *p 139*

Oregon Caves National Monument★★ (OR) *p 140*

William L. Finley National Wildlife Refuge★ (OR) *p 151*

Wolf Haven International★ (WA) *p 202*

Nisqually National Wildlife Refuge★★ (WA) *p 202*

Lake Roosevelt National Recreation Area (WA) *p 212*

Turnbull National Wildlife Refuge★ (WA) *p 220*

McNary National Wildlife Refuge★ (WA) *p 221*

Toppenish National Wildlife Refuge★ (WA) *p 228*

North Cascades National Park★★ (WA) *p 232*

Ross Lake National Recreation Area★ (WA) *p 233*

Lake Chelan National Recreation Area★★ (WA) *p 234*

San Juan Island National Historical Park★ (WA) *p 240*

Ebey's Landing National Historical Reserve★ (WA) *p 245*

Olympic National Park★★★ (WA) *p 248*

Dungeness National Wildlife Refuge★ (WA) *p 257*

Mount Rainier National Park★★★ (WA) *p 262*

Mount St. Helens National Volcanic Monument★★★ (WA) *p 266*

Pacific Rim National Park Reserve★★★ (BC) *p 328*

Denali National Park and Preserve★★★ (AK) *p 353*

Gates of the Arctic National Park and Preserve (AK) *p 363*

Glacier Bay National Park and Preserve★★★ (AK) *p 367*

Misty Fjords National Monument (AK) *p 376*

Wrangell-St. Elias National Park and Preserve★ (AK) *p 386*

Kenai National Wildlife Refuge (AK) *p 386*

Kenai Fjords National Park★★ (AK) *p 389*

View from Harts Pass, North Cascades Range

© Dianne Dietrich Leis

Washington

Introduction to Washington

Wedged into the far northwest corner of the contiguous 48 states, Washington claims a mixed population of back-to-the-earth naturalists, weekend hikers and tough-minded entrepreneurs who proudly call the Evergreen State home. That mix is evident in the ambience of the state. Even in the urban enclaves of Puget Sound, where there is enough good coffee, cuisine and art to satisfy diehard cosmopolites, suits and ties are the exception rather than the rule, and a small-town easiness is cultivated by corporate powerbrokers and corner shopkeepers alike.

Washington State Facts

Capital: Olympia

Land Area:
66,583 square miles

Population: 5,689,263

Nickname: Evergreen State

Motto: *Al Ki* ("By And By")

State Flower: Coast Rhododendron

Part of the easygoing style is no doubt due to the epic grandeur that surrounds residents on almost every side. The state's 66,583sq mi define an irregular rectangle, its northwestern Pacific coast filigreed by the waters of Puget Sound, the Strait of Juan de Fuca and their smaller waterways. The mountainous Olympic Peninsula juts out from the rest of the coast, extending an arm out into the Pacific, virtually within waving distance of Canada's Vancouver Island. To the south, the Columbia River carries the waters of faraway and nearby mountains to the sea, its famous gorge forming the boundary with Oregon. Along Washington's northern border sprawls British Columbia; at the western edge of the state, the Rocky Mountain foothills mound into Idaho.

Owing to its remote geographic position, Washington was slow to fill with settlers, but today it is one of the fastest growing states in the Union. Nearly 5.7 million people now call the state home, and more move here daily, anxious to live in sight of towering mountains, a sweeping coastline and one of the most livable metropolises (Seattle/Tacoma) in the United States.

Geographical Notes

Geologic Past – Riding a tectonically active seam of the earth, present-day Washington has been heaving and reforming for some 90 million years. Here at the junction of continent and ocean, the deep tectonic plates on which the landmasses float push and screech against each other. As the North American plate has inched west, the Pacific plate and the much smaller Juan de Fuca plate have been subducted, or shoved down under it. This tension and the resulting heat in the Earth's mantle have created a surface volcanic terrain alive with the dynamism of creation. For the last 15 to 20 million years, molten rock has been bubbling to the surface, feeding the Cascade Range, particularly such volcanic pyramids as mounts Rainier, Baker and Adams. In addition, basaltic lavas have spread and thickened across the land to form the Columbia River Plateau. And the earth shaking and shattering continues, due to the fact that Washington lies within the Pacific Ring of Fire, a circle of active volcanoes that extends from the tip of South America north to Alaska then south and west to the south end of New Zealand. The volatility of this fiery arc was brought dramatically home to Washingtonians in 1980, when the perfect pyramid of Mt. St. Helens erupted with cataclysmic fury, imploding one side of the volcano.

Ice as much as fire has shaped the land during recurring ice ages. About 18,000 years ago, glaciers covered the Northwest, gouging great holes in the earth as they advanced. When the glaciers began to retreat about 12,000 years ago, the holes slowly filled with water, accounting for such current marvels as Puget Sound. Though Washington is no longer sheathed in ice, its Cascade and Olympic high country boasts more glaciers than any other area in the contiguous US.

Regional Landscapes – Washington's terrain covers several distinctive areas. The lush Pacific Coast curves up into the Olympic Peninsula, whose rain-shrouded Olympic Mountains support the continent's only temperate rain forests. North of the peninsula, the Strait of Juan de Fuca sweeps in from the ocean to Puget Sound, whose bays and inlets etch the northern coastline of the state. The upper sound is dotted by the San Juan Archipelago and the long finger of Whidbey Island, second longest island in the nation. On the mainland nearby, the Skagit Valley stretches in a fertile swath, beneath the forbidding serrations of the glacier-mantled North Cascades. In this 100mi-wide swath of mountains, 10,778ft Mt. Baker reigns. South of the tightly packed northern peaks, the South Cascade volcanoes, mounts Rainier, St. Helens and Adams rear up in splendid snow-capped isolation, surrounded by ranchlands and forests. Along the southern edge of the state flows the mighty-but now dammed-

Columbia River. Northeast of the river the naturally semiarid lands are made productive by irrigation from the Columbia and its tributaries. The largest of these, the Snake River, twists through the southeast corner of the state. Washington's dry basin Inland Empire is bordered in the northeast by the Kettle River Mountains, which curve down from Canada, and in the far eastern side of the state, the Rocky Mountain foothills loom above the landscape.

Climate – The infamous climate of the state's western realm ensures Pacific and Puget Sound coast dwellers rain-sodden weather from late fall until the beginning of spring. Some spots here average up to 85in a year, depending on where they are situated in relation to either the Olympic or Cascade Mountains. Both ranges cause the warm, wet ocean air to dump its moisture as it climbs up their peaks, resulting in a rain shadow on the east side of the ranges. With the Olympics, the shadow cast is small, but the Cascades shadow blocks out much of eastern Washington, keeping rainfall to a scant 8in a year.

Temperatures, too, vary greatly on the east and west sides of the state, though the greatest weather changes are dependent on elevation. West of the Cascades mild temperatures prevail, rarely topping 80°F in the summer nor dipping much below freezing in the winter. However, by October the mountains can be getting snow and winter weather that will last well into June; despite the extreme snowfall (world records have been set in the Cascades), temperatures are not extreme, generally hovering between 20-30°F. The expansive east experiences a much broader range, with summer highs in the southeast sometimes climbing to 100°F and frequently remaining below 20°F in winter.

Historical Notes

A Land of Plenty – The first humans wandering into Washington probably came from the north, ancestors of the Asian hunter-gatherers who, sometime between 30,000 and 14,000 years ago, followed wild game across the Bering land bridge that formed when frozen ocean water created a walkway at a narrow point between the continents. Ample archaeological evidence suggests that humans were hunting and gathering in this area as early as 13,000 years ago, maybe earlier. The fossilized skeleton of A 12,000-14,000-year-old mastodon uncovered on farmland near Sequim had a human-honed bone point embedded in it, and fossilized human remains found in a cave in the southeastern corner of the state date back roughly 10,000 years.

Life here, particularly along the seafood-abundant coast, was good, and in the millennia that followed, Native Americans of the Coast Salish and Athabaskan linguistic groups drifted in from the north and west. These coastal Indians became some of the wealthiest in North America, putting to sea in elaborately carved canoes and building enormous longhouses out of the abundant wood of the local forests. Inland, to the southeast, other tribes congregated along the Columbia River, where the salmon harvest was virtually inexhaustible, and game animals such as bear, elk and deer were plentiful. But the paradise they had lived in for as long as memory served came to an abrupt end with the arrival of settlers.

The first European forays into the area were generally harmless sea expeditions. Juan Perez, reconnoitering for Spain, sailed past in 1774, and a year later, Bruno de Heceta actually stepped ashore at Point Grenville and claimed the entire region for Spain. South of the point, another contingent went ashore to collect water and firewood and were promptly massacred by the local natives. Close on the Spaniards' heels came the Russians under Vitus Bering, who sailed from Alaska as far south as the mouth of the Columbia in the mid-1770s. Not to be outdone, the English came too. Most prominent among the latter was George Vancouver, whose 1792 expedition charted in some detail the waters and lands of Puget Sound. But it was an American merchant sea captain, Robert Gray, who became the first to sail into the great river that same year. In 1805 the US Corps of Discovery, led by Meriwether Lewis and William Clark, reached the end of its epic cross-continent exploration by following the Columbia through the southeast corner of present-day Washington, then on to the Pacific coast. On the west side of the Rockies, in the Columbia River basin, they encountered the Nez Perce, good horsemen who helped the explorers recover from the ordeal of their Rockies crossing. As the corps headed down the Columbia, they encountered the Chinook-speaking peoples, who dominated the banks of the river, and on the Pacific, they traded with the Clatsops as well, wintering on the coast before they began the long overland trek east.

The Oregon Country Decades – In the early years of the 19C, what is now Washington State was included within the informal boundaries of the Oregon Country, which extended across the Northwest from the Rockies to the Pacific. British and American fur interests, notably the British North West Company and John Jacob Astor's Pacific Fur Company, vied for control of trading rights in the area. In 1810, the North West Company established Spokane House, the first fur-trading enterprise in what is now the state of Washington. In 1818, after the

American victory in the War of 1812, a treaty between the two countries arrived at conditions for their joint occupation of the Pacific Northwest. Soon thereafter, the British Hudson's Bay Company established a thriving headquarters for the region at Fort Vancouver, on the north bank of the Columbia 100mi inland from the Pacific. As a counter to British dominance in the area, American Charles Wilkes' worldwide scientific expedition spent time exploring and charting the lands of Puget Sound and the Columbia in 1841.

In addition to fur traders, settlers had discovered the area by the 1840s and were streaming west over the Oregon Trail, bringing with them diseases like measles and smallpox, which proved deadly to the native populations. Many newcomers settled south of the Columbia in the fertile Willamette Valley, but some ventured north, and soon settlements grew up along the coast at Seattle, Port Townsend and Oysterville. At the same time, Walla Walla and Centralia experienced their own growth. This wave of new immigrants put increasing pressure on the conflicting claims of Britain and America. (Spain and Russia had by then relinquished any claims to the region.) In 1846 a treaty recognized the region south of the 49th parallel as American land.

For almost a decade prior to the treaty, American settlers in the region had lobbied the US Congress to make Oregon an official territory of the US. In 1847 a Cayuse massacre of missionaries Dr. Marcus Whitman and his wife, Narcissa, as well as other settlers in the Walla Walla area, convinced lawmakers that the people in the far reaches of the Pacific Northwest needed the protection of federal government. A year later, the vast Oregon country became a US territory.

Dividing the Spoils – In the year following the creation of the Oregon Territory, roughly 300 people lived north of the Columbia. That population quickly swelled as newcomers headed into the Northwest, drawn by the free acreage guaranteed in the federal Organic Act of 1843 and the later Donation Land Claim Act of 1850. As more and more settlers ventured farther north, they felt isolated from the territorial government centered south of the Columbia. Hoping to remedy this, they petitioned for the formation of their own Territory of Washington, and in 1852 Congress granted their petition.

The new territory extended from the Columbia to the Canadian border and east to the Rockies. But the territorial status only encouraged neglect of the Native American populations and their rights, and throughout the 1850s politicians made bad-faith treaties with the Indians that essentially deprived them of more and more of their traditional lands. Washington Territory, too, was deprived of some of its own acreage, when in 1863 Idaho calved off into its own territory, taking the eastern side of Washington with it.

What was left, however, was vast and rich in resources. In the coastal area, the wealth of timber had brought prosperity and rapid growth to cities like Tacoma and Seattle, and in 1872, the Northern Pacific Railroad chose the former as its Pacific terminus, thus sparking a rivalry between the two cities that remains to this day. The coming of the railroad also assured Washington a solid link with the East, and in 1889 Congress admitted it to the Union as the 42nd state.

Four years later, the Great Northern Railroad gave Seattle its own transcontinental terminus, but it arrived in the wake of a serious nationwide depression and even the Iron Horse could not pull the state out of its economic slump. What did get the Seattle economy rolling again was the Klondike Gold Rush, which began in 1897. Seattle's role as a staging point and supplier to those infected with gold fever turned the town overnight into a burgeoning metropolis.

In 1909 Seattle and the State of Washington had sufficient international recognition to host a world's fair, the Alaska-Yukon Exposition. Prosperity continued as the growing Weyerhauser company made timbering big business again, while a smaller concern, Bill Boeing's airplane manufacturing company, began to produce planes for World War I.

Though the state suffered with the rest of the nation during the Depression, huge dam projects along the Columbia (Bonneville and Grand Coulee) helped bring employment to out-of-work laborers. World War II brought booming prosperity as Boeing became a major supplier of planes to the military, and state shipyards hummed with the industry of war. Another, more secretive industry brought jobs to Hanford, in the central desert, where a hastily assembled military-industrial plant created the plutonium for the bomb that destroyed Nagasaki.

After the war the state continued to thrive, with Boeing and Weyerhaeuser providing large stabilizing forces in the economy. Washington's reputation for progressive social and political action, established early in the century, continued to grow. The state's penchant for forward thinking was symbolized in its second world's fair. Held in Seattle in 1962, the fair celebrated a rosy, high-tech future. In 1974 Spokane, too, hosted an Expo, this one more soberly focused on preserving the environment. Nature staged its own exposition in 1980, when Mt. St. Helens erupted, spewing inches of ash on nearby cities and towns and capturing the world's attention.

Economy

Washington's traditional industries—logging, farming and fishing—still hold their own in the state's economy, but they are now backed by the modern behemoths of aerospace, high-tech and hydroelectric-power production. Almost all of the heavy industrialization centers on the Puget Sound megalopolis and along the Columbia, while the central inland remains a land of farmers and ranchers. In recent years, tourism, understandably, has emerged as a major economic force, now ranking among the top five industries.

Natural Resources – The Evergreen State got its start on timber and, even today, Weyerhaeuser's many tree farms are evident wherever forestlands predominate. Log-laden trucks are constant reminders that the timber industry is alive and well, now accounting for about 2.4 percent of the state economy.

Fishing has not fared so well, as environmental factors, damming and protective legislation have radically affected salmon harvests. Still, the largest commercial fishing fleet in the West calls Seattle home, and the fleet's small sole proprietors and commercial trawlers fish coastal waters as far north as Alaska for salmon, pollock, cod, perch, sole, flounder and rockfish. Another of the state's abundant resources, coal supplies the thermal-electric power plant in Centralia, just south of Olympia.

Lumber Industry, Aberdeen

Manufacturing – If the name Weyerhaeuser is virtually synonymous with Washington logging, Washington's aerospace industry immediately conjures the name Boeing. Though the company remains the state's largest employer, it is a volatile one, subject to the whims and conditions of world markets. In the late 1990s, for example, the downturn in the Asian economies and competition within the industry led to layoffs. Despite that, aircraft manufacture accounts for eight percent of the state economy. Another larger-than-life Washington player in world industries is Microsoft, the computer software giant birthed by Seattle natives Bill Gates *(p 195)* and Paul Allen. Its presence has brought other high-tech companies to the Seattle/Bellevue area, and now the industry fuels 2.7 percent of the state's gross business income.

Since the 1880s, Washingtonians have realized what a powerful source of energy their rivers, if harnessed, could provide. Today, 14 dams take advantage of the Columbia's might, and the hydroelectric power they produce creates the electricity for much of the Pacific Northwest and for parts of California. Both Tacoma and Seattle have their own dams farther north and rely on hydroelectric power to light and fuel their cities.

Service Industries – In the service industries, tourism contributes a healthy 9.1 percent of the total economy, as visitors come to enjoy the urban offerings of Seattle and other cities or to revel in the splendor of the state's oceanfront, islands and mountains. Financial institutions contribute another 3.4 percent, but the largest player in this field is transportation, particularly shipping, as the ports of Seattle and Tacoma do a bustling business with the Pacific Rim and Alaska. The value of foreign waterborne trade through all Washington ports totaled almost $58 billion in 1997.

Agriculture – The hardscrabble farming and ranching that took place east of the Cascades in the 19C and early 20C got a lot easier with the coming of dams along the Columbia and its tributaries. In 1952 the Columbia Basin Irrigation Project channeled water to half a million acres, and now eastern Washington's farmers do a brisk production in wheat, hay and potatoes, as well as some cattle and sheep, apples, pears and other fruits and vegetables. In the last two decades, grapes have become a highly visible crop, as Washington State wines have received increasing national and international acclaim. Nurseries and flower-bulb production, too, have become big business, especially in the Skagit Valley, one of the world's largest tulip-bulb-producing regions.

The State Today

One of the fastest growing states in the country, Washington, and particularly the Seattle-Tacoma area, are greatly esteemed for their livability, natural beauty, growing economies, and friendly, low-key ambience. Throughout the state, dramatic scenery is always within eyeshot, and beyond the cities many Washingtonians have chosen communities simply to live in constant awe of their surroundings. Even the Sea-Tac (Seattle-Tacoma) corridor is overseen by the immense splendor of Mt. Rainier. That kind of natural beauty, along with the urban pleasures-the cafes, lively nightlife, museums and restaurants—of Seattle, Tacoma and Bellingham, draw some 83.7 million visitors to the Evergreen State annually. They flock here to ski on the daunting slopes of the snow-mantled peaks, to hike through the pristine wilds of the North Cascades, to bike the pastoral hills of the San Juans, to kayak and whale-watch in Puget Sound, and of course to sample the almost profligate bounty of Northwest cuisine—salmon, halibut, oysters, clams and an endless array of fresh fruits and vegetables. In the last century, different ethnic groups have brought their own touches to the cuisine. The Asian-Pacific Island population, now accounting for about 5.6 percent of the total, has long been strong in the urban areas, but the state remains predominantly Caucasian (83.5 percent), with Hispanics making up another 6.1 percent. Though American Indians account for only 1.6 percent of the population, more than 20 reservations, some very small, are scattered throughout the state.

Addresses, telephone numbers, opening hours and prices published in this guide are accurate at press time. We apologize for any inconvenience resulting from outdated information, and we welcome corrections and suggestions that may assist us in preparing the next edition. Please send us your comments:

Michelin Travel Publications
Editorial Department
P. O. Box 19001
Greenville, SC 29602-9001

Seattle and Puget Sound

View of Seattle from Queen Anne Hill / © Robert Holmes

A rare blend of breathtaking natural scenery and urbanity, the Puget Sound mega-lopolis stretches along inlets and bays from Everett in the north to the state capital of Olympia in the south. Seaside parks, nearby mountain wildernesses and endless other outdoor opportunities characterize the area as much as the high rises that now punctuate its skylines, always competing with incomparable Rainier, on the eastern horizon. Sprawling Seattle, in the north, reigns as undisputed cosmopolitan queen of the area, renowned for its cafes and performing-arts venues, its mix of modern office towers, funky marketplaces, waterside neighborhoods and fabulous views of the mountains and Puget Sound. As one of the country's most heralded and livable cities, Seattle and its energetic street scene have begun to rival San Francisco and New York. In many ways, its restaurants, though, are unrivaled. Seattle chefs pioneered the acclaimed Northwest cuisine, which makes innovative use of the area's bountiful fresh seafood and produce.

Seattle and its longtime rival, Tacoma, about 40mi to the south along the heavily trafficked I-5 corridor, have come a long way since their early 20C days as rough-and-tumble logging and railroading towns. Though both are still major port cities servicing Alaska and the Pacific Rim, and though the Weyerhaeuser logging giant and the Boeing aircraft behemoth contribute greatly to the area economy, the Sea-Tac megalopolis has developed an increasing number of white-collar industries in the past decade, with the computer leviathan Microsoft making a major presence in the Seattle suburbs. Equally prosperous, though decidedly more compact and sedate, Tacoma has been in the process of re-envisioning itself and its downtown in the past decade, and new museums, restaurants and performance halls are continually adding to its appeal. Smallest of them all is modest but charming Olympia. Dominated by the grand dome of the state capitol, the little town lines the shores of Budd's Inlet, content apparently to lead a quiet life away from the hubbub of its northern neighbors.

SEATTLE★★★

Michelin map 493 B 3 and map pp 184-185
Population 536,978
Tourist Information ☎ 206-461-5840 or www.seeseattle.org

Blanketing high hills overlooking Puget Sound, Seattle has grown from a hardworking lumber town to one of the nation's cultural trendsetters. Noted for its livability and natural beauty, the city is backdropped by spectacular vistas in almost every direction, from Mt. Rainier in the southeast and the Olympics in the southwest, to the Cascades in the northeast. Ample lakes and waterways add to its al fresco charms. Always a mecca for outdoors enthusiasts, the city in recent decades has cultivated its own distinctive brand of living well. Street-corner coffee bars have encouraged a cafe society, and the abundance of Northwest seafood and produce are celebrated in a regional cuisine that has vaulted local restaurants to world-class status. In the last decade, the city has become a center of the high-tech industry, thanks to local software giant, Microsoft. With so much in its favor, only the weather dampens Seattle's attractiveness—but rarely its spirits.

Historical Notes

A Northwest New York – Tribes of Coast Salish Indians roamed the shores of what is now Elliott Bay and lakes Union and Washington long before Capt. George Vancouver and the crew of *Discovery* sailed into the waters of Puget Sound and anchored within sight of Alki Point in 1792. For some reason, Vancouver eyed the future townsite from a distance but found it unworthy of exploration. Following Vancouver's brief foray, few settlers interrupted the hunting-and-gathering lifestyle of the area's Salish Indians for several decades. Hudson's Bay Company explorers wandered into the region in the 1820s, but they did not stay. They established their fur-trading post farther south.

No serious settlers made their way to this region until the 1850s, when disappointed `49°rs from the California goldfields and homesteaders from the OLYMPIA area began filtering north. A handful settled in the fertile Duwamish River bottomlands, traditional home of the Duwamish Indians. Their tyee, or chief, was **Seatlh**, a respected native leader who was friendly to the newcomers. In 1851, both the Duwamish and the new settlers found themselves with neighbors—a group of Illinoisans lead by Arthur Denny. The party had struggled west across the Oregon Trail, drawn by letters extolling the "wonders of the Pacific; the grandeur of the mountains; the vastness of the untouched forests; but best of all …the mild climate and the fertile soil and the flowers that bloom in the winter time."

Denny's group had gone first to Portland, then sent a scouting party—brother David Denny, Lee Terry, and John Low—north to find a suitable settlement site. The three chose Alki Point, a peninsula jutting between Elliott Bay and Puget Sound. Backed by rich forests, it was bordered on the east by the Duwamish River. The three men were' in the process of building a log cabin when their comrades anchored off the point aboard the schooner *Exact*.

The date was November 13, 1851, a chill gray day typical of Northwest autumns and hardly auspicious for the anxious new settlers. Still, it became the acknowledged birth date for the founding of a city that began with the unlikely dual name of New York-Alki—New York because the Illinois natives had such high hopes for it and Alki after the Duwamish word for "by and by."

Across Elliott Bay – The "by and by" of success came sooner perhaps than skeptics among the group might have expected. The following month the brig *Leonesa*, empty and bound for San Francisco, hove to off New York-Alki, and Capt. David Howard inquired whether the"townsfolk" (whose numbers totaled 7 men, 5 women and 12 children) could provide him with a cargo of pilings to ship back to San Francisco. Give them a little time, they assured Howard, and they would have the lumber ready. Howard sailed for Olympia, then returned for the lumber. The episode made two points clear to the locals: Whether they liked it or not, timber would prove one of their most lucrative assets; and their beachside settlement, plagued by shallow water offshore, was no good as a port for loading ships.

In February, Arthur Denny and two companions set off to find a suitable deepwater site for a new settlement. They soon discovered that the bay waters to the east and north were deep indeed, but in most places fronted by steep, red-clay cliffs. There was one promising site, however, where the cliffs sloped gently down to the water; furthermore, a wild fire had naturally cleared the forests and left a meadowland. Immediately the three men each claimed the portion they wanted, and David Denny soon paddled over to lay his own claim. The bulk of the settlement made plans to move, while two families decided to stay at Alki Point.

At about this time, a promising newcomer arrived on the scene. **David Swinson "Doc" Maynard**, a Vermonter by birth, had spent most of his adult life in Ohio. At the age of 42 and in debt—owing in part to his propensity for generosity—he had headed for the California goldfields. But he never quite made it there. By 1851, he had established a trading post in the burgeoning settlement of Olympia, up the sound on Budd Inlet.

When the Duwamish leader Seatlh came to town one day looking for a merchant willing to set up a trading post farther north for his people, Maynard agreed to move. He would prove an invaluable asset to the newly forming town, the town whose name he himself would choose. To counter the name Duwamps that had been attached to the settlement, Maynard proposed instead Seattle, after Chief Seatlh. While the new community was happy with the name, Seatlh himself was not; the Salish believed that speaking a person's name after his death would disturb his spirit.

Nevertheless, the name Seattle prevailed and Maynard and his fellows were convinced that their newly christened town had limitless potential. Still, the town needed something more than their enthusiasm to attract new businesses and new settlers. They soon got it. An Ohio businessman named Henry Yesler was exploring Puget Sound, looking for a likely spot on which to build a new steam-powered sawmill. Maynard and his fellow claimants were willing to sacrifice land to Yesler in order to get his mill in Seattle. When Yesler agreed to their proposal, the fortunes of the town were launched.

A year later, in 1853, Seattle was platted, though a dispute between Maynard and Denny created a strange street pattern that persists to this day, with Yesler Way, the "skid road" he used to roll his logs downhill, cutting through it. Despite this, the town was prospering so remarkably that in 1854, with the formation of the new Washington Territory, Arthur Denny proposed Seattle as the new capital. That suggestion, however, made little headway with the territorial legislature, who still considered the older settlement of Olympia a more appropriate site.

Seattle's growth had one negative, but inevitable, consequence. As the pressure for more land and resources grew, so did the pressure on the traditional Salish lifestyle. The forests the Indians had used as fertile hunting-and-gathering grounds were felled to feed Henry Yesler's sawmill, and their lands were taken whether they agreed to the transfer or not. In the fall of 1854, the pressure became too much, and trouble broke out in the eastern part of the territory.

In order to protect the friendly tribes around Seattle, both from hostile tribes and from hostile settlers, Doc Maynard, ever a friend of the Salish, convinced them to move across the sound in November. He even used his own funds to help them with supplies they needed for the move. The short-lived Indian War that followed had little effect on the town, save to brand Maynard an "Indian lover," disfranchising him and causing him to move to Alki Point. The anti-Indian sentiment also affected the Duwamish Indians, who were permanently forced off their native lands and on to reservations.

Years of Turmoil – Throughout the late 1850s, Seattle continued to grow, and in 1861, the city was chosen as the site for the new Territorial University. Denny, a town booster like Doc Maynard, donated land for the new institution, and Denny's Knoll (now University Street between Fourth and Fifth Streets) served as the campus for the school for more than 30 years. By the end of the decade the town had two newspapers and an official charter from the territorial legislature. But the coming decades would prove hard for Seattle.

In 1872 the first blow fell when the Northern Pacific Railroad chose TACOMA rather than Seattle as its western terminus, thus encouraging a rivalry between the two major Puget Sound cities that continues to this day. But Seattle would not be daunted. It began building its own modest line linking the coal deposits that had been discovered on the south shore of Lake Washington with the port area. With local timber now depleted, coal became the city's major export.

Despite this boon, unrest had been steadily growing between the immigrant Chinese who had settled in the city and other groups of laborers. Much of the resentment centered on the willingness of the Chinese—coolies, as they were derisively called—to work for such low wages that it forced out other laborers. By the early 1880s growing anti-Chinese sentiment and the passage of the federal Restriction Act led Henry Yesler, then mayor, and other city fathers to insist on the expulsion of all Chinese from Seattle. When leading Chinese businessmen did not comply in a timely fashion, a self-appointed group of like-minded citizens entered Chinatown in February 1885 and began forcibly evicting the residents, hauling their belongings down to the waiting *Queen of the Pacific*. The steamer could carry only 200 passengers back to China, forcing the rest of the Chinese community to wait in Chinatown until another ship arrived. During the waiting, mob violence against the "Yellow Peril" briefly broke out, but it was quickly quelled. Within a few days, most Chinese had been banished from Seattle.

That unfortunate episode was followed a few years later by early Seattle's greatest tragedy. On the fateful morning of June 6, 1889, a pot of glue boiled over in James McGough's basement paint shop, located in the Pontius Building near Pioneer Square. Owing to the flammable materials in the shop and an unusual dry spell the city had been experiencing, the fire spread with devastating speed. Firemen frantically hooked up hoses and began spraying, but the city's water system could not sustain such use, and the pressure fell till the hoses were spurting little more than a dribble. As luck would have it, the tide was out and the hoses could not even pump the waters of Elliott Bay into the raging flames, now fanned by a rising wind.

All day long and into the night, citizens formed bucket brigades and fought on. A few houses were saved, but little else. By three o'clock in the morning, the fire was at last flickering out; there was virtually nothing left to burn. The flames had ignited 125 acres—25 city blocks—destroying the business district, the waterfront and Skid Road. The very heart of Seattle was gone. Gradually, but with great fervor, the town rebuilt itself, brick buildings rising on the sites of the former tinderbox wooden ones. Fire would not take Seattle unaware again.

In the meantime, major railroad interests, including James Hill's Great Northern, had been vying for control of Seattle's port connections. In 1893 Hill won, and Seattle had its first link with transcontinental lines, just as a financial panic swept the country. Seattle's fortunes then rose abruptly and unexpectedly in 1897, when the S.S. *Portland* steamed up to Schwabacher's Wharf on July 17. Though almost empty of passengers, the steamer carried a reported two tons of gold, recently discovered in the Klondike. Gold fever struck Seattle like an epidemic, quickly spreading throughout the region and far into the American interior. Virtually overnight, Seattle became the "gateway to the Klondike," swarming with men headed for the goldfields. Merchants grew rich selling the hopefuls supplies, hotels were quickly built and mining schools opened. Though many returned from the Klondike empty-handed, there was indeed gold in the subarctic wilds, and the assayers office in Seattle weighed in $174 million worth of the precious metal in four years.

Beginning to Soar – Even as the gold was petering out, an Illinois lumberman, **Frederick Weyerhaeuser**, arrived in the Northwest and with his partners bought up some 900,000 acres of Northern Pacific Railroad land. The name Weyerhaeuser would come to dominate timber interests in the Pacific Northwest and eventually throughout much of the US. At about the same time another timber baron moved to Seattle. His name was **William Boeing**, and fortuitously for Seattle he eventually switched his attention from timber to a new technology—flight. Like Weyerhaeuser's interests, Boeing's airplane factories would fuel the area's economy for a century to come. Another critical name entered the Seattle scene in 1903, when the city hired respected East Coast landscape architects· **Frederick Law Olmsted, Jr., and John Olmsted**. For the first decades of the 20C, the Olmsted brothers' vision imprinted the city with a system of parks and greenswards that took advantage of its hills and sweeping sea and mountain views.

In 1909 Seattle had achieved sufficient international prominence to host a World's Fair, and the city again called on the Olmsteds to design the fairgrounds. The Alaska-Yukon-Pacific Exposition opened on the new but undeveloped University of Washington campus on the northeast side of the city. The exposition's dramatic buildings were designed mostly by San Francisco-based architect Édouard Frère Champney, and the entire enterprise was a rousing success.

Meanwhile, new development gradually filled in the 10-acre swath opened by the university's move to the city outskirts. During the early decades of the century, Seattle's downtown office and business structures shot up as steel-framed infrastructures faced with a decorative exterior of terra-cotta tiles, most of them produced by the Denny-Renton Clay & Coal Company. Even today terra-cotta facades predominate on such exceptional old buildings as the Smith Tower. When it was completed in 1914, it ranked as the tallest building west of the Mississippi and became symbolic of Seattle's growing status.

As Seattle burgeoned, "streetcar" suburbs expanded the city well beyond its original waterfront boundaries and drew an increasingly mixed influx of hopeful immigrants.

Scandinavians poured into the Ballard area northwest of downtown, working in the salmon-fishing and canning industry, while Asians flocked to the International District east of downtown. The successes of German brewmaster Andrew Hemrich drew more of his countrymen to the Georgetown neighborhood surrounding his Rainier Beer brewery. So many Italians flocked to southeast Seattle's Rainier Valley that it became known as "garlic gulch." While each group preferred its own neighborhood, there was a common meeting place: **Pike Place Market**. Established in 1907 as a produce market, it quickly grew to encompass fishmongers, butchers and other purveyors of Northwest bounty. As an institution, Pike Place became emblematic of the independent, egalitarian spirit of Seattleites.

During World War I, Seattle enjoyed the same boomtimes that briefly infected the rest of the country, and the city seemed destined for unending success. But labor problems engulfed the city with the war's end.

Pike Place Market

© Robert Holmes

In 1919 prominent Marxist and school-board member Anna Louise Strong became a national figure when she helped organize the city's militant "Wobblies." In defiance of the city's entrenched special interests, they staged the nation's first general labor strike. The event cemented Seattle's reputation for social and political activism. Ten years later the Great Depression created more long-lasting havoc. The unemployed and homeless erected their own shanty town—dubbed Hooverville—south of Pioneer Square, and Yesler's old Skid Road soon became Skid Row. In the 1920s and `30s, Seattle's population grew only slightly.

World War II ended the idle years, and William Boeing's Seattle factories alone employed some 50,000 people. In Bremerton, the Puget Sound Naval Shipyard also leapt into high gear, and Seattle became a major Army transport center. But the war was not kind to all the city's residents. When Japan bombed Pearl Harbor in December 1941, some 7,000 ethnic Japanese lived in Seattle, representing the city's largest minority population. In 1942, in response to anti-Japanese sentiment, the government herded them up and shipped them to detainment camps for the remainder of the war. The end of the war created a serious slump in the economy, exacerbated in 1949 by the worst earthquake in Seattle history. Measuring 7.1 on the Richter scale, it claimed eight lives and did its greatest damage to the aging buildings of Pioneer Square. The quake sealed the neighborhood's fate, at least for the next decade. Buildings that had long been landmarks were not resurrected to their former glory, lapsing instead into bordellos and flophouses.

■ William Boeing

William Boeing was already rich from lumber when he took up the fledgling "sport" of flying in 1916. That year he founded a small Aero Club in a boathouse on Lake Union, and he and his partner, Navy Lieutenant Conrad Westervelt, built a floatplane here. It lifted off successfully that year, and airplanes became Boeing's—and Seattle's—future. A man of action, Boeing established the Pacific Aero Products Company a month later. With the coming of World War I, he quickly outgrew the Lake Union site and shifted operations to a shipyard he owned on the shores of the Duwamish. Here, in the famous Red Barn factory, William Boeing's company took off, soaring far beyond the predictions of his skeptics. In 1926, after winning a bid for a major airmail contract, he began lobbying city fathers for a true airfield, threatening to move his operations to Los Angeles if his demands weren't met. By then Boeing's company was the area's largest employer, so the city complied, building Boeing Field in south Seattle. Now one of the world's largest aircraft companies and the linchpin of area economy, William Boeing's company and the Boeing name have become synonymous with Seattle.

Gateway to the Future – The early 1960s brought futuristic "progress" to the city with two distinct events: the building of Interstate 5 along the eastern edge of downtown and the opening of Seattle's second World's Fair, Century 21. The effects of the former have been hotly debated since I-5 opened. While it alleviated some of the congestion in downtown streets, it severed off the once fashionable First Hill neighborhood and created a noisy, unattractive river of traffic threading the city. The World's Fair, on the other hand, endowed the city with one of its most treasured attractions—Seattle Center, home of the Space Needle, the Monorail and a wealth of cultural venues still in use, and growing, today.

The wisdom shown in preserving and recycling the fair buildings was not indicative of attitudes of that period. In the mid-1960s, as downtowns nationwide lost business to suburban malls, Seattle's Central Association eyed some of the area's most historic neighborhoods as ripe for urban renewal. Plans were put forth to raze the old buildings of both Pike Place Market and Pioneer Square and replace them with parking garages, high rises and apartment buildings. The proposed redevelopment spurred a sudden preservation consciousness, and grassroots groups quickly formed to protect the historic heart of the city. In 1969 the Pioneer Square area became the city's first designated National Historic District; in 1971, Pike Place Market followed with its own historic designation.

Meanwhile, the central business district continued to puncture the Seattle skyline with new high rises. In 1968, the Seafirst Building surpassed the old 1914 Smith Tower as the tallest building west of the Mississippi. As the latter half of the century unfolded, the city continued to seek a happy medium between continued growth and preservation.

In the last decades of the 20C, Seattle has once again become one of the nation's leading cities—and one of its fastest growing. Now a casually cool style-maker, the once gritty lumber town has given the country a craze for coffee, grunge rock music and youthful entrepreneurism—symbolized by Microsoft co-founder, Bill Gates *(p 405)*. While Boeing has seesawed back and forth between hirings and layoffs in recent years, its status as the area's economic mainstay remains, with Costco, a membership warehouse retailer headquartered here, as number two. Weyerhaeuser holds the number three spot, while number four is occupied by upstart Microsoft. Founded by Bill Gates and Paul Allen in the mid-1980s, the company has become a world-class industrial giant. Microsoft monies shore up not only the local economy, but also local museums, schools and other institutions. In addition, the Port of Seattle continues to

PRACTICAL INFORMATION ... ...Area Code: 206

Getting There

By Air – **Seattle-Tacoma International Airport** (SEA) 13mi south of downtown; serviced by major international and domestic airlines. Information: ☎ 431-4444. Traveler's Aid *(open Mon–Fri 9am–9pm, weekends until 6pm;* ☎ *433-5288)*. Transportation to downtown: GrayLine Airport Express *(daily 5am–midnight; $7.50;* ☎ *626-6088)*; Metro Transit buses *(*☎ *553-3000)* leave from baggage areas. Shuttle Express offers 24-hour van service within Seattle metro area *(by reservation only;* ☎ *622-1424 or 800-487-7433)*. Taxi to downtown *($25)*. Rental car agencies *(p 405)* located at main terminal.

By Train and Bus – Amtrak **train** station: 3rd Ave. S. & S. King St.; reservations ☎ 800-872-7245. Greyhound/Trailways **bus** station: 811 Stewart St.; information ☎ 628-5526; reservations ☎ 800-231-2222.

Getting Around

By Public Transportation – The Seattle Metropolitan Transit System operates **buses** and **trolleys** in the city and suburbs *($1/bus, $1.25/trolley during rush hour; exact change required; transfers valid 2 hrs)*. Metro buses in the downtown area bounded by Jackson St., Battery St., the Waterfront and transit tunnel are free *(6am–7pm)*. A vintage **streetcar** runs along the waterfront from Broad St. to Pioneer Square *(every 20–30min;)*. Day pass *($2)* available on holidays and weekends. Route information: ☎ 553-3000. Downtown's **Westlake Center** *(400 Pine St.)* is connected to Seattle Center via **monorail** *(p 183)*.

© Robert Holmes

By Car – Two interstate highways lead into downtown: I-5 runs north-south from Canada to Portland OR; I-90 traffic flows east-west. Route 520 connects with I-405 crossing Lake Washington. Most avenues run north-south while streets run east-west. Downtown area and its access roads are best avoided during rush hours *(Mon–Fri 6am–9am and 3pm–6pm)*. Downtown metered **parking**: 25¢ for 15min, limit 2 hrs. Parking lots and garages in business district average $3/hr or up to $12/day.

By Ferry – **Washington State Ferries** service the Puget Sound and San Juan Islands offering extended schedules to the commuters and tourists. Walk-on passengers can board up to 5min prior to departure; bicycles and kayaks are permitted on board. On summer weekends expect long waits, especially when bringing a vehicle on board. **Note:** Some routes require 24 hr advance reservations for vehicles; check well in advance, especially when traveling between Memorial Day and Labor Day. Passengers on the Anacortes-Sidney route will be subject to US and/or Canadian Customs and Immigration Service inspection. Not all ferries are wheelchair accessible. Schedules & fares: ☎ 464-6400 or 800-843-3779.

By Taxi – Farwest Taxi ☎ 622-1717; Graytop Cab ☎ 282-8222; Yellow Cab ☎ 622-6500

prosper from its Pacific Rim and Alaska trade, and the city is stretching again toward the waterfront. With the building of two new stadiums (baseball and football) near the **Kingdome**, "SoDo," south of downtown, is fast becoming an enclave for retail businesses and condominiums.

Despite its growth, Seattle still exudes a pioneering hopefulness, a zest for new ideas and innovative approaches, and a surprisingly well-entrenched love of law and order. Their town may now be a big city, but Seattleites maintain a small-town warmth and a welcoming friendliness for all comers.

General Information

Visitor Information – For information and brochures on points of interest, seasonal events, accommodations, shopping, entertainment, recreation and tour operators, contact the **Seattle-King County Convention & Visitors Bureau**, 520 Pike St., Ste. 1300, Seattle WA 98101, ☎ 461-5840, www.seeseattle.org. Or stop by their downtown location at Washington State Convention & Trade Center, 800 Convention Place *(open year-round Mon–Fri 8:30am–5pm, weekends 10am–4pm; closed Jan 1, Thanksgiving Day, Dec 25)*.

Accommodations – Area visitors' guide including lodging directory available *(free)* from Seattle-King County Convention & Visitors Bureau *(above)*. Accommodations range from luxury hotels to modest hotels and motels. Bed-and-breakfast inns can be found in downtown and surrounding neighborhoods. Apartments and condos are also available for rent.

Reservation services: Seattle Supersaver *(☎ 461-5882 or 800-535-7071)* and Pacific Reservation Service *(☎ 784-0539)* offer free bookings *(Mon–Fri 8:30am–5pm)*.

Youth Hostel: Hostelling International, 84 Union St., ☎ 622-5443. There is A 14.2% hotel tax in Seattle.

Local Press – Daily news: *Post Intelligencer (morning)* and *Seattle Times (afternoon)*. Periodicals distributed free: *Seattle Quick Guide* and *Seattle in Your Pocket (monthly)*; *WHERE Seattle* magazine.

Foreign Exchange Office – Thomas Cook Foreign Exchange, 906 Third Ave., ☎ 682-4525; airport location in ticket area *(open daily 6am–8pm; ☎ 248-0401)*.

Sports and Leisure

Sightseeing – CityPass *($23.75, valid for 7 days)*, available from many hotels and participating attractions, offers a savings of 50% off regular admission fees. Take one of the many **walking tours** that highlight the city's history and architecture: See Seattle *(☎ 425-226-7641)*; Seattle Walks & Talks *(☎ 282-2209)*; Scapes Walking Tours *(☎ 517-5432)*. Discover Chinatown on a guided walking tour and savor dim sum for lunch; for reservations, contact Chinatown Discovery, Inc., ☎ 236-0657. Explore the other Seattle with **underground tours** *(daily; $6.50)*; for reservations contact Bill Speidel's Underground Tour, ☎ 682-4646. Enjoy a panoramic view from a **hot-air balloon** *(reservations required)*; Rainbow Balloon Flights ☎ 364-0995.

Harbor cruises, lake and locks cruises by Argosy Cruises *(departs year-round from Pier 55; $13.50-$23; schedules & reservations ☎ 623-4252)*. Explore the sights of Seattle, take a day trip to Victoria or Vancouver, or enjoy an **overnight excursion** to Mount Rainier National Park or the coastal region via GrayLine of Seattle *(☎ 626-5208 or 800-426-7532)* or Victoria Clipper *(☎ 448-5000 or 800-888-2535)*. Visit the San Juan Islands by seaplane and spend the day biking, fishing, sailing or whale-watching *(year-round; 5 flights/day; $112;)*; for reservations, call Kenmore Air ☎ 425-486-1257 or 800-543-9595. Coastal **cruises** from Seattle to the Strait of Georgia include many port towns in the San Juan Islands *(Apr–mid-Oct; 8 days; reservations required; Alaska Sightseeing Cruise West, 4th & Battery Bldg, Ste. 700, Seattle WA 98121, ☎ 206-441-8687 or 800-426-7702)*.

Entertainment – Consult the arts and entertainment section of local newspapers *(Thu & Fri)* for schedules of cultural events and addresses of theaters and concert halls. To purchase tickets, contact the box office or Ticketmaster *(☎ 628-0888)*. **Ticket/Ticket** *(☎ 324-2744)* sells **half-price tickets** *(cash only)* on day of show at outlets located at Broadway Market and Pike Place Market.

Venue	Performances	☎
Charlotte Martin Theater	Seattle Children's Theatre *(Sept–Jun)*	441-3322
Opera House at Seattle Center	Seattle Opera *(Aug–May)*	389-7676
	Pacific Northwest Ballet	441-9411
Benaroya Hall *(p 175)*	Seattle Symphony Orchestra *(Sept–Jun)*	215-4747
Bagley Wright Theatre	Seattle Repertory Theatre, classic and contemporary theater *(Oct–May)*	443-2222
Fifth Avenue Theatre	Fifth Avenue Theatre Company productions, traveling musical and theatrical productions	625-1900 or 625-1418
Paramount Theatre	Best of Broadway shows, national pop music events	682-1414

Spectator Sports – While their new stadium is being built (scheduled for completion in 2002), the **Seattle Seahawks** will play NFL football at the University of Washington *(☎ 425-827-9777)*. The **Seattle Mariners** baseball team *(☎ 346-4000)* plays at Safeco Field. The **Seattle Thunderbirds** *(☎ 448-7825)* play ice hockey and NBA's **Supersonics** *(☎ 281-5800)* play basketball at Key Arena. The **Seattle Sounders** *(☎ 622-3415)* play professional soccer at Renton Memorial Stadium. Emerald Downs offers thoroughbred **horse racing** *(Apr–Sept)*; for racing dates, call ☎ 253-288-7000 or 888-931-8400. Order **tickets**: from Ticketmaster Sportsline *(☎ 622-4487)*.

Shopping – Downtown's Pioneer Square offers a large selection of **antique shops**, fashionable boutiques, **art galleries** and jewelers. Many galleries hold openings on the first Thursday of each month *(5:30pm–8pm)*. Upscale shops are located in **Rainier Square** neighborhood *(on 4th & 5th Aves. between Union & University Sts.)*. **Westlake Center** *(400 Pine St.)* incorporates more than 80 specialty shops. Fifth and Sixth Avenues are lined with specialty stores offering an array of merchandise from fashion to rainwear, and climbing gear to rainwear. Imported goods from Asia can be found in the International and University districts. Seattle's **Pike Place Market** sells fresh produce, seafood, baked goods, flowers and souvenirs. Pike Place merchants will be glad to ship fresh fish home for visitors.

Bellevue Square Mall *(☎ 425-454-8096)*, on Seattle's eastside across Lake Washington, houses over 200 fine shops, cafes, restaurants and department stores. This neighborhood is known for its drive-through **espresso stands** and excellent **ethnic restaurants**. Redmond Town Center *(☎ 867-0808)* houses a unique outdoor shopping mall. More than 50 **outlet stores** are located at Factory Stores of America in North Bend *(☎ 425-888-4505)*.

Recreation – A popular summer activity is **biking** on the Burke-Gilman Trail *(12.5mi)*, along the shore of Lake Washington and Green Lake, or on the Waterfront Park Bike Path. Bike rentals: Al Young Bike & Ski *(☎ 524-2642; $15/day)*; and Greeg's Greenlake Cycle *(☎ 523-1822; $10-$15)*. Take a scenic **hike** along miles of marked trails that lace the national forests; picnic in the park near Snoqualmie Falls; or hike on the beach on Vashon or Bainbridge islands. The many trails in Bridal Trails State Park allow **horseback riding** *(☎ 470-4060)*. Municipal **golf** courses: Jackson Park *(☎ 301-0472)*, Jefferson Park *(☎ 762-4513)*, West Seattle *(☎ 935-5187)*. The Seattle Parks & Recreation Dept. *(☎ 684-4075)* offers information on activities and events.

Water sports abound and many outfitters offer excursions that include sailing, white-water rafting and kayaking. Paddle the waterways near Washington Park Arboretum; canoe rentals available from Waterfront Activities Center *(Feb–Oct; $4/hr; ☎ 543-9433)*. Rent canoes, pedal boats and windsurfing equipment from Green Lake Boat Rentals *(May–Sept; ☎ 527-0171)*; they also offer lessons. For additional information, contact the National Park Service Outdoor Recreation Information Center, 222 Yale Ave. N, ☎ 470-4060. For a listing of outfitters, contact the Seattle-King County Convention & Visitors Bureau *(above)*.

Winter activities include skiing, snowshoeing and sleigh rides.

© Robert Holmes

Useful Numbers

24-hour pharmacy:
Bartell Drugs, 600 1st Ave. N....284-1353 or 54

Chamber of Commerce..389-7200

Dentist Referral...800-336-8478

Doctor Referral 800-362-8677

Weather 526-6087

ADDRESS BOOK

Staying in Seattle

Most of Seattle's accommodations are in and around downtown, convenient to the city's best-known attractions: Pike Place Market, Seattle Center, Pioneer Square and Washington State Ferries. Visitors should reserve well ahead for summer travel.

The accommodations listed below have been chosen for their location, character, or value for money. All venues listed are located in Seattle unless otherwise specified. Rates are for a standard room, double occupancy in high season; some hotels offer lower weekend rates.

$$$$	over $250
$$$	$175-$250
$$	$100-$175
$	under $100

Four Seasons Olympic – *411 University St.* ✗ ♿ 🅿 ☎ *206-621-1700, 800-821-8106. Fax 206-623-2681. www.fshr.com.* **$$$$** Monument-like 1924 Italian Renaissance-style property is Seattle's only true landmark hotel. Grand but understated, its excellent service makes it a favorite of business travelers. 450 rooms.

Alexis Hotel – *1007 1st Ave.* ✗ 🅿 ☎ *206-624-4844 or 800-426-7033. Fax 206-621-9009. www.alexishotel.com.* **$$$** A pioneer in the boutique hotel trend, this lower-downtown inn features quiet charm and personal service. 109 rooms.

Edgewater Inn – *2411 Alaskan Way.* ✗ ♿ 🅿 ☎ *206-728-7000. Fax 206-441-4119. www.noblehousehotels.com.* **$$$** Northwest lodge-style inn on Elliott Bay. 238 rooms.

Mayflower Park Hotel – *405 Olive Way.* ✗ 🅿 ☎ *206-623-8700. Fax 206-382-6996. www.mayflowerpark.com.* **$$$** Boutique 1927 hotel has fine central downtown location for shopping, near Nordstrom and Westlake Center. 173 rooms.

Sorrento Hotel – *900 Madison St.* ✗ ♿ 🅿 ☎ *206-622-6400. Fax 206-343-6155. www.hotelsorrento.com.* **$$$** Elegant small 1908 hotel with a Mediterranean ambience nestled inconspicuously on First Hill just above downtown. 76 rooms.

Woodmark Hotel – *1200 Carillon Pt.* ⚜ ♿ 🅿 ☏ *425-822-3700 or 800-822-3700. Fax 425-822-3699. www.thewoodmark.com.* **$$$** Classy modern property on the east shore of Lake Washington offers great views of Seattle. 100 rooms.

Salish Lodge & Spa – *6501 Railroad Ave. S.E., Snoqualmie WA.* ⚜ ♿ 🅿 ☏ *425-888-2556. Fax 425-888-2420. www.salishlodge.com.* **$$$** Perched on a cliff above Snoqualmie Falls, this romantic countryside getaway offers deluxe accommodations and a restaurant famed for Northwest cuisine and big breakfasts. 91 rooms.

Inn at the Market – *86 Pine St.* ⚜ ♿ 🅿 ☏ *206-443-3600 or 800-446-4484. Fax 206-448-0631. www.innatthemarket.com.* **$$** Small, exclusive hotel with fabulous views of Elliott Bay and the Olympic peninsula, located at Pike Place Market. 65 rooms.

Inn at Queen Anne – *505 1st Ave. N.* ♿ ☏ *206-282-7357 or 800-952-5043. Fax 206-217-9719. www.innatqueenanne.com.* **$$** Ivy-covered 1928-vintage brick apartment building converted to a quiet inn across the street from Seattle Center. Each room has a small kitchenette. Free continental breakfast. 68 rooms.

MV Challenger – *1001 Fairview Ave. N.* 🅿 ☏ *206-340-1201. Fax 206-621-9208. www.vacationspot.com.* **$$** Restored tug and 46ft yacht moored in Lake Union feature 8 cozy cabins and 2 staterooms. Breakfast included.

Pioneer Square Hotel – *77 Yesler Way.* ♿ ☏ *206-340-1234. www.pioneer-square.com.* **$$** Nicely restored 1914 hotel with compact but comfortable rooms and period furnishings. Close to Pioneer Square and the new baseball stadium. 75 rooms.

Ace Hotel – *2423 1st Ave.* ♿ ☏ *206-448-4721. Fax 206-374-0745. www.theacehotel.com.* **$** Hip, sleek new hotel with high-tech amenities in the heart of the Belltown restaurant district. 18 rooms.

Dining in Seattle

Seafood and fresh ingredients epitomize Seattle cuisine. Pioneered in the 1980s as "Northwest contemporary" cooking, the city's style incorporates many Asian and European influences. Although fine restaurants are found throughout the city—and small, neighborhood spots have much to offer—Seattle's highest-profile restaurant district is the hip Belltown area, between downtown and Seattle Center.

The list below represents a sample of some of the city's more popular establishments. Prices indicate the average cost of an entree, an appetizer or dessert, and a beverage for one person (not including tax and tip, or alcoholic beverages). Reservations are highly recommended for $$$ and $$$$ restaurants.

$$$$ = deluxe (over $50)
$$$ = expensive ($30-$50)
$$ = moderate ($15-$30)
$ = inexpensive (under $15)

★★**DOWNTOWN**   *1 day. Map p 174.*

In the last several years Seattle's central city has emerged as one of the most vibrant downtowns in the country. Towering high-rise office buildings house inviting street-level shops, galleries and cafes that keep the district lively even after the business day ends. In the late 1990s, **Nordstrom** *(p 173)*, a traditional downtown landmark made the decision to keep its flagship department store in the city center, further strengthening the area's retail viability.

An eclectic architectural mix, the downtown intersperses newly designed office high rises, such as the 78-story **Columbia Seafirst Tower** *(701 5th Ave.; 73rd-floor observation deck)*—at 943ft the city's tallest building—with preserved architectural gems like the **Fifth Avenue Theatre** *(1308 5th Ave.).* Housed within its sedate Renaissance Revival exterior is a lavishly fantastical rendition of the imperial chambers in Beijing's Forbidden City. Many downtown buildings also celebrate Native American or contemporary visual arts. The public spaces of the **City Centre** *(1420 5th Ave.)* feature an impressive public collection of contemporary glass art by artists affiliated with the Pilchuk Art School founded by Dale Chihuly, whose own works are also prominently featured.

A central gathering place in downtown since 1989, **Westlake Center** *(400 Pine St.)* is a brightly lit arcade of some 80 shops, chain retailers and a food pavilion. The center also serves as the downtown terminus of the **Seattle Monorail** *(p 183).*

Rover's – *2808 E. Madison St., Madison Park.* ♿ 🅿 ☎ *206-325-7442. www.rovers-seattle.com.* **$$$$** **Northwest contemporary**. Effervescent Thierry Rautureau is Seattle's top celebrity chef. Tues–Sat.

Campagne – *86 Pine St., Pike Place Market.* ♿ ☎ *206-728-2800.* **$$$** **Provençale**. Relying on ingredients from neighboring Pike Place Market, Campagne offers sumptuous French cuisine in low-key, refined surroundings. Dinner only. Its downstairs bistro serves three meals a day.

Dahlia Lounge – *1904 4th Ave.* ♿ ☎ *206-682-4142. www.tomdouglas.com.* **$$$ Northwest contemporary**. Chef/owner Tom Douglas pioneered Northwest cuisine; his food is as inventive as ever.

El Gaucho – *2505 1st Ave., Belltown.* ♿ ☎ *206-728-1337. www.elgaucho.com.* **$$$ Supperclub**. High-style dining room is a see-and-be-seen hangout. Adjoining cigar lounge is Seattle's most popular. Dinner only.

Georgian Room – *411 University St., in the Four Seasons Olympic Hotel.* ♿ 🅿 ☎ *206-621-7889.* **$$$ Northwest/Continental**. Sumptuous, elegant surroundings and refined service mark Seattle's renowned high-end dining room. Dinner only. Closed Sun.

Metropolitan Grill – *820 2nd Ave.* ♿ ☎ *206-624-3287.* **$$$ Steakhouse**. Seattle's top expense-account restaurant offers excellent food in a clubby atmosphere. No lunch Sat & Sun.

Ray's Boathouse – *6049 Seaview Ave., Shilshole Bay.* ♿ 🅿 ☎ *206-789-3770. www.rays.com.* **$$$ Seafood**. The view across Puget Sound, especially at sunset, is unsurpassed, and the seafood is great, too.

Space Needle Restaurant – *219 4th Ave. N., Seattle Center; at the top of the Space Needle.* ♿ 🅿 ☎ *206-443-2100. www.spaceneedle.com.* **$$$ Continental**. The 360-degree view is what draws diners here. Good breakfast.

Flying Fish – *2234 1st Ave., Belltown.* ☎ *206-728-8595.* **$$ Seafood**. Innovative chef/owner Christine Keff was the 1999 James Beard Foundation Northwest honoree. Her hugely popular restaurant is one of the centers of the Belltown dining scene. Dinner only.

Ivar's Acres of Clams – *Pier 54, Central Waterfront.* ♿ ☎ *206-624-6852. www.keepclam.com.* **$$ Seafood**. Quirky impresario Ivar Haglund was a quintessential Seattle character; look for the nearby statue of Ivar feeding the gulls. Popular tourist stop.

Wild Ginger – *1400 Western Ave., Pike Place Market.* ♿ ☎ *206-623-4450.* **$$ Asian fusion**. Wildly popular with travelers, celebrities and locals alike, Wild Ginger's ever-excellent food makes it a culinary landmark. No lunch Sun.

Dilettante – *416 Broadway, Capital Hill.* ♿ ☎ *206-329-6463. www.dilettante.com.* **$ Desserts**. Tom Davenport's ancestors made chocolate for the czars; today, his desserts are an incomparable indulgence. They also serve light fare (soups, salads, sandwiches).

Sit & Spin – *2219 4th Ave., Belltown.* ♿ ☎ *206-441-9484.* **$ Diner food**. A hangout for artists and musicians, this hip Belltown eatery/laundromat is a grunge-culture shrine.

❶ Nordstrom

Map p174. Pine St. between 5th and 6th Aves. ☎ *206-628-2111.* When young Swedish immigrant John W. Nordstrom opened a Seattle shoe store in 1901, he could never have imagined what the Nordstrom name would come to symbolize. The roughly 100 Nordstrom stores now operating in more than 20 US states are synonymous with outstanding service and quality fashion; fourth-generation family members are still actively involved in the business. In 1998 the flagship Nordstrom store moved across the street from its longtime location to its current home, the former Frederick & Nelson department store (1918). Nordstrom's extensive renovation of the building returned the façade to its original terra-cotta veneer and restored the marble floors.

With a flair for nostalgic elegance, Nordstrom welcomes its visitors with a liveried doorman at the Pine Street entrance. Throughout the store, glass cases display the store's **shoe collection** spanning a century of foot fashion.

Seattle Architectural Foundation Gallery – *1333 5th Ave., Level 3. Open year-round Mon–Fri 10am–4pm. Closed major holidays. ♿ ☐ ☎ 206-667-9184.* Housed among the lower-level atrium shops of Rainier Square, the foundation's small museum highlights a hundred years of the city's architectural history. The spaces that residents used for work and commerce, social and recreational pursuits, learning and enlightenment, and personal and family endeavors are depicted through historic photographs, blueprints, building models and furniture. The foundation also offers guided walking tours "celebrating the contributions of architecture and urban design." Tours sometimes focus on a single building or design firm, at other times on a historic commercial district or residential neighborhood. *Call for tour schedules and topics.*

SEATTLE

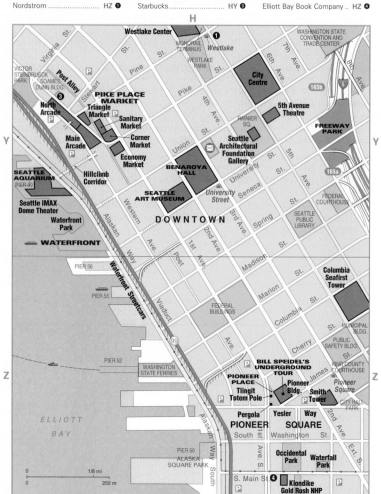

★ **Freeway Park** – *6th Ave. and Seneca St.* The rift across northern downtown caused by the construction of I-5 was at least partially healed by the establishment of this park in 1976. Designed by Lawrence Halprin and Angela Danadjieva, the five-acre oasis bridges the canyon created by the freeway and reconnects downtown with First Hill. Greenery, plazas for outdoor concerts, ponds, plantings of flowers and a series of soothing water cascades create an atmosphere in contrast to the high speed of the interstate.

★★ **Seattle Art Museum** – *1st and 2nd Aves. at University St. Open year-round Tue–Sun 10am–5pm (Thu 9pm). Closed Jan 1, Thanksgiving Day, Dec 25. $7.* ✗ ♿ ☎ *206-654-3100. www.seattleartmuseum.org.* In 1991, the Seattle Art Museum (SAM) moved much of its collection from its original home in Volunteer Park to this new downtown building. Philadelphia architect Robert Venturi's design for the downtown facility juxtaposes a lower-level facade of granite, marble and colored terra-cotta with an upper facade of smooth fluted limestone curves. Fronting the entrance is the 48ft-tall mechanical **Hammering Man** by Connecticut sculptor Jonathan Borofsky. The museum's permanent collection includes some 21,000 paintings, artifacts and works on paper.

Visit – *3 hrs.* The two entrances on First and Second Avenues are connected by a grand stairway, with monumental Ming Dynasty sculptures guarding the landings. The exhibit galleries begin on the second floor, where space is devoted to traveling and special exhibits. On the third floor you'll find rotating pieces from the museum's extensive collection of non-Western art. A strong **Asian art**★ collection features works from Korea, Japan and China, including porcelains, carved screens, textiles and Buddhist figures. A re-created **Chinese Scholar's Studio** captures the aesthetics of a 17C Ming Dynasty man of letters, depicting his interests in calligraphy, poetry and music. **African art**★ has a strong representation in wood sculpture and ceremonial masks and headdresses, while **Pacific art** encompasses weavings and native paintings from Australia, Oceania and Indonesia. **Northwest Coast** art and artifacts include wood and stone sculptures, masks, buttonwork, basketry and 14ft red-cedar carved house posts from British Columbia. Glass, textiles, Persian miniatures and pottery are the focus of **Near Eastern art**.

The fourth-floor galleries are devoted to the full span of **Western art**, displaying varying pieces from the permanent collection. **Ancient Mediterranean** strengths include pottery and coins; **Medieval and Renaissance** religious works include *The Judgement of Paris* (1518-18) by Lucas Cranach the Elder. The **Baroque** collection is notable for Peter Paul Rubens' *Last Supper* and a Van Dyck portrait of *Pompone II de Bellièvre*. The **18C** gallery often displays European porcelain, Italian glass, American silver and furniture. The **19C** collection includes portraiture, and the **20C** galleries exhibit contemporary art, both domestic and international, including Jackson Pollock's large canvas entitled *Sea Change*.

★★ **Benaroya Hall** – *3rd Ave. between University and Union Sts. Visit by guided tour (1 hr) year-round Thu 1pm–5pm, Fri 10am–2pm, first Sat of the month 10am–4pm.* ✗ ♿ 🅿 ☎ *206-215-4800. www.seattlesymphony.org. For ticket information, see p 170.* The new home of the Seattle Symphony, this state-of-the-art performance hall opened in 1998. Occupying an entire block in the middle of downtown, it features a circular window façade that achieves the effect of a giant chandelier when lit at night. Built mostly from private funds but owned by the City of Seattle, the hall is named in honor of its two most generous benefactors—Rebecca and Jack Benaroya, self-made business-park developers and personal friends of symphony conductor Gerard Schwarz. The hall's two performance spaces—the 2,502-seat Taper Auditorium and a more intimate 541-seat Nordstrom Recital Hall—have received acclaim for their acoustical qualities and their comfort, both of which far surpass those of the symphony's former home at the Seattle Center. The glass-enclosed Boeing Company Gallery links the two auditoriums and is anchored by 20ft **Dale Chihuly chandeliers**★, best appreciated at night when their tumble of blown-glass shapes shimmer in the light. Also featured is a massive art mélange entitled **Echo**, by Robert Rauschenberg—nine panels depicting pastoral, urban and musical topics.

② REI

Map p 185. 222 Yale Ave.N. ☎ *206-223-1944.* The small Recreational Equipment Inc. founded in 1938 by a group of regional mountaineers is now a nationwide retail co-op frequented by a loyal clientele of outdoors enthusiasts. REI's new flagship store offers much more than a retail experience. Sitting on two acres landscaped with a waterfall and pond and threaded by trails, the 80,000sq ft facility simulates the atmosphere of a mountain lodge with stone fireplaces, high ceilings and even a kids' camp that simulates a Northwest forest. A glass tower encloses A 65ft climbing pinnacle, where both experienced climbers and novices can test their abilities (with supervision).

Additional Sight *Map p 185.*

★★**Frye Art Museum** – *704 Terry Ave. at Cherry St. Open year-round Tue–Sat 10am–5pm (Thu 9pm), Sun noon–5pm. Closed Jan 1, Thanksgiving Day, Dec 25.* ✗ ♿ 🅿 ☏ *206-622-9250. www.fryeart.org.* A small jewel set amid the streets of First Hill, the newly expanded museum showcases 19C and 20C realist works by American and European artists. The galleries, lit by natural light, offer an intimately appealing space for the quiet appreciation of art.

The museum exists through the bequest of Charles and Emma Frye, who moved to Seattle in the 1880s. The Frye-Bruhn meatpacking company, of which Charles was a founder, prospered dramatically, and in 1893, the Fryes purchased their first painting. In the coming decades, the couple became serious collectors of realist art, traveling to the East Coast and to Europe to purchase paintings. Both of German extraction, the Fryes were particularly drawn to the works of German artists, and avidly acquired pieces by Munich Secession School painters. Their large First Hill mansion soon took on the appearance of an art salon, with skylights providing natural illumination. At Charles Frye's death in 1940, the collection along with his fortune went to the creation of a free public museum of art. Opened in 1952, the original museum building recently underwent an expansion and renovation. The current structure, completed in 1997, includes workshop studios, a museum store and auditorium.

The museum's permanent collection comprises 232 19C and 20C American, German and French representational paintings, including the most complete collection of Munich School paintings in the US. American artists represented in the rotating collection include Albert Bierstadt, Winslow Homer, John Singer Sargent, Thomas Eakins and John Singleton Copley. Paintings from the Munich School collection are permanently exhibited in the museum's **Frye Galleries**. Painters of this school, active in the Bohemian capital in the late 19C and early 20C, were renowned for their unromanticized portraiture. The works of such prominent artists in the movement as Franz Seraph von Lenbach and Franz von Stuck are well represented. In the **Viewpoints and Graphics Galleries**, the museum focuses on the works of contemporary or regional realists or on theme-oriented works from the permanent collection. The **Greathouse Galleries** are devoted to national and international touring exhibitions.

★★★PIKE PLACE MARKET *1 1/2 days. Map p 174.*

Information booth located at 1st Ave. and Pike St. Open year-round Mon–Sat 9am–6pm, weekends 11am–5pm. Closed Jan 1, Easter Sunday, Thanksgiving Day, Dec 25. ✗ 🅿 ☏ *206-682-7453. www.pikeplacemarket.org.*

Distilling the essence of Seattle, this "public market center," as its landmark neon sign proclaims it, has been a revered city institution for most of the 20C. Funky, feisty and infinitely appealing, the market has maintained its salty egalitarianism despite the gentrification of the rest of the city. Its abundance of farm-fresh

Pike Place Market

vegetables, seafood and flowers dazzle the eye and have tempted many a traveler to cart bags of market produce aboard home-bound planes as they depart the city.

Pike Place got its start in 1907, when Seattle decided to host an open-air market that would enable farmers to sell their produce directly to consumers without sharing profits with middlemen. Farmers were invited to bring their wagons to the market site on August 17, 1907, the opening day. Though only a few wagons showed up, thousands of eager shoppers thronged the market site. By the next market day, the farmers, too, were there in force. Within the year, the market had such a following that real-estate speculator and visionary, Frank Goodwin, recently returned from the Klondike with gold to invest, created a market syndicate and built an arcade to shelter buyers and sellers from capricious Seattle weather. Gradually, fishmongers and butchers added their wares to the bounty, and Goodwin took over nearby structures and built more to accommodate the market's monumental growth. In 1925 he sold his Pike Place interests to his nephew, Arthur Goodwin. In the coming Depression, the new Goodwin owner found himself in financial straits, and controlling interest in the marketplace was gradually acquired by Joe Desimone, an Italian immigrant whose success as a farmer had led him into real estate.

Despite depressions, wars and urban flight, the market survived its first half-century, welcoming respectable housewives and street people alike. Then in the early 1960s, urban renewal advocates eyed the rundown market buildings, still owned by the Desimone family, and began to press for demolition. Seattleites responded overwhelmingly in 1971, voting for a public initiative to preserve the market and surrounding blocks as a historical

③ Starbucks

Map p 174. Pike Pl. and Stewart St. ☎ *206-448-8762.* The modest but cozy little store where cafe giant Starbucks got its start still does business at 1912 Pike Place. Crowds queue up on its polished plank floors on weekends for one of its famous lattés or espressos. Locals opened the store in 1971, then four years later hired Howard Schultz to direct their retail and marketing operations. In 1976 Schultz returned from a trip to Milan, determined to make espresso bars the kind of corner establishment they were in Italy. In the last two decades, he has succeeded. Now chairman and CEO, as well as the founder of the Starbucks Corporation, Schultz oversees an empire of 28,000 employees in some 1,900 locations from Seattle to the eastern US and from Asia to the UK. A staggering seven million customers a day visit Starbucks cafes, buying everything from a fresh-brewed latté to a pound of Arabica beans to Starbucks coffee mugs.

district. Now, a nine-acre swath and a collection of a dozen buildings are protected in a national historic district that extends from First to Western Avenues and from Pike to Virginia Streets. Hundreds of food vendors, eateries and small shops line the boisterous, crowded streets. But the district is more than a marketplace. Since the mid-1970s, the nonprofit Market Foundation has helped fund social-service centers and low-income housing within the historic district. In mid-century, artist Mark Tobey, a great champion of the market and painter of its scenes, called Pike Place "a most human growth, the heart and soul of Seattle." So it remains today.

© Robert Holmes

Main Arcade – *Pike Pl. between Pike and Stewart Sts.* Heart of the market area, this is the original building designed and built by Frank Goodwin, and rehabilitated in a massive project headed up by Seattle architect George Bartholick in 1978. The neon Depression-era Public Market Center sign and clock above the northeast entrance have long been a popular meeting place for market visitors. Guarding this entrance to the market is a relatively new landmark, Rachel, a life-size bronze pig (and piggy bank) sculpted by Georgia Gerber and placed here in 1986. Donations to Rachel net the Market Foundation several thousand dollars annually. Inside the arcade, the street-level stalls are vibrant with seasonal vegetables, stands of fresh and dried flower bouquets, and fish shops where fresh salmon, halibut and Dungeness crabs glisten in beds of ice. A crowd usually collects around Pike Place Fish, where mongers provide endless entertainment by loudly hawking their wares and throwing sizable whole fish to each other over customers' heads.

The two lower levels of the main arcade, known as **Down Under**, have a labyrinth of more traditional shops and small restaurants, most devoted to seafood.

The adjacent **North Arcade**, built in 1922 in response to demand for more market space, houses some 200 vendors, from farmers offering local honeys, jams and specialty foods to craftspeople. The latter are particularly in evidence on weekends, selling an imaginative array of handmade clothing, jewelry, leatherwork and general Northwest exotica.

Post Alley – *Pike to Virginia Sts. between Pike Pl. and 1st Ave.* Separating the **Corner Market** (1912) and **Triangle Market** (1908) buildings, picturesque Post Alley is a Europeanesque pedestrian walkway lined with shops and eateries. At its north-west corner, the Soames-Dunn Building combines two historic structures, the Soames Paper Company and the Dunn Seed Building, into a renovated home for scores of restaurants and shops. Predating the Main Arcade building by seven years, the **Economy Market** building *(Pike St. and 1st Ave.)* was leased by Frank Goodwin in 1916 and turned into another market structure. Across Pike Street is another vintage market building, the **Sanitary Market** (1910), so named because it prohibited horses and other livestock within its halls.

THE CENTRAL WATERFRONT *Map p 174.*

Once a working port area where a century ago the small ferries of the Mosquito Fleet put in, the Elliott Bay shoreline at the foot of downtown has become a long, continuous festival marketplace, the old pier sites along Alaskan Way now home to endless pubs, hotels, eateries, cafes and several serious tourist attractions. Harbor cruise ships dock at Pier 56 and at Piers 90 and 91, at the northern end of the waterfront. At the southern end, Piers 50-52 serve as terminals for busy Washington State Ferries, which link Seattle with Bremerton on the Olympic Peninsula, and with Bainbridge and Vashon Islands. Pier 58, now demolished, was the site of Schwabacher's Wharf, where in 1897, the S.S. *Portland* steamed into port with two tons of Klondike gold onboard. In 1974 city planners tore down the pier, but the hole it left, as well as adjacent Pier 59, became part of **Waterfront Park**. Its boardwalk and raised walkways offer views of the city and the bay. Proposed redesigns of this area of the waterfront have been circulating for several years and reconfigurations could occur early in the coming century.

Built into the steep hill that ascends from the waterfront to Pike Place Market, the series of 169 stairs called **Hillclimb Corridor** allows pedestrians to huff back and forth between the market and Waterfront Park (an elevator helps out along one leg of the journey). The well-landscaped stairs, built in 1973, replaced A 1912 wooden overpass that allowed pedestrian access to the waterfront. Shopkeepers have taken advantage of the hillside location (hillclimbers need to rest now and then) by flanking the steps with shops and cafes.

★ **Seattle Aquarium** – Kids *Pier 59. Open Memorial Day–Labor Day daily 10am–7pm. Rest of the year daily 10am–5pm. $8.25, children $5.50.* & ☎ *206-386-4320. www.seattleaquarium.org.* Some 380 species of fish, birds, plants, marine inver-tebrates and mammals are housed in this city-run aquarium's two buildings. In the first building a tunnel-like walkway leads through the world of a **Pacific Coral Reef**, where sharks cruise and colorful tropical fish flutter amid the coral. In the **Discovery Lab**, visitors can touch marine critters before moving on to tanks filled with such local invertebrates as geoduck (pronounced GOO-ee-duck), anemones, crabs, sea stars, nudibranchs and octopus. In the **Principles of Survival** section, creatures like lungfish, seahorses and an electric eel are highlighted for their distinctive adaptive features.

The second building, cantilevered above the waters of Elliott Bay, houses a net-roofed, **Northwest Shores** re-creation, with such shorebirds as ruddy ducks, puffins, godwits and guillemots in residence, and a tide pool with sea stars, urchins and limpets. A salmon hatchery and ladder are actually used to release salmon fry into the waters of Puget Sound; adult fish return here to breed. In the **marine mammal tanks**, harbor seals, northern fur seals and sea otters cavort. The aquarium's most recent addition, **Sound to Mountains: A Watershed Journey**, takes visitors from mountain watersheds downstream to the sound. On the lower level, an underwater viewing area gives a submarine glimpse of the marine mammal tank.

Seattle IMAX Dome Theater – Kids *Pier 59. Open May–Oct daily 10am–9pm. Rest of the year daily 10am–7pm. Closed Dec 25. $6.95.* ✗ & ☎ *206-622-1868.* Featuring a domed overhead screen, six "surround-sound" speakers and reclining seats, this theater offers a changing series of movies that generally celebrate the wilderness, whales and other natural subjects. A mainstay is *The Eruption of Mount St. Helens (30min).*

★★ Odyssey: The Maritime Discovery Center

★★ Odyssey: The Maritime Discovery Center – Kids *Map p. 184. Pier 66. Open year-round daily 10am–5pm. $6.50.* ✗ ♿ ☎ *206-374-4000. www.ody.org.* An innovative new addition to the Seattle waterfront rises in glass-walled modernism on the newly renovated Bell Street Pier (Pier 66), at the northern end of the waterfront. A non-profit museum funded by private and public monies, Odyssey offers a wide range of imaginative hands-on exhibits that explore Seattle's maritime life. The **Ocean Trade Gallery** traces the connection between Puget Sound and markets worldwide. Visitors can try their skill at working a simulated loading crane, operating a remote-control tug and pedaling a propeller; and they can learn what a Plimsoll line is or the route taken by cargo from the interior US to the Port of Seattle. **Sharing the Sound** explores the many things that Puget Sound means to the many people using it. Here, visitors paddle a simulated kayak or try to dock an 850ft tanker. They also learn how the National Oceanic and Atmospheric Agency maps the sound and what environmental and safety issues affect these waters and their users. The lives and skills of salmon fishermen, clammers and the snowcrabbers that work the treacherous waters of the Bering Sea are highlighted in the **Harvesting the Sea** section of the museum. On decks outside, visitors may watch Russian and other fishing vessels that often dock here; information boards provide interesting facts.

Waterfront Streetcars – *Cars run every 20min; transfers allowing passengers to re-board are good for 90mi;* $1 In 1982, a city councilman revived the romantic age of the streetcar by importing two vintage Australian models dating to the late 1920s. Since then, these elegant renditions, of white ash and Tasmanian mahogany, have been joined by three more streetcars. The cars trundle along the waterfront, from Pier 70 to Pier 48 at Main Street, where they turn inland and continue through Pioneer Square to the International District.

■ Cruising Seattle

In Seattle you're almost never out of sight of water. For those seeking a water's-eye view of the city, a number of cruises offer tours of the city's waterways:

Harbor Cruise – *1 hr. Argosy Cruises, Pier 55.* ☎ *206-623-4252.* This narrated cruise takes in the shoreline of Elliott Bay from Piers 90 and 91 south to the Duwamish Waterway.

Locks Cruise – *2.5 hrs. Argosy Cruises, Pier 57.* ☎ *206-623-4252.* A narrated cruise plies the northern end of Elliott Bay, then through the Hiram Chittenden Locks and the Lake Washington Ship Canal to Lake Union. Passengers disembark here and travel overland back to the Seattle waterfront.

Lake Cruise – *2 hrs. Argosy Cruises, Lake Union's AGC Marina Dock E (1200 Westlake Ave.).* ☎ *206-623-4252.* Leaving from the south end of Lake Union and passing the lake's famed houseboat district on the way to Lake Washington, the narrated cruise crosses the lake to its eastern shore at Evergreen Point, and returns along the same route.

Cruise to Tillicum Village, Blake Island *(p 198).*

★PIONEER SQUARE   *1/2 day. Map p 174.*

The city's first permanent settlement, the Pioneer Square neighborhood retains the nostalgic appeal of an older, less refined Seattle. Tracing its roots to the mid-19C logging days, the roughly 18-block area is still cut by the long downhill incline of **Yesler Way**—the original "skid road," where logs were slid downhill to Mayor Henry Yesler's sawmill. After the Great Seattle Fire of 1889 destroyed the original buildings here, the rebuilt neighborhood became a jumping-off point for fortune seekers caught up in the 1897 Klondike Gold Rush. In this century, as the town pushed inland and to the north, Pioneer Square lapsed into a neglected "skid row" notorious for its houses of prostitution and gambling. After the Seattle earthquake of 1949 demolished many of the old buildings, little was done to reconstruct the area until preservationists became interested in its historic worth in the 1960s. In 1969, a 30-acre National Historic District was established to preserve the Victorian buildings and character of Pioneer Square. Today, its venerable structures house galleries and restaurants; in its parks and squares, street people now lounge side-by-side with young professionals. **Occidental Park** *(Between S. Washington and S. Main Sts. above 1st Ave.)* is notable for its totem poles, while the semi-enclosed **Waterfall Park** *(2nd Ave. and S. Main St.),* which commemorates the site where United Parcel Service began, offers a quiet corner to contemplate a series of low

Pioneer Square

cascades set amid green landscaping. The circular **Kingdome** stood at the southeast edge of Pioneer Square from 1976 to 2000, when it was imploded. Covering seven acres, the Kingdome boasted the world's largest single-span roof, measuring 650ft in diameter. A new stadium for the Seattle Seahawks is scheduled to open on the site in 2002. A new exhibition center adjacent to the Kingdome site hosts ongoing consumer shows, and the Seattle Mariners play baseball in **Safeco Field**, which opened in July of 1999 just south of the old Kingdome.

★★ **Pioneer Place** – *1st Ave. and Yesler Way.* At the site of the city's first intersection, this brick-paved triangle holds two neighborhood landmarks: the wrought-iron **Pergola** erected in 1909 to shield streetcar and cable-car passengers from the weather, and a Tlingit **totem pole** commissioned in the late 1930s to replace an earlier one destroyed by an arsonist. Fronting the square is the much photographed **Pioneer Building** *(610 1st Ave).* Commissioned by Henry Yesler after the Great Seattle Fire of 1889 and built on the site of his first Seattle home, the six-story Victorian Romanesque Revival building, with its heavy ashlar entryway, was long a city centerpiece. After its completion in 1892, the American Institute of Architects called it "the finest building west of Chicago."

★ **Bill Speidel's Underground Tour** – *Begins at Doc Maynard's Public House in the Pioneer Bldg. on Pioneer Place. Visit by guided tour (90min) only, year-round daily 10am–5pm every hour; additional tours during Jun–Aug. $8. ☎ 206-682-4646. Undergroundtour.com.* A ribald recounting of Pioneer Square's history makes for an entertaining and informative introduction to downtown. Groups are taken down to the original street levels, 8-35ft below today's streets. After the Great Seattle Fire in 1889, the street level was rebuilt on top of the rubble, in part to allow underground space for the sewage system. Here, storefronts that that have been abandoned since that time can still be seen, giving tour participants a sense of life in Seattle from the mid-19C to the Prohibition era. Among the deserted establishments covered on the tour are remnants of brothels, small shops, a dance hall and a large emporium. The 90min tour ends in Bill Speidel's **museum**, where artifacts and photographs trace the history of Seattle.

(4) Elliott Bay Book Company

Map p 174. 101 S. Main St. ☎ 206-624-6600. Packed with floor-to-ceiling books, this family-run store has operated since 1973, offering a refreshing contrast to the modern mega-chain bookstores. Its exposed brick walls, cedar shelves and pleasant cafe create an inviting setting for book lovers and browsers, and its 150,000 titles cover topics from accounting and applied art to occult studies and espionage.

Klondike Gold Rush National Historical Park – *117 S. Main St. Open year-round daily 9am–5pm. Closed Jan 1, Thanksgiving Day, Dec 25. & ☎ 206-553-7220. www.nps.gov/klse/home.html.* The small National Park Service museum here—the Seattle unit of the national park in Alaska—houses artifacts and historic photographs detailing the Klondike gold rush and its impact on the city of Seattle. Seattleites first heard of the Klondike strike on July 17, 1897, when the steamship *Portland* arrived in town from Alaska, carrying men hefting sacks of gold. Overnight, the city was struck with gold fever, and many residents quit their jobs to get rich quick in the northern hinterlands. At the same time, Seattle merchants got rich themselves by outfitting the prospectors. Two park service audiovisual presentations—*Days of Adventure, Dreams of Gold (27min)* and *Seattle: Gateway to the Goldrush (15min)*—convey the excitement and hardships of those heady days.

Smith Tower – *2nd Ave. and Yesler Way.* ☎ *206-682-9393.* Anchoring the northest corner of Pioneer Square since 1914, the white, 42-story, 522ft Smith Tower ranked as the tallest building west of the Mississippi for almost half a century. Lyman C. Smith, the Smith-Corona typewriter tycoon, commissioned the terra-cotta facaded, steel building as an office headquarters. Though many other city buildings now rise above it, the Smith Tower is still remarkable for its small but ornate lobby, whose eight brass-ornamented elevator cages are overlooked by sculptures of Indian heads.

International District – *Map p. 185. 4 blocks south of Pioneer Square.* The heart of this compact multi-ethnic district centers around South Jackson Street, between Fifth and Sixth Avenues. Traditionally home to the Chinese and Japanese populations that have been a mainstay of the city for more than a century, the current International District is still predominantly Chinese in character, with other Asian and African-American restaurants and businesses now represented as well. A hub of activity here is the ever popular **Uwajimaya** *(6th Ave. S. and S. Weller St.)*, a cavernous emporium selling Asian foodstuffs, curios, clothing and books, as well as fresh Northwest produce. The Moriguchi family has operated the store since 1928, moving to this location in 1970. A block away small **Hing Hay Park** *(Maynard Ave. S and S. King St.)* holds a Chinese pavilion constructed in Taipei and presented as a gift by the people of Taiwan.

■ Caffeine Capital

Seattleites claim that the area's long, rainy winters are responsible for their love affair with coffee. Be that as it may, a fresh-brewed latté, espresso or plain old coffee is always within reach—even at drive-in cafes. The small, neighborhood coffeehouse has become an institution here in the last decade, and most Seattleites would admit it was Starbucks that started the trend. Ironically, though, the independent city spirit has given rise to an upsurge of resentment against the coffee giant, and many locals now prefer to patronize the many other coffee chains that have locations around the city. Any visitor who wants to appreciate Seattle life at its relaxed best should seek out a neighborhood coffeehouse, settle back with a newspaper or a book, and sip an aromatic cup of:

© Robert Holmes

Espresso – a thick, strong shot of caffeine, served in demitasse quantities

Latté – a frothy version of espresso spiked with steamed milk

Cappuccino – like a latté but frothier, with twice as much foam on top

Mocha – another espresso-based concoction, with mocha flavoring and a whipped cream-cocoa powder topping

Americano – a watered-down version of espresso that feels like the classic, American-style "cuppa Joe"

Chai latté – spicy black Indian tea made with steamed milk

★**Wing Luke Asian Museum** – *Map p. 185. 407 7th Ave. S. Open year-round Tue–Fri 11am–4:30pm, weekends noon–4pm. $2.50.* ⚐ ☎ *206-623-5124. www.wingluke.org.* This museum is devoted to the history and culture of the Chinese, Japanese, Filipino, Southeast Asian and Pacific Island immigrants who have settled in America. Its permanent exhibit, "The Asian Pacific American Experience," traces their contributions to agriculture, canning, fishing, mining and other industries, as well as detailing family traditions, celebrations and other distinctive aspects that make each of these cultures unique. The museum's namesake, Wing Luke, became the first Asian-American elected to office in the continental US when he won a seat on the Seattle City Council in 1962. His vision of strong community involvement and pride remains a hallmark of the museum.

★★**SEATTLE CENTER AREA** *1 day. Map pp 184-185.*

The high hopes that the city of Seattle periodically had for this area at the northwestern edge of downtown were a long time in coming to fruition, and even today, the potential of the old Belltown neighborhood remains unrealized. But the full potential of the area northwest of it has been more than amply realized by Seattle Center, site of the 1962 World's Fair. A museum, sports and performing-arts mecca for the city, the center is lively with school children during the day, and with sports, theater– and concert-goers well into the night.

Belltown

The early 19C claimants to this part of Seattle bordered by Pine Street, Westlake Avenue and Denny Way were city father Arthur Denny and William Bell, a short-lived pioneer who had left the city by the 1850s. Throughout the late 19C, Denny Hill stood precipitously at the northern edge of downtown, thwarting any serious city expansion to the north. Finally, in the early years of the 20C, Seattle's Scotch-Irish city engineer, R.H. Thomson, took on the hill as his mission. By 1911, much of it had been leveled into the "Denny Regrade," a term now often used interchangeably with Belltown. The few stubborn property owners who refused to move were left with unreachable homes on mounds 100ft above the hosed-away earth; steam shovels later leveled them. Architect Virgil Bogue's ambitious plan to ornament the newly flattened real estate with a Civic Center and a cluster of Beaux-Arts government buildings failed with voters in 1912, and the area never attracted any serious development. The inexpensive land here gradually became taken up with working-class neighborhoods, warehouses and apartment buildings. In recent decades, Belltown has developed a bohemian reputation, with bookstores, secondhand shops and alternative galleries. In the last several years the area, particularly along Second Avenue, has become a popular night spot, with a number of restaurants, live-music clubs and bars along First and Second Avenues.

> **Belltown Nightlife**
>
> **Crocodile Cafe** – *2200 2nd Ave.* ☎ *206-441-5611.* One of the birthplaces of grunge, this trendy rock club attracts a young audience willing to stand while they listen to some of the region's hottest young performers.
>
> **Lava Lounge** – *2226 2nd Ave.* ☎ *206-441-5660.* The cushy red booths here quickly fill with a hip young crowd on weekends, come to take in the city's rising stars. Live music includes surf bands, jazz and local rock.
>
> **Jewelbox Theater** – *In the rear of the Rendezvous bar, 2320 2nd Ave.* ☎ *206-441-5823.* A shabby charm gives this live-music bar its enduring appeal.

★★★Seattle Center

With more than a dozen structures—from theaters and museums and to an amusement park and sports arena, the 74-acre "campus" of the Seattle Center is bordered by Denny Way, Broad Street, Fifth Avenue, Mercer Street and First Avenue. This entertainment hub for the upper Northwest draws over nine million visitors a year. *For a recorded schedule of daily and weekly events, call* ☎ *206-684-8582 or www.seattlecenter.com.*

The so-called Potlatch Meadows of early Seattle, traditionally used by the Indians as a hunting ground, were slow to develop, but by 1928 the city had erected a Civic Auditorium here. In the next two decades, an ice arena, an athletic field, an armory and Memorial Stadium followed. These large public gathering places made the area a natural choice for the site of the 1962 Seattle World's Fair.

Called the Century 21 Exposition, the fair took modernism as its theme and such futuristic landmarks as the Monorail and Space Needle added atmospherics to the site. Along with the construction of new fair buildings, such as a state-constructed coliseum (now the Key Arena) and a federally built pavilion (now the Pacific Science Center), several of the existing buildings were transformed and renamed. The remodeled Civic Auditorium became the Opera House and the armory was converted to a "food circus." During its six-month life (April 21 to October 21), the Century 21 Exposition was visited by 10 million fairgoers.

At fair's end, many of the buildings, as had been intended, were put to good use as permanent city facilities. The recent wave of money that has washed over the city has helped the center as well, and in the mid-1990s, a number of its buildings were renovated and modernized; a **sculpture garden** and **Peace Garden** (both adjacent to the Space Needle) were added to the center's 20 acres of landscaped grounds. The rough edges of the **International Fountain**, considered something of an eyesore by many, have been smoothed out and a sound-and-light system now makes the fountain a showy nighttime feature of the center. The nostalgic, child-oriented rides of the **Fun Forest Amusement Park** [Kids] also received a boost, with the addition of teen thrillers like the Windstorm roller coaster.

In mid-2000, the new **Experience Music Project** is scheduled to open on the Seattle Center campus. Housed in a psychedelically colored 140,000sq ft building, designed to look like a smashed guitar, the museum is dedicated to "celebrating and exploring creativity and innovation in rock `n roll and other forms of American popular music." The museum will feature interactive exhibits, a ride called Artist's Journey and live music performances.

★★**Space Needle** – [Kids] *Southeast corner of Seattle Center. Open Memorial Day–Labor Day daily 8am–midnight. Rest of the year Sun–Thu 9am–11pm, Fri–Sat 9am–midnight. $9. ✕ ⅋ ⓟ ☎ 206-443-2100 or 800-937-9582. www.spaceneedle.com.* Seattle's signature landmark, the Space Needle embodies A 1960s vision of the future brought to fruition by World's Fair architects Victor Steinbrueck and John Graham, Jr. A graceful metal tripod rising 602ft is topped by a revolving, two-story flying saucer-like observation room and restaurant. Anchoring the precarious structure to earth was no small feat and required burrowing foundations 30ft deep and pouring almost 6,000 tons of concrete. As its designers intended, the needle sways in the wind 1in for every 10mph—and was built to withstand hurricane-force winds of up to 150mph.

Glass-walled elevators whoosh guests to the observation level in just 43 seconds. From this 520ft vantage, panoramic **views**★★ of the city (south/east), Elliott Bay and the Olympic Mountains (southwest/west), and Lake Washington and the Cascade Mountains (east) spread below, weather permitting.

★★**Monorail** – *Entrance north of the Space Needle. Departs every 15min Memorial Day–Labor Day daily 9am–midnight. Rest of the year Mon–Fri 7:30am–11pm, weekends 9am–11pm; $1.25. ☎ 206-441-6038.* Designed by the Swedish firm Alweg Systems for the World's Fair, the two sleek, almost silent, elevated trains of the Monorail travel the 1.3mi between Seattle Center and downtown's Westlake Center in under 2min. Some 7,000 passengers a day take advantage of this easy link between downtown and the center. Elvis Presley gave the monorail lasting fame in his early-1960s movie, *It Happened at the World's Fair.*

★★**Pacific Science Center** – [Kids] *South end of Seattle Center, entrance on Denny Way. Open mid-Jun–Labor Day daily 10am–6pm. Rest of the year Mon–Fri 10am–5pm, weekends 10am–6pm. Closed Thanksgiving Day & Dec 25. $7.50. ✕ ⅋ ⓟ ☎ 206-443-2001. www.pacsci.org.* Built as the US pavilion for the World's Fair, the striking complex is fronted by arches that sweep up in airborne splendor. The U-shaped center has six interconnected buildings surrounding a fountained central pavilion. A non-profit foundation now operates the center, with generous support from such Seattle corporate behemoths as Boeing and Microsoft. State-of-the-art interactive exhibits entice children of all ages. A **Laser Theater** features shows for families during the day and laser-light shows set to rock and pop music at night. In the new **Boeing IMAX Theater** large-format films are shown on a screen six stories high and 80ft wide.

Visit – *3 hrs.* Begin on the lower level with a **Science Playground** aimed at older children and technologically curious adults. Featured here are a gigantic interactive lever, a pitching cage, pulleys, gears and a Probability Machine.

Upstairs follow the exhibits clockwise through the interconnected exhibit buildings. A large, state-of-the-art **Tech Zone**★★ offers computers where visitors can compose music or create art; a place to play virtual baseball or try virtual hang gliding; and A 10ft-tall robot ready to take on all comers in tic-tac-toe. **Body Works** is a colorful, action-packed gallery where visitors can test their own bodies' abilities, from their strength to their hearing range to their vision and lung capacity. In the **Willard Smith Planetarium** a changing series of shows are featured daily. **Kids Work** offers school-age children and toddlers a chance to explore waterpower, create music (in a soundproof room), catch their shadow on the "shadow wall," and climb the PSC Starship. A 600-gallon tide pool houses tidal creatures of Puget Sound, and Animal Attractions shows naked mole-rats and other animals. The **K5 First Alert Weather Center**★ offers the opportunity to become a virtual meteorologist, with all the

SEATTLE

necessary tools—weather maps, satellite tracking and more. **The Dinosaurs: A Journey Through Time★** exhibit features a full-size robotic model of a Pachycephalosaurus, as well as a half-size Tyrannosaurus rex and Apatosaurus; visitors can even operate the controls of these roaring, lifelike robots.

Continue around to the new Ackerley Family Exhibit Gallery, featuring a **Tropical Butterfly House★** where visitors stroll through a garden with a constant temperature of 80°F amid exotic butterflies from around the world. In the new **Insect Village**, elaborate homes built by various insects are featured, and insect marvels (the jumping power of fleas, for example) are illustrated. In the zoo area here, visitors can touch giant centipedes, walking sticks and other creeping critters.

On the plaza outside, visitors may operate hoses to hit targets in a large fountaining pool.

Children's Museum – 🧒 *Lower level of Center House. Open year-round daily 10am–6pm (weekends until 7pm). $4.* ✕ ⅃ 🅿 ☎ *206-441-1768. www.thechildrensmuseum.org.* Geared mostly to toddlers and elementary age children, the hands-on exhibits here focus on arts and humanities with multi-cultural themes. The Mountain, a simulated Pacific Northwest wilderness, boasts a waterfall and campsite, and in **Global Village**, the cultures of many countries are represented. The MindScape technology studio houses computers with educational games and a studio where kids can make their own music video. The museum also hosts national traveling exhibits.

Additional Sights *Map pp 188-189.*

Maritime Heritage Center – *12 blocks (about 1mi) northeast of Space Needle. South end of Lake Union at Valley St. and Westlake Ave.* Long the site of the Navy Reserve Center, this prime piece of lakeshore has recently come under city control, and plans to incorporate the existing sites below into a much expanded facility are underway. The new heritage center and park are scheduled for completion in the coming decade. The attractions below are currently operating.

Center for Wooden Boats – *S. Lake Union, 1010 Valley St.* ☎ *206-382-2628.* This boat livery rents vintage wooden rowing and sailing boats for use on the waters of Lake Washington. The center's 20-some craft include peapods, dories, catboats, skiffs, kayaks and canoes, all on view in the lake waters beside the center. Non-boating observers are welcome to watch the staff at work maintaining this museum-quality "fleet."

Northwest Seaport – *S. Lake Union, 1002 Valley St. Open year-round Tue–Sun noon–5pm. Closed Jan 1, Thanksgiving Day, Dec 25.* 🅿 ☎ *206-447-9800. www.nwseaport.org.* Along the south edge of Lake Union, the "seaport" offers a look at the maritime heritage of Seattle via three vintage ships. Visitors may take self-guided tours above– and below-decks of all three. The 1897 schooner **Wawona** carried lumber along the coast early in this century and later became a Bering Strait fishing vessel. During World War II, the US military used the 165ft-long vessel to supply lumber to the burgeoning regional aircraft industry. The 120ft-long tug **Arthur Foss** was built in 1889 in Portland and worked as a barge tug on the Columbia River, then as a lumber tug hauling logs. It served as Washington's Centennial Flagship for the Expo '86 World's Fair in Vancouver, British Columbia. Built in 1904, the 129ft-long lightship **Swiftsure** was stationed along the California coast prior to World War II; during the war it served as an armed marine patrol boat.

Queen Anne District – *Bordering Seattle Center to the northwest.* Set atop 450ft Queen Anne hill, this affluent neighborhood northwest of Seattle Center is considered one of the city's hippest new night spots, with an abundance of fine restaurants and cafes along lower Queen Anne Street North. The plethora of Queen Anne-style mansions built here in the late 19C earned the neighborhood its name. Though most are gone now, the area is still a haven of respectability. The showiest pieces of architecture can be found along **West Highland Drive**, particularly between Seventh and Eighth Avenues West. A walkway follows the bluffs here with fine Puget Sound views. At the **Marshall Viewpoint** *(7th Ave. W. and W. Highland Dr.)*, a retaining wall with stairs dates to 1913. Across the street, the intimate walled **Parsons Garden** makes an enticing place to stop.

★CAPITOL HILL & UNIVERSITY DISTRICT
1 1/2 days. Map pp 188-189.

A boisterous, eclectic mix of tastes, lifestyles and neighborhoods enliven these two areas, where you can find the mansions of old Seattle not far from bohemian coffeehouses, and university student hang-outs around the corner from working-class taverns. Though it never became the site of the state capitol as city planners had hoped, the high ground of Capitol Hill was the first of the two areas to develop, and by the early 20C the streets south of Volunteer Park had given rise to a Millionaire's Row. Many of the mansions from that era still stand, but the current commercial and nightlife hub of Capitol Hill is unquestionably Broadway.

Northeast of Capitol Hill, across Montlake Portage, the University District had begun to develop before the University of Washington moved here, but the institution's arrival in the 1890s, along with the 1909 World's Fair staged on the university grounds, encouraged the area to develop rapidly. Throughout the 20C, as the university has grown, so has the activity on its adjoining streets, particularly University Way and 45th Street. The energizing street scene here offers a good place to observe au courant attitudes and trends among university students.

★**Volunteer Park** – *E. Prospect St. between 11th & 15th Ave. E.* Established in the 1880s and now the centerpiece of Capitol Hill, this 43-acre park crowns a high point overlooking the city. In 1901 it became the site of a city reservoir and at the same time received its current name, to honor the men who had volunteered in the 1898 Spanish-American War. Two years later, the Olmsted brothers turned the natural forestlands here into a landscaped space of fountains, promenades and formal plantings. In 1906 a brick-faced Water Tower was constructed in the park. Today, a narrow, 106-step stairway winds around the interior of the 75.5ft tower, leading to an observatory with panoramic **views**★ of the city. Along the wall of the observatory, photographs and story boards explain the influence that the Olmsted Brothers had on the landscape design of Seattle's city parks.

The park's **conservatory**, completed in 1912, is a classic Victorian-style garden house. Its glass walls enclose palm, fern, bromeliad and cactus plantings, as well as a pavilion devoted to seasonal displays.

★★ **Seattle Asian Art Museum** – *1400 E. Prospect St., in Volunteer Park. Open year-round Tue–Sun 10am–5pm (Thu 9pm). Closed Jan 1, Thanksgiving Day, Dec 25. $3.* & 🅿 ☎ *206-654-3100. www.seattleartmuseum.org.* From 1933 to 1991, this stately Art Moderne structure on a park promontory overlooking the city functioned as the Seattle Museum of Art. Designed by local architect Carl Gould, the museum owed its origins in large part to Dr. Richard E. Fuller and his mother, philanthropists and collectors whose donation of some 1,700 objects of Asian art to the city in the early 1930s formed the museum's core collection. With the 1991 completion of the new downtown Seattle Art Museum facility, the original museum split into two entities. The Volunteer Park structure is now devoted solely to displaying the institution's extensive holdings of **Asian art**, ranked among the top 10 collections outside Asia. Less than a quarter of the museum's more than 7,000 objects are displayed at any one time.

Haniwa Warrior Figure, Pottery, Tumulus Period

From the entry foyer, stairs ascend to a cavernous garden court, lined with large pieces of **South Asian sculpture★★** reflecting the Buddhist and Hindu traditions. Galleries to the right display **Japanese art★★**, including earthenware vessels and figurines of prehistoric and early Japan; finely wrought ceramics, calligraphy and ink painting of the 17C–19C; and Buddhist temple art and folk art. Galleries to the left of the garden court house **Chinese art★**: metalwork, Buddhist sculpture, ceramics and small ornate bibelots of jade. Early Chinese vessels, figurines and censers are found in a gallery to the left of the entry foyer; to the right is a gallery devoted to **Korean art**.

Lake View Cemetery – *1554 15th Ave. E.* This high, grassy bluff with lake views is the final resting place for such Seattle greats as "Princess" Angeline, Chief Seatlh's Daughter (her coffin is canoe shaped); city pioneer "Doc" Maynard; 19C mayor and city founder Henry Yesler; and kung fu film star, Seattle native Bruce Lee, and his son Brandon.

★★ **Washington Park Arboretum** – *2300 Arboretum Dr. E. Open year-round daily 8am–dusk.* 🅿 ☎ *206-543-8800. weber.u.washington.edu/~wpa.* Preserving 230 acres of woodlands extending south from Union Bay, the parkland was set aside by the city in 1904. Soon thereafter, the Olmsted brothers designed a curving roadway, Lake Washington Boulevard East, aesthetically integrated into the natural contours of the land. In the mid-1930s, an arboretum was established and laid out, again by the Olmsted brothers. Today, it is administered jointly by the Seattle Department of Parks and Recreation, the University of Washington and the Arboretum Foundation. Some 5,500 different kinds of plants are nurtured here, including towering evergreens, firs, ashes and oaks. Trails lace the park, leading through woodlands, and through such specialty areas as a rock garden, a pinetum, a rhododendron glen, a honeysuckle hill and an azalea way, whose floral spring display also includes dogwoods and flowering cherries.

Lake Washington

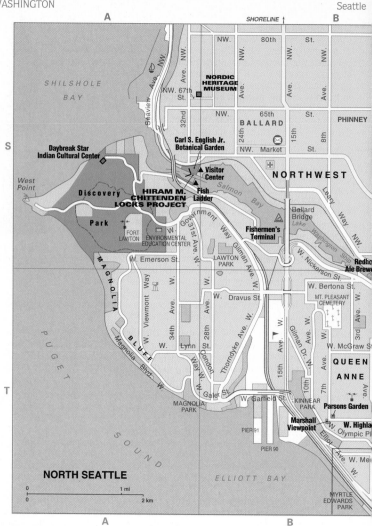

★**Japanese Garden** – *Open Mar–May & Sept–Nov daily 10am–7pm. May–Aug daily 10am–8pm. Graham Visitor Center open year-round daily 10am–4pm. $2.50.* & ☎ 206-684-4725. www.ci.seattle.wa.us\parks. A serene haven of boulders, waterways, plantings and a traditional teahouse, the 3.5-acre garden was designed in 1960 by Juki Iida, a respected Japanese landscape architect who had created more than 1,000 such gardens before being commissioned for this one. Iida personally chose over 500 granite boulders from the nearby Cascade Range to punctuate the garden landscape. The large central pond is crossed by an earthen and a plank bridge, and Japanese lanterns, gates and a "moon-viewing stand" add to the contemplative atmosphere. Among the botanical species are pines, cherries, maples, rhododendrons and bamboos.

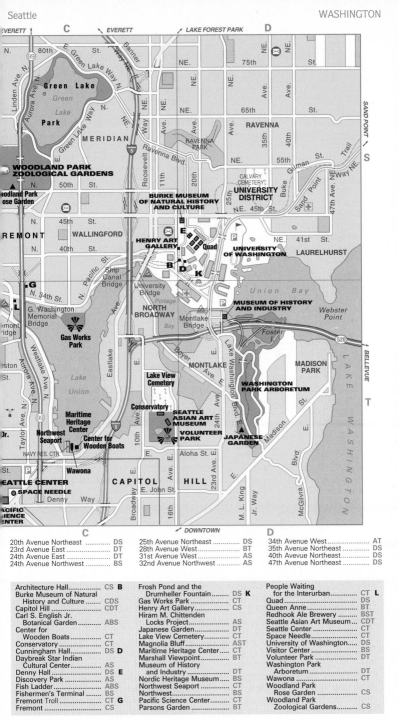

★**Museum of History and Industry** – *2700 24th Ave. E. Open year-round Mon–Fri 11am–5pm, weekends 10am–5pm. Closed Jan 1, Thanksgiving Day, Dec 25. $5.50.* ♿ ▯ ☎ *206-324-1126. www.seattlehistory.org.* Since its opening in 1952, the museum has been the keeper of Seattle's past. Among its collection are vintage aircraft (including A 1920s Boeing mail plane), boats, and ship figureheads. The "Seattle in the 1880s" exhibit re-creates a city street with print, hardware, barber, blacksmith and other period shops, as well as a saloon and bank. In "Salmon Stakes: People, Nature and Technology" life aboard a fishing boat and in a cannery are detailed. "Seattle Roots" is another street scene, based on the city's appearance before the Great Seattle Fire of 1889.

★University of Washington

This respected university, sprawling across almost 700 acres on the north shores of Portage and Union bays, educates some 35,000 students a year, making it one of the largest campuses of higher learning on the West Coast. Roughly 82 percent of its student body is composed of Washington State residents. Of its 16 different schools and colleges, it is best known for its schools of computer science, engineering and health sciences.

"U Dub," as the university is known locally, began life in 1861 as the Territorial University, located on Denny Knoll in downtown Seattle. In 1891, the state legislature voted funds for a new campus, and four years later the site's first building, Denny Hall, opened its doors. Several other buildings followed in the coming decade, before the campus area was chosen as the site for the 1909 Alaska-Yukon-Pacific Exposition, Seattle's first World's Fair. John Olmsted was retained to lay out the exposition's grounds, which were to become a framework for the growing campus. With the exposition's conclusion, Olmsted returned again to develop a new and more lasting plan.

Throughout this century, the school has grown by fits and starts, gradually extending onto a South Campus. Its presence defines the neighboring area far beyond the campus limits, and the lively streets surrounding the university offer an abundance of cafes, restaurants and specialty shops.

Campus – *Maps and a Campus Walk booklet highlighting significant buildings are available from the Visitor Information Center at University Way N.E. and N.E. Campus Pkwy.* ☎ *206-543-2100.* The mixture of building styles on this large campus reflects the last hundred years in academic architecture. The first building to be erected, **Denny Hall**, still stands in turreted French Renaissance splendor. How the site for the hall was chosen has become one of the university's enduring legends. Frustrated by delays and quibbling over where to locate the building, Regent David Kellogg finally stabbed his umbrella into a rotting log and declared that the hall would be built there. Named for Arthur Denny, who donated a downtown tract for the original university campus, the rambling Tenino sandstone and pressed-brick structure opened its doors in 1895. At that time Denny Hall constituted the sum total of the university; the building held classrooms, a teaching museum, laboratories, recital rooms and A 736-seat assembly hall. The belfry topping the building still holds the 1861 **Varsity Bell** originally installed in the Territorial University.

To the southeast of Denny Hall lies the "**Quad**," the Liberal Arts Quadrangle envisioned by the Olmsteds and flanked by buildings dating from the early decades of the 20C. On the southwest side of the campus stand two survivors of the 1909 Alaska-Yukon-Pacific Exposition: the classical revival **Architecture Hall** and **Cunningham Hall**, named for 1907 university alumna, photographer Imogen Cunningham. Also a relic of the exposition, **Frosh Pond** is now ornamented with the spraying jets of the **Drumheller Fountain**, added in 1961 to commemorate the university's centennial.

★**Burke Museum of Natural History and Culture** – *N.E. 45th St. and 17th Ave. N.E. Open year-round daily 10am–5pm (Thu 8pm). Closed Jan 1, July 4, Thanksgiving Day, Dec 25. $5.50.* ✗ ⚿ 🄿 ☎ *206-543-5590. www.washington.edu/burkemuseum.* The Northwest's premiere natural science museum, the Burke celebrates the cultures of the Pacific Rim and the diverse natural history of the Pacific Northwest. Opened in 1885, the museum had, within four years, been designated the Washington State Museum by the legislature. In 1962 the museum moved to its current imposing brick building and was renamed in honor of Judge Thomas Burke, a visionary Seattleite whose wife had liberally endowed the new edifice.

Today, the lower level of the Burke celebrates the cultures and histories of **Pacific Rim peoples** with exhibits of archaeological and ethnological artifacts and historic photographs. Cultures featured include those of China, Japan, Southeast Asia, the Philippines, the Pacific Islands and the Northwest Coast.

The main floor exhibit, **Life & Times of Washington State**, details the geologic processes that have formed the region, from its submarine beginnings to the plate tectonics that gave rise to the Cascade volcanoes. Along with appropriate mineral specimens, the exhibit displays a variety of **dinosaur skeletons**—some casts and some the actual fossilized bones. Another gallery on this level hosts changing exhibits, often of Northwest native art.

On the museum grounds, *Single Fin* is a replica of a killer whale erected as a Haida grave monument in Alaska. Two **totem poles** replicate a Haida House Front Pole and a Tsimshian Memorial Pole, honoring a deceased chief. Both poles are the work of contemporary carver Bill Holm, now a curator emeritus at the Burke. An **ethnobotanic garden** displays some 100 species important to Northwest Coast native cultures.

★★**Henry Art Gallery** – *15th Ave. N.E. and N.E. 41st St. Open year-round Tue–Sun 11am–5pm (Thu 8pm). Closed Jan 1, Thanksgiving Day, Dec 25. $5.* ✗ ⚿ ☎ *206-616-8674. www.henryart.org.* The official art museum of the university, the Henry ranks as one of the country's most progressive small museums, with a reputation for encouraging and exhibiting cutting-edge art. While its primary mission is research, it offers the visiting public an eclectic look at movements and innovations in art over the past century. The museum's founder, railroad and real-estate magnate **Horace C. Henry**, was so eager to share his collection of 19C and early 20C paintings with the people of Seattle that he occasionally opened his Capitol Hill home for public viewing. In the mid-1920s, the president of the university, Henry Suzzallo, persuaded Henry to donate his collection of 158 paintings to the university and to finance a museum to house them. The red-brick Gothic-style structure (designed in 1927 by Carl Gould) was adjoined in 1997 by the South Gallery, a Modernist creation of glass, textured stainless steel and cast stone by New York architect Charles Gwathmey; the museum now boasts a total of 46,000sq ft of exhibit space.

Exhibits in the original North Galleries and the new South Gallery are in constant flux and feature both visiting exhibits and art from the permanent collection. The original core collection donated by Henry focuses on 19C and 20C French and American paintings by such masters as Winslow Homer and Gilbert Stuart. European art acquired since the museum's founding concentrates on Barbizon School paintings and other mid-19C and 20C landscapes. Artists represented in the contemporary collection include Robert Motherwell, Morris Graves, Marsden Hartley, Robert Rauschenberg and Max Weber. The museum's photography collection includes works by Edward Weston, Ansel Adams, Man Ray, Imogen Cunningham and Diane Arbus; the Monsen Photography collection traces the evolution of the art form from its mid-18C infancy to its role in contemporary art. A textile collection of some 16,000 objects spans 1500 BC to the present.

NORTHWEST SEATTLE *1 1/2 days. Map pp 188-189.*

An area of discrete neighborhoods graced by parklands, this section of the city encompasses the upscale contemporary homes of Magnolia Bluff, the proud Scandinavian-American community of Ballard, the quiet streets bordering Green Lake, and the rambunctiously liberal enclave of Fremont. At the southern edge of the district, the quaint houseboats featured in the popular 1993 movie *Sleepless in Seattle* (one served as co-star Tom Hanks' home) still dot Lake Union.

Discovery Park – *Entrance at W. Government Way and 36th Ave. W. Maps and other information available at the Environmental Education Center. Open year-round daily 8:30am–5pm. Closed major holidays.* ♿ ☎ *206-386-4236.* Occupying part of the windswept **Magnolia Bluff** peninsula above Puget Sound, this 534-acre wilderness of forests, meadowlands and beaches is home to eagles, raccoons, birds and marine mammals. Looped by more than 7mi of hiking trails and 5mi of paved biking trails, the park is also interspersed with the former facilities of Fort Lawton (now mostly private residences), designed at the turn of the century by the Olmsted brothers. The city's largest park, Discovery is reputedly named after the ship of 18C explorer George Vancouver. In the northwest corner of the park, the **Daybreak Star Indian Cultural Center** *(open year-round daily 9am–5pm; ☎ 206-285-4425)* houses the United Indians for All Tribes Foundation Center and features large works by contemporary artists in its public spaces.

★★ **Hiram M. Chittenden Locks Project** – [Kids] *3015 N.W. 54th St. Also accessible via Commodore Park on W. Commodore Way.* ☎ *206-783-7059. www.nws.usace.army.* On the Lake Washington Ship Canal, this multipurpose site is maintained by the US Army Corps of Engineers. It comprises two navigational locks, a dam and spillway, a fish ladder, the Carl S. English Jr. Botanical Garden and a visitor center. The **Hiram M. Chittenden Locks** (called the Ballard Locks by locals) and the 8mi Lake Washington Canal were completed in 1917, allowing access from Puget Sound to Lake Union, then on to larger Lake Washington. The locks' namesake and engineering visionary, Brigadier General Hiram M. Chittenden, was a respected officer of the US Army Corps of Engineers. Prior to his Seattle posting, he had surveyed Yellowstone National Park and worked on other federally significant engineering projects. At his insistence, the Seattle project featured two locks instead of one (the larger measures 825ft by 80ft; the smaller is 150ft by 30ft) and was built of enduring concrete rather than wood. At the locks' official opening, the *Roosevelt*, flagship of polar explorer Adm. Robert E. Peary, led a procession of ships through the canal.

Initially planned to provide ship access to the rich coal and timber resources on the eastern shores of Lake Washington, the project also had the effect of lowering lake and bay levels by up to 20ft and thus helped with flood prevention. A **spillway** to the south of the smaller lock regulates the flow of freshwater from the lakes and saltwater from the sound. Today, some 100,000 pleasure, sightseeing and fishing boats, as well as barges and container and research vessels are "locked through" annually, providing almost constant entertainment for the spectators that line the north side of the canal, where the two locks lie. At their edge a **visitor center**

Hiram M. Chittenden Locks

(open Jun–Sept daily 10am–7pm; rest of the year Thu–Mon 11am–5pm; closed Jan 1, Thanksgiving Day, Dec 25; & ▣*)* is housed in a structure with displays on the history of the canal and lock and its current operations, also explained in A 12min film, *Where the Activity Never Stops*.

Behind the visitor center, the **Carl S. English Jr. Botanical Garden** takes in seven acres of walking paths beneath shade trees and past plantings of shrubs and flowers that represent some 500 species from around the world. The romantic-style

---

■ Salmon

The life cycle of the salmon begins in mountain-fed streams and rivers, where spawning adults lay fertilized eggs in gravel beds. Because of predators, pollution, temperature changes and disturbances of the gravel beds, only about 20 percent of the eggs hatch out as alevins. For 50 more days these tiny three-quarter-inch creatures remain buried in the gravel, feeding off the egg's yolk sac. After that time, a two-inch fingerling, or fry, emerges and continues to feed on freshwater insects and plankton. If they survive their many predators (fish, birds, frogs), the fry will begin the journey to saltwater as smolts. (When they actually begin that journey depends on the species). Once in the ocean, adult salmon spend anywhere from one to five years fattening up on smaller fish, squid and plankton. Then they begin the long journey back to their original birthplace to spawn. In the spawning phase, most of them change appearance. Adult males develop a hooked jaw, and their flesh rapidly deteriorates as they move upstream. Once they have spawned, the adults die, but the cycle begins anew with their offspring.

Four kinds of salmon are commonly found in Northwest streams and rivers:

Chinook (or King) – King of the salmon, chinooks reach an average weight of 20 pounds, though some have tipped the scales at over 120. The king's size makes it a prized catch for sportfishermen.

Coho (or Silver) – These salmon look like smaller versions of the king, reaching an average weight of between 6 and 12 pounds. After sockeye, coho are most highly valued for their tastiness.

Sockeye (or Red) – Curiosities in the salmon family, these fish may stay in freshwater rivers and streams for as long as three years, and some never choose to make the journey into the ocean. Prized for their flavorful flesh, sockeye average 8 pounds and reach up to 33 inches long. During the spawning phase, the males become a spectacle of color, with bright red bodies and green heads. They are the only Pacific salmon to spawn in lakes.

Steelhead – Actually a sea-running rainbow trout, the silvery steelhead is a long, narrow fish identifiable by its square tail and is highly sought after by anglers. These fish make the longest upstream journey to spawn, moving high into the headwaters of streams and rivers. Unlike true salmon, after spawning they do not necessarily die. Adult steelhead average 26 inches long and weigh as much as 20 pounds.

---

gardens were laid out by Army Corps of Engineers member Carl English, Jr., who spent 43 years transforming the barren area created during construction of the locks into this botanical haven.

On the south side of the canal, a **fish ladder**, constructed in 1976, replaces the original 1917 version. Its series of weirs allows spawning salmon to swim upstream to the freshwater lakes, rivers and bays where they were born and where they themselves will spawn, then die. Young salmon smolts swim downstream and enter the ocean waters, where they will live several years before repeating the process. Human visitors may descend to a submarine viewing window to watch adult steelhead, coho, chinook and sockeye salmon making their way upriver during the spawning season.

★**Nordic Heritage Museum** – *3014 N.W. 67th St., entrance to parking lot off 68th St. at Webster Park. Open year-round Tue–Sat 10am–4pm, Sun noon–4pm. Closed Jan 1, Thanksgiving Day, Dec 24-25. $4.* ♿ 🅿 ☎ *206-789-5707.* Appropriately situated in the Ballard neighborhood where many Scandinavian immigrants settled at the turn of the century, the museum celebrates the traditions and histories of all five northern European countries—Denmark, Norway, Sweden, Finland and Iceland. In 1979 the museum leased the 1907 Webster Elementary School from the Seattle school district, and its exhibits now fill three floors and more than 51,000sq ft.

Visit – *2 hrs.* Originally created by the Danish National Museum in Copenhagen and the Moesgaard Museum in Aarhus, Denmark, the **Dream of America** exhibit *(1st floor)* details the hopes, dreams and hardships of the Scandinavian immigrants who migrated to America in the late 19C and early 20C. Re-created farmhouses, rooms and street scenes trace their odyssey, from the harsh poverty of rural Scandinavia to the rigors of the Atlantic crossing and the arduous cross-country journey to the Pacific Northwest. A final area developed by the Nordic Museum itself depicts life in the Ballard neighborhood for the immigrant community.

Two **Heritage Rooms** on the second floor display such traditional Scandinavian crafts as hand-painted furniture and utensils and folk costumes. Two other galleries are devoted to the Northwest industries that attracted many Scandinavian laborers—fishing, along with boat building, canning and logging. In five separate **Ethnic Heritage Galleries** *(3rd floor)* designed by local groups, the culture and traditions of the five countries are represented by clothing, home interiors and other artifacts.

Fishermen's Terminal – *15th Ave. N.W. at Emerson and W. Nickerson Sts. tel 206-728-3395.* This facility on Salmon Bay is a good place to get a taste of the North Pacific fishing fleet, one of the world's largest. The marina here on the south side of the Ballard Bridge is home port for some 700 commercial fishing boats—from small, family-owned vessels to enormous factory trawlers. The vast terminal building houses several casual and crowded seafood restaurants and a seafood market. A 30ft-tall bronze and concrete statue overlooking the marina commemorates fishermen lost at sea.

★★**Woodland Park Zoological Gardens** – *Phinney Ave. N. between N. 50th and N. 59th Sts. Entrance gates to the zoo are located on all three streets. Open mid-Mar–mid-Oct daily 9:30am–6pm. Rest of the year daily 9:30am–4pm. $8.50.* ✗ ♿ 🅿 ☎ *206-684-4800. www.zoo.org.* A regional showpiece, this nationally acclaimed zoo houses animals in environments that closely simulate their native habitats—savannas, tundras, tropical rain forests, marshlands and more. Of the zoo's 92 acres, 65 are now allocated to exhibits housing 1,100 animals that represent more than 300 species; tree and shrub species number over 1,000.

The zoo traces its origins to **Guy Phinney**, an Englishman who, after making a fortune in Canadian real estate, moved to Seattle in the 1880s and attempted to repeat his Canadian successes. Developing the current zoo neighborhood for residential lots, Phinney built a private park and menagerie on his own Woodland Park estate and offered its use to potential buyers. After Phinney's death, his widow sold the 200-acre estate to the city in 1899. Recognizing its potential, city landscape consultant John Olmsted turned it into a "proper" zoo, with cages typical of such early 20C establishments. Improvements to Olmsted's 1909 buildings were made during the 1930s WPA era, but it was not until the early 1980s that serious efforts were undertaken to revitalize the facility. In November 1985, King County voters approved zoo bonds that guaranteed $31.5 million for a re-envisioned zoo; the Woodland Park Zoo Society committed to raise another $10 million from private and corporate donations. The results of this funding are evident in the zoo's state-of-the-art, cageless spaces for its large animals.

Visit – *3 hrs.* A highlight of the zoo, the open **African Savanna**★★ area encompasses the largest space in the park. Within its naturalistic grasslands setting, giraffes browse side by side with zebras, while lions look on from a distance. Trenches and other concealed barriers separate predators from prey. Walls of bamboo in **Tropical Asia**★★ separate the Thai Village—with its simple raised structures—from elephants cooling themselves in a large pool. Macaques, tapirs, siamangs, orangutans and pythons have homes in this lush area. Committed to animal conservation, the zoo uses the **Conservation Yards** to house injured raptors, the long-haired goat known as the takin and endangered gorals. In the popular new **Northern Trail**★★ area, gray wolves pose against the horizon and elk graze on the taiga behind them. The main inhabitant of the **Australasia** area, the tree kangaroo is represented by several varieties. The zoo's latest addition, the **Butterflies & Blooms** space allows visitors to walk through a flurry of color, as some 1,000 butterflies waft by.

The nearby **Day and Night** exhibits lead visitors inside small buildings where animals are kept at their natural light levels. Next comes the **Tropical Rain Forest**, where western lowland gorillas lounge about; a variety of monkeys, lemurs and guenons do high-wire acrobatics in their own habitats. In the leafy **Temperate Forest**, the red panda roams, but it is mostly an avian world, populated by cranes, members of the pheasant family and marsh birds. A farm allows young people a place to encounter barnyard animals up close.

Adjacent to the zoo, the 2.5-acre **Woodland Park Rose Garden** *(same hours as above)* features 260 varieties of roses as well as other botanical specimens, some sculpted into topiary.

Green Lake Park – *E. Green Lake Dr. N. and W. Green Lake Dr. N.* An Ice Age glacier sculpted the depression now filled by the well-named lake that is the centerpiece of this popular, 323-acre park. A 1910 city project blocked the natural drainage into the lake, exposing an additional 7ft of shoreline for green spaces and a boulevard, but an unanticipated result was the explosive growth of algae, already prevalent in lake waters. Bathers in Green Lake complain of "swimmer's itch," caused by a parasite associated with waterfowl. But joggers and walkers are happy to enjoy the two paths that encircle the lake.

Fremont – *West of Aurora Ave. N. between Aurora Bridge and Woodland Park Zoo.* This neighborhood lying on the north side of the Fremont Bridge is a blend of playful funk and intellectual liberalism. As an example of its outré attitude, Fremont declared in 1994 that it was seceding from Seattle and the State of Washington to form its own Republic of Fremont, "Center of the Known Universe." Laid-back restaurants, shops and taverns line its streets, particularly around the intersections of Fremont Avenue North and North 35th and 36th Streets. Seattle's first microbrewery, the **Redhook Ale Brewery** *(3400 Phinney Ave. N.;* ☎ *206-548-8000)*, opened in an old red-brick streetcar barn in this neighborhood in 1988. It still operates a brewery and the Trolleyman Pub here, but public tours of its brewing operations are now given only at its facility in Woodinville. Aside from Fremont watering holes, the area is famous for its outdoor sculpture. The main stem, Fremont Avenue North, boasts one of the city's most popular artworks: **People Waiting for the Interurban**. The whimsical cast-aluminum sculpture by local artist Richard Beyer depicts a group of people queuing for public transportation; Fremont residents love to adorn the sculpted would-be passengers with hand-lettered signs, scarves and other accoutrements. A few blocks away stands a bronze Lenin *(N. 36th St. and Fremont Pl.)*, brought over from Eastern Europe. Another piece of neighborhood self-expression, the 18ft concrete **Fremont Troll**★ lies in wait under the Aurora Bridge *(at N. 36th St.)*, clutching a Volkswagen Bug in his grip.

Gas Works Park – *N. Northlake Way at Wallingford Ave. N.* Remnants of the Seattle Gas Company Plant that operated here from 1907 to the 1960s have been allowed to stand amid the green space that now blankets this small point on the north shore of Lake Union. **Richard Haag**, the architect who turned the former World's Fair site into the Seattle Center, was the mastermind behind this compelling mixture of industrial artifacts and parkland. The park also offers wide-angle **views**★★ of the Seattle cityscape.

© Robert Holmes

Fremont Troll

■ Bill Gates

The youngest billionaire ever, Microsoft mogul Bill Gates (b.1955) had made his first billion by the age of 31. Known as a scrappy and highly competitive entrepreneur, William Henry Gates III grew up in Seattle, his father a lawyer and his mother an educator. In his early teens, he discovered computers and began learning on his own to program. With a small group of like-minded friends (including Paul Allen, who became a co-founder of Microsoft), Gates began developing salable computer programs that did everything from handle payrolls to help monitor highway traffic. As a rising high school senior, Gates was offered a programming position at TRW—with an annual salary of $20,000—and he took a year off from his studies to work. After attending Harvard for two years, he dropped out to pursue programming development full-time. Gates correctly anticipated a coming revolution in technology that would "put a computer in every home." In 1975 Gates and his old friend Paul Allen established a New Mexico-based programming company called Microsoft. In 1980 Microsoft was hired by IBM to develop a disk-operating system for personal computers, and MS-DOS was born. The rest is corporate history. For more than a decade Microsoft has dominated the software industry and often incurred the wrath of competitors and the scrutiny of the Federal Trade Commission. So far, Gates and his company have emerged from most disputes victorious. He and his family live in a 37,000sq ft home on the shores of Lake Washington.

SOUTH SEATTLE *1 day. Map 196.*

Birthplace of the city, this corridor, dominated by the commercial piers along the south shore of Elliott Bay and the Duwamish River Valley, represents the industrial heart of working Seattle. But along with the beat of industry, the area enfolds as well one of the city's favorite gathering places, the sound-facing sweep of Alki Beach.

★**Puget Sound Vessel Traffic Service** – *4th floor, 1519 Alaskan Way S. at Pier 36. Open year-round daily 8am–4pm.* & ▣ ☎ *206-217-6040.* Since 1972, the Puget Sound VTS has monitored some 3,500sq mi of waterways, from Olympia in the south to the Canadian border in the north, and from the Pacific Ocean to the eastern bays of Puget Sound. This area ranks as the largest VTS jurisdiction in the country, and together, Seattle and Tacoma rank as one of the busiest port areas in the US. Operated jointly by the Coast Guard and a local civilian staff, the service relies on banks of computers to monitor and guide the vessel traffic moving through congested regional waters. Visitors are welcome to observe the activities of the service, housed on the fourth floor of a government building among the portside hubbub of Elliott Bay. From here you have a working perspective into the complexities of bringing huge ships in and out of Puget Sound waters.

The **Coast Guard Museum Northwest** *(beside the VTS building; open year-round Mon–Fri 9am–3pm, weekends 1pm–5pm; closed major holidays; ☎ 206-217-6993)* offers exhibits of model ships; Coast Guard uniforms; and historic photographs. It also preserves the lens from the Dungeness Lighthouse (1857-1976), the first built in the Strait of Juan de Fuca.

Alki Beach – *North of Alki Point along Alki Ave.* This 2.5mi-long stretch of sand at the conjunction of Elliott Bay and Puget Sound attracts a lively crowd during sunny summer days. Preserved as a city park, the beach parallels a boardwalk frequented by walkers and joggers in almost any weather. Aside from its obvious seaside pleasures, the beach looks out on the open waters of Puget Sound or east across Elliott Bay to the Seattle skyline. Alki Drive Southwest, which hugs the beach, ends at **Alki Point**, the birthplace of Seattle. Here, on November 13, 1851, Arthur Denny rowed ashore to make his first landfall. To commemorate the moment, Arthur's daughter Lenora dedicated a concrete pylon *(Alki Dr. S.W. at 63rd Ave. S.W.)* to the city in 1905. In 1913 the current **Alki Point Light Station** was erected at the tip of the peninsula. Now automated, it continues to guide ships between the sound and Elliott Bay.

★★ **Museum of Flight** – ⊞ᵈˢ *9404 E. Marginal Way S. (.5mi northwest of I-5, Exit 158). Open year-round daily 10am–5pm (Thu 9pm). Closed Thanksgiving Day & Dec 25. $8.* ⊁ & ▣ ☎ *206-764-5720. www.museumofflight.org.* The largest air and space museum in the western US was founded in 1964 by the Pacific Northwest Aviation Historical Foundation. The large, contemporary museum building, which opened in 1987, overlooks Boeing Field (the King County Airport) and features interactive exhibits that realistically re-create the adventure of flight and a collection of aircraft ranging from early gliders and biplanes to space capsules.

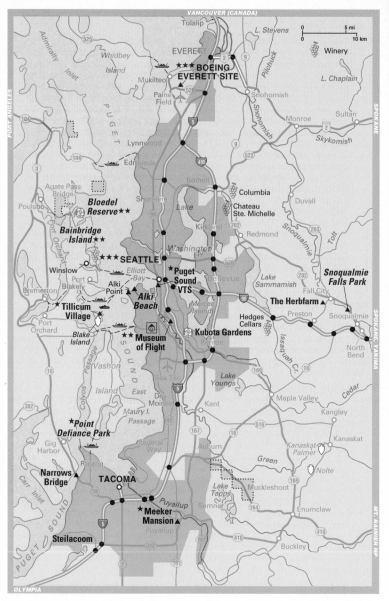

Visit – *2 hrs.* The steel-and-glass architecture of this tremendous space makes it feel open to the skies through which the aircraft now on display once soared. Among about 50 planes and other flying vehicles parked on the ground level or suspended at "cloud level" are such rarities as a World War II Goodyear FG-1D Corsair; the Boeing VC-137B delivered to President Dwight Eisenhower in 1959 (the first presidential jet); an M/D-21 Blackbird spy plane; and a working replica of the B&W, Boeing's first airplane. The **Apollo exhibit** details the history of the US space program, and the small **Murdock Challenger Theater** has a live link to NASA satellite reception and shows Landsat and other images as they are received by NASA. A **flight tower** area features simulators that allow visitors to try their hands as pilots and air-traffic controllers, monitoring actual landings and take-offs at Boeing Field. The 268-seat **William M. Allen Theater** shows a changing selection of films related to flight.

Built in 1909 on the shores of the Duwamish River, the **Red Barn** was the central building in the Pacific Aero Products Company founded by William E. Boeing. In 1975, the appropriately named "barn" was floated up the Duwamish River to this location and opened as the museum's first building in 1983. An exhibit here details the building's legendary past; the Aero Club headquarters, founded by William

Boeing in a converted boathouse, is also re-created, as are an early Boeing wood-shop and the Wright Brothers' wind tunnel. A reproduction of the historic 1902 glider the Wrights launched from Kitty Hawk, North Carolina, is also displayed, along with a reproduction of the equally historic German Lilienthal Glider.

Kubota Gardens – *Renton and 55th Aves. S. Open year-round daily dawn-dusk.* ⚐ ☎ *206-725-5060.* An unexpected haven in the midst of the Rainier Beach neighborhood, the Kubota Gardens owe their existence to their namesake designer, Japanese immigrant Fujitaro Kubota. In the late 1920s, Kubota purchased five acres of logged marshland and began transforming it into a botanical showplace for his business, the Kubota Gardening Company. The gardens, which gradually expanded to 20 acres, also served as a hub of social and cultural events for Seattle's Japanese community until World War II, when all Japanese, including the Kubota family, were forced into internment camps. Following this, the gardens suffered years of neglect. Now a city-owned park, they have been restored by volunteers and city staff. Paths again weave through a landscape of ponds and waterfalls, past feathery Japanese pines, a bamboo grove and a traditional Japanese garden.

EXCURSIONS

★★**Bainbridge Island** – *5 hrs. Accessible via Washington State Ferries from Pier 52 on Alaskan Way. Ferries depart from both directions roughly every 50 min year-round daily 6am–2am. 35min one-way. $8:25 car & driver, $3.70 each additional passenger.* ✗ ♿ ☎ *206-464-6400 or 800-843-3779.* Separated from the mainland by Puget Sound on the east and Port Orchard Bay on the west, 48sq mi Bainbridge Island has traditionally maintained an atmosphere distinctly its own. Squamish Indians hunted and gathered in its forests and beaches for centuries before George Vancouver sailed into the sound and anchored off it in 1792. In the late 19C, the southern end of the island was dominated by the Port Blakely operations of one of the world's largest sawmills and the nearby Hall Brothers Shipyard. The rough-and-tumble atmosphere that characterized the lower island in those days was interrupted in the 1920s, when ferry service linked the island to the mainland. The influx of a more peaceful populace ensued, and farmers, including many Japanese, moved here to become vegetable and berry growers. Island growth again increased with the 1950 completion of the Agate Pass Bridge, connecting to the Olympic Peninsula.

In the 1960s, hippies discovered the sylvan delights of the island, and it briefly became a haven for those pursuing alternative lifestyles. Though the current population is more sedate than alternative, they still covet the island's unique atmosphere, and in 1991, residents on the northern, unincorporated end of the island voted to join with incorporated Winslow to from an island-wide city. A few malls and developments have sprung up recently on Bainbridge, as land prices have soared, and the population has become increasingly affluent. Still, much of the island maintains a rural feel.

Located directly west of the ferry terminal, **Winslow** is the commercial hub of the island. It maintains a nostalgic, small-town mien, despite the decidedly upscale trendiness of the shops, cafes and galleries that line its main stem, Winslow Way. A small farmers' market takes place on Winslow Green *(Winslow Way and Madison Ave.)* on Saturdays, from mid-spring to fall.

★★**Bloedel Reserve** – *6.5mi north of Winslow. Take Rte. 305 north, then right on Agate Wood Rd. 1mi to 7571 N.E. Dolphin Dr. Limited number of visitor; call for advance reservations. Open year-round Wed–Sun 10am–4pm. Closed major holidays. $6.* ♿ ⚐ ☎ *206-842-7631. www.bloedelreserve.org.* The 150-acre reserve on the northern coast preserves meadowlands, forests and glens that epitomize the natural beauty of the Northwest. Allowing the native flora to thrive in its own setting, the human touch and sense of landscaping here is deft and extremely subtle. The reserve occupies land known as Agate Point, a tract presented in 1856 by President James Buchanan to the Washington Territories to be used as the site of a territorial university. Mrs. John Collins, wife of an early city mayor, purchased 67 acres on Agate Point in 1904 and built a small beach cottage retreat. **Collinswood**, the imposing French château-style home that Mrs. Collins built here in 1932, now serves as the reserve's visitor center. In the early 1950s Collinswood was sold to Prentice and Virginia Bloedel, whose fortune derived from timber. Over the next three decades, the Bloedels established many of the botanical areas that grace the grounds today.

Visitors check in at the stately 1888 gatehouse, where a blazing fire often greets guests and a guide is available with maps and information. From the gatehouse a trail leads through the west meadow; to cover the whole site requires about 2mi of walking.

About 1/3mi south of the gatehouse, two connecting ponds fringed by bog-loving shrubs provide habitat for migratory waterfowl, such as merganser ducks, king-fishers, herons and Canada geese. From the marsh the trail loops north through a wetland forest and emerges into an open area dominated by **Middle Pond**. The pond and nearby pair of empress trees provide a formal setting for Collinswood. Farther on, a simple gate leads into the **Japanese Garden**, where a Zen rock garden engenders a mood of contemplation. The rest of the garden is the work of Fujitaro Kubota, responsible for the gardens of the same name in west Seattle. Heading southwest, the trail passes through the winsome **Moss Garden**, where native mosses carpet a soft green forest floor, offset by skunk cabbage and huckleberry.

★**Tillicum Village** – *4 hrs. On Blake Island in Puget Sound. Commercially operated tours to the village depart from Piers 55 & 56 on Alaskan Way. Visit by guided tour (4 hrs including meal) only, May–early Oct daily. Call ahead for specific hours. Rest of the year weekends only. $55.25.* 🍴 ♿ ☏ *206-443-1244. www.tillicumvillage.com.* Brainchild of Seattle caterer Bill Hewitt, Tillicum Village offers a commercialized but sincere attempt to celebrate the native cultures of the Northwest. Built in the 1960s, Tillicum—whose name derives from Chinook jargon for "friendly"—consists of a single longhouse in Kwakiutl style. Tour participants are treated to a traditional salmon bake, with the whole fish splayed open on cedar planks and cooked over an alderwood fire. Following the meal, native performers enact a stage presentation, based on Northwest myths; afterwards, such traditional crafts as wood carving are demonstrated.

The surrounding **Blake Island State Park** encompasses 476 acres of Northwest trees and shrubs and 5mi of beaches. Some 15mi of trails loop through and around the island.

Boeing 777 Factory Floor

★★★**Boeing Everett Site** – *1 hr. 22mi north of Seattle in Everett. Follow I-5 north and take Exit 189, then west on Rte. 526 3.5mi to plant entrance. Visit by guided tour (65min) only, Jun–Sept Mon–Fri 8:30am–3pm. Rest of the year Mon–Fri 9am–3pm. Closed major holidays & last 2 weeks in December. $5.* ♿ 🅿 ☏ *425-544-1264 or 800-464-1476. www.boeing.com/companyoffices/aboutus/tours.* At its Everett plant, the aeronautical giant officially known as the Boeing Commercial Airplane Group assembles its wide-body commercial jetliners—the 747, 767 and 777. The facilities necessary to produce these airborne behemoths rack up some impressive statistics *(p 199)*. Since William Boeing founded his Pacific Aero Products Company in 1916 in Seattle, the aircraft industry has been a bulwark of the regional economy. The Everett plant, one of the company's largest, now employs thousands of people. Worldwide demand for aircraft impacts the site directly, resulting in growth or layoffs. In late 1998, for example, this plant reduced personnel in response to a downturn in the economies of Asia, which account for the greatest percentage of Boeing's current business.

One-hour tours of the facility begin with a film explaining the process of assembling a jumbo jet. Guides then take visitors by bus to the spacious main assembly building. From a viewing area overlooking the assembly floor, guides explain the

■ Boeing Statistics

- It takes four to five months to assemble a wide-body jet; in 1998 the Everett plant turned out approximately 550 jets.

- Everett's main assembly building ranks as the largest building by volume in the world, with a 472-million-cubic-foot capacity. It rises 11 stories and covers an area equivalent to 74 football fields.

- The wire fabrication plant is the world's largest plant of its kind.

- Four times more earth (8.5 million cubic yards) was moved in the grading and leveling of this site than in the construction of the Grand Coulee Dam.

- The steepest standard-gauge rail line in the nation is the 3mi spur built to move materials and airplane parts from the main track up 600ft to the plant.

- A small man can stand upright inside the wing of a wide-body jet.

- The world's largest commercial jet, the 747-400, has A 211ft 5in wingspan and a length of 231ft 10in; it can carry up to 568 passengers.

- The 767, smallest of the wide-body jets, is used on more North American routes than any other aircraft.

- The newest addition to the Boeing jumbo jet family, the 777 began commercial service in 1994 and is sized between the 747 and 767.

work teams and stations where various parts of the aircraft are assembled. Four fully assembled jets can occupy the final bays at the same time. From the assembly building, a brief, narrated bus tour passes the paint hangars and the bridge that crosses Route 526 to Paine Field, where the assembled airplanes are flight-tested and delivered to customers.

The Herbfarm – *1/2 hr. 23mi east of Seattle. Take I-90 east to Exit 22 and go through Preston. After 3mi, bear left at the Y-intersection that crosses the bridge on S.E. 328th Ave. The nursery is located at 32804 Issaquah-Fall City Rd. Open May–Sept daily 10am–6pm. Rest of the year daily 10am–5pm Closed Jan 1, Thanksgiving Day, Dec 25.* ♿ 🅿 ☎ *425-222-7103. www.theherbfarm.com.* This popular commercial nursery grew up almost by accident in the mid-1970s, when Bill and Lola Zimmerman retired to Fall City, bought an old dairy farm and began growing plants, mostly for their own consumption. When Lola offered a handful of chives from her garden for roadside sale, they were so quickly purchased that

■ Wineries

In recent decades, Washington wines have become increasingly well-respected nationwide. Though most of the wines (and many of the grapes for locally produced wines) come from the warmer and drier eastern part of the state, the Puget Sound area also claims ideal cool-climate grape-growing conditions that are similar to the Loire Valley in France. In the greater Seattle area, several wineries offer tasting rooms and tours.

Bainbridge Island Vineyards & Winery – *682 Rte. 305, .5mi north of ferry terminal, Bainbridge Island.* ☎ *206-842-9463.* This family-owned island winery grows the grapes it produces for its European-style wines, available only here and at local shops and restaurants. A wine museum and tasting room are also on the premises.

Chateau Ste. Michelle – *2mi south of Woodinville on Rte. 202, 14111 N.E. 145th St.* ☎ *425-488-4653.* One of the first wineries in the state producing European vinifera, the winery offers complimentary tours, tastings and wine classes in a French château-like setting.

Columbia Winery – *14030 N.E. 145th St., Woodinville.* ☎ *425-488-2776.* Another pioneering Washington winery and the producer of well-respected vintages, the Columbia facility features weekend tours and the state's largest tasting bar.

Hedges Cellars – *195 N.E. Gilman Blvd., Issaquah.* ☎ *425-391-6056.* A new tasting room opened at this small winery provides a European atmosphere in which to sample the wares.

the couple decided to offer a few more. Now the former dairy farm is the site of the family's thriving mail-order operation and 17 gardens and greenhouses devoted largely to herbs, sedums and succulents; other specialty gardens include an "edible Eden," featuring food-bearing trees, shrubs, vines, groundcovers, vegetables and herbs. The Herbfarm is also known for its **restaurant**, which prides itself on its fresh ingredients *(reservations required well in advance)*.

Snoqualmie Falls Park – *1/2hr. 25mi east of Seattle via I-90 to Exit 27; follow signs north of Snoqualmie on Rte. 202 to the falls. Open year-round dawn-dusk.* In spring and fall, the swollen Snoqualmie River makes quite a spectacle here as it free-falls 270ft from a ledge (100ft farther than Niagara Falls), then continues on through a rock-rimmed gorge. Since the turn of the century, generators have harnessed the river's energy. Snoqualmie's Plant 1, hidden underground behind the falls, was the world's first underground electric-generating facility. Puget Sound Energy now operates two plants on the site, generating enough power to supply 16,000 homes. The company has also set aside a two-acre park for public enjoyment of the falls. From the observation platform at road level, the .5mi River Trail descends the cliffs toward Plant 2, at river's edge.

OLYMPIA

Michelin map 493 B 3 — and map p 251
Population 39,188
Tourist Information ☎ 360-357-3362 or www.olympiachamber.com

Washington's small, pleasant capital on **Budd Inlet** is dominated by the striking dome of the state capitol. Bureaucratic concerns have characterized the town almost from its inception in the 1840s, when it was called Smithfield and boasted the first US customs house in the Northwest. A pioneer from Maine, Edmund Sylvester, platted it in 1850, and three years later it ranked as the largest town on Puget Sound and the meeting place for the newly formed territorial assembly.

In 1856 a wooden Territorial Capitol was built, and for the next three decades Olympia fought hard to fend off claims by rival cities Yakima, Vancouver, Seattle and Tacoma to have the capital moved. With statehood in 1889, Olympia was chosen by the electorate as the permanent state capital, but by then its boom days were long gone. Railroads had made their way to other towns and commerce had followed. Throughout this century, Olympia has remained a quiet backwater whose main business revolves around state government. No area of town is far out of sight of **Capitol Lake** or Budd Inlet. Fronting the inlet, **Percival Landing** *(4th Ave. between Sylvester and Water Sts.)* offers a 1.5mi waterside boardwalk, as well as shops and restaurants. The nearby **Olympia Farmers' Market** *(north end of Capital Way.; open year-round Thu–Sun 10am–3pm)* attracts some 80 produce, crafts and food vendors, making it the second-largest farmers' market in the state.

The current **Board of Education Building** *(Legion Way between Franklin and Washington Sts.)* began life as the Thurston County Courthouse, but was used for the first decades of this century as chambers for the state legislature; it is frequently called the **Old State Capitol**. The striking Romanesque Revival structure was designed by W. A. Ritchie, who received his architectural training through a correspondence course that educated him so well he went on to design imposing courthouses for Spokane and Port Townsend.

SIGHTS *1 day*

★★**State Capitol** – *Off Capitol Way between 11th and 16th Aves. Open year-round Mon–Sat 8am–5pm, Sun 10am–4pm. Closed Jan 1, Thanksgiving Day, Dec 25.* ✗ ♿ 🅿 ☎ *360-664-2700.* A long time in the making, Washington's state capitol building got off to a sluggish start. When the 42nd state was admitted to the Union in 1889, the US government granted it revenues from 132,000 acres of federal land to use in building a permanent state capital building. A design competition held in 1893 awarded acclaimed New York architect Ernest Flagg the contract for the building, based on his Neoclassical, heavily ornamented design. Soon after excavations for the foundation began, however, a nationwide depression struck and funds for further construction dissolved. The **Thurston County Courthouse** was pressed into use as an interim capitol and not until 1911 did work resume on the new capitol. This time a new Romanesque design by Walter Wilder and Harry White was chosen, to rise on the incomplete foundations of Flagg's building. The Wilder-White plans were influenced by the Rhode Island capitol building, which had been designed by their former colleague, Stanford White, of the prestigious New York firm McKim, Mead, and White. Their plan saw the Legislative Building surrounded by five other government structures; four were built and more were added later to the eight-acre greensward now called the **Capitol Campus**. Also gracing the sweeping campus are a conservatory, the Tivoli Fountain (modeled on the one in Copenhagen) and memorials honoring Washingtonians who served in World War I, World War II, Korea and Vietnam.

Visit – *1/2 hr.* Completed in 1928 and renovated in 1986, the capitol boasts a gleaming white dome that rises 287ft above its base, making it the fourth-highest all-masonry, domed building in the world. The 42 steps of local sandstone that lead to the north-facing main entrance commemorate Washington's place as the 42nd state admitted to the Union. Below the entrance pediment, six bronze doors are embossed with scenes symbolizing the state's history and industry. From the entrance, the view to the northwest looks out on the Olympic Mountains.

Inside the capitol, the north vestibule is offset by two statues of Washingtonians, replicas of works created for Statuary Hall in the US Capitol. One is of Marcus Whitman, the first medical doctor in the region; the other is Mother Joseph, a Catholic nun who spearheaded the development of charitable institutions in the state in the late 19C.

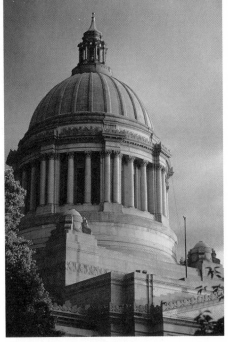

State Capitol

© Robert Holmes

Beyond the vestibule, the soaring **capitol dome** overhangs the rotunda. Suspended from it, a five-ton crystal Tiffany chandelier is centered above the state seal inset in a marble floor. Other public areas include the ornate **State Reception Room** and the house and senate **legislative chambers**. The interior corridors and stairs of the building are fashioned of marble from Alaska.

State Capital Museum – *211 W. 21st. Ave. Open year-round Tue–Fri 10am–4pm, weekends noon–4pm. Closed major holidays. $2. & 🅿 ☎ 360-753-2580.* The Italian Renaissance-style home, built by late-19C Olympia banker and mayor C.J. Lord, now houses exhibits devoted to the political and cultural history of both Olympia and the state. Second-floor exhibits focus on the traditions, past and present, of the Native Americans of Puget Sound and the ramifications of 19C contact on their culture.

Bigelow House Museum – *918 Glass Ave. N.E. Visit by guided tour (40min) only, year-round weekends & holidays 1pm–3pm; Thur–Fri by appointment. Closed Easter Sunday. $3. & 🅿 ☎ 360-753-1215.* This Carpenter Gothic-style frame house was built by Harvard-educated lawyer Daniel Bigelow in 1854 and remains the home of his descendants. An early advocate for creating Washington Territory, Bigelow was also a supporter of civil rights, temperance and public education. The parlor, dining room and kitchen now display original Bigelow family furnishings.

EXCURSIONS

Tumwater Falls Historical Park – *1 hr. 1mi south of Olympia on Deschutes Pkwy. in Tumwater. Open year-round dawn-dusk. ☎ 360-754-4160.* Located along the banks of the Deschutes River, the park offers picnic and children's play areas and looks out to Olympia's old redbrick brewery, across the river. Above the riverfront, the **Historic Crosby House** (now one of the state's oldest surviving wood frame homes) was built in 1858 by Nathaniel and Cordelia Crosby, grandparents of actor Bing Crosby. A grand piano shipped by sea to the Crosbys still dominates the parlor. The nearby Victorian **Henderson House Museum** (1905) was originally the home of an Olympia Brewery brewmaster. It now features changing exhibits of works by local artists *(open year-round Mon–Fri 9am–5pm).*

Mima Mounds Natural Area – *1 1/2 hrs. 12mi south of Olympia via I-5. Take Exit 95, then follow signs west to Littlerock. Continue through town, and turn right on Waddell Creek Rd. for .9mi. Open daily year-round; walking access only. & 🅿 ☎ 360-748-2383.* This area of expansive prairie-covered mounds south of Tumwater has been a scientific curiosity since 1841, when Capt. Charles Wilkes of the US Exploring Expedition made a special trip to see it. Theories on the creators of these abundant earthen mounds range from gophers to glaciers. Many scientists believe they may have been created by freezing and thawing conditions when the last ice age glaciers retreated from the area some 10,000 to 15,000 years ago. In 1967 they were designated a National Natural Landmark, and in 1976 the state purchased A 445-acre tract as a Natural Area Preserve; the paved Mima Mounds Natural Trail (.5mi) leads through the mounds; A 2mi loop extends south. The mounds support a native prairie grassland which includes wildflowers, butterflies and birds.

★**Wolf Haven International** – *1 1/2 hrs. 10mi southeast of Olympia via Old Rte. 99 (Capital Blvd.; then go east .3mi on Offut Lake Rd. Visit by guided tour (1 hr) only, May–Sept Wed–Mon 10am–4pm. Mar–May & Oct Wed–Mon 10am–3pm. $6.* 🅿 ☎ *360-264-4695 or www.wolfhaven.org.* Founded in 1983 to provide a sanctuary for unwanted captive wolves and to re-educate the public concerning the animals, an 80-acre site nestled into a forest amid the Mima Mounds houses more than a dozen gray wolves bred in captivity. Guided tours among the large, open-air animal enclosures explain wolf behavior and socialization. The facility is also the major breeder of the extremely endangered Mexican gray wolf (enclosures not on view). An ongoing program to re-introduce animals from the center into their natural habitat has thus far met with little success, owing to human predation.

★★**Nisqually National Wildlife Refuge** – *2 hrs. 8mi east of Olympia via I-5. Take Exit 114, then go east .5mi on Brown Farm Rd. Trails open year-round daily dawn-dusk. $3/car. www.rl.fws.gov.* Preserving natural habitat in the Nisqually River Delta, the refuge wetlands attract some 300 species of birds, mammals, reptiles, amphibians and fish. Remnants of the dairy farm that once claimed this area can be seen in an extensive dike built to keep out saltwater and in two renovated barns used for educational groups. A series of trails follow the dike through forest and marshland to the barns and beyond. Loons, grebes, cormorants, harriers, hawks and a variety of ducks, geese and songbirds are frequently spotted. A new **Visitor Center** explains the natural history of the area *(open year-round daily 9am–4pm; closed Jan 1, Thanksgiving Day, Dec 25;* ♿ 🅿 ☎ *360-753-9467).*

TACOMA

Michelin map 493 B 3 and map p 206
Population 179,814
Tourist Information ☎ 253-627-2836 or www.tpctourism.org

Hailed as the "City of Destiny" in the late 19C, the old railroad/port city of Tacoma has been busily brushing up its somewhat tarnished "aging industrial town" image in the past decade. A reinvigorated downtown now boasts notable museums, galleries, a new University of Washington campus and a lively theater district, all within a few walkable blocks of one another. Throughout Tacoma, parks, restaurant districts and fine old neighborhoods lend Washington's third largest city a livable charm and small-town friendliness.

Historical Notes

For centuries before the arrival of Europeans, Nisqually and Puyallup tribes lived in this coastal area virtually in the shadow of the looming mountain (Rainier) they called "Tacobet"—Mother of Waters. The British, following in the steps of Captain George Vancouver, arrived in the area in 1833 and established a Hudson's Bay Company fur-trading post called Fort Nisqually.

About 20 years later, the first independent settlers arrived, mostly lumbermen intent on extracting the area's forested wealth. By 1865 a lumber town had grown up on Commencement Bay. It was called Tacoma, a corruption of the native word "Tacobet." From the outset, city founders had hopes that their town would be chosen as a likely western terminus for the Northern Pacific Railroad, and in 1873 their dreams were realized. A decade later, with rail lines linking it to eastern markets, Tacoma became the "City of Destiny," and new settlers spilled in seeking their own fortunes. For another 10 years, Tacoma sustained the excitement of a boomtown, until the nationwide depression of 1893 briefly interrupted its growth. By the turn of the century, however, it was quickly recovering, thanks in large part to the establishment of the Weyerhaeuser Timber Company, with headquarters in downtown.

The opening of the Panama Canal in 1914, offering a much easier shipping link between eastern and western markets, further spurred development, as did the dredging of the city's Thea Foss Waterway. Meanwhile, the railroads maintained a strong presence in the city, with the Milwaukee, Great Northern, Union Pacific and Northern Pacific Companies vying for city land and shipping.

While the world wars added ever more economic opportunity to Tacoma, at the end of World War II, the city's long-running boom began to tail off, and downtown Tacoma became a graying, over-industrialized remnant of an earlier age. But with the 1980s restoration of the old Pantages and Rialto theaters and the 1992 renovation of Union Station, Tacoma's downtown began a revitalization that continues today. In 1996 the Washington State History Museum opened a new 106,000sq ft facility, and a year later the University of Washington Tacoma Branch opened directly across from it. The first phase of the 46-acre campus is also across from Union Station, and plans for more museums and development at this south end of downtown are underway.

Despite this development, the city has worked to preserve its history as well. Northwest of downtown, **Stadium Historical District** protects stately Victorian and early 20C homes that crowd the hills overlooking Commencement Bay. The area is named for its château-like Stadium High School *(N. 2nd St.)*, built as a luxury hotel and locally known as the "Castle."

Tacoma recently moved up in rank to the fifth-largest container port on the continent, and shipping, much of it coming or going to Pacific Rim countries or Alaska, is still much in evidence on Commencement Bay. But such white-collar industries as the Frank Russell Company, an international pension and investment concern, have recently edged into the blue-collar base of city employment, and deal-makers can often be seen meeting in the upscale waterfront restaurants along **Ruston Way**. Joggers and walkers, too, take advantage of the 2mi paved path that bends along the bay shoreline here.

SIGHTS *2 days*

Downtown – On the bluffs above the Thea Foss Waterway, Tacoma's revitalized downtown is justifiably proud of its **theater district** *(Broadway and S. 9th St.)*. The **Broadway Center for the Performing Arts** houses three theaters: the Classical Revival **Pantages Theater** (1918), which hosts the Tacoma Symphony; the Beaux-Arts 1918 **Rialto Theater**, where two ballet companies and a chamber orchestra perform; and the **Theatre on the Square**, home to the Tacoma Actors Guild. Nearby, the small but whimsical **Children's Museum of Tacoma** [Kids] *(936 Broadway)* holds hands-on changing exhibits and activities for children up to 12 years of age. The city's **Antique Row** *(Broadway between S. 7th and 9th Sts.)* is lined with galleries, small restaurants and antique shops. Anchoring the east side of downtown is the red-brick **Old City Hall Clock Tower** *(Pacific Ave. between S. 8th and 9th Sts.)*, an 1886 Italian Renaissance-style structure; and A 105ft **totem pole★** *(Fireman's Park at S. 9th St.)* carved by Native Americans from southeast Alaska, ranks as one of the largest such totems in the US.

★**Tacoma Art Museum** – *1123 Pacific Ave. Open year-round Tue–Sun 10am–5pm (Thu 8pm), and Monday holidays. $5.* &. ☎ *253-272-4258. www.tacomaartmuseum.org.* One of the world's largest public collections of **glass art★★** by **Dale Chihuly**

TACOMA

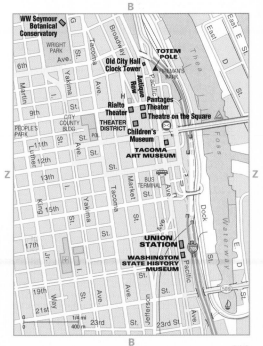

© Robert Holmes

Dale Chihuly Window at Union Station

(p 204) highlights the permanent collection of this small museum. has a strong showing among 19C European and American Impressionists. Also featured are Japanese woodblock prints The museum presents changing exhibits of works by Northwest artists and hosts national and international traveling exhibits.

★**Union Station** – *1717 Pacific Ave. Guided tours begin at visitor kiosk in rotunda. Open year-round Mon–Fri 8am–5pm. Closed major holidays.* ✗ ᕀ 🄿 🕾 *253-572-9310.* Completed in 1911, this impressive domed, Beaux-Arts structure is fronted by a Larry Anderson bronze entitled *New Beginnings.* The sculpture, depicting A 19C traveler with valise, recalls the romance of rail travel.
The last train pulled out of Union Station in 1984, and thereafter the structure was left to languish for a number of years. An extensive 1992 restoration replaced the copper roof of the large dome and transformed the station into an entrance building leading to the new US Courthouse. The rotunda now displays monumental Dale Chihuly **glass art**★★. A public contest held to name the large glass installation hanging below the dome resulted in the title *Cobalt Blue Chandelier.* Each of the four mezzanine-level bays also frame Chihuly works: the east bay features a work from his "Persian spinners" series; the west is from his Venetian series; the south bay is known as the Lackawanna Ikebana Installation, as it incorporates the metal grid of an Erie/Lackawanna Railroad sign; an abstract acrylic painting hangs in the north bay.
Plans are underway for a new **International Glass Museum**, to be situated on nearby Dock Street. A 575ft-long "bridge of glass" walkway will span I-705 and provide access from Union Station to the museum; completion is expected in 2002.

★★**Washington State History Museum** – *Pacific Ave. and S. 19th St. Open Memorial Day-Labor Day Mon–Sat 10am–6pm (Thu 8pm), Sun 11am–6pm. Rest of the year Tue–Sat 10am–5pm, Sun 11am–5pm. $7.* ✗ ᕀ 🄿 🕾 *253-272-3500 or 888-238-4373. www.wshs.org.* Inspired by the renovation of Union Station, the Washington State Historical Society built this museum facility adjacent to it on the former depot grounds. Opened in 1996, the museum is notable for its ground-level **Great Hall of Washington History**★, a comprehensive look at the state's past, from the pre-contact Native American period through the current computer age. The Great Hall's nine thematic exhibit areas include: "Encounters," life-size dioramic settings where

---

▪ Dale Chihuly

Born in Tacoma in 1941, Dale Chihuly graduated from the University of Washington, then received an M.F.A. from the prestigious Rhode Island School of Design, where his gifts as a glass artist blossomed. Now an internationally recognized force in the arts, Chihuly founded his own acclaimed **Pilchuck Glass School** in 1971 in Stanwood, Washington. His influence has led to the burgeoning of glass art in the Northwest during the past 25 years, and his own dramatic works can be seen in a host of public places, museums and galleries.

mannequins and voice-overs dramatize early interactions between Euro-Americans and local Native Americans; a re-created Southern Coast Salish plank house, with life-size figures poised in everyday tasks; "Natural Setting," detailing the state's geography; "Native Heritage," featuring a Petroglyph Theater and recorded Native American storytellers; "Railroads" and "Frontier Towns," focusing on 19C settlement and development; "Wageworkers Frontier, Logging and Lumber," detailing major state industries over the last century; "Modern Washington," a leap ahead to the state's high-tech present, complete with a 42ft transmission tower and the Columbia River Theater, with changing films; "Homefront and Hard Times," recapturing the Depression and war eras, and related government projects, such as the Hanford nuclear site, Grand Coulee Dam and the rise of Boeing; and, finally, "Inviting the Spirit," changing exhibits of works by state artists.

Upper-level galleries are devoted to temporary regional history exhibits.

W. W. Seymour Botanical Conservatory – *Wright Park at S. 3rd and G Sts. Open year-round daily 10am–4:30pm. Closed Thanksgiving Day & Dec 25.* ☎ *253-591-5330.* Built in 1908, the Victorian-style conservatory supports 200 species of tropical plants, notably orchids, cacti and bromeliads. An exhibit area celebrates the seasons with changing floral displays of spring-blooming bulbs; summer annuals; fall chrysanthemums; and winter poinsettias.

Narrows Bridge – *Rte. 16, west edge of city.* This dramatic, 5,979ft-long bridge ranks as the fifth-largest suspension bridge in the world. Hovering 188ft above the Narrows, a narrow water passage in southeastern Puget Sound, it boasts a center span measuring 2,800ft in length. The bridge's predecessor was the star-crossed and now legendary "Galloping Gertie," so named for the way it swayed in the wind. Opened in 1940, Gertie lasted only four months before it collapsed. Today's rendition has spanned the Narrows since 1950.

© Robert Holmes

Point Defiance Park and Narrows Bridge

★**Point Defiance Park** – *Pearl St. at N. 54th St., 3mi north of Exit 132 off Rte. 16.* Taking full advantage of its setting on the lush Point Defiance Peninsula between Commencement Bay and Puget Sound, this 700-acre city greensward incorporates miles of trails through old-growth forests, interrupted by gardens, a zoo and historic attractions. A one-way road circles the park, with access to peaceful **Owen Beach** on Commencement Bay. Near the park entrance are several lovely **gardens**, including a hillside native garden, rose gardens backed by an 1898 stone-and-wood lodge, a Japanese garden with a pagoda and a woodland rhododendron garden.

★**Point Defiance Zoo and Aquarium** – **Kids** *5400 N. Pearl St. Open Memorial Day-Labor Day daily 10am–7pm. Rest of the year daily 10am–5pm. Closed Thanksgiving Day & Dec 25. $7.25.* ✕ & 🅿 ☎ *253-591-5337. www.pdza.org.* This small but well-done facility traces its origins to the efforts of two young city residents who built a saltwater aquarium on a pavilion overlooking Commencement Bay in 1930. Their endeavor ultimately inspired the creation of a non-profit Zoological Society that resulted in the current 29-acre zoo and aquarium complex, which houses more than 5,000 animals representing almost 300 species. A nationally recognized leader in the captive breeding and re-introduction of **red wolves**, the zoo sometimes echoes with their howls.

Rocky Shores, the zoo's signature attraction, features sleek white beluga whales swimming through cold, rock-edged pools. **Arctic Tundra** contains large habitats for polar bears, musk oxen and Arctic foxes. At **Discovery Reef**, a simulated South Pacific environment is home to seven species of sharks. An abrupt change of atmosphere heralds the **North Pacific** area, dominated by a large open pool with marine creatures of that region.

TACOMA

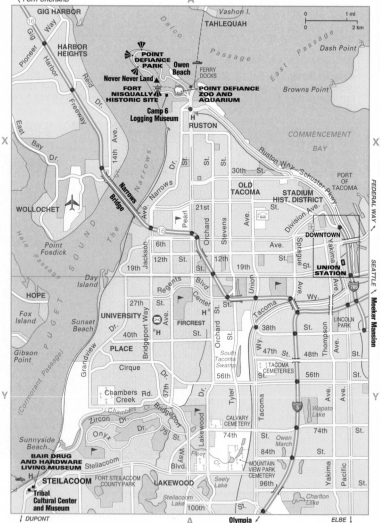

★★ Fort Nisqually Historic Site – ▥ *Five Mile Dr., southwest corner of the park. Open Memorial Day-Labor Day 11am–6pm. Rest of the year Wed–Sun 11am–5pm. Closed major holidays. $2.* ▯ ☎ *253-591-5339. www.fortnisqually.org.* Britain's Hudson's Bay Company established its first outpost on Puget Sound in 1833, about 17mi south of this location. The re-created, palisaded fort depicts life at the company's fur-trading post in the year 1855, after the fort had been moved a mile inland. By 1869, the outpost had ceased to function, owing to increased harassment by American interests determined to drive British traders from the area. The majority of the half-dozen buildings now overlooking the fort's grassy central expanse are re-creations of period buildings, but the post-and-sill **New Granary**, considered one of the state's oldest extant structures, contains 60 percent of its original timbers. Other structures include a trade store displaying firearms, blankets and other items; a blacksmith shop where demonstrations are given; a simply furnished laborers' dwelling; and a clap-board kitchen with an adjacent garden. Costumed interpreters explain the activities that took place in the buildings during the mid-19C and demonstrate crafts and other skills of the period. The white frame, picket-fence-enclosed factor's house has a period dining room decorated with the kind of furnishings that would have been used by Dr. Tolmie, the Scottish physician who became the post's chief factor; the house also contains visitor services and exhibits on the fur-trading era.

Just beyond the fort, on the cliffs overlooking Puget Sound, is a **view★** of the Narrows Bridge. Adjacent to the fort lies **Never Never Land** *(open Memorial Day-Labor Day daily 11am–6pm; $3;* ☎ *253-591-5845)*, a 10-acre storybook environment featuring fiber-glass nursery rhyme characters and some thirty scenes well-known to young children.

Camp 6 Logging Museum – *Southeast corner of park, near Fort Nisqually. Open year-round daily dawn-dusk.* ☎ *253-752-0047.* Set amid the peninsula's forests, this open-air museum re-creates conditions in a lumber camp during the steam-logging era (1880-1950). Five raised red camp cars house displays of logging tools and historic photographs. A group of Kapowsin Bunkhouses on timber skids depict liv-ing conditions for loggers; these transportable accommodations could be moved to a new logging site as required. A vintage steam locomotive offers visitors short rides through the forest in summer months and during the Christmas season *(Memorial Day-Sept weekends & holidays; round-trip 30min; $2.50)*.

EXCURSIONS

Steilacoom – *45min. 14mi southwest of Tacoma via Steilacoom Blvd. or Grandview Dr.* Overlooking Puget Sound, this tidy little village holds the distinction of being the state's oldest incorporated town (1854). As such, it also had Washington's first library, territorial jail and courthouse. The quiet, almost nostalgic ambience of the town is particularly apparent at the 1895 **Bair Drug & Hardware Living Museum★** *(1617 Lafayette St.;* ☎ *253-588-9668)*, which functions as an old-fashioned cafe and soda fountain and displays historic hardware merchandise and pharmaceutical equipment in wall cases. Housed in a white clapboard, 1903 church a block away, the **Steilacoom Tribal Cultural Center and Museum** *(1515 Lafayette St.; open year-round Tue–Sun 10am–4pm; $2;* ♿ ☎ *253-584-6308)* has three exhibit areas that focus on the his-tory and craft traditions of the Steilacoom tribe and other Coast Salish groups. The permanent collection contains clothing, basketry, tools, historic photographs and ornamental items ranging from the pre-Columbian era to the present.

★ **Meeker Mansion** – *1 hr. 10mi southeast of Tacoma via Rte. 167. Take Bay St. Exit and follow signs to 312 Spring St. in Puyallup. Open mid-Mar–mid-Dec Wed–Sun 1pm–4pm, holidays 1pm–6pm. Closed Easter Sunday & Thanksgiving Day. $4.* ♿ ☎ *253-848-1770.* Completed in 1890, this 17-room Italianate Victorian mansion was home to Washington legend **Ezra Meeker** (1830-1928) and his wife, Eliza Jane, for 20 years. Mrs. Meeker was the force behind the house, choosing its architects and decor. After his wife's death in 1909, Meeker ceased to live in the house. In subse-quent years, it was used as a hospital, retirement home for Civil War widows and nursing home. In 1970 the Meeker Historical Society acquired it and has since been completing a slow restoration. Decorated in turn-of-the-century furnishings, the house is notable for its woodwork of various native woods and its hand-painted ceilings.

■ Ezra Meeker and the Oregon Trail

An early settler in Washington, Ezra Meeker brought his young family west across the rough Oregon Trail in the mid-19C. At a time when the inter-national hops market was severely affected by the hop louse, Meeker pio-neered hops farming in the Puyallup Valley and transformed it into the short-lived "hops capital of the world." By 1892, however, the louse had decimated crops here as well. Undaunted by severe financial reversals, Meeker ventured to Alaska, hoping to supply gold-rush miners with neces-sities. Though this project failed financially, Meeker remained energetic and in 1906 at the age of 76 he embarked on his greatest adventure. "I longed to go back over the Old Oregon Trail and mark it for all time for the chil-dren of the pioneers who blazed it, and for the world." In an oxen-pulled prairie schooner, Meeker set out East to fulfill his dream. The trip earned him national publicity and an audience with President Theodore Roosevelt, who supported Meeker's efforts to preserve the trail.

In 1912 Meeker made the trek a second time, searching for obscured por-tions of the trail. He received congratulations from another president in 1926, when Calvin Coolidge signed a bill Meeker had pressed for in the US Congress authorizing the minting of 50-cent Oregon Trail memorial coins to be sold for a dollar. The proceeds went to pay for monuments along the trail. When Meeker died just before his 98th birthday, he was preparing a third transcontinental trip, this one in an automobile donated by Henry Ford.

Eastern Washington

Winter Wheat near Waitsburg/© Dick Dietrich

Open, dry and rugged, Eastern Washington takes in a vast expanse of largely desert terrain stretching from the foothills of the Cascade Range to the Idaho border and from Walla Walla to the Okanogan Highlands north of Coulee Dam. The region encompasses three important rivers—the Columbia, Snake, and Yakima—which cut deep, meandering canyons across the arid land. Throughout the region, coarse basalt rock lies close to the surface of the ground and is often exposed as gnarled outcroppings, or as high, nearly vertical cliffs that line the river gorges and dry-bed canyons. Everywhere, the sense of a grand landscape pervades, and there are many natural areas to visit. Spokane and a handful of other cities also offer a fine variety of parks, museums and historic sites.

Known collectively as the Plateau Indians, various groups of indigenous peoples have inhabited the region for at least 10,000 years. Though they have separate tribal names and distinct histories, they shared a common, pre-settlement material culture and, in many cases, a common language. Lewis and Clark passed through Eastern Washington in 1805 on their historic journey to the Pacific Coast. Wars with various Plateau tribes discouraged settlement in Eastern Washington until the 1860s, when cattle ranching began. Soon, farmers, especially in the Yakima Valley, were planting fruit orchards and shipping their produce to market on railroads, which penetrated the region in the 1880s. But it was wheat that became the region's cash crop, particularly in the Palouse area northeast of Walla Walla. During the late 19C, Spokane prospered as a railroad town and banking center for agriculture, logging and mining. In the midst of the Great Depression, dam building along the Columbia River put thousands of unemployed men back to work, brought a major source of power to the region, and provided irrigation to hundreds of thousands of acres of land. During World War II, the federal government established the Hanford site in the Tri-Cities area in order to produce plutonium for nuclear weapons. Today, Eastern Washington's economy continues to rely on agriculture, transportation, manufacturing and government. Tourism also plays a growing role as visitors discover the region's fruit farms, wineries, unique museums, historic sites and awesome landscapes.

Bounded by the Grand Coulee gorge on the east and the foothills of the Cascade Range to the west, the Grand Coulee area takes in a wide swath of sagebrush flats, desert hills and spectacular dry-bed canyons lined with precipitous basalt lava cliffs. The Columbia River corridor bends in from the northeast, then carves around the northern and western perimeters of the region to link two landmark communities, Coulee Dam and Wenatchee. Immense Grand Coulee Dam, constructed during the Great Depression, spans the Columbia, impounds Lake Roosevelt reservoir and pumps water into Banks Lake, which stretches south from the dam and occupies much of the Grand Coulee gorge.

The region's dry-bed canyons, called coulees, were formed during cataclysmic Ice Age floods that scoured out long channels in the underlying layers of basalt. Grand Coulee is perhaps the most spectacular example. During the floods, cliffs at its southern end formed a colossal waterfall 3.5mi wide and 400ft high. The cliffs, now dry, stand over Sun Lakes State Park southwest of Coulee City.

Various Plateau Indians lived in the region for thousands of years, hunting in the coulees and harvesting salmon from the Columbia and its tributaries. Settlement came slowly, but picked up dramatically during and after the construction of Grand Coulee Dam, which now irrigates 500,000 acres of the region's cropland.

COULEE DAM *1 day*

A Depression-era boomtown, the small community of Coulee Dam was built along the Columbia River during the 1930s to house the workers and engineers who built Grand Coulee Dam, which now looms over the town. Originally, the community was divided into two towns: the "engineer's camp," on the west bank, which housed the project's engineers and foremen; and Mason City, on the east bank, built for the construction workers. Today, the economy of Coulee Dam—and of the neighboring towns of Grand Coulee and Electric City—still relies on the dam and its reservoirs for local jobs. Much of the activity relates to tourism, a fact brought home by the town's 36min **Laser Light Show** *(Memorial Day–Jul daily 10pm; Aug daily 9:30pm; Sept daily 8:30pm; ☎ 509-633-9265)*, a narrated extravaganza which uses the dam's spillway as a giant projection screen and fills the canyon with light and reverberating music nightly during summer.

About 20mi north in Nespelem, on the Colville Indian Reservation, is the grave of Nez Percé leader Chief Joseph who led 800 of his people on a long series of marches across eastern Oregon, Washington, Idaho and Montana in the late 1870s. Apprehended by the US cavalry only 40mi short of the Canadian border, he gave a stirring speech that endured:

"Hear me, my chiefs; my heart is sick and sad. From where the sun now stands, I will fight no more forever."

Crown Point – *6mi west of Coulee Dam, via Rte. 174 toward Bridgeport.* A good place to start a visit to Grand Coulee, this vantage point atop the west bluffs offers a grandstand **vista★★★** of the dam, the gorge, the town and the river. Across the river stands an enormous mound of sand left over from concrete production for the dam. Measuring 12 million cubic yards, the sandpile takes up as much space as the dam itself.

★★**Grand Coulee Dam** – *Above the town of Coulee Dam. Visitor Arrival Center on the west bank open Jun–Jul daily 8:30am–11pm.*

© Robert Holmes

Grand Coulee Dam

Aug daily 8:30am–10:30pm. Sept daily 8:30am–9:30pm. Rest of the year daily 9am–5pm. Visit of dam interior by guided tour (40min) only, year–round starting at 10am; stop at visitor center for schedules. & ⚑ ☎ *509-633-9265.* The mammoth 550ft-high wall of sloped concrete, measuring 500ft wide at its base, stretches across the Columbia River for nearly a mile, spanning the rugged cliffs of a deep desert canyon and backing up the waters of the Columbia for 151mi to create Lake Roosevelt. Built during the Great Depression under the auspices of the Public Works Administration, it put thousands of unemployed men to work from 1933-42 and began operating shortly after Japan bombed Pearl Harbor. Electricity from its turbines powered aircraft assembly plants and other crucial war industries in the Northwest. After World War II, its operations expanded to include irrigation. Water impounded behind the dam as Lake Roosevelt was pumped onto the bed of Grand Coulee to create Banks Lake, 30mi long, which now irrigates a half million acres of farmland. Today the dam has the largest power-generating capacity in the US at 6,809 megawatts. These benefits, however, have come at significant cost to the environment. Lake Roosevelt submerged more than 150mi of riparian and wetland habitat, and the dam itself destroyed a rich salmon run.

Exploration of the dam starts on the west side of the canyon at the Visitor Arrival Center, a circular concrete building overlooking

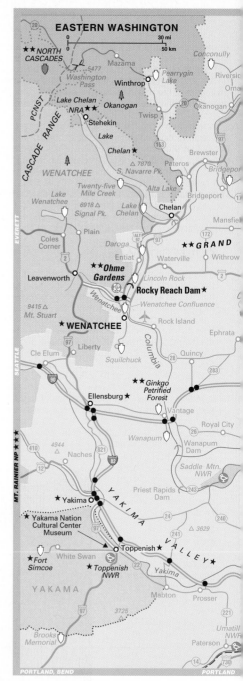

the dam and its tailwaters. A film *(50min)* employs original newsreel footage to chronicle the dam's construction. Exhibits include historic photos and the wheelchair President Roosevelt sat in while visiting the construction site in August 1934. Here, too, is the control booth for Coulee Dam's nightly Laser Show.

Three guided tours investigate sections of the dam's labyrinthine interior, leading visitors through long hallways of gleaming tile and across terrazzo floors—some of which include full-scale inlaid diagrams of the generators' working components. Tours of the Third Powerhouse *(30min)*, completed during the 1970s, include a glimpse of its colossal generator shafts and a ride down the face of the dam in a glass-enclosed incline elevator that offers spectacular **views**★★ and provides a sense of the structure's awesome scale. The Left Powerhouse tour *(30min)* explores the dam's first powerhouse, and the Right Powerhouse tour *(45min)* visits the second.

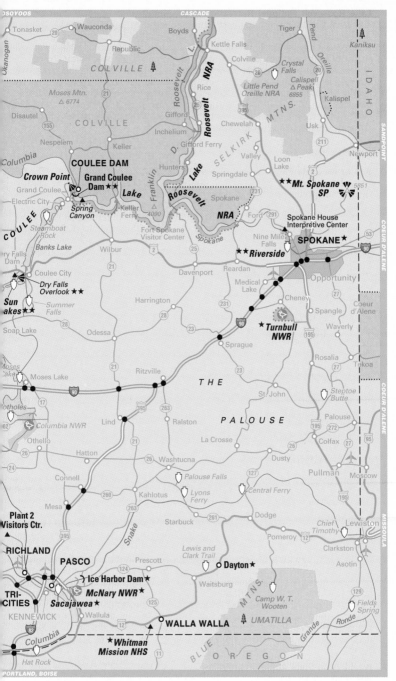

Colville Confederated Tribes Museum – *East bank, 512 Mead Way. Open year-round Mon–Sat 10am–6pm.* ♿ 🅿 ☏ *509-633-0751*. Housed in a modest A-frame building, a small museum provides a brief cultural overview of the Colville Confederated Tribes, which include some of the Nez Percé tribe as well as the Okanogan, Methow, Wenatchi, Moses/Columbia, Nespelem and Colville peoples. A large central exhibit displays woven baskets, beaded buckskin clothing, a Jefferson Peace Medal carried by the Lewis and Clark Expedition (1804-06), and copies of Matthew's Gospel translated into Nez Percé. There are also many historic photos, arrowheads and other flaked stone points, and a small exhibit on Chief Joseph's 1877 fighting retreat across the West with his band of Nez Percé. A tribal gift shop full of contemporary native arts and crafts occupies the lower level.

Lake Roosevelt National Recreation Area – *Information at 1008 Crest Dr. The lake stretches 151mi east and northeast of Coulee Dam. Spring Canyon is 7mi east of town via Rtes. 155 and 174.* ⚠ 🅿 ☎ *509-633-9441.* Best suited for visitors with boats, this national recreation area extends for roughly 130mi along the shores of Lake Roosevelt and takes in 28 campgrounds, 22 boat ramps and dozens of beaches. Few roads within convenient reach of Coulee Dam approach the lake, but one of the recreation area's most popular campgrounds—**Spring Canyon**—lies just 7mi from town and offers a large beach, lawns and shaded picnic areas. Near the campground, you'll find the start of the self-guiding **Bunchgrass Prairie Nature Trail★** *(.75mi)*, which explores a section of the shrub-steppe ecosystem that once covered most of eastern Washington.

Excursion

★★Sun Lakes State Park – *2 hrs. 31mi southwest of Coulee Dam via Rtes. 155, US-2 and Rte. 17. Open year-round daily dawn–dusk.* ⚠ 🅿 ☎ *509-632-5583.* Located within the spectacular rock-lined gorge of Grand Coulee, Sun Lakes State Park takes in the site of an immense Ice Age waterfall as well as a series of nine small lakes that lie beneath the cliffs on the old riverbed. The waterfall that once thundered over these now-dry faces of basalt measured 3.5mi wide by 400ft high and was created by the great Spokane Floods of the Pleistocene era. Dozens of times, floodwaters roared along the route of the Columbia River and then south past this point. They scoured out the broad, flat-floored trough of Grand Coulee, crashed over these cliffs and then raced down the canyon. After the floods, the Columbia River resumed its normal course and left the coulee and the site of the ancient cascade high and dry.

The drive south from Coulee Dam follows the shoreline of Banks Lake through the rugged beauty of Grand Coulee, where nearly vertical cliffs rise from the water and huge knobs of basalt protrude from the lake as islands of bare, black rock. At **Dry Falls Overlook★★** *(3mi southwest of Coulee City)*, a Civilian Conservation Corps shelter perches at the rim of the cliffs and offers a splendid **vista★★** of the waterfall site. Signs explain the formation of the falls, and a painted rendition helps visitors imagine what they might have looked like. A **visitor center** here also overlooks the gorge and offers exhibits on the geology of the falls, the Columbia Plateau and the Spokane Floods. Two miles farther south off Route 17, state park roads descend to the floor of the gorge and double back among the sagebrush and protrusions of basalt to what was once the base of the falls (follow signs to Dry Falls Lake). The park also offers beaches, picnic grounds and boat rentals.

★WENATCHEE   *1/2 day*

Located at the confluence of the Wenatchee and Columbia rivers, Wenatchee stretches for miles beneath a line of spectacular, semiarid mountain ridges that rise above the rooftops as a vast, deeply furrowed wall, studded with rock outcrops and largely bare of trees. From some points, a cluster of peaks in the Cascade Range jut above the ridges as a reminder of the alpine beauty that exists west of town within the Wenatchee National Forest. A fishing and hunting ground for Plateau Indians for thousands of years, the Wenatchee Valley was settled during the 1870s by ranchers, traders and apple growers. With the arrival of the railroad in 1892, it became an important shipping hub for the region's agricultural produce. Irrigation began in 1904, greatly expanded the valley's arable land, and helped boost it to the forefront of Washington's apple industry. Wenatchee remains an important agricultural center, but its economy has diversified to include manufacturing, medical services, utilities and government service. About 25mi northwest, the popular Bavarian-style tourist village of **Leavenworth** has dozens of shops and motels; outfitters here offer white-water rafting trips along the scenic Wenatchee River.

Washington State Apple Commission Visitor Center – *2900 Euclid Ave., off US-2/97 in north part of town. Open May–Dec Mon–Fri 8am–5pm, Sat 9am–5pm, Sun 10am–4pm. Rest of the year Mon–Fri 8am–5pm.* ♿ 🅿 ☎ *509-663-9600. www.bestapples.com.* Located in the lobby of the Washington State Apple Commission, the center offers a 17min video and several small exhibits that cover the growing, harvesting and marketing of apples. Most of the space is devoted to a gift shop selling T-shirts, sweatshirts, cookbooks and trinkets incorporating an apple motif.

★North Central Washington Museum – *127 S. Mission St. Open year-round Mon–Sat 10am–4pm. Closed Jan 1, Thanksgiving Day, Dec. 25. $3.* ♿ 🅿 ☎ *509-664-3340.* Located downtown in Wenatchee's historic Post Office buildings (1917, 1937), this excellent regional history museum focuses on farm and town life of the early 20C and includes an outstanding depiction of the apple industry past and present. Exhibits begin inside the marble-lined lobby of the building with a series of re-created settings c.1910 that include the interior of a typical home and various

Main Street businesses such as a general store, bank and printing shop. Here, too, are displayed a gleaming Oldsmobile Palace Touring Car and a massive pipe organ rescued from Wenatchee's Liberty Theatre. Upstairs, an exhibit on the Great Northern Railway includes an elaborate, coin-operated **model train★★**, that winds through a spectacular and meticulously detailed re-creation of the three mountainous railroad routes over Stevens Pass northwest of Wenatchee. On the first floor of the museum annex, the **Apple Industry Exhibit** displays a fascinating array of 1920s farm equipment, including a fully operational **packing line★**. Roughly 45ft long, this contraption of wood, canvas, whirling rope and gears polishes, sorts, and flings apples into their proper bins.

★★Ohme Gardens County Park – *North Wenatchee, off US-2/97, follow signs. 3327 Ohme Rd. Open mid-Apr–mid-Oct daily 9am–6pm. $6.* 🅿 ☎ *509-662-5785. www.ohmegardens.com.* A masterpiece of landscape architecture, Ohme Gardens is an enticing pocket of shade, water, lawn and stone perched atop a rocky bluff overlooking Wenatchee and the Columbia River Valley. Its sinuous flagstone paths wander among a pleasing blend of tall evergreens, natural rock formations, lovely blue-green pools, tiny sun-dappled lawns, stone fireplaces and rustic shelters. Viewpoints open vistas of the river and its long line of rumpled hills as well as a glimpse of the Cascade Range. Begun in 1929 by the Ohme family and tended by them for more than 60 years, the gardens are now managed by Chelan County. The nine acres of grounds were intended to suggest a natural mountain setting, and, to a large extent, they succeed. The abundant use of native stone for walkways, benches and tables, the groves of mature evergreens transplanted from neighboring mountains, the trickle of water, and the use of native perennials all combine to produce an idealized alpine scene. A color map helps visitors navigate the 1mi network of trails and to find such highlights as Totem Pole Lodge, Hidden Pool, Sylvan Pool, Canadian Point and Wishing Well.

Excursion

★Rocky Reach Dam – *1 1/2 hrs. 7mi north of Wenatchee via Alt. US-97. Open May–Oct daily 8am–6pm. Rest of the year daily 8am–4pm. Closed Jan–mid-Feb, Thanksgiving Day, Dec 25.* ✗ ♿ 🅿 ☎ *509-663-7522. www.chelanpud.org.* Spanning the Columbia River north of Wenatchee where two sets of high stone bluffs converge on the water, Rocky Reach Dam was constructed between 1956 and 1961 and can generate 1,280 megawatts of electricity. It offers 18 acres of pleasantly landscaped grounds, a visitor center, fish ladder viewing area and extensive exhibits covering the geology and history of the Columbia Plateau as well as the long history of electric power generation. Self-guided tours of the facility begin at the visitor center, where an auditorium screens 11 different videos covering such topics as the construction of the dam, hydroelectric generation and salmon migration. One floor down, you'll find the fish ladder viewing room, with its row of windows embedded into the concrete so visitors can watch migrating salmon make their way around the dam. A short walk along the top of the dam leads to the powerhouse, which contains the dam's interpretive museum, art gallery and gallery of electricity. All feature worthwhile exhibits, especially the latter, which traces the history of electric power generation and use from the electrostatic generators of the 1750s to the hydroelectric and nuclear power plants of today. Throughout, you hear and feel the constant thunder of the spinning turbines. Balconies at each end of the powerhouse allow visitors to look down on the row of 11 generator housings, some of them running, others in various states of repair.

SPOKANE★

Michelin map 493 D 3 and map pp 218-219
Population 184,058
Tourist Information ☎ 888-776-5263 or www.visitspokane.com

Settled during the 1880s as a transportation hub and trading center for the agricultural, mining and logging industries, Spokane sprawls along the steep, wooded slopes of the Spokane River Valley in northeastern Washington. Its vibrant downtown area encompasses dozens of historic buildings, an impressive urban park that hosted the 1974 World's Fair, and a spectacular stretch of the river where waterfalls crash over magnificent basalt lava cliffs. To the south and west of downtown lie Spokane's earliest residential neighborhoods, which line the shaded bluffs of the valley with Victorian-era mansions and well-kept Craftsman-style bungalows and cottages. Scattered throughout the metropolitan area are several fine parks offering a variety of settings, from formal gardens brimming with flowerbeds to the rugged terrain of the river corridor.

Historical Notes

Nature's Bounty – Prior to the arrival of outsiders, various indigenous peoples, known collectively as the Plateau Indians, had been living in the Spokane region for at least 10,700 years. Dwelling in tule-mat lodges, they made seasonal rounds of the rivers, forests and prairies of the Columbia Plateau. They depended heavily on the abundant salmon runs for protein but also hunted deer, elk and waterfowl, and gathered roots, nuts and berries.

In 1810 the North West Company established a fur trading post at the confluence of the Spokane and Little Spokane rivers (within today's Riverside State Park). The outpost, known as Spokane House, operated for just 15 years before the traders dismantled it and rebuilt at Kettle Falls, on the Columbia.

Settlers began filtering into the Spokane area during the 1870s, but it was only after the Northern Pacific Railroad's arrival in 1881 that the city firmly established itself as a transportation hub and began to boom. Between 1880 and 1910, its population grew from 350 to more than 104,000. The discovery of rich silver and lead mines in nearby northern Idaho and British Columbia spurred its growth, as did its location near the vast timber lands and rich farm country of the Inland Northwest. Sawmills, flour mills and railroad yards were built along the river, and construction began on a series of hydroelectric dams.

In 1889 fire destroyed 32 blocks of central Spokane. The city rebuilt in grand style, funded by the deep pockets of mining magnates, timber barons, railroads, bankers and shipping companies. Elegant brick, stone and terra-cotta facades rose throughout the downtown area as storefronts, tall office buildings, hotels and warehouses. During the same era, Spokane's wealthiest citizens built themselves ornate mansions in what is now called the Historic Browne's Addition Neighborhood, just west of downtown.

Downtown Spokane (c.1900)

Settling Down – During the early decades of the 20C, Spokane became a settled community of pleasant tree-lined neighborhoods built around a bustling downtown core. A series of inviting neighborhood and community parks were also built to preserve and enhance the quality of Spokane's public places.

During World War II, the region saw an influx of people who staffed the nearby military bases, supply depots and aluminum mills. After the war, tracts of new homes sprang up around Spokane on what had been small farms. In time, much of the city's business began to move to the suburbs, and the neglected downtown area slipped into decline.

The Expo '74 World's Fair reversed that slide. Held in Riverfront Park, which was specially built for the occasion, the fair led to the removal of urban blight, and a renewal of commercial interest in the downtown area resulted in rejuvenation of the Spokane River. Today, the rushing river, the abundance of interesting restaurants, pubs and shops, the presence of attractive historical buildings, and a wonderful network of pathways along the river corridor make the heart of Spokane a joy to visit.

Practical Information

Getting There – **Spokane International Airport** (GEG) ☎ 455-6455: 7mi west of city. Transportation to downtown via shuttle service *(by appointment ☎ 535-6979)*, hotel courtesy shuttles and taxis *($16)*. Rental car agencies *(p 405)* are located at the airport. Amtrak **train** station at 221 W. 1st Ave., ☎ 624-5144 or 800-872-7245. **Bus** service by Greyhound Bus Lines *(☎ 624-5251 or 800-231-2222)* and Northwestern Trailways *(W. 221 1st; ☎ 838-5262)*.

Getting Around – Local **bus service**: Spokane Transit Authority *(Mon–Sat 6am–midnight, Sun 8:50am–7pm; 75¢)*. Schedule and route information: ☎ 328-7433. Metered street and garage **parking** is available downtown.

Visitor Information – For information on points of interest, seasonal events, accommodations and recreation, contact the **Spokane Area Convention & Visitors Bureau** *(open year–round Mon–Fri 9am–4:30pm)*, 201 W. Main St., Spokane WA 99201; ☎ 747-3230 or 800-248-3230; www.visitspokane.com.

Accommodations – Area visitors' guide including lodging directory is available *(free)* from Spokane Area Convention & Visitors Bureau *(above)*. Accommodations range from hotels, motels and B&B's to guest ranches, as well as a full range of campgrounds including backcountry camping and RV parks.

Entertainment – Consult the arts and entertainment section of the *Spokesman-Review* (Friday) for schedules of cultural events. The **Spokane Symphony** performs classical, pops and family concerts at the Opera House *(Sept–May)*, 601 W. Riverside Ave., ☎ 624-1200. Musicals and plays are staged at the Spokane Civic Center, 1020 N. Howard, ☎ 325-2507. For tickets: ☎ 800-325-7328.

Sports and Leisure – Many public **golf courses** are located near or within one hour of downtown, for a listing, contact the visitors bureau *(above)*. Downtown Riverfront Park is the city's main recreational space; it offers carousel rides, an IMAX Theatre, a gondola ride over falls and a skating rink *(Oct–Mar daily)*. A narrated park train tour gives a history of the area. For activities and schedules: ☎ 625-6943. You can hike, bike and in-line skate along the **Centennial Trail** that follows the Spokane River from Riverside State Park to Coeur d'Alene, Idaho. Other **outdoor activities** include mountain biking, hiking, and camping at Riverside State Park *(☎ 456-4386)*. Area ski resorts are within a 2 hr drive from downtown, as are miles of cross-country and snowmobile trails *(season: Thanksgiving-Easter)*. Mount Spokane Ski & Snowboard Park, located 30mi from Spokane, offers downhill **skiing**, snowboarding, five lifts, equipment rental and lessons; call ☎ 238-2200 for more information.

Shopping – Covered skywalks in the downtown area connect specialty shops, department stores, art galleries and restaurants. Spokane Market Place, a farmers' market *(1202 W. 1st Ave. at Jefferson St.; Wed–Sat 9am–5pm, Sun 10am–4pm; ☎ 482-2627)* features local produce, ethnic foods, and crafts.

SIGHTS *2 days*

For an overview of Spokane and its layout, start with a self-guided one-hour **City Drive Tour** *(brochures available at Spokane Visitor Information Center, 201 W. Main St.; ☎ 509-747-3230 or 888-776-5263)*. A lovely driving loop, it follows brown directional signs from downtown and leads to the town's significant sights. Next, consider a self-guided 90min walking tour of the downtown area. The Visitor Information Center publishes a free pamphlet covering 49 historic sites and buildings within a 50-square-block area. The buildings represent all of Spokane's major architectural styles, from Victorian-era fortresses to streamlined Art Deco facades. Begin your walk at **Riverfront Park** and follow Spokane Falls Boulevard west. Highlights include the 1931 **Fox Theater** *(Monroe St. and Sprague Ave.)*, with its magnificent Art Deco interior; and the c.1895 **Spokane County Courthouse** *(W. Broadway Ave. and Jefferson St.)*, a veritable castle built in the French Renaissance style.

★★ **Riverfront Park** – *Spokane Falls Blvd. between Post and Washington Sts. Open year-round daily; hours vary with season.* ⚔ ♿ ☎ *509-456-4386. Hours of operation for attractions vary, attractions hotline ☎ 509-625-6943.* Taking in both banks of the Spokane River as it flows through the heart of the city's downtown, this outstanding urban park combines the relaxing atmosphere of a pedestrian mall with thundering waterfalls and the gleeful presence of a carnival midway. Site of Expo '74 World's Fair, the park grounds were once a filthy expanse of industrial blight, but the prospect of the world's fair—the first ever to embrace the environmental cause-led not only to the transformation of the fairgrounds and the river but also to the revitalization of the entire downtown. Today the park itself lies at the core of a bustling downtown full of interesting shops, ethnic restaurants, pubs, hotels and office buildings.

© Robert Holmes

Riverfront Park

Several footbridges lead from the north and south banks onto **Havermale Island** and **Canada Island**, which form the heart of the park. At the lower end of Havermale, just off Post Street, the **Gondola Skyride★** *(hours vary with season; narrated ride; round-trip 20min; $3.50)* descends into a deep gorge where the river suddenly drops 132ft over Lower Spokane Falls, now topped by the Monroe Street Dam and its red-brick powerhouse. Visitors can walk down along the same thundering stretch of whitewater on a series of concrete stairways beginning at the parking lot on the south side of the powerhouse.

Farther east along Spokane Falls Boulevard stands the 1909 **Looff Carrousel★★**. Completely restored to its original operating condition, it consists of 54 hand-carved horses and other animals, all gaily painted and whirling merrily to tunes played on a 200-pipe band organ.

At the center of Havermale Island rises the giant, asymmetrical canopy of the **US Pavilion**. Designed to suggest a Plains Indian tepee, the pavilion houses a modest assortment of standard amusement park rides and coin-operated games. Here, too, is the entrance for the **IMAX Theatre**, which screens a variety of its trademark 70mm films.

Bing Crosby Collection – *E. 502 Boone Ave., on the campus of Gonzaga University. Open year-round daily 7am–noon. Closed major holidays.* 🅿 ☎ *509-328-4220.* Bing Crosby (1904-77), the popular American singer and film actor, grew up in Spokane in a house adjacent to Gonzaga University. A modest collection of his memorabilia now resides in the university's Crosby Student Center, which was completed in 1957 with funds donated by the singer. Inside, a small anteroom contains photos of Crosby both before and after he rose to stardom, including shots of him playing baseball as a member of Gonzaga's Class of 1924. Glass cases display Crosby mementoes and gold records awarded for some of his hit albums and singles ("White Christmas," "True Love," "Swinging on a Star").

★**Cathedral of St. John the Evangelist** – *Grand Blvd. and E. 12th Ave.* ♿ 🅿 ☎ *509-838-4277.* Begun in 1925 and completed in 1961, this magnificent English Gothic-style cathedral rises from a wooded bluff overlooking downtown Spokane. Massive, ornate, crowned by a 180ft carillon tower and resplendent with glittering stained-glass windows, the cathedral is the seat of the Episcopal Bishop of Spokane. Each Sunday, its glistening stone and wood interior reverberates with the sound of a 1960 Aeolian-Skinner organ that has 4,095 pipes; before services, the 48-bell carillon peals over the surrounding neighborhood. Weekday tours are offered, and a free pamphlet for self-guided tours is also available *(year-round Mon–Tue, Thu & Sat noon–3pm; none on major holidays).*

★**Manito Park** – *Grand Blvd. and 18th Ave. Park and conservatories open year-round daily dawn-dusk.* ♿ 🅿 ☎ *509-625-6622.* A gardener's delight and inspiration, Manito Park presents four lovingly cultivated landscapes from diverse horticultural traditions—a fine Japanese garden, an immense rose garden, a perennial garden and a large classical garden planted in the European Renaissance style. In addition to these, the park offers a small, glassed-in conservatory jammed with flowering plants, a lilac garden, play areas and a duck pond.

Start at the centrally located Gaiser Conservatory *(off 21st Ave. and Park Dr.)*, two interconnected greenhouses that display tropical, subtropical and temperate plant specimens from around the world. The conservatory overlooks **Duncan Garden★★**.

Designed and built in 1913 and expanded in 1996, this three-acre garden incorporates a large central fountain and geometric planting beds. On the opposite side of the conservatory, the colorful **Joel E. Ferris Perennial Garden** gracefully drapes a gentle slope. A short stroll northwest of the conservatory leads to **Rose Hill★**, a colorful and fragrant landscape graced with formal beds of 1,500 rose bushes in more than 150 varieties. West of Rose Hill, a high wooden fence encloses **Nishinomiya Japanese Garden★** built in 1974 to coincide with Expo '74 and named in honor of Spokane's Japanese sister city. It centers around a large, sinuous pond stocked with fish and fed by a tumbling waterfall.

★**Cheney Cowles Memorial Museum** – *2316 W. 1st Ave. The museum is temporarily closed for expansion. Call for special events ☎ 509-456-3931*. Located in Spokane's Historic Browne's Addition Neighborhood and surrounded by wonderful Victorian and Craftsman-style homes, this polished stone museum perches atop the bluffs overlooking the Spokane River and offers a brief overview of the region's past, from prehistory to the present day. The museum's central exhibit, "**Portraits of the Inland Empire**," employs artifacts, historic photos, film clips, maps and excerpts from diaries and tribal oral histories to sketch the prehistory of the Plateau Indians, and the various eras that followed. Much of the space is devoted to the history of Spokane. Admission includes a tour of the adjacent **Campbell House** (c.1898), a massive Tudor-style home furnished with period pieces.

★**John A. Finch Arboretum** – *3404 Woodland Blvd. Open year-round daily dawn-dusk. 🅿 ☎ 509-625-6657*. Nestled among the wooded foothills of southwest Spokane, Finch Arboretum's 65 acres of sloping terrain blend attractive, formally landscaped grounds with settings more characteristic of the region's natural areas. A creek trickles through the center of the arboretum, pooling in shaded glens, curving past large outcroppings of coarse basalt and tumbling over miniature cascades. Trees and shrubs include many species native to the inland Northwest as well as others from around the world. Planting began in 1949 on land largely donated by John A. Finch, a pioneer mining investor, and D.H. Dwight, who owned a summer cottage in the area. Today the arboretum offers more than 2,000 labeled trees and shrubs, representing 600 species. Highlights include **Bamboo Springs**, a small artificial pond with a narrow, 6ft waterfall; the **Lilac Collection**; intimate Corey Glen, with its birches, wildflowers and blossoming trees; and **Lookout Point**, which overlooks the margin between the formally landscaped grounds and a ponderosa pine forest.

Cliff Park – *13th Ave. and Grove St.* Thrust above a tidy neighborhood of Craftsman-style bungalows, this pocket park perches atop a massive protrusion of basalt called Review Rock, the highest point in the city. A short footpath leads to a grassy space at the top of the rock and opens up a grandstand **vista★★** of Spokane, the Spokane River Valley, Mt. Spokane and the creamy spires of the Cathedral of St. John the Evangelist.

---

1 Birkebeiner Brewing Company

Map p 219. 35 W. Main St. ☎ 509-458-0854.
Brewpubs—small, independent breweries serving food and fresh, British-style beers fermented on the premises—have long been a mainstay of dining in the Northwest. They became popular here long before the brewpub concept became a marketing ploy and spread to the rest of the US. Northwest standards remain higher, generally, for the quality of both the beer and the food. There are several pubs in Spokane, but locals persistently rank one—the Birkebeiner Brewing Company—ahead of the rest, and for good reason. Unafraid to experiment with its beers and equally courageous in its cuisine, it routinely offers 10 of its own outstanding ales, porters and stouts as well as a good selection of Northwest wines. The food, never routine, borrows often from Creole and Southwest traditions but always with a Northwest flair.

EXCURSIONS

★★**Riverside State Park** – *1 1/2 hrs. 7mi northwest of Spokane. Go north on Monroe St., left on Northwest Blvd., left on Meenach St., right on Downriver Dr. Open Apr–Sept daily dawn-dusk. Rest of the year 8am–dusk. ⚠ 🅿 ☎ 509-456-3964*. An invigorating, conveniently located 7,655-acre parcel stretches for miles along the wooded banks and spectacular basalt lava cliffs gripping the Spokane River. Footpaths and roads follow the swift clean river through forests of mature ponderosa pine and lead to overlooks of spectacular whitewater and to the site of Spokane House, an important fur-trade outpost. At the park's entrance, a short path leads to the top of a stout knob of rock that provides an excellent **view★** of

SPOKANE

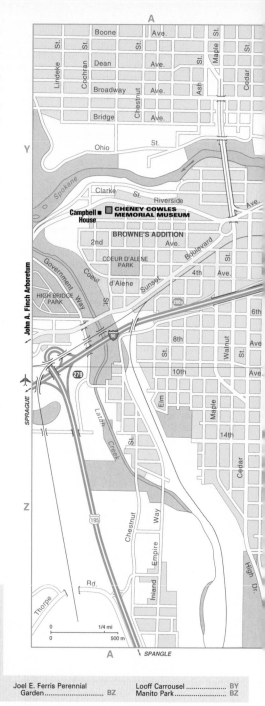

a furious whitewater stretch called the Bowl and Pitcher, where the Spokane River dashes between massive lumps of basalt that rise dozens of feet from the water. A trail starting from the picnic area below the overlook crosses the river on a footbridge, wanders among the rock formations and connects with the Centennial Trail, which leads upstream to the streets of Spokane, or downstream approximately 5mi to the Nine Mile Falls Dam.

Located elsewhere in the park, **Spokane House Interpretive Center** *(5.5mi north on Rte. 291; open Memorial Day–Labor Day Wed–Thu 10am–6pm)* stands in an open parkland meadow near the confluence of the Spokane and Little Spokane rivers. The outpost was built by the North West Company in 1810 to trade manufactured goods for furs brought in by the region's Indians. In 1821 the rival Hudson's Bay Company merged with the North West Company. It took control of Spokane House and, in 1826, shut it down in order to move operations to Kettle Falls, on the

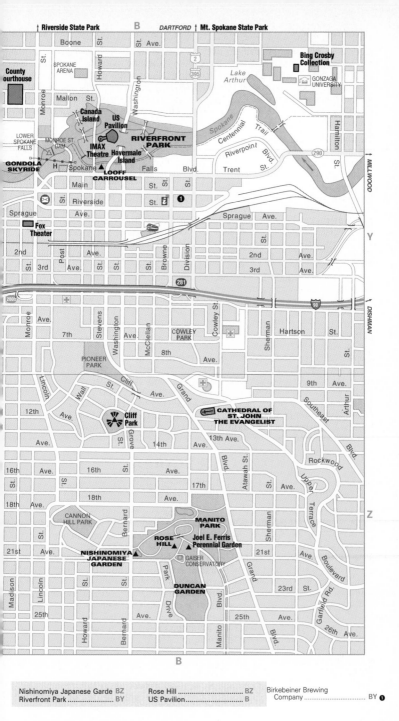

Columbia River northwest of Spokane. Apart from the setting, virtually nothing of the old trading post survives; the interpretive center provides a brief overview of the Northwest fur trade and displays some of the few artifacts unearthed at the site by archaeologists during the 1950s and 1960s.

★★**Mount Spokane State Park** – *1/2 day. 25mi northeast of Spokane via US-2 and Rte. 206. Open year-round daily dawn-dusk.* ⚠ 🅿 ☎ *509-238-4258.* This inviting high-country preserve takes in nearly 14,000 acres of wooded mountain terrain, including the summit of Mt. Spokane (5,851ft) and portions of Mt. Kit Carson (5,306ft). The narrow park road winds 5mi up through forests of cedar and Engleman spruce to the very top of Mt. Spokane, where **Vista House**, originally a fire lookout constructed of native stone by the Civilian Conservation Corps, commands an unparalleled **view**★★ of Spokane and the Columbia Plateau as well as mountains and lakes in northern Idaho, Montana and British Columbia. Worth a trip for the vista alone *(call first; snow often closes the road until late June)*, the park also offers many hiking and mountain biking trails and excellent wildlife viewing for moose, bear, deer, cougar and many species of birds. Because of its location between two of the continent's major mountain ranges, the park's slopes contain all of the plant species common to both the east slope of the Cascades and the west slope of the Rockies.

★**Turnbull National Wildlife Refuge** – *2 hrs. 22.5mi southwest of Spokane via I-90 and Rte. 904 through Cheney, following signs. Open year-round daily dawn-dusk. $3/car from Mar–Oct.* ⏣ ▣ ☏ *509-235-4723.* Speckled with dozens of lakes, ponds and marshy areas, a 15,468-acre sanctuary southwest of Spokane takes in a gently rolling and exceedingly rocky landscape of expansive ponderosa pine forests and open grasslands. An important nesting and migratory site for waterfowl in the Pacific Flyway, the refuge is home to diverse species of migratory waterbirds at the height of the fall migration. But it is also home to many other animals, including elk, white-tailed deer and coyotes. The underlying rock is basalt that formed roughly 17 million years ago as part of the great Columbia Plateau lava flows, cropping up as low cliffs and ledges around some of the lakes and as large, coarse protrusions throughout the forests and meadows. A quick glance at a map shows that the refuge's elongated lakes all orient in roughly the same direction—evidence that Turnbull lies on the Channeled Scablands that were scoured out by immense Ice Age floods. In the late 19C, settlers began draining the lakes to expose the beds as cropland. By the 1920s, most of the lakes on the refuge were dry. But crop yields were low, so the area was allowed to return to its natural state.

Today, visitors can sample some of the refuge's terrain on the 5.3mi **Pine Creek Auto Loop★**, which starts near the refuge headquarters, circles several of the lakes and offers a handful of casual but rewarding strolls. **Kepple Lake** offers two short trails: the first to Kepple Lake Overlook *(.25mi one-way)*, where a stout brow of basalt overlooks the water; the second around Kepple Lake Peninsula *(.5mi loop)*, where the lake narrows to about 75ft. Both trails provide good chances of seeing hooded mergansers, canvasbacks and other diving ducks. Near the end of the auto loop, the short **Blackhorse Lake Boardwalk** crosses upland and wetland habitats.

TRI-CITIES AREA

Michelin map 493 C 4 and Principal Sights map p 13
Tourist Information ☏ 509-735-8486 or www.cbvcp.com/tcvcb

The Tri-Cities area encompasses the adjacent communities of Richland, Pasco and Kennewick, which sprawl over a high desert landscape at the confluence of three important waterways—the Columbia, Snake and Yakima rivers. Remote and sparsely populated until 1942, the area expanded rapidly as a key site for the US Army's Manhattan Project, which built the world's first atomic weapons with plutonium produced on the Hanford Nuclear Reservation north of Richland. Today, the Tri-Cities comprise one of the largest metropolitan areas in the state.

Plateau Indians, including the Yakama and Wanapum peoples, lived here for at least 10,000 years before Lewis and Clark passed by in 1805. Cattle ranchers arrived during the 1860s and the Northern Pacific Railway followed in 1871, platting the twin towns of Pasco and Kennewick. Pasco became a transportation hub, Kennewick a small agricultural center after irrigation made farming possible during the 1890s.

Richland, a tiny crossroads town in 1942, was evacuated, along with Hanford and White Bluffs, to make way for 51,000 construction workers who descended on the Hanford Site to build the plutonium production reactors that yielded nuclear material for the atomic bomb dropped on Nagasaki in 1945. Production continued until 1988. Today, Hanford is the nation's largest hazardous waste site. The cleanup is expected to pump more money into the local economy than producing weapons-grade plutonium ever did.

RICHLAND *1/2 day*

Incorporated in 1910, the small agricultural community of Richland mushroomed in 1943 to accommodate the US government's plutonium-production facility just north of town in Hanford. From its 1940s peak of over 50,000 people, Richland's population has declined to a steady level of 37,291, with the Hanford Nuclear Reservation continuing as a major player in the region's economy. Several national high-tech businesses have laboratories and testing facilities in the area, and vineyards and fruit orchards flourish here. Built for the Hanford plant's employees during World War II, modest "alphabet houses,"—each design based on a letter of the alphabet—are sprinkled throughout town.

Columbia River Exhibition of History, Science and Technology – *95 Lee Blvd. Open year-round Mon–Sat 10am–5pm, Sun noon–5pm. Closed Jan 1, Easter Sunday, Thanksgiving Day, Dec 25. $3.50.   ☎ 509-943-9000. www.crehst.org.* This relatively small museum overlooks Richland's riverside greenbelt and focuses almost exclusively on the history of the Hanford Site, the vast tract of federal land northwest of Richland which played a vital role in the production of nuclear weapons and which has exerted such an enormous influence over life in the Tri-Cities area. Established during World War II as part of the Manhattan Project, Hanford's reactors produced plutonium for the first atomic bombs and continued to supply radioactive material for nuclear weapons throughout the Cold War. The work required tens of thousands of laborers and engineers, who flocked to this sun-baked and once remote section of Washington's desert during the 1940s. Exhibits include a plethora of historic photos and excerpts from newspapers and personal diaries that depict life and work in the area during World War II. Visitors can manipulate a robotic arm used to handle radioactive materials, look at models of nuclear reactors and inspect cutaway sections of the controversial single-layer storage tanks that have leaked millions of gallons of radioactive waste.

★Columbia River Journeys – *Columbia Park Marina, 1229 Columbia Dr. S.E. Depart daily May–Oct 8am–12:30pm. Round-trip 1 hr30min. Commentary. Reservation required. $36. ☎ 509-943-0231.* A charter jetboat service offers half-day excursions through the Hanford Reach, one of the last free-flowing stretches of the Columbia River. Largely undeveloped before World War II and then placed off-limits throughout the Hanford Site's status as a nuclear weapons facility, the desert lands bordering the Hanford Reach are still wild, mostly roadless, and rich in wildlife. Cruises travel upriver from Richland through the reservation, passing a vast field of sand dunes, two wildlife refuges and sets of 500ft cliffs in the White Bluffs area.

Excursion

Plant 2 Visitors Center – *1/2 hr. 12mi north of Richland on the Hanford Nuclear Reservation via Rte. 240 and Stevens Dr. Open Thu–Fri 11am–4pm, weekends noon–5pm.   ☎ 509-372-5860. www.wnpa.com.* Parked on the asphalt in front of Energy Northwest's Plant 2 nuclear power plant, this small modular building offers an 8min video outlining the history of the plant's construction, operation and benefits. Exhibits include a diagram of how the plant harnesses nuclear fission to generate electricity, a half-life demonstration and cutaway diagrams of the plant building. This may not seem like much of a reward for driving from Richland, but the trip through a high desert landscape studded with the pale gray domes of reactor vessels does help one get a feel for the bleak landscape where plutonium was first produced for nuclear weapons.

PASCO *1 hr*

With the arrival of the railroad in the 1890s, this small burg sealed its future as a transportation center for the region's agricultural products. World War II brought further growth with the Hanford site and the building of a US Naval Air Station; the station has since been converted into the Tri-Cities airport, the state's third-largest commercial airport. Agribusiness and food processing bolster the local economy, and most of the area's large pool of laborers call Pasco home.

★Sacajawea State Park – *1 hr. 3mi southeast of town off US-12. Open year-round daily dawn-dusk. ☎ 509-545-2361.* Peaceful, breezy and shaded by a canopy of tall hardwood trees, this 284-acre park lies on the point of land between the Snake and Columbia rivers and offers long vistas across the water to the high, bare hills that rise above the Tri-Cities area. The area was once a rich fishery where the Yakama, Wanapum and other Sahaptian-speaking Indians gathered to harvest and dry salmon. Lewis and Clark camped on the point October 16-18, 1805, marveled over the abundance of salmon and visited with the Indians who lived nearby. The small, Art Deco **Sacajawea Museum** overlooks the confluence and offers modest but worthwhile exhibits on Lewis and Clark and their female Indian guide, Sacajawea. A 10min video summarizes the expedition's story.

Excursions

★McNary National Wildlife Refuge – *1 1/2 hrs. 6mi southeast of Pasco on US-12, then .2mi north. Open year-round daily dawn-dusk. ☎ 509-547-4942.* Rich in bird life and within easy reach of Pasco, the pleasant wildlife refuge near the confluence of the Snake and Columbia rivers takes in a rich variety of habitats—reedy marshlands, groves of cottonwood, sagebrush steppe and even sand dunes. It attracts many different species of waterfowl during the autumn migratory season, and provides a summer home for nesting Canada geese, white pelicans and various ducks. The **McNary Environmental Education Center** *(corner of Maple St. and South Lake Rd.; ☎ 509-543-8322)* is located in a small farmhouse overlooking a portion of the refuge and offers a spotting scope and a handy stack of bird books. Just below the center, the 1mi **Burbank Slough Wildlife Trail**★ skirts the wetlands and passes through ribbons of shrubs and trees to a south-facing slope of sagebrush. Along the way are interpretive signs and a bird blind.

★**Ice Harbor Dam** – *1 hr. 12mi east of Pasco via US-12 and Rte. 124. Visitor Center open Apr–Oct daily 9am–5pm. Closed major holidays. Park is for day use only.* ⚠ ♿ ▣ ☎ *509-547-7781.* Set in a high desert landscape of rolling sagebrush hills studded with basalt lava outcroppings, this massive concrete barrier spans the Snake River east of Pasco, impounding the waters of Lake Sacajawea. The dam generates electricity and helps to irrigate many of the region's wineries and fruit orchards. An adjoining lock, 103ft deep, allows large vessels to navigate the waterway. Visitors can browse through exhibits in the visitor center, view migrating salmon (in season) through large glass panels, and walk into the powerhouse. At the Indian memorial above the dam, a circular rock wall surrounds a large boulder adorned with petroglyphs and offers a fine **vista** of the river, the dam, and the countryside. Across the dam, an observation deck allows visitors to peer over the rim of the navigation lock and into the turbulent waters beneath the spillway.

WALLA WALLA   *3 hrs*

An appealing agricultural hub and college town, Walla Walla stands amid rolling hills and farm fields at the foot of the Blue Mountains, which rise south of town as a long, darkly wooded mass. Irrigation, fertile soil and a long growing season account for the valley's impressive yields of wheat, wine grapes and vegetables (including the famous Walla Walla sweet onion). Walla Walla also boasts three college campuses, lovely parks and an interesting assortment of old houses and public buildings.

The Walla Walla area had been home to the Cayuse Indians for generations before Marcus and Narcissa Whitman arrived in 1836 and built their Presbyterian mission 7mi west of the present town. Although the mission became an important stopover on the Oregon Trail, the nonnative population declined in the area in 1847 when the Whitmans and others were killed by the Cayuse. The present town grew up around Fort Walla Walla, established in 1856. It prospered during the 1860s as a supply center for Idaho gold miners, and later as a commercial, banking and manufacturing center.

A 2mi walking tour of downtown Walla Walla *(1 1/2 hrs)*, outlined in a free booklet available at the **Visitor Information Center** *(416 N. Second Ave., ☎ 509-525-0850)* takes in a scattered procession of Victorian-era buildings constructed after various fires destroyed whole blocks of the city's early wooden structures. Stops include: the **Whitman Statue** *(Main St. and Boyer Ave.)*, a heroic bronze of Marcus gazing west; the 1926 **Liberty Theater** *(54 E. Main St.)*, with its twin towers that look like Dutch windmills; the Italianate 1899 **Dacres Hotel** *(Main and 4th Sts.)*; and the magnificent 1916 **Walla Walla County Courthouse**★ *(300 block of Main St.)*, featuring a polished marble interior as ornate as any state capitol. North of downtown, the Italianate **Kirkman House**, dating to the 1880s, has been restored and furnished in period style *(N. Colville and Cherry Sts.; open late Mar–early Dec Wed–Sun 1pm–4pm; $2; ▣ ☎ 509-529-4373.*

★**Pioneer Park** – *Alder and Division Sts.* A rare oasis of shade trees and cool breezes in an otherwise arid region, this splendid city park was designed by the Olmsted brothers, and the touch of those master landscape architects remains evident. The central drive, lined with blossoming trees, flower beds and pruned shrubs, leads to an elevated bandstand framed by the spreading branches of enormous sycamores. Shaded lawns stretch off in all directions, and sidewalks lead through an **aviary** *(☎ 509-527-4403)* full of exotic birds (mostly colorful varieties of pheasant) and to a cacophonous duck pond crowded with mallards, domestic geese and gulls. The park's west side faces one of the nicest clusters of Arts and Crafts-style homes in Walla Walla.

Fort Walla Walla Museum – *755 Myra Rd. in Fort Walla Walla Park. Open Apr–Oct Tue–Sun 10am–5pm. Closed rest of the year. $5.* ♿ ▣ ☎ *509-525-7703.* Located along a large grassy hillside on the southern fringe of Walla Walla, this museum combines an enormous collection of antique farm implements and horse-drawn vehicles with a group of 14 historic pioneer buildings that are furnished in period style. Visits start with a stroll through the Pioneer Settlement, which includes log cabins, a one-room school, a tiny railroad depot, a doctor's office and a little girl's playhouse complete with dolls and toys. Behind the museum store, a short path climbs to the crest of the hill and a semicircle of six exhibit buildings. Don't miss the 1919 Harris combine with its team of 33 fully-outfitted fiberglass mules; a surrounding mural puts visitors in the middle of a period wheat harvest.

■ Amber Waves of Grain: Washington's Wheat Region

Though apples garner much of the agricultural attention in Washington, wheat has been its largest cash crop for generations, thanks to an exceptionally fertile, well-watered region in the southeastern portion of the state known as the **Palouse**. Stretching from the foothills of the Blue Mountains north almost to Spokane, and from western Idaho to the high deserts of central Washington, the billowing, asymmetrical hills of the Palouse produce some of the highest wheat yields per acre in the world.

The Palouse hills are actually a sea of dunes composed of rich silt blown in from the southwest. The age of the dunes is unknown, but they are thought to have formed before the ice ages. The silt lies 150ft deep in some places, though the fertile upper layer of loam averages only 2ft-4ft deep. The Palouse receives twice the annual precipitation of dry wheat regions to the west, and its soil retains moisture better than the soil of other regions.

The hills originally bore a tallgrass prairie, which early French traders called *pelouse* (meaning"lawn"). The name stuck after settlers arrived in the region during the late 1870s. Within a couple of generations, farms and towns in the Palouse were exporting bountiful harvests of wheat around the world. Teams of horses and mules pulled huge combines, plow rigs, harrows and seed-drillers over the steep slopes until the 1930s, when tractors took their place. With the widespread use of fertilizers and herbicides during the 1960s, average yields on the Palouse doubled from 40 bushels per acre to 80. Whitman County often harvests more wheat than any other single county in the nation. Almost all of it is shipped down the Snake and Columbia rivers on immense barges; it eventually finds its way overseas to Japan, Korea, Taiwan, the Philippines and other Asian markets.

But, soil scientists warn, erosion on the Palouse is greater than in any other farming region in the country. During the 1980s, the Palouse was losing an estimated 17 million tons of topsoil every year. Unless farming practices change, productivity on the Palouse will dwindle.

Excursions

★**Whitman Mission National Historic Site** – *1 1/2 hrs. 7.7mi west of Walla Walla via US-12. Open Jun–Aug daily 8am–6pm. Rest of the year daily 8am–4:30pm. Closed Jan 1, Thanksgiving Day, Dec 25. $2. & ▣ ☎ 509-522-6360. www.nps.gov/wmmi.* This evocative historic park preserves the site of Marcus and Narcissa Whitman's Presbyterian mission to the Cayuse Indians and describes how they lived and died here at the hands of those they had hoped to help. The park's shaded grounds embrace a swath of rich bottomland along the Walla Walla River and offer splendid vistas of the Palouse prairie landscape and the foothills of the Blue Mountains. A 10min slide show outlines the Whitman's story, beginning with their 1836 journey west from upper New York state and ending with their deaths in 1847. Excellent exhibits, supported by artifacts and journal excerpts, deepen the tale by illuminating the profound cultural gulf that existed between the Whitmans and the Cayuse. Outside, a 1mi loop trail climbs past the mass grave where the Whitmans are buried to a monument at the top of a bare prairie hill. The trail then descends to the Mission Site, where paving stones outline the foundations of the buildings. Interpretive signs explain each building's purpose and identify the locations where the Whitmans died.

★**Dayton** – *1 hr. 29mi northeast of Walla Walla on US-12. Walking-tour maps available at the Dayton Depot, ☎ 509-382-2026.* The drive from Walla Walla to this pleasant small town in the heart of Washington's wheat country winds among billowing Palouse prairie hills and follows the route Lewis and Clark took as they returned from the Pacific Coast in 1806. An agricultural hub established in 1872, Dayton nestles into the hills at the confluence of the Touchet River and Patit Creek and reflects the early prosperity of the region's farmland in its concentration of attractive Victorian-era houses and public buildings. More than 85 structures have been placed on the National Register of Historic places, including the 1881 **Dayton Depot★**, at the corner of Second Street and Commercial Avenue, and the Italianate **Columbia County Courthouse** (c.1887), at Third and Main Streets. Both have been carefully restored inside and out. Of particular interest is the third-floor courtroom, with its 22ft cove ceilings, spectator galleries, and antique jury chairs.

YAKIMA VALLEY★

Michelin map 493 C 4 and map below
Tourist Information ☎ 509-575-3010 or 800-221-0751

Stretching in a long southeastern arc from Ellensburg to the Horse Heaven Hills west of the Tri-Cities, the Yakima Valley runs as a verdant, tree-lined river corridor through a thirsty landscape of sagebrush flats and rumpled brown hills. Home to the Yakama Indians for countless generations, the valley was settled beginning in the 1860s by cattle ranchers and, during the late 19C, by fruit farmers. Today, the Yakima ranks as one of the richest fruit growing regions in the US; it is also the nation's top producer of hops and home to dozens of the state's best wineries. From Yakima to Walla Walla, wine growers take advantage of the region's irrigation-controlled moisture, late growing season, and alkaline, disease-resistant soil to produce award-winning vintages. Culturally diverse, the valley takes in a portion of the Yakama Indian Reservation west of Toppenish and also includes a large and vibrant Hispanic population, which handles most of the manual farm labor and deeply influences the valley's cuisine. Many of the towns, especially Ellensburg and Toppenish, have retained some of their early 20C atmosphere by preserving important historical buildings.

★ELLENSBURG *3 hrs*

This relaxed college town of 14,419 lies nestled between the wooded foothills of the Cascade Range and a sea of high desert hills that sprawls eastward to the canyon country of the Columbia River. Once a rich hunting and fishing ground shared by the Nez Percé, Yakama and Wenatchee tribes, the Ellensburg area attracted its first settlers during the late 1860s. With the arrival of the Northern Pacific Railroad, the town grew rapidly during the 1880s. A devastating 1889 fire gutted the downtown area, but residents soon rebuilt in brick and stone, leaving the town a rich architectural legacy of attractive Victorian-era storefronts and office buildings. Ellensburg lost an early bid to become the state capital, but it did garner one of the state's first colleges, Central Washington University, founded in 1891 and surrounded today by shaded neighborhoods of Craftsman-style homes.

★★**Chimpanzee and Human Communication Institute** – *Central Washington University, 400 E. 8th Ave. Visit by guided tour (1 hr) only, Mar–Nov Sat 9:15am & 10:45am, Sun 12:30pm & 2pm. Jan–Feb Sat 10:45am, Sun 12:30pm. Reservations suggested. Closed Thanksgiving weekend; Easter Sunday. $10.* ♿ ☎ *509-963-2244. www.cwu.edu/~cwuchci.* This extraordinary facility provides a home for a family of five chimpanzees who use American Sign Language to converse with humans and among themselves. Raised from infancy in the same manner as deaf children, the chimps have acquired roughly 200 different signs; they compose simple sentences and are the subject of non-invasive research studies. Visitors attending 1 hr weekend "chimposiums" can watch them sign as they run, play and climb about their spacious enclosure, which includes a large outdoor area

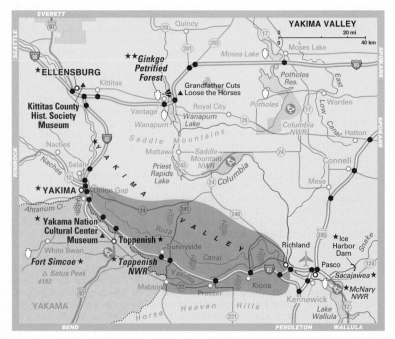

with plenty of vertical space and elaborate climbing structures. The visit starts with a 30min lecture that sketches the chimps' background and teaches visitors to recognize some of the more common sign gestures. The lecture is followed by a half hour of observation, and, to some extent, interaction with the chimps through large plate-glass windows. Some of the chimps come up to the glass and sign at visitors, who are encouraged to sign back; a docent is present to interpret what the chimps say. There is no other place in the world that offers such an opportunity.

★**Clymer Museum of Art** – *416 N. Pearl St. Open year-round Mon–Thu 10am–5pm, Fri 10am–8pm, weekends noon–5pm.* ♿ 🅿 ☎ *509-962-6416.* Housed in one of Ellensburg's historic downtown buildings, the Clymer focuses on the life and work of John F. Clymer, an Ellensburg native who became one of America's premier painters of Western landscapes, wildlife and historical subjects. Exhibits, illustrated with examples of his work, follow Clymer's life from his boyhood in Ellensburg to his triumphant years as a celebrated painter living in Jackson Hole, Wyoming. They cover his years as an illustrator for such magazines as *Field & Stream* and the *Saturday Evening Post*, explain his approach to art, and describe the deep professional collaboration he shared with his wife, Doris. Here too, are some of Clymer's belongings—a heavily used portable easel, fishing net and fly rod.

Kittitas County Historical Society Museum – *E. 3rd. and Pine Sts. Open May–Sept Mon–Sat 10am–4pm. Rest of the year Tue–Sat 11am–3pm. Closed major holidays.* ♿ 🅿 ☎ *509-925-3778.* The county history museum in downtown Ellensburg occupies the ground floor of the 1889 Cadwell Building, a pleasant red-brick structure with fanciful windows shaped like horseshoes. The museum offers five big rooms of pioneer memorabilia—antique china, crosscut saws and musical instruments. It also displays a fine collection of rocks and minerals, petrified wood and arrowheads.

Excursion

★★**Ginkgo Petrified Forest State Park** – *2 hrs. 27mi east of Ellensburg on I-90 to Vantage, and follow signs. Open Apr–Sept daily 6:30am–dusk. Rest of the year daily 8am–dusk.* ⚠ ♿ 🅿 ☎ *509-856-2700.* Stretching back from the rim of a dramatic desert canyon carved by the Columbia River, this 7,500-acre state park preserves a remarkable variety of petrified trees which were buried within the massive lava flows that created the Columbia Plateau about 17 million years ago. It is one of the most extensive, and certainly the most varied petrified forest ever discovered in the US. Perched at the edge of the canyon, the **interpretive center** *(open Apr & early Sept–Oct Friday–Sun 10am–6pm; mid-May–Labor Day Thu–Mon 10am–6pm; $1)*, houses exhibits that explain the petrifaction process and advance theories for how so many different species of trees came to rest here within a deep layer of lava rock. Displays include more than 50 varieties of petrified wood, some presented as logs and stumps, others as crosscut sections which reveal intriguing details such as growth rings and cracks. Four videos recount the discovery of Ginkgo Petrified Forest and cover the area's geography and history. Outside, more petrified stumps stud the parking lot and observation area, which offers a tremendous **vista**★★ of a sprawling landscape of sagebrush hills, precipitous basalt lava cliffs, and the great void of the canyon itself. A short path leads beneath the building to a display of Indian petroglyphs salvaged from riverside cliffs when the Wanapum Dam was constructed downstream. Three miles west on the old Vantage highway, a .75mi **interpretive trail** switchbacks up a steep desert slope and loops past examples of petrified tree species.

Across the river from Vantage *(Exit 3.2mi east on I-90)* and high atop the bluffs stands the sculpture **Grandfather Cuts Loose the Horses**, a line of 18 life-size, weathered steel horses that trot as silhouettes along the rim of the canyon. When complete, the sculpture will include a 36ft basket, tilted as if the horses had just spilled from it. Inspired by Native American spirituality, the sculpture is David Govedare's rendition of the Great Spirit putting horses onto the Earth.

★YAKIMA   *1 day*

Located at the confluence of the Yakima and Naches rivers, Yakima is one of the largest cities in eastern Washington. It serves as the commercial hub for the entire Yakima Valley, and its outlying areas sprawl south along the Yakima River to Union Gap as a nearly continuous swath of commercial development. Even so, Yakima is not without scenic appeal. An excellent system of greenbelt pathways runs for miles along the rivers, and the city faces a long row of high desert ridges—wrinkled, velvety and especially attractive in the evening as they catch the glow of sunset. Settlers first arrived in the area after a war with the Yakamas ended in the late 1850s. They established cattle ranches at first but then planted fruit orchards as irrigation became available. In 1884 the Northern Pacific Railroad arrived but had

■ Yakima Valley Fruit Farms

Fragrant with blossoms in the spring, heavy with fruit throughout the summer and fall, the Yakima Valley's orchards, vineyards and farms stretch for dozens of miles along the Yakima River and its tributary streams. They form a wide band of green foliage and shade that stands in sharp contrast with the rolling brown hills that rise beyond the reach of irrigation.

Thanks to fertile volcanic soils, an unusually long growing season (200 days), and an intricate network of irrigation canals and ditches, these small acreages harvest an astonishing variety and volume of fruits, vegetables and other produce. Yakima County contains more fruit trees than any other county in the nation. It produces more apples than any other, more winter pears, more mint and more hops. It also ranks high in the production of wine grapes, sweet cherries, peaches and apricots.

The first settlers arrived in the Yakima Valley during the 1860s and established themselves as open-range cattle ranchers. Soon, though, farmers who recognized the fertility of the soil brought water to the land through various small-scale irrigation projects. In 1870 John Beck planted the first orchard with 50 apple trees and 50 peach trees. During the late 19C, the valley's irrigation network expanded, cold storage became available and the railroad linked major markets. The valley shipped its first railroad car of apples in 1894.

Today the valley's status as a fruit-growing center is apparent at every turn. Neatly planted orchards and vineyards nestle among the dry hills. Stacks of crates as high as small buildings stand beside the packing plants. In the spring, the heady scent of flowering trees sifts along the river. Perhaps best of all, though, the valley has a long tradition of selling its produce directly to the public at dozens of roadside stands and farmers' markets. These range from painted plywood shacks to veritable supermarkets. Whatever the venue, the bottom line for visitors translates to one word: fresh. The sweet cherries you bite into on a June afternoon may have been picked that very morning.

An excellent map and guide to 22 produce outlets is available at public places throughout the valley, including the **Yakima Valley Visitors and Convention Bureau** *(10 N. 8th St., Yakima;* ☎ *509-575-3010 or 800-221-0751)*. A small sampling of these outlets follows:

Thompson's Farm – *14mi northwest of Yakima in Naches.* ☎ *509-653-2589.* Owned and operated by the Thompson family for more than 100 years, this 45-acre fruit farm sells its sweet cherries, peaches, pears and apples from a gift shop in the original farmhouse as well as from a roadside stand in Naches. At the farm *(Shaffer Rd., east of Rte. 12)*, visitors can watch a cider press in action, and sample milkshakes and ice-cream sundaes-flavored with the Thompson's fresh fruit—from a replica 1890s soda fountain.

Cherry Harvest

Johnson Orchards – *Summitview and 49th Aves., Yakima.* ☎ *509-966-7479.* An outpost of the country in the city, this neatly planted plot of fruit trees stands amid a busy residential neighborhood in west Yakima. Established in 1904 and operated by the same family ever since, the orchard sells cherries, apricots, nectarines, peaches, pears, plums and apples from a stand and warehouse.

© Robert Holmes

trouble acquiring land from some Yakima property owners. So it bypassed the town, established its terminal 4mi north and offered to move all of the town's buildings to the terminal. Most of "Old Yakima" accepted the railroad's offer, and soon more than 50 buildings had been moved to what is now Yakima. In 1919 "Old Yakima" was renamed Union Gap.

★**Yakima Greenway** – *Through Yakima along the banks of the Yakima and Naches rivers.* Paved, patrolled and very popular, Yakima's Greenway meanders along the banks of the Yakima and Naches rivers for more than 10mi, passing through riverine forests and offering good vistas of the volcanic hills and bluffs around town. Suitable for bikes, in-line skates, strollers and wheelchairs, the pathway connects the city's riverside parks, leads to interesting natural areas, and takes in several excellent playgrounds and swimming areas. The route extends from Harlan Landing (north end of 16th Ave.) to Valley Mall Boulevard south of town, but there are many intermediate access points that make it possible to enjoy short outings or to reach specific sites. *Maps are available at the Yakima Foundation Visitor Center, 111 S. 18th St.* ☎ *509-453-8280.*

Yakima Electric Railway Museum – *306 W. Pine St. Open May–Oct Mon–Fri 8am–4:30pm, weekends 9:45am–6pm. Rest of the year Mon–Fri 8am–4:30pm. $4.* 🅿 ☎ *509-575-1700.* Housed in a weathered 1910 stone-and-brick train depot, the museum serves as a departure point for 2 hr rides on vintage electric trolley cars that clatter through Yakima and out into the countryside. Exhibits consist mainly of the train cars themselves—a c.1909 freight locomotive, a c.1923 Steeplecab locomotive and streetcars from different eras. The museum also contains a c.1910 belt-driven machine line still used today to maintain the equipment. The rides take in much of Yakima, then head north through fruit country to the town of Selah.

Yakima Valley Museum – *2105 Tieton Dr. Open year-round Mon–Fri 10am–5pm, weekends noon–5pm. Closed major holidays. $3.* 🍴 ♿ 🅿 ☎ *509-248-0747. www.yakimavalleymuseum.org.* A large, red-brick building in Franklin Park depicts life in the Yakima region from prehistory to the present through the use of artifacts, historic photos and interpretive notes. Exhibits start with an overview of the tribes of the Inland Northwest, then focus on Anglo history: fruit farming, settlement and the growth of Yakima. Included are a balanced view of native son and US Supreme Court Justice William O. Douglas (1898-1980), an impressive array of horse-drawn vehicles, and an extensive collection of apple-crate labels. On the lower level, the museum operates a fully restored 1930s soda fountain, with an Art Deco interior of gleaming chrome, neon and tile.

★**Washington's Fruit Place** – *105 S. 18th St. Open Memorial Day–Labor Day Mon–Sat 10am–5pm. Rest of the year Mon–Fri 10am–5pm.* ♿ 🅿 ☎ *509-576-3090.* The visitor center, located just off the Yakima Greenway near Sarg Hubbard Park, showcases the state's commercial fruit industry. Hands-on exhibits, photos and a short video describe how the industry cultivates, harvests, processes and ships to market an abundant variety of fruits including peaches, pears, plums, apricots, nectarines, cherries and apples. Free fruit samples are offered.

Yakima Area Arboretum – *Nob Hill Blvd., south side of town off I-82. Open year-round daily dawn-dusk. Visitor Center open year-round Tue–Fri 9am–5pm, Sat 9am–4pm. Closed major holidays.* ♿ 🅿 ☎ *509-248-7337.* Tucked between I-82 and the Yakima River just south of town, this relatively young arboretum adjoins the Yakima Greenway and offers a pleasant stroll that takes in many varieties of flowering trees and an interpretive center where you can pick up a self-guided-tour map. Landscaped with patios, walkways, a large fountain and planting beds hemmed in by large rock borders, the low, red-roofed interpretive center houses a horticultural library. A short walk toward the river leads to the Japanese Garden, laid out around a small central pond fed by a small waterfall. Closer to the river, a wetland trail loops through a small section of freshwater swamp and marsh frequented by wood ducks, painted turtles and great blue herons.

★TOPPENISH *1/2 day*

Located on the Yakama Indian Reservation and in the heart of fruit country, Toppenish stands on a broad, relatively flat-floored basin, well watered by a web of creeks and surrounded by high desert ridges. Far to the west rises the snowy volcanic dome of Mt. Adams (12,276ft), an isolated and, to the Yakama, sacred summit. During the 1850s, the Yakama stoutly defended their land, conducting a two-year war against the US before accepting reservation status in 1858. The same year, the US Army built Fort Simcoe 27mi west of town. It later became the Yakama Indian Agency and then a boarding school for Indian children. After the war, settlers moved into the valley, established cattle ranches, developed irrigation and built the dozens of fruit, vegetable and hops farms that stretch off in all directions from town. Today, most of the people living in Toppenish are Hispanic, a fact evident in street conversations and in the abundance of excellent Mexican restaurants.

★**Yakama Nation Cultural Center Museum** – *West edge of town, off US-97. 100 Spilyiy Loop. Open year-round daily 8am–5pm. Closed Jan 1, Thanksgiving Day, Dec 25. $4.* ⅄ ⅍ 🅿 ☎ *509-865-2800. www.wolfenet.com.* This outstanding cultural museum presents the history of the Yakama peoples through their own eyes, starting with a vivid depiction of the lifeway they enjoyed prior to European contact and ending with the present day. Housed in a tall, A-frame structure suggestive of a Yakama winter lodge, the museum stands on the western edge of town facing Mt. Adams. Inside, a central display of traditional tule-mat dwellings is surrounded by excellent exhibits that form a loose timeline highlighting important eras in Yakama life. Petroglyphs, dioramas, photographs, paintings and an abundance of craft items and tools serve to illustrate the Yakamas' traditional lives as hunters, gatherers and fishermen. Other exhibits cover the the treaty and settlement eras of the late 19C, and the sad years of the 1920s and 30s, when children were ordered to attend boarding schools in an attempt, the Yakama maintain, to break down family ties and destroy their culture. The exhibits conclude with a collection of color photographs of contemporary Indians wearing splendid ceremonial clothing.

American Hop Museum – *22 S. B St. Open May–Oct daily 11am–4pm. Donation requested.* ⅍ ☎ *509-865-4677.* Set in a neatly renovated creamery building in downtown Toppenish, a small museum outlines the process of growing and harvesting hops, an important ingredient in beer-making and one of the principal agricultural commodities of the Yakima Valley. A 10min video presents the various steps in modern cultivation, from preparing the fields with tall poles to baling the dried hops cones for shipment to breweries throughout the world. Exhibits focus on the past, displaying industry trappings and equipment from the early 20C.

★**Yakima Valley Rail and Steam Museum** – *10 S. Asotin Ave. Open May–Nov Sat 10am–5pm, Sun 1pm–5pm. $2.* ⅍ 🅿 ☎ *509-865-1911* A train buff's delight, this collection of railroad memorabilia is displayed in the town's red-brick 1911 Northern Pacific Railroad depot, which has been lovingly restored. Items such as place settings and china from various railroads are neatly arranged in glass cases, along with telegraph keys, train whistles, plaques and signs advising passengers not to flush the toilets while the train is standing in the station. The Agent's Office has been restored to its c.1911 condition and furnished with bentwood office chairs and antique typewriters. The depot also serves as the home base for an active freight line, the Toppenish Simcoe & Western Railroad.

★**Toppenish National Wildlife Refuge** – *5.5mi south of Toppenish on US-97. Open year-round daily dawn-dusk.* 🅿 ☎ *509-865-2405. www.fws.gov.* Located south of town at the foot of Toppenish Ridge, an extensive wetland area offers a refreshing prospect of the valley floor and surrounding landscape as well as a chance to see a wide variety of birds. An elevated gazebo overlooks a section of Toppenish Creek and several of the wetland ponds which were created to help offset the loss of habitat due to agriculture. It's a lovely setting, with a gurgling bend of the creek at your feet and a broad vista of the valley floor and the velvety hills that embrace it. The refuge also offers a bird checklist and an excellent, full-color brochure with photos of some of the birds visitors are likely to see—American avocets, black-necked stilts and northern harriers, to name a few.

Excursion

★**Fort Simcoe State Park** – *1 hr. 27mi west of Toppenish via Rte. 220. 5150 Fort Simcoe Rd. State Park open Apr–Sept daily dawn-dusk. Rest of the year weekends & holidays only. Interpretive Center and historical buildings: open Apr–Sept Wed–Sun 9:30am–4:30pm.* ☎ *509-874-2372.* This pleasant, shaded park west of Toppenish takes in the grounds and surviving buildings of a frontier Army fort built in 1856 as tensions rose between the region's Indians and the settlers. In 1859 it became the Indian Agency and, later, a detested boarding school for the Yakama. The surviving buildings include a row of four wood-frame houses that stand in the shade of tall oak trees and overlook the fort's parade ground. Built for the post's officers, the homes—especially the large commandant's house—have been restored and furnished in period. Some of the other buildings, including block-houses and an infantry barracks, have been reconstructed and remain unfurnished.

The 𝕂𝕚𝕕 *symbol indicates areas of special interest to children.*

Northwest Washington

Deception Pass State Park, Whidbey Island/© Robert Holmes

A land apart from the rest of the Pacific Northwest, the northwest corner of Washington prides itself on its spectacular, unsullied natural beauty. Puget Sound funnels past the region, spilling around myriad islands and into bays, inlets and straits created by long-gone glaciers. In the middle of the sound, the scores of isles and islets in the San Juan archipelago—popular with bicyclists, kayakers and nature enthusiasts—serve as stepping stones connecting the Upper Northwest with Canada's VANCOUVER ISLAND. Canada's snow-shrouded mainland Coast Range rears up on the northern horizon, as do the North Cascades to the west. But the monarch of mountains here is 10,750ft **Mount Baker**, a pyramid of white that dominates the northeastern landscape.

Lummi, Samish and Squamish Indians hunted, fished in this area's long before Spanish and British explorers arrived in the 1770s. Permanent settlement did not begin in earnest until the mid-19C. Late in the century, towns around present-day Bellingham boomed, as rumors spread that the Great Northern Railroad was considering Bellingham Bay for its western terminus. Those hopes were dashed when Tacoma was chosen, and in the following decades, farming and ranching became mainstays of the Upper Northwest economy.

Around Mt. Baker and the North Cascades, pockets of traditional farming and ranching remain, and scattered small towns add to the rural ambience. But today, the area is more famous for its recreational opportunities than for its agriculture. Hikers and skiers flock to Mt. Baker, and to the craggy wilderness of **North Cascades National Park**, a world of daunting peaks, lakes and glaciers accessible only to adventurers willing to explore them by boat or on foot. The tamer coastal lands flatten out toward the sound, their mild winters and fertile soils a gift to the nurseries that have turned the Skagit Valley into a gigantic spring bouquet. Quaint villages along the coast and on Whidbey and Fidalgo islands attract their own contingent of weekend vacationers and resident artists. And the San Juan Islands, once sleepy and rural, are now a prime travel destination. Even the region's major city and commercial center, Bellingham, maintains the relaxed demeanor that makes Northwest Washington a delight.

NORTH CASCADES★★

Michelin map 493 C 3 and map p 233
Tourist Information ☎ 360-856-5700 or www.nps.gov/noca

The rugged, almost impenetrable peaks of the North Cascades sprawl across north-central Washington in remote, wild splendor. Since 1968, much of the area has been protected in the North Cascades National Park and the adjacent Ross Lake and Lake Chelan National Recreation Areas, but only in 1972 was a roadway, the North Cascades Highway (Route 20), completed across the daunting terrain. In 1988 Congress further protected 93 percent of these lands, designating them the Stephen Mather Wilderness in honor of the founding father and first director of the National Park Service. All three areas, a total of 684,000 acres, offer superb high-country wilderness and a host of recreational opportunities. The 300 or so glaciers here and on adjacent public lands account for more than half the glaciers in the contiguous United States.

The older part of the Cascade Range, the North Cascades began to rise some 90 million years ago with the collision of tectonic plates at the edge of the continent. The resulting intense pressure created metamorphic rocks and pushed the Pacific farther west. Much of the North Cascades visible today is volcanic, formed only a few million years ago; but in the north part of the range erosion has already worn down the volcanic rock, exposing the older layers. Over the past several thousand years, glaciation and stream erosion have adding the finishing touches, carving out U-shaped valleys, cirques, craggy peaks and other awe-inspiring features visitors may behold on a hike or a drive-through.

PRACTICAL INFORMATION ....Area Code: 360

When To Go

The mountains, forests, alpine meadows, glaciers, lakes and rivers of North Cascades National Park offer unlimited recreational opportunities in all seasons. The park is open year-round; admission is free. Owing to the rugged terrain, only one road, the North Cascades Highway/Route 20 *(closed in winter from Ross Dam to Silver Star Creek)*, leads through the park. In Marblemount the Cascade River Road *(unpaved, round-trip 46mi)* is a narrow, steep road that leads to a parking area at 3,660ft with spectacular views of glaciers. Trails and lakes at lower elevations can be enjoyed from early April through mid-October, although snow can block trails even in July.

Getting There

By Car – The region is accessible via I-5, which extends from the Canadian border south to Seattle and Portland.

By Air – Closest airports: **Seattle-Tacoma International Airport (SEA)**, international and domestic flights; and **Bellingham Airport**, serviced by Horizon Air *(☎ 800-547-9308)* and United Express *(☎ 800-241-6522)*.

By Bus and Train – Greyhound *(☎ 733-5251 or 800-231-2222)* provides daily bus service from Seattle and Vancouver to Bellingham. Closest Amtrak train station is in Burlington/Mount Vernon *(☎ 800-872-7245)*.

General Information

Visitor Information – To obtain maps and information on accommodations, recreation and seasonal events, contact **North Cascades National Park Headquarters**, 2105 State Rte. 20, Sedro-Woolley WA 98284-9394, ☎ 856-5700, www.nps.gov/noca. Maps, weather and trail information, and backcountry camping permits *(free)* are available at: **Wilderness Information Center** in Marblemount *(open mid-May–mid-Oct Sun–Thur 7am–6pm, Fri & Sat 7am–8pm;* ☎ 873-4500, ext. 39)*; **North Cascades Visitor Center** in Newhalem *(open mid-Apr–mid-Nov daily 8:30am–6pm; rest of the year weekends only;* ☎ 206-386-4495)*; **Golden West Visitor Center** in Stehekin, Lake Chelan National Recreation Area *(open mid-Mar–mid-Oct daily 8:30am–5pm; rest of the year reduced hours;* ☎ 856-5700)*; and **Bellingham/Whatcom County Convention & Visitors Bureau**, 904 Potter St., Bellingham WA 98227, ☎ 671-3990 or 800-487-2032.

Accommodations – Ross Lake Resort on Rte. 20 *(☎ 206-386-4437)*, North Cascades Stehekin Lodge on Lake Chelan *(☎ 509-682-4494)* and Stehekin Valley Ranch, Stehekin *(☎ 509-682-4677)* offer year-round accommodations in the park. Stehekin can be reached by ferry, boat, floatplane from Chelan or on foot along numerous trails. For **cabin rentals** check with park headquarters. Baker Lake Resort *(☎ 888-711-3033)* operates mid-Apr–Oct near Mt. Baker Wilderness. For other accommodations contact: **Sedro-Woolley Chamber of Commerce**, 714 B. Metcalf St., Sedro-Woolley WA 98284, ☎ 855-1841; **Concrete Chamber of Commerce**, P.O. Box 743, Concrete WA 98237, ☎ 853-7042; **Methow Valley Central Reservation Service**, P.O. Box 505, Winthrop WA 98862, ☎ 509-996-2148 or 800-422-3048; **Chelan Chamber of Commerce**, P.O. Box 216, Chelan WA 98816, ☎ 509-682-3503.

Camping – Permits, required for all backcountry overnight stays, are available on a first-come, first-served basis at visitor centers. Campfires are not allowed in many backcountry areas. Ross Lake National Recreation Area offers five campgrounds *(year-round)*. Goodell Creek Campground *(tent & RV, but no hookups; $7/night)* is open year-round. For additional camping information, contact North Cascades National Park Headquarters *(above)*. Camping in the National Forest does not require a permit.

Sports and Leisure

Sightseeing – The **Outdoor Recreation Information Center** *(year-round daily; ☎ 206-470-4060)* can help you plan a visit to the area. Ride a historic incline lift, **cruise** Diablo Lake, visit the Ross Powerhouse or take a tugboat from Diablo Dam to the base of Ross Dam. **Narrated tours** *(mid-Jun–Sept; reserve at least one month in advance)* are offered by Seattle City Light, 500 Newhalem St., Rockport WA 98283, ☎ 206-684-3030. For visitors who want to explore Lake Chelan, Lake Chelan Boat Co. offers **boat rides** *(depart from Chelan year-round daily; round-trip 8 hrs plus 2 hr layover; commentary; reservations suggested; $22; ✗ ♿ ; schedules & reservations, ☎ 509-682-2224)*. Lake Chelan Tours offer boat tours dinto the Stehekin Valley *(depart from Chelan year-round daily; round-trip 6 hrs including transportation to Rainbow Falls; $40/person; reservations required; ♿ ☎ 509-682-8287)*. Lodges, cabins and backcountry camping offer a variety of accommodations. The valley offers nature and hiking trails of varying difficulty, overnight horseback trips, bike rentals and rafting trips. Along Stehekin Valley Road, shuttle buses provide access to trailheads and **campgrounds** *(mid-May–mid-Oct; reservations recommended; ☎ 856-5700)*. View the fjordjlike valley on a **scenic flight** *(year-round, round-trip 1 hr; reservations: Chelan Airways, Chelan WA 98816, ☎ 509-682-5555)*.

Boating and Rafting – A multitude of activities are available along the many lakes and rivers. Boat ramps and rentals are available at Baker Lake, Ross Lake and Lake Chelan. Experienced outfitters offer rafting trips on the Skagit, Nooksack and Stehekin rivers. For a listing of **outfitters** who offer float and canoe excursions, as well as alpine, backpacking and climbing trips, contact park headquarters *(above)*.

Hiking and Climbing – Day hikes do not require a permit. Interpretive signs are posted along many self-guided trails. Take Trail of the Cedars *(.5mi)* or the **hike** from the parking lot at the end of Cascade River Road to Cascade Pass *(3.7mi)* at 5,384ft. The more avid hiker will enjoy Thunder Creek Trail *(19mi)*, which ascends to Park Creek Pass at 6,300ft starting at Colonial Creek Campground on Rte. 20. Entering wilderness areas requires additional preparation. Even on day hikes, each person should carry plenty of drinking water, warm clothing, rain gear and a first-aid kit; and don't forget a trail map and compass. Check with rangers for hiking conditions before setting out. Hiking in national forests, including Mt. Baker Wilderness, requires a Trail Park Pass *($3/day)*; inquire at Mt. Baker-Snoqualmie National Forest *(☎ 425-775-9702)*. Mountain and glacier **climbing** excursions into the North Cascades National Park. For a list of outfitters conducting mountain and glacier **climbing** excursions, contact park headquarters *(above)*.

Other Outdoor Activities – The North Cascades Highway and Mt. Baker Scenic Byway *(Rte. 542, 24mi)* are ideal for **biking** excursions, while side roads challenge the experienced mountain biker. All hiking trails in the park and the Mt. Baker Ranger District are closed to bicycles. **Llama trekking/hiking trips**, limit six participants, include camping equipment and all meals *(late May–Sept; day long/$45 or up to 9-days/$170 per person/day)*; reserve well in advance from High Valley Llama Treks *(☎ 826-4133)*. Sawtooth Outfitters in Pateros, WA offers pack trips on horseback into the wilderness *(all-inclusive; $150 per person/day; ☎ 509-923-2548)*. Trails that accommodate **horseback riding** in the national park and national forest are restricted; check with the ranger station for regulations and trail conditions.

The many lakes and rivers are home to a variety of salmon and trout. A valid Washington State **game-fishing** license, available at local bait shops, is required. For seasons, catch limits, and other regulations, call ☎ 902-2700.

Winter Sports – *For a list of ski areas, see p 420 [ref to Gen Pl]*. To the north near the Canadian border, the Mt. Baker Ski Area *(on Rte. 542; ☎ 734-6771)* boasts large snowfalls and an extended ski season *(Nov–Apr)*. To the south, the Bavarian-style town of **Leavenworth** and Stevens Pass *(equipment rental, ski & snowboard school; night skiing, sleigh rides; ☎ 206-812-4510; www.stevenspass.com)* both on Rte. 2, offer **downhill ski**, **snowboarding** and cross-country trails. Other terrain suitable for **cross-country skiing** in the North Cascades are: Methow Valley and Sun Mountain *(for information contact Sport Tails Assn., ☎ 800-682-5787)* and the Stehekin Valley *(☎ 509-682-4494)*. **Heli-skiing** excursions *(all-inclusive 1-3 days)* are led by professional mountain guides and require ski experience. For reservations, contact North Cascade Heli-Skiing, P.O. Box 367, Winthrop WA 98862, ☎ 509-996-3660 or 800-494-4354, www.methow.com/~heli-ski.

★★NORTH CASCADES NATIONAL PARK

Visit time varies, depending on allotment for hiking or backpacking.

About 120mi northeast of Seattle, the old-growth forests, waterfalls, lakes, sub-alpine meadows, and glaciated peaks that rear from 7,000ft-9,000ft fill this park's 505,000 acres, most of which is accessible only by foot. Such endangered animals as the grizzly bear and gray wolf inhabit its backcountry, generally far from human eyes. The 2,600mi **Pacific Crest National Scenic Trail** (PCT), running from Canada to Mexico, traverses 14mi in the southern unit of the park. The few developed areas of the park are actually in Ross Lake National Recreation Area, which runs along Route 20 and divides the north and south sections of the park, and in Lake Chelan National Recreation Area to the south.

North Cascades Highway

© Robert Holmes

North Cascades Visitor Center – *1mi west of Newhalem, off Rte. 20. Open mid-May daily 8:00am–4:30pm (Fri 6pm). Rest of the year Mon–Fri 8am–4:30pm. Closed major holidays.* ⚠ ♿ 🅿 ☎ *360-856-5700.* Surrounded by towering evergreens, this new center-opened in 1993-offers information on hiking, backpacking and fishing. Two innovative audiovisual presentations are shown in its theater: **Return to Wilderness**★ *(25min)*, a film on the history and natural history of the park, and a more artistic slide presentation, *A Meditation on Wilderness (20min)*. A short boardwalk trail behind the visitor center ends at a **viewpoint**★ looking north to 6,805ft Pinnacle Peak in the Picket Range.

★★NORTH CASCADES HIGHWAY   *1/2 day*

An impressive feat of engineering, this portion of Route 20 follows the corridor formed by the Ross Lake National Recreation Area, which separates the north and south units of North Cascades National Park. As it enters the recreation area from the west, the highway parallels the tumbling **Skagit River**. After passing Diablo and Ross lakes, where overlooks offer fine views, the roadway enters the **Okanogan National Forest** and a terrain of high peaks and lakes so spectacular that in 1984 Congress designated this roughly 38mi section the **North Cascades Scenic Highway**. Along the way, it passes a number of trailhead turnouts and traverses two mountain passes—the first, 4,860ft Rainy Pass marks the rain shadow divide; on the east side the landscape becomes markedly more arid. The second pass is 5,477ft Washington Pass, after which the road begins a steep descent toward the **Methow Valley**.

★**Rainy Lake Trail** – *Rainy Pass, Rte. 20.* The paved trail *(2mi round-trip)* through high coniferous forests offers the casual visitor an opportunity to experience the North Cascades wilderness on a short, level hike. The trail leads to small, sapphire blue **Rainy Lake**★, set in a glacial cirque and fed by a waterfall plunging from a distant cliff.

★★★**Washington Pass Overlook** – *Rte. 20, 35mi east of Marblemount.* A .5mi round-trip trail twists around a cliff face, offering views of towering Early Winter Spires and the heart-stopping descent of the highway through the arid landscape surrounding the steep mountain pass.

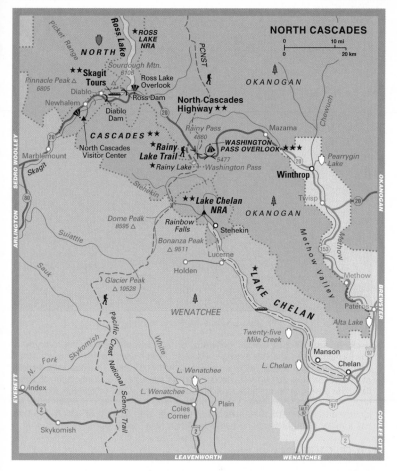

★ROSS LAKE NATIONAL RECREATION AREA *1/2 day*

Encompassing 118,000 acres, three hydroelectric dams, three lakes, and two small company towns (Newhalem and Diablo), this multi-use area is intended both for recreation and to perpetuate the operations of Seattle City Light, whose facilities provide the metropolitan area with electricity.

With the turn-of-the-century interest in hydroelectric power, utility companies began to vie for control of water rights. To thwart excessive pricing by private industry, the City of Seattle formed its own publicly held and administered company, Seattle City Light. Petitioning the US Secretary of Agriculture, it received rights to harness the upper Skagit River for hydroelectric power. In 1924, a temporary Gorge Dam was completed and the Gorge Powerhouse came on line. Problems with the temporary dam led to the construction of a second dam, Diablo, between 1927 and 1930. In 1936 its powerhouse was completed, and the following year a third dam was begun upstream. Completed in 1939, Ross Dam was named after J. D. Ross, known as the "Father of Seattle City Light." Later, the level of the dam was raised to create an enlarged reservoir with more generating capacity. In 1961, the new Gorge High Dam was completed. On the National Register of Historic Places, the Skagit Hydroelectric Project drains a watershed area of 1,175sq mi and generates 784 megawatts of electricity.

★★**Skagit Tours** – *Off Rte. 20. In Diablo, follow signs to parking area. Depart from Diablo Tour Center mid-Jun–Aug Thu–Mon 11am. Commentary. For reservations: Seattle City Light ☎ 206-684-3030. www.ci.seattle.wa.us/light/tours.* Since the mid-20C Seattle City Light has been conducting these highly popular tours of its various facilities. Informative guides outline the purpose, construction and operation of the two massive dams—Diablo and Ross—that supply Seattle's electricity. Tours include an orientation film, powerhouse tour, boat cruise, and a ride on a 1920s incline railway, built to carry dam workers 570ft up the 57 percent grade of Sourdough Mountain. The 3.5 hr tour of **Ross Dam** *($25)* also includes a boat tour and an all-you-can-eat lunch. Ross Dam, 540ft high, 1300ft long, and 208ft

Ross Lake National Recreation Area

© Robert Holmes

thick, is Skagit Project's major generator of hydroelectric power. The reservoir it has formed, Ross Lake, fills a gorge between forested Cascade peaks and stretches from the dam for 24mi, with a maximum width of 2mi. The **Ross Lake Overlook** *(Mile 135 on Rte. 20)* affords views down on the lake. The 90min tour of **Diablo Dam** *($5)* gives you an up-close look at the 1930 dam. When completed, the 389ft-high, 1,180ft-long dam ranked as the highest arch-type dam in the world. It curves picturesquely above the 910-acre lake it created. With a depth of 330 ft, the lake has a milky blue-green color, caused by "rock flour" from glacial runoff.

★LAKE CHELAN *1 1/2 days*

This narrow, 50mi-long lake occupies a glacially gouged trough that plunges to depths of 1,500ft, making the lake one of the deepest in the US. In 1927 a dam was built near the southern end of the lake, raising its level a further 21ft. In the rain shadow of the Cascades, the lower end of the lake is surrounded by arid hills covered with a plethora of apple orchards that make this area one of the state's largest producers. The fairly constant sunlight here also attracts watersports enthusiasts, and the lakeside towns of **Chelan** and **Manson** have become popular resort communities.

★★**Lake Chelan National Recreation Area** – *Accessible only by boat (see practical information). Open mid-May–mid-Oct daily 8:30am–5pm. Call ahead for reduced hours in spring and fall.* ⚠ 🍴 ♿ ☎ *360-856-5700 ext. 340 & 14.* Protected within the 62,000-acre national recreation area, the fjord-like upper end of the lake nestles between sawtooth peaks that soar 8,000ft above its narrow waterway. The hub of activity centers on the village of **Stehekin** *(pop. 100)*, whose charm lies in its quiet remoteness from any extensive development. The National Park Service's **Golden West Visitor Center** offers information on hiking, boating, biking and natural history; a gallery in the center features crafts, artworks and programs by regional artists. The park also offers **narrated shuttle bus tours** along the gravel Stehekin Valley Road that follows the Stehekin River north from the head of the lake; another shuttle bus makes a 3.5mi trip to 312ft **Rainbow Falls**.

Excursions

Winthrop – *1/2 day. 60mi north of Chelan on Rte. 20. Visitor information ☎ 509-996-2125 or 888-463-8469. www.winthropwashington.com.* Recapturing the spirit of the Old West, the Main Street of Winthrop boasts wooden sidewalks and nostalgic, early 20C storefronts. The visionary behind returning the town to its appearance as an early western mining town was local lumber baron Kathryn Wagner, who, with the completion of the North Cascades Highway in 1972, hoped to draw travelers here. Her vision proved a success, and today Winthrop is a tourist mecca amid the arid farm country of the Methow Valley.

White Buck Museum – *Main St. Open May–Sept daily 9am–7pm. Rest of the year daily 9am–6pm.* ☎ *509-996-3500.* This local history facility exhibits personal memorabilia, as well as the tools, pharmaceuticals and housewares of yesteryear. A 1938 Dodge sedan, old carriages and engines are featured on the basement level.

★**Shafer Museum** – *Castle and Corral Aves. Open May–mid-Sept Thu–Mon 10am–5pm.* ☎ *509-996-2712.* Re-creating a turn-of-the-century pioneer village, the museum's nine buildings—reproductions and historic structures moved to the site—include shops, a schoolhouse, a doctor's office, a stable and carriage house, and the "**Castle.**" On its original site, the latter is the lodgepole pine home built by Guy Waring, a Bostonian who founded the town in the 1890s and operated an outfitters store for miners in the area.

NORTHWEST COAST

Michelin map 493 B, C 2, 3 and map p 242
Tourist Information ☎ 360-671-3990 or www.bellingham.org

Beyond the pale of the Seattle-Tacoma megalopolis, Washington's quiet northwest corner is wedged into the foothills between Mt. Baker and the coastal bays and inlets of Puget Sound. At its north lies the Canadian border, and the local populace's ties to its Canada neighbors are almost as strong as their ties to fellow Washingtonians. Like Seattle and Tacoma, this coast area developed in the mid-19C along with logging and maritime concerns; in addition, some coal mining occurred in the area of present-day Bellingham. Hopes that the Great Northern Railroad would establish its western terminus here never came to fruition. But the long-range result was to ensure the low-key loveliness of the area, with farmlands inland and marinas and small port facilities along the coast and coastal islands. The Skagit Valley, east of Anacortes, boasts a spectacular spring display of **tulips and daffodils★★**. Now, as in the past, Bellingham serves as the cosmopolitan hub of the area and a jumping-off point for travelers headed to Canada, both by car and ferry. The smaller city of Anacortes also functions as a port and ferry terminal.

ANACORTES *2 1/2 hrs*

Anchoring the northwestern tip of Fidalgo Island, this coastal town is best known as the terminus for Washington State Ferries heading to the San Juan Islands and VICTORIA, British Columbia. The town's name evolved from that of Anna Curtis Bowman, the wife of 19C town founder Amos Bowman. A working port city, Anacortes (ana-COR-tes) has preserved its mid-19C-style downtown, including the landmark 1889 **Majestic Inn** *(419 Commercial Ave.)*, built to house a pioneering business and moved to different town locations throughout its long career. Old buildings and storefronts are often adorned with murals designed by local artist Bill Mitchell and representing individuals from the town's past. Walking tour maps of the murals are available at the **visitor center** *(819 Commercial Ave.; open May–Sept Mon–Sat 9am–5pm, Sun 10am–3pm; rest of the year Mon–Fri 9am–5pm, Sat 10am–3pm; closed Thanksgiving Day, Dec 25;* ♿ 🅿 ☎ *360-293-3832; www.anacortes.org).* **The Depot** *(7th St. and R Ave.),* built in 1911 as the Great Northern Railway Depot, now serves as a gallery showcasing the works of local artists. Several miles from town, 1,273ft **Mount Erie**, now a city-owned park, is switchbacked by a steep road that leads to 360-degree **views★★** of Puget Sound and its waterways, Mt. Baker, the sawtooth crenellations of the North Cascades,

---

■ Skagit Valley Tulips

One of the largest tulip bulb cultivation areas in the world, the Skagit Valley between the towns of La Conner and Mount Vernon stretches in a spring dazzle of color, its flat expanses backed by the towering snow-rimed summits of the North Cascades. Thousands of acres are planted in the majestic flowers, which are cultivated here for their bulbs rather than their blooms. The tulip frenzy culminates in a two-week-long **Skagit Valley Tulip Festival** in mid-April, when bus tours of the fields are given, special performances staged, arts and crafts fairs held in neighboring towns and barbecues thrown by community groups. Preceding the tulip bloom, fields of daffodils begin blooming in early March, and in May irises reach their peak. Among the largest commercial growers in the valley is the family-owned, 1,200-acre **RoozenGaarde** *(Beaver March Rd. between McLean and Calhoun Sts., Mount Vernon; open year-round Mon–Sat 9am–5pm; closed major holidays;* ☎ *360-424-8531),* which also offers a display garden and store.

and on a clear day, even Mt. Rainier. The mount's craggy sides are popular with rock climbers and day hikers. Northeast of town, along Padilla Bay, the 2.4mi-long **Padilla Bay Trail** leads along dike tops with views out across the bay waters.

Anacortes Museum – *1305 8th St. Open year-round Thu–Mon 1pm–5pm. Closed major holidays. $2.* ▣ ☎ *360-293-1915. www.anacorteshistorymuseum.org.* The former 1909 Carnegie Library now features frequently changing exhibits related to the history and culture of Fidalgo and Guemes Islands. A section devoted to the Fidalgo Island Canning Company Office recalls the salmon-canning industry that prospered in Puget Sound early in the 20C. The museum collection includes the **W.T. Preston**, which occupies a dry berth along R Avenue near Seventh Street. One of only two extant snagboats operated by the Army Corps of Engineers to keep Puget Sound waters and tributaries clear of navigational hazards, the 1939 vessel saw service until 1981. When decommissioned, she was the oldest stern-wheeler operating in Puget Sound. The 163.5ft vessel now interprets life aboard a stern-wheeler snagboat.

★LA CONNER   *1/2 day*

On the National Register of Historic Places, this picturesque village and artist community edging the Swinomish Channel dates to the late 1860s and ranks as Skagit County's oldest community. In the 1930s artists Guy Anderson, Morris Graves and other pioneers of the now famous Northwest style, lived here, and since the 1970s, novelist Tom Robbins has also made the town his home. Today, La Conner's waterfront galleries and craft shops along South First Street, the town's three museums and its charming ambience make it a popular weekend destination.

La Conner Quilt Museum – *703 S. 2nd St. Open Apr–Oct Wed–Sun 11am–5pm. Nov, Feb–Mar Wed–Sun 11am–4pm. Closed major holidays. $3.* ☎ *360-466-4288.* Located in the Victorian Gaches Mansion (1891) that was formerly the home of the Museum of Northwest Art, the museum displays a changing series of quilts by artists from around the world in its second-floor exhibit rooms. The first-floor rooms reflect the turn-of-the-century furnishings that would have originally decorated the mansion.

★★ **Museum of Northwest Art** – *121 S. 1st St. Open year-round Tue–Sun 10am–5pm. Closed Jan 1, July 4, Thanksgiving Day, Dec 25. $3.* ♿ ▣ ☎ *360-466-4446. www.museumofnwart.org.* Though founded as recently as 1981, MoNA, as locals call it, has acquired a strong reputation for its focus on Northwest contemporary artists. Its small but select permanent collection *(second floor)* includes works by the four mid-20C artists credited with fathering the Northwest style: Mark Tobey, Morris Graves, Guy Anderson and Kenneth Callahan. The museum's **Benaroya Glass Gallery** features works by Dale Chihuly and other outstanding regional glass artists. MoNA's aggressive schedule of changing exhibits features traveling exhibits and shows highlighting the works of individual artists.

Skagit County Historical Museum – *501 S. 4th St. Open year-round Tue–Sun 11am–5pm. Closed major holidays. $3.* ♿ ▣ ☎ *360-466-3365.* This well-displayed local history museum tops a small hill with **views** east across the Skagit Valley to the North Cascades. The permanent Skagit Legacy galleries focus on Native American and pioneering traditions in the region. Farming, logging, merchandising and blacksmithing are covered in exhibits, as are personal memorabilia; several late-19C rooms are also re-created.

★BELLINGHAM   *1 day*

A pleasant, well-heeled city in the foothills of Mt. Baker, Bellingham wraps itself around a bay by the same name. Its earliest settlements, based on coal mining and sawmills, formed in the mid-19C. In 1903 the adjacent communities of New Whatcom, Fairhaven and Whatcom consolidated to form the city of Bellingham. Today, the town is both a maritime and university community, focused around Western Washington University. Its proximity to the Canadian border also creates a strong link with that country. In the last decade, the downtown has developed a significant arts focus, with the growth of the **Whatcom Museum Campus** *(p 337)* and the **Mount Baker Theatre** *(104 N. Commercial St.).* Opened in 1927 as a vaudeville venue and later a movie palace, the Spanish-Moorish-style theater continues to feature films, as well as live stage performances and community events.

The western suburbs of Bellingham are dominated by the long, narrow curve of **Lake Whatcom**, fifth-largest lake in the state. Curving along Chuckanut Bay and Puget Sound to the south of town, **Chuckanut Drive** *(west on Rte. 11, off I-5 at Exit 250)* weaves in and out of forested bluffs for almost a dozen miles, with lovely **views** of the island-dotted coastal waters.

Western Washington University – *South of downtown on Bill McDonald Pkwy. Walking-tour maps available at visitor center, S. College Dr. and College Way; open mid-Sept–mid-Jun Mon–Fri 7am–8pm. Rest of the year Mon–Fri 7am–5pm. Closed* *major holidays.* ☎ *360-650-3424. www.wwu.edu.* Established in 1893 as a "normal school" to train teachers, this institution now serves as the major state university in northern Washington. Some 10,600 undergraduate students are enrolled in the university's five colleges, with an additional 800 students attending the graduate school. Though the campus sprawls across 190 acres, most academic buildings are compacted around contiguous plazas, showcasing the university's famous outdoor **sculpture collection★**. Now grown to more than 24 pieces and still growing, the collection began in 1960 with the installation of Rain Forest, by northwest artist James Fitzgerald. Among the works, some monumental, others small-scale, is a walk-in piece, **Skyviewing Sculpture★** *(in Red Square)* by artist Isamu Noguchi. Other sculptors represented include Alice Aycock, Richard Serra, George Trakas and Mark di Suvero. The university's **Western Gallery★** sponsors six changing exhibits a year, featuring the works of regional, national and international artists *(in the Fine Arts Building, east side of campus; open late–Sept–mid-Jun Mon–Fri 10am–4pm, Sat noon–4pm; closed major holidays;* ♿ ▣ ☎ *360-650-3900).*

Sehome Arboretum – *25th St., off Bill McDonald Pkwy.* ☎ *360-671-3990.* On Sehome Hill adjacent to the Western Washington University campus, 70 acres of forests provide a quiet natural reserve. Seven miles of trails now loop through the mostly evergreen forests. A summit-top tower affords views of Bellingham Bay and the San Juan Islands, as well as the Canadian Coastal Mountains and Mount Baker.

★Fairhaven Historic District – *Between 13th and 20th Sts. Walking tour brochures available at area businesses.* Along Bellingham Bay south of downtown, Fairhaven was established by smuggler "Dirty" Dan Harris in the 1870s. By the 1890s, with the area in a wild economic boom over speculation that the Great Northern Railroad would locate its terminus here, construction sprang up and more than 35 hotels and boardinghouses were built within the decade. Now little remains from its 19C past, though granite plaques throughout its streets recall historic spots, such as the site where a freight wagon sank in quicksand. Most of the historic buildings now standing date to the town's 1890s economic boom, though the liberal, neighborly atmosphere is decidedly 1990s. Charmingly preserved red-brick storefronts house small cafes, restaurants, galleries and bookstores that provide low-key, friendly meeting places for locals. Several classic Victorian homes are scattered through the streets, notably the 1892 **Roland G. Gamwell House** *(1001 16th St.)* and the 1890 **Wardner's Castle** *(1103 15th St.).* The **Fairhaven Terminal** *(4th and Harris Sts.)* at the foot of town on Bellingham Bay services vessels plying the Alaska Marine Highway System and ferries heading to the San Juan Islands and Victoria, British Columbia.

Roeder Home – *2600 Sunset Dr. Open Jan–Nov Mon–Thu 9am–4pm.* ☎ *360-733-6897.* Now owned by Whatcom County, this substantial 1908 sandstone-and-brick home was built by Victor Roeder, son of one of the county's pioneering settlers, Henry Roeder. The house exemplifies what was considered the most modern of features for its time, including a house-wide vacuum system, brass light fixtures with Steuben glass shades and an original furnace made from a Great Northern Railway boiler. The dining room is decorated with romantic wall murals and oak paneling. The spare furnishings reflect the period; only two pieces, a parlor couch and a hall cabinet, are original to the home. An upstairs gallery hosts changing art exhibits.

★Big Rock Garden – *Off Alabama St. at Sylvan St. and Balsam Lane. Open Apr–Oct daily 10am–6pm.* ☎ *360-676-6985.* A former nursery, the small, serene city-owned garden occupies a high wooded plot in a suburban neighborhood. Ferns, evergreens, rhododendrons, azaleas and Japanese maples are grouped in a naturalistic style reminiscent of Japanese gardens and broken here and there by pieces of sculpture. Benches face out from a hillside, with a contemplative view down to Lake Whatcom.

★Whatcom Museum of History & Art – *121 Prospect St. Open year-round Tue–Sun noon–5pm. Closed major holidays.* ♿ ▣ ☎ *360-676-6981. www.cob.org/museum.htm.* This four-building museum complex is devoted to the region's cultural and artistic history centers. Its main building is the eye-catching former **Old City Hall★** dominating Prospect Hill. Built in 1892 in the ornate style of Victorian civic architecture, the turreted red-brick structure, trimmed in sandstone and topped by a bell tower, opened as a museum in 1941. In 1992 the museum expanded into two additional buildings and took over management of the Whatcom Children's Museum. Centered around a stately oak-and-maple staircase and entry hall, the galleries on the lower two floors are devoted to changing exhibits of contemporary art and photography, often curated by leading art authorities nationwide. The third floor displays a permanent collection of antique clothing, toys, tools and other local memorabilia, as well as **clockworks★** that regulate the Tosco Tower Clock now installed in the bell tower.

The museum's **Syre Education Center** *(201 Prospect St.)* houses permanent displays of Native American tools, chests and **basketry★** by First Nations Peoples from the West Coast (mostly Lummi and Coast Salish) and Alaska (Aleut and Eskimo), and exhibits tracing the history of Northwest logging and pioneering. An extensive collection of mounted **birds of the Pacific Northwest**★ offer the visitor an opportunity to study the plumage, beaks and other identifying details of the waterbirds, birds of prey, gallinaceous birds, shorebirds, owls and perching birds that inhabit the Northwest. Also considered part of the Whatcom "campus," the nearby **ARCO Exhibition Gallery** *(206 Prospect St.)* features major changing exhibits of art and history, and the **Whatcom Children's Museum** *(227 Prospect St.; same hours as above; $2;* ☎ *360-733-8769)* entertains and educates children two to eight years old with its hands-on play areas.

Maritime Heritage Center – *1600 C St. Park open year-round dawn-dusk. Information Center open Oct–mid-Dec daily 9am–3pm.* 🅿 ☎ *360-676-6806.* Below the Prospect Street bluffs, this 10-acre park along Whatcom Creek was the site of the city's first settlement (1852), a sawmill fueled by the Whatcom (a Lummi word meaning "noisy water"). Trails landscaped with native flora now follow Whatcom Creek and feature interpretive stations that explain the life cycle of the salmon that are annually released into the creek and return here to spawn. The best time to view salmon is mid-October to mid-December.

Squalicum Harbor – *Roeder Ave.* ☎ *360-676-2500 or 2542.* On Bellingham Bay, this large marina area is fronted by working terminal and administrative buildings related to the city's maritime industry. The small **Marine Life Center** *(1801 Roeder Ave.; open year-round daily 8am-dusk;* ♿ 🅿 ☎ *360-671-2431)* holds several touch pools with anemones, starfish and other marine life. In summer months, **Island Mariner Cruises** offers daylong wildlife-watching cruises and shorter sunset cruises, both aimed at spying whales and other marine mammals *(depart from 5 Harbor Esplanade May–Sept daily 8am; rest of the year daily 9am; round-trip 7 hr 30min; reservations recommended; $55, children $35;* ✕ 🅿 *Island Mariner Cruises, Bellingham* ☎ *360-734-8866 or 877-734-8866; www.orcawatch.com).*

● Regional Restaurants

The Bay Cafe – *Lopez Village, Lopez Island.* ☎ *360-468-3700.* The only fine restaurant on Lopez, this newly renovated waterfront cafe is renowned for its well-prepared local seafood.

Downrigger – *10 Front St., Friday Harbor on San Juan Island.* ☎ *360-378-2700.* On the waterfront, this large, boisterous restaurant features hearty seafood standbys, like steamed clams and grilled fish.

The Majestic Inn – *419 Commercial Ave., Anacortes.* ☎ *360-293-3355.* Both the main dining room and the Rose & Crown Pub (with authentic English pub decor) of this historic hotel serve superb Northwestern cuisine (including mouth-watering Padilla Bay oysters).

Mannino's Italian Restaurant – *130 E. Champion St., Bellingham.* ☎ *360-671-7955.* A small, low-key downtown restaurant offers reasonable and well-prepared Italian pastas, veals and other classics.

The Place – *1 Spring St., Friday Harbor on San Juan Island.* ☎ *360-378-8707.* Right next to the ferry terminal on the waterfront, this intimate little restaurant is a favorite of locals, and for good reason. Its entrees combine unusual ingredients with fresh local seafood.

Rosario Resort – *East side of Orcas Island off Horseshoe Hwy.* ☎ *360-376-2222.* Lovely resort dining room stretches across the waterfront and the appetizers and entrees, in classic Northwest style, are prepared with flair.

Wild Garlic – *114 Prospect St., Bellingham.* ☎ *360-671-1955.* Across from the Whatcom Museum, the small, casual restaurant is deserving of its name, as it features garlic in many guises—combined with burgers, chicken, pork, scampi, vegetables, salads, and even roasted on its own.

Excursion

★**Ferndale** – *1/2 day. 8mi northwest of Bellingham via I-5.* A farming center for the Upper Northwest, this small town proudly celebrates its past and its geography in three historic sites.

★**Pioneer Park** – *1st Ave. and Cherry St. Open mid-May–mid-Sept Tue-Sun 11:30am-4:30pm. $3.* 🅿 ☎ *360-384-0792.* The largest collection of historic log homes in the state, this site was begun by the Whatcom County Settlers Association, founded in 1895 and devoted to celebrating the pioneer past. In 1930, the association moved the first 19C building to the site. Since then 13 more log structures have been acquired, and the park has been deeded to the City of Ferndale. The buildings, dating from the 1870s-90s, include homes, a church, granary, barn, post office, jail, inn and schoolhouse. During summer months, guided tours are given by costumed interpreters.

★ **Hovander Homestead** – *Nielsen Ave. off Hovander Rd. Grounds open year-round dawn-dusk. $3. House open May weekends noon–4:30. Jun–Labor Day Thu–Sun noon–4:30pm. $3/car.* ⅃ 🄿 ☏ *360-384-3444.* An impressive interpretation of an immigrant farmstead, this working, turn-of-the-century farm centers around the 1903 Hovander home, whose gables, gingerbread trim and interior period furnishings bespeak the Swedish background of its owners. Flanking it is a large dairy barn with a milking parlor and harness and tack rooms, and a farmyard full of hoofed animals, ducks, geese and even peacocks. Surrounding fields are cultivated in hay, and both children and adults are invited to savor the smells and sights of this historic farm.

Tennant Lake Natural History Interpretive Center – *Hovander Rd., adjacent to Hovander Homestead. Open mid-Jun–Labor Day Thu–Sun noon–5pm. Labor Day–Nov Wed–Sat noon–4pm.* ⅃ 🄿 ☏ *360-384-3064.* Now an environmental education center with exhibits on local flora and fauna, an early 20C home is fronted by an extensive fragrance garden. A .5mi boardwalk trail leads from the home out across the wetlands formed by the Nooksack River.

SAN JUAN ISLANDS★★

Michelin map 493 B 2, 3 and map p 242
Tourist Information ☏ 360-468-3663 or www.guidetosanjuans.com

This 172-island archipelago floats between the Washington mainland and Vancouver Island like an ephemeral, often fog-shrouded armada. Actually the tops of submerged mountains, the island chain was scoured by glaciers during the ice ages, then eons later used by the Lummi Indians as a hunting ground. In 1791 the Spanish sailed through the islands, and a year later Capt. George Vancouver followed in their wake, claiming the islands for Britain; in 1841 Capt. Charles Wilkes claimed them for the US. Not surprisingly, the disputed ownership escalated into a conflict in the late 19C. Now called the **Pig War** *(p 240)*, the altercation lasted 12 years but cost no casualties, save the namesake pig. At its end, the islands became internationally recognized as US territory, and as farmers from the mainland settled in earnest here, the islands became famous for their apples. Today in 175sq mi San Juan County, smallest in the state, little land is commercially cultivated. Instead the islands attract artists, crafts-folk and others seeking quiet and scenic beauty. That quiet is broken in the warm-weather months, when the islands maintain a thriving tourist trade. Visitors, both regional and international, flock to the islands to kayak, bicycle, beachcomb, and whale– and bird-watch. Though each of the islands offers such outdoor activities, each also provides its own distinctive ambience, assiduously cultivated by the local residents. Only four of the islands are serviced by commercial ferry and of these, only the three below offer visitor accommodations and amenities. Washington State Ferries run several times daily among the islands and the mainland *(p 240)*.

Friday Harbor

© Robert Holmes

★★SAN JUAN ISLAND *1 1/2 days*

The second-largest, westernmost, and most populous island in the archipelago, 35,448-acre San Juan was once the home of farmers and fruit growers. Though it has few agricultural concerns left, much of the island still sweeps across pastoral open spaces. Tourism is a burgeoning industry, with travelers flocking here to whale-watch along Haro Strait; bike the scenic country roads; kayak; walk the long beaches along the southern end of the island; or visit sites associated with the strange Pig War that occurred here between the US and Britain in the late 19C. San Juan's main commercial center, the pleasant town of **Friday Harbor** on the south end of the island, is also the most westerly ferry stop in the islands, and its shops cater both to browsing tourists and the needs of locals. At the north end of the island, the town of **Roche Harbor★**, with its manicured lawns and cobblestoned waterfront, centers around the old 1886 resort by the same name; in a nearby grove stands the **Mausoleum**, designed by the hotel builder and the founder of the island limeworks, John McMillan. The monument's Winding Stairs and Brazen Pillars, as well as other features, are symbolic of the Masonic ideals that McMillan espoused. At the center of the mausoleum, six stone chairs surrounding a round table presumably are emblematic of the meeting of members of the McMillan family in the afterlife.

★San Juan Island National Historical Park – *English Camp on northwest end of island (10mi from Friday Harbor); American Camp on southeast tip (6mi from Friday Harbor). Park open year-round dawn-dusk.* 🅿 ☎ *360-378-2240. www.nps.gov/saju/home.htm.* The 1,250-acre park preserves coastal swatches of the

Practical Information ....Area Code: 360

Getting There – Closest airports: **Seattle-Tacoma International Airport** (SEA) and **Bellingham Airport**. Connecting flights to islands via Harbor Airlines (☎ *800-359-3220)* and West Isle Air (☎ *800-874-4434)*. Ground transportation from both airports to ferry terminal in Anacortes via Airporter Shuttle *(pre-paid 24 hr reservations suggested; ☎ 380-8800)*. Lopez, Orcas, Shaw and San Juan islands are accessible via **ferry** *(year-round; daily)* from Anacortes WA. Ferry lines can be long during rush hour or peak weekend times. The ferries leaving Anacortes for the San Juans can generate three-hour-long lines on weekends, so plan ahead. For schedules: **Washington State Ferries**, Coleman Dock, Seattle WA 98104, ☎ 206-464-6400, www.wsdot.wa.gov/ferries. Puget Sound Express runs between Port Townsend and Friday Harbor *(Mar–Oct; ☎ 385-5288)*.
Closest Amtrak **train** station: Burlington/Mount Vernon, ☎ 800-872-7245. Greyhound **bus** service *(☎ 733-5251 or 800-231-2222)* runs to Bellingham.

Getting Around – Ferry access *(year-round)* between islands in the archipelago is free for walk-ons. San Juan Transit *(☎ 800-887-8387)* provides public transportation on San Juan Island. Taxi service *(Apr–Sept)*: Orcas Island, Orcas Taxi, ☎ 376-8294; San Juan Island, San Juan Bus & Taxi, ☎ 378-8887. **Car rental**: Orcas Island, West Isle Air, ☎ 800-874-4434; San Juan Island, M&W Rental, ☎ 378-2794. The best way to explore the islands is by **bicycle** or **scooter**: San Juan Island, Island Bicycles in Friday Harbor, ☎ 378-4941; Lopez Island, Bike Shop, ☎ 468-3497. Bike rentals average $25/day. Some companies will deliver bikes to the ferry terminal.

Visitor Information – For information and brochures on points of interest, accommodations, sightseeing, tour companies and seasonal events, contact **San Juan Islands Visitor Information Service**, P.O. Box 65, Lopez Island WA 98261, ☎ 468-3663 or 888-468-3701; www.guidetosanjuans.com.

Accommodations – A variety of lodgings including hotels, small inns, bed-and-breakfast inns, beachfront cottages or cabins, as well as resorts, is available on Lopez, Orcas and San Juan islands. **Camping** facilities are plentiful; reservations during summer are strongly recommended. Some campgrounds offer RV hookups. Off-road camping is prohibited. For a listing of camping facilities and vacation rental properties, contact the San Juan Islands Visitor Information Service *(above)*.

Recreation or Sightseeing – The islands are easily accessible by ferry for day trips *(above)* from the mainland. Recreational activities abound in the summer. Outdoor activities include **hiking**, **bicycling**, fishing, **scuba diving**, boating and swimming. Boat rentals are readily available. A variety of charter companies offer **sailing**, **fishing**, **whale-watching** and sportfishing. A license is required for all fishing. For a listing of outfitters for outdoor activities, contact the San Juan Islands Visitor Information Service *(above)*.

island associated with the 1859-72 occupation by English and American troops during the Pig War. The conflict was sparked in 1859, when an American farmer on the island, Lyman Cutlar, shot a pig rooting in his potato patch. Unfortunately, the pig belonged to British Hudson's Bay Company agents, and soon the pig shooting had escalated into an international incident. US infantry under Capt. George Pickett (who would later lead the infamous Pickett's Charge at the Civil War Battle of Gettysburg) were dispatched to the island, as were three British warships. The US Army dug in along the Cattle Point Peninsula, as the British Navy faced them offshore. The standoff continued for two months, until Gen. Winfield Scott, commander of all US forces, arrived and negotiated a joint occupation agreement with the British. For the next dozen years, the two occupation forces remained, the Americans at the original camp along Cattle Point and the English at the northern end of the island. Finally, in October 1872, German Kaiser Wilhelm was asked to arbitrate in the conflict, and he declared in favor of the US, thus ending the conflict and the occupation, and placing the islands within America's domain.

Visit – *3 hrs.* The park headquarters, located at the entrance to **American Camp** *(Cattle Point Rd.; open Memorial Day–Labor Day daily 8:30am–4:30pm; rest of the year Thu–Sun 8am–4:30pm; closed major holidays)*, presents a 12min slide show on the Pig War. A self-guided walking-tour pamphlet leads visitors through the former campsite, where only two wooden buildings-an officers' quarters and a laundress' quarters—still remain (the others were torn down). However, bulges from the redoubts erected by the Americans still etch the open, windswept hills overlooking the Strait of Juan de Fuca on the south and Griffin Bay to the north. Along Griffin Bay lagoons interrupt the park's curving beach and the **lagoon trail** weaves through

From Seattle, **sightseeing cruises** take visitors to many of the islands and combine whale-watching with a stop in Friday Harbor *(depart Seattle from Pier 69 mid-May–Sept daily 6:45am; 13 hr round-trip; reservations required; $72, $36 child;* ⚓ ♿ ▣ *Gray Line of Seattle;* ☎ *800-426-7505).* To explore the abundant marine wildlife-sea lions, harbor seals, porpoises, whales-as well as myriad seabirds, engage the services of a tour operator. Sports enthusiasts can partake in exciting **kayaking** tours led by experienced guides from April to October *(rental included; schedules & reservations: Lopez Kayaks, Lopez Island;* ☎ *468-2847).* Guided 3 hr tours *($39),* all-day trips *($75)* or multi-day excursions with overnight camping leave from Orcas Island *(reservations: Shearwater Adventues Inc., P.O. Box 787, Eastsound WA 98245;* ☎ *376-4699).* Sea kayaking outings combine the excitement of watching marine wildlife close-up and exploring the rocky shoreline while camping *(mid-May–Sept; all-inclusive 1, 3 & 5-days; $75-$605; schedules & reservations: Outdoor Odysseys Inc., 12003 23rd Ave. N.E., Seattle WA 98125;* ☎ *206-361-0717 or 800-647-4621; www.pacifi-crim.net~bydesign/odyssey.html).* Scheduled **whale-watching cruises** accompanied by a naturalist leave from Orcas Island *(May–Sept; daily; round-trip 4 hrs; commentary; binoculars & rain gear provided; reservations required; $46.50; Orcas Island Eclipse Charters;* ☎ *376-4663 or 800-376-6566)* and Friday Harbor on San Juan Island *(May–Sept daily; round-trip 4 hrs; commentary; $45; schedules & reservations: Western Prince Cruises, Friday Harbor;* ☎ *378-5315 or 800-757-6722).*

© Robert Holmes

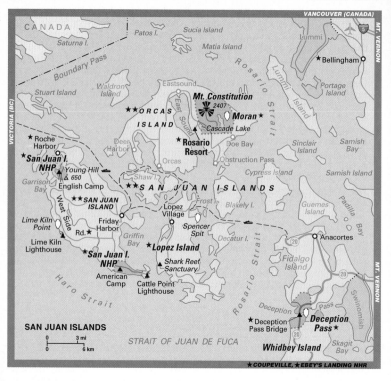

SAN JUAN ISLANDS

0 ———— 3 mi
0 ———— 6 km

★COUPEVILLE, ★EBEY'S LANDING NHR

the woods above the lagoons; beyond the broad sand **beaches★** along the south coast orcas glide offshore in their seasonal migrations.

Outside the park boundary, at the east tip of Cattle Point, the **Cattle Point Lighthouse** continues to flash a warning to mariners. At quiet **English Camp** *(off W. Valley Rd.)* several clapboard buildings and a formal English garden still overlook protected Garrison Bay. In the **Barracks**, historical photographs are displayed. A trail leads .75mi uphill through the forest to **English Camp Cemetery**, where a few headstones mark the graves of men who died during (but not because of) the occupation. Beyond the cemetery, the trail loops to the summit of 650ft **Young Hill**, with views of the island and west toward Vancouver Island.

San Juan Historical Museum – *405 Price St., Friday Harbor. Open May–Sept Thu–Sun 1pm–4pm. Oct, Mar–Apr Sat 1pm–4pm. Nov–Feb by appointment only. $2.* 🅿 ☎ *360-378-3949. www.sjmuseum.org.* This local history museum preserves historic buildings that once stood in various locations throughout the island, including the former county jail, a milk house, a 19C log cabin and weatherboard barn, a carriage house and stone root cellar. A 19C clapboard farmhouse is furnished in period style and exhibits local memorabilia. The resource center houses rotating exhibits and research facilities.

The Whale Museum – *62 1st St. N., Friday Harbor. Open Memorial Day–Labor Day daily 9am–5pm. Rest of the year daily 10am–5pm. $5.* ☎ *360-378-4710. www.whale-museum.org.* Dedicated to raising public awareness about the marvels of whales and the threats to them and their environment, a grass-roots-style museum offers simple but educational exhibits on the behavior and unique physiology of these marine mammals. Echolocation, mating, calving and "singing" are among the topics covered, as is an explanation of the vastly different kinds of cetaceans, from porpoises and dolphins to deep-diving behemoths like the sperm whale. Naturally, Puget Sound's most famous denizen, the orca (formerly called the killer whale) is prominently featured.

Lime Kiln Point State Park – *Off Lighthouse Rd. Open year-round daily dawn-dusk.* 🅿 ☎ *800-233-0321. www.parks.wa.gov.* The drive along **West Side Road★** leading to the park hugs the rocky coastline of the island dramatically. In the small park, anchored by the 1917 **Lime Kiln Lighthouse**, you can walk down along the cliffs and tide pools and take time out for **whale-watching★★**. The park faces Haro Strait, a favorite cruising spot for pods of orcas and minkes who spend their summer months in Puget Sound waters. Locals suggest late afternoon to sunset as the best time for spottings.

Whale Watching at Lime Kilin Point State Park

★★ORCAS ISLAND *1 day*

Largest island in the San Juans, 36,431-acre Orcas is a horseshoe whose middle is cloven by the long, beautiful blue gash of East Sound. Hills, forests and low mountains, including 2,407ft Mount Constitution, characterize the landscape. While several major resorts are scattered through the island, Orcas remains a haven for those seeking a more alternative lifestyle. The studios of potters and other craftspeople nestle into the woods around the island, with outdoor displays of crafts often surrounding them. A number of crafts galleries also front the few streets of Eastsound, the island's only town. Fronting the sound itself, small **Emmanuel Church** *(Horseshoe Hwy.)* is the island's most historic structure. Englishman Sidney Gray, one of Orcas' most ardent early boosters, pressed for the founding of the parish, and the church was built in the 1880s, with Gray serving as its reverend. Also built in the 1880s, six log cabins have been moved to Eastsound and interconnected to house the **Orcas Island Historical Society Museum** *(North Beach Rd.; open Memorial Day–Sept Tue–Sun 1pm–4pm, Fri til 8pm; $2;* ☎ *360-376-4849; www.orcasisland.org)*, where Native American and pioneer artifacts and memorabilia trace the island's past.

★Moran State Park – *Horseshoe Hwy., on the island's east peninsula. Open year-round daily dawn-dusk.* ⚠ ♿ 🅿 ☎ *360-376-2326*. Robert Moran, former mayor of Seattle and builder of the nearby Rosario mansion (now the centerpiece of Rosario Resort), donated the original 2,000 acres for this preserve. Now grown to encompass 5,200 acres (one-seventh of the island), it is the largest state park in western Washington. Thirty miles of hiking trails thread the wooded mountain park, passing five lakes. The park road (an extension of the Horseshoe Highway)

■ Orcas

Orcinus orca—popularly known as the killer whale, or "wolf of the sea"—is a regular denizen of the waters of Puget Sound. Its distinctive black-and-white coloring and high dorsal fin, sometimes jutting 6ft above its body, is a thrilling sight to behold. Toothed whales, or odontocetes, orcas belong to the same phylogenetic group as dolphins and porpoises but grow much larger than their cousins. A full-grown male can measure 22ft long and may weigh more than two tons. They can swim at speeds of 30mph, surfacing every two to four minutes; males live about 50 years, females can reach 100. Though orcas are ferocious animals, even hunting down other, larger whales by orchestrating group attacks, they are not the belligerently aggressive marauders that their name implies. In fact, recent researchers who have studied them closely have found them to be highly intelligent, affable and deeply committed to their family units. Small groups of interrelated orcas, called pods, will travel, hunt and nurture their young together. Though Puget Sound is famous for the orcas that migrate to its waters from mid-summer through fall, the whales can actually be found in oceans worldwide, from the arctic waters to the tropics.

hugs the shores of capacious **Cascade Lake** before intersecting Mountain Road, whose switchback curves climb 2,407ft **Mt. Constitution**, passing several turnoffs for other lakes on the way. From the parking area at road's end, a short trail leads to the summit, topped by a stone observation tower built in the mid-1930s by the Civilian Conservation Corps. The staircase to its top is well worth the climb for the panoramic **views★★★** of the islands, the Cascade (east) and Olympic (south) ranges, the Canadian Coast Range (north) and Vancouver Island (west).

★**Rosario Resort** – *Rosario Rd., off Horseshoe Hwy. on the island's east peninsula.* ☎ *360-376-2222 or 800-562-8800.* In 1904 shipbuilding magnate and former mayor of Seattle, Robert Moran (1857-1943), then 47, retired in poor health and began planning his final home, an Orcas Island mansion on the secluded banks of Cascade Bay. By 1909, the eclectic five-story structure, wrapped by a verandah and with interior touches recalling Moran's shipbuilding past (including the exterior maroon paint normally used for ships' bottoms), was complete and heralded as the showplace of the region. Outliving his doctor's prophecies, Moran resided at his Rosario estate for almost 30 years. The second owners, Donald and Alice Rheem, painted the mansion its signature white color. Since 1960 it has functioned as a resort; today, additional guest lodgings flank the main mansion, whose rich woodwork and elaborately ornamented **Music Room★** with its own pipe organ bespeak the elegance of a former age.

Bicycling in Orcas Village

© Robert Holmes

★LOPEZ ISLAND *1/2 day*

The least developed of the "tourist" islands, Lopez has preserved its low-key, rural ambience, and proudly bills itself as the "friendliest island." Long the haunt of Samish and Lummi Indians, the island received its current name in 1846 from a British naval officer, who wanted to honor the pilot of the 1790 Quimper Expedition, Gonzola Lopez de Haro. As with other islands in the archipelago, the late 19C and early 20C settlers here fished for salmon and grew fruit, but they also became famous for the rich cream they exported, earning Lopez the sobriquet of the "Guernsey Island." Today, though only a few farms remain, the rural character has been preserved. Small **Lopez Village**, on the northwest side of the island, offers limited commercialism, the only visible anywhere on the island. Elsewhere, quiet beaches and rocky inlets afford endless opportunities to contemplate seascapes that look out on San Juan Island to the west or the mainland Cascades to the east. The north end of the island is blessed with sandy stretches of beach, while the south end is cragged by a more dramatic shoreline. At **Shark Reef Sanctuary** *(Shark Reef and Burt Rds.)*, a .2mi trail through a dense forest leads to rocky cliffs with close-up views of San Juan Island and opportunities to sight seals and other marine life. At the northeast corner of the island, 130-acre **Spencer Spit State Park** *(off Baker View Rd.)* is named for the .75mi sand spit that hooks out toward small Frost Island, which lies across a narrow, fast-flowing channel.

■ Washington State Ferries

With the myriad islands and peninsulas that lace Puget Sound, water travel has long been a way of life here. It was the British Hudson's Bay Company that began operating the first commercial steamer service in 1836, its one vessel, the *Beaver*, plying the waters of Puget Sound. In the mid– to late-19C other steamers, side-wheelers and stern-wheelers sprang into operation, offering cross-sound service to the area's burgeoning population. By 1903 such a busy swarm of small, independently owned ferries shuttled commuters in and out of Seattle that the entire armada was dubbed the "Mosquito Fleet." (Popular legend traces the origins of the term to a newspaper article of the period: "At five o'clock in Seattle, the little commuter steamers scurry off to their destinations like a swarm of mosquitoes.")

Today, as then, for residents of the Puget Sound area hopping a ferry is an integral part of getting around. But now the state of Washington owns and operates most of this regularly scheduled water transportation. The state's fleet of 28 ferries, the largest in the US, functions as a well-run extension of the transportation system, servicing 20 different ports of call along the sound, as well as a few in British Columbia. The 11 different classes of ferry that characterize the fleet range from the 460ft-long Jumbo Mark II class to the 94ft, passenger-only Tyee class. Roughly 23 million passengers a year take the ferries, some as commuters and some as sightseers. *For further information see p 240.*

Lopez Historical Museum – *28 Washburn Pl., Lopez Village. Open Jul–Aug Wed–Sun noon–4pm. Rest of the year Fri–Sun noon–4pm. Closed Memorial Day weekend & Jul 4. $1.* & 🅿 ☎ *360-468-2049.* Regional artifacts and native stone and antler tools speak to the long human occupation on the island and its maritime focus. Among the museum's highlights is a 1903 Orient buckboard, first "car" in San Juan County and equipped with a tiller for steering. A series of **ship models** by respected model-builder and longtime Lopez resident, Ralph Hitchcock, replicate the historic passenger ferries and other vessels that once plied the waters of Puget Sound. Also in the museum's collection are three dugout canoes and a gill-net boat used by a local fisherman from the 1930s to 1980s.

WHIDBEY ISLAND

Michelin map 493 B 3 and map p 242
Tourist Information ☎ 360-675-3535

A popular weekend getaway for Seattle residents, Whidbey Island arcs in a narrow 60mi curve off the mainland coast, making it the second longest island in the contiguous US, after New York's Long Island. Its bucolic tumble of hills, small towns and verdant fields is interrupted only in the north by Whidbey Island Naval Air Station (the island's largest employer), and the suburban commercialism of Oak Harbor. North of Oak Harbor the narrow, deep channel of Deception Pass is traversed by **Deception Pass Bridge★**, actually two coterminous stone bridges built in the mid-1930s by the Civilian Conservation Corps to connect Whidbey and Fidalgo islands. Viewpoint pullouts and a pedestrian walkway allow sightseers to walk across the bridge and admire the surrounding rocky cliffs and the spectacular gash that connects the Strait of Juan de Fuca with Skagit Bay.

★COUPEVILLE *1/2 day*

Walking-tour brochures of the town are available at Island County Historical Museum (Alexander and Front Sts.; ☎ 360-678-3310).

Oldest town on the island and one of the oldest in the state, Coupeville was established in the early 1850s on the south shore of Penn Cove in central Whidbey. Along the waterfront, small galleries and restaurants specializing in Penn Cove shellfish fill up on weekends with passing travelers; the former town wharf and warehouse have been converted into more shops. Imposing **Victorian houses**, built by 19C sea captains, line the town's side streets; a number of them now function as inns. The surrounding countryside is blessed with exceptionally fertile prairie lands that attracted many settlers in the mid-19C and continue to be used as farmland to this day.

★**Ebey's Landing National Historical Reserve** – *Information at 23 Front St. Open May–Sept daily 10am–5pm. Rest of the year Fri–Mon 10am–5pm. $2.* & 🅿 ☎ *360-678-6084 or 678-3310.* This sprawling 17,400-acre reserve represents a pioneering cooperative effort between a local community and the National Park Service "to preserve and protect a rural community." The concept for the reserve began with a grass-roots effort in the 1970s to preserve prairie land on the outskirts of Coupeville. In 1978 the US Congress officially recognized these efforts by designating a number of parcels in the area as the nation's first historical reserve, named in honor of mid-19C pioneer Col. Isaac Neff Ebey. The reserve's mission is to preserve the land and spirit of the past and the various cultural and geographical elements that formed the community and its traditions. Some 90 percent of the reserve encompasses private lands, still put to use in farms and other traditional rural activities. Two state parks are also fall within the preserve: Fort Casey and 645-acre Fort Ebey State Park, where trails lead through coastal woodlands bordering Admiralty Inlet and Lake Pondilla.

Visit – *3 hrs.* **The Island County Historical Museum** serves as the visitor information center for the reserve *(908 N.W. Alexander St., at Front St. in Coupeville; open May–Sept daily 10am–5pm; rest of the year Fri–Mon 10am–5pm; ☎ 360-678-3310).* A 15min video narrates community efforts involved in founding the reserve and gives a brief history of the area. Artifacts and memorabilia, including the 1902 Holsman that was the island's first car, are displayed. Beside the museum stands the 1855 **Alexander Blockhouse**, built to protect settlers from the Coast Salish Indians. At the heart of the reserve lies some 5,000 acres of prairie land, the remnants of ancient lake beds created by receding glaciers. The sweeping natural expanse of **Ebey's Prairie** sprawls between Penn Cove and the Strait of Juan de Fuca, bisected by a 1mi trail that leads from Ebey's Landing beach *(foot of Ebey Rd.)* through the prairie to hilltop **Sunnyside Cemetery** *(Cook & Sherman Rds.).* The cemetery offers **views★** of the prairie and surrounding seas and contains the headstones of some of the region's pioneer families, as well as the 1855 James Davis Blockhouse. Two smaller prairies—Crockett and Smith—lie to the east and are also protected within the preserve.

Fort Casey State Park – *Fort Casey Rd., 3mi south of town off Rte. 20. Open year–round daily 8am–dusk.* △ ♿ ℙ ☎ *360-678-4519.* Lying within the national historical reserve but administered by the state, this blufftop park occupies Admiralty Head, where a 19C fort was built as part of a three-fort "Iron Triangle" defense system guarding the entrance to Admiralty Inlet. The fort's substantial gun batteries were completed in 1905 and, though the guns were never fired in actual conflict, the fort was used as a training site during both world wars. In 1956, the US government sold the site to Washington State Parks and Recreation, which has preserved its batteries and two rare 10in "disappearing guns." The **Admiralty Head Lighthouse**, which operated only briefly in the early 20C, now serves as an interpretive center for the fort's history *(open Wed–Sun & holidays 11am–5pm).*

Excursions

Meerkerk Rhododendron Gardens – *1 hr. 13.5mi south of Coupeville. Follow Rte. 525 south to Resort Rd., turn left and proceed .2mi to Meerkerk Lane. Open May–Oct daily 9am–4pm. $3.* ℙ ☎ *360-678-1912.* Although these gardens are noted for their 10 acres of rhododendrons, the forests of fir, hemlock, cedar and lush ferns on the remaining 43 acres are equally inviting. On the bluffs above Holmes Harbor, the gardens were initially planted by Ann and Max Meerkerk in the 1960s. Now administered by the Seattle Rhododendron Society, they boast a collection of almost 2,000 rhododendrons from throughout the world. A **harborside trail** through a lush fern grotto offers a good vantage for spotting the whales and bald eagles that frequent the area.

★ Deception Pass State Park – *2 hrs. 23mi north of Coupeville on Rte. 20, on north and south sides of Deception Pass Bridge. Open daily year-round dawn-dusk.* △ ✗ ℙ ☎ *800-223-0321.www.parks.wa.gov.* Along the rocky coastline of Rosario Strait, the 4,128-acre park lies on both Whidbey (south) and Fidalgo (north) islands.

Its 15mi of shoreline, much of it in gravel beaches strewn with the sculpted shapes of driftwood, is popular with picnickers who come to build late afternoon fires and enjoy the sunsets on Bowman Bay and Rosario Strait. Trails plunge into thickets of madrona trees or thread past freshwater lakes and coastline. The .8mi round-trip Rosario Head Trail on the north side of the park offers views out across the sound; nearby stands the popular 1983 wooden carving of Ko-Kwal-Awoot (Samish for "maiden of the sea"), by local artist Tracy Powell. A low stone building constructed in the mid-1930s serves as the Civilian Conservation Corps Interpretive Center *(north side of park on Fidalgo Island, overlooking Bowman Bay).* Exhibits there tell the story of the corps' public works projects (they built the interpretive center) and relate what camp life was like for the workers of the Civilian Conservation Corps.

Greenbank Farm

11mi south of Coupeville on Rte. 525, then east on Wonn Rd. ☎ *360-678-7700.* In 1904 a dairy farm operated here, and one of its barns functioned as the area's first schoolhouse. In subsequent years mainland winemaker Stimson Lane Ltd. purchased the site and began producing loganberry wine and liqueur. Stimson put the property up for sale in 1997 and Island County purchased it. Since then, volunteers have reintroduced loganberry cultivation, and the gift shop offers loganberry jams and other products.

Olympic Peninsula & Pacific Coast

Hoh Rain Forest, Olympic National Park/© Robert Hommes

The thumb of Washington state, the Olympic Peninsula extends from the jigsaw puzzle of islands and waterways in Puget Sound west to the Pacific Ocean. The Strait of Juan de Fuca forms its northern boundary, the Columbia River separates it from Oregon to the south, and Hood Canal, an 80mi-long inlet of Puget Sound, divides it from the mainland to the east. The glacier-sheathed peaks of the Olympic Mountains rear up in the north-central portion of the Peninsula, trapping wet Pacific air on their western slopes and creating a rain shadow to the east. The difference in rainfall is remarkable: Up to 150in falls in the Pacific-facing valleys, yet only 16in in the **Sequim** (pronounced "squim")–Dungeness Valley to the east.

A vast portion of the Peninsula's rugged and extraordinarily diverse terrain lies within Olympic National Park, the major tourist destination in western Washington. Port Angeles, the peninsula's largest town, serves as a convenient point of entry to the park. And the Long Beach Peninsula to the south is a popular resort area along the Pacific coast.

For millennia these flat coastal regions were home to several Native American tribes, each speaking their own language but sharing common cultural characteristics. Among the principal tribes were the Makahs at Cape Flattery; the Chinooks along the Lower Columbia River; and the Quileutes, Quinaults and Copalis, whose villages were found along Pacific beaches and rivers. The largest tribe was the S'Klallam, mostly scattered along the strait. British captain George Vancouver became the first European mariner to sail up the strait as far as Puget Sound in 1792, but permanent settlement, most of it concentrated along the shores of the strait, had to await overland travel and did not begin until the 1850s. Farming, logging, fishing and sea trade formed the basis of the economy.

Efforts to protect the remaining resources of the peninsula have led to economic hardship and environmental conflicts in recent years. The once-prodigious salmon runs have dwindled, and clear-cutting old-growth forests and damming the Elwha and Dungeness rivers have destroyed fish and wildlife habitat. With both industries now curtailed by federal regulations, local economies have become more dependent on tourists who seek the varying wonders of primordial rain forests, snow-skirted mountains and wild and wave-tossed beaches.

OLYMPIC NATIONAL PARK★★★

Michelin map 493 B 3 and map p 251
Tourist information ☎ 360-452-0330. www.nps.gov/olym

One of the most diverse ecosystems in the contiguous United States, the 922,000-acre Olympic National Park was designated an International Biosphere Reserve by UNESCO in 1976 and recognized as a World Heritage Site in 1981. The park is noted for its natural beauty and remarkable variety of wilderness communities. Rising up from the center of the park are the craggy, glaciated peaks of the Olympic Mountains, with 7,965ft Mt. Olympus the highest summit. The Olympics' wet, western-facing valleys shelter one of the largest old-growth temperate rain forests in the Western Hemisphere. And the last primitive US coastal habitat outside Alaska unfurls along the park's Pacific coastline.

The Olympics, with their sharply folded valleys and alpine lakes, were formed some 12-30 million years ago by tectonic upthrust. Their glaciers feed 12 major rivers and 200 streams, and their slopes and valleys are covered by the largest intact stand of coniferous forest in the lower 48 states. Over 300 species of birds and 70 species of mammals—including 5 found only on the Olympic Peninsula—live within the park's boundaries. Though US-101 encircles the perimeter, with spur roads branching off to scenic highlights, there are no roads through the wild interior. Yet except for Hurricane Ridge, the major sights are normally accessible year-round.

Historical Notes

Although newcomers began arriving and settling along the coastline of the Olympic Peninsula in the mid-19C, the rugged Olympic Mountains remained unexplored by anyone except the indigenous peoples who had hunted here for thousands of years before the white man came. The first well-documented expedition into the interior was led by US Army Lt. Joseph P. O'Neil in 1885. It took O'Neil and his party of enlisted men from Vancouver Barracks about a month to forge a trail to Hurricane Ridge, from which point O'Neil headed south and explored as far as Mt. Anderson before being ordered to return to Fort Leavenworth. A second attempt to penetrate the interior was made in December 1889, when James Christie, an enthusiastic but inexperienced young man volunteered to organize and lead an expedition financed by the *Seattle Press* newspaper. In May 1890, after nearly six months in the mountains, Christie and his four men became the first group to cross the Olympics from the strait to the Pacific Ocean. In a later report, Christie proposed that the interior be set aside as a national park to protect the "numerous elk—that noble animal so fast disappearing from this country."

The Olympic Forest Reserve, which included most of the forested land on the Olympic Peninsula, was established in 1897, later becoming Olympic National Forest. Attempts to establish a national park began in the early 1900s but remained unsuccessful until 1909, when President Theodore Roosevelt issued a proclamation creating Mount Olympus National Monument within the national forest. The act was designed to protect the summer range and breeding grounds of the Olympic elk (now called Roosevelt elk). A bill proposed in 1935 by Washington Congressman Monrad Wallgren and a 1937 visit by President Franklin D. Roosevelt led to the establishment of Olympic National Park in 1938, with the park's more than 60mi of coastline following 15 years later.

Once threatened with extinction, some 5,000 **Roosevelt elk**—the largest unmanaged herd in the world—now roam the lowland forests and snowy mountain passes of Olympic National Park. Other mammals found here include black bears, cougars, bobcats, black-tailed deer, marmots, beavers and river otters. Steller sea lions, harbor seals, orcas, and gray, humpback and Minke whales inhabit or migrate along coastal waters. Some 4.5 million annual visitors explore this unparalleled sea of wilderness, mostly sampling along its periphery. The climate is generally mild year-round, but visitors should take note that rainfall is prodigious, particularly on the Pacific side of the park. July and August, the most popular months, are also the driest.

SIGHTS *3 days*

Olympic National Park Visitor Center – *3002 Mt. Angeles Rd. (just south of US-101), Port Angeles. Open Jun–Sept daily 8:30am–6pm. Rest of the year daily 9am–4pm.* ☎ *360-452-0330.* Located on the road to Hurricane Ridge, the main visitor center is the best place to stock up on information about the sites in Olympic National Park. In addition to providing free maps and brochures, the center has a 12min slide show introducing visitors to the park's diverse habitats, and exhibits on the area's natural and human history. Remnants of old-growth forest can be seen on the **Peabody Creek Trail**, an easy .5mi loop that begins next to the visitor center.

Getting There – **Horizon Air** (☎ 800-547-9308) provides regularly scheduled flights to Port Angeles from Seattle-Tacoma International Airport. Closest Amtrak train station (☎ 800-872-7245) is in Seattle. Year-round **ferry** service across the Puget Sound is provided by Washington State Ferries (☎ 206-464-6400). Service from Victoria, BC to Port Angeles is available from Black Ball Transport, Inc. (☎ 457-4491). Victoria Express operates a walk-on ferry (mid-May–mid–Oct; ☎ 452-8088).

Access to the Olympic Peninsula from Seattle (90mi) is via US-104 and US-101. Some roads may close in winter. The only gas stations in the park are located at Kalaloch Lodge (☎ 962-2271) and at Fairholm. From Seattle, **bus** service to Port Angeles is offered by Olympic Bus Lines (☎ 417-0700). Olympic Van Tours offers charter bus tours into the park and trailhead pick-up from Port Angeles (Apr–Oct by reservation only; P.O. Box 2201, Port Angeles WA 98362; ☎ 452-3858). Gray Line offers sightseeing excursions from Seattle (summers only; reservations: ☎ 206-626-5208 or 800-426-7532).

Visitor Information – The park is open year-round daily. $10/car, $5 on foot or bike (admission valid for 7 days; △ ⚔ ⅄ ▣). For information and brochures on points of interest, accommodations, recreation and seasonal activities, contact **Olympic National Park**, 600 E. Park Ave., Port Angeles WA 98362-6798, ☎ 452-4501; www.nps.gov/olym. **Olympic National Park Visitor Center** (p 248), located on the north side of the park, issues wilderness permits and provides maps and information on weather and trail conditions. **Hoh Visitor Center**, located in Hoh Rain Forest off US-101 on the west side of the park, houses exhibits on plants, wildlife and ecology (same hours as above; ☎ 374-6925). Additional visitor centers: **Hurricane Ridge Visitor Center** (south of Port Angeles at the top of Hurricane Ridge Rd.; open daily Apr–Oct weather conditions permitting; rest of the year weekends & holidays only; ☎ 360-452-0330) and **Storm King Visitor Center** (summer only; ☎ 928-3380) at Lake Crescent.

Accommodations – There are four lodges located within the park; rates for a double room range from $75 to $130: Kalaloch Lodge (year-round; ☎ 962-2271); Lake Crescent Lodge (Apr–Oct; ☎ 928-3211); Log Cabin Resort (Apr–Oct; ☎ 928-3325); and Sol Duc Hot Springs Resort (May–Sept, Apr & Oct weekends only; ☎ 327-3583). A wide range of accommodations can be found throughout the area year-round, including historic lodges, log cabins, seaside resorts, bed-and-breakfast inns, hotels and motels. For information, contact the **North Olympic Peninsula Visitor & Convention Bureau**, P.O.Box 670, Port Angeles WA 98362, ☎ 452-8552. **Youth Hostel**: Olympic Hostel, Port Townsend, ☎ 385-0655.

Numerous **campgrounds** are located within park boundaries. Most offer drinking water and fire pits, but no RV hookups or showers. Some are closed during winter months. All are available on a first-come, first-served basis and most charge a fee ($8-$12/night). For further information and camping restrictions, call ☎ 452-0330. For campsites and **RV parks** outside the park, check with local chambers of commerce.

Recreation – Olympic National Park offers year-round recreational opportunities. Guided rain forest and ecology hikes, beach and tide-pool walks and campfire programs are available (free) from park visitor centers. Many of the marked **hiking** trails are also used for **horseback riding**. All-inclusive hiking excursions (Jul–Sept; 5 days; reservations required) are offered by Backroads, 801 Cedar St., Berkeley CA 947710, ☎ 510-527-1555 or 800-245-3874. **Biking** is permitted only on paved roads. A **wilderness permit** is required for all trail and beach camping as well as for backcountry hiking (contact Wilderness Information Center; ☎ 452-0300). The many lakes, rivers and ocean areas allow a variety of water activities such as **kayaking**, **canoeing**, **white-water rafting** and **sailing**. A license is not required for **fishing** in the park's lakes and rivers, but you must have a punch card (available at most sporting-goods stores) for salmon or steelhead. Check with ranger station about regulations for ocean fishing. Mountaineering is allowed year-round; climbers should register with the ranger station. For outfitters, check with tourist offices in local communities.

During the **winter** season, hiking trails become **cross-country skiing** trails. Guided snowshoe walks depart from Hurricane Ridge Visitor Center (late Dec–Mar, weekends only) and a small **downhill ski** area offers ski instruction, equipment rental and snack bar. For more information, call ☎ 452-0330.

© Robert Holmes

Hurricane Ridge

★★★ **Hurricane Ridge** – *17mi south of park visitor center via Heart O' the Hills/Hurricane Ridge Rd.* ☎ *360-452-0329 (24 hr road and weather conditions). Portions of the road may be closed Oct–late–Apr, though it is generally open on weekends throughout winter.* The magnificent scenery that unfolds along Hurricane Ridge makes it one of the most popular destinations in Olympic National Park. A paved 17mi road to the ridge passes through dense forest, skirts lush sub-alpine meadows, and offers dramatic vistas of crenellated, snow-crusted peaks and the distant sea.

From the Olympic National Park Visitor Center a 5.3mi parkway slices through a forest of Douglas fir, western hemlock and western red cedar to the park's entrance station at **Heart O' the Hills**. A railed turnout at **Lookout Rock** *(3.7mi from Heart O' the Hills entrance)* provides a panoramic **vista★★** north to the Strait of Juan de Fuca, Dungeness Spit, the San Juan Islands, Vancouver Island and Mt. Baker, 90 mi to the northeast. After tunneling through a massive outcropping of basalt, the road continues its steady ascent up the east shoulder and south flank of Klahhane Ridge to **Hurricane Ridge Visitor Center** *(☎ 360-452-0330)*. Here, at an elevation of 5,230ft, there are unobstructed **views★** of the peaks, ridges and deep valleys of the Olympic Mountains, including Mt. Olympus and the Elwha River Valley. From the parking area, paved **Meadow Loop Trails** traverse subalpine meadows covered in mid-summer with low-lying sedges, grasses and a profusion of colorful wildflowers. Black-tailed deer and marmots are sometimes seen in the vicinity. The visitor center contains exhibits on the geology and wildlife of the Olympics and a snack bar; during the snow-packed winter months it rents cross-country skis and snowshoes. Two rope tows and a ski lift with a 665ft vertical rise service downhill skiers.

Elwha River Valley – *7mi southwest of Port Angeles on US-101 to turnoff for Elwha River Valley.* Fed by glaciers and rushing along its rocky bed past banks of red alders, the 45mi-long Elwha River runs north to empty into the Strait of Juan de Fuca. This lovely river valley is accessed by a well-paved road that follows a 5mi stretch of the river, the largest watershed in Olympic National Park. Before it was dammed, the Elwha was one of the great fishing rivers of the Olympic Peninsula. The Klallam Indians subsisted on the river's vast runs of salmon. Settlers arrived in the 1880s and were followed by anglers lured by the river's reputation for producing 100-pound chinook. Two dams, completed in 1913 and 1927 and built without fish ladders, prevent native fish from reaching 70mi of their original spawning habitat in the Elwha and its tributaries. A 1992 act of the US Congress authorized the removal of the dams so that the Elwha would once again become a free-flowing river. Removal of the dams is dependent on funding, however, and to date both remain in place. The Elwha River Valley drive winds up to **Lake Mills**, created by the lower dam.

★★ **Lake Crescent and Marymere Falls** – *18.3mi west of Port Angeles (to Lake Crescent Lodge) on US-101.* US-101 runs along the southern shore of a serenely beautiful alpine lake, providing easy access from Port Angeles. One of two large lakes in Olympic National Park, Lake Crescent provides visitors with a cluster of resorts, restaurants, picnic areas, hiking trails and campgrounds; in the summer it is a popular place for canoeing, swimming, hiking and fishing. Cupped within steep forested hillsides, Lake Crescent was carved out by glaciers during the last ice age. Kokanee, a small landlocked species of wild salmon, inhabits the lake's deep, cold waters; beavers, river otters, bald eagles and black-tailed deer reside along its 12mi shoreline. **Lake Crescent Lodge★** *(416 Lake Crescent Rd; ☏ 360-928-3211)* was the scene of a 1937 meeting between President Franklin D. Roosevelt, US senators and Parks Department officials that led to the creation of Olympic National Park.

Marymere Falls Trail★ *(2mi)* makes a circuit through old-growth forest to 90ft-high Marymere Falls, one of the most beautiful cascades in Olympic National Park. **Moments in Time Nature Trail,** a .7mi loop from the lodge, also winds through old-growth forest, passing old homestead sites and providing views of Lake Crescent.

Sol Duc Hot Springs – *52mi southwest of Port Angeles. Take US-101 to marked turnoff. ☏ 360-327-3583.* The sulphurous smell emanating from these naturally occurring hot springs on the Sol Duc River caused the Quileute Indians to call them *si'bi'*, or "stinky place." After Theodore Moritz staked a claim to the hot springs in the 1880s, settlers began arriving for therapeutic soaks in hand-hewn cedar-log tubs. By 1912 an elegant hotel/sanitorium with landscaped grounds and beds for 100 patients had opened, but it burned down four years later.

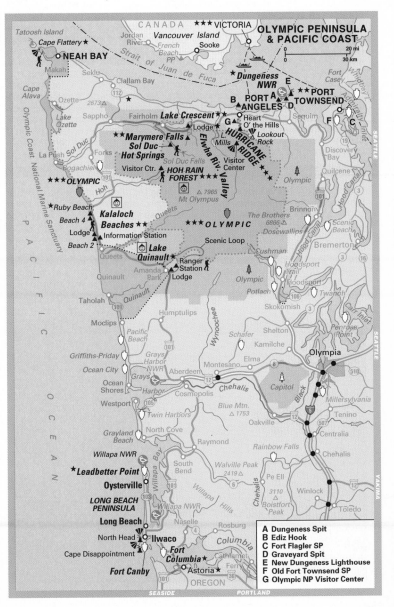

Today visitors may swim in a large open pool or soak in one of three smaller mineral-water pools. The site also features a rustic lodge and restaurant. Well-graveled .8mi **Sol Duc Falls Trail**★ winds through an old-growth forest of hemlock and Douglas fir to lovely Sol Duc Falls.

★★★**Hoh Rain Forest** – [Kids] *91mi southwest of Port Angeles; entrance station 12mi east of US-101.* In this lush, dripping, primeval world, where rainfall averages 140-150 inches a year, some of the largest examples of Sitka spruce, western hemlock, Douglas fir, and western red cedar loom 200-300ft above a forest floor cushioned with mosses and giant sword ferns. Soft green swags of spike moss, epiphytes that gain their nourishment primarily from the moisture-saturated air, hang from tree limbs and cover the massive, lichen-covered trunks, while licorice ferns take root in the mosses and grow up the sides of the trees. Roosevelt elk grazing on the plants and red alder in the understory keep the forest from becoming an impenetrable thicket. The rain forest is also home to the spotted owl and marbled murrelet, endangered bird species that require old-growth forest to survive.

Three self-guided interpretive trails begin at the **visitor center** (☎ *360-374-6925*), 6mi beyond the entrance station. The 1.25mi **Spruce Nature Trail**★ circles through old-growth forest to the Hoh River, the sound of its rushing waters providing accompaniment along the way. An old-growth forest, by definition, is at least 200 years old. Most of the giants found here are more than twice that age, some of them 12ft in diameter. Though many are as tall as a 20-story building, the trees have shallow root systems. When a tree falls, it becomes a "nurse log" for the seedlings that take root on its decaying trunk. Over time the seedlings send down roots to the forest floor, straddling the nurse log and forming a colonnade of trees along its length. As the nurse log decays, the trees are left standing on their huge, stilt-like roots. A few trees take root directly in the soft, spongy forest floor.

The .75mi **Hall of Mosses Trail**★ is an easy loop through a segment of forest on higher, better established ground. The same cathedral-like calm pervades this ancient sanctuary. A dim, vaporous light filters through the canopy, giving a soft green glow to the wild profusion of spike mosses hanging in dripping festoons from big-leaf maples and cloaking the sides of trees. Luxurious mats of mosses cushion the forest floor. A paved .25mi **Rain Forest Mini Trail** makes a circuit through a portion of old-growth forest just off the parking lot.

★★**Kalaloch Beaches** – [Kids] *95mi southwest of Port Angeles (to Kalaloch Information Station) on US-101.* The most easily accessible portion of Olympic National Park's 57mi strip of primitive Pacific coastline lies along the 10mi stretch of US-101 that runs parallel to the beaches north and south of the year-round beach resort of **Kalaloch Lodge** *(157151 US-101 at mile marker 157; ☎ 360-962-2271)* and **Kalaloch Information Station** *(just south of Kalaloch Lodge; ☎ 360-962-2283; staffed in summer).* From the highway, short trails lead down through a narrow corridor of Sitka spruce and western red cedar to a half dozen separate beaches.

Kalaloch (ka LAY-lock), Quinault for "land of plenty," sports pounding waves and glistening tide pools, with bald eagles perching above on cliffs and treetops, swooping down to snatch trout and steelhead from the rivers and streams. The offshore waters, part of a National Marine Sanctuary, are a protected haven for

Kalaloch Beach

© Robert Holmes

seabirds, seals and sea lions, and more kinds of whales and dolphins than anywhere else in the world. In the spring and fall, the Kalaloch beaches provide good vantage points for viewing gray whales on their annual migrations between Alaska and Mexico.

Ruby Beach★ *(8mi north of Kalaloch Information Station on US-101)*, with its towering offshore seastacks and rocky shoreline heaped with driftwood logs, is the most scenically distinctive of the Kalaloch beaches. Just north of **Beach 4** *(3.5mi north of information station)*, sculptured rocks provide rich tide-pool habitats. For a wide, sandy spread, try **Beach 2** *(.8mi south of information station)*. The 1.2mi **Kalaloch Nature Trail**, which begins at the south end of Kalaloch Campground *(2.9mi north of Kalaloch Information Station)*, crosses US-101 and winds through the forest along Kalaloch Creek.

The more rugged and remote segment of the park's south coastline lies north of the Hoh River and can only be reached by hiking in from La Push *(14mi west of Forks)*, at the end of Route 110.

★ Lake Quinault – [Kids] *120mi south of Port Angeles; 30mi east of Kalaloch, off US-101.* Sitting in a low basin in the Quinault Valley, Lake Quinault measures 6mi in circumference and 250ft in depth. Like the Hoh and Queets valleys to the north, this area receives some 14ft of rain a year and is noted for its giant old-growth trees and green, cushioning profusion of mosses and ferns (only the lake's north shore lies within the national park boundaries). Formed by a glacier that plowed out the valley and receded back into the mountains about 11,000 years ago, the lake is home to bald eagles, wintering trumpeter swans and loons, which fill the summer air with their strange cries. A legend of the Quinault Indians, who traditionally used the lake and its environs for summer salmon fishing, hunting and berry-picking, says that a monster so big it can swallow a cedar canoe lives in the lake's deep blue waters.

Settlers came to the valley in the 1880s but the first road to Lake Quinault was not built until 1914. Twelve years later the lake's most famous tourist destination, the two-story, cedar-shingled **Lake Quinault Lodge** (☎ *360-288-2571 or 800-562-6672*), was built on the south shore. President Franklin Roosevelt stayed here in 1937.

Branching off from US-101, North Shore and South Shore Roads form a 30mi **scenic loop** around the lake, passing through the rain forest and along the Quinault River at its northern end. On the South Shore, near **Quinault Ranger Station** (☎ *360-288-2444; infrequently staffed)*, there are several interconnecting hiking trails; the easiest is a .9mi **lakeside trail** that hugs the south shore between Falls Creek Campground and Willaby Campground. Directly across from the lodge is a trailhead for the 1.6mi **Cascade Falls Trail**, which loops through the forest and passes the tumbling waters of Cascade Falls. Big-leaf maples draped with green club moss can be seen on the .5mi, self-guided **Maple Glade Rain Forest Trail** on the lake's northern shore.

PACIFIC COAST★

Michelin map 493 B 2, 3 and map p 251
Tourist Information ☎ 360-289-2451 or www.oceanshores.com

Stretching from Cape Flattery to Kalaloch, the northern section of Washington State's 260mi-long Pacific coastline paints a wild and rocky picture of forested headlands, offshore islands and sea stacks, tide pools, and beaches heaped with kelp and driftwood logs. A 57mi stretch of this primitive coastline is contained within Olympic National Park. The beaches south of Kalaloch, from Queets to Moclips, are part of the Quinault Indian Reservation and not open to the public. Farther south, between Gray's Harbor and the Long Beach Peninsula, the Pacific shoreline becomes markedly different, with smooth, flat, sandy beaches and estuaries that attract thousands of migrating shorebirds. This is the most commercially developed portion of the coast. The Lewis and Clark expedition arrived at the south end of the Long Beach Peninsula in November 1805, firming up American claims to the region. Clark wrote that the "men appear much satisfied with their trip beholding with astonishment the high waves dashing against the rock and this emence Ocian." Those waves and the dangerous bar extending from the mouth of the Columbia River have wreaked havoc with area shipping. In the past 300 years, nearly 2,000 vessels and 700 lives have been lost in these treacherous seas. Lighthouses built in the latter 19C have helped somewhat, as have jetties, buoys and constant dredging of the bar.

NEAH BAY *1/2 day*

Located on the Strait of Juan de Fuca a few miles east of Cape Flattery and the Pacific Ocean, Neah Bay is the only town in the Makah Indian Reservation. Archaeological research indicates that the Makahs have inhabited this coastal region at the northwestern tip of the Olympic Peninsula for at least 4,000 years. Carved totem poles rise above the gravestones in the town's small cemetery and

another tall painted totem stands near the marina. Every August the tribe celebrates Makah Days with costumed dancing, canoe races and a traditional salmon
bake.

In 1998 the Makahs in Neah Bay became embroiled in controversy when they
announced plans to resume whale hunting after a self-imposed moratorium dating
back to the 1920s. Up until that time, hunting whales from dugout canoes was
an integral part of Makah culture; they are the only tribe in the US to retain whale-
hunting rights by treaty. Their plan to hunt one gray whale using traditional
methods was met with fierce opposition from non-native environmentalists and
animal-rights groups. Amid much publicity, the tribe ultimately cancelled the hunt
when the whales failed to appear on their usual migratory route. In the spring of
1999, however, the hunt resumed, and the Makah—none of them experienced
whalers—killed a gray whale.

★★**Makah Museum** – 🄺🄸🄳🅂 *Open Memorial Day–mid–Sept daily 10am–5pm. Rest of
the year Wed–Sun 10am–5pm. Closed Jan 1, Thanksgiving Day & Dec 25. $4.* &
🄿 ☎ *360-645-2711.* The history and traditions of the Makahs—traditionally
known as "The People Who Live By the Rocks and Seagulls"—come into sharp
focus in this fine museum. Carefully displayed in a modern building are the remains
of a Makah coastal village buried in a mudslide 500 years ago and exposed by tidal
erosion in 1970. Remarkably preserved baskets, textiles, harpoons, spears and
wood carvings were recovered during the Ozette dig, an 11-year excavation led
by Washington State University. Ozette, near Cape Alava on the Pacific coast 15mi
south of Neah Bay, remained a tribal home of the Makahs well into the 20C.

The galleries are designed to re-create the ancient seasonal rhythm of the Makahs
before their contact with Europeans. Objects on view reveal the tribe's skillful use
of indigenous materials—wood (particularly cedar), grasses and mussel shells—
and their daily lives as hunters, gatherers and artisans. In addition to items from
the Ozette dig there are replicas of traditional eight-man **whaling canoes**★ hand-
carved from cedar logs and a full-sized reconstruction of a cedar-planked Ozette
longhouse. The final section of the museum showcases fine baskets made by Makah
weavers from the end of the 19C to the present.

★**Cape Flattery** – *7mi west of Neah Bay on Cape Flattery Trail Rd.* Dense coastal
forest and dramatic ocean views draw visitors to Cape Flattery, the rocky headland that forms the northwesternmost point in the lower United States. James
Cook, who stopped at the northwestern tip of the Olympic Peninsula in
March 1788, named it Cape Flattery because an opening along the coast flattered
the captain with the hope of finding a harbor.

The .5mi **Cape Flattery Trail**★, recently renovated by the Makah tribe, provides relatively easy access. The muddiest parts of the trail are covered by a sturdy, raised
boardwalk made from cedar slabs. Passing through towering stands of western
red cedar and Douglas fir with a green understory of ferns, salal, mosses and
grasses, the trail culminates in four clifftop **observation platforms**, providing **views**★ of
the turbulent blue-green waters of the Pacific; wild, rocky inlets pierced by sea
caves; Tatoosh Island with its lighthouse; and the mouth of the Strait of Juan de
Fuca. Seals can sometimes be seen on offshore rocks. It was at Cape Flattery in

Anemones in Tide Pool

© Robert Holmes

1788 that the Makahs had their first glimpse of "the house on the water people," as they called the Americans exploring the coast in a ship manned by Capt. Robert Gray.

In 1994, in an effort to preserve the area's rugged character and marine life, the coastal waters around Cape Flattery became part of the 3,300sq mi Olympic Coast National Marine Sanctuary administered by the National Oceanic and Atmospheric Administration. Closed to seabed mining and oil and gas exploration, the sanctuary extends some 135mi from Cape Flattery south to Ocean City, protecting one of the largest concentrations of seabirds in the continental US, the world's largest octopus species, transplanted sea otters (hunted to extinction locally in the 19C), migrating gray whales, seals, sea lions and other coastal wildlife.

LONG BEACH PENINSULA *1 day*

Stretching from the Columbia River to the mouth of Willapa Bay, the Long Beach Peninsula provides access to 28mi of surf-pounded Pacific coastline in the south-western corner of Washington State. The area, originally inhabited by the Chinook Indians, occupies a special place in the annals of Northwest exploration for it was here, in 1805, that the Lewis and Clark Expedition finally reached the shores of the Pacific. North of Cape Disappointment, the rocky headland separating the Columbia from the open sea, the peninsula narrows to a flat, 2mi-wide strip of land between the Pacific and Willapa Bay. A handful of small towns, such as **Ilwaco** and **Long Beach**, cater to today's visitors, who come to enjoy the Peninsula's relaxed seaside ambience. Historic sites, sportfishing, hiking trails and miles of sandy (and often windy) beaches are all part of its appeal.

Ilwaco Heritage Museum – *115 S.E. Lake St., Ilwaco; 1 block south and 1/2 block east of stoplight on US-101. Open Apr–Oct Mon–Sat 9am–5pm, Sun noon–4pm. Rest of the year Mon–Sat 10am–4pm. Closed Dec 24–25. $3. ♿ 🅿 ☎ 360-642-3446.* The rooms in this local museum are devoted to early Chinook Indian culture, Hudson's Bay Company forts and fur trapping, the Columbia River Estuary and other aspects of peninsula life over the last century. Outside the museum you can visit the former Ilwaco train depot and view a reconstructed saw-cutter's shop with examples of the 7ft crosscut saws used in early logging operations.

Fort Canby State Park – *2mi southwest of Ilwaco on Rte. 100 loop road. Open year-round daily dawn-dusk. ⛺ ♿ 🅿 ☎ 360-642-3078.* Fort Canby, established in 1862 to protect the Columbia River, remained in use until the end of World War II. Today it is a 1,700-acre park used for camping, picnicking and hiking. The self-guided tour in the **Lewis & Clark Interpretive Center★** *(open year-round daily 10am–5pm)*, located in the park, culminates in a vista of Cape Disappointment, where the explorers obtained their first, awe-inspring view of the tumultuous Pacific. The cape received its name in 1788 when English sea captain John Meares was disappointed in his attempt to locate the mouth of the then-unnamed Columbia River. From the interpretive center a .75mi path leads to **Cape Disappointment Lighthouse**, completed in 1856 and today the oldest operating light-house on the West Coast. A tour of nearby **North Head Lighthouse** *(visit by guide tour only, Apr–Oct daily 10am–6pm; $1)* offers outstanding **views★** of wave-lashed coastline. High winds and treacherous currents have led to so many wrecks that this portion of the coast is referred to as the "Graveyard of the Pacific."

Long Beach – *3mi north of Ilwaco on Rte. 103.* The commercial hub of the penin-sula, Long Beach provides unobstructed views of the Pacific along its .5mi-long oceanfront **boardwalk**. Windy conditions make this beach popular with kite fliers, who gather here every August for the annual Washington International Kite Festival. In town, the **World Kite Museum and Hall of Fame** *(3rd St.; open Jun–Sept daily 11am–5pm; rest of the year Fri–Mon 11am–5pm; $1.50; ♿ 🅿 ☎ 360-642-4020; www.worldkitemuseum.com)* offers a modest display of historic kites from around the world.

★**Fort Columbia State Park** – *1 hr. 8.1mi east of Ilwaco on US-101. Open May–Sept daily dawn-dusk. 🅿 ☎ 360-642-3078 or 800-233-0321. www.parks.wa.gov.* Started during the Spanish-American War and completed in 1904 atop Chinook Point overlooking the mouth of the Columbia River, Fort Columbia is one of the best-preserved historic coastal defense sites remaining in the Northwest. **Fort Columbia Interpretive Center**, housed in the former barracks, has exhibits on local Chinook Indian culture and the daily operations of the fort. The handsome two-story **Commanding Officer's House★** has been restored to reflect the tastes and lifestyle of a military officer in the early part of this century. A .5mi interpretive walk covers bunkers, gun batteries and lookouts.

Oysterville – *18.2 mi north of Ilwaco on Rte. 103 (Sandridge Rd.).* The discovery of prodigious oyster beds in Willapa Bay sparked off an "oyster boom" and resulted in the founding of Oysterville in 1854. The town's prosperity was short-lived and by the 1880s it was in decline. In 1976 the community, with its bevy of mid-19C to early-20C buildings, was placed on the National Register of Historic Places. Historic buildings include homes, a church, an oyster cannery and the oldest continuously operating post office in Washington. Oysters are still harvested in Willapa Bay, one of the cleanest estuaries in the country.

★**Leadbetter Point State Park** – *21.4mi north of Ilwaco on Stackpole Rd. Open year-round daily dawn-dusk.* 🅿 ☎ *360-642-3078.* Hiking trails in this day-use park at the northern tip of the Peninsula traverse thick coastal forest, dunes, ocean beaches and the mudflats and pristine shoreline of Willapa Bay.
The adjacent Leadbetter Point Unit of **Willapa National Wildlife Refuge** *(☎ 360-484-3482)*, the open dune area on Leadbetter Point, functions as an annual stopover for more than 100 migratory bird species, including sandpipers, yellowlegs and sanderlings. *The refuge is closed March 15 through August to protect the endangered snowy plover, which nests on the dunes.*

PORT ANGELES

Michelin map 493 B 3 and map p 251
Population 18,769
Tourist information ☎ 360-452-8552 or www.olympicpeninsula.org

Located on the Strait of Juan de Fuca, about midway along the northern shoreline of the Olympic Peninsula, Port Angeles is the Peninsula's largest town and a major gateway to Olympic National Park. US-101, which encircles much of the park, runs right through town, and a ferry service links Port Angeles to VICTORIA, British Columbia, directly across the strait.
The first land claim in Port Angeles was staked in 1857 but the town was not officially organized until 1890. In 1862, after an executive order from President Abraham Lincoln established Port Angeles and Ediz Hook as a military reservation, the town became known as the Second National City; the American government planned to move its capital to Port Angeles if Washington, DC, was destroyed. During the 1880s the Puget Sound Cooperative Colony, a socialist collective, established a shipyard and lumber mill. When the Pacific Fleet anchored here in the 1920s and 1930s, Port Angeles' summertime population swelled with an influx of some 30,000 sailors.
Although Port Angeles claims an undeniably scenic setting, with the Olympic Mountains looming up to the south and the Cascades visible across the strait to the north, the town itself is not particularly attractive or architecturally noteworthy. In the 1980s, in a bid to increase tourism, the downtown area was renovated and a new **pier** with shops, restaurants and an **observation tower** was constructed next to the ferry dock. **Ediz Hook**, a sand spit formed by the Elwha River west of town, forms one arm of Port Angeles Bay.

SIGHTS *2 hrs*

Arthur D. Feiro Marinelife Center – 🔳 *City Pier, 1 block east of ferry terminal. Open mid–May–mid–Sept Mon, Wed–Sat 10am–6pm. Rest of the year weekends 10am–6pm. Closed major holidays. $2.50.* ⛇ 🅿 ☎ *360-417-6254.* Opened in

© Robert Holmes

Mural on Arthur D. Feiro Marine life Center

1981, a small marine lab and teaching facility for Peninsula College contains open tanks filled with local marine life (including an octopus); a touch tank where visitors can stroke starfish, sea anemones and sea cucumbers; and a new jellyfish exhibit. Two exterior walls of the building are covered with **murals** completed in 1998 by Port Townsend artist Corey Ench. The paintings, highly detailed but considerably idealized, depict nearby Hollywood Beach in the 17C, when it was used by Native Americans, and in the late 1800s with settlers.

Port Angeles Fine Arts Center – *1203 E. Lauridsen Blvd. Open year-round Tue–Sun 11am–5pm. Closed major holidays.* & P ☎ *360-457-3532. www.olympus.net/community/pafac.* A small gem of Northwest architecture, the Fine Arts Center occupies a semicircular Modernist house designed by Seattle architect Paul Hayden Kirk and built in 1951 for Esther Barrows Webster, a local artist who became editor of the town's newspaper. The house sits on a bluff overlooking Port Angeles and has a circular sculpture garden planted around a towering madrona tree. Regular exhibits feature the work of Northwest artists. Five acres of forested grounds include trails with marine and mountain views.

EXCURSION

★**Dungeness National Wildlife Refuge** – *3 hrs. 15.1mi east of Port Angeles. Take US-101 east towards Sequim; turn north on Kitchen-Dick Rd. for 3.3mi; left on Voice of America Rd. and continue through Dungeness Recreation Area 1mi to parking lot. Open year-round daily dawn-dusk.* P ☎ *360-457-8451.* A narrow finger of land with sand and gravel beaches, a protected bay and tide flats rich in marine life, 5.5mi-long **Dungeness Spit,** (encompassed by the wildlife refuge) ranks as one of the longest natural sand hooks in the world. Originally established to protect the Pacific black brant (a small, migrating sea goose), the refuge is also home to harbor seals and 250 different species of seabirds and shorebirds.

An easy .5mi path from the parking lot takes visitors through a fragrant patch of evergreen coastal forest to a blufftop overlook. From here you can observe the spit extending into the Strait of Juan de Fuca and notice how it was formed by the outpouring and tidal reshaping of sand and sediment from the Dungeness River. **Graveyard Spit,** its southern appendage, was named for a group of Tshimhian Indians killed by a raiding party of S'Klallams in 1868.

From the overlook, you can continue down to the spit and walk 4.5mi down the wave-lapped, driftwood-strewn **beach★** to **New Dungeness Lighthouse** *(visit by 30min guided tour only, May–Sept daily 9am–6pm; rest of the year daily 9am–3pm;* ☎ *360-683-9166).* When it was completed in 1857 the lighthouse sat at the very end of the spit; since that time an additional .5mi of sand has accumulated beyond it. The spit continues to grow by about 30ft a year. The area beyond the lighthouse, along with the entire inner shoreline (including Graveyard Spit) is closed to the public to protect wildlife.

PORT TOWNSEND★★

Michelin map 493 B 3 and map p 259
Population 8,259
Tourist Information ☎ 360-385-2722 or 888-365-6978

One of the best-preserved examples of a Victorian seaport in the US, Port Townsend in its entirety is a National Historic Landmark. With its placement on the northwest corner of the peninsula at the mouth of Puget Sound, the town claims a distinct maritime charm, a relaxed but sophisticated atmosphere and an abundance of cultural events that make it a favorite Northwest getaway.

Historical Notes

Port of Entry – Before the arrival of settlers, the S'Klallam Indians used the Admiralty Inlet area as a place to portage their canoes from the strait to the bay, thus bypassing the treacherous currents at the tip of the peninsula (today known as Point Wilson). Capt. George Vancouver noted the presence of a large, sheltered harbor in 1792 and named it Port Townshend, after the Marquis of Townshend.

The first town site on the Olympic Peninsula, Port Townsend was founded in 1851, after Olympia but six months before Seattle. In 1854 the US government moved its headquarters for the Puget Sound customs district from Fort Vancouver to Port Townsend, thus establishing the town as the area's most important commercial maritime center. It was also designated as the official Port of Entry for the Northwest United States. From a small settlement of log cabins Port Townsend quickly grew into an international seaport with a reputation for bawdiness rivaling that of San Francisco's Barbary Coast. Old Fort Townsend, the first fort in the area, was erected

in 1856 to protect the town from Indian raids; it burned down in 1895 and the site is now **Old Fort Townsend State Park** *(3mi south of town off Rte. 20 on Old Fort Townsend Rd.; open Apr–Sept daily dawn-dusk; closed rest of the year;* △ & 🄿 ☎ *360-385-3595).*
Maritime businesses flourished as more and more European and Chinese immigrants arrived. Great Britain, France, Germany, Norway, Sweden and Hawaii opened consulates and agencies. By 1889 the town was second only to New York in the number of ships tying up in its harbor. Cargo and passenger ships sailing into Puget Sound picked up their crews in Port Townsend, shanghaiing them if necessary. Recognizing the area's strategic importance, the US government established three major artillery batteries—known collectively as the "Iron Triangle"—to protect the Puget Sound area from invasion. Two of these coastal defenses, now state parks, are in the vicinity of Port Townsend. **Fort Flagler** *(16.4mi east of Port Townsend off Rte. 116; open Mar–Oct daily 6:30am–10pm; rest of the year daily 8am–5pm;* △ ✗ 🄿 ☎ *360-385-1259 or 800-233-0321)* was established in 1899 on the tip of Marrowstone Island across the bay. Fort Worden, just north of town, was in operation by 1902. The third unit, Fort Casey stands on Whidbey Island, across Admiralty Inlet.

Downtown and Uptown – The burgeoning town became stratified into a "Downtown" waterfront business district and a genteel "Uptown" residential section on the bluff above. **Water Street** and other Downtown streets contain fine blocks of two- and three-story stone and red-brick commercial and civic buildings from the town's boom years. A former territorial courthouse, the 1874 **Enoch S. Fowler Building** *(226 Adams St.)* is the oldest two-story stone structure in Washington. Many of the Victorian homes on the Uptown streets were built for sea captains and maritime merchants and command fine views of the harbor. Port Townsend's oldest surviving blufftop residence is the c.1858 **Captain Enoch S. Fowler Home** *(Jefferson and Polk Sts.)*, built in a plain, Federal-style reminiscent of New England. The Greek Revival-style **Captain Tibbal House** *(1208 Franklin St.)* was completed in 1860. Horace Tucker, a local architect, designed and built the 1872 **R.C. Hill House** *(611 Polk St.)* and the simple, unornamented **St. Paul's Episcopal Church**, built in 1865 *(Jefferson and Tyler Sts.).*

Waiting for the Railroad – By the late 1880s, anticipating the arrival of a transcontinental railroad, Port Townsend was poised to become a major West Coast city. Land speculators drove up prices; houses, churches and other buildings became grander and more stylistically complex. The **Hastings Building** *(Taylor and Water Sts.)* became Port Townsend's most elegant retail store when it was completed in 1869. The 100ft clock tower of the 1892 **Jefferson County Courthouse** *(Jefferson and Walker Sts.)* acted as a landmark for mariners.
Economic disaster set in when the eagerly awaited transcontinental railroad was routed to Seattle instead of Port Townsend. This, coupled with a worldwide depression in 1893, put an end to the town's glory days. By the turn of the century, the once-vital port town was in serious decline. A pulp and paper mill erected in 1927 provided work through the Great Depression and remains the county's single largest employer.
Efforts to preserve Port Townsend's outstanding architectural heritage began in the 1950s with the restoration of the 1883 **Bartlett House** *(Polk and Jefferson Sts.)*, a 14-room Italianate villa overlooking the bay. The process gained momentum in 1976 when the Downtown waterfront district and the blufftop residential area were designated a National Historic Landmark. The lower part of town, along the harbor, is lined with an impressive array of 19C buildings housing galleries, restaurants and shops, while the residential area on the bluff above holds a treasure trove of Victorian homes, many converted into B&Bs. The town remains a center for marine trades—rope-making, sail-making, boat repair and the like are practiced here and taught at regular apprentice workshops.

SIGHTS *1 day*

Historical Sidewalk Tours – *Depart from Jefferson County Historical Museum (Madison and Water Sts.). Guided 1 hr tours offered year-round daily (minimum of 2 people). $10/person.* & 🄿 *Call Guided Historical Tours for appointment* ☎ *360-385-1967.* Led by local historians, this lively, informative guided walking tour (1 hr) through the Victorian waterfront district is a good way to acquaint yourself with Port Townsend. The artsy, upscale and well-heeled town of today was once a lusty Victorian port city with more than its share of sailors, "parlor houses" and opium dens. Tours showcasing the historic homes on the bluff above can also be arranged.

★ **Jefferson County Historical Museum** – *210 Madison St. at Water St. Open Feb–Dec Mon–Sat 11am–4pm, Sun 1pm–4pm. Jan Sat 11am–4pm, Sun 1pm–4pm. Closed Jan 1, Thanksgiving Day, Dec 25. $2.* 🄿 ☎ *360-385-1003. www.olympus.net/arts/jcmuseum.* A four-floor store of memories, the museum occupies the original Judge's Chambers, City Jail and Fire Hall of Port Townsend's

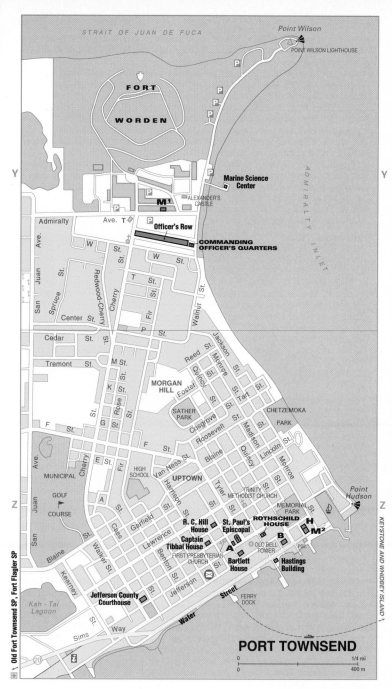

PORT TOWNSEND

0 — 1/4 mi
0 — 400 m

City Hall, dedicated in 1892. The building's **exterior★**, with its red-brick basket-weave patterns, forms a two-story façade divided into four architecturally distinct sections, each with its own cornice detail.

Visitors enter what was originally a courtroom, with the judge's bench and chair at one end. Among the objects displayed in old-fashioned glass cases are baskets, tools and carvings of the Peninsula's Hoh, S'Klallam, Makah, Quileute and Queets tribes. Stairs from the courtroom lead down to the dark, primitive cells in the City Jail, which held prisoners until the 1940s. Writer Jack London (1876-1916), who stopped in Port Townsend on his way to the goldfields in the Klondike, reputedly got into a brawl and spent one night in this gloomy lockup. Also in this area is an exhibit on prostitution, which flourished in the town's heyday.

Adjacent to the courtroom, the Fire Hall had horse stables on the first floor and firemen's quarters on the second with a hayloft between. The high-ceilinged stabling area, which today houses volumes of historic photographs, has a white beaded-board interior; the hole where firemen slid down on a brass pole is still visible. Collections of 19C artwork, furniture, stuffed birds and coral are displayed in the hayloft and second-floor firemen's quarters.

★**Rothschild House** – *Jefferson and Taylor Sts. Open May–Sept Wed–Sun 10am–5pm. Rest of the year call ahead for hours. $2.* ◘ ☎ *360-379-8076. www.olympus.net/ftworden/rh.* Sitting on a bluff overlooking the harbor, this simple, white-frame house—one of the oldest in Port Townsend—was completed in 1868 for D.C.H. Rothschild, a German immigrant who became a prosperous merchant. Mrs. Rothschild's restored herb garden is planted near the small back-entry porch; an open porch with an expansive harbor view spans the front. The virtually unchanged **interior★** contains original family furniture and memorabilia. The first-floor dining room and parlor retain their original wallpaper; the hand-grained woodwork throughout the house was the work of Chinese artisans. Three upstairs bedrooms can also be seen. Occupied by the Rothschild family for nearly a century, the house was given to the Washington State Parks and Recreation Commission (and became Washington's smallest state park) in 1959. The flower garden behind the house contains many old varieties of peonies, roses and lilacs.

★★**Fort Worden State Park** – *Entrance on W St. at Cherry St. at the northern limits of Port Townsend. Open May–Oct Mon–Thu & Sun 8:30am–4:30pm, Fri–Sat until 7:30pm.* ⚠ ☓ ◘ ☎ *360-385-4730. www.olympus.net/ftworden.* Authorized in 1896 and in use through World War II, Fort Worden was headquarters for Puget Sound Harbor Defenses. Along with Fort Flagler and Fort Casey, it formed part of the "Iron Triangle" defense system built to protect Puget Sound from invasion by sea. The fort, with its gun emplacements and late-Victorian buildings, overlooks Admiralty Inlet on the northern end of Quimper Peninsula. From its beaches and crisp green parade ground there are wonderful **views★** north across the Strait of Juan de Fuca to the San Juan Islands and the Cascade Mountains beyond. The 454-acre park is frequently used for festivals and concerts.

The large, wood-framed houses along **Officer's Row** were built in a style inspired by Jeffersonian Classicism, with pedimented roofs, colonnaded porches and Palladian windows. Standing at the end of the row is the impressive **Commanding Officer's Quarters★** *(open Apr–May & Sept–Oct weekends noon–4pm; Jun–Aug daily 10am–5pm; $2)*, completed in 1902. The 12-room house, with its late-Victorian (1890-1910) furnishings, is decorated to look as though it were still lived in. Across the parade grounds separating Officer's Row from the barracks stands the **Coast Artillery Museum** *(open early May–mid–May weekends noon–4pm; mid–May–mid–Sept daily 11am–4pm; $2)*. Two 16-inch practice projectiles flank the front steps of this museum, which contains weapons, uniforms and military artifacts pertaining to the fort's history. The building and adjacent grounds were used in the movie *An Officer and a Gentleman* (1982).

Further north, housed in a former warehouse on the fort's dock, is the small, child-friendly **Marine Science Center** *(open Apr–mid–Jun & mid–Sept–Oct weekends noon–4pm; mid–June–mid–Sept Tue–Sun noon–6pm; $2;* ◘ ☎ *360-385-5582)*. Touch tanks contain starfish, anemones, sea cucumbers and other living specimens found in the area's intertidal habitats.

Sights described in this guide are rated:
   ★★★   *Worth the trip*
    ★★   *Worth a detour*
     ★   *Interesting*

South Cascades

Mount St. Helens National Volcanic Monument/© Robert Holmes

Traditionally a wilderness playground for the urbanites of Puget Sound, the mighty South Cascade volcanoes—**Mount Rainier** and **Mount St. Helens**—raise their snow-capped summits high above the sprawling ranchlands of south-central Washington. Very different in character, the two mountains have increasingly attracted international admirers. One of the nation's first national parks and the highest volcano in the lower 48 states, Rainier is an island of its own, far removed from the nearby Seattle-Tacoma megalopolis. Its broad girth encompasses thick Northwest forests, and its high-country slopes gleam with glaciers. Small ranch towns nestle around its base, choosing to ignore the threat that this slumbering volcanic giant poses.

That threat became a vivid reality for Americans living in the shadow of Mt. St. Helens in May 1980. The volcano, long an outdoor paradise carpeted in evergreen forests, blew away its northern face. Now, the swath of destruction created by lava, pyroclastic blasts and mudflows has become a phenomenon in itself, drawing thousands of visitors a year. Protected as a national volcanic monument, Mt. St. Helens offers a rare look at geology in the making.

Long before George Vancouver sailed into Puget Sound in 1792, Native American tribes of the area knew these peaks well. Though the Indians hunted on the mountains' lower slopes, they rarely ventured high up, recognizing that "smoking" mountains might be dangerous. Settlers who ventured into the area in the mid-19C had no such reservations, and several attempted to climb Rainier. Others developed the resort potential of the more accessible lower slopes, and in this century Mt. St. Helens' Spirit Lake and Rainier's Paradise Valley became popular vacation destinations. On its way from Mexico to Canada, the **Pacific Crest National Scenic Trail** threads the meadows, streams and woodlands of the surrounding 1.3-million-acre **Gifford Pinchot National Forest**, passing under the shadow of the often overlooked 12,276ft volcano, Mt. Adams.

With advances in the science of seismology, leading volcanologists have begun predicting that Mount Rainier is due for a major explosion. Even though Mount St. Helens leaped to life first, scientists still hold to their belief that Rainier harbors the engines of massive destruction within its bulk.

MOUNT RAINIER NATIONAL PARK★★★

Michelin map 493 B, C 3, 4 and map p 265
Tourist Information ☎ 360-569-2211 or www.nps.gov/mora

The highest volcano and fifth highest peak in the contiguous United States, 14,410ft Mount Rainier dominates the landscape of central Washington, forming a majestic backdrop to the Puget Sound megalopolis. The national park now preserving the volcano encompasses 235,612 acres, much of it in high-country wilderness. A half million years old, "the Mountain," as Washingtonians call it, is relatively young by Cascade Range standards. Two craters crown the summit, flanked on the north and south by two lower summits, remnants of older, higher cones. An arctic island in the midst of a temperate zone, Rainier is covered in more than 36sq mi of ice and snow. Its 25 major glaciers afford it the ranking of the most glaciated peak in the lower 48 states. Meltwater from the glaciers filigrees the landscape with fast-running rivers and streams; on the high slopes near the summit the volcano's steam vents have carved a labyrinth of ice caves into the glaciers. Considered "episodically active" by geologists, the volcano vented with minor eruptions in the 19C. Its last major one was 2,000 years ago, but scientists believe Rainier could roar to life again at any time.

Historical Notes

The Nisqually, Yakama and other Native American tribes who lived in the shadow of Mount Rainier feared the mountain and mostly confined themselves to its thickly forested lower slopes, where hunting and foraging were good. In 1792 Capt. George Vancouver sighted the volcano when he sailed into Puget Sound and named it for Rear Admiral Peter Rainier. In 1857 US Army Lt. August Valentine Kautz made a six-day climb that took him within 400ft of the summit. The first successful climb was completed in August 1870 by two Olympia men, Hazard Stevens and Philemon Van Trump.

Widespread public interest in Rainier came after conservationist **John Muir** (1838-1914) climbed it in 1888 and wrote of its splendors: "Of all the fire mountains which, like beacons, once blazed along the Pacific Coast, Mount Rainier is the noblest." During the same period **James Longmire**, a guide who had established a route between the coast and Rainier's accessible southwestern flank, began developing a rustic mineral springs resort on its slopes. Longmire Medical Springs became a popular destination and

© Dianne Dietrich Leis

Reflection Lake

Practical Information

Getting There – Access to Mt. Rainier from Seattle *(87mi)* via I-5 and Rte. 706 to Paradise. Route 123 reaches the park from the southeast. There is no public transportation to the park. The closest Amtrak **train** station is in Tacoma *(☎ 800-872-7245)*. Daily **shuttle** service from Seattle-Tacoma International Airport by Rainier Overland Transportation Co. *(reservations required: ☎ 569-2604)* and Rainier Shuttle *(☎ 569-2331)*. Gray Line Tours of Seattle offers **bus tours** into the park *(spring–mid-Oct; reservations ☎ 206-626-5208 or 800-426-7505)*. The closest gas station is located in Ashford. In winter, chains are often required to reach Paradise.

Visitor Information – The park is open year-round daily from Ashford to Longmire; $10/car, $5 on foot or bike *(admission valid for 7 days; △ ⚔ ₺ ⛫)*. In winter, snow closes most of the other park roads except the stretch from Longmire to Paradise *(weather permitting)*. For information and brochures on points of interest, recreation and seasonal activities, contact Mount Rainier National Park Headquarters, Tahoma Woods, Star Rte., Ashford WA 98304, ☎ 569-2211, www.nps.gov/mora. Visitor centers offer exhibits, ranger-guided walks, campfire and children's programs, backcountry permits, maps and the park newspaper, *Tahoma News* – all available free. Other visitor centers: **Henry M. Jackson Memorial Visitor Center**, on Nisqually Paradise Rd. in Paradise *(p 265)*; **Ohanapecosh Visitor Center**, southeast of Paradise on Rte. 123 at Stevens Canyon entrance *(p 266)*. **White River Wilderness Information Center** *(open Memorial Day–Labor Day daily 9am–5pm; ☎ 569-2211, ext. 2356)*, **Sunrise Visitor Center** *(p 266)*, northeast of Paradise at the end of Sunrise Rd. via the White River entrance, where telescopes allow visitors a close-up view of glaciers.

Accommodations – **Paradise Inn** *(open late May–early Oct; p 265)* and the **National Park Inn** *(open year-round)* are located within the park; for reservations, contact Guest Services, Inc., P.O. Box 108, Ashford WA 98304, ☎ 569-2275. Visitors can choose among lodges, resorts and chalets in surrounding communities. For information, contact Tacoma-Pierce County Visitor and Convention Bureau, 1001 Pacific Ave., Tacoma WA 98401, ☎ 253-627-2836 or 800-272-2662. There are four **campgrounds** *($10-$14/night)* located within park boundaries. All offer drinking water, toilets and fireplaces. Sunshine Point Campground is open year-round. During peak season *(Jun–Aug)*, campsites at Cougar Rock and Ohanapecosh are by reservation *(☎ 800-365-CAMP)*; rest of the year, campsites are available on a first-come, first-served basis. Camping outside designated campgrounds requires a wilderness permit *(free)*, available from visitor centers and wilderness information centers. For campsites and **RV parks** outside the park, check with local chambers of commerce.

Recreation – Three hundred miles of **hiking** trails allow visitors to explore forests, meadows and glaciers. Interpretive signs are posted along many self-guided trails. Burroughs Mountain Trail *(5mi round-trip)* leads through meadows to alpine viewpoints. The more strenuous Skyline Trail *(5mi round-trip)* offers panoramic views of Nisqually Glacier. The Wonderland Trail *(93mi)* is for experienced hikers only and can take from 10-14 days. Steep slopes, glaciers and variable weather require proper equipment and training for **climbing**; watch for falling rocks and avalanches. Climbers planning to go above 10,000ft must register at the ranger station *(fee $15)*. For road, weather and trail information, call ☎ 569-2211. Other activities include **horseback riding** and **fishing** *(no fishing license required in the park)*.
Guide services, summit climbs and five-day seminars are offered through Rainier Mountaineering Inc., 535 Dock St., Tacoma WA 98402, ☎ 569-2227 (summer) or 253-627-6242 (winter). Backpacking trips along Northern Loop Trail and portions of Wonderland Trail, and climbing seminars are organized through REI Adventures, P.O. Box 1938, Sumner WA 98390, ☎ 206-395-8111; www.rei.com/travel *(Jul–Sept; 7-day all-inclusive $895; reservations required)*. Take a steam-powered train through the forest, across high bridges to Mineral Lake for a scenic 7mi round-trip *(mid-June–Labor Day daily, early May & until Sept 30 weekends only; Mt. Rainier Scenic Railroad; ☎ 569-2588)*.

Winter Activities – Many trails are used for **cross-country skiing**. Equipment rental and lessons are offered at Longmire Ski Touring Center, next to the National Park Inn *(mid-Dec–early Apr daily; ☎ 569-2411)*. Ranger-led **snowshoe walks** leave from Henry M. Jackson Memorial Visitor Center *(Dec–Apr weekends & holidays only)*.

spurred further interest in the volcano. In 1899, Mount Rainier became the fifth national park in the US. Several years later, engineer Eugene V. Ricksecker began designing a road that would connect Longmire to the spectacular subalpine meadows of Paradise Valley, 13mi up the mountain. Ricksecker's road, opened to cars in 1911, was intended "to follow ...the graceful curves of the natural surface ..." and set a precedent for future park design. Now the 147mi system of roads and bridges encircling Rainier's lower slopes flow with the natural landscape through meadowlands and forests of cedar, hemlock, and Douglas fir, providing spectacular views.

SIGHTS *3 days*

★Longmire – *Elevation 2,761ft. 6.4mi northeast of the Nisqually Entrance on Nisqually-Paradise Rd.* Owing to the quantity of large, smooth rock used in its construction, Longmire is sometimes called a village of stone. It preserves a cluster of historic park buildings in the original rustic style, including a historic museum, and offers a first **view** of the mountain. The **National Park Inn** here was originally built in 1916 as an annex to a larger inn destroyed by fire in 1926. The small building that served as the park headquarters from 1916-28 now houses the **Longmire Museum** *(open late-Jun–Labor Day daily 9am–6pm; rest of the year daily 9am–4pm;*

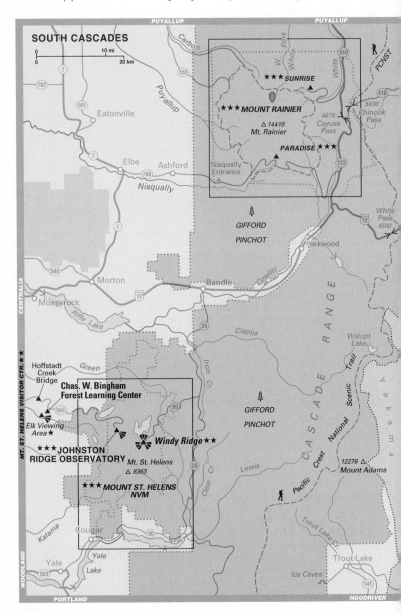

[P] ☎ *360-569-2211)*, with exhibits detailing the natural history and the early days of the area. A 6ft cross section of Douglas fir at the center's entrance highlights the longevity of these trees; spanning 1293 to 1963, the trunk's concentric rings are marked with major events in human and geologic history. The rustic-style 1929 **gas station** now features exhibits on park road-building and early transportation. Behind the village, the **Nisqually Suspension Bridge** is a reconstruction of the park's oldest suspension bridge, built across the Nisqually River in the early 1920s. Across the main park road, the **Trail of Shadows** *(.7mi)* loops through the former site of the Longmire Springs Hotel, passing a natural mineral spring pool and an 1888 cabin built by the Longmire family; interpretive signs explain natural and human history. The 13mi drive that climbs from Longmire to Paradise passes a turnoff for the 1mi **Ricksecker Point Road** *(one way, 6.5mi from Longmire)*, which curves around a precipice with **views★** of Mount Rainier and the glacial-carved Nisqually River Valley. Farther on, **Narada Falls** *(9mi from Longmire)* plunges 168ft over a cliff of andesite lava. A steep .2mi trail leads from the parking area to a lower viewpoint of the falls.

★★★**Paradise** – *Elevation 5,400ft. 19.5mi from Nisqually Entrance on Nisqually-Paradise Rd*. The most popular area in the park, Paradise Valley's subalpine meadows nestle into the volcano's southern flank, offering intimate views of the

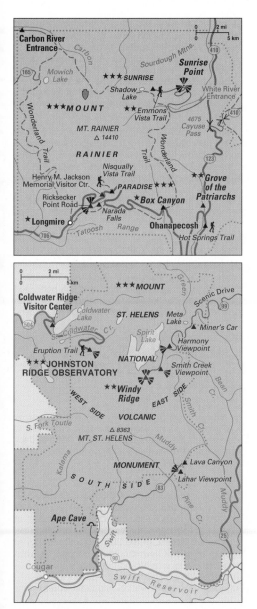

summit and the Nisqually Glacier. Spring wildflowers fill the meadows in late July and August, but during the long winter an annual average of 680in of snow covers Paradise.

The **Henry M. Jackson Memorial Visitor Center** *(open May–Labor Day daily 9am–7pm; rest of the year weekends & holidays 10am–5pm; ☎ 360-569-2211, ext. 2328)*, a circular, modern building named for the state's influential former US senator (1912-83), features exhibits on the park's geology and human and natural history. Films are shown in the auditorium throughout the day. The visitor center's upper level is devoted to an observation room whose wrap-around windows take in uninterrupted views of the volcano on the north and the jagged peaks of the Tatoosh Range on the south. Beside the visitor center, the rolling terrain of the 1.2mi **Nisqually Vista Trail** bends through the forests to an overlook **view** of the glacier's snout and the classic U-shaped valley it has scoured.

The historic **Paradise Inn★★** *(☎ 360-569-2275)*, designed by the Tacoma firm of Heath, Grove and Bell, was built of Alaska cedar salvaged from a fire-damaged area near Narada Falls. The original portion of the inn was completed in 1917, with an annex added in the 1920s. The hand-hewn log furniture that complements the soaring lobby's rustic character is the work of a single craftsman, German carpenter Hans Fraehnke, who carved the pieces in 1917. Since the 1920s, the nearby rustic-style **Guide House** has helped outfit mountaineers experienced or fit enough to make the hazardous two-day climb to the summit.

★**Box Canyon** – *10mi east of Paradise, on Stevens Canyon Rd.* A branch of the Cowlitz River has cut this narrow cleft into the rock face. Ferns sprout from crevices in the canyon, which plunges to depths of 115ft and narrows in some places to only 13ft across. Paved trails edge either side of the canyon and connect to each other via an upstream footbridge and the auto bridge on Stevens Canyon Road.

★★**Grove of the Patriarchs** – *Just inside the Stevens Canyon entrance on Stevens Canyon Rd., accessible via trail (1mi round-trip).* Situated on a small island in the Ohanapecosh River is one of the best surviving groves of lowland, old-growth forests in the Northwest. The island setting protected the conifers from recurring forest fires, and many have survived a thousand years. Among these "patriarchs" are western red cedar, western hemlock, and a 250ft-high Douglas fir. Named for Scottish naturalist David Douglas, who botanized through the Pacific Northwest from 1825-26, Douglas firs proliferate in the park's lowland forests. Not true firs, the trees are taxonomically placed in the pine family.

Ohanapecosh – *Elevation 1,900ft. 2mi south of the Stevens Canyon entrance on East Side Rd./Rte. 123.* This former hot-springs area now functions as the hub of visitor services in the southeast end of the park, providing information, camping facilities and ranger aid. Earlier in the century, a health resort developed the natural hot springs in this heavily forested area, but the springs have been returned to their natural state and provide no bathing opportunities. A **visitor center** *(open Memorial Day-Labor Day daily 9am–5pm, until mid–Oct weekends 9am–5pm; △ ✗ 🄿 ☏ 360-569-2211 ext. 2352)* houses exhibits on the natural history of the area, and the .5mi **Hot Springs Trail** leads through the forest, past the site of the former resort. *A booklet available at the visitor center interprets the natural and human history along the trail.*

★★★**Sunrise** – *Elevation 6,400ft. 14mi from White River entrance on White River Sunrise Rd.* The highest point in the park accessible to cars, Sunrise offers breathtaking **views**★★ of the volcano summit and its heavily glaciated northwestern slopes. The **Sunrise Visitor Center** *(open Jul–mid–Sept daily 9am–5pm; ☏ 360-569-2211, ext. 2357)* houses natural history exhibits and provides information on the hiking trails that web the area. The **Emmons Vista Trail**★★ follows the fairly level rim of White River Canyon, affording views down into the canyon and onto the Emmons Glacier, at 4sq mi Rainier's largest. After about 1.2mi, the trail descends to small, serene **Shadow Lake**, a good turnaround point for the hike.

Sunrise Point, a roadside pull-off 2.7mi from the visitor facilities, affords exquisite **views**★★★ of Rainier *(west)*, Sunrise Lake and the Sourdough Ridge *(north)* and conical Mount Adams *(south)*.

Carbon River Entrance – *Elevation 1,880ft. On Carbon River Rd.* The northwestern corner of the park is historically subject to flooding, and the park road here washed away several years ago and has only recently reopened to high-clearance vehicles. The road leads to trailheads for the **Wonderland Trail** and others.

MOUNT ST. HELENS NATIONAL VOLCANIC MONUMENT★★★

Michelin map 493 B 4 and maps pp 264-265
Tourist Information ☏ 360-274-2100

One of the world's most famous volcanoes, Mount St. Helens erupted with the energy of several atomic bombs in 1980, destroying its northern flank. Now preserved as a 110,000-acre national volcanic monument, the eviscerated mountain and the decimated landscape it created have become one of the region's leading visitor attractions.

Historical Notes

Only 40,000 years old, Mount St. Helens is the youngest of the major Cascade volcanoes. To Native Americans, it was Fire Mountain, a towering symmetrical cone of white that sometimes spewed steam and ash from its summit. On his exploration of Puget Sound in 1792, **George Vancouver** (1757-98) gave the volcano its current name, in honor of his friend, the English Baron St. Helens. In the 20C, the volcano was so quiescent that volcanologists only began to realize how dangerous it might be when studies were done in the 1960s. Its lack of glacial erosion and the dispersion of botanical communities led them to conclude that Mt. St. Helens had "been more active and more explosive during the last 4,500 years than any other volcano in the coterminous United States."

In the spring of 1980, the mountain verified these scientific conclusions when it rumbled slowly awake. On March 20, seismometers recorded a 4.1 magnitude earthquake on the mountain, followed by more quakes in the coming days. On March 27, a loud boom was accompanied by a column of steam and ash that shot 7,000ft into the air. Similar eruptions continued for days, coming from two craters that had appeared on the mountain and left gaping black holes in the ice cap. By late April a large "bulge" had appeared on Mt. St. Helens' north face, growing at the rate of five feet a day. A cadre of scientists and sightseers had descended on the area to monitor the waking giant, and landowners on the north flank of the mountain had been asked to leave, because of the threat posed by avalanches. One colorful local figure—Harry Truman, the longtime manager of Spirit Lake Lodge—refused.

On the morning of May 18, an earthquake loosened much of the north flank, and the entire side of the mountain began collapsing downhill into Spirit Lake, the North Fork Toutle River, and Coldwater Creek. Almost immediately, a blast cloud roared out of the mountain, outracing the avalanche as it reached speeds of up to 600mph. Filled with hot rock fragments, the stone-filled avalanche knocked down the lush forests in its path, searing their leaves and creating a jackstraw litter of fallen timber in the blow-down zone. This initial destruction took only five minutes to accomplish, but for nine hours afterward, a column of ash spewed 15mi high from the crater, blanketing eastern Washington in gloom.

Pyroclastic flows of hot rock, pumice, ash and gases melted snow and ice and began to cause mudflows that looked, as one observer described them, "like a wall of warm, fluid, brown concrete." The mudflows, filled with increasing amounts of debris, created severe flooding as they moved downstream, particularly along the Toutle River. As it entered the Columbia, the debris mass filled the river channel and temporarily shut off shipping. At day's end, Mt. St. Helens had gone from an elevation of 9,677ft to 8,363ft; its crater measured 2,000ft deep and about 1mi wide. It had devastated 250sq mi, blown down four billion board feet of timber, sent a blanket of ash 150mi east, and left 57 people dead or missing. Harry Truman was never found; his lodge lay buried under 200ft of mud and water.

Despite the devastation it wrought, the mountain quickly became an awe-inspiring symbol of nature's powers, both in destruction and rejuvenation. Some forms of wildlife protected in underground burrows actually survived the eruption, and within months after the disaster, plants had begun to recolonize, attracting more animal life. Since the eruption, a lava dome within the crater has slowly grown and now measures 1,000ft high and 3,000ft across. On August 26, 1982, Mt. St. Helens and much of the area affected by its explosion, was declared a National Volcanic Monument, under the aegis of the National Forest Service. Today, the volcano itself ranks as the second most climbed mountain in the world, after Japan's Mount Fuji.

WEST SIDE *1/2 day.*

Accessible via Rte. 504 from the town of Castle Rock. Two dramatic areas associated with the 1980 eruption have been interpreted for visitors: one along the **West Side**, and the other along **Windy Ridge** on the east side. No road connects the two areas directly; they lie a half-day's drive apart. The **South Side** of the mountain also offers several points of interest. *Monument passes, required for all developed areas, may be purchased ($8) at visitor centers and information stations.*

★★**Mount St. Helens Visitor Center** – *Rte. 504 5mi east of I-5 Exit 49 at Castle Rock. Open late Apr–late Sept daily 9am–6pm. Rest of the year until 5pm. Closed Jan 1, Thanksgiving Day & Dec 25* ✗ ♿ 🅿 ☎ *360-274-2100.* Set in wooded surroundings, this impressive center serves to

© Roger Werth /Woodfin Camp

Mount St. Helens Erupting, May 18, 1980

Getting There – Access to Mount St. Helens National Volcanic Monument from the west *(Seattle, 120mi)* or south *(Portland, 50mi)* via I-5; at Castle Rock (Exit 49), Rte. 504 extends 52mi and leads to the three main visitor centers. This road is accessible year-round, although chains or snow tires are recommended from late October to April. To reach the park from the north, take Forest Service Road 5 off US-12 in Randle; from the south, take Forest Service Road 90 at the town of Cougar. Both roads are closed in winter. Gasoline and groceries are available at Swift Reservoir. The closest Amtrak **train** station is in Kelso *(☎ 800-872-7245)*. Greyhound **bus** service *(☎ 423-7380 or 800-231-2222)* runs to Kelso.

Visitor Information – The forest is open year-round daily. $8; children under 15 years free *(admission valid for 3 days; ⛺ ✗ ♿ 🅿 ☎ 274-2103)*. For information and brochures on points of interest, recreation and seasonal activities, contact Mount St. Helens National Volcanic Monument Headquarters, 42218 NE Yale Bridge Rd., Amboy WA 98601, ☎ 247-3900; www.fs.fed.us/gpnf. **Mount St. Helens Visitor Center** on Rte. 504 *(p 267; ☎ 274-2100)* is located 5mi east of Castle Rock and offers interpretive exhibits, video presentations and guided nature walks. **Coldwater Ridge Visitor Center** *(✗ ☎ 274-2131)*, located 7mi west of Mt. St. Helens on Rte. 504, affords panoramic views of the volcano and the Toutle River Valley. At the end of Rte. 504, **Johnston Ridge Observatory** provides the closest views of Mt. St. Helens of any of the visitor centers *opposite; ☎ 274-2140)*. On the east side, **Woods Creek Information Center** *(open mid-May–Sept daily 9am–4pm)* is located on Forest Road 25.

Accommodations – There are no overnight accommodations within the park. For information on lodging in the surrounding communities, contact **Cowlitz County Dept. of Tourism**, 207 Fourth Ave., Kelso WA 98626, ☎ 577-3137; **Castle Rock Chamber of Commerce**, P.O. Box 721, Castle Rock WA 98611, ☎ 274-6603; or **Woodland Chamber of Commerce**, 1225 Lewis River Rd., Woodland WA 98674, ☎ 225-9552. Most campgrounds and RV parks are open June–October. Iron Creek campground is located within park boundaries. Forest Service campground reservations: ☎ 800-452-5687.

Recreation – There are many **hiking** trails of various difficulty levels that allow visitors to explore the park and its craters, lakes and ancient lava flows. Before setting out, check with park officials regarding weather conditions and obtain trail maps *(free)* from visitor center. Interpretive walks leave from all visitor centers *(daily mid-Jun–Sept)*. Trails are generally accessible from June–October, except at lower elevations where trails are open year-round. West-side trails such as Winds of Change and Birth of a Lake are wheelchair accessible and offer close-up views of the crater. East-side trails lead into the heart of the blast area, with ranger-led walks to Meta Lake. Windy Ridge Viewpoint is open daily mid-May to early fall. On the south side hikers can explore Ape Cave and Lava Canyon. Some trails are open to **mountain bikers** and **equestrians**. Check with park headquarters *(above)* for **fishing** and **hunting** regulations. Permits are required to **climb** above 4,800ft *(season May 15-Oct 31; $15)* and are available by advance reservation from the monument headquarters *(above)* or by lottery *(daily 6pm for next day's climb)* at Jack's Restaurant on Rte. 503, 23mi east of Woodland. Information and climbing conditions: ☎ 247-3961. **Helicopter** rides depart from Hoffstadt Bluffs Visitor Center, Rte. 504 at Milepost 27 *(mid-May–mid-Sept daily; 25min; $89; for schedules, contact Hillsboro Helicopters ☎ 274-7750 or 800-752-8439)*.

During the **winter** season, **snowmobiling**, **cross-country skiing** and **snowshoeing** are practiced throughout the park and in nearby Gifford Pinchot National Forest. Cougar Sno Park and Marble Mountain Sno Park are reached via Rte. 503. Vehicle parking permits are required, available at Jack's Restaurant *(above)* or by mail from Washington State Parks & Recreation Commission, 7050 Clearwater Lane KY-11, Olympia WA 98505. Snow, avalanche & weather information: ☎ 326-2400.

orient visitors to the park through its detailed exhibits on the geologic history of the volcano, a timeline of events surrounding the recent eruption, and a dramatic, live-footage movie **This Place in Time**★ *(22min)*. A seismograph allows visitors to record mini-earthquakes they can create themselves by stomping their feet.

From the visitor center, Route 504 continues east 48mi. Known as the Spirit Lake Memorial Highway, the road was built between 1992-95, on a ridge following the valley of the Toutle River, with clear views—weather permitting—of Mt. St. Helens on the eastern horizon. About 5.5mi from the visitor center, a new bridge spans the Toutle, just below the confluence of the north and south forks of the river. It replaces a bridge destroyed by 1980 mudflows and the debris they carried.

At Mile 16 the highway begins to roughly parallel the North Fork of the Toutle, and at Mile 24.5, it crosses **Hoffstadt Creek Bridge**, spanning a gorge that plunges 370ft below it. Now devastation from the eruption becomes apparent; trees in this area were fatally scorched by the heat. Farther on begins the blow-down zone-where trees were actually leveled by the blast.

Charles W. Bingham Forest Learning Center – *Mile 33, Rte. 504. Open mid-May–Oct daily 10am–6pm. Closed major holidays.* ♿ 🅿 ☎ *360-414-3439. mountsthelens.weyerhaeuser.com.* Largely funded and operated by the Weyerhaeuser timber company, this exhibit facility explains the life cycle of forests, forestry techniques and conservation issues—all in relation to the 1980 eruption. A theater shows changing audiovisual presentations related to the volcano and to elk that inhabit the region. The **Elk Viewing Area★** behind the center overlooks the devastated valley of the North Fork Toutle, where a resident herd of animals can often be seen grazing.

Coldwater Ridge Visitor Center – *Mile 43, Rte. 504. Same hours as Mount St. Helens Visitor Center.* ✗ ☎ *360-274-2131.* Focusing on the recovery of the Mt. St. Helens habitat, the center offers distant views of the crater and of the newly created Coldwater and Castle Lakes. A 7min video, *A Change of Scenes*, explains the survival and recovery of local flora and fauna. Rangers also deliver **lectures** on related topics, held in the pavilion or on the deck of the center.

★★★**Johnston Ridge Observatory** – *Mile 52, Rte. 504. Open late Apr–late Sept daily 9am–6pm. Rest of the year 10am–4pm.* ☎ *360-274-2140.* This visitor center, opened in May 1997, is located only 5mi from the crater and offers spectacular **views★★** of the steaming lava dome, as well as the collapsed flank of the mountain. The facility and the ridge on which it is located are named for **David Johnston**, a US Geological Survey scientist who was monitoring the volcano from a spot 25mi from the center on the morning of May 18, 1980. His now legendary last transmission-"Vancouver, Vancouver, this is it!"—alerted the world to the explosion and cost Johnston his life. A 16min film, **A Message from the Mountain★★★**, shown in the large, state-of-the-art observatory theater, relives the drama of that day through live footage and ends with a surprise flourish. The large **electronic topographical model★★** of the volcano and surrounding area uses serial lights to explain the often confusing sequence of events—ash, mud and pyroclastic flows, landslides and flooding. A working observatory, the facility also houses publicly displayed seismographic monitors that keep constant tabs on the mountain's activity. Beginning at the visitor center, the 25mi **Eruption Trail** leads back to the parking lot.

■ Pacific Northwest Volcanoes

Young by geologic standards (compared to the Appalachian Range, which began forming 250 million years ago), the volcanic Cascade Range began to form in a lowland coastal region some 50 million years ago. Over eons, eruptions spread lava and ash, creating mountains that through uplifting and faulting eventually formed a 600mi-long corridor, stretching from present-day Canada into northern California.

Sometime between a half-million and a million years ago, the great volcanic cones that tower above the Pacific Northwest today began to grow. Classified by geologists as stratovolcanoes, they comprise layers of pumice and lava ejected during eruptions. By 75,000 years ago, **Mount Rainier**, the giant among them, had reached its full height. This was the Pleistocene Epoch, the time of the great Ice Age, when glaciers further scoured and sculpted the volcanic landscape. Many of the glaciers formed in that period continue to this day, though recent warming trends have caused them to recede significantly in the last 60 years.

But the ice masses add their own element of danger to the eruption potential. All of the southern Cascade peaks are seismically active, and lie within the **Ring of Fire** that curls around the Pacific from the tip of South America to Alaska and from northern Asia to New Zealand. In the Cascades themselves, more than 6,000 small earthquakes are recorded each year. But increased seismic activity can signal that a major event is on the way. A volcanic eruption has particularly cataclysmic results, melting glaciers and adding floods to the destruction. Early in this century, California's Mount Lassen, one of the 18 volcanic cones in the Cascades, awoke violently and destructively. More recently, in 1980, Mt. St. Helens paralyzed the region with a massive eruption that created flooding, pyroclastic "blow-down" (leveling of trees), and wide-ranging ash fallout. Geologists carefully monitor the seismic activity of the threatening Cascade peaks, checking for any changes that might herald disaster for the human populations that now live near the fiery breath of these volcanoes.

EAST SIDE *1 day*

Scenic Drive – *16mi from Randle on Rte. 12, Forest Rd. 25 leads south 20mi to Forest Rd. 99, which then twists 16mi up to Windy Ridge.* Unpopulated back-country, this area offers no gas stations after Randle. Starting out in coniferous forest, Route 99 enters the blowdown zone in about 7mi. From here, the road winds precipitously along sere cliff edges denuded by the eruption. After 2.5mi the road passes the **miner's car**, which belonged to a family of three who hiked to a nearby miner's cabin prior to the eruption. The hikers were killed and their car was hurtled 60ft to this location. Just beyond the car is small **Meta Lake**. Some 4.5mi farther along, **Harmony Viewpoint** offers a distant glimpse of log-choked Spirit Lake. Continue 1.5mi to the turnout for **Smith Creek Viewpoint**, which affords a **view★** of **Mount Adams** in the east. Follow the road 1mi farther to its end at Windy Ridge.

★★**Windy Ridge** – *At the end of Forest Rd. 99.* On this 4,000ft wilderness ridge 5mi east of Mt. St. Helens' crater, the volcano takes on a looming immediacy, untempered by any human development. A steep, stepped trail climbs to the top of the ridge for **views★★★** of the still-steaming, horseshoe-shaped crater of the mountain and down onto the full expanse of Spirit Lake. Rangers periodically offer outdoor lectures on various topics here.

SOUTH SIDE *2 hrs*

Forest Rd. 83, off Forest Rd. 90, 55mi southwest of Windy Ridge. Except in the town of Cougar, this backcountry area offers no running water, gasoline or other amenities.

Ape Cave – *Off Forest Rd. 83, 3mi north of the junction with Forest Rd. 90. Information station open daily year-round. Lantern rental: late-May–Sept daily 10am–5:30pm only.* 🅿 ☎ *360-247-3900. Ranger-led hikes of the cave are available; for those exploring the caves on their own, lanterns are available for rent at the information station.* One of the longest continuous lava tubes in the continental US, 12,810ft-long Ape Cave reaches depths of 60ft. The hollow tube, formed 1,900 years ago from Mt. St. Helens lava, is 45ft high at its highest point. Discovered by a logger in the late 1940s, the cave was first explored in the early 1950s by a group of young nature enthusiasts who called themselves the St. Helens Apes. The lower passage offers an easy .75mi hike; the more rugged upper passage is 1.25mi long.

Forest Road 83 continues 10mi beyond the Ape Cave turnoff to **Lahar Viewpoint**, an area flooded by water, stone and mud during the 1980 eruption. A mile farther on, **Lava Canyon** was formed 3,500 years ago, when another Mt. St. Helens eruption filled a small valley with lava. Mudflows scoured the valley in the recent eruption.

SOMETHING FOR EVERYONE

■ Museums

Oregon History Center★ Portland (OR) *p 66*
Portland Art Museum★ Portland (OR) *p 66*
Oregon Museum of Science and Industry★★ Portland (OR) *p 78*
Maryhill Museum★ East of The Dalles (OR) *p 88*
High Desert Museum★★ Bend (OR) *p 93*
Museum of Art★★ Eugene (OR) *p 154*
Seattle Art Museum★★ Seattle (WA) *p 175*
Frye Art Museum★★ Seattle (WA) *p 171*
Seattle Asian Art Museum★★ Seattle (WA) *p 187*
Henry Art Gallery★★ Seattle (WA) *p 190*
Tacoma Art Museum★ Tacoma (WA) *p 203*
Clymer Museum of Art★ Ellensburg, (WA) *p 225*
Museum of Northwest Art★★ La Conner (WA) *p 236*
Vancouver Art Gallery★★ Vancouver (BC) *p 289*

■ Indian Heritage

The Museum at Warm Springs★★★ Warm Springs (OR) *p 96*
Manuel Museum★ Joseph (OR) *p 108*
Tamastslikt Cultural Center★ East of Pendelton (OR) *p 112*
Favell Museum of Western Art and Indian Artifacts Klamath Falls *p 139*
Tillicum Village★ Seattle (WA) *p 198*
Colville Confederated Tribes Museum Grand Coulee Dam Area (WA) *p 211*
Yakama Nation Cultural Center Museum★ Toppenish (WA) *p 228*
Makah Museum★★ Neah Bay (WA) *p 254*
UBC Museum of Anthropology★★★ Vancouver (BC) *p 301*
Royal British Columbia Museum★★★ Victoria (BC) *p 316*
Cowichan Native Village Duncan (BC) *p 324*
Secwepemc Museum and Native Heritage Park★★ Kamloops (BC) *p 337*
Alaska State Museum★★ Juneau (AK) *p 372*
Sheldon Jackson Museum★ Sitka (AK) *p 375*

■ Halls of Fame

State of Oregon Sports Hall of Fame Portland (OR) *p 68*
Round-Up Hall of Fame★ Pendelton (OR) *p 112*
BC Sports Hall of Fame★ Vancouver (BC) *p 291*

View of Vancouver from Stanley Park

© Robert Holmes

British Columbia

Introduction to British Columbia

Shaped like an ax head placed upright along Canada's Pacific Coast, the province of British Columbia stretches north-south 1,200km (744mi), from the 49th to the 60th parallels, and east-west 600km (372mi). At 948,596sq km (364,640sq mi) it is a huge province, bigger than California, Oregon and Washington combined—and four times as large as Great Britain. It borders Alberta, the Yukon, the Northwest Territories, Alaska, Idaho, Washington and Montana. Ranging from 114 to 139 degrees west longitude, the province lies almost entirely within the Pacific time zone.

British Columbia is astoundingly diverse, embracing a vast range of climates, topographies, ecosystems, peoples and economic activities. Here you'll find sagebrush deserts and gla-

British Columbia Provincial Facts

Capital: Victoria

Land Area: 948,596 square kilometers (364,640sq mi)

Population: 3,724,500

Motto: *Splendor Sine Occasu* ("Splendor Without Diminishment")

Provincial Flower: Pacific Dogwood

cier-clad peaks; storm-tossed maritime islands and deep-grass inland prairies; cosmopolitan urban centers and vast cattle ranches where cowboys still drive herds to the high country each spring. Lavished by nature with incomparable scenery, the province's land is its greatest wealth. Traditionally dependent on its natural resources, British Columbia's economy and lifestyle are shifting from mining, fishing and forest products to tourism and technology. Its four million residents are concentrated in the southwest portion, where Vancouver and Victoria comprise Canada's Pacific gateway.

Geographical Notes

Geologic Past – British Columbia's position along the Pacific Rim "Ring of Fire," the most geologically active area on earth, explains its complex and fascinating geology. Most of the province lies within the Western Cordillera, an area of uplift encompassing most of western North America. Composed of several eastward-thrusting terranes (large "island" rock fragments carried up against the North American plate by earth surface movement), ranging in age from 30 to 180 million years, the topography of British Columbia makes a convoluted picture. It includes the Monashee, Stikinia, Quesnellia, Cache Creek, Alexander and Wrangellia terranes, along with a large eastern section of the ancestral North American plate. Terrane collision continues today in the Northwest corner of the province, where British Columbia, Alaska and the Yukon meet; here the coastal mountains are rising 4cm (1.6in) a year. In contrast, one of the world's most distinctive geologic features, the Rocky Mountain Trench stretches along the west face of the Rockies more than 1,400km (868mi) from Montana to the Liard River in the north part of the province. Here, the earth's crust has literally cracked open as it stretches. One of the world's major subduction zones (where oceanic crust is carried beneath the continental mass) occurs off the coast of British Columbia, creating a potential major fault line.

The mountains produced by all that tectonic action include two major ranges, the Rocky Mountains and the Coast Range, plus several smaller ones in between. Running approximately north-south, these mountains constitute the majority of the province's interior, except for a large central highland plateau bordering the Fraser River from Cache Creek north to Fort St. James. The province's northeast corner, the Peace River country, is the northwesternmost angle of the Great Plains that run all the way down to the Gulf of Mexico. Several major rivers arise in the interior-the Columbia, Peace, Fraser, Stikine and Skeena-and the latter three penetrate the jagged, 4,000m (13,120ft) heights of the Coast Range, forming the only gaps in that formidable chain.

Various glaciations—2,000,000, 400,000 and 15,000 years ago—have carved their marks into the landscape, with glacial moraines, high mountain cirques, kettle lakes and long U-shaped valleys common throughout the province. Volcanic activity is pronounced, and especially evident in Wells Gray Park, Garibaldi Provincial Park and far north in the Skeena Mountains.

Regional Landscapes – The fractured shape of the land, more than three-quarters of it mountainous, means most of the province is little developed, and much of it—about 50 million acres—is roadless wilderness. Forest covers 40 percent of the land, and 75 percent lies above 1,000m (3,280ft). The British Columbia coast is a lengthy, perilous but beautiful stretch of inlets, bays, islands and fjords that add up to 27,800km (17,236mi) of shoreline. One-third of Canada's freshwater is also located in British Columbia.

Rain Forest Trail, Pacific Rim National Park

© Robert Holmes

Dozens of geographic regions spread over the province, from coastal rain forests and inland desert canyons to high-country wilderness and alpine tundra. British Columbia includes every major North American habitat except subtropical.

The **Lower Mainland**, or lower Fraser Valley, lies pressed between the Coast and Cascade mountains and the US border. It contains two million people, about half of British Columbia's population. To the west, **Vancouver Island** ranks as one of North America's largest islands. Measuring 460km (285mi) long, it is roughly the size of Holland. A steep chain of mountains runs along its spine, leaving human settlement largely confined to the protected east coast. The **Okanagan** region in south-central British Columbia centers on the Okanagan Valley, a land of huge lakes, orchards and vineyards. To the north, the mountainous Cariboo was once the scene of a fervid gold rush; it is now cattle and timber country. The **Kootenay** region stretches east from the Okanagan to the Continental Divide along the Rockies, embossed with narrow valleys and steep mountain ranges. The **Chilcotin** is a vast plateau extending west from the Fraser River, north of Lillooet all the way to Burns Lake, bordered on the West by the impenetrable Coast Range. A vast land of mountains, forests and lakes, **North British Columbia** remains largely undeveloped, with half the province's land area and less than two percent of its people. Its northeast corner, the relatively flat **Peace River** country, is the only area where extensive grain farming takes place.

Climate – Offering some of the most diverse weather in the Western Hemisphere, British Columbia's meteorological landscape is controlled by two key features—its mountains and the Pacific Ocean. Areas directly exposed to Pacific weather experience temperate maritime climates, with cooler temperatures and greater rainfall than areas sheltered by mountains from Pacific exposure, which are warmer in summer, colder in winter, and receive less rainfall.

The climate in any particular spot is determined by exposure and orientation, and variations are sometimes just a matter of miles, with astonishing extremes. Lowland canyons and valleys stay semiarid, with warm summers; west-facing slopes catch rain coming off the Pacific and remain cool; mountainous heights are snowbound much of the year. At HOPE, in the eastern end of the lower Fraser Valley, the climate is maritime, with about 100cm (39in) of rain a year and moderate temperatures. At Ashcroft only 180km (112mi) up the Fraser canyon, rainfall drops to less than 15cm (5.9in) a year, and summer temperatures regularly climb past 35°C (95°F). High above both locales, glacier-clad peaks bear huge amounts of snowfall, sometimes building depths of 10m (33ft). The entire portion of British Columbia west of the Coast Range is temperate rain forest, some spots along Vancouver Island ranking among the wettest on earth, with more than 5m (16.4ft) of rain a year. At one long-abandoned island weather station, Henderson Lake, 8.1m (26ft) of rain fell in 1931. By contrast, portions of the interior canyons are Canada's hottest, driest spots—at Lytton, just past Hell's Gate, the Canadian temperature record of 44.4°C (112°F) was set. Despite the prevailing Pacific influence, parts of the province are far from mild: The mercury once registered -58°C (-61°F) at Smith River, in the extreme northeast corner. Yet in Vancouver, in the southwest, non-native palm trees thrive.

Nor is British Columbia entirely dominated by clouds. Cranbrook, in the Rockies, is a beautifully sunny spot with more than 2,200 hours of sunshine a year. On the other hand, Prince Rupert, on the north-central coast, enjoys less than half that amount.

275

Historical Notes

First Nations – The first human inhabitants probably reached British Columbia about 12,000 years ago, after the last glaciation's ice sheets had mostly receded. Isolated by the area's rugged topography, the province's indigenous people segmented into numerous bands; anthropologists have identified approximately three dozen distinct languages and dialects, making this one of the most linguistically diverse areas on earth. The First Nations inhabitants probably lived a generally peaceful existence heavily dependent on salmon and cedar. Coastal people traveled by canoe; a few took difficult routes into the interior, carrying fish oil as the chief item of trade.

European Settlement – Spanish explorer **Juan Perez Hernandez** claimed British Columbia for Spain in 1774, but he did not actually land. British Capt. **James Cook** arrived four years later on Vancouver Island, and shortly thereafter British traders began developing a fur trade in the province. By 1792, Capt. **George Vancouver** had mapped the entire Northwest coast from Oregon to Alaska, solidifying the British claim to the region; and in 1793, **Alexander Mackenzie** crossed the province from the Canadian plains by following a traditional First Nations trade route. In the first half of the 19C, the **Hudson's Bay Company** established control of the region, which remained sparsely settled. Then, in 1846, a treaty divided the region between British and US interests along the 49th parallel. Hudson's Bay Company official James Douglas became governor of a small colony on Vancouver Island three years later.

Cariboo Gold – A pivotal event in British Columbia history took place in 1858, when gold was discovered along the Fraser River, precipitating a worldwide sensation. The mainland was declared a British colony that year at Fort Langley, and Douglas—put in charge of both the mainland and Vancouver Island—is credited with imposing order on the rowdy scene. The California gold rush had largely played out; adventurers were ready for a new frontier. It opened up in 1860 when gold was found in the Cariboo Mountains in the British Columbia interior. Construction of a dependable highway into the interior, the famed **Cariboo Road**, was begun in 1862 and completed in 1864.

British Columbia and Vancouver Island were united into one colony in 1866, with VICTORIA becoming the provincial capital two years later. By then, Barkerville, in the Cariboo, was the largest community in Western Canada, at 25,000 people. New Westminster, the former capital of the mainland colony, was the major city in the lower Fraser Valley. A few hundred sawmill workers lived on the shores of Burrard Inlet, near the heart of present-day Vancouver. As late as 1881, the province's 24,000 European residents were still outnumbered by its 25,000 First Nations. Yet federal authorities suppressed the indigenous culture, making the traditional **potlatches** (gift-giving feasts, *p 35*) illegal and seizing ceremonial gear. (Restoration of Native rights did not take place until the late 20C.)

The Coming of the Rail – With the **Confederation of Canada** forming in 1867, British Columbia was soon mulling an invitation to join. The westerners agreed, on condition that Canada build a rail line across the continent and, most challenging, the mountains of British Columbia. It took 15 years to accomplish, entailing harrowing construction over two major passes and down the treacherous Fraser Canyon. The delays created an attitude of suspicion toward Eastern Canada politics that persists today. When the Canadian Pacific finally reached the lowlands in 1886, and Burrard Inlet was chosen as its terminus, the new city of Vancouver began to grow. Meanwhile, the gold rush had panned out, and with the fur trade long dead, the economic emphasis slowly shifted to timber. What was left constituted the future: vast forests, copious amounts of water, rich mineral deposits and seemingly limitless salmon runs.

20th Century – The turn of the 20C brought on the resource extraction economy that dominated British Columbia for most of the 1900s. Huge salmon canneries were established along the coast; mills began to process vast quantities of timber from the province's deep forests; and orchards began prospering in the southern interior valleys. A second national rail line reached the Lower Mainland, and the decline of timber supplies elsewhere made the province's huge reserves more valuable. The province's first pulp mill opened in Powell River in 1909, while across the Strait of Georgia more than 40 percent of the old-growth forest on the east slope of Vancouver Island was cut between 1918 and 1937. The Great Depression and World War II slowed economic growth, but the postwar boom across North America brought renewed demand for British Columbia's forest products.

The second half of the 20C garnered increased trade with Asia and a huge influx of new residents whose arrival created economic growth by itself. In the early 1990s, an exodus from Hong Kong brought thousands of new residents—and millions of dollars in capital—to Vancouver, which experienced a sharp real-estate boom as a result. British Columbia's population, just 2.5 million in the mid-1970s, passed 4 million (about 13 percent of the Canadian total) at the dawn of the 21C, at which time the gross domestic product surpassed $110 billion.

Economy

Blessed with abundant natural resources, British Columbia has long depended upon its salmon-rich waters, thick forests and mineral-laden hills. Petroleum reserves, coal, natural gas and water provide the power for the province's engines of commerce. Recent decades have seen an increasing awareness of the value of tourism, resulting in a growing concern for protecting the natural environment.

Timber – Once the paramount fact of life in British Columbia, the forest products industry remains crucial but not dominant. The annual harvest is 60-70 million cubic meters (78-91 million cubic yards), worth about $17 billion. Virtually all the wood cut is softwood, with lodgepole pine, spruce, hemlock and Douglas fir the leading species. Mills convert about 20 percent of this wood into pulp and paper products; the vast majority, $15 billion worth, is exported to the rest of Canada, the US and overseas. More than 95 percent of the province's roughly 50 million hectares (125 million acres) of productive forestland are owned by the British Columbia government; logging takes place under leases granted to timber companies.

Trade – Trading fish oil, jade and other goods kept First Nations bands in touch. Fur trade brought the first European settlers to the province, and gold, fish and timber in succession bought them prosperity. Today trade remains the linchpin of British Columbia's economy. Vancouver is by far Canada's most active port, shipping huge exports of forest products, grain and mine ores, and handling significant imports of cars, electronic goods and other finished products. The port handles about 75 million tons of cargo a year; more than 63 million tons of that is in bulk commodities such as wheat (from the prairie provinces), ore and timber products.
British Columbia also trades power. Rich in hydroelectric resources, the province transmits more than 12,000 megawatts of electric power to Canada and the US.

Mining – Although gold is still mined in British Columbia, the focus long ago shifted to lesser-value commodities such as copper and coal. The overall value of mineral production is about $5 billion; coal, natural gas, copper and zinc all exceed gold in revenues. Although not in British Columbia, a recent major diamond strike in the Northwest Territories has had a ripple effect in Vancouver, whose stock exchange is a leading capital market for mining ventures.

Agriculture – Despite the relatively small amount of land available to British Columbia farmers (just 3 percent of the total), their contribution to Canada's produce bins is huge. The province leads in production of apples, peaches, pears, grapes and numerous other fruits; the greenhouses of the Fraser delta ship tomatoes, peppers, cucumbers and other produce throughout North America. Overall, dairy products and fruits are the agricultural leaders in British Columbia. Ginseng *(p 336)* has recently assumed great importance in the interior canyons, supplementing the hay and cattle that had been dominant for a century. Although not in the same class as those from California or Europe, Okanagan Valley wines *(p 342)* are gaining recognition. Overall, agriculture accounts for a $17 billion industry in British Columbia.
Fisheries contribute another $1 billion to the provincial economy, with more than 80 species of fish, shellfish and marine plants harvested. Salmon account for half the industry's receipts; the rest encompasses everything from halibut to sea cucumbers.

Tourism and Services – Film and tourism benefit from the province's scenery and diversity and continue to grow in importance. Vancouver has stood in for dozens of other world cities, and British Columbia's islands, coast, mountains and wildlife draw more than 20 million visitors each year, who pour almost $10 billion into the provincial economy. Film contributes another $1 billion or so. The great majority of visitors are Canadian or US residents, the latter having for years taken advantage of the exchange premium the US dollar enjoys over the Canadian.
With more than 17 million passengers a year, Vancouver International Airport ranks as the West Coast's second-busiest (after Los Angeles, California). And the port of Vancouver is a major debarkation point for cruise ships, with nearly 850,000 passengers utilizing British Columbia docks annually.

British Columbia Today

Even after a century and a half of development, British Columbia remains a rugged, dynamic province dominated by its spectacular landscape. There are still just three places, for instance, where modern highways reach from the interior to the coast: down the Fraser River to Vancouver, across the Chilcotin to Bella Coola, and down the Skeena River Valley to Prince Rupert. Relatively unspoiled, the province remains rich in wildlife, with vast numbers of bears—10,000 grizzly and 100,000 black—bald eagles, cougars, deer, wolves, moose, wild sheep and goats, migratory birds and waterfowl. Although in decline, up to 20 million salmon a year course the Fraser River system. And large numbers of gray whales and orcas patrol the coasts.

Planning Your Trip

Citizens of the US visiting Canada need proof of citizenship (a valid **passport**, or a driver's license together with a birth certificate or a voter's registration card). Persons under 18 who are not accompanied by an adult should carry a letter from a parent or guardian stating name and duration of travel in Canada. Students should carry their student identification. All other visitors to Canada must have a valid passport and, in some cases, a **visa**. No vaccinations are required.

For **entry into Canada via the US**, all persons other than US citizens or legal residents are required to present a valid passport. It is advisable to ask the Canadian embassy or consulate in your home country about entry regulations and proper travel documents before traveling.

Customs – Nonresidents may import personal baggage temporarily without payment of duties. Persons of legal age as prescribed by the province or territory may bring into Canada duty-free 200 cigarettes, 50 cigars and some other forms of **tobacco** (contact Revenue Canada at address below). **Alcohol** is limited to 1.14 litres (40 imperial ounces) of wine or spirits, or 24 bottles (355ml or 12 ounces) of beer or ale. All **prescription drugs** should be clearly labelled and for personal use only; it is recommended that visitors carry a copy of the prescription. Canada has stringent legislation on **firearms**. Contact the Automated Customs Information Service ☎ 604-666-0545 (Vancouver) or write Revenue Canada, Customs and Excise, Ottawa, ON, K1A 0L5 for more details.

Getting There

By Air – International and domestic flights to **Vancouver International Airport** (YVR) *(15km/9mi south of downtown;* ☎ *276-6101)* via Air Canada, ☎ 688-5515 or 800-776-3000 (US), Canadian Airlines International, ☎ 800-426-7000 (Canada/US) and other major carriers. Affiliated airlines offer connections to Victoria: Air BC, ☎ 688-5515 and Canadian Regional Airlines, ☎ 800-665-1177 (Canada) or 800-426-7000 (US). **Taxi** to downtown Vancouver *($20-$25)*. Airport **shuttle** Vancouver Airporter *($10;* ☎ *946-8866)*. Airport Limousine Service: ☎ 273-1331. Car rental agencies are located at the airport.

By Bus and Train – Greyhound **bus** service within BC: ☎ 482-8747 (in Vancouver). Greyhound, Maverick Coach Lines *(☎ 662-8051)* and other bus companies serve Vancouver Island *(consult the telephone directory)*. **VIA Rail** connects Victoria to Courtenay and links Vancouver to Toronto, ☎ 800-561-8630 (in BC), or ☎ 800-561-3949 (US); www.viarail.ca. **BC Rail** *(☎ 631-3500)* services Whistler and Prince George from Vancouver .

By Car – Foreign **driver's licenses** are valid for a period of three months. Drivers must carry vehicle registration information and/or rental contract at all times. Vehicle **insurance** is compulsory in BC. US visitors should obtain a Canadian Non-Resident Inter-Province Motor Vehicle Insurance Liability Card (**yellow card**), available from US insurance companies.

By Boat – **BC Ferries** operates 25 different routes connecting 42 ports of call on the coastline and many of the islands. For routes & schedules: BC Ferries, 1112 Fort St., Victoria, BC, V8V 4V2, ☎ 250-386-3431; www.bcferries.bc.ca.

General Information

Visitor Information and Accommodations – The government tourist office produces annually updated guides on accommodations, camping, fishing, skiing and vacation planning. The *BC Travel Guide* suggests driving tours and gives general travel tips. All publications and a map are available free of charge from: **Tourism British Columbia**, Parliament Buildings, Victoria, BC, V8V 1X4; ☎ 250-387-1642 or 800-435-5622 (Canada/US); www.travel.bc.ca. For a listing of **Youth Hostels** contact Hostelling International, #402-134 Abbott St., Vancouver BC, V6B 2K4, ☎ 604-684-7111, www.hihostels.bc.ca.

Currency and Banking – Canadian currency is based on the decimal system (100 cents to the dollar). Bills are issued in $5, $10, $20, $50, $100, $500 and $1,000 denominations; coins are minted in 1 cent, 5 cents, 10 cents, 25 cents, 50 cents, $1 and $2. It is recommended that visitors exchange money at banking institutions to receive the most favorable exchange rate.

Banks are generally open Monday to Friday 9am-5pm. Some banks are open on Saturday morning. Banks at large airports have foreign-exchange counters and extended hours. Traveler's checks in Canadian or American currency are accepted universally. Some institutions may charge a small fee for cashing traveler's checks. Most principal bank cards are honored at affiliated Canadian banks.

Language – English and French are the official languages for all federal and judicial bodies, federally mandated administrative agencies and Crown corporations.

National and Provincial Holidays – The following holidays are observed throughout Canada. Most banks, government offices and schools are closed on these days:

New Year's Day	January 1
Good Friday	Friday before Easter Sunday
Easter Monday	Monday after Easter Sunday
Victoria Day	closest Monday to May 24
Canada Day	July 1
BC Day	1st Monday in August
Labor Day	1st Monday in September
Thanksgiving	2nd Monday in October
Remembrance Day	2nd Wednesday in November
Christmas Day	December 25
Boxing Day	December 26

Road Regulations – Unless otherwise posted, speed limits are 80km/h (50mph) on provincial highways and 50km/h (30mph) in cities. For information on road conditions, call ☎ 604-299-9000 ext. 7623. **Seat belt** use is mandatory. Right turn on red is allowed after coming to a complete stop. The **Canadian Automobile Assn. (CAA)** maintains a 24 hr emergency road service (☎ *800-222-HELP*) for its members. These services are extended to members of the American Automobile Assn. (AAA).

Time Zones – BC is on Pacific Standard Time. Daylight Saving Time is observed from the first Sunday in April to the last Sunday in October.

Taxes – In addition to the national 7% **Goods and Services Tax (GST)**, BC levies a 7% provincial sales tax, and a 3% accommodation tax. Foreign visitors can request a cash **rebate** of the GST of up to $500 for short-term accommodations and for most consumer goods taken out of Canada within 60 days of purchase by submitting original receipts and identification to any participating Canadian Duty Free Shop or by mail. Rebate claims above $500 must be mailed with an application and original receipts. For additional information and rebate forms, contact Revenue Canada, Visitor Rebate Program, 275 Pope Rd., Summerside, PEI C1N 6C6, ☎ 800-668-4748 (in Canada) or 902-432-5608; www.rc.gc.ca.

Liquor Laws – The legal drinking age is 19. Liquor is sold in government stores.

Recreation

Outdoor Activities – The rivers, mountains and many parks of this vast and sparsely populated region offer the outdoor enthusiast a variety of recreational activities. Many **fishing** lodges arrange fly-in packages to remote lakes that attract anglers from around the world. Licenses are required for both saltwater and freshwater fishing, and can be obtained locally. Daily entrance fees to the region's **National Parks and Reserves** range from $2.50-$5. Additional fees are charged for camping, fishing and guided programs. Visitor centers *(open daily late–May–Labor Day; reduced hours the rest of the year)* are usually located at park entrances. All **hikers** in backcountry areas are required to register at the park office before setting out and to check in upon completion of their trip. For additional information, contact Parks Canada, Box 129, Fort Langley, BC V1M 2R5, ☎ 604-666-1280.

Special Excursions – The **Rocky Mountaineer** train journeys through some of the most spectacular mountain scenery in North America during a two-day trip from Vancouver to Jasper or Banff *(departs from Vancouver May–Oct; reservations required; ✗ ⅙ ◻; Rocky Mountaineer Railtours, 1150 Station St., Suite 130, Vancouver, BC, V6A 2X7 ☎ 606-7245 or 800-665-7245 (Canada/US); www.rkymtnrail.com.*

The 21C dawns on a province keenly aware of its prime position along the Pacific Rim—and of both the perils and potential that accompany its shift from past to future, with an ever-growing international visibility. British Columbia forest-product exports have suffered under a European boycott aimed at the still-common (though now considerably less extensive) practice of clear-cutting, leading the largest timber company (MacMillan-Bloedel, recently acquired by Weyerhaeuser) to announce a plan to phase out clear-cuts. Another early 1990s international protest led to curtailment of timber harvest along Clayoquot Sound, the beautiful area on Vancouver Island's west shore that has become a major tourist attraction.

This new focus on renewable values has created a vibrant modern society in which conservation is as important as extraction. The provincial government, which owns more than 90 percent of the land, intends to fold 12 percent of the province into conservation reserves. Ecotourism and outdoor adventure are now key activities in every corner of British Columbia, which boasts some of the world's best fishing, camping, hiking, canoeing and kayaking opportunities.

With an unemployment rate that hovers around 8 percent, British Columbia possesses in reality two separate economies—the healthy economy of Vancouver and Victoria, and the depressed natural-resource-driven economy of the rural areas. Fueled by growth in trade and population, Vancouver is booming; hardly a block in the city's downtown lacks a construction project and Victoria thrives on tourism and government. Elsewhere, the long decline in mining, logging and fishing has led to more than 20 percent unemployment in some isolated areas, though growth in tourism is beginning to help. Throughout the province, trade remains constant, be it logs bound for Asia or Europe or a film shoot in Vancouver. The waterways and river valleys that served as conduits a century ago remain central to British Columbia life, yet modern commerce more and more often revolves around the huge numbers of people who make their way to British Columbia simply to experience the virtues that have drawn so many people to this marvelous land for centuries.

Humpback Whale Breaching

Stuart Westmorland /Tony Stone Images

Vancouver Area

Downtown Vancouver/© Robert Holmes

Perched on a scenic lowland peninsula in the Strait of Georgia, with the spectacular North Shore mountains backing the skyline, the thriving city of Vancouver ranks as the capital of the Pacific Rim at the start of what is widely expected to be the Pacific century. Its magnificent setting offers countless breathtaking views, and it functions as an economic, cultural and artistic bellwether, filling much the same role as San Francisco does in the US. Canada's third-largest city, Vancouver claims one of the continent's most diverse populations, with dozens of European, Asian and First Nations ethnic groups. Its museums hold some of Canada's most important artworks and cultural artifacts; and its glistening steel-and-glass skyline challenges the nearby mountains for visual interest. Traditionally a major shipping and timber industry center, Vancouver now counts tourism as its top employer: More than eight million visitors a year revel in its varied cuisine, parks, shopping and arts.

The greater Vancouver area, a lengthy belt of suburban cities spread along the Fraser River eastward 100km (62mi), holds almost two million people—half the population of British Columbia. Once a pastoral patchwork of farms, fields and forests, the Lower Mainland is now one of Canada's top urban growth areas. The area's mild, but famously rainy, maritime climate is characterized by long, dark, wet winters, ameliorated by lack of snow and glorious light-filled summers. Whether drawn by scenery, weather, recreational or economic opportunity, Vancouver's many new residents are a well-satisfied lot; an international survey in 1997 rated it second in the world for quality of life. As cosmopolitan as the Vancouver metropolis has become, residents remain fond of pointing out that unlimited outdoor recreation—even real wilderness— is just a few miles away, and no amount of growth will change that. In early July, when all the city's gardens are in bloom, sailboats ply the Strait of Georgia, and the late evening sun splashes vermilion across the water and over the tops of The Lions (the twin North Shore mountain knobs). At such times, a more appealing place is hard to imagine.

VANCOUVER★★★

Michelin map 493 B2 and map pp 298-299
Metropolitan Area Population 1,831,665
Tourist Information ☎ 604-683-2000 or www.tourism-vancouver.org

Occupying 113sq km (44sq mi) on a tongue of land between the Fraser River and Burrard Inlet, Vancouver's location affords both aesthetic and practical virtues. The North Shore Mountains provide the scenery, while blocking Arctic weather; and the Strait of Georgia helps moderate the climate. Burrard Inlet is a natural deep-water harbor, the home of Canada's largest port. Like many port cities, Vancouver acts as both a gateway and an ethnic and cultural mixing bowl. Originally founded by Canada's Scotch-English settlers, the city has experienced successive waves of immigration from West and East, all converging on the grounds of numerous First Nations' tribes. Walking Vancouver's streets you are likely to hear English, French, Spanish, German, Japanese, Mandarin, Dutch, Russian, Ukrainian, Italian, Korean, Punjabi and Pharsee, as well as a dozen other tongues, representing both residents and visitors. Luring this polyglot mass is a richly varied menu of mountains and beaches, cafes and seafood restaurants, theaters and sports venues, shops and galleries.

Historical Notes

Of Furs and Gold – Captain George Vancouver first sailed into the Strait of Georgia in 1792; he had been preceded by one year by José Maria Narvaez, a Spanish pilot. Neither at first thought much of the region—an impression not shared by the local Indians, mostly Coast Salish, who had inhabited the area for 9,000 years, peacefully enjoying the sea's rich bounty.

Though Vancouver did not find the fabled Northwest Passage, he did chart Burrard Inlet and claimed the territory for Britain. The next European to pass through was Simon Fraser, the diligent Scot who had painfully fought his way down the Fraser. Despite the fact that early fur traders preferred the Columbia Basin route into the rich northern forests of the interior, Europeans came back to the Fraser Valley two decades later. The present site of Vancouver was not the first focus of settlement in the area. Fort Langley, 25km (15.5mi) up the Fraser, was established by the Hudson's Bay Company as a trading post in 1827. VICTORIA, across the Strait of Georgia on Vancouver Island, also considerably predates Vancouver, and long nurtured dreams of becoming the major city of New Caledonia (as the territory was first named). But the ascendance of railroads made it clear the mainland would ultimately dominate development, and when gold was discovered in the provincial interior in 1858, the Fraser Valley earned instant international attention.

Coming on the Rails – British Columbia was declared a Crown colony in 1858. Its political godfather and first territorial governor, James Douglas, determined to establish the Fraser Valley (not the American Columbia Basin) as the thoroughfare to the goldfields and to ensure the region remained British, set about building the legendary Cariboo Road north to the Cariboo Mountains. Settlers thronged to the area, many turning to more reliable occupations such as farming and logging. The lower Fraser Valley soon became the shipping, agricultural and commercial center of the colony. Still none of this activity focused on Vancouver, which did not even exist until the early 1860s, when a small sawmill was established at Burrard Inlet. Though little timber grew here, what did was high-volume: An 80-acre parcel on English Bay produced nine million board-feet of Douglas fir, including massive 34m (112ft) beams used in Beijing's Imperial Palace. The long-anticipated arrival of the railroad two decades later thrust this obscure site into prominence. British Columbia had agreed to join the Canadian federation if the new country would build a transcontinental rail line. Originally slated to terminate in Port Moody at the east end of Burrard Inlet, the line was pushed through to Vancouver when Canadian Pacific officials became alarmed at rampant land speculation in the former, which had little land to develop. Overnight, Vancouver boomed-and was quickly erased when a June 13, 1886 conflagration leveled the city in less than an hour. Rebuilding began on the spot, and the city's future was foretold that July when the first inbound shipment arrived in Burrard Inlet-tea from China. By the end of 1886 the town had 8,000 residents. The first Canadian Pacific train actually arrived in Vancouver in May 1887; by then the fledgling city had begun to outpace towns such as Port Moody and New Westminster.

The Klondike gold rush of 1897 solidified Vancouver's position as a shipping and supply center; World War I enhanced its importance as an industrial gateway, cementing the city's dependence on resource-based industries such as timber and mining that continues today, although diminished. It was during the early 20C when the three forerunners of MacMillan Bloedel, Canada's largest forest products company, began operating in Vancouver. North Vancouver shipyards supplied boats for the war effort, and a second transcontinental railroad, Canadian National, reached Vancouver in 1916. The next 60 years brought steady, if unspectacular, growth, as the city asserted its position as Western Canada's economic and cultural capital. As Vancouver entered the 1980s, the city yearned for greater prominence outside the confines of the Pacific Ocean and Rocky Mountains, and it settled on a tactic used successfully by many cities before.

Showing Off the City – Expo '86, the massive fair staged around False Creek, vaulted Vancouver into international prominence and indelibly altered its character from a timber and shipping center to a preeminent Pacific Rim metropolis. International attention returned when the city hosted the US-Russia summit between Bill Clinton and Boris Yeltsin in 1993, and its status was solidified by the Asia-Pacific Economic Cooperation summit in 1996. Expo '86 drew 22 million people, the start of a tourism tide that has resulted in approximately 4,000 restaurants, 11,000 hotel rooms, and the second-busiest airport on the West Coast (after Los Angeles). Vancouver is now frequently rated one of the top five destination cities in North America.

The city's growth, already boosted by Expo, reached the boiling point in the early 1990s as wealthy Hong Kong residents, wary of that city's impending transfer to Chinese control, exercised their Commonwealth passports and immigrated to Vancouver (which became briefly known as "Hongcouver"). Hundreds of millions—perhaps billions—of dollars of investment money poured into the city, both in business and real estate; the new immigrants made a practice of purchasing modest existing homes and replacing them with "monster homes" encompassing entire lots and costing $1 million or more. As a result of this influx, North Shore real estate, especially in view-rich West Vancouver, is Canada's most expensive, with hundreds of million-dollar properties. West Vancouver and its neighbor along the road to Whistler, Lions Bay, are both among Canada's top 10 most prosperous communities. Within Vancouver, a tidal wave of condominium construction led to a similar real-estate frenzy; in one year, one broker sold 1,305 condominiums worth a total of $127 million.

The boom years lasted from 1990-96; during the last five years of that period, the Greater Vancouver population rose 230,000, a 14 percent growth rate that made the metropolis the fourth fastest-growing in North America. The Hong Kong influx slowed in 1996, and even reversed after normalcy returned to the Asian city, but Vancouver had been transformed. Today it is more popular with Asian visitors than European; about 500,000 visitors annually come from Asia, most from Japan and Taiwan, compared with 300,000 from Europe.

As Canada's only major Pacific port, Vancouver handles an annual shipping volume of better than $40 billion, making trade the area's second-largest employer. Some 3,000 foreign vessels a year from more than 90 nations make port here, providing jobs for 10,000 locals as shipping agents, chandlers, terminal workers and employees in related marine services. About 85 percent of the container ships transport coal, grain and sulphur. A further 300 cruise ships pass through here every year. The Vancouver Stock Exchange is a world leader for mining company issues and start-up firms, and was the first North American exchange to become fully electronic, abandoning its trading floor in 1990. Vancouver also remains a center for timber industry management, holding the headquarters of MacMillan-Bloedel.

Despite all this economic energy—or perhaps because of it—Vancouver residents thoroughly demonstrate the famous Canadian courtesy and friendliness. You hardly ever hear a car horn, for instance—it's considered rude to honk. The city is quite pedestrian-friendly, especially true downtown, where parking is scarce, traffic is tricky and the visitor is best advised to see the city on foot.

■ MOWtown

With more than $1 billion of activity and up to 200 productions per year, Vancouver ranks with Los Angeles, San Francisco, New York and Toronto as a North American leader in film and video production. When *The X-Files* television series left Vancouver for Los Angeles in 1998, after five years in British Columbia, Vancouverites were chagrined not so much by the show's departure as by the fact that the event earned as much publicity as any other facet of the city's film industry. With so many television movies and series produced here, the city has acquired the nickname, "MOWtown" (for Movie Of the Week). Furthermore, the number of feature films has actually eclipsed that of television movies. Popular films shot in the area include *Carnal Knowledge* (1971), *McCabe and Mrs. Miller* (1971), *The Accused* (1988), *Legends of the Fall* (1994) and *Little Women* (1994); television series include *Millennium* and *Viper*.

US-Canadian exchange rates and cheaper production costs help drive the city's popularity with filmmakers, as does a tax break for foreign-film investors. And moderate weather and a great variety of shooting locations also play leading roles. Vancouver and its surroundings have stood in for locales ranging from Manhattan to Russia. Viewers with sharp eyes may have noticed that some early *X-Files* episodes are set in supposed "Southern" forests that look suspiciously like the Douglas fir fastness of Lighthouse Park. In addition, the legendary Canadian courtesy and restraint have a strong appeal to Hollywood personalities-Vancouverites go quietly about their business when they encounter celebrities. Providing technical support, the Vancouver Film School is a highly regarded institution that helps supply the roughly 30 film crews working at the same time in the city.

Meanwhile, although *X-Files* is gone, it continues to draw money into the city's economy: A local entrepreneur offers half-day tours of locations featured in the series, including the apartment complex where Dana Scully lived. *For information on the "X-Tour," call ☎ 604-609-2770.*

Getting Around

By Public Transportation – Vancouver Regional Transit System operates an integrated network of rapid transit, ferries and buses. Hours of operation vary among the different services. **SkyTrain**, the city's rapid transit, services downtown, Burnaby, New Westminster and Surrey *(daily 5:30am-1am; every 2-5 min)*. **SeaBus**, passenger harbor ferries, operates between Vancouver and the North Shore *(Mon–Sat 6am-12:30am, Sun 8am–11pm; every 15–30min)*. Adult fare during off-peak hours is $1.50; weekdays before 6:30pm fares are based on zone boundaries. Fares are the same for all services; exact fare is required. FareSaver books of 10 tickets *($13.75)* and a DayPass *($6)* are available from ticket machines and outlets. Transfers are free for 90min of unlimited travel. **Bus** service connects SkyTrain and SeaBus at all stations. Buses operate 7 days/week. A *Transit Guide* map *($1.50)* is sold at Ticketmaster outlets and convenience stores. Route information and schedules: ☏ 521-0400.

By Car – Use of public transportation or walking is strongly encouraged within the city, as roads are often congested and street parking may be difficult to find. Metered and garage parking available. Car rentals: Avis, ☏ 606-2847; Hertz, ☏ 688-2411; Tilden, ☏ 685-6111.

By Taxi – Advance Cabs, ☏ 876-5555; Black Top Cabs, ☏ 731-1111; Yellow Cabs, ☏ 681-1111.

General Information

Visitor Information and Accommodations – For information and brochures on points of interest, seasonal events, accommodations, shopping, entertainment, recreation and tour operators, contact Tourism Vancouver, 200 Burrard Street, Vancouver, BC, V6C 3L6, ☏ 683-2000; www.tourism-vancouver.org. **Vancouver Tourist InfoCentre**, 200 Burrard St., plaza level *(open mid-May–Sept daily 8am–6pm; rest of the year Mon–Fri 8:30am–5pm, Sat 9am–5pm)*.
For a listing of **hotels/motels**, contact Tourism Vancouver *(above)*. Reservation services: Beachside B&B Registry, ☏ 922-7773; AAA B&B Ltd.. ☏ 872-0938; Best Canadian B&B Network, ☏ 738-7207. **Youth Hostel**: Hostelling International Vancouver Downtown, ☏ 684-4565 and Vancouver Jericho Beach, ☏ 224-3208.

Local Press – Daily: *The Vancouver Sun* and *The Province. Where Vancouver*, a monthly guide *(free)* to entertainment, shopping and restaurants is available at most hotels.

Entertainment – Consult arts and entertainment supplements in local newspapers *(Thursday edition)* for schedule of cultural events and addresses of principal theaters and concert halls, or call **Arts Hotline** *(☏ 604-684-ARTS)*. The Vancouver Symphony Orchestra plays at Orpheum *(Sept–Jun)*; for schedules & tickets, call ☏ 876-3434. Events are listed weekly in the *Georgia Straight*, the city's alternative newspaper. To purchase tickets, contact the box office or **Ticketmaster**, ☏ 280-4444 (major credit cards accepted).

Sports – BC Lions Football Club play at BC Place Stadium *(Jun–Nov; schedules*, ☏ 583-7747). Vancouver Canadians play baseball at Nat Bailey Stadium *(Apr–Sept; schedules* ☏ 872-5232). Vancouver Canucks stage ice hockey games at GM Place Stadium *(Oct–Apr; schedules* ☏ 899-7400). Vancouver Grizzlies play NBA basketball at GM Place Stadium *(Oct–Apr; schedules* ☏ 899-4667). Hastings Park Race Course offers thoroughbred racing with pari-mutuel betting *(for tickets: Ticketmaster, ☏ 280-4400)*.

Useful Numbers

	☏
Police	911 (emergency) or 717-3321
BC Rail (North Vancouver), *1311 W. 1st St.*	984-5246
VIA Rail, *1150 Station St.*	800-835-3037
BC Ferries (in province)	888-223-3779
Greyhound Lines of Canada (bus)	482-8747
Vancouver International Airport	276-6101
Canadian Automobile Assn., *999 W. Broadway*	268-5600
Shoppers Drug Mart (24 hr pharmacy), *1125 Davie St.*	669-2424
Weather (24 hr)	664-9010

Address Book

Staying in Vancouver

With thousands of hotel rooms, most downtown, Vancouver offers a huge range of accommodation alternatives–elegant and historic, modern and high-tech, hip and stylish. In the summer, the options don't include economy: High season brings high prices and equally high occupancies; summer travelers must reserve well ahead.

The accommodations listed below have been chosen for their location, character, or value for money. All venues are in Vancouver unless otherwise specified. Rates are for a standard room, double occupancy in high season; prices are indicated in US dollars.

$$$$	over $250	$$	$100-$175
$$$	$175-$250	$	under $100

Chateau Whistler – *4599 Chateau Blvd.* ✗ & 🄿 ☎ *604-938-8000 or 800-606-8244. Fax 604-938-2099. www.cphotels.ca.* $$$$ Canadian Pacific property offers upscale elegance at the foot of Blackcomb Mountain in Whistler. 342 rooms.

Hotel Georgia – *801 W. Georgia St.* ✗ & 🄿 ☎ *604-682-5566 or 800-663-1111. Fax 604-642-5579.* $$$$ Recently renovated Art Deco lobby is a decorative marvel at this historic property. 313 rooms.

Hotel Vancouver – *900 W. Georgia St.* & 🄿 ☎ *604-684-3131 or 800-441-1414. Fax 604-662-1924. www.cphotels.ca.* $$$$ Copper-roofed landmark château (1939) epitomizes the Canadian Pacific style; recently renovated. 550 rooms.

Four Seasons – *791 W. Georgia St.* ✗ & 🄿 ☎ *604-689-9333 or 800-268-6282. Fax 604-684-4555.* $$$$ Excellent service and amenities mark one of Vancouver's premier business hotels. 385 rooms.

Sutton Place Hotel – *845 Burrard St.* ✗ & 🄿 ☎ *604-682-5511 or 800-543-4300. Fax 604-682-5511. www.travelweb.com/sutton.html.* $$$$ This glamorous upscale property is favored by members of the film industry. 397 rooms.

Waterfront Centre Hotel – *900 Canada Place Way.* ✗ & 🄿 ☎ *604-691-1991 or 800-441-1414. Fax 604-691-1999. www.cphotels.ca.* $$$$ Classy modern business hotel, this Canadian Pacific property is located across the street from Canada Place. Most rooms have a view of the water. 489 rooms.

Wedgewood – *845 Hornby St.* ✗ & 🄿 ☎ *604-689-7777. www.travel.bc.ca/w/wedgewood. Fax 604-689-7777.* $$$$ Friendly, comfortable boutique hotel just steps away from Robson Street. Comfortable, distinctive rooms were personally decorated by owner Eleni Skalbania. 89 rooms.

Metropolitan Hotel – *645 Howe St.* ✗ & 🄿 ☎ *604-687-1122 or 800-667-2300. Fax 604-643-7267. www.metropolitan.com.* $$$ High-style small hotel focuses on business travelers and has an exceptional health club. 197 rooms.

Residences on Georgia – *1288 W. Georgia St.* & 🄿 ☎ *604-688-0461 or 800-663-1815. Fax 604-891-5141.* $$$ Sophisticated high-tech twin towers; excellent for extended stays. 100 units.

Edgewater Lodge – *8841 Rte. 99, Whistler, BC.* ✗ & 🄿 ☎ *604-932-0688. Fax 604-932-0686. www.edgewater-lodge.com.* $$ Fine lake and mountain views characterize this quiet Whistler retreat on the shores of Green Lake. 12 rooms.

Sylvia Hotel – *1154 Gilford St.* ✗ & ☎ *604-681-9321.* $$ Ivy-covered, 1920s brick landmark along English Bay, near Stanley Park; many kitchenettes. 119 rooms.

© Robert Holmes

Thistledown House – *3910 Capilano Rd., North Vancouver.* ♿ 🅿 ☎ *604-986-7173. Fax 604-980-2939.* **$$** Superbly renovated 1921 Craftsman-style mansion offers elegant, quiet rooms near Grouse Mountain and Capilano Canyon. Free breakfast, tea & cocktails. 5 rooms.

Hostelling International Vancouver – *1114 Burnaby St.* ☎ *604-684-4565. Fax 604-684-4540.* **$** Not only is this the best choice for budget travelers in downtown Vancouver, its West End location is convenient to Stanley Park and Granville Island. 226 beds.

Dining in Vancouver

"West Coast cuisine" is the appellation given to the distinctive British Columbia culinary style that melds Asian and Continental influences with the fresh seafood and the Fraser Valley produce available year-round to Vancouver chefs. Many of Vancouver's most noteworthy restaurants offer some version of this approach. Informality is widespread; business casual dress is acceptable in most restaurants.

The list below represents a sample of some of the city's more popular establishments. Prices (in US dollars) indicate the average cost of an entree, an appetizer or dessert, and a beverage for one person (not including tax and tip, or alcoholic beverages). Reservations are highly recommended for $$$ and $$$$ restaurants.

$$$$ = deluxe (over $50)   **$$** = moderate ($15-$30)
$$$ = expensive ($30-$50)   **$** = inexpensive (under $15)

Bishop's – *2183 W. 4th Ave., Kitsilano.* ☎ *604-738-2025.* **$$$ Continental**. A hospitable atmosphere and dependable elegance mark this high-end Vancouver institution. Dinner only.

C Restaurant – *1600 Howe St., on False Creek.* ♿ ☎ *604-681-1164. www.crestaurant.com.* **$$$ Seafood**. Asian influences melded with Northwest ingredients distinguish this hugely inventive restaurant.

Diva – *645 Howe St., in the Metropolitan Hotel.* ♿ 🅿 ☎ *604-602-7788. www.metropolitan.com.* **$$$ West Coast**. Glitzy décor and flashy cuisine have brought Diva national renown as a capital of West Coast innovation. Favorite pre-theater stop for Vancouverites.

Fleuri – *845 Burrard St., in the Sutton Place Hotel.* ♿ 🅿 ☎ *604-682-5511. www.suttonplace.com.* **$$$ West Coast/Continental**. Sumptuous Sunday brunch. The lounge, Gerard's, is a film-industry hangout.

Lumiere – *2551 W. Broadway.* ☎ *604-739-8185.* **$$$ French**. Chef/owner Robert Feenie incorporates Continental touches in his innovative cuisine. Prix-fixe menu. Dinner only.

Raincity Grill – *1193 Denman St., West End.* ☎ *604-685-7337. www.raincity.com.* **$$$ West Coast**. Owner Harry Kambolis pioneered West Coast cuisine at this English Bay culinary landmark.

Bacchus – *845 Hornby St., in the Wedgewood Hotel.* 🅿 ☎ *604-608-5319.* **$$ Northern Italian**. Mediterranean accents spice the cuisine in this excellent dining room. The lounge is a popular after-work gathering spot; adjoining is a quiet cigar lounge favored by celebrities.

LaRua – *4557 Blackcomb Way, in the Le Chamois Hotel, Whistler, BC.* ♿ ☎ *604-932-5011. www.whistler.net/larua.* **$$ Northern Italian**. Tasty West Coast cuisine with Mediterranean touches make up the menu at this Whistler standout. Dinner daily; lunch summers.

Lilliget Feasthouse – *1724 Davie St., West End.* ☎ *604-681-7044 or 888-681-7044.* **$$ first Nations (Native American)**. Diners here are introduced to a modern take on traditional Coast Salish food, focusing on Northwest seafoods. Dinner only.

Pink Pearl – *1132 E. Hastings St., East Vancouver.* ♿ 🅿 ☎ *604-253-4316.* **$$ Cantonese**. This cavernous East End restaurant, much favored by locals, is a dim sum shrine.

Star Anise – *1485 W. 12th Ave., Broadway district.* ☎ *604-737-1485.* **$$ Indian**. Flavors of the Indian subcontinent embellish West Coast ingredients at this intimate southside dining room. Dinner only.

Buddhist Vegetarian Restaurant – *137 E. Pender St., Chinatown.* ♿ ☎ *604-683-8816.* **$ Asian**. Inconspicuous Chinatown eatery offers highly flavored soups, stews and stir-fries. Great value for the money.

Stepho's Souvlakia – *1124 Davie St.* ♿ ☎ *604-683-2555.* **$ Greek**. Locals love this West End restaurant for its dependable food and great value; lines often wind out the door and down the street.

Vancouver Today – In a city this diverse and energetic, the cultural ferment is dizzying. Sometimes the contrasting dynamics are profound: Vancouver is Canada's timber capital, the headquarters for a half-dozen major forest-products companies; it is also where, in 1971, environmental activists founded Greenpeace. Here, in 1993, city voters endorsed closing down the Stanley Park Zoo, not wishing to keep wild animals caged; yet the beloved Vancouver Aquarium thrives. The West End includes a flourishing gay community, one of the largest in Canada, and several crime-ridden block of Hastings Street *(between Homer and Main Sts.)* is the provincial headquarters of a lucrative marijuana industry—a dubious distinction the city's business establishment would understandably love to change. Yet young Vancouverites are politically and economically motivated, and jobs in the fast-moving high-tech sector have recently surpassed those in the resource industries.

Heading the list of city cultural institutions, the **Vancouver Symphony Orchestra** *(☎ 604-876-3434)*, which plays in the gorgeous Baroque-style Orpheum Theatre, has achieved new stature under the direction of Sergiu Comissiona, who, despite his European background, regularly programs works by British Columbia composers. Likewise, the **Vancouver Opera** has gained much notice for its willingness to stage ground-breaking productions, including a sensational version of Strauss' *Salomé* directed by famed Canadian film director Atom Egoyan. A half-dozen active theater groups, film societies and a thriving nightlife round out the entertainment universe in Vancouver. On any given night visitors can avail themselves of cultural presentations ranging from chamber music to improv comedy to Hong Kong hip-hop.

Although chain-store excess has invaded the Vancouver suburbs, the central city offers hundreds of small shops, cafes and independent enterprises, more resembling a European city than the North American norm. The best shopping is found downtown along **Robson Street** *(between Burrard and Denman Sts.)* and south of False Creek in the **Broadway and Fourth Avenue** districts.

Vancouver has been sardonically described by local writer Allan Fotheringham as the Canadian city with the best climate and the worst weather. It does rain frequently from November to May, and when it is not raining, gray skies are common. However, Canada's major eastern seaboard cities actually receive more precipitation (including much more snow) than Vancouver's 91cm (36in) annual average, and temperatures are moderate year-round, rarely dipping below freezing, rarely rising above 32°C (90°F). Snowfall is unusual in the city, and the hard-earned reward for unremit-ting months of damp weather comes in July, August and September, when rain is rare, the sky is an infinite blue and temperatures are balmy during blissfully long days. May, June and October offer much pleasant weather also, although not as reliably. Even in summer, bring at least a windbreaker; the cooling breeze off the water means nighttime temperatures hover consistently around 15°C (50°F).

All these facets add up to a vigorous, delightful city, rich in cultural attractions, rel-atively prosperous and unsurpassably blessed by nature. City advocates are fond of pointing out that the Vancouver visitor can ski, sail and golf all in the same day; have dinner in a national-class restaurant that evening; and retire to a room in one of the city's many deluxe hotels. And when such full days deplete your supply of energy, vigorous Vancouver has a way of re-supplying you as you start over again the next day.

★★DOWNTOWN
2 days. Map pp 292-293

Downtown Vancouver is an ever-bustling metropolitan center that manages to maintain a very human ambience. The 40-story office towers of the financial dis-trict between Granville and Burrard Streets, north of Georgia Street, are interspersed with numerous fountains, plazas and gardens, and some heritage buildings remain along Georgia and Hastings. Nearby huge condominium com-plexes enable thousands of people to live within blocks of downtown. Despite the high-energy atmosphere, Canadian manners are in force: Most drivers will stop on secondary streets to let pedestrians cross, though don't expect the same cour-tesy on the main thoroughfares. **Robson Street** from Burrard west to Denman is a popular shopping district packed with boutiques, gift shops, cafes and people, day and night. At least a dozen very good restaurants are found along this stretch, as are several of the downtown area's huge selection of excellent hotels. A few blocks east stands **The Bay** *(Georgia and Granville Sts.)*, a massive stone Neoclassical building housing the Hudson's Bay Company store, a direct descen-dant of the company that inaugurated Canada's development more than 300 years ago.

Three blocks northeast on Granville, the venerable former **Canadian Imperial Bank of Commerce** *(Hastings and Granville Sts.)* dates from 1908 and boasts Neoclassical arches and columns worthy of this stalwart Canadian institution. Just across to the north, the **Sinclair Centre** *(757 W. Hastings St.)* is Vancouver architect Richard Henriquez' handsome and respectful restoration of four historic buildings (constructed 1910-37)-the Post Office, Customs Examining Warehouse, Federal Building and Winch Building-joined by a two-level atrium courtyard. At the foot of Granville, the grand 1912 **Waterfront Station** *(601 W. Cordova St.)* once served as the western terminus of the Canadian Pacific Railway; a 1978 restoration converted it into an office-retail complex and SeaBus station; interior murals depict Canadian landscapes. The **Dominion Building,** *(207 W. Hastings St. at Hamilton St.),* claimed the title of tallest building in the British Empire at its completion in 1908. Its distinctive, orange-hued facing and bizarre turban-shaped brass cap were designed to make it stand out; it still does today. Two blocks east, the **Sun Tower** *(100 W. Pender St.)* also briefly became the tallest in the Empire, in 1914. The extravagant copper dome atop the building competes for attention with the nine caryatids (maidens) supporting an entablature halfway up the 17-story tower.

Tourism Vancouver InfoCentre, a massive compendium of information about the city and the whole province, is located in the Waterfront Centre complex at the foot of Burrard Street *(p 285).*

★★**Canada Place** – *999 Canada Place Way.* ☎ *604-775-8687.* If any physical edifice is Vancouver's symbol, it's this three-block-long sail-topped structure that extends into Burrard Inlet on a 1927-vintage pier supported by 6,000 concrete pilings. The facility's striking design, by architect Eberhard Zeidler, recalls the days when clipper ships sailed across the Pacific into Burrard Inlet. The most prominent remnant of Expo '86, Canada Place now houses the city's convention and exhibition center; the deluxe Pan Pacific Hotel; the city's Board of Trade and World Trade Center; an **IMAX Theatre** with a five-story screen and seat-shaking digital sound *(located on the upper deck at the extreme north end of the pier; open Apr–Oct daily noon–10pm; rest of the year daily noon–4pm & 7pm–10pm; closed Dec 25; $8-$12;* ☎ *604-682-4629 or 800-582-4629; www.imax.com/vancouver);* and various offices and stores. The **promenade** level that circles the pier affords excellent **views**★★ of downtown, Stanley Park, North Vancouver and the often snow-capped mountains beyond. Numerous information panels offer a concise overview of the history of Vancouver and British Columbia. With the building's tall white sails at your back and flags snapping in the breeze, you almost feel as though you're on one of the many vessels that ply the inlet.

Owned by a Canadian federal agency, Canada Place serves as the home dock for Vancouver's thriving cruise industry. The five sails that crown the building are Teflon-coated fiberglass (the same material that roofs B.C. Place Stadium), and have surpassed the designers' original expectations for longevity. Long thought to be a knock-off of Sydney's famed Opera House, the Canada Place design now strikes most observers as the inspiration for Denver International Airport, the sails atop which mimic the peaks of the Rockies as well as Canada Place. The latter's sails enclose the vast 16,000sq m (172,000sq ft) exhibit space beneath them; a 244m (800ft) pier extension that will house expanded cruise ship and convention space is scheduled for completion in 2003.

© Robert Holmes

Canada Place

★**Marine Building** – *355 Burrard St.* Formerly the dominant building on the Vancouver skyline, this 1930 Art Deco edifice was also briefly the tallest building in the British Empire. Though somewhat dwarfed now by the taller glass-and-metal towers that surround it, the 21-story building retains the distinction of its remarkable design. Considered one of the finest Deco office buildings in the world, it boasts terra-cotta and tile embellishments in the form of bas-reliefs, friezes, gargoyles, statues, frescoes and inlaid and embossed figuring. Builder J.W. Hobbs told architects McCarter & Nairne "the sky's the limit," and they took him seriously. The overall theme is the sea and its gifts to Vancouver, ranging from food to trade goods; the arch over the Burrard Street main entrance depicts a ship's prow with Canada geese outlined against the sunset, while around the building's exterior runs a masterful frieze of sea horses and dozens of other marine creatures. Inside the lobby, which was intended to evoke a Mayan temple, a stunning **floor mosaic** delineates the zodiac.

① Dorothy Grant Boutique

Map p. 293. Sinclair Centre, 757 W. Hastings St. ☎ 604-681-0201. Haida artist Dorothy Grant translates traditional First Nations designs into "wearable art" decorated with tribal regalia. The high-fashion apparel is colorful and dramatic, sure to make the wearer stand out. With a small and pricey inventory, the store's carefully chosen selection is as entertaining to view as gallery art: Her flowing felt and wool coats and dresses feature appliqués in customary tribal patterns, with the more vivid articles fetching up to $300. The boutique occupies a space on the promenade level of Sinclair Centre.

Canadian Craft Museum – *639 Hornby St. Open Jun–Aug Mon–Fri 10am–5pm (Thu 9pm). Sat 10am–5pm, Sun noon–5pm. Rest of the year Mon & Wed–Sat 10am–5pm (Thu 9pm), Sun noon–5pm. $5.* ♿ ⊡ ☎ *604-687-8266.* Located in the courtyard behind Cathedral Place, an airy, light-filled modern structure is devoted to ceramic, textiles, glass, jewelry, metal, wood and other fine crafts from Canada and abroad. Four to five exhibits are shown each year; the gift shop has a well-chosen selection of objects.

Across the street at the **Hong Kong Bank of Canada** *(885 W. Georgia St.)*, the vast three-story atrium lobby is used as a space for art exhibits. Swinging above is Allan Storey's **Pendulum★**, a 1986 installation rated one of the most popular pieces of modern art in Vancouver. The 1,600kg (3,250lb), 27m (89ft) buffed-aluminum tube describes a 6m (20ft) arc through the air.

★**Christ Church Cathedral** – *Georgia and Burrard Sts. Open year-round Mon–Wed & Fri 10am–4pm, Thu 7:30am–4pm, Sun 7:30am–10pm. Sat & holiday hours vary.* ♿ ☎ *604-682-3848.* Vancouver's oldest church building maintains a low but solid profile opposite the towering Hotel Vancouver. The 1889 Gothic-style stone structure conveys the odd impression of being much larger once you're inside. Its Douglas-fir framing and elaborate woodwork are warmly lit by numerous stained-glass windows, some imported from England. Next door, **Cathedral Place** (1990) is a modern office tower that was expressly designed to mirror the styles of its venerable neighbors: The copper roof and carved stone lions reflect the Hotel Vancouver across the street, and the massive stone first story melds with the cathedral.

★**Hotel Vancouver** – *900 W. Georgia St. at Burrard St. ☎ 604-684-3131.* Long considered one of Vancouver's quintessential institutions, the 15-story Hotel Vancouver (1939) is a copper-roofed stone massif built in the French château style by Canadian National Railways. The lengthy construction period, owing to the Depression, means the hotel contains elements of several ornamental styles, including Art Deco and Art Moderne; the stonework of the former and polished metal of the latter are both evident in the lobby. Outside, the lion gargoyles represent the two Lions peaks on the North Shore skyline; other gargoyles portray Indian chiefs and mythological figures.

One block down, the 1927 **Hotel Georgia** *(Georgia and Howe Sts.; ☎ 604-682-5566)* features a handsome lobby, lavishly decorated with brass, hand-carved mahogany and marble. The hotel's second-floor ballroom contains an interior balcony, and the basement lounge presents good live jazz and R&B.

★★**Vancouver Art Gallery** – *750 Hornby St.; entrance on Robson between Hornby and Howe. Open Apr–Oct daily 10am–5:30pm (Thu 9pm). Rest of the year Tue–Sun 10am–5:30pm (Thu 9pm). Holidays noon–5pm. $8.* ✕ ☎ *604-662-4719. www.vanartgallery.bc.ca.* This massive 1911 Neoclassical structure was, like so many British Columbia edifices, designed by Francis Rattenbury of Victoria, who also designed the Empress Hotel and Parliament Buildings in VICTORIA. The granite-block building served as the Vancouver Courthouse until 1974, and was

Courtesy Vancouver Art Gallery VAG 42.3.11

Big Raven (1931) by Emily Carr

transformed into the city's art museum in 1983. Part of the attraction itself, the imposing building soars to a seven-story-high domed center with a skylight. The back, or southern section of the complex, the annex designed by British architect Thomas Hooper, houses administrative offices; the steps along Robson are a hugely popular site for demonstrations and youthful hanging out. The building and its grounds have appeared in innumerable films and television movies.

On three levels, spacious exhibit rooms are devoted to traveling shows and to leisurely examination of a few Canadian artists at a time—some from the permanent collection of 7,000 works—recently including an intriguing photo/video exhibition by local artist Stan Douglas. One of the museum's highlights is an extensive **collection★** of the works of acclaimed British Columbia artist **Emily Carr** *(p 302)*, whose distinctive approach incorporates both First Nations decorative styles and Carr's personal, somewhat dark vision of British Columbia's natural world. Her depictions of deep, dusky old-growth forests, native villages and the ravages of logging helped form indelible public impressions of British Columbia. With her work long ignored, Carr willed her vast store of paintings to the Vancouver Art Gallery, largely because it had been one of the few institutions willing to show her art.

★**Robson Square and Law Courts** – *Bounded by Robson, Howe, Nelson and Hornby Sts.* A lovely terraced oasis surrounded by office buildings and restaurants provides midday respite for office workers and a gathering place for public events. Vancouver architect Arthur Erickson's 1979 design gives the square numerous steps and levels, interspersed among garden beds, pools and waterfalls, in a style reminiscent of Frank Lloyd Wright's Fallingwater. The courthouse squats south of the square, enclosed on one side by a huge, slanting steel-framed panel of glass.

★**Orpheum Theatre** – *884 Granville St. For performance schedule check the Talking Yellow Pages ☎ 604-299-9000 or www.city.vancouver.bc.ca/theatres.* Vancouver's grande dame of vintage theaters, the ornate 1927 Orpheum was designed by vaudeville circuit architect Marcus Priteca in a Spanish Baroque style, with numerous "Moorish" columns and arches, crystal chandeliers, decorative wall sconces, faux brass embellishments, etched-glass panels and a barreled and coffered lobby ceiling. In the 2,780-seat auditorium, a gargantuan chandelier is suspended beneath a muraled dome in which, legend has it, some of the angels and cherubs depict actual Vancouverites. Bought by the city of Vancouver in the mid-1970s, the Orpheum is now the home of the **Vancouver Symphony Orchestra** *(☎ 604-876-3434)*, and is usually open to the public only during scheduled performances.

★★**Library Square** – *350 W. Georgia St. at Homer St. Open year-round Mon–Thu 10am–8pm, Fri–Sat 10am–5pm. Sun 1pm–5pm Sept–May only. Closed major holidays.* ✗ ♿ ▣ *☎ 604-331-3600. www.vpl.vancouver.bc.ca.* Renowned Canadian architect Moshe Safdie's breathtaking nine-story 1995 building, based on the Roman Colosseum, houses the main branch of the Vancouver Public Library. The semicircular library, made of concrete mixed with crushed granite, is offset by a semicircular annex and office tower. Between them an enclosed arcade holds shops and cafes; even when the weather is poor, library patrons can savor a cup of coffee at cafe tables flooded by natural light. The whole is surrounded by a brick plaza that sets the library off from the streetscape. Built over 26 months at a cost of $156 million—the largest publicly-funded project in Vancouver history—the 36,270sq m (390,000sq ft) library holds 1.2 million items and can accommodate 1,200 patrons at tables and chairs scattered throughout, including delightful, unique reading nooks secreted in the odd-angle corners.

Holy Rosary Cathedral – *646 Richards St. at Dunsmuir St. Open year-round Mon–Sat 6:15am–6pm, Sun 7am–9:30pm.* 👤 ☎ *604-682-6774.* The site for this sturdy sandstone and granite edifice was selected in 1885 when the parish priest picked out the tallest tree on the skyline. That long-ago fir has been replaced by the Catholic cathedral's 66m (217ft) steeple, which tops the building that was completed in 1900. Fifteen exceptional stained-glass windows light the interior, where Pope John-Paul II sang Mass on his Vancouver visit in 1984. The cathedral's pillars exhibit a common late-19C technique in which paint was applied to ordinary stone to simulate marble. The massive organ has 2,468 pipes.

★**Lookout! at Harbour Centre Tower** – *555 W. Hastings St. at Seymour St. Open Apr–Oct daily 8:30am–10:30pm. Rest of the year daily 9am–9pm. $9.* ⅄ 👤 ☎ *604-689-0421. www.harbourcentretower.com.* A heart-stopping exterior elevator whisks visitors up 167m (551ft) to the top of Vancouver's tallest building for expansive, 360-degree views★★★ from the observation deck (just under a revolving restaurant), which take in the business district, Chinatown, Stanley Park, the mountains and the harbor. Informative panels provide an overview of the city and its port.

Additional Sights

West End – *Downtown northwest of Broughton St.* City officials proudly advertise the West End as the most densely populated urban neighborhood in North America, with its towering apartment and condominium complexes vying for views of Stanley Park, False Creek and the North Shore. **Denman Street**, with myriad small stores and cafes, is a worth a stroll. At **St. Paul's Anglican Church** *(1130 Jervis St., ☎ 604-685-6832)* parishioners have painted a Medieval labyrinth, patterned after one in Chartres Cathedral, on a gymnasium floor; walking it is an intense meditative exercise *(Mon–Fri daily 8:30am–9:30am, Sat 10am–noon, Sun 9:30am–noon).* At **English Bay Beach**★★ *(Beach Ave. and Denman St.)* parks officials maintain a series of palm gardens here as testimony that this is ground zero for Vancouver's balmy climate—and lifestyle. On a sunny summer afternoon, with the gardens in bloom, the palms reaching skyward and the westering sun warming the sand, hundreds of West End residents enjoy the languorous, almost Mediterranean scene. Along the promenade, which connects to the Stanley Park seawall, artists and craftmakers set up shop on fair days. At the **English Bay Bathhouse**, swimmers may change and shower; kayak and sailboard rentals are available here as well.

Roedde House – *1415 Barclay St. at Broughton St. Visit by guided tour (45min) only, year-round Tue–Fri and 2nd & 4th Sun of every month 2pm. $4.* ☎ *604-684-7040. www.roeddehouse.org.* This 1893 Queen Anne mansion with a polygonal tower was built to afford views of the bay for bookbinder Gustav Roedde. Supposedly designed by Francis Rattenbury, the famed architect of Victoria's Parliament and Empress Hotel, the house functions as a museum to late-19C West End life. Restored in 1984, the three-story house is furnished in period with nine rooms on the ground and second floors open to the public. The house is part of **Barclay Heritage Square**, which includes a charming Victorian garden.

★**BC Sports Hall of Fame & Museum** – 🧒 *B.C. Place, 777 Pacific Blvd. S., Gate A. Open year-round daily 10am–5pm. $6.* ⅄ 👤 ▣ ☎ *604-687-5520.* An exhaustive compendium of sports memorabilia includes an entertaining look at the history of sports in the province, from gold-miner snowshoe races to the 1994-95 Stanley Cup excitement (in which the Vancouver Canucks lost to the New York Rangers). Two inspirational exhibits depict the exploits of Terry Fox and Rick Hansen, the latter a British Columbia resident and paraplegic who spanned the globe on his wheelchair. Vancouver-area resident Fox fired the world's imagination with his 1979 campaign to run across Canada after losing a leg to cancer; he made it from Nova Scotia to Alberta before his advancing disease forced him to abandon the run. The museum is found on the northwest side of the 1983 **B.C. Place Stadium**★ a 60,000-seat facility designed by Phillips Barratt and considered the world's largest air-supported domed amphitheater *(visit by 1 hr 30min guided tour only early–Jun–Labor Day Wed & Fri 11am & 1pm; $6;* 👤 ▣ ☎ *604-669-2300; www.bcplacestadium.com).* The stadium's Teflon and fiberglass roof is inflated by huge fans and secured with steel cables. Containing heating elements to melt winter snow, the roof is self-cleaning with the aid of rainfall and translucent enough that artificial lighting is rarely required. A glass-enclosed concourse on the upper level offers panoramic city **views**. With a circumference of 360m (1,181ft) and a height of 60m (197ft), the stadium is home to the BC Lions professional football team, and countless trade shows and exhibitions are held here.

VANCOUVER

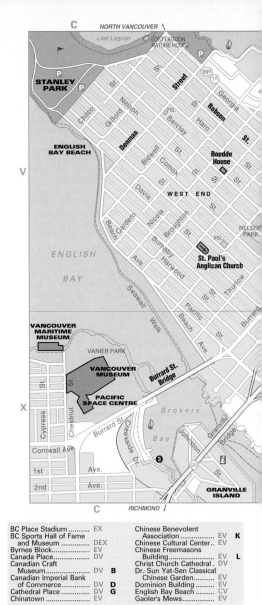

Science World – 🧒 *1455 Quebec St. at Terminal Ave. Open year-round Mon–Fri 10am–5pm, weekends 10am–6pm. Closed Dec 25. $11.75, children $7.75.* 🍴 ♿ 📶 ☎ *604-268-6363. www.scienceworld.bc.ca.* One of the last major legacies of Expo '86, Science World's 47m (155ft) geodesic dome, popularly called the "golf ball," was the fair's Expo Centre. Today, this is the sort of educational experience kids (and parents) love, because almost everything within is some sort of game. The fun starts at the entrance with the Tower of Bauble, a whimsical kinetic sculpture moved from an inland British Columbia shopping mall. Inside, two levels of exhibits offer scores of games, puzzles, projects and other interactive attractions, covering topics that range from math to mining. Visitors can learn how optical illusions work, how waves sweep the ocean and how gold ore is processed. Highlights include a 3D laser theater, a stage devoted to daily science demonstrations, and the **Alcan Omnimax Theatre**, containing a five-story-high domed screen.

GASTOWN & CHINATOWN *1 day. Map p 293.*

Visitors should exercise caution traveling Hastings Street between Homer and Main. Hastings is the center of Western Canada's drug traffic—especially for heroin and marijuana—and prostitution and violence have become common. Best to avoid this neighborhood after dark. In the daytime, it's safe to walk from Gastown to Chinatown along Carrall Street.

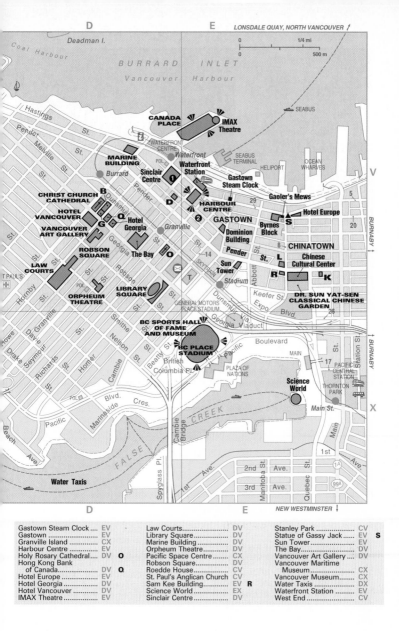

★**Gastown** – Running along Water Street between Richards and Carrall Streets, the well-known Gastown district encompasses the original site of settlement in Vancouver. Here the city's first mills processed timber cut along nearby shores and rivers; mill workers had to go all the way to New Westminster to carouse, until "Gassy Jack" Deighton—so-called owing to his garrulousness—opened a saloon here in 1867. Today, the site of the Globe Saloon is marked by a **statue** of Gassy Jack in a small plaza at the intersection of Carrall and Water Streets. Threatened by demolition proposals, the area was designated a historic district by the provincial government in 1971 and transformed into a thriving three-block area of shops, galleries and cafes. Though Gastown is generally assumed to be named after Jack Deighton, a story persists that a pocket of natural gas in the area originally produced its name. The attractive area between Carrall and Richards Streets combines restored buildings of the late 19C with modern structures that blend with their surroundings; gaslights and shops lend the area a quaint atmosphere.

Gastown Steam Clock – *Cambie and Water Sts.* This local landmark was built in 1977 as part of the district's restoration. Its whistle, which marks the quarter-hour, runs on waste steam from nearby building heating systems; the much-photographed clock itself is actually electric.

Gastown

A block east, the **Gaoler's Mews** *(north side of Water St.)* was the site of a 19C customs house, constable's cabin and log jail; today it holds a compact warren of shops and cafes, as well as several galleries devoted to First Nations arts and crafts, selling totem poles, ceremonial masks, carved soapstone and many other items, at a wide range of prices.

Byrnes Block – *South side of Water St. between Carrall and Abbott Sts.* Just behind the Gassy Jack statue, Byrnes Block ranks as the premier historic building in the area. The 1886 brick structure is ornamented with pediments and pilasters. Across the small square at the intersection of Water, Carrall and Powell Streets, the **Hotel Europe** *(43 Powell St.)* was Vancouver's first reinforced-concrete building (1908); though the lobby is closed to the public, you can peer in at a glistening tile frieze and ornate brass stairway banister.

★★**Chinatown** – North America's second largest such district (after San Francisco's) is best visited afoot. Its two main streets—Pender and Keefer, from Carrall to Gore—are a wondrous cacophony of sights, sounds, smells, tastes and textures, and a morning spent wandering up one and back down the other not only leads past the few notable sights, it takes you by dozens of small shops, restaurants and food vendors that make up the real character of the district. Bins of exotic fruits and vegetables spill out on the sidewalk; the musty scent of mysterious herbs and spices fills the air, while the aroma of fried and roasted food tempts the taste buds. Here, foreign adventure is as simple as sampling tiny, whole spit-roasted quails basted with tamarind and honey, or the golden-skinned sweet-and-sour "dragon fruit." Wind the journey up with a tea ceremony at one of a half-dozen tea shops, with ginseng tea, perhaps, or a rare jasmine blend—and you'll have truly traveled to a different land, all in the space of a few blocks.

During the 1880s, some 17,000 Chinese immigrants arrived in British Columbia to work on the Canadian Pacific Railway. With the railroad completed and no provision made to take the laborers back home, many Chinese settled in this part of Vancouver, taking up such occupations as logging, farming, peddling and laundry cleaning. Though this bachelor

2 Sikora's Classical Records

Map 293. 432 W. Hastings St. ☎ *604-685-0625.* An inconspicuous storefront at the edge of the Gastown district opens into a serious music lover's treasure trove with bin after bin of CDs, almost exclusively of classical music. With approximately 10,000 titles, Sikora's offers more than five times the usual inventory of mainstream music stores. Not only can customers browse among a dozen versions of, say, Mahler's "Resurrection Symphony" (Tragic Symphony No. 6), they can ask the store's staff which is best and receive knowledgeable answers. There are smaller sections devoted to Celtic and New Age music as well, plus used CDs, vinyl records and classical music books.

society was at first crowded, the population began to decline with the passage of the restrictive Chinese Immigration Act of 1923. After World War II, the act was repealed, and Chinatown again bustled with activity as families began to grow and prosper. Chinese celebrations, restaurants and grocery stores soon began attracting tourists, further strengthening the bonds of this ethnic community. Chinatown was formally designated a historic district in 1971.

Pender Street – One of Chinatown's main thoroughfares, Pender Street contains some of the district's most interesting architecture. The **Sam Kee Building** *(southwest corner of Pender and Carrall Sts.)*, considered by Ripley's Believe It or Not the thinnest building in the world, measures a mere 1.8m (6ft) wide and two stories tall, so built because of a property dispute. Farther along Pender stand several examples of early 20C buildings—some still housing tongs, or benevolent associations—exhibiting the recessed balconies that are distinctive to Chinatown. One of the best is the **Chinese Freemasons Building** *(northwest corner of Pender and Carrall Sts.)*, a 1907 three-story structure, reputed to be the secret residence of Dr. Sun Yat-Sen when he visited Vancouver; here Sun Yat-Sen and the freemasons worked to overthrow the Manchu government in China. Between Columbia and Main Street is the **Chinese Benevolent Association** *(no. 108)*, a lavishly painted four-story 1909 structure.

★ **Dr. Sun Yat-Sen Classical Chinese Garden** – *578 Carrall St. (behind Chinese Cultural Centre on Pender St.). Open May–mid-Jun daily 10am,–6pm. Mid-Jun–Sept daily 9:30am–7pm. Rest of the year daily 10am–4:30pm. Closed Jan 1 & Dec 25. $7.50. ⑤ ☎ 604-689-7133. www.discovervancouver.com/sun.* This serene and graceful $5 million homage to classical Chinese garden design was built by artisans from Suzhou, using materials shipped from China to create the first such garden outside that country. The courtyards, colonnades, pavilions, meditation rooms, pools and plantings represent a Ming Dynasty (14C-17C) garden; the four elements of classical Chinese garden design—buildings, rocks, plants and water—are evident at every turn. Pine, bamboo and flowering plum trees grow amid sculpted rocks, water, arched bridges and covered walkways. Thick masonry walls, topped by intricately curved, hand-fired roof tiles, keep the city noise at bay. The garden is part of the larger, equally serene **Dr. Sun Yat-Sen Park**, which houses the **Chinese Cultural Center** and its own meditation garden with a large, placid pond and weeping willows. Both gardens honor **Sun Yat-Sen** (1866-1925), the father of modern China, whose efforts as a statesman and revolutionary led to the downfall of the Manchu dynasty in 1911.

★★★STANLEY PARK *1 day. Map p 298.*

Vancouver's most outstanding attraction occupies a matchless 405 ha (1,000-acre) **site**★★★ at the tip of a peninsula east of downtown Vancouver, with the North Shore Mountains in the background. Home to deep forests and thousands of animals, as well as horticultural gardens, activity centers and innumerable small delights, the park is crisscrossed by hiking trails built on old logging skid roads. Most human activity is confined to the outer perimeter, especially the hugely popular seawall promenade, the formal gardens and the Vancouver Aquarium.

Considerable legend attends to Stanley Park's establishment, often cited as an astounding example of frontier foresight. For centuries a popular spot with aboriginal inhabitants, the peninsula was declared a military reserve in 1859 by colonial authorities mindful of the rumored imminence of American incursion. In the decades following, contract loggers "high-traded" the area, selectively removing the best trees in many spots. The Vancouver City Council displayed progressive thinking in 1886 by petitioning Ottawa to convert the reserve to a city park—the council's very first resolution. The park was also the key facet of a real-estate development scheme: Speculators allied with the Canadian Pacific Railroad offered for sale choice West End lots, advertising their location near the park.

Stanley Park was opened in 1888, and was formally dedicated the following year by its namesake, Lord Peter Stanley, Canada's governor-general. According to contemporary accounts, during the dedication ceremony Stanley "threw his arms to the heavens, as though embracing within them the whole of one thousand acres of primeval forest, and dedicated [the park]: 'To the use and enjoyment of people of all colors, creeds and customs, for all time.'" A statue of Stanley commemorating the occasion occupies a small rise just past the Georgia Street entrance to the park, near the Rose Garden.

More than a century of uninterrupted growth has transformed the woods here into mature maritime forest. Red alder and big-leaf maple are the dominant hardwoods. Douglas fir, western hemlock and the occasional Sitka spruce tower skyward, but the showpiece trees of Stanley Park are its **Western red cedars**, many mature specimens of which stand like red-barked beacons approaching 3m (10ft) in diameter. The park's finest trees can be seen along the Beaver Lake, Bridle Path, Third Beach and Merilees trails. Common throughout the park are the **remnant stumps** left by early loggers, still exhibiting the notches for springboards on which fallers perched to saw through the trees. Many of these stumps have become "nurse logs" on which young trees take root.

Totem Poles in Stanley Park

© Robert Holmes

Park officials manage 600 acres of forest as wilderness and 400 acres, most of those at the southeastern end, as cultivated parkland. Much loved by residents and visitors alike, Stanley Park today attracts more than eight million visitors a year.

Visiting the Park – *Open daily year-round.* ⚓ ♿ ☐ ☎ *604-257-8400. www.parks.vancouver. bc.ca. Note that it is illegal to feed Stanley Park's wild animals. The Lost Lagoon Nature House (just past the end of Alberni St.) offers park maps and informational brochures. To access the park by car, stay in the far right lane of Georgia Street and follow the overhead sign. Traffic is mostly one-way counterclockwise; parking is metered and difficult to find on weekends and throughout the summer. A daylong pedestrian circuit, following the seawall, will take* the visitor to the park's best features, including the separately run Vancouver Aquarium and most of those described in the scenic drive. The free **Stanley Park Shuttle** *(Jun–mid-Sept daily 10am–6:30pm)* circles the park, stopping at 14 key spots.

★**Scenic Drive** – *About 1 hr. 10km (6mi).* Circling the park in a counterclockwise direction, the drive begins and ends at Georgia Street. The **totem poles**★ near Hallelujah Point include examples of work representing the Kwakiutl, Nisga'a and Haida Nations. Local inhabitants harvested herring and shellfish from the tideflats and shallow waters of nearby Coal Harbour. A bit farther along, **Lumberman's Arch**, a 1948 construction made of Douglas fir logs occupies the site of a historic Coast Salish village. **Prospect Point**★, at 64m (210ft) the park's highest spot, affords a splendid **view**★ of the Lions' Gate Bridge, First Narrows and the North Shore. **Ferguson Point** offers **views** across the Strait of Georgia, and access to **Third Beach**★, a quarter-mile expanse of west-facing golden sand and a choice, relatively uncrowded spot on a warm afternoon. Park officials position drift logs along the sand to provide privacy for sunbathers; a concession stand above the beach offers refreshments. The **Teahouse Restaurant** *(☎ 604-669-3281)* at Ferguson Point offers fresh, well-prepared food and fine vistas from nearly every table. **Second Beach**★ is known more for its swimming pool than for the beach itself, which is a short expanse of sand. The heated freshwater pool replaced the original saltwater draw-and-fill impoundment in 1994. A putting course lies nearby, surrounded by rhododendrons.

Pipeline Road cuts north across the park's eastern half, enabling vehicle access to the Vancouver Aquarium, and the **Variety Kids Farmyard** 🧒 *(open Apr–Sept daily 11am–4pm; rest of the year weekends 11am–4pm; ☎ 604-257-8530)* a small domestic animals petting zoo. Close by, a **miniature railway** features locomotives which are replicas of historic engines, including Engine 374 from the first Canadian Pacific Railway transcontinental train in 1887; children enjoy rides through the forested area.

★**Formal Gardens** – The **Rose Garden** and landscaped hillock just north of the Georgia Street entrance to Stanley Park are at their best in May and June, with numerous beds of roses ranging from traditional floribundas to modern hybrid teas. The **Ted & Mary Greig Rhododendron Gardens**★, across Lost Lagoon south of the rose gardens, contain hundreds of hybrid rhododendrons and azaleas that bloom from January to June in a myriad of colors and blossom formations. Throughout the southeastern portion of the park, flowering cherries, plums, crabapples and other trees and shrubs brighten the grounds from January (witch-hazel and winter-cherry season) to June.

★★Stanley Park Seawall – Conceived in 1916 by early park commissioner M.S. Logan, this marvelous promenade was the lifework of master stonemason James Cunningham (1878-1963). Working 46 years (long past his official retirement) Cunningham and his colleagues carefully placed thousands of 46kg (101lb) blocks along the seawall's 9.5km (5.9mi) length. The result is a magnificent accomplishment artfully molded to the park's meandering shoreline but able to withstand winter's worst. Offering easy access to many points of interest not on the road, a walk (or bike or run) around the seawall is an exhilarating experience that begins with stupendous **views★★** of the downtown skyline; swings around to reveal Burrard Inlet, North Vancouver and the North Shore Mountains; then passes under the Lions' Gate Bridge; turns south to open up views across the Strait of Georgia to Vancouver Island; then heads east along English Bay. Traveling counterclockwise, points of interest include the **9 o'clock Gun** at Hallelujah Point, fired every evening since 1894 to mark a former fishing curfew; the replicated prow of the **Empress of Japan**, one of the first Pacific traders to call at Vancouver; the **Girl in a Wet Suit** statue, placed on a subtidal rock in 1972; a children's **water-play park**; and **Siwash Rock★**, a small but impressive andesite seastack right next to the seawall. A memorial to **James Cunningham**, the stonemason, is mounted in a rock face nearby. His ashes are buried at an undisclosed location in the wall itself.

★★Vancouver Aquarium – 🄺🄸🄳🄴 *East side of Stanley Park, just off Avison Way. Open late Jun–early Sept daily 9:30am–7pm. Rest of the year daily 10am–5:30pm. $12.95.* 🍴 ♿ 🅿 🖨 *604-659-3474. www.vanaqua.org.* Canada's largest marine-life facility has achieved international prominence since its opening in 1956. Beautifully designed to conform to its park setting, it contains 166 aquatic displays whose 54,000 occupants depict sea life in the North Pacific, Arctic Canada, tropical oceans and the Amazon Basin. At the entrance to the aquarium, Haida sculptor Bill Reid's bronze **orca statue** has a wonderfully fluid aspect.

Inside, the **Amazon Gallery** is highlighted by the daily feeding of the caimans. Several tanks offer an underwater look at the river's exotic denizens. In this steamy environment live crocodiles, anacondas, turtles, lizards and two-toed sloths, complete with suitable vegetation and a multitude of brightly colored birds. The adjacent **Tropical Gallery** explains the significance of coral reefs to the world's oceans; tanks contain sharks, piranhas, electric and moray eels and other creatures. The **Pacific Canada★** wing sports dozens of tanks illustrating the rich, colorful and varied life of the ocean's near shore. From the high-beach zone through tide pools and subtidal habitats, anemones, sea pens, starfish and nudibranchs lend the exhibits as many hues as the better-known tropical reefs. Concise illustrations explain the life cycle of British Columbia's salmon as they hatch in freshwater, mature in saltwater and return inland to spawn; aquarium operators have inaugurated a small stock of salmon that will return annually to the facility along a manmade stream. A nearby **wetlands** hall displays a variety of frogs and other amphibians.

The **Marine Mammal Deck★** outside presents beluga whales housed in a large tank with both above-ground and underwater viewing window. Excellent exhibits detail the short summers and long winters of the belugas' home in the Arctic. Nearby tanks hold amazingly acrobatic **sea otters**, **harbor seals** and **Steller's sea lions**. The daily **killer whale shows** are tremendously popular.

© Robert Holmes

Vancouver Aquarium

■ West Coast Seafood

Vancouver's location along the rich and productive North Pacific has long made the city a natural for superlative seafood, served in a variety of styles from simple to gourmet. Oysters, clams, Dungeness crabs, halibut and a half dozen kinds of salmon are grown and/or harvested in British Columbia, along with more exotic sea dwellers such as prawns, sea cucumber, squid and octopus. Traditional preparations are notably simple: salmon grilled over maple-wood fires, clams steamed in big pots, halibut broiled or oven-roasted. Modern variations add Asian and Continental influences—curried salmon filets, for example, or Northwest-style cioppino—seafood cooked with tomatoes, wine, herbs and spices. Diners should be sure to ask their server which menu items are freshest and from where they originate. And note that lobster, which many visitors expect to find, must be shipped clear across Canada from the Maritime provinces, as there is no Northwest species.

The native Northwest salmon types are chinook, coho, sockeye, pink, chum and steelhead, which is actually a sea-running form of rainbow trout. Farm-grown salmon is usually Atlantic salmon; the "farms" are pens in protected inland waters along the central British Columbia coast and Vancouver Island. Much controversy rages about the wisdom of raising a non-native salmon species in Pacific waters. King salmon is traditionally considered the top choice, but many connoisseurs prefer sockeye or coho, which tend to have higher natural oils, greater color and stronger flavor. Halibut is usually moist and mild, cod smoky and oily. Whatever you order, if it is fresh, of Northwest origin and properly prepared, it's certain to be memorable.

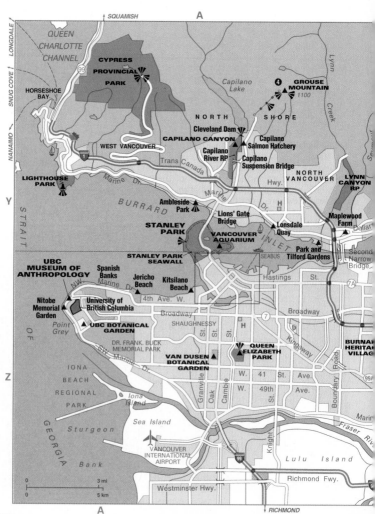

Lions' Gate Bridge – *Rte. 99 from Stanley Park to North Vancouver.* Also called the First Narrows Bridge, this 1938 structure was built, at their own expense, by the Guinness beer-making family to enable development of their North Shore properties. The provincial government bought it for $6 million in 1963. Although there are much bigger and longer suspension bridges, this structure's three suspended spans form a graceful arch that gives ships a clearance of 61m (185ft) from waterline to bridge deck; the center span is 472m (1,548ft) long. The bridge's three lanes have proved inadequate for modern commuting; tie-ups are lengthy during morning and evening rush hours. *Visitors are best advised to cross the bridge from 9am to 3pm.*

SOUTH OF FALSE CREEK 2 days. Map pp 292-293.

False Creek, the short tidal inlet that separates downtown Vancouver from the southern part of the city, was not long ago a decaying industrial area. Expo '86, built along False Creek, changed things considerably: Now expensive apartments and condominiums line the water on both sides, and a promenade edges the inlet from Stanley Park all the way out to the University of British Columbia. The Granville Bridge and the **Burrard Street Bridge** both cross False Creek. The latter is a marvelous 1932 span whose Art Deco portals bear the motto: "By Land and Sea We Prosper."

The area just east and west of Burrard Street along Fourth and Broadway Avenues is Vancouver's most important **shopping district**, thronged with small stores, cafes and vendors. North of Fourth Avenue lies the **Kitsilano** neighborhood, a counter-culture center in the 1960s and now a gentrified residential area. Many of the neighborhood's homes are Craftsman-style gems, especially several large ones near the Maritime Museum.

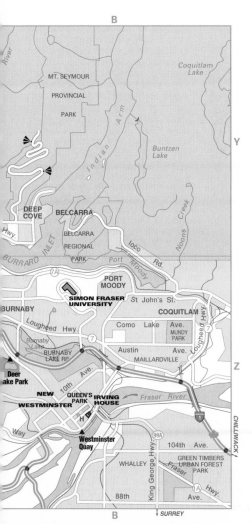

VANCOUVER

The shoreline west from Burrard encompasses a string of well-known public beaches, each with its own character. **Kitsilano Beach**, the first, has a large outdoor pool and is a hot spot for beach volleyball. **Jericho** and **Spanish Banks** come next, the favored locales for windsurfing and skimboarding. Finally, at the foot of a bluff below the University of British Columbia, the clothing-optional **Wreck Beach** is not marked on maps (ask for directions).

The **University of British Columbia** occupies the high ground at the tip of Point Grey, the Vancouver area's westernmost extension into the Strait of Georgia. The 35,000-student institution, founded in 1915, is noted for its cultural anthropology, Pacific Rim studies, political science and ecological studies programs. The university has also long been a hotbed of student activism—recent protests include student-police clashes during an Asia-Pacific Economic Cooperation Group conference in 1996.

★**Granville Island** – *On False Creek beneath the Granville Bridge; vehicle access via W. 2nd Ave. Granville Island Infocentre is on Johnston St. across from the public market. Open year-round daily 9am–6pm. Closed Jan 1, Dec 25–26.* ♿ 🅿 ☎ *604-666-5784.* Created in the early 20C by dredging sea mud into wooden forms, what was then called Industrial Island reached its heyday during World War II, when its factories helped produce naval stores for the war effort. In the 1950s most of the island's business customers departed the False Creek basin for cheaper environs elsewhere, and the area entered a period of decline until imaginative civic activists conceived the notion that warehouses and factory buildings are perfectly good for other uses. Now operated by Parks Canada, the island (actually a peninsula since the tiny southern channel was filled in) is a delightful 12 ha (29-acre) bustle of shops, cafes, vendors and visitor attractions on cobblestone streets, drawing up to nine million visitors a year and easily covered on foot. Parking is limited, especially on weekends, but you can park nearby or arrive on one of the whimsical little **water taxis** on False Creek *(False Creek Ferries depart from the Aquatic Centre at south end of Thurlow St.; daily 7am–10:30pm; every 5min;* ☎ *604-684-7781; Aquabuses depart from south end of Hornby St.; daily 7am–10:30pm;* ☎ *604-689-5858).* Afoot is how you'll want to see Granville anyway, sampling ethnic food, eyeing fresh fruits and vegetables, pausing for coffee or ice cream, and shopping in the numerous studios and galleries. Three theaters keep the island active at night.

> **3 False Creek Fishermen's Wharf**
>
> *Map p 292. East end of W. 1st St. near Granville Island.* Though there are many places in Vancouver to buy fresh seafood, here you can buy from the folks who actually catch the fish and shellfish. Not only does that usually mean it's incomparably fresh, it also means you can learn exactly where it's from, how long ago it was caught and how this difficult trade is practiced. Seafood is available in all seasons, the offerings often including crab and salmon, as well as rarities such as shrimp, steelhead, octopus and rockfish.

The focal point for many visitors, the **Granville Island Public Market**, dating from 1979, spurred the development of the rest of Granville. By 8:30am on weekends the market is abuzz with shoppers amid stands of fresh vegetables, fruits, breads, meats, cheeses, seafood, flowers and crafts. The **Emily Carr Institute of Art & Design** *(east end of Johnston St., next to the cement plant,* ☎ *604-844-3800)* is Vancouver's top art school. Its lobby serves as a gallery for intriguing student artworks. At the nearby **Granville Island Brewery** *(1441 Cartwright St.; open year-round daily 9:30am–7pm, Fri & Sat til 8pm; closed Jan 1, Dec 25-26; $7;* ♿ 🅿 ☎ *604-687-2739)*, the originator of British Columbia's craft-brewing industry, visitors receive a brief exposure to the brewing process, and a tasting session that focuses on the test brews now made at this plant. (The company's main brewing plant is elsewhere.) The brewery's inception in 1984 made it Canada's first modern microbrewery. Around on Dunleau Street, the **Granville Island Sport Fishing Museum** *(open year-round daily 10am–5:30pm; $5.* ✂ ♿ 🅿 ☎ *604-683-1939; www.sportfishingmusuem.bc.ca)*, holds several wonders, including an extensive collection of fly rods and reels, hand-tied flies and fly-fishing "plates" (fishing photos mounted with flies), as well as a large collection of **model ships**, concentrating on warships.

★★**Vancouver Museum** – *1100 Chestnut St., in Vanier Park. Open Jul–Aug daily 10am–5pm. Rest of the year Tue–Sun 10am–5pm. Closed Dec 25. $8* ♿ 🅿 ☎ *604-736-4431. www.vanmuseum.bc.ca.* Housed with the Pacific Space Centre in a single complex whose entranceway wraps around a massive fountain and sculpture, the Vancouver Museum was founded in 1894, making it the city's oldest. Representing the creature that guards the harbor in Indian legend, a large stainless-steel **crab**★—an 1958 work of sculptor George Norris—dominates the front entrance in an ornamental pool. The conical shape of the museum's roof represents a traditional Coast Salish cedar-bark hat. Inside, visitors see only a tiny fraction of its 100,000 items as they wind their way through connecting halls that delineate the city's history, passing through representations of sawmills and trading enterprises.

★**Pacific Space Centre** – 🌐 *1100 Chestnut St., in Vanier Park. Open Jul–Aug daily 10am–5pm. Rest of the year Tue–Sun 10am–5pm. Closed Dec 25. $12.50.* 📶 ☎ *604-738-7827.www.pacific-space-centre.bc.ca.* A compact facility geared to children holds interactive exhibits in a carpeted, dark, space-station-shaped gallery. Displays focus on Canada's role in space research. The extremely invigorating **virtual voyages simulator**★ takes passengers on 15min "trips" to Mars, the moon and other extra-terrestrial destinations. The new **MacMillan Planetarium** offers music-driven laser light shows along with the traditional explorations of the heavens, and in the Southam Observatory visitors can look through the giant telescope at the sun, moon, planets and stars.

★★**Vancouver Maritime Museum** – *1905 Ogden Ave., in Vanier Park. Open Victoria Day–Labor Day daily 10am–5pm. Rest of the year Tue–Sat 10am–5pm, Sun noon–5pm. $6.* ♿ 📶 ☎ *604-257-8300. www.vmm.bc.ca.* Ship models and artifacts illustrate the maritime history of Vancouver and British Columbia. This compact waterside museum was designed to accommodate the 19m– (62ft) high mast of the wood-hulled **St. Roch**★★, a restored Royal Canadian Mounted Police arctic patrol ship that was the first to make the difficult Northwest Passage in both directions, during World War II. To assert sovereignty over the northland, the Canadian government decided to send a ship through the passage. Under Capt. Henry Larsen, the *St. Roch* left Vancouver in June 1940 and—after being frozen in several times—reached Halifax in October 1942. In 1944, the return trip of 13,510km (7,295 nautical mi) in ice-strewn waters took only 86 days. Visitors may tour the 32m (104ft) vessel, and imagine for themselves how confining the cramped quarters were during the two-year voyage; a radio plays tapes of war news dispatches and quarters are furnished with authentic items. Elsewhere in the museum, a hands-on **children's maritime center** includes a full-scale replica of the pilot-house on the tugboat *Seaspan Queen*; telescopes provide close-up viewing of ships in the harbor; and informative exhibits examine Northwest exploration, pirates and famous shipwrecks in literature and art.

In a small plaza outside, the **Centennial Pole**★ was carved for the British Columbia centennial in 1958 by famous Kwakiutl artist Chief **Mungo Martin** (1879-1962). The 30m (100ft) pole, depicts the 10 mythical ancestors of the 10 bands in the Kwakiutl nation.

★★★**UBC Museum of Anthropology** – *Map p 298. 6393 N.W. Marine Dr., on the University of British Columbia campus. Open mid-May–Labor Day daily 10am–5pm (Tue 9pm). Rest of the year Tue–Sun 11am–5pm (Tue 9pm). Closed Dec 24-25. $6.* ✗ ♿ 📶 ☎ *604-822-3825. www.moa.ubc.ca.* Housed in a lauded concrete-and-glass **building**★★ designed by Vancouver architect Arthur Erickson, the museum contains major collections of Northwest Coast First Nations art. The building itself reflects the traditional Northwest Coast architectural style; opened in 1976 to instant acclaim, it incorporates Erickson's interpretation of First Nations designs and British Columbia's natural environment. A cast-concrete exterior represents traditional post-and-beam longhouse construction. The massive cedar doors, carved by Gitksan artists, open onto a ramp leading the visitor downward into increasingly spacious galleries.

The **Great Hall**★★ of totems, canoes and other aboriginal carved works is naturally lit by 15m– (50ft) high glass walls. The wood carvings, many from the mid-19C, represent many of the major coastal nations, chiefly Haida, Kwakwaka'wakw, Nisga'a, Gitksan and Coast Salish styles. The stirring atmosphere created by these powerful works is palpable; one can imagine the artisans of generations ago at work. A short passage leads to a small rotunda devoted to the sculpture **Raven and the First Men**★ by Haida artist Bill Reid *(p 302)*. This massive work, carved from a 3,636kg (4-ton) block of cedar

© Robert Holmes

Raven and the First Men (1980) by Bill Reid

gracefully depicts a Haida creation story featuring a huge raven standing on a clamshell that is being pushed open by a series of small figures. It was unveiled by Prince Charles at a 1980 ceremony to which Haida people brought the sand that surrounds the sculpture. Farther down the hall, visitors are encouraged to touch Reid's **Haida bear**, a squat 1962 piece carved from a single cedar stump.

Much of the rest of the museum is given over to numerous **visible storage galleries**, in which cultural and archeological works from around the world are displayed in glass-fronted cases. Some 15,000 items are on view, ranging from South Seas artifacts to Inuit carvings. Outside the museum, a reconstruction of a **Haida Village★** features a longhouse, mortuary house and several totems, all depicting a 19C Haida community. Two of the totems are by Chief Mungo Martin, the legendary Kwakwa'wakw carver.

★**UBC Botanical Garden** – *Map p 298. 6804 S.W. Marine Dr. (on the University of British Columbia campus, 2km (1.2mi) south of Anthropological Museum). Open mid-Mar–mid-Oct daily 10am–6pm. Rest of the year daily 10am–2:30pm. $4.50.* 🅿 ☏ *604-822-9666. www.hedgerows.com.ca.* This 28 ha (70-acre) largely informal garden is set within a mature forest that, unlike most others in the Vancouver area, contains large numbers of Western hemlocks, the theoretical "climax" species of the Pacific Northwest maritime forest. Nestled beneath the sheltering trees are more than 400 **rhododendron** varieties (Canada's largest collection); springy, bark-paved pathways wind through the woods. Gardens embrace eight separate themes: alpine, native British Columbia, contemporary, arbor, food, Asian, winter and physick gardens-the latter a 16C medicinal herb collection surrounding a sundial. In all more than 10,000 plant species are represented.

Nearby, the **Nitobe Memorial Garden** *(Marine Dr. near UBC Gate 4; open mid-Mar–mid-Oct daily 10am–6pm; rest of the year Mon–Fri 10am–2:30pm; $2.50)* is a serene, compact Japanese tea garden, widely considered the most genuine in North America. Its stucco garden walls enclose strolling paths, ponds and meditation benches amid many formal plantings.

★★**Van Dusen Botanical Garden** – *Map p 298. 5251 Oak St. at 37th Ave. Open Jun–mid-Aug daily 10am–9pm. May & mid-Aug–Labor Day daily 10am–8pm. Rest of the year daily 10am–6pm; in winter gardens close 4pm. Closed Dec 25. $5.50 (winter $2.75).* ✗ ♿ 🅿 ☏ *604-878-9274. www.vandusengarden.org.* Location of the Shaughnessy Golf Club until 1964, this rolling 22 ha (55-acre) expanse was

---

■ The Art of Bill Reid and Emily Carr

The two artists most associated with Vancouver, **Bill Reid** (1920-1998) and **Emily Carr** (1871-1945), could hardly be more dissimilar. She was a girl of the Victorian age, born in Victoria, who did not outlive the era of prejudice against women artists. Her dramatic work achieved international fame only long after her death. Bill Reid, by contrast, was a Haida descendant, also born in Victoria after his mother Sophie Gladstone left behind her Haida roots to marry William Reid, an American of Scotch and German descent. During his life, Bill Reid achieved worldwide fame as the popularizer of his ancestral Haida artistic style, to which he brought modern design sensibilities and a bit of celebrity savvy.

But under the surface many similarities remain. Carr and Reid both crystallize the human and natural landscape of British Columbia in their work, and both were heavily influenced by journeys made up the Northwest coast. In 1943 Reid visited Skidegate, a Haida village in the Queen Charlotte Islands and met his maternal grandfather, Charles Gladstone— one of the few remaining practitioners of traditional Haida carving arts. Although a short career in radio in Toronto preceded Reid's entry into the artistic world in the 1950s, the visit to Skidegate was pivotal: From the beginning, his work reflected the Haida tradition.

Carr's pivotal journey came in 1907 when a trip up the coast to Alaska exposed her for the first time to the monumental carved artwork of Northwest Coast tribes. For the rest of her life she adopted a somewhat phantasmagoric style reflecting First Nations life and design traditions, as well as the British Columbia environment, particularly its forests.

Carr's finest work, now world-famous and often compared to that of Georgia O'Keeffe, is in the collection of the Vancouver Art Gallery, which was one of the few institutions to support her art during her lifetime. Reid's work is scattered around the globe, but the sculpture most consider his masterpiece, *Raven and the First Men*, is in the UBC Museum of Anthropology *(p 301)*, as are several other sculptures and a collection of his jewelry. Reid's 6m (20ft) *Jade Canoe* is the centerpiece at Vancouver International Airport; and his depiction of a killer whale guards the entrance to the Vancouver Aquarium.

acquired by the VanDusen Botanical Garden Association to forestall conversion of the site into housing and turned into a remarkably rich and mature garden. More formal than the UBC Botanical Garden, VanDusen holds 7,500 different kinds of plants, ensuring that something is in bloom, or at least in color, every month. The entrance to the main building offers a taste of what's inside, and of what is possible in Vancouver's maritime climate: Palm trees and bamboo cluster beneath a large Douglas fir. Highlights are the heather garden and witch hazels in winter; a Canadian heritage garden; several Oriental gardens, including a serene meditation garden in a Douglas fir grove; a maze; an Eastern North America garden; a lush fern dell; and a long rhododendron-bordered walk.

The nearby hilltop neighborhood of **Shaughnessy** *(east of Granville St., south of 16th Ave.)* contains many fine early-20C upper-class homes.

★**Queen Elizabeth Park** – *Map p 298. Cambie St. and 33rd Ave. Open daily year-round.* ✗ &. ▯ ☞ *604-257-8584. www.parks.vancouver.bc.ca.* The highest spot within Vancouver at 153m (501ft), the 53 ha (130-acre) park offers an excellent **panorama**★★ of the gleaming towers of downtown, False Creek and Burrard Inlet, and the North Shore. On clear days you can see the two Lions—twin peaks in the Coast Range to the north. Atop the hill, the **Bloedel Floral Conservatory** *(open Apr–Sept Mon–Fri 9am–8pm, weekends 10am–9pm; rest of the year daily 10am–5pm; closed Dec 25; $3.50;* &. ▯ ☞ *604-257-8570)* houses 500 species of tropical plants, as well as 150 tropical birds in a dome made of 1,490 plexiglass bubbles. Late-19C rock quarries have been converted to attractive **quarry gardens** that cascade down the northwest slope of the hill; most of the rest of the northern section of the park functions as an arboretum containing trees native to Canada, as well as exotic species from around the world. **Seasons in the Park** restaurant *(☞ 604-874-8008)* serves fine food with spectacular views; it hosted US President Bill Clinton and Russian President Boris Yeltsin during their 1993 Vancouver summit. At the northern foot of the park's hill, **Nat Bailey Stadium** is the summertime home of the Vancouver Canadians AAA baseball team *(☞ 604-872-5232)*.

NORTH SHORE *1 1/2 days. Map pp 298-299.*

The North Shore communities of **North Vancouver** and **West Vancouver** hug the rapidly rising slopes of the Coast Range foothills. Much of the area's property was originally developed by the Guinness brewing family, which built the Lions' Gate Bridge in 1938 to provide access to its housing developments. The distinct demarcation line between suburbs and forests at about 245m (800ft) elevation is the highest point served by water lines, and is frequently the snow line in winter and early spring. Directly above, the ski areas at Grouse Mountain, Mount Seymour and Mount Cypress often register snowfalls of 9m (30ft) or more.

North Shore residents enjoy the best of both worlds—wilderness hiking and skiing next door, and quick access to the city center. Though the three-lane Lions' Gate Bridge is often clogged by traffic, the Second Narrows Bridge (Hwy. 1) to the east provides an alternative. After long public discussion, the provincial government decided in 1998 to invest $120 million in upgrading (but not expanding the capacity of) the Lions' Gate Bridge. Nonetheless, living on the North Shore is so popular that West Vancouver claims the most expensive real estate in Canada. Within West Van (its common appellation) the hugely popular **Ambleside Park** begins at the Capilano River and follows the shoreline west about 6km (3.7mi); the **views**★ of English Bay, Stanley Park and Vancouver are superlative throughout the park's length.

Scenic Highway 1 (which becomes Route 99) follows the North Shore slope about a half-mile above the water, winding up 12km (7.4mi) west at **Horseshoe Bay**, the BC Ferries departure point for Vancouver Island, Bowen Island and the Sunshine Coast, north of Howe Sound. Ferry line-ups on Fridays and major holidays can be extensive; travelers are advised to proceed cautiously, as the lines frequently spill back onto the main highway.

The **SeaBus**, a BC Ferries operation, offers transit across Burrard Inlet roughly every half hour from a terminal near Canada Place to **Lonsdale Quay**, a North Shore counterpart to Granville Island with numerous shops, cafes, vendors and craft galleries. A few kilometers east, **Park & Tilford Gardens** *(Brooksbank Ave., North Vancouver; open year-round daily 9:30am–dusk; closed Dec 25;* ✗ &. ▯ ☞ *604-984-8200)* is a handsome facility built as a community gift from a local brewery. The brewery is long gone, and the shopping center that replaced it now surrounds the garden, replete with roses, herbs and native plants.

★**Cypress Provincial Park** – *12km/7mi from downtown by Lions' Gate Bridge and Hwy. 1. Open daily year-round.* ✗ &. ▯ ☞ *604-924-2200.* This 3,000 ha (7,400-acre) expanse includes Hollyburn Ridge and Cypress Bowl, popular local ski areas. The access road leads through a forest of Douglas fir and western hemlock to Highview Lookout, which permits a breathtaking **view**★★★ of the Vancouver area. On clear days Mt. Baker adds its stunning snow-clad mass to the scene. At 1,300m (4,264ft) above sea level, the ridgetops here abound with amabalis fir, mountain hemlock and yellow cypress, for which the park is named.

Capilano Suspension Bridge

★★ Lighthouse Park – *On Marine Dr. 8km (5mi) west of Lions' Gate Bridge; watch for entrance on the south side.* Situated on a headland protruding into Howe Sound, this 79 ha (185-acre) park harbors one of the last major parcels of untouched old-growth forest in the immediate Vancouver area and provides stunning **views★★★** across the Strait of Georgia to Stanley Park and Vancouver. The trees were given protected status when the first lighthouse was built in 1874 to mark an especially dangerous hazard, rocky Point Atkinson; the dark background of the forest helped the light stand out in fog, and the wood was earmarked to supply fuel for the lighthouse steam plant. Later declared a park, the area is forested with immense, **Douglas firs**, cedars and hemlocks. Numerous trails lead through the forest and down to the current lighthouse (1912) a half-hour walk in, widely considered the best place to watch sunsets over Georgia Strait. Near the parking lot you can see some ancient trees whose trunks have been scarred by the attempts of vandals to burn them down. Lighthouse Park, its sunlight filtered through thick forest, has frequently been used as a film set.

★ Capilano Canyon – Kids *9km (6mi) from downtown by Lions' Gate Bridge and Capilano Rd.* The Capilano River pours out of the Coast Range through a spectacular gorge that has been drawing visitors for more than a century. **Capilano Suspension Bridge and Park** *(3735 Capilano Rd.; open Mar–Oct daily 8:30am–dusk; rest of the year daily 9am–5pm; closed Dec 25; $10.75; ✗ ◪ ☏ 604-985-7474; www.capbridge.com)* has been a tourist attraction since 1889; the current bridge stretches 137m (449ft) across the 70m– (230ft) deep canyon. The heavily promoted, old-fashioned attraction draws hordes of visitors in the summer; walking trails and a gift shop are also featured.

Just up Capilano road from the suspension bridge, **Capilano River Regional Park** *(open year-round daily 8am; closing times vary, but are posted at park entrance; ☏ 604-224-5739)* covers 142 ha (350 acres), in which hiking trails cross the river and climb into deep forest. A few old-growth trees remain, including an 86m (281ft) fir near the parking lot (the tallest tree in the Vancouver area) and a 300-year-old Pacific yew. The nearby **Capilano Salmon Hatchery** *(4500 Capilano Rd.; open Jun–Aug daily 8am–8pm; rest of the year daily 8am–6pm; closing hours in winter vary; ⅚ ◪ ☏ 604-666-1790)* contains exhibits explaining the salmon life cycle and the hatchery's role. A small park farther up Capilano Road at **Cleveland Dam**, which impounds part of Vancouver's water supply, offers excellent **views** of the North Shore Mountains, including the twin Lions peaks.

④ Hiwus Feasthouse

Map p 298. Atop Grouse Mountain; access by aerial tram. ☏ 604-980-9311. Featuring massive cedar beams, totem poles and posts hand-carved by First Nations craftsmen, this mountaintop retreat is architecturally impressive, its appeal enhanced by the entertainment offered visitors. A six-course feast includes cedar-plank salmon, forest mushrooms, berries and other traditional dishes, accompanied by native chants, songs and tales performed by Coast Salish dancers. After guests have learned how Salmon Woman convinced Raven, Bear, Eagle, Wolf and Thunderbird to let Man join the world, everyone joins in one last dance around the longhouse.

★Grouse Mountain – *13km (8mi) from downtown by Lions' Gate Bridge, Capilano Rd. and Nancy Greene Way. Tram operates year-round daily 9am–10pm. $16.95.* ✗ ᨈ ▯ ☎ *604-984-0661.* The aerial tram rises 854m (2,800ft) to an elevation of 1,100m (3,700ft), offering a splendid **view★★** of the city en route. From the summit on a clear day you can see Vancouver Island, the Fraser delta and Burrard Inlet. The mountain is Vancouver's oldest ski area, offering quick access and night skiing to city residents. The lodge at the top shows a free 15min video, *Born to Fly*, with aerial views of the province. In summer, hang-glider pilots and hikers use Grouse as a jumping-off point; the **Grouse Grind** trail ascends the mountain in 3km (1.9mi).

★Lynn Canyon Regional Park – *17km (10.5mi) from downtown by Lions' Gate Bridge; follow Lynn Valley Rd. north of Hwy. 1 to Peters Rd. Park hours: summer daily 7am–9pm, spring & fall daily 7am–7pm, winter daily 7am–6pm.* ✗ ᨈ ☎ *604-981-3103. www.dnv.org/parks/funparks.htm.* Much quieter but no less scenic than Capilano Canyon, this North Shore gorge is almost as deep as Capilano and boasts a more spectacular waterfall. The park encompasses 250 ha (617 acres); logged long ago, the mature second growth forest is attractive, but the highlight is the 33m– (109ft-) long **suspension bridge★**, which swings over a 52m (172ft) defile. The bridge is part of a trail network that stretches along the entire North Shore and ultimately reaches into Garibaldi Provincial Park. A short walk across the bridge takes you upstream to the river's edge and a large natural pool; other trails wind through the forest to good views of tumbling water. A compact but thorough **Ecology Centre** near the bridge details the area's wildlife and natural habitats *(open Mar–Sept daily 9am–5pm; Oct–Feb Mon–Fri 9am–5pm, weekends noon–4pm; closed Jan 1, Dec 25–26).*

Maplewood Farm – 🄺🄸🄳🅂 *405 Seymour River Pl., North Vancouver. Open year-round daily 10am–4pm. Closed Dec 25. $2.25.* ᨈ ▯ ☎ *604-929-5610. www.maplewoodfarm.bc.ca.* This peaceful petting zoo holds ponies, sheep, ducks, dairy cows, goats and dozens of other animals. Once a thriving dairy, the farm was acquired by North Vancouver Parks in the early 1970s.

LOWER MAINLAND

Michelin map 493 B, C 2 and map pp 298-299
Tourist Information ☎ 604-683-2000 or www.tourism-vancouver.org

The long expanse of lowland that runs from Hope west to the Strait of Georgia, popularly called the Lower Mainland, compresses half of British Columbia's four million residents into less than four percent of its land area. Even so, much of this picturesque delta still seems rural, an impression reinforced by the timbered shoulders of the Coast Range and Cascade foothills that rise abruptly at the valley's edges. In the background, snow-mantled peaks are always present; in the foreground, farms and fields spread across the valley loam, and innumerable groves of tall black cottonwoods provide shade, wildlife habitat and bald eagle perches.

Though urban growth is rapidly overtaking the rich farmland, this narrow belt has become Canada's leading producer of crops ranging from blueberries to tomatoes, with 6,000 farms encompassing more than 101,215 ha (250,000 acres) and 1.4 million square meters (15 million square feet) of greenhouse space. Today it ranks as one of the fastest-growing urban areas in Canada, and prime farmland and valuable wetlands are being converted to urban uses at a rate that alarms conservationists. The issue was brought into sharp focus in 1999 by a proposal to convert a large part of the 4,000-acre Burns Bog in Delta, one of the largest intact peat bogs in North America, into a theme park—a plan that aroused fierce and immediate controversy. The major Vancouver satellite cities of Richmond, Burnaby, Coquitlam and Surrey are urban areas in their own right, with more than 100,000 residents apiece. Notable visitor attractions are sprinkled here and there, and each city holds several major regional parks. The Tourism Vancouver regional visitor map specifies the location of most of these parks, all of which offer pleasant picnicking, walking and wildlife watching opportunities.

SIGHTS *1 day*

★George C. Reifel Bird Sanctuary – *Westham Island. 11km (7mi) west of Ladner, following signs from Rte. 99, south on Rte. 17, then west. Open year-round daily 9am–4pm. $3.25.* ✗ ᨈ ▯ ☎ *604-946-6980.* An important migratory habitat, the cottonwood-lined marsh here annually hosts the greatest variety of birds in the Lower Mainland; more than 260 species have been observed on this 360 ha (890-acre) parcel, including peregrine falcons, bald eagles, owls, herons and swans. Peak birding season is October to March, although visitors will see birds any time of year. An observation tower, trails and picnic facilities are available.

Richmond Buddhist Temple

★**Richmond Buddhist Temple** – *9160 Steveston Hwy. near No. 4 Rd., Richmond. Open year-round daily 10am–5pm. closed Dec 25.* ⭑ 🅿 ☏ *604-274-2822.* Richmond, one of Vancouver's largest and fastest-growing suburbs, is home to an extensive Asian population, with its own Chinatown, as well as one of the largest Buddhist temples in North America. Built to represent Chinese palatial architecture, the temple has graceful tiled roofs, courtyards and lavishly decorated meditation halls of gilt, brass, tilework, porcelain and marble. A bonsai garden borders the entrance.

★**Gulf of Georgia Cannery** – *12138 4th Ave., Steveston Village, Richmond. Open Jun–Labor Day daily 10am–5pm. Apr–May & Labor Day–Oct Thu–Mon 10am–5pm. Closed major holidays. $5.* ⭑ 🅿 ☏ *604-664-9009. www.harbour.com/parkscan/ggc.* Fishing boats still moor at the docks behind this historic facility on the lower Fraser, but the cannery industry has moved to other shores (and offshore to factory fishing boats). A tremendous factory, at one point the leading salmon canner in the province, operated here from 1894-1979. Converted into a heritage site, it was opened to the public in 1994. Highlights include a **salmon canning line**, complete with an automatic fish-gutter whose 60-fish-a-minute capability replaced 16 workers. Several examples of the Easthope engine, which revolutionized commercial fishing, round out the equipment. A 120m (40ft) fishing skiff is open to visitors, and multimedia presentations explains the history and significance of the fishing industry to the province.

Steveston★, the erstwhile fishing village around the cannery site, is slowly embracing its heritage character and morphing into a day-trip tourist attraction where boutiques and cafes now outnumber fishing industry supply stores. The **Steveston Museum** *(3811 Moncton St.; open year-round Mon–Sat 9:30am–1pm & 1:30pm–5pm; closed major holidays;* ☏ *604-271-6868)* is housed, along with the village post office, in a handsome former bank building. At **Britannia Heritage Shipyard** *(foot of Railway Ave., open year-round Mon–Fri 9am–5pm;* ☏ *604-718-1200)*, volunteers use an intact ship-chandler's facility to work on boat restorations. On shore, a restored shipyard worker's home contains exhibits about the industry. **London Heritage Farm** *(6511 Dyke Rd.; open Jul–Labor Day daily 10am–4pm; rest of the year weekends noon–4pm; closed Dec 25–mid-Jan;* ☏ *604-271-5220)*, a restored Victorian farmhouse, makes a good picnic spot.

★**New Westminster** – The "Royal City" once aspired to be British Columbia's major urban area. Founded by the Royal Engineers, who had come west to build the Cariboo Road, the city was named by Queen Victoria and served briefly as the mainland colony's capital (1860-68) until colonial administration was consolidated in Victoria. New Westminster today hews to its British heritage as one of just two British Columbia communities to continue the **May Day** tradition, with a citywide festival, May Queen and Maypole dance. **Westminster Quay**, on the shores of the Fraser, is a charming agglomeration of shops and vendors; a tugboat pilot house mounted on the dock reflects the city's continuing dependence on river commerce.

★**Irving House** – *302 Royal Ave. Open May–mid-Sept Tue–Sun 11am–5pm. Rest of the year weekends 1pm–5pm. $2.* ☏ *604-527-4640.* Built in the San Francisco Gothic Revival style for riverboat captain William Irving, this 14-room 1865 mansion on the hill above downtown has been maintained remarkably close to its original condition. Furnishings are from 1865-87, and two rooms contain the original 1865 wallpaper. Behind the house, the **New Westminster Museum** focuses on the Royal Engineers and their efforts on the Cariboo Road, as well as the city's May Day history. Farther up the hill, the **Queen's Park** neighborhood, between Third Street and the park, contains many restored Victorian and Craftsman-style homes.

★**Burnaby Heritage Village** – *In Deer Lake Park, just south of Hwy. 1 in Burnaby. Open May–mid-Sept & late-Nov–Dec 11am–4:30pm. Closed Dec 24–25. $6:45.* ✗ ♿ 🅿 ☎ *604-293-6501. www.burnabyparksrec.org.* The bustling complex contains a replica early 20C village with dozens of historic structures, replicas and exhibits. Costumed interpreters perform tasks ranging from blacksmithing to printing, and visitors can buy such treats as sarsaparilla sodas and ice-cream sundaes. Highlights include the Chinese herbalist's store; Elworth, the estate residence of railway executive Edwin Bateman; the music store, with its player piano; the movie theater, which runs 1920s short films; and the ice-cream parlour. Near the complex entrance, the 1890s **Love Farmhouse** is the oldest remaining building in Burnaby, and contains many original furnishings, including the embossed tin ceiling in the two front rooms. The village's showpiece is the restored 1912 **C.W. Parker carousel**★, one of 200 such carousels remaining in North America. Accompanied by a 1925 Wurlitzer organ, the carousel offers rides on three dozen intricately decorated horses.

The heritage village is contained within **Deer Lake Park**, known for the wonderful views across its namesake lake toward downtown Vancouver. On the hill above the museum, the **Shadbolt Centre for the Arts** is a handsome modern performance venue; behind it, the Century Garden becomes a delightful spot in April, May and June when its dozens of rhododendrons bloom. Topping all, the 1912 **Fairacres** mansion now serves as an art gallery. Especially notable are several brass fireplaces, backed by floor-to-ceiling ceramic tile.

★**Simon Fraser University** – *On Burnaby Mtn., north of Hwy. 1, Burnaby. Grounds are open daily year-round. Information:* ☎ *604-291-3210. www.sfu.ca.* Designed by Vancouver architect Arthur Erickson, the mountaintop complex with its many concrete levels and cantilevered layers has remained a focus of aesthetic debate since the university's opening in 1965. Erickson's intent was to create a singular whole in which students and staff would be able to walk from one end of the university to the other under cover. Though problems with leaking arose, they have been fixed, and Erickson's striking design now looks far more familiar after numerous imitations. Home to 23,000 students, Simon Fraser was known for radicalism and social action in the 1960s and for college athletics and its world championship pipe band since; its academic strengths are ecology, political science and outreach education.

★**Fort Langley National Historic Site** – *6.5km (4mi) north of Langley, off Hwy. 1 to 23433 Mavis Ave. Open Mar–Oct daily 10am–5pm. $4.* ♿ 🅿 ☎ *604-513-4777.* Founded in 1827 as a Hudson's Bay Company outpost, the fort was moved to this spot in 1839 from its original site 4km (2.5mi) downstream. It was a remote and little-known spot, shipping farm products and salt salmon as well as furs, until gold was discovered up the Fraser, and in 1858 30,000 prospectors (mostly from the played-out California fields) swarmed the area. Fort Langley is also where British Columbia was declared a crown colony in November of 1858, to forestall territorial ambitions by American gold seekers. Afterwards, the fort fell slowly into disuse, eclipsed by newer settlements up and down the Fraser. Visitors may explore the re-created buildings of the wooden-palisaded fort. The only original building remaining is the **storehouse**, a low-slung, adzed-beam blockhouse in which costumed interpreters explain the fur trade. The **Big House**, a 1958 reconstruction of the original in which the colony of British Columbia came into being, overlooks this pleasant site above an arm of the Fraser River. A blacksmith shop, servant's quarters, cooperage and heritage gardens round out the fort. Visitors may try their luck at panning for "gold" (actually melted brass), hand-sawing or toting fur bales.

A block away, the **Langley Centennial Museum** offers an exemplary depiction of pre-settlement Coast Salish life in the area, as well as exhibits on 19C trading and logging. The museum also contains a fine replica of a 19C Langley-area general store. Next door, the **BC Farm Machinery and Agricultural Museum** stockpiles equipment derived from the Langley area's long tradition of farming. Antique tractors and horse-drawn farm machinery are supplemented by a restored 1890s sawmill.

Greater Vancouver Zoo – 🄺🄸🄳🅂 *5048 264th St., Aldergrove. Open year-round 9am–dusk. $10.50.* ✗ ♿ 🅿 ☎ *604-856-6825. www.greatervancouverzoo.com.* a 48 ha (120-acre) facility holds more than 125 animal species, ranging from exotics such as zebras and tigers, to Northwest natives like elk and bears; many of the animals roam freely in large, natural enclosures. Children will enjoy the petting zoo and miniature-train rides.

★**Minter Gardens** – *Hwy. 9 just north of Hwy. 1 (Exit 135), east of Chilliwack. Open Apr–mid-Oct daily 9am–5:30pm. $11.* ✗ ♿ ▯ ☎ *604-794-7191. www.minter.org.* Hundreds of thousands of blooms spread over nearly 11 ha (27 acres) in 11 thematic areas make this a garden of delights. Pathways wind along streams, over footbridges, by fountains and past benches. Highlights include rose and fragrance gardens, a formal garden, a Chinese garden, topiary and a maze. Brian Minter, creator of the attraction, is a well-known Lower Mainland commercial-gardening expert.

NORTH BANK EXCURSIONS

From Fort Langley, a short jaunt across the roiling Fraser River on the free Albion ferry leads to **Route 7**, a scenic secondary road through the pastoral, less developed north bank of the Fraser Valley. Thick groves of tall cottonwoods line the river and surrounding farm fields, with the flanks of the Coast Range thrusting up just north. Several spots along the road afford splendid views of the Fraser, and in summer fresh fruit and vegetable stands are common—the valley's sweet corn is legendary. Harrison Hot Springs, reached through a narrow mountain gap, is roughly an hour's drive from Fort Langley.

★**Westminster Abbey** – *1 hr. 23km (14.3mi) east of Fort Langley via Albion ferry and Rte. 7. Turn north on Stave Lake St. just east of Mission, travel about 2mi and turn right on Dewdney Trunk Rd. Watch for sign on right to 34224 Dewdney Trunk Rd. Open year-round daily 8:30am–noon & 1:30pm–4:30pm.* ♿ ▯ ☎ *604-826-8975.* A small group of Benedictine monks came here in 1953 to establish a retreat and worship center. To the spectacular 81 ha (200-acre) site, on a high promontory overlooking the Fraser River, they have added an abbey, seminary, church and bell tower. An airy concrete structure incorporating Gothic elements such as flying buttresses, the church is a handsome example of modern ecclesiastical architecture. A footpath leads across the property to an overlook with a riveting **view**★★ of the Fraser Valley. Visitors are welcome weekdays and Sunday afternoons, and for worship during the five daily services.

Kilby Historic Store and Farm – *1/2 hr. About 50km (31mi) east of Fort Langley via Albion ferry and Rte. 7, just west of Harrison Mills. 1.6km (.9mi) south of Rte. 7.* ✗ ☎ *604-796-9576.* An authentic 19C roadhouse turned into a heritage site, this enterprise was operated by the Kilby family until 1971. The building is reached by ramps, as floods drove vital operations to the second story. Livestock and poultry sheds illustrate typical farm operations, and the country store is laden with typical 1920s goods. The site includes a restaurant and picnic facilities.

★**Harrison Hot Springs** – *1/2 day. 72km (45mi) from Fort Langley via Albion ferry. Follow Rte. 7 east 66km (41mi) to Kent, then north on Rte. 341 for 6km (3.7mi). Chamber of Commerce Information Centre: May–early Sept daily 9am–5pm. Rest of the year Wed–Fri 10am–4pm.* ☎ *604-796-3425.* Legend tells of a passing prospector who swamped his canoe in Harrison Lake in 1859, and was surprised to land in hot water. The mineral-laden hot waters at this homey resort are widely considered restorative, and the town's prospect-looking past beautiful Harrison Lake to the peaks of the Lillooet Range—is splendid. Sand sculpture artists descend on the broad beach in September for a world championship competition, creating fantastic tableaux from the lakebed's heavy brown sand. From nearby mountains come frequent reports of **Sasquatch**, the mythical mountain creature reportedly spotted from northern California to Alaska. In the winter, thousands of bald eagles flock to the lake's outfall, the Harrison River, to feed on a chinook salmon run. The **Harrison Hot Springs Resort** (*100 Esplanade Ave.* ☎ *604-796-2244 or 800-663-2266*) is a 1927 resort with modern conveniences; it owns the lakeside spring from which the 74°C (148°F) water is drawn. A public **hot pool** is located at Harrison Hot Springs Road and Esplanade Avenue.

SEA TO SKY HIGHWAY★★

Michelin map 493 B, C 2 and map opposite
Tourist Information ☎ 250-387-1642 or www.travel.bc.ca

Route 99, the 102km (63mi) highway that runs from Horseshoe Bay, west of Vancouver, to Whistler is a constantly scenic ribbon of road that hugs a narrow shelf along Howe Sound, then casts upward into the Coast Range fastness that holds one of North America's most popular ski resorts. Running from sea level into the mountains, the highway takes in a remarkable coast-to-range panorama that compares in visual impact with California's famous Highway 1. Extending some 48km (30mi) into the Coast Mountains, the deep fjord of **Howe Sound** provides some of the province's most dramatic coastal scenery. Route 99, a road built through virtually sheer cliffs, offers incredible **views**★★★ of the mountains and the blue-green waters of the sound between the picturesque ferry port of Horseshoe Bay and Squamish. An alternative

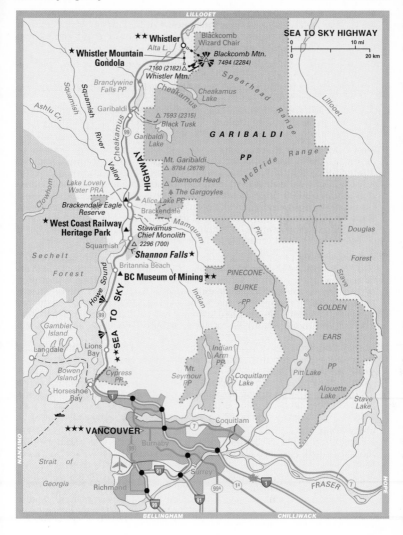

to the highway, the **Royal Hudson 2860** steam engine travels regularly in the summer from North Vancouver to Squamish (☎ *604-688-7246*). The return trip aboard the **MV Britannia** is a spectacular voyage through the fjord and back to Vancouver harbour. Once it leaves the upper reaches of Howe Sound, Route 99 follows the **Squamish River Valley**, known for the high numbers of bald eagles—sometimes more than 3,000— that winter along its banks, feasting on a late salmon run and roosting in the tall cottonwoods. The small community of Brackendale is the center for wintertime eagle-watching, the best starting point an interpretive center along the river dike that marks the 486 ha (1,200-acre) **Brackendale Eagle Reserve** *(Brackendale exit off Rte. 99; turn left at first stop sign and travel 2km to interpretive center).* Several Vancouver-area adventure companies mount float trips down the Squamish to view the eagles.

SIGHTS *1 day*

★★BC Museum of Mining – *38km (24mi) north of Horseshoe Bay on Rte. 99, in Britannia Beach. Open Jul–Aug daily 10am–4:30pm. Early May–Jun & Sept–mid-Oct Wed–Sun 10am–4:30pm. $9.50.* ✗ ☎ *604-896-2233.* Copper was first discovered here in 1888, but the mines enjoyed marginal success until World War I, when Britain and her allies needed industrial heft as much as military might. Several decades of intense production ensued, and by 1929 the Britannia complex was the largest copper mine in the British Empire. Closed in 1974, it became a historic museum in 1975. Visitors tour industry-friendly exhibits on provincial mining and the colorful Britannia Beach history, then pile into ore cars for a trip into an old 671m (2,200ft) **supply shaft** in which workers demonstrate the operation of mining equipment. The highlight of the complex is the massive, eerie **concentrator building**, an eight-level steel-and-concrete industrial megalith that descends the hill above the complex. Incomparably spooky, the concentrator building has often been used as a film set. The old mines themselves, 242km (150mi) of shafts and tunnels, honeycomb the mountains above Britannia Beach.

★**Shannon Falls** – *45km (28mi) north of Horseshoe Bay.* A short hike from the parking lot leads to a viewing point at the base of these impressive falls, which cascade 335m (1,100ft) over a cliff here. Along the trail is an old **steam donkey**, the 19C machine that made horse teams obsolete in the logging industry.

Just up the highway, on the east side, stands the 700m (2,296ft) granite monolith known as **Stawamus Chief**. Its sheer cliff face attracts rock climbers from around the world; a new, steep 3km (1.9mi) trail leads to the top.

★**West Coast Railway Heritage Park** – *1km (.6mi) west of Rte. 99 on Government Rd. in Squamish. Open May–Oct daily 10am–5pm. Rest of the year Wed–Sun 10am–5pm. Closed Jan 1 & Dec 25. $4.50.* ✗ 🔒 ☎ *604-898-9336. www.wcra.org.* a 5 ha (12-acre) museum devoted to Western Canada's trains features the painstakingly restored 1890 **British Columbia★★**, a Canadian Pacific business car. Inlaid Honduran mahogany combines with genuine leather to create a posh ambience. There are 60 other cars and engines, most open to visitors, including a huge snowplow used to clear snowdrifts on British Columbia mountain passes. The chugging of locomotives is heard constantly from the active rail yard just down the way.

★★**Whistler** – *Visitor center in Whistler Conference Centre.* ☎ *604-932-3928 or 800-944-7853. www.whistler-resort.com.* This well-planned resort community with its three alpine hamlets (Whistler Village, Village North and Upper Village) is dominated by two massive peaks, **Blackcomb Mountain** (2,284m/7,494ft) and **Whistler Mountain** (2,182m/7,160ft), groomed for state-of-the-art skiing. Regularly voted the top ski area in North America, the town held just a few backwoods residents before the first mountain, also named Whistler, was opened to skiing in 1966. Blackcomb, the second ski area, occupying its own mountain, was added in 1980. Most of the resort village's present character dates from 1979, when the Whistler Resort Association adopted development standards that have led to today's compact, mountain-village-style resort, with a pedestrians-only core. The ski area does offer grand scenery, dependable volumes of snow, and the greatest lift-served vertical drop in North America (exactly one mile on Blackcomb Mountain), but the village holds its own charms and the area offers plenty of year-round outdoor recreation. Hiking and biking trails abound, as do opportunities for fishing, riding, tennis, golf, sailing and kayaking.

Whistler Village, the original development, boasts shops, restaurants, hotels and other enterprises on a grid of cobbled and brick-paved walkways and plazas; cars are shunted to back passageways, out of sight. **Blackcomb** (Upper Village), a newer development, follows a similar design philosophy. Main lifts to both mountains depart from within 200m (650ft) of each other, and there are thousands of hotel rooms touting ski-in-and-out access.

With 5,000 visitor rooms, ranging from budget hostels to luxury hotels, Whistler somehow manages not to seem either overbuilt or crowded (except during major holidays). Now incorporated as a resort municipality, the village has adopted a

Skiing at Whistler

growth limit of 80,000 beds, which it expects to reach by 2003. Despite its popularity, Whistler remains surprisingly economical compared to similar high-profile
resorts elsewhere in North America. Summer visitors can, among other things,
canoe down a nearby stream long ago named, presciently, the River of Golden
Dreams by early settlers. No treasure ever turned up in the surrounding mountains—until the late 20C leisure economy made this valley a real gem.

★**Whistler Mountain Gondola** – *Lift runs daily July–mid-Sept. $21. Rest of year operating
as ski lift. For hours of operation and lift prices call ☎ 800-944-7853.* Though
high season here is mid-winter, this lift runs all year, providing skiers and non-
skiers alike a stunning **view**★★ from the top of Whistler Mountain. In summer you
can hike or bike down, or use the lift as a departure point for hang-gliding and
parasailing.

Garibaldi Provincial Park – *Open daily year-round.* △ 🅿 ☎ *604-898-3678. Day hikers
and overnighters should be properly equipped with good footwear, clothing, food
and water.* Wilderness trekkers head up into one of British Columbia's wildest parks
from the resort. Though covered with snow much of the year, this 195,000 ha
(482,000-acre) wilderness park is stippled with wildflowers in late summer and
favored by mountain goats, deer and bears. The most prominent peak, 2,678m
(8,784ft) Mt. Garibaldi, was named in 1860 for the Italian statesman. Other features include a 1.5km (.9mi) lava flow west of Garibaldi Lake, rock formations
called the Gargoyles on the park's south side, and the 2,315m– (7,593ft) high
basalt outcrop called the Black Tusk. Some 58km (36mi) of developed trails head
out from five main access points off Route 99 (from south to north): Diamond
Head, Black Tusk/Garibaldi Lake, Cheakamus Lake, Singing Pass and Wedgemont
Lake.

Michelin Green Guides available in English include:
North America:
California
Canada
Chicago
Florida
Mexico, Guatemala and Belize
New England
New York City
New York, New Jersey, Pennsylvania
Quebec
San Francisco
Washington DC
Outside North America:
Amsterdam
Austria
Belgium-Luxembourg
Berlin
Brussels
Disneyland Paris
Europe
France
Germany
Great Britain
Greece
Ireland
Italy
London
Netherlands
Paris
Portugal
Rome
Scandinavia Finland
Scotland
Sicily
Spain
Switzerland
Thailand
Tuscany
Venice
Vienna
Wales
The West Country of England
Regions of France:
Alsace Lorraine Champagne

Vancouver Island

Parliament Building, Victoria/© Robert Holmes

The major puzzle piece in the archipelago along British Columbia's corrugated west coast, Vancouver Island nuzzles between mainland Canada and the Olympic Peninsula of northwest Washington. The Strait of Juan de Fuca flows around its western coast from the Pacific; the Georgia, Johnstone and Queen Charlotte Straits, laced with piney islands, separate it from the rest of the province. Victoria, the capital of British Columbia and the island's largest city, occupies its southeast corner.

The largest island on North America's Pacific Coast at over 31,000sq km (12,000sq mi), Vancouver Island is part of a submerged mountain range that runs parallel to the Canadian coast. Ancient glaciers receded 15,000 years ago carving and molding the landscape with their tremendous weight and depth—1,500m (4,920ft) in places. High peaks bisect the island from northwest to southeast, making the seaside climate wild and wet, the lee side mild and dry. The Pacific's warm Japanese Current tempers the weather, which can alternate rapidly between "sunny breaks" and downpours, especially in the winter.

Largely wilderness, the most northerly part of the island is endowed with abundant wildlife and rugged scenery, lashed by strong winds and rainfall enough to make it among the wettest regions in Canada. In the south, lush temperate rain forests of fir, cedar and hemlock march down to the sea. Routes 1, then 19, skirt the eastern coast from Victoria to Port Hardy, the largest town in the north; Routes 4 and 28 climb over the central mountains from east to west. In the center of the island, Strathcona Provincial Park, British Columbia's oldest, spans over 253,000 ha (625,000 acres) and includes Mt. Golden Hines, the island's highest peak at 2,200m (7,216ft), and its last ice field, the Comox Glacier. Cape Scott hunkers at the north-westernmost tip of Vancouver Island, some 460km (285mi) up island, inaccessible except by two-day hike. A litter of small Gulf Islands range up the eastern coast between Swartz Bay and Nanaimo. Ferries ply the Georgia Strait making connections among Vancouver Island, the Gulf Islands and mainland British Columbia.

Living off the rich land and fruitful sea, Vancouver Island's "First Peoples" developed sophisticated societies and elaborate artistic, religious and cultural traditions. While humans have probably lived on the island for 10,000 years, it was the Kwakiutl, the Nootka and the Coast Salish whom the first European explorers encountered in the 18C. In the ensuing years, Spain, England, Russia and the US tussled over the island, and the discovery of its wealth in furs by Capt. James Cook in 1778 upped the stakes. Captain George Vancouver sailed to assure Spain's agreement to share the territory with Britain in 1791, spending considerable time the following year charting the island's ragged coast. Spain and Russia eventually capitulated their claims, leaving Britain and America to sort out their border disputes, accomplished in 1846 when they agreed on the 49th parallel as the international boundary. The British received all of Vancouver Island in the deal, even though it straddles the parallel. In 1849 they made Vancouver a colony and leased it to the Hudson's Bay Company to settle and develop. Seventeen years later, it joined the province of British Columbia, and Victoria was made the capital.

The island's economy has long been based on its ample resources—first furs, then gold and coal, fishing, farming and forestry, which remain the prime industries today. Tourism thrives here too and no wonder, since urbanity and wilderness coexist within such easy reach of one another.

Practical Information ....Area Code: 250

Getting There – Vancouver Island is accessible by air, ferry and bus. Flights originating from Vancouver and Seattle service Nanaimo Airport while several major airlines offer frequent scheduled flights into Victoria International Airport *(20km/ 13mi from downtown Victoria)*. For short flights from the mainland: via helicopter Helijet Airways (from Seattle, WA and Vancouver) ☎ 250-382-6222; float plane service is available through several operators including Pacific Spirit Air ☎ 250-247-9992 or 800-665-2359 and Harbour Air ☎ 800-665-0212 www.harbour-air.com.

Bus service from Vancouver: Pacific Coach Line ☎ 604-662-8074 (Vancouver) ☎ 250-385-4411 (Victoria) offers scheduled service to Victoria via BC Ferries; Maverick Coach Tours ☎ 604-662-8051 connects Vancouver to Nanaimo.

BC Ferries *(☎ 888-724-5223 or 604-444-2890; www.bcferries.bc.ca)* provides ferry service for passengers, vehicles, RV's and bikes to Nanaimo, including the new Duke Point terminal, and Victoria. Ferry service orginating from the US: The Victoria Clipper *(departure schedules from Seattle, WA; call for schedule & rates ☎ 250-382-8100 from Victoria or 206-448-5000 from Seattle; www.victoriaclipper.com)* and Washington State Ferries *(☎ 250-381-1551 from Victoria or 206-464-6400 from Seattle)*.

Getting Around – Via **bus**: Island Coach Lines ☎ 205-385-4411. BC Transit ☎ 250-382-6161 offers scheduled daily bus service for Victoria and its immediate surroundings. By **train**: for service between Victoria and Nanaimo VIA Rail ☎ 800-835-3037; E & N Railiner *(☎ 250-953-9000 ext 5800 or 800-561-8630)* allows unlimited stops on its scenic daily routes along the island's east coast.

Visitor Information and Accommodations – Tourist information and vacation planners, including the *Islands Vacation Guide, Islands Golf Vacation Guide* and *Islands Diving Guide*, are available through **Tourism Vancouver Island**, #302-45 Bastion Square, Victoria, BC V8W 1J1 ☎ 250-382-3551; www.islands.bc.ca. **Tourism Victoria** *(812 Wharf Street, Victoria, BC V8W 1T3 ☎ 250-382-6539; www.tourismvictoria.com)* offers detailed tourist information for Victoria.

Accommodations range from resorts to hostels and camping; the *Islands Vacation Guide* offers listings.

Youth Hostel: Hostelling International Victoria, 516 Yates Str. ☎ 250-385-4511.

VICTORIA ★★★

Michelin map 493 B 3 and map p 317
Population 73,504
Tourist Information ☎ 250-953-2033 or www.tourismvictoria.com

Situated at the southeastern tip of Vancouver Island, the city of Victoria overlooks the confluence of the Straits of Juan de Fuca and Georgia. To the south tower the Olympic Mountains of Washington State, and east lie the San Juan Islands. Northwest stretches the rugged interior of Vancouver Island. Hospitable Victoria crowns this majestic natural setting with color and charm, a few commercial corners notwithstanding. Though famous for its British atmosphere, much of the city's allure lies in its distinctive blending of cultures, its comfortable elegance and its friendly climate. Greater Victoria extends as far north as Sidney on the Saanich Peninsula and west to Metchosin. Closer in, hilly residential neighborhoods encircle the central city; Victorian-era homes, stucco cottages, board-and-batten Tudors share the meandering streets with awkward apartment buildings and a profusion of exotic and flowering trees. Victoria's signature gardens—from expansive public plots to miniature hanging baskets—bring color and fragrance to the city air. Encircling this urban oasis, the sea cradles Victoria in its watery palm.

Historical Notes

First Peoples – Though evidence exists of ancient settlement in southern Vancouver Island, the Salish people migrated from the interior of Canada only centuries ago. They settled amid the rich abundance of wildlife and natural resources along the coasts and on the islands, favoring especially those around present-day Victoria. At the time of European contact in the late 18C, many different bands of Coast Salish—Lekwungen, Songhees, Sooke and Saanich among them—occupied the region. Their fertile surroundings afforded them a comfortable existence and enough leisure time to develop a rich artistic tradition. Salish women were renowned as basketmakers and weavers; native carvers crafted totem poles plainer but more sculptural than those of other Pacific Coast peoples. They practiced complex social and religious rituals, celebrating important occasions with the **potlatch** *(p 34)*, a ceremony involving a complicated round of gift giving that reflected the prosperity of the culture. European settlers and missionaries changed the lives of the Coast Salish people forever. Though no wars were fought, assimilation and subjugation nonetheless diminished their native culture.

Next Peoples – Spanish explorer Manuel Quimper was probably the first European to explore the coast of Victoria in 1790, but serious settlement took another 40 years. In 1843, James Douglas established Fort Victoria (named for the recently crowned Queen of England) as the headquarters of the fur-trading Hudson's Bay Company. Douglas exerted considerable influence over the growing town, becoming its wealthiest resident and the first governor of both Vancouver Island and British Columbia. His determination to civilize and anglicize the remote outpost put Victoria on the cultural and commercial map. Indeed, Victoria reigned as capital of the island colony (1848-1866) and beginning in 1868, of the province of British Columbia. Gold fever in the late 1850s swelled the population, and in 1862, Victoria became the first incorporated city in western Canada. Its ideal location between land and sea ensured its status throughout the 19C as it grew from trading post to international entrepôt. The wealth of the land—furs, coal, gold, timber, produce—passed through Victoria. The Royal Navy base at Esquimalt established its military and shipbuilding importance. Victorians anticipated that Canada's transcontinental railroad, constructed in the 1880s, would guarantee the city's future, but railroad officials decided to end the line in tiny Vancouver instead.

Empress Hotel

Modern Peoples – Victoria fought back from this isolating blow, and by the turn of the century, streetcar lines, a local railroad and electricity kept life moving. And when shipping and manufacturing faded, tourism began its rise. In the early 1900s, fast ferry service and the Empress Hotel put Victoria on elite itineraries. Meanwhile, across the harbor at Esquimalt, shipbuilders hammered away, kept busy by two world wars. Government work increased, too, along with the service and retirement industries. In 1960, B.C. Ferries launched the first full-scale assault on the island by autos and trucks and ended Victoria's lingering isolation. The influx prompted road building and suburban sprawl, along with urban beautification and preservation efforts. Today, its island location, rich history, and composite culture spiced with Native, British, Asian, French, American and Canadian influences, give contemporary Victoria a rhythm and texture all its own.

DOWNTOWN WALKING TOUR

1 day. 2.5km (1.5mi). Begin at the Inner Harbour.

Victoria Visitor Information Centre – *812 Wharf St. (at Government and Humboldt Sts.). Open mid-Jun–mid-Sept daily 8:30am–7:30pm. Rest of the year daily 9am–5pm. Closed Dec 25. ♿ ☎ 250-953-2033. www.tourismvictoria.com.* An Art Deco tower tops the Information Centre on the north edge of the Inner Harbour. Its beacon guided seaplanes into the harbor when the building was originally constructed in 1931 as a service station. Today the center provides brochures for local attractions, and helpful counselors can answer questions, make reservations and offer suggestions for a Victoria visit.

Walk south along Government St. or descend to the Causeway at sea level.

The **Inner Harbour**, Victoria's historic front yard, occupies one corner of the capacious basin that made the port city's fortunes. Long the site of native settlements, the harbor swelled with upwards of 700 Songhees villagers after the establishment of the fort in the 1850s. The Songhees' village shared the harbor with the growing city until 1911 when the band gave up the land and moved to a reserve on Esquimalt Harbour. Today the Inner Harbour graciously receives visitors who arrive by land (from elsewhere on the island) or by sea. In good weather the promenade here is abuzz with tourists, sidewalk musicians, chalk artists and other street performers. At night the scene is equally welcoming, illuminated by 3,330 sparkling lights that trim the Parliament Buildings.

Cross Government St.

⋆**The Empress Hotel** – *721 Government St. ☎ 250-384-8111.* All care is taken to cultivate the Empress's eminence as Victoria's grande dame and a cornerstone of the city's mannerly reputation. Envisioning a rush of tourists to the Pacific Coast, city boosters at the turn of the 20C struck a deal with the Canadian Pacific Railroad to establish fast ferry service to Victoria from the mainland and to build there another in its series of choice hotels. The project began in 1904. It involved filling in the mudflats to the east of the present Inner Harbour (then the malodorous dumping grounds for local manufactories) and building a stone causeway (now Government Street). English architect Francis Rattenbury designed the Empress's original château-like structure, which was subsequently surrounded by several wings. The original building opened its 116 rooms with much fanfare in 1908. The hotel became famous for its gardens, ivy-covered walls and potted palms, its afternoon tea and its lavish evening entertainment. Well-used by royalty, celebrities, elite travelers and honeymooners over the years, the hotel underwent an extensive renovation in 1989, restoring such common spaces as the Palm Court, the Crystal Ballroom, the Empress Dining Room and the Tea Lobby to their original elegance.

© Robert Holmes

1 **Tea Lobby at the Empress Hotel**

Map opposite. 721 Government St. Reservations required. ☎ 250-384-8111. Among the numerous tearooms in Victoria, there is none more venerable than the Tea Lobby at the Empress Hotel. Once the main lobby of the hotel, this space was dedicated to formal afternoon tea service with the hotel's renovation in 1989. Decorated in full Victorian splendor and set about by immense potted palms, the room oozes gracious elegance and offers a lovely view of the Inner Harbour. Reservations and appropriate attire ("smart casual") are required to take tea here, but the atmosphere is relaxed and welcoming. Friendly waitstaff serve the luscious tea with all the trimmings—dainty sandwiches, scones, cream, preserves and fruit—at several sittings each afternoon. Tea is not the total here, however; besides the Empress's specially blended brew, non-teetotalers can partake of champagne, sherry or a kir royale that complements perfectly the rosy hues of the room.

Cross Government and then Belleville Sts.

Government buildings have occupied this 5 ha (12.5-acre) site overlooking the harbor since 1859 when Vancouver Island was a British Crown Colony. The provincial government outgrew the original structures, called the Birdcages, by the 1890s. Bricks from the Birdcages pave the driveway of the current Parliament Buildings. Gardens and native trees now ornament the grounds, and around back, a plaque identifies the important Victorians who are represented in statuary on the south wing. A bronze likeness of **Queen Victoria** stands prominently out front, while a gilt statue of Capt. George Vancouver tops the Parliament's central dome.

★ **Parliament Buildings** – *501 Belleville St. Open Jun–Labor Day daily 9am–5pm. Rest of the year Mon–Fri 9am–4pm. Cosed major holidays. ☎ 250-387-3046.* The imposing Romanesque Parliament Buildings, seat of the provincial government of British Columbia, embody the province's motto: "Splendor Without Diminishment." The first Victoria commission of young architect Francis Rattenbury, the main building was completed in 1897, its three additions by 1915. Public spaces inside the sprawling complex are elegantly appointed with a blend of indigenous and imported materials. Paintings in the lower rotunda depict events in British Columbia's history; above, the soaring dome features four monumental murals illustrating the province's main industries—logging, mining, fishing and agriculture. Upstairs, the stately legislative chamber opens off a small gallery *(closed during sessions)* set about with stunning stained glass from Leeds, England. One particularly notable window marking the diamond jubilee of Queen Victoria in 1897 had been dismantled and forgotten for 62 years until workers rediscovered it in 1974. Original light fixtures still illuminate the rooms; the lights that decorate the outside were installed in 1897 to honor Queen Victoria's 60th anniversary on the throne. During assembly sessions, visitors may observe the proceedings from public galleries on the third floor.

Cross Government St. and walk east on Belleville St.

★★★ **Royal British Columbia Museum** – *675 Belleville St. Open year-round daily 9am–5pm. closed Jan 1, Dec 25. $9.65, IMAX $9, combination ticket $16.40.* 🍴 ♿ ☎ *250-387-3701. http://rbcm1.rcbm.gov.bc.ca.* Conceived in 1886, this museum of British Columbia's natural and human history aimed to "preserve specimens of the natural products and Indian Antiquities and Manufactures of the Province" for study and exhibit. From the start, its mission depended upon amateur collectors, but over the years the museum has amassed an important array of artifacts. Originally housed in a corner of the Parliament Buildings, the museum moved into its current quarters in 1968. Faced with the daunting task of filling two extensive floors of exhibit space, curators used the opportunity to develop a series of exhibits that combine the finest diorama-making with skilled set design. Opened in phases beginning in 1972, the exhibits have been acclaimed for the blend of art and craft, illusion and reality they employ to convey the history of the land and the people. The largest carillon in Canada stands in front of the museum. A gift from the city's Dutch community to mark Canada's centennial in 1967, the tower contains 62 bells that toll every 15 minutes throughout the day.

Visit – *2 hrs. Check the admission desk for regular show times in the National Geographic IMAX Theatre.* Begin your museum tour in the **Natural History Gallery** on the second floor. A majestic life-sized **woolly mammoth**★ greets visitors to "Living Land, Living Sea." Meticulously researched down to eye color, the long-extinct mammoth

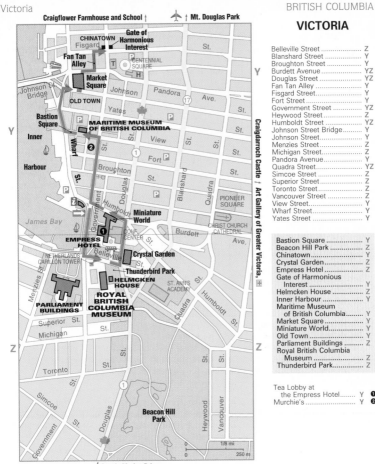

VICTORIA

has fabricated muscles that ripple under his woolly coat, made from nine musk ox hides. He occupies a chilly-looking glacial terrain of about 10,000 years ago. Other dioramas within the gallery represent various indigenous habitats in the life zones of British Columbia. Of particular interest to Vancouver Island visitors are the full-scale replicas of island forests, including the ancient giants of Cathedral Grove (p 327). Each tree in the gallery was painstakingly cast from a living specimen in the wild. Enter the "**Open Ocean**" exhibit for a simulated journey through the upper, middle and lower ocean. Ten visitors at a time proceed through the gallery guided by a fictitious story line, recorded narration, and simulated undersea scenes. Though theatrical, the exhibit conveys well the marvels of deep-sea life.

The tour takes 30min and involves entering some small, enclosed spaces.

Exhibits continue on the third floor with galleries devoted to British Columbia's human history. "**First Peoples**"★ contrasts the lifeways of prehistoric, pre-contact and post-contact native

Masks in Cave of Supernatural Treasures

peoples in the interior and along the coasts of the province. Exhibits devoted to technologies, food gathering, transportation, cosmology and society illustrate the richness and complexity of life among the region's diverse First Nations before the coming of Europeans. Note especially, on the exhibit's mezzanine level, a beautifully arranged grouping of **ceremonial masks** eerily animated through intermittent lighting and narration. Half a flight down, displays depicting the challenges and changes of post-contact life open with photographer Edward Curtis' famous 1914 film of Kwakiutl war canoes. The exhibit's centerpiece (and the museum's) is a central gallery devoted to the artistic traditions of British Columbia's far-flung native peoples, including the major groups of Vancouver Island—the Coast Salish, the Nuu-chah-nulth and the Kwakiutl. Behind a forest of totem poles stands an authentic **bighouse**, carved in the 1970s by the grandson of Kwakiatl chief Kwakwabalasami of Fort Rupert.

Across the hallway, a series of **Modern History galleries** depicts British Columbia's discovery, settlement and growth as an agricultural and industrial society. The exhibits feature large walk-in dioramas, including the captain's quarters of explorer George Vancouver's vessel, *Discovery*, a full-size Cornish waterwheel, and the corner of a milling operation.

★**Helmcken House** – *Douglas and Belleville Sts. Open May–Oct daily 10am–5pm. Rest of the year Thu–Mon 10am–5pm. Special hours during December. Closed Dec 25. $5.* 🅿 ☎ *250-361-0021.* Located just east of the Royal British Columbia Museum, Victoria's oldest house still on its original site began as a log cabin in 1852, built by Dr. John Sebastian Helmcken, a Hudson's Bay Company surgeon who served the city with a distinguished political and medical career. Original furnishings, 19C medical instruments and personal belongings from the doctor's residence (he died in 1920) fill the house. Informative 20min audio tours give insight into early life in Victoria. In addition to the Royal British Columbia Museum and the Helmcken House, the block bounded by Government, Belleville, Douglas and Superior Streets includes tiny **Thunderbird Park**, bristling with **totem poles** modeled after historic poles in the museum's collection by noted artist and Kwakiutl Chief Mungo Martin and his artisans. Evoking an authentic village landscape, the poles surround a half-size replica of a ceremonial house and a carvers' workshop, used for gatherings and demonstrations.

Walk east across Douglas St. and north across Belleville St.

Crystal Garden – *713 Douglas St. Open Apr–Oct daily 9am–6pm. Rest of the year daily 10am–4:30pm. Closed Dec 25. $7.50.* ✗ ♿ ☎ *250-381-1213. www.bcpcc.com/crystal.* This European-style glass hall was designed by Francis Rattenbury in 1925 as a center of recreation and social life in Victoria. When built it housed the largest saltwater pool in the British Empire along with ballrooms and tearooms that enticed a generation of Victorians to swim, dance and frolic. As the years passed, the structure began to fail until it closed in 1971. Public outcry prompted a renovation by the provincial government, and today the garden—minus its famous pool—is home to 350 species of tropical plants, free-flying butterflies and a roster of small mammals, reptiles and birds. An active participant in survival programs for golden lion tamarins, the Bali mynah and several other species, this small facility even sponsors a breeding program for hyacinth macaws. The conservatory makes a nice stop on a chilly Victoria afternoon, with the faded elegance of its bygone days still peeking through the palm trees.

Walk north on Douglas St. and turn left on Humboldt St.

Miniature World – 🄺🄳🅂 *649 Humboldt St. Open Jul–Sept daily 8:30am–9pm. Rest of the year daily 9am–5pm. Closed Dec 25. $8.* ♿ 🅿 ☎ *250-385-9731.* Found on the north side of the Empress Hotel building, a collection of more than 80 small-scale dioramas includes a futuristic space world, a working sawmill, a detailed scene of Canadians taking the ruined town of Caen in 1944, fairyland and literary setups, and a miniature circus display.

Continue west on Humboldt St. and turn right on Government St. Walk north four blocks.

② Murchie's

Map p 317. 1110 Government St. ☎ *250-381-5451.* Munching at Murchie's makes a great interlude to an Old Town expedition. Known as makers of fine teas and coffees since 1894, the Murchie family also offers a smorgasbord of delectables for breakfast and lunch to take away or eat in. Choose from a scrumptious selection of light fare, pastries and sweets—and of course, a variety of brewed and blended beverages. If you need more, browse the adjacent shop for specialty teas, fresh-ground coffees, pungent herbs and spices, and all the accoutrements of an afternoon tea (down to the tea cozy). Peruse the china and tableware for a nice selection of decorative Canadian-made items.

Victoria's **Old Town** consists of scattered blocks of historic buildings bounded roughly by Wharf, Humboldt, Douglas and Fisgard Streets. Once home to busy wharfside traders, saloons, hotels, groceries and warehouses, nearly 200 old buildings now house retail outlets, offices and restaurants. A walk north from the Inner Harbour may turn into a wander among purveyors of chocolate, tea, books and clothing, or a stop at a pub. Government Street is Old Town's main thoroughfare.

Turn left into Bastion Square at View and Government Sts.

The two blocks between Government and Wharf were closed to motor traffic in the 1960s as part of the redevelopment of **Bastion Square**. Here James Douglas built Fort Victoria as a fortified trading post for the Hudson's Bay Company in 1843 with the help of native laborers who dragged logs from Mt. Douglas. The fort comprised two "bastions," corner watchtowers connected by wooden fencing. One stood at Government and Bastion; its outlines are marked on the sidewalk. The other stood at the water's edge near Wharf and Broughton Streets. Fort Victoria lasted 20 years, just long enough for the city to rise up around it. Victoria's early office district took root here; most buildings in the square today date from the late 19C.

★**Maritime Museum of British Columbia** – *28 Bastion Sq. Open year-round daily 9:30am–4:30pm. Closed Jan 1 & Dec 25. $5.* ☎ *250-385-4222. www.mmbc.bc.ca.* A handsome beige edifice, once the Provincial Court House, now houses collections, exhibits and archives pertaining to British Columbia's extensive maritime heritage. The turreted building was constructed in 1889 and remodeled 11 years later by Francis Rattenbury, who added a marvelous birdcage lift, the oldest operating elevator in Canada today. Exhibits here present an excellent interpretation of local history from sea level, an important point of view considering the province's 32,000km (20,000mi) of coastal waters and its several port cities. New exhibits on the first of the museum's three floors focus on exploration, maritime commerce and adventure in roughly chronological order. Human sagas abound, including that of John Antle, a missionary mariner who brought religion by boat to remote logging camps at the turn of the century. Adventurer John Voss converted a 38ft war canoe into a sailboat and set sail around the world from Victoria in 1901. His sturdy little *Tilikum* is now docked here. Upstairs, a sampling of the museum's 400 ship models shows off the wonderful variety of craft. Informative galleries describe the history of getting around British Columbia's watery byways on the classic Canadian Pacific Steamship Lines and the B.C. Ferries "Dogwood Fleet." On the third floor, the museum has made good use of the old Vice Admiralty Courtroom where bewigged jurists once conducted inquests into marine disasters. Restored to its original appearance, the chamber now serves as a theater.

Walk west through Bastion Square to Wharf St. and proceed north.

Wharf Street once bustled with warehouses and waterfront activity, sealers, sailors and Klondikers. Buildings dating to the 1860s still line the street; the oldest, at no. 1218, went up about 1858. Just east of Wharf at Johnson and Store Streets, **Market Square** makes an interesting study in urban restoration. In the 1970s developers linked the historic buildings around this colorful block with walkways, enclosing the block's interior as a pleasant public courtyard. Shops and cafes open into the courtyard, and the surrounding blocks swarm with shoppers in the nice weather; information boards offer tidbits on Old Town, Indians, the seaport, gold rush days and Chinatown.

Exit Market Square to the north and cross Pandora Ave. Enter Fan Tan Alley on the north side of the street.

Chinatown – *Bounded by Pandora Ave. and Store, Government and Herald Sts.* Chinese miners from San Francisco came to Victoria in 1858, settling Canada's first Chinatown. In the ensuing years, native Chinese came in droves to build the Canadian railroads. Mostly men made the journey; steep head taxes kept all but the wealthiest merchants from bringing their families. Small but populous, Victoria's Chinatown evolved into a self-contained community that intrigued the outside world with its exoticism. Narrow alleyways, concealed courtyards and hidden passageways created a secret streetscape. While groceries, herbalists and benevolent associations did business on the main streets, a demimonde thrived amid gambling and opium dens along claustrophobic corridors like **Fan Tan Alley**. Restored in the 1970s, the alley today (named for a popular late-19C gambling game) is lined with offbeat boutiques and curio shops. At Government and Fisgard Streets, the **Gate of Harmonious Interest** was erected in 1981 as part of a Chinatown redevelopment project. The gate makes permanent the tradition of constructing elaborate temporary arches to honor visiting dignitaries.

ADDITIONAL SIGHTS *1 day*

Beacon Hill Park – *Foot of Douglas St.* a 75 ha (185-acre) greensward tames a portion of Victoria's windswept waterfront in lovely 19C style. Once an Indian burial ground, the high point of the park offers a sweeping vista of the Strait of Juan de Fuca and the snow-capped Olympic Mountains beyond. A warning light burned here beginning in the 1850s to guide ships around the coastal hazards. The modern park began to take shape with a racecourse in 1860, and its picturesque land-scaping was underway by 1889. John Blair designed the lakes and gardens, groves and fountains that are laced together with footpaths and stone bridges. Among the formal plantings remain remnants of meadows and grasslands and swaths of wildflowers, along with a dwindling number of old growth Garry oaks. The park also offers a petting zoo, playground, cricket pitch, soccer fields and a band shell. Across Dallas Road, a footpath rims the rugged water's edge for several kilome-ters. Walk or drive out to Clover Point and enjoy the seaside views.

★★**Scenic Marine Drive** – *Starting at Dock St. and Dallas Rd., the drive heads east, then cuts north on Richmond St. and east on Beach Dr. At 12.6km you reach Landsdowne St. (between Oak and Cadboro bays), a good place to head west back to town. Or you can continue another 9km through a mostly residential area to Mt. Douglas Park.* This lovely drive skirting land and sea offers glimpses into Victoria's waterfront communities and **vistas**★★ of the surrounding seascape. Beginning at Fisherman's Wharf Park, Dallas Road winds around the James Bay residential neighborhood, past Ogden Point Wharves where ferries and cruise ships berth. A marine sanctuary makes Ogden Point Breakwater a wonderful diving spot; walkers enjoy strolling the 800m (2,624ft) jetty. The intersection of Douglas Street and Dallas Road marks Mile Zero of the Trans-Canada Highway; beyond that point, Beacon Hill Park slopes gently away from the water. From here the drive makes its way along the shore, outlining Ross Bay, Foul Bay and MacNeill Bay and past Gonzales Point, the island's furthest point southeast and today part of Victoria Golf Club. The Trial Islands lie to the south. The road now turns north and passes through the district of Oak Bay, Victoria's most residential—and most English—municipality, a tidy neighborhood of Tudor-style stucco houses with flower gardens. Willows Beach is a popular spot on expansive Oak Bay. Beyond lies Haro Strait and Chatham and Discovery Islands. The route continues past Uplands Park and around Cadboro Bay, where the largest native village in the area once stood; then past the University of Victoria on the left. A longtime resort area, the bay fea-tures a lovely beach at Gyro Park.

★**Mount Douglas Park** – *About 8km (5mi) northeast of downtown, off Royal Oak/Cordova Bay Rd. Open daily year-round.* ♿ 🅿 ☎ *250-744-5341.* This easily accessible park, founded in 1858 and named for Gov. James Douglas, feels more remote than it is. Mt. Douglas itself is a monadnock, an ancient hill so sturdy that even glaciers failed to mow it down. From its 227m (745ft) summit to the beach below, the 182 ha (450-acre) refuge encompasses an extraordinary diversity of habitats. A visit here makes for a good introduction to Vancouver Island's many ecosystems. From the summit parking lot it's an easy climb to the hilltop where stunning 360-degree **views**★★ include the Gulf and San Juan Islands, the Olympic Mountains of Washington, downtown Victoria and points up island. A lower parking lot *(Ash and Cordova Bay Rds.)* gives access to the beach and several hiking trails that wind around the 6-8km (3.7-5mi) base of Mt. Douglas. A large posted map charts the routes and describes the park's habitats.

Art Gallery of Greater Victoria – *1040 Moss St. Open year-round Mon–Sat 10am–5pm (Thu 9pm), Sun 1pm–5pm. $5.* ♿ 🅿 ☎ *250-384-4101 aggv.bc.ca.* The small gallery offers an eclectic blend of East and West, ancient and modern. Eight temporary gallery spaces are housed in an 1889 mansion and its recent addi-tions. The museum is known for its collection of Asian art, which includes the only Shinto shrine outside of Japan. Gallery shows also feature native art, contempo-rary Canadian works and western paintings, sculpture and decorative arts from various historical periods.

★**Craigdarroch Castle** – *1050 Joan Crescent. Open mid-Jun–Labor Day daily 9am–7pm. Rest of the year daily 10am–4:30pm. Closed Jan 1, Dec 25-26. $7.50.* 🅿 ☎ *250-592-5323. www.craigdarrochcastle.com.* Though the surrounding res-idential neighborhood has somewhat diminished the prominence of this baronial stone pile, it still commands a fine vantage point overlooking the city. Such was the effect intended by Scotland-born coal baron Robert Dunsmuir when he built the mansion from 1887-90. Though he didn't live to see Craigdarroch's comple-tion, his widow Joan and three daughters (they had eight, along with two sons) did. After Joan's death in 1908, the edifice passed through several owners to be reincarnated as a house museum in 1979.

To build his 39-room castle, Dunsmuir hired American architects Warren H. Williams and Arthur L. Smith, who designed it of sandstone and brick, and crowned it with a roofline crowded with turrets, chimneys and gables. Inside, the finest oak, cherry and cedar paneling line the walls, and an 87-step staircase soars up through four floors to the tower. Lovely stained– and leaded-glass windows throughout are among the largest in situ in Canada. Transoms of etched glass and lincrusta—a 19C faux surface that mimics carved wood or embossed leather—top doorways. Celtic symbolism (the castle's name means "rocky oak place") abounds throughout the house. Furnishings, though not original, have been carefully collected to represent the period. The fourth floor houses a small exhibit about restoring the Castle. On one wall hangs a charming collection of dance cards, reminders of occasions that Joan Dunsmuir and her daughters must have enjoyed in the house. Be sure to climb the last few stairs to the **tower**, which offers a sweeping panorama of the city and the distant Olympic Mountains.

Craigflower Farmhouse and School – *Admirals Rd. at Hwy. 1A (Craigflower Rd.), View Royal. Call ahead for hours.* ☎ *250-356-5137.* In 1849 the British government established Vancouver Island as a colony, leasing it to the Hudson's Bay Company. Having agreed to settle the island in five years, the company imported indentured farm workers from Scotland. A hearty band of 60 arrived in 1853, and after a long winter in Fort Victoria, went about settling 280 ha (692 acres) along the Victoria Gorge Waterway. This and several other such settlements marked the transition from fur trading to colonization in the region. Heritage gardens, orchards and fields surround bailiff Kenneth McKenzie's 1856 manor house, the only farm building standing today and a good example of early domestic Canadian architecture. Just across the bridge in West Saanich stands the original Craigflower schoolhouse *(2755 Admirals Rd.)*, the oldest in the province, erected by the farm's workers in 1855. The one-room school stands on the site of an ancient Kosapsom village undergoing archaeological investigation.

EXCURSIONS

Sooke – *1 hr. 29km (18mi) west of Victoria on Rte. 14.* The forest industry of British Columbia began here in 1849, when the province's first independent settler, Walter Colquhoun Grant, constructed a water-powered sawmill on the basin not far from a village of the native T'Sou-ke people. Grant's stay was brief, though he left a lasting impression by planting the rampant yellow broom bushes that have widely overtaken the native flora of southern Vancouver Island. The Muir family next established a mill in 1855 and began to build the industry by logging tall, straight Sitka spruce for the spars of sailing ships. Sooke is today a center of sport and commercial fishing; picturesque Government Wharf at the foot of Maple Street serves Sooke Harbour, the farthest south in Canada. West from Sooke, the beauty of Vancouver Island's west coast unfolds. Beaches and scenery grow ever more wild as narrow Route 14 (also known as the West Coast Highway) makes its rugged way toward Port Renfrew and the Pacific Ocean.

Across Sooke Basin, **East Sooke Regional Park** *(off E. Sooke Rd.; ☎ 250-478-3344)* covers 1,400 ha (3,560) acres with trails, beaches, bluffs and bays along the Strait of Juan de Fuca.

Sooke Region Museum – *2070 Phillips Rd. at Rte. 14, 1km (.6mi) east of town. Open Jul–Aug daily 9am–6pm. Rest of the year daily 9am–5pm. Donation requested.* ♿ 🅿 ☎ *250-642-6351.* A visit here gives a good overview of the region, since it is both a rustic, small museum and a well-stocked visitor center. Crowded indoor exhibits display a wealth of artifacts and photographs related to the history of Sooke, where logging, fishing, mining, sealing and farming blended into an economy based on the wealth of local natural resources. A particularly detailed description of logging camps gives a good sense of the life led by loggers (never "lumberjacks"). On the grounds stand several outdoor exhibits and buildings, including Moss Cottage (1870), Sooke's oldest building. A "round" or slice of a giant spruce felled in 1979 measures 4.2m (14ft) at its widest and gives only a mild impression of how tall and dignified that tree must have been.

★★**Fort Rodd Hill and Fisgard Lighthouse National Historic Sites** – *2 hrs. 14.5km (9mi) west of Victoria. Follow Hwy. 1, take Colwood Exit onto Hwy. 1A, turn left at Ocean Blvd. and go 2.6km (1.6mi) to Fort Rodd Hill Rd.; turn left for fort. Open Mar–Oct daily 10am–5:30pm. Rest of the year daily 9am–4:30pm. Closed Dec 25. $3.* 🅿 ☎ *250-478-5849. www.parkscanada.pch.gc.ca.* The fort and the lighthouse, though neighbors at the entrance to Esquimalt Harbour, represent two very different shoreline sites—one to protect the coast from ships and one to protect ships from the coast. Southern Vancouver Island's splendid natural harbors and their protected location so close to the Pacific Ocean made them at once safe and vulnerable. The British Royal Navy dropped anchor in Esquimalt Harbour in 1848. Before 1900, a base, dry dock and shipyard took up residence, and in 1910 the Royal Canadian Navy took over. Today the heir to that military activity is the 2,000 ha (4,949-acre) Canadian Forces Base at Esquimalt. Fort Rodd Hill represents only one part of the Victoria-Esquimalt Fortress, a system of defensive works situated to protect this coast from 1878 to 1956. As a "coast artillery battery," the fort included big guns and the buildings and equipment to support them. A visit here entails scrambling around empty gun emplacements, barracks and earthworks and perhaps a walk along the old sentry path through mossy woods. The earliest buildings of the Upper and Lower Batteries were built in 1895; subsequent installations reflect the changing technology of coastline defense before radar came into wide use after World War II. Gunners relied on large diesel-powered searchlights hidden along the fort's seaward perimeter to illuminate enemy warships. The lights were turned off for the last time in 1954, and only vestiges remain standing today. Excellent audio presentations spoken in the words of former personnel can be heard in several of the fort's buildings. From its beginnings until its decommissioning in 1956, Fort Rodd Hill never fired an angry shot.

A short walk along the beach below the fort ends at **Fisgard Lighthouse**. A working lighthouse since 1860, picturesque Fisgard is the oldest on Canada's west coast. The light marks the entry to Esquimalt Harbour as well as the expanse of water known as Royal Roads where ships can anchor safely in darkness or heavy weather. Its light can be seen for 16km (10mi) out to sea. Though the last keeper left in 1929, the keeper's house has been converted into a small museum with fascinating exhibits about lighthouses, lenses and coastal history. Note the original hand-painted checkerboard flooring in one corner and the handsome spiral stairs that lead 51 steps up to the light *(not open to the public).*

★★★ **Butchart Gardens** – *2 hrs. 21km (13mi) north by Rte. 17 and Keating X Rd. Open year-round daily 9am. Closing times vary. $15.50.* ✗ ♿ ▣ ☎ *250-652-5256. www.butchartgardens.com.* It's hard to imagine a more inviting blend of landscapes than an old limestone quarry, a cement factory and a spectacular garden. However, blend they do at this wonderfully inviting site. Robert Pim Butchart, a pioneer of Canada's cement industry, established the Vancouver Portland Cement Company at Tod Inlet in 1904 amid the rich limestone deposits of the Saanich Peninsula. So enamored were he and his wife Jennie of the location that they built their villa-style home, Benvenuto, close by the plant. Though not then a gardener, Jennie Butchart began slowly to fill in 53 ha (131 acres) around the residence with various gardens, and the property soon bloomed with color and style. Jennie reveled in her discovered talent, opening her gardens—and serving tea—to anyone who came to see them. Over the years she earned a reputation for the breadth and rarity of her collections. After she died in 1950, the gardens remained in the family, and, in the hospitable spirit of his grandmother, R. Ian Ross made them the gracious public attraction they are today. Over 5,000 varieties of plantings blanket the grounds in a handsome collection of specialty gardens created by Mrs. Butchart over her lifetime and linked together by charming walkways. Statues, fountains, ponds and meadows punctuate the floral profusion against a lush green backdrop of indigenous and exotic trees.

Visit – *2 hrs.* Visitors are invited to stroll the gardens at their leisure; a plant identification center on the piazza and a free flower guide can help answer questions. Butchart Gardens also offers several dining experiences, including an elegant lunch or afternoon tea in the Butchart villa.

Butchart Gardens

Butchart Gardens' undisputed centerpiece is the breathtaking **Sunken Garden★★**. Between 1908 and 1921, Jennie Butchart transformed the cement factory's spent limestone quarry into this pocket Eden. She planted graceful Lombardy poplars to mask the factory's smokestack and spent hours suspended in a small seat sowing ivy in the tall quarry walls. Horses and wagons hauled in topsoil and rock debris, and Mrs. Butchart landscaped the pit to take advantage of waterfalls and a spring-fed lake. In 1964 the delightful **Ross Fountains** were added in an adjacent quarry to the south. The garden is best viewed from above or from the rock island at its center. Other delights include the old-fashioned **Rose Garden★** *(in full bloom late June)*, added in 1930, which contains some 6,500 types of roses. The **Japanese Garden★**, begun by Mrs. Butchart and landscape architect Isaburo Kisheda in 1906, comprises a wonderland of Japanese plants and decorative elements. A carefully placed window cut in the bordering hedge offers a small glimpse of cozy Butchart Cove below. The formal **Italian Garden★** contains statues and a star-shaped lily pond. Butchart Gardens has something to offer in each season. At Christmas and during the summer, nighttime illuminations cast the landscape in a different light. Thousands of bulbs color the grounds in spring, and fireworks and concerts enliven summer evenings. Brilliant autumnal colors paint the grounds from late September through November, and winter showcases the evergreens, sometimes lightly seasoned with snow.

★**Malahat Drive** – *30min. About 19km (12mi) of Rte. 1 between Goldstream Provincial Park and Mill Bay Rd., starting about 18km (11mi) north of Victoria.* The first road connecting Victoria with the agricultural Cowichan Valley to the west was made in 1861. Though narrow and unsuitable for anything but driving cattle, few improvements were made until one J. F. L. MacFarlane plotted a new road along the Malahat Ridge in 1911. Today this stretch of road is part of Route 1, the 7,821km (4,849mi) Trans-Canada Highway completed in 1962, also known as the Island Highway. From Goldstream Provincial Park, the road climbs to the Malahat Summit, through a corridor of towering trees. At the top, a scenic turnout commands a spectacular **view★** of the Finlayson Arm of the Saanich Inlet and the lumpy hills of the surrounding countryside. Stately firs march up the steep slopes, nearly to the top of the 352m (1,187ft) summit. Descending the summit, vistas to the north to encompass the widening expanse of the inlet below.

SOUTHEAST COAST

Michelin map 493 B 2, 3 and map p 325
Tourist Information ☏ 250-746-4636

The Southeast Coast, cluttered with islands and inlets, occupies the lee side of Vancouver Island along the Strait of Georgia. Sheltered by the island's central mountains, this region receives a fraction of the rain that saturates the Pacific coast. Though the winters are mild and moist, the summers are the driest in Canada. Douglas fir forests thrive here, along with groves of gnarly Garry oak, the island's only native oak. The lovely arbutus, whose red bark peels away to reveal a smooth green skin, clings to hillsides and headlands. Coastal waters teem with life, including harbor seals and porpoises, sea lions and a veritable melting pot of sea creatures that flourish along the shorelines and intertidal zones. Not far offshore lie the Gulf Islands, miniature replicas of the big island but wilder yet. For centuries this part of Vancouver Island has been occupied by the Coast Salish people, including the Cowichan band, the largest in British Columbia today with nearly 3,200 members. The Trans-Canada Highway (Route 1) skirts the southeast coast, connecting seaside towns that once thrived on sawmills, coal mines and fishing. Many are now retooling their faltering economies to build a flourishing tourist and resort trade.

DUNCAN *2 hrs*

On the banks of the Cowichan River, Duncan is the first sizable town north of Victoria, lying 60km (37mi) up Route 1. Founded as a railway stop in 1886, Duncan remains a crossroads in this rural area where agriculture and forestry predominate. The region is home as well to the Cowichan people, whose nine reserves in the valley comprise 2,400 ha (6,000 acres). In 1985 city fathers elected to celebrate the local native heritage by collaborating with native carvers to re-invigorate the art of totem-pole making. Now known as the "City of Totems," Duncan proudly displays around 60 **totem poles** in buildings, parks and along city streets. Traditional poles, usually carved from the sturdy, long-lasting trunks of red cedar trees, exhibited a family's crests or legends, honored the living and the dead, and welcomed guests. Visitors to a native village might well encounter a forest of poles, and so it is in Duncan, though here they spread over several square blocks. While these modern totems incorporate traditional symbolism—the raven, killer whale, bear and so on—they also blend contemporary elements. To view the totems, follow the yellow footprints on the sidewalks, or pick up a guide at the Duncan-Cowichan Chamber of Commerce **Travel Infocentre** *(381 Trans-Canada Hwy.; open Apr–Oct Mon–Sat 9am–5:30pm;* ☏ *250-746-4636)*. Guides are also available at the Cowichan Native Village.

Cowichan Native Village – *200 Cowichan Way. Open year-round daily 9am–5pm. Closed Jan 1 & Dec 25. ✗ ⅅ ℙ ☎ 250-746-8119.* Upon arriving at this art center and living-history replica village, ask to see the 22min multimedia presentation for a good overview of the Cowichan people. Formed in the mid-1800s, the Cowichan (meaning "basking in the sun") are part of the Coast Salish Nation that populates the coastal regions of British Columbia. From 19C immigrant Scots, skillful Cowichan weavers learned to knit and a century later still produce cozy woolen goods that blend native motifs with European styles. They are also expert carvers, and in the warm months, the village's seven structures hum with activity, including native artisans at work in the world's largest carving house. The complex also includes a crafts gallery, a reconstructed bighouse, and a restaurant that serves native fare.

★**BC Forest Discovery Centre** – *2892 Drinkwater Rd. Open mid-May–Labor Day daily 10am–6pm. Labor Day–mid-Oct daily 10am–4pm. $8. ℙ ☎ 250-715-1113.* Covering 40 ha (99 acres) this museum provides some background

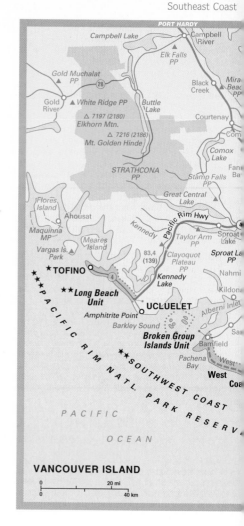

VANCOUVER ISLAND

to the province's most important industry. Visitors can walk through a forest of Douglas fir trees, visit a log museum displaying the evolution of logging techniques, see a reconstructed logging camp and ride the narrow-gauge steam railway *(runs mid-May–Labor Day daily 10:30am–5pm; every 30min).*

CHEMAINUS *2 hrs*

Dependent upon forest industries since 1858, tiny Chemainus suffered economic setbacks with the downsizing of the local sawmill in the 1980s. To counteract the crisis, locals created a tourist destination here by honoring its mill-town heritage in a series of expansive outdoor **murals**. Painted by a variety of artists, the 33 murals that today decorate storefronts and building walls around town depict everything from Indian princesses to lumber barons. Boutiques, antique stores, art galleries and cafes have since taken root along the town's streets. To view the murals and browse the shops, follow the footprints painted on the sidewalks or pick up a map at the information kiosk at Willow and Legion Streets, or any of several shops in town. The small **Chemainus Valley Museum** in Heritage Park explores the history of the mill town and exhibits the original maquettes for many of the murals. Also in the park stands a replica of the waterwheel that powered the town's first mill in 1862. To the north of the park is Old Town, the original town center, where more murals and shops are located. Ferries depart for Thetis Island, a good place to bike and picnic, from the foot of Oak Street. Despite its hardships, the local sawmill still operates on Chemainus Bay *(tour information: ☎ 250-246-3221)*, and when the wind is right, the pungent aroma of cut wood hangs in the air as it has for over a century. For information and maps, contact the **Chemainus Chamber of Commerce** *(9796 Willow St.; open May–Aug Mon–Fri 9am–5pm, weekends 9am–6pm; rest of the year Mon–Fri 9am–4pm; ⅅ ℙ ☎ 250-246-3944; www.chemainus.com).*

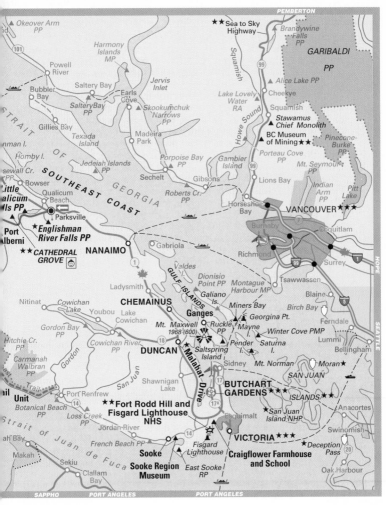

NANAIMO *1/2 day*

Nanaimo lies due west of mainland Vancouver across the Georgia Strait and is the second-largest city on Vancouver Island. Sheltered by a close-in archipelago, the "Harbour City" has long offered protected waters and a broad anchorage to its inhabitants. Spanish explorers in 1791 found five Coast Salish bands here, known as the Snuneymuxw, from which the modern "Nanaimo" is derived. When the English arrived in 1852, the native people shared their "black rocks" with the newcomers and then sold 19km (12mi) of waterfront land to the Hudson's Bay Company for 688 blankets. Over the next hundred years, mining of the "black rocks" (coal) built the city. At the height of production in 1923, the mines employed 3,400 men and produced nearly 1.3 million tons of coal. Today the city depends on forest industries and commercial fishing, as well as tourists and outdoor enthusiasts who come to dive, kayak, hike, fish and boat. A 4km (2.5mi) **Harbourside Walkway** takes in waterfront sights, from the commercial boat basin up the Newcastle Island Channel to Departure Bay, where ferries come and go from Vancouver. In town, several eateries and shops line the promenade, and the water churns with seaplanes and fishing boats. From docks along the walkway, ferries depart for Gabriola, Newcastle and Protection Islands. Overlooking the marina stands the **Bastion** *(Bastion and Front Sts.)*, built in 1853 by the Hudson's Bay Company to protect its growing mining community; it is the oldest of the company's structures in North America and houses a museum that is open in summer. Three self-guided **walking tours** of the harbor and downtown begin at the Bastion; pick up a Heritage Walk Guide there or at the Nanaimo District Museum. **Petroglyph Provincial Park** *(Hwy. 1 just south of town)* contains ancient rock carvings representing real and mythic humans, animals and denizens of the deep.

325

■ The Gulf Islands

Islands aplenty swarm the southeast coast of Vancouver Island north of the Saanich Peninsula. Called the Gulf Islands because early explorers mistook the Strait of Georgia for a large inlet, the archipelago creates a maze of waterways for ferries and other mariners to navigate. Little replicas of their large neighbor, the Gulf Islands enjoy the drier, milder climate of eastern Vancouver Island. A matching shag of Douglas fir blankets their heights and valleys; huge stars bespeckle their clear, and very dark, night skies. For their small size, the Gulf Islands feature an amazing range of topography and a veritable bestiary of birds (Galiano alone boasts 130 species). Indeed, the islands' lure lies in their unspoiled natural beauty, conducive to superb cycling, hiking, swimming, camping, kayaking, diving, fishing and beaching. The islands can be visited year-round, but since accommodations are limited, it is best to call ahead for reservations to avoid both off-season closings and high-season crowds. For, while the Gulf Islands usually provide a quiet refuge for residents, visitors and wildlife alike, summer vacationers do descend in abundance.

Throughout most of their human history, the Gulf Islands have been accessible only by small boat or canoe. Native Coast Salish visited them for hunting and fishing, and later settlers came in small numbers to farm, grow fruit and raise livestock. They made good stepping stones for travelers between Vancouver Island and the mainland, though their lack of harbor facilities kept large boats away. Concern over real estate development prompted the founding of the Gulf Islands Trust in 1974 to preserve and protect the islands from unregulated growth.

Today, though these islands number over 200, only the major southern Gulf Islands—Saltspring, Mayne, Galiano, the Penders and Saturna—can be reached by ferry from Swartz Bay on Vancouver Island or Tsawwassen on the mainland. There is inter-island service as well, but sailing schedules, especially in the off-season, make it difficult to island hop, so visitors should budget several days for a leisurely tour of the archipelago. If time is short, a round-trip can be made to any island in one day. Or, a long weekend could easily be spent exploring a single island.

The largest at 185sq km (71sq mi) and most populous with 10,000 residents, **Saltspring Island** attracts artists and craftspeople, writers and recluses. Tall hills, rocky bluffs and rugged coastline characterize the island's dramatic geography, and its winding, wooded roads are a delight to drive. In the southwest, peaks rise to over 600m (1,968ft). A provincial park tops **Mt. Maxwell**, and though the logging road to the summit is rough, the **panorama★** is breathtaking. In the southeast corner of the island, **Ruckle Provincial Park** encompasses one of the oldest family farms in British Columbia, run by the Ruckle family since 1872. Visitors are welcome to explore the farm without disturbing the animals or operations. Farther north, harborside **Ganges**, the only true town in the islands, features art galleries, boutiques, restaurants and nearby accommodations. Across the Swanson Channel from Saltspring lie the two **Pender Islands**, north and south. Most of the 2,000 residents live on North Pender, which connects to South Pender by bridge. Both islands are known for secluded coves and quiet harbors. A climb to the summit of **Mt. Norman** rewards the hardy with a sweeping vista of surrounding land and sea.

Southeasternmost of the Gulf Islands, sparsely populated **Saturna Island** exudes a remote charm. East Point Road follows the coast along the Strait of Georgia from **Winter Cove Provincial Marine Park** to lonely East Point, where a small park surrounds the lighthouse built here in 1888. **Mayne Island** lies northeast of Saturna. Once the social center of the Gulf Islands, its port at **Miners Bay** was a lively enclave in the 19C. **Georgina Point**, where the first lighthouse was constructed in 1885, overlooks Active Pass. Long, lean **Galiano Island** is located across the pass, stretching 26km (16mi) to the northwest. Mt. Galiano and high ridges in Bluffs Park, Montague Harbour Provincial Park and Bodega Ridge afford good views and excellent hiking.

*For ferry information, call **B.C. Ferries**, ☏ 250-386-3431; toll free in British Columbia at ☏ 888-BCFERRY. For Gulf Island information, call Tourism Vancouver Island, 302-45 Bastion Square, Victoria, BC V8W 1J1, ☏ 250-382-3551; the Salt Spring Tourist Information Centre, 121 Lower Ganges Rd., Salt Spring Is., BC V8K 2T1, ☏ 250-537-5252; or the Galiano Chamber of Commerce, P.O. Box 73 Galiano Is., BC V0N 1P0, ☏ 250-539-2233.*

Nanaimo District Museum – *100 Cameron Rd. Open late May-Labor Day daily 9am–5pm. Rest of the year Tue–Sat 9am–5pm.*   📆 *250-753-1821.* This small museum makes a good introduction to the history of Nanaimo beginning with a look at the changing lives of the native Snuneymuxw people upon whose ancestral lands the city stands. A walk-through replica of a mine tells the coal story, showcasing gear (note the miner's cap with fish-oil headlamp), tools and rescue equipment used until the last mine closed in 1953. Upstairs, full-scale dioramas replicate a typical street in late 19C Nanaimo, including shopfronts, a schoolroom and business offices. The windows of Chinatown are noteworthy for their detail and color. As the Chinese came to labor in the coal mines they built a large community in Nanaimo, and, though Chinatown burned in 1960, the Chinese influence here lingers on. Many of the artifacts on display survived the 1960 fire.

★FROM PARKSVILLE TO PACIFIC RIM

Allow 1/2 day, including visits. 154km (95mi) by Rte. 4.

Winding Route 4 traverses the mountain backbone of the island through lovely scenery. Some parts are wild and untouched by mankind; other parts are the scene of great activity, particularly that of the logging industry. Just north of Parksville, the busy summer resort of Qualicum Beach was developed in the early 20C by real-estate investors; it now supports a diverse community of artisans and is a favorite haven for retired Canadians. The town offers broad, sandy beaches at its front door and a panoply of forest parks to explore in its backyard. In recent years, government-run fish hatcheries have been established nearby to stem the decline of the salmon brought on by overfishing.

★**Englishman River Falls Provincial Park** – *From Parksville, take Rte. 4 west. After 5km (3mi), turn left and continue 8km (5mi). Open daily year-round.* ⚠ 📆 *250-954-4600. www.elp.gov.bc.ca/bcparks.* Relatively small at 97 ha (240 acres), this park nonetheless contains two mighty waterfalls buried deep in the mixed hemlock, fir and cedar forest. Within 1km (.6mi) of each other on the Englishman River, both are easily accessible on foot from the park's farthest parking lot.

★**Little Qualicum Falls Provincial Park** – *26km (16mi) west of Parksville. Open daily year-round dawn-dusk.* ⚠ & 📆 *250-752-6305.* The sprightly Little Qualicum River tumbles down two sets of falls here as it churns its way through a narrow gorge. At the far side of the spacious picnic grove adjacent to the parking lot, well-groomed gravel paths and stairways lead to both falls. For a nice **view** up and down the boisterous waterway, cross the bridge that spans it near the lower falls. The larger **upper falls★** are accessed by a pleasant 30min round-trip forest walk. The Little Qualicum River flows out of lovely Cameron Lake, an idyllic setting for fishing and swimming just a short drive west of the park on Route 4.

★★**Cathedral Grove** – 🧒 *35km (22mi) west of Parksville in MacMillan Provincial Park. Open daily year-round.* & 📆 *250-954-4600.* The congregation of stately giants that straddles Route 4 includes many of earth's oldest and tallest living inhabitants. While the youngsters here sprouted in the wake of a fire some 300 years ago, certain elders have endured for eight centuries. The tallest, a Douglas fir, stretches up 76m (250ft). A walk among these arboreal behemoths is a treat for all senses: A creaking of ancient limbs fills the moist pungent air and it takes a moment for the eye to adjust to their towering scale in the dappled light of the thicket. Route 4 bisects the grove; both sides of the highway are well worth a look. To the north, dirt paths lead between the giants—western red cedars, Douglas fir, western hemlocks among them—and occasional interpretive signs point out interesting details. Across Route 4 to the south, the forest reveals another side. In 1997 an intense burst of winter wind (called a "Qualicum wind") howled through the old growth leveling scores of the giants, whose shallow root systems make them unstable under such conditions. Much of the destruction occurred in this part of the grove, and most of the trees lie where they fell, as impressive reclining as they are upright. New boardwalks wind through the woods, and excellent signage describes the chaotic scene in terms of the forest life cycle. Aside from lessons learned, however, this breathtaking landscape appeals most for its primordial beauty, draped as if in green snow by mosses and lichens and shimmering with the ubiquitous moisture of the rain forest.

Port Alberni – *48km (30mi) northwest of Parksville via Rte. 4.* Its strategic location at the tip of the tall Alberni Inlet, an arm of the Pacific that reaches inland 40km (25mi), made Port Alberni a historic logging and commercial fishing crossroads. Set against a mountainous backdrop, this hardworking town of nearly 20,000 also functions as a deep-sea port and gateway to the Pacific Rim. The first sawmill was established here in 1861—lumber, pulp and paper are still the primary exports from the port. Famous for salmon fishing, the local waters attract sportsmen and women eager to hook a prized chinook. The Alberni Harbour Quay at the foot of Argyle Street is a center of harbor activity; the top of the clock tower amid the shops and cafes offers a panoramic view and on summer weekends a steam train tours the waterfront. Adventuresome travelers with a day to spare can book passage on the **MV Lady Rose** or **MV Frances Barkley** *(☎ 250-723-8313 or 800-663-7192)*, working freight and mail packets that take passengers on their rounds down the inlet and around the Broken Group Islands of Barkley Sound *(accessible only by boat)*, with stops at Ucluelet or Bamfield. The compact **Alberni Valley Museum** *(4255 Wallace St.; open year-round Tue–Sat 10am–5pm; closed major holidays;* ⚐ ▣ ☎ *250-723-2181)* runs the gamut of local history, exploring both native and non-native cultures.

Just west of Port Alberni on Route 4 (Pacific Rim Highway), **Sproat Lake Provincial Park** makes an interesting stop. The beach there offers a good view of the docked **Martin Mars Water Bombers**, mammoth airborne fire fighters that carry over 6,000gals (7,200 US gals) of water. The last two World War II troop carriers of their kind, the bombers have a 61m (200ft) wingspan.

After leaving the lake, Route 4 begins to climb Klitsa Mountain along the valley of the Taylor River. From its peak, the road starts a curving descent to the Pacific along the Kennedy River, offering **views★** of snow-capped peaks. The river widens into **Kennedy Lake**, the largest stretch of freshwater on the island. The road follows the lake, alternately rising above it and dipping to water level. Between Port Alberni and Long Beach is an 85km (53mi) stretch of backcountry with no services.

SOUTHWEST COAST★★

Michelin map 493 B 2 and map p 324
Tourist Information ☎ 250-726-4701

Across Vancouver Island's central spine of mountains a tangle of land and sea comprises the Pacific coast. From Sooke in the south to windswept Cape Scott, the shoreline makes its tortured way northwest. Fjords and inlets pierce the island's side carving a complicated puzzle of islands, bays, capes and promontories. This side of Vancouver Island is as wet as it is wild since humid air off the Pacific drops its moisture before crossing the mountains. While Canada's annual precipitation averages 119cm (47in), this waterlogged coast receives over 250cm (98in) yearly and in places twice that much. The lush coastal rain forests support western hemlocks and red cedars fringed along the beaches by the salt-loving Sitka spruce. Sea creatures of all sizes swarm the ocean waters warmed by the Japanese Current; the annual springtime migration of **gray whales** attracts a host of whale-watchers, and beach visitors delight as well in tide pools crowded with starfish and other seaside dwellers. The seafaring Nootka people, historic inhabitants of this coast, gathered a rich diet from the sea and from the inlets where commercial and sport fishermen still harvest spawning salmon, shellfish and crab. Moist winds and warm currents of the Pacific moderate the temperature here, but massive ocean storms pound the shore between November and February and have themselves become a popular tourist attraction. Local hostelries even offer **storm-watching** packages. The treacherous coast and brutal seas make this edge of Canada particularly dangerous for mariners. So many ships have foundered here that the shoreline has earned a reputation as a "Graveyard of the Pacific."

★★★PACIFIC RIM NATIONAL PARK RESERVE *2 days*

Pacific Rim National Park Reserve clings to the edge of the continent between, Tofino on the north and Port Renfrew on the south. Bearing the full brunt of the Pacific Ocean, the park pulses with the raw energy of wind and waves. Set aside in 1970 to protect and preserve the many littoral ecosystems that share this disjointed 130km (81mi) stretch of coast, the park covers more than 500sq km (190sq mi) of beach, forest, islands and water. Indeed, its reach extends into the Pacific Ocean in order to protect the sea life that inhabits the shallows. The weather here is eminently changeable, especially during the stormy winter months when sun, rain, ice, fog and mist come and go in a twinkling. Three separate units make up the park; each is a world unto itself and, though adjacent, must be accessed separately. For general information about the park, the **Administration Office** is open year-round *(☎ 250-726-7721)*.

West Coast Trail Unit – *Located between Port Renfrew and Bamfield. ☎ 250-647-5434 in Port Renfrew; ☎ 250-728-3234 in Pachena Bay.* This rugged 75km (47mi) wilderness track between Port Renfrew and Bamfield on the southeastern corner of Barkley Sound follows the route of the old lifesaving trail. So many boats sank in these remote waters that authorities widened an existing telegraph trail in

Pacific Rim National Park Reserve

© Robert Holmes

1907 and equipped a cabin every 6mi with blankets, emergency provisions, a telephone and instructions in several languages. The cabins offered some refuge and the hope of rescue to shipwreck survivors who might scramble ashore. Today the trail remains remote, both challenging and rewarding experienced hikers. Hiking the West Coast Trail requires total self-sufficiency *(there are no facilities)* and at least six days to make the one-way trip. The hike can be made in either direction, winding through rain forests and along beaches, across rivers and down cliffs. *Limited permits are available to hike the West Coast Trail (open May–Sept).*

Broken Group Islands Unit – *Barkley Sound.* Dollops of pine and rock in the middle of Barkley Sound, the Broken Group Islands are accessible only by boat. Once home to native peoples, the islands today—they number about 100—are uninhabited and support a profusion of sea and bird life. Human visitors seeking a day or two of wilderness camping, kayaking, canoeing and exploring drive to launch sites or arrive on the *MV Lady Rose (☎ 250-723-8313)* from Ucluelet or Port Alberni. Day trips from Ucluelet are also available.

★★**Long Beach Unit** – *Between Ucluelet and Tofino along Rte. 4.* ☎ *250-726-4212 or 726-7721.* The 25km (16mi) of the Long Beach Unit are by far the most accessible and popular in Pacific Rim National Park. Broad, hard-packed beaches—**Long Beach★★**, **Combers Beach**, and **Wickaninnish Beach**—form a continental threshold of about 11km (7mi) where the pounding Pacific comes and goes in its endless round of tides. Marking the ocean's winter heights are piles of drift logs, beached survivors of a century of wrecked log rafts. Windblown spruce, sculpted by driven sand and spray, trim the beach's edge and protect the old-growth forest beyond. Twenty-one species of whales ply these waters; during migration season *(Mar–Apr)*, some 20,000 gray whales move north along the shore and can sometimes be seen from these beaches. To complement walks on the beach, the Long Beach Unit includes several kilometers of well-maintained **boardwalk trails** into the surrounding forests. Parking areas are located at intervals off Route 4 with access to beaches and trails.

In season, the **Wickaninnish Centre★** *(open daily mid-Mar–mid-Oct; ✗ &. ▣)* presents exhibits, films, artifacts and information about the Pacific Ocean and the natural and human history of the area. Interpreters are on hand to answer questions, and the center also features a restaurant. From there A 1.5km (.9mi) round-trip along the **South Beach Trail** follows the edge of the forest and climbs the headland for panoramic **views** before descending to South Beach. The 5km (3.1mi) **Wickaninnish Trail** was once part of the old footpath between Tofino and Ucluelet; the original plank road can be seen in places through the moss. The **Spruce Fringe Trail★**, at Combers Beach, makes A 1.5km (.9mi) loop through the tangled Sitka spruce fringe at the edge of the beach and then up into the older forest where 300-year-old Sitka giants live. Amazing "aerial gardens" of epiphytes populate the gnarled branches, along with moss and fungi. Near the northwest border of the park, remnants of a radar installation built atop **Radar Hill★★** during the Cold War speak to the strategic importance of this remote stretch of coast. The area was originally developed as a defensive zone during World War II and local fishermen even formed a naval militia. No equipment remains on this lonely hill now, but the **vista★★★** of wild coastline backed by mountains is breathtaking.

329

★TOFINO *1/2 day*

At the end of the peninsula stands friendly little Tofino. Settlement on the Clayoquot Sound began with a Nootka band under the leadership of Chief Wickaninnish. The native people still populate his village of Opitsat across Tofino Inlet on Meares Island. Though Capt. Cook landed here in 1778, the town is named for a seafaring Spaniard. Quiet and low-key in the winter, Tofino is a busy staging area for local adventures the rest of the year—whale-watching in the spring, exploring Pacific Rim National Park Reserve, charter fishing, sailing, surfing, kayaking and hiking. Wonderful fresh oysters and Dungeness crab come out of the local waters, and of course delicious fresh fish. To the southeast, between Tofino and Pacific Rim National Park, the deep crescent of **Chesterman Beach** offers splendid walking and a view of the Lennard Island lighthouse just offshore.

© Robert Holmes

Tofino

UCLUELET *1 hr*

Named for its early inhabitants, the "people with a safe landing place," Ucluelet indeed occupies a fine harbor northwest of Barkley Sound. The town makes a convenient embarkation point for kayaking the Broken Group Islands or hiking Pacific Rim National Park Reserve. Fishing charters and whale-watching excursions can also be arranged from here. For a taste of the fury that earned this coast the name "Graveyard of the Pacific," visit **Amphitrite Point** south of town on Coast Guard Road on a stormy day. The squat lighthouse was built on this headland in 1906 to help guide ships through the rocky waters and into Barkley Sound and the Ucluelet Inlet; a foghorn blasts intermittently through stormy weather. The Coast Guard station next door monitors traffic in the area.

South-Central British Columbia

Fraser River Canyon/© Robert Holmes

Between the towering granite wall of British Columbia's Coast Mountains, and the equally imposing barrier formed by inland ranges, lies a spectacular landscape defined by staggering geographic contrasts. Dense rain forests, prodigious canyons, unexpected deserts, glacier-clad peaks, huge lakes and rich orchards and vineyards all lie within miles of each other. These features are what shaped life here ages ago—native inhabitants depended for ten millennia on salmon in the rivers, cedar and cottonwood from the forests, and berries from native plants.

As productive as South-Central British Columbia is today, riches elsewhere originally attracted European adventurers to the area. Surveying routes to transport beaver pelts from distant northern forests to the Pacific Coast, adventurer **Simon Fraser** and geographer **David Thompson** were among the first to explore the area's fearsome chasms; the canyons named for Fraser and Thompson bear tribute to those early-19C expeditions. The next wave of visitors came in the 1860s as gold rushers sought the rich fields of the Cariboo Mountains to the north. Construction of the **Cariboo Road** through the Fraser Canyon (1862-64) was one of the great Canadian engineering feats of the 19C; some of the original roadbed is still in use. Its pulse-quickening adherence to steep mountainside slopes amazes travelers even today. The interior's agricultural potential was realized by settlers such as Father Charles Pandosy, an Oblate priest who planted the area's first fruit trees at his Kelowna mission.

Today the Fraser Canyon remains a transportation corridor; high above the canyon, huge mines extract copper. Cedar and Douglas fir are the foundations of an active, although declining, wood-products industry, and salmon runs numbering millions of fish still pump life into inland rivers. In the Okanagan beats the heart of Canada's orchard and vineyard industries, and huge cattle ranches blanket the highland plateaus. An energetic traveler can, in a couple of days, take a desert hike; visit a top-notch vineyard; go sailing; play golf; take a high-country trail ride; and raft down the same river canyon that Simon Fraser struggled through so perilously almost two centuries ago.

FRASER CANYON COUNTRY★★

Michelin map 493 C 2 and map below
Tourist Information ☎ 604-739-0823 or www.coastandmountains.bc.ca

Stretching 193km (120mi) from Hope to Cache Creek, the gorges the Fraser and Thompson Rivers have cleaved through the Coast Range are geologically remarkable chasms enhanced by modern works of engineering. At Lytton, epicenter of the two gorges, the riverbed lies just 90m (300ft) above sea level, while glacier-wrapped Mt. Lytton looms above at 2,010m (6,700ft) and Skihist Mountain, 16km (10mi) west, approaches 3,000m (10,000ft). Lytton is also in the transition zone between desert and rain forest: In a span of about 65km (40mi), from Boston Bar to Spences Bridge, the environment changes from lush rain forest, with more than 250cm (98in) of rain a year, to stark desert, with less than 26cm (10in).

Although Simon Fraser traversed this passage in 1808, no meaningful traffic used it until colonial Governor James Douglas embarked on construction of the Cariboo Road in 1862. Determined that the newfound goldfields 500km (310mi) north would draw fortune-seekers through Vancouver rather than up the Columbia through the United States, British authorities sent an army of workers (including two contingents of Royal Engineers) into the canyon to build a 5m- (18ft) wide throughway sufficient for wagon traffic. With rickety-looking plank trestles cantilevered out from nearly vertical canyon walls in the worst stretches, the 650km (400mi) road was finished in 1864. Most of the present-day TransCanada Highway (Highway 1) from Yale to Cache Creek—a more modern but equally impressive piece of construction—follows the original Cariboo Road. Just a half-century ago it was a single track; converting it to two lanes required seven tunnels between Hope and Boston Bar, just past Hell's Gate. The road's utility as a passage to the interior has been circumvented by the Coquihalla superhighway, which crosses the mountains from Hope to Kamloops, cutting more than an hour off the transit time. Still, the canyon remains one of the most scenic routes in North America. Although most visitors to British Columbia drive up the canyon, it is perhaps equally impressive traveled from north to south, as the sense of descending into a vast defile from the plateau outside Cache Creek is profound.

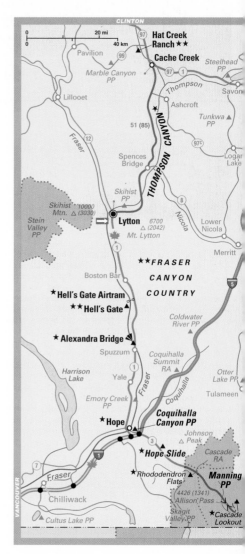

★HOPE 1/2 day.

Hope's idyllic setting at the foot of Fraser Canyon offered gold rushers a century and a half ago a somewhat misleading idea of the rugged trek ahead. The town occupies a small, gentle delta at the juncture of the Coquihalla and Fraser Rivers; passing showers paint rainbows on the peaks that encircle the valley. Founded by the Hudson's Bay Company in 1848 as Fort Hope, this was an inconsequential trade depot until gold was found on nearby Fraser River gravel bars a decade later. When that gold played out in a few years, and its source was discovered in the Cariboo, Hope became a center for gold-rush traffic, undergoing several boom-and-bust cycles as the rush waxed and waned. In 1886 construction of the Canadian Pacific Railroad once again brought prosperity. Today Hope is still a crossroads town, trying to shift its livelihood from timber to tourism. Visitors here can pan for gold on nearby Fraser gravel bars, or go soaring in gliders on the constant thermal uplifts.

Hope's spectacular surroundings have from time to time been the setting for films, including the original Rambo movie, *First Blood* (1982). Several other films requiring steep, deeply forested mountain backgrounds have been made in this area, including portions of a movie about K2 in the Himalayas.

Hope Visitor InfoCentre and Museum – *919 Water Ave. Visitor center open May–Jun & Sept–Oct daily 8am–6pm. Jul–Aug daily 8am–8pm. Rest of the year Mon–Fri 10am–4pm. Closed major holidays.* 🅿 ☎ *604-869-202. Museum open May–Sept Thu–Mon 9am–5pm. Donation requested.* Here you'll discover aboriginal and pioneer artifacts, the most interesting of which is a restored 19C ore concentrator found buried in mud nearby in 1981. The center also offers maps and information on hiking, rafting, gold panning, chainsaw carvings, and Rambo film locations—such as the sidewalk where star Sylvester Stallone rode his stolen motorcycle. Hope aspires to the title of "Chainsaw Carving Capital of Canada"; attractive artworks by local sculptor Pete Ryan are on display throughout the town. The largest number of sculptures can be found in **Memorial Park** *(Wallace and 3rd Sts.)*, where dying Douglas firs have been transformed into eagles, bears and salmon.

★**Christ Church** – *Park and Fraser Sts. Open for church services only.* This tidy building was consecrated in 1861 and thus lays claim to the title of oldest church in British Columbia on its original site. Well-kept and still in active use, its

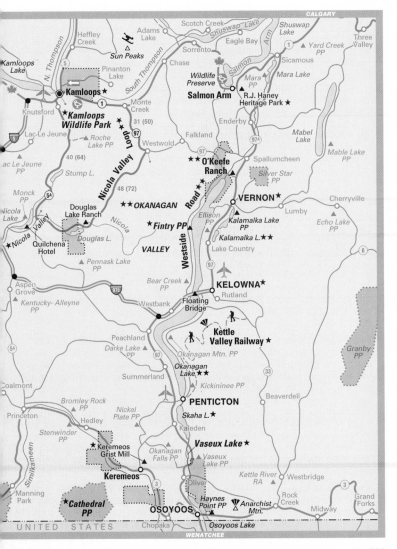

compact, Gothic-influenced design features an unusual set of metal tie-rods across the vaulted roof, used for supporting the walls. Most of the church and its furnishings, such as the leaded-glass, diamond-patterned windows and fir floors are original. The huge Douglas firs outside were planted when the church was built; their present size bears witness to the fertility of Hope's rain-forest climate.

Excursions

Coquihalla Canyon Provincial Park – *1 hr. 9km (5.6mi) east of Hope on Tunnels Rd. Open May–Oct daily. Closed in winter when the tunnels are unsafe.* 🅿 ✆ *604-824-2300.* When early 20C builders of the Kettle Valley Railway *(p 341)* came down out of the forbidding mountains to the east, they faced one last obstacle, this narrow chasm in the Coast Range foothills. The solution was an impressive set of five tunnels pushed through the rock toes of the slopes above. The railroad was shut down in 1961; today the railbed provides a pleasant stroll through the cottonwood-lined canyon and the somewhat eerie tunnels.

★**Hope Slide** – *1 hr. 18km (11mi) east of Hope along Rte. 3.* Geologists believe a small earthquake in January 1964 caused a 600m (2,000ft) face of Johnson Peak to collapse into the valley below, burying a lake, the existing highway and a mile of the valley floor. The viewing area is built on the highest point of the fallen rubble; the barren face that sheared off lies directly across the valley.

Manning Provincial Park – *1 day. 26km (16mi) southeast of Hope via Rte. 3 to park's west gate. Park open daily year-round. Visitor center open mid-May–mid-Oct daily 8:30am–4:30pm. Rest of the year Mon–Fri 9am–4:30pm. Closed holidays in the winter.* △ ✗ ♿ 🅿 ✆ *250-840-8836. www.e/p.gov.bc.ca/bcparks.* Set above Fraser Canyon, and divided by Highway 3, 66,802 ha (165,000 acre) Manning Park is one of British Columbia's oldest and—owing to its proximity to Vancouver—most popular mountain parks. **Rhododendron Flats★** *(7km/4.3mi from west gate)* is a beautiful grove of old-growth Douglas fir and cedar along the Skagit River, with hikes from 15min to three days possible in the valley. Atop the Cascades above, in the heart of the park, hiking, camping, canoeing, horseback riding and biking are popular summer activities; downhill and cross-country skiing and snowshoeing take over in winter. The 8km (5mi) **Cascade Lookout★** drive affords views of the mountainous terrain that stretches from the lower Fraser River Valley eastward to the Okanagan. Just beyond, Blackwall Peak meadows brighten with wildflowers in July and August.

★★HELL'S GATE   *3 hrs. 50km (31mi) north of Hope on Rte. 1.*

The Fraser River is Canada's fifth largest, draining one quarter of British Columbia and spanning 1,368km (848mi). At Hell's Gate this huge torrent of water crashes through a 60m– (198ft) high rock portal that narrows to less than 33m (110ft) wide, creating an awe-inspiring chasm. Hell's Gate was not the only obstacle for early travelers through the long and perilous Fraser Canyon, but it was the most fearsome; Simon Fraser described his passage here along sheer ledges and down primitive ladders with legendary restraint: "We had to pass where no human being should venture." In 1913, landslides set off by railroad construction blocked the way for the Fraser's annual migration of 20 million salmon. Fishways built in the late 1940s by US and Canadian officials have since restored the salmon runs.

★**Hell's Gate Airtram** – *Operates mid-June–Labor Day daily 9am–6pm. Call for off-season hours. $10.* ✗ ♿ 🅿 ✆ *604-867-9277. www.hellsgate.bc.ca.* Because this part of the canyon is still rain forest, views of the actual gap are difficult from the highway. The airtram, whose upper terminal is on Highway 1, offers a quick but stunning 153m (510ft) descent across the chasm to a tourist village where small shops tempt souvenir-seekers; and exhibits depict the history of the canyon, railroad and highway construction, and the restoration of the river's salmon runs. South of the airtram entrance, a steep .5mi **trail★★** follows an access road to the fishways, bringing you to a rock ledge across from the airtram terminus. Whether you hike or ride the airtram down, the spectacle of a major river surging through such a narrow passage, at speeds approaching 48km/h (30 mph), is unforgettable.

★**Alexandra Bridge** – *7km (4.3mi) south of Hell's Gate on Rte. 1.* A free and easy 10min walk down through second-growth forest takes visitors to a handsome steel suspension bridge built in 1926 to carry traffic across the Fraser. Although the gap here is not as formidable as Hell's Gate, the **view★** of the Fraser from the bridge is still spectacular.

★THOMPSON CANYON – LYTTON TO CACHE CREEK *1 hr*

Twisting east and north away from the Fraser Valley, the Thompson River cleaves another deep canyon that joins with the Fraser at Lytton. As you follow the TransCanada Highway upstream, the canyon widens to a valley and the climate grows drier until you slowly emerge into a high semidesert region of sagebrush and other scrub plants. This sparsely settled area holds a rugged beauty, with here and there a green tract of irrigated land. Just south of Cache Creek the Thompson shoots east, gradually opening up to make **Kamloops Lake**, set amid an arid, rocky terrain that gives way a mere hour to the east to the pine foothills and lush shores of Shuswap Lake.

Lytton – *105km (65mi) north of Hope on Rte.1.* The mountains are responsible for the contrast in climate between this hot spot at the heart of the Fraser Gorge and the temperate rain forest just an hour downstream at Yale. With the Coast Range blocking cool Pacific air, and summer's long hours of sunshine focused by the canyon walls, Lytton vies with Lillooet (64km/40mi north) as Canada's hottest place. Both recorded a temperature of 44°C (112°F) in July 1941. Here the Thompson River, the Fraser's largest tributary, flows in from the northeast, its green waters remaining visible in the Fraser mainstream for about a mile downstream. Founded as yet another fur-trade depot in the 1840s, Lytton today is a timber industry center and the capital of British Columbia's whitewater-rafting business. From here Highway 1 veers east up the Thompson Canyon, a desert gorge just as impressive as the Fraser Canyon. Instead of tunneling, the highway clings like tape to the toes of huge scree slopes. The **Lytton Infocentre** *(400 Fraser St. in the center of town; open May–Sept daily 9am–5pm; rest of the year Mon–Fri 11am–2pm; closed Dec 20–Jan10; ☎ 250-455-2523),* offers information on rafting and gold panning in the area.

Cache Creek – *193km (120mi) northeast of Hope, at the junction of Rtes. 1 and 97; visitor information ☎ 250-457-9566.* When Cariboo gold rushers reached this point they were halfway to the goldfields-and, more important, they had traversed the most rugged part of the route. Today it remains a crossroads, the gateway to the famous ranch country of the Cariboo beyond, although the town itself is a somewhat tawdry strip of fast-food joints and bargain motels. Here, too, the climate is quite hot and dry; nearby Ashcroft holds British Columbia's record for least rain in a year—less than 7.1cm (2.8in) in 1931.

★★**Hat Creek Ranch** – *11km (6.8mi) north of Cache Creek, junction Rtes. 97 and 99. Open mid-May–Sept daily 10am–6pm. Restaurant open year-round. $5.* ✕ 🅿 *☎ 250-457-9722 or 800-782-0922.* More than a century after it was first settled,

Hat Creek Ranch is still such a lovely spot that it's obvious what attracted a Cariboo Road entrepreneur, Donald McLean, to open a roadhouse on this site in 1861 to serve travelers to the goldfields. Here, where cottonwoods and willows shade Hat Creek as it burbles down from the Marble Mountains into the Cache Creek meadows, the canyon-weary traveler finds the first hints of the gentle, forest-bordered prairies of the Cariboo highlands that lie to the north. Although it was always both an operating ranch and a roadhouse, the latter business dominated until vehicle traffic began to supplant horse-drawn travel. Eventually the road was moved across the valley, and by 1930 Hat Creek's days as a way station were done. The ranch stands now essentially as it did in 1901, its roadhouse heyday.

© Robert Holmes

Freight Horse Barn

Guided tours explain the heritage of the site's 16 major buildings. The splendidly restored Victorian **Hat Creek House★** is a massive example of 19C pioneer travel accommodations, luxurious for the times. In the **Freight Horse Barn★**, whose ancient planks betray a century of hoof-wear, is a fine collection of antique saddles and leather goods. The ranch maintains a stable of draft horses, and summer visitors can take a stagecoach or trail ride along the original **Cariboo Wagon Road**, which runs through the site. Also in summer, the Bonaparte band of the Secwepemc (Shuswap) nation operates a **traditional summer camp** in a pretty grove of cottonwoods along Hat Creek, with tribe members on hand to explain their quiet early lifestyle.

■ Ginseng

The explosion of interest in herbal medicine has had a profound impact on the agriculture of British Columbia's hot interior valleys. Long valued by Asian cultures as a general health tonic, ginseng grows wild in British Columbia. Now largely a cultivated crop, ginseng was first planted near Kamloops in 1982; it currently encompasses more than 5,000 acres in the Thompson, Fraser and Okanagan valleys. Grown in raised beds under black net shade canopies, ginseng is expensive to plant but hugely profitable, with yields on the order of $150,000C per acre. It takes five years for the plants to mature their roots, which are processed into teas, medicinal powders and other products. Two of Kamloops' major ginseng processors open their facilities for tours and product sampling; for information visit the **Kamloops Infocentre** *(1290 W. TransCanada Hwy., Kamloops; open mid-May–mid-Sept daily 8am–6pm; rest of the year Mon–Fri 9am–5pm; closed Easter Sunday, Nov 11, Dec 25-26; ☎ 2,50-374-3377 or 800-662-1994).* Because the crop is most often planted on what used to be hayfields, livestock owners have seen the price of hay escalate nearly $10C a bale—a sharp dislocation in the economy of British Columbia's cattle country.

★KAMLOOPS *1 day.*

Tucked in a wide valley at the confluence of the North and South Thompson rivers, Kamloops (Shuswap for "meeting of the waters") had long been a major Shuswap village when fur traders established a fort here in 1812. Situated to serve as a way station on the long fur-brigade canoe route from the forests of northern British Columbia down the Okanagan and Columbia valleys to Astoria, Oregon, Kamloops was one of the most remote outposts in Canada—until gold strikes in the Cariboo brought a wave of fortune seekers and settlers to the British Columbia interior. Kamloops then evolved into what it has been ever since, a crossroads and commercial center—the arrival of the Canadian Pacific Railroad in 1886 cementing this identity—and the capital of the interior cattle country. The ranches founded in the 1860s in the highlands north and south of Kamloops—most notably the Douglas Lake and Gang Ranches—were, and still are, among the largest in the world.

Despite the timber industry's slow decline and the perennial struggles of cattle ranchers, Kamloops continues to grow as a government and commercial center. The town sits roughly halfway along the TransCanada Highway between Vancouver and Jasper (440km/273mi east); a tedious string of gas stations, motels and other roadside enterprises stretches from the middle of town eastward for several miles. All the more reason to get off the TransCanada and venture into a town just beginning to make the most of its colorful heritage.

Like many other inland communities, Kamloops banks heavily on tourism; its attractions range from superb fishing in hundreds of high-country lakes to peaceful horseback rides on area ranches. **Sun Peaks**, 50km (31mi) northeast of the city, is developing into a major ski resort, and the annual **Kamloops Cattle Drive**, a five-day trek across the high-country wilderness in July, draws participants from throughout North America. At **Riverside Park**, an attractive greenbelt along the Thompson River, the reconstructed sternwheeler **Wanda Sue** offers 2 hr summertime cruises on the river *(depart from Old Kamloops Yacht Club mid-May–Sept daily; round-trip 2 hrs; commentary; day cruises $11.50; ＆ ▣ for schedules of day & dinner cruises call Wanda Sue Sternwheeler, ☎ 250-374-7447).*

★**Kamloops Museum & Archive** – *207 Seymour Street. Open year-round Tue–Sat 9:30am–430pm. Closed major holidays. ☎ 250-828-3576.* Dating from 1937, this major historical facility ranks as one of the province's oldest. Its spacious second-floor main hall is filled with reconstructed historic storefronts and shops, as well as the 19C cabin long occupied by "St. Paul" (area pioneer Jean Baptiste Lolo), which served as the city's museum until it moved to its present location. Especially interesting is the exhibit detailing the local history of outlaw **Billy Miner**, who robbed a Canadian Pacific train nearby in 1906, was captured in the highlands and was tried and convicted in Kamloops. A fly-fishing exhibit on the lower floor honors one of the area's best-known recreational activities. The museum offers pamphlet guides to a 2 hr **historic walking tour★** of nearby neighborhoods, leading past a turn-of-the-century courthouse (now a hostel), Federal Building, two banks, fire halls, churches and a dozen heritage homes.

© Robert Holmes

Fields South of Kamloops

St. Andrews on the Square – *159 Seymour St.* ☎ *250-377-4232.* Local volunteers accomplished this gorgeous 1998 restoration of an 1887 Presbyterian church; the Gothic clapboard structure, the oldest public building in Kamloops, now serves as a community hall. Its pine-plank floors glisten in the light let in by high windows under the vaulted ceiling.

St. Joseph's Church – *End of Chilcotin St. Open Jul & Aug. For hours, call Kamloops Infocentre* ☎ *250-374-3377.* St. Joseph's served as the parish church for Chief Louis, the remarkable Kamloops Indian who led his tribe for 60 years (1855-1915) and who once traveled to Great Britain to plead his group's cause. The present church was completed in 1900 and completely restored by Indian members in 1985. In the **cemetery** across the street, ribbon-wrapped rings hanging on the crosses exemplify renewed native interest in traditional beliefs; the rings represent the four cardinal directions.

★★Secwepemc Museum and Native Heritage Park – *355 Yellowhead Hwy. OpenJun–Aug Mon–Fri 8:30am–8pm, weekends 10am–6pm. Rest of the year Mon–Fri 8:30am–4:30pm. Closed major holidays. $6.* ✗ ⅃ 🄿 ☎ *250-828-9801. www.secwepemc.org.* One of the best Native heritage sites in the province offers a frank, evenhanded look at the Shuswap people, one of British Columbia's largest and most dynamic Indian groups. A video explores the Shuswap people's ties to the land and traditional culture, and their sentiments about what has happened to both. (Shuswap, an anglicization of Secwepemc, means "scattered people") Exhibits depict traditional lifestyles, including an explanation of the uses of indigenous fish, game and plants.

On the riverside flats below the museum, the band has constructed a marvelous 4.9 ha (12-acre) representation of a historic **Shuswap village**, with several walk-in examples of the traditional winter pit house. The **T'kumlups Marshes** around the heritage village, and across Yellowhead Highway, constitute a wetlands restoration project undertaken jointly by the Kamloops Band, Ducks Unlimited and provincial and national environmental officials. The marshes are home to dozens of species of birds.

★Kamloops Wildlife Park – 🄺 *TransCanada Hwy. 17km (11mi) east of Kamloops city center. Open year-round daily 8am–4:30pm. Closed Dec 25. $6.75.* ✗ ⅃ 🄿 ☎ *250-573-3242. www.kamloopswildlife.com.* An eclectic array of animals inhabit this 26 ha (65-acre) park-like facility in the pine-clad foothills of the South Thompson River Valley. Most major Canadian mammals are represented, as well as birds of prey, Siberian tigers, zebra and antelope, and oddities ranging from pheasants to camels. (Actually, wild camels briefly populated the Cariboo. They were imported to serve as draft animals, but proved unacceptably cranky and were set free; the last feral Cariboo camel died nearly a century ago.) A miniature train, the **Wildlife Express**, carts children around the park, and a short trail leads through native bunchgrass prairie habitat to a nearby waterfall. The nonprofit park earned a national award in 1990 for its educational programs; another award in 1995 honored its program to breed endangered burrowing owls.

Excursion

★★**Nicola Valley Loop** – *1/2 day. 188km (117mi). From Kamloops, follow Rte. 5A south out of Kamloops about 66km (41mi), then turn east on Douglas Lake Rd. 70km (42mi) to Westwold (the middle 25km/16mi of this road are unpaved). Go northwest on Rtes. 97 and 1 for 53km (33mi) back to Kamloops.* Highway 5A climbs rapidly from Kamloops into the upper reaches of the Nicola highlands, a beautiful rolling prairie of high bunchgrass, which lured early ranchers who figured there was ample gold to be won selling beef to miners. Once you crest the high ridge above Kamloops, the road drops down into the **Nicola Valley**★, a picturesque vale whose five lakes gleam golden as the bunchgrass ripens in midsummer. Halfway along Nicola Lake, the Edwardian **Quilchena Hotel** (1908) is still owned and operated by the local ranching family that built it; rooms are furnished with original antiques. Various stories circulate about the bullet holes in the hotel saloon's bar.

The road to **Douglas Lake Ranch** leads through highlands that hold what is now Canada's largest ranch, a 200,000 ha (500,000-acre) enterprise on which cowboys still drive cattle in traditional fashion from winter pasture into high summer ranges. Coyotes, cougars and bears still roam the countryside, while eagles and ospreys throng to the sparkling, trout-rich lakes. The ranch operates a summer family-oriented lakeside resort and an exclusive fishing lodge for tourists. Long owned by a British Columbia family, the ranch was bought in 1998 by a Canadian telecommunications tycoon.

OKANAGAN VALLEY★★

Michelin map 493 D 2 and map p 333

Tourist Information ☎ 250-860-5999

Running north-south between two highland mountain plateaus, the Okanagan Valley slants southward into the sun, creating a gentle, warm climate much appreciated by the valley's original inhabitants. In fact, the major town in the south part of the valley, Penticton, takes its name from a Salish Indian word that means "a place to stay forever." That's exactly what the first European settlers did in the 1860s when they stopped for a good look at the valley's long clean lakes, rich grasslands and mild climate. Cattle ranchers and missionaries were first. Oblate Father Charles Pandosy established his mission at Kelowna in 1860, and although his assignment was to found the church in the wilderness, the area's pastoral appeal must have been too much to resist. Pandosy immediately planted an orchard. He was followed in 1867 by Cornelius O'Keefe, who built a cattle ranch at the north end of Okanagan Lake.

The orchard industry was boosted by personal interest on the part of Lord and Lady Aberdeen, Canada's Governor-General and first lady in the 1890s, who bought up local ranches, planted orchards and attempted to sell parcels to British crofters (tenant farmers). Although neither railroads nor highways had yet flanked the steep-sided expanse of Okanagan Lake, paddlewheel steamboats plied the lake to haul commercial goods and orchard crops between the valley and the railhead at Vernon.

Today the Okanagan climate fosters many different crops, ranging from the traditional apples, peaches and apricots to the newly popular wine grapes. The valley's warm lake waters, golden beaches and 40 golf courses make it one of Canada's most popular summer recreation areas. During peak season (July and August) virtually every campsite, hotel room and resort cabin in the valley is likely to be booked. For those wishing to avoid crowds, June and September offer ample warm weather, and October—when the cottonwoods and cherry and apple orchards turn vivid colors—is exceptionally beautiful. Three ski resorts draw winter visitors from hundreds of miles away.

★VERNON *1 day*

This low-key town lies in the heart of the north Okanagan, a broad pastured valley in which the traditional activities—cattle ranching and dairying—are giving way to subdivision development. **Polson Park**, which lies right along Highway 97 in the center of town, is a handsomely landscaped greenbelt along Vernon Creek. The **Vernon Museum**★ *(3009 32nd Ave., City Hall complex; open May–Oct Mon–Sat 10am–5pm; rest of the year Tue–Sat 10am–5pm; ♿ ☎ 250-542-3142)* contains locally significant artifacts, including a rare cottonwood dugout canoe unearthed nearby, and a sizable exhibit about James Cameron Dunwaters, founder of the Fintry estate across the lake from Vernon. **Kalamalka Lake**★★, just south of town, is renowned for its beauty—reflected light, clear water and constant breezes paint its surface shifting hues of blue, green, indigo and lavender. A good viewpoint *(5km/3.1mi south of Vernon on Rte. 97)* affords vistas across the north end of the lake, overlooking **Kalamalka Lake Provincial Park**, a marvelous 850 ha (2,100-acre) pitch of Okanagan prairie, marsh and headland with numerous hiking trails and swimming beaches.

Interior Space & Science Centre – Kids *2704 Rte. 6, at Polson Park. Open year-round Tue–Sat 10am–5pm. Closed major holidays. $3. ☎ 250-545-3644.* Housed in a nondescript wing of an old schoolhouse, this hands-on learning center contains three main rooms jammed with games, devices, experiments and machines that demonstrate principles of natural science and mathematics. Exhibits range from robots and optical illusions to fossils and a Tesla coil (arc generator). A new planetarium upstairs unfolds the secrets of the heavens, focusing on constellations and their legends.

Excursions

Salmon Arm – *1/2 day. 65km (40mi) north of Vernon on Rtes. 97A, 97B, and 1. Visitor information ☎ 250-832-6247.* This pleasant small town is the commercial and government center of the Shuswap Lake region, with logging as the region's major employer. The town's Salmon Arm Bay shoreline constitutes a key **wildlife preserve** that hosts dozens of types of migrating birds, including the "dancing grebes" waterfowl, whose late spring mating dance is considered superior to the more famous ritual of loons. **R.J. Haney Heritage Park**★ *(3km/1.9mi east of Salmon Arm on Rte. 97B; open May–Sept Wed–Sun 10am–4pm; ⚄ ▯ ☎ 250-832-5243)* harbors the 1908 Haney House, a marvelous mansion showing the transition from Edwardian to Craftsman-style home design. Included in the complex are a compact museum, historic schoolhouse, church, fire hall and gas station. South of town, **Gort's Gouda Cheese** *(1km/.6mi on Salmon River Rd.; open year-round Mon–Fri 10am–10:30am; closed Jan 1 & Dec 25; $2; ⚄ ▯ ☎ 250-832-4274; www.gortsgoudacheese.bc.ca)* keeps generations of Dutch-descended cheese-making techniques alive and well. Visitors can tour the dairy barn and cheese-making plant, and load up on especially fine mild, medium and aged Gouda cheese and spiced cheeses.

★★**O'Keefe Ranch** – *2 hrs. 14 km (8.7mi) northwest of Vernon along Rte. 97 in Spallumcheen. Open May–Oct daily 9am–5pm. Rest of the year Mon–Fri 9am–5pm. $6. Closed Jan 1 & Dec 25. ⚄ ▯ ☎ 250-542-7868. www.okeeferanch.bc.ca.* Founded in 1867 by Cornelius O'Keefe on the grass prairie of the upper Okanagan Valley, a small cattle ranch grew into a 8,000 ha (20,000-acre) complex that also served as a small town and way station. The O'Keefe family began restoring their ranch as a heritage attraction in the 1960s; it was sold to a private foundation and given to the town of Vernon in 1977.

Among more than a dozen restored heritage buildings on the ranch grounds are several stand-outs. **O'Keefe Mansion**★, built in 1887, belies the notion that ranch life was primitive. This opulent, sprawling Victorian house contains hand-tooled woodwork throughout. The **General Store** is stocked with genuine 19C articles—some of which are unsold O'Keefe store inventory. A spare 1889 structure overlooking the ranch, **St. Anne's Church**, retains its original pews, furnishings and pump organ. A small cowboy museum holds an exquisite jade-crusted ceremonial saddle; and an outbuilding behind the museum houses the ranch's exceptional collection of woodstoves, ranging from cast-iron potbellies for line shacks, to huge, nickel-plated contraptions designed for both aesthetics and function.

★★**Westside Road** – *2 hrs. Westside Rd. traverses the shore of Okanagan Lake from O'Keefe Ranch 80km (50mi) south to Westbank. From Vernon, go 14km (8.7mi) northwest on Rte. 97 to Spallumcheen, then south on Westside Rd.* This winding back road—the most scenic route to Kelowna from the north Okanagan—runs along the steep west shore of Okanagan Lake, roughly following the route taken by fur brigades in the early 19C as they trekked pelts to the Columbia Valley. Not meant to be driven fast, the road provides ample reason to enjoy the constant panorama of the huge lake. A 128km (79mi) glacial basin, **Okanagan Lake**★★ forms the geophysical and spiritual center of the Okanagan. Geographically it divides the valley, with its steep-sided shores relieved on the north end only at Spallumcheen and Vernon, in the middle at Kelowna, and on the south end at Penticton. Until Highway 97 was built along the lake from Penticton to Kelowna in the 1950s, steamboats linked lakeside communities.

The shimmering, cliff-sided lake seems to draw down the vast Okanagan sky and lakeside desert to create a world that far exceeds the lake's tremendous size (352sq km/135sq mi). Fed largely by underwater springs, the lake at one point plunges 550m (1,830ft). This is where legend places the home of **Ogopogo**, the mythical lake monster that has been seen by thousands of witnesses over the years—not one of whom, oddly enough, has had a camera at hand to record their sighting. Modern representations of the serpent-like creature largely call on centuries-old native pictographs of Ogopogo. Efforts to find Ogopogo have at times reached such a frenzy that the provincial government in 1991 added the creature to its protected-species list. As for the lake's other denizens, the only salmon in Okanagan Lake are kokanee (access for others is blocked by dams downstream), landlocked sockeye that spawn in the modest streams that spill down from the highlands on either side.

At **Fintry Provincial Park**★ *(open May–Sept daily dawn–dusk; △ ▯ for all other information ☎ 250-494-6500)* about halfway along the road, a magnificent stand of ruby-colored old-growth ponderosa pines includes specimens that number among the largest in Canada.

★KELOWNA *2 days*

Rivaling Kamloops as the interior's economic locus, Kelowna stands as a bustling commercial center. Its airport is the third busiest in the province; and a super-highway, the Okanagan Connector (Highway 97C), was built across the mountainous plateau between here and Hope specifically to cut two hours from the travel time to Vancouver.

First settled by Father Charles Pandosy in 1860, the area slowly grew into a commercial hub; a major boost came with the arrival of Lord and Lady Aberdeen in the 1890s. The pair launched an orchard-development venture that achieved far more publicity than financial success. Today, economic activity ranges from shopping to tourism to orchard and vineyard operations, with logging and cattle ranching in the highlands around the city. Tacky commercial strips along Highway 97 north and south of Kelowna are not truly representative of the overall community, which is pleasantly residential and friendly. Connecting Westbank to the city, the 640m (2,130ft) **Kelowna floating bridge** was the first of its kind in North America; it was opened in 1958 by Princess Margaret, rendering obsolete the car ferries that had served the community for more than half a century. The success of its concrete pontoons led to construction of much longer floating bridges across Seattle's Lake Washington and Puget Sound's Hood Canal.

Kelowna's downtown lakeshore section is a compact but bustling area of shops, hotels and municipal facilities. Flashbulbs sparkle around the **Ogopogo statue** *(foot of Bernard Ave. in City Park)*, as this is the only sure picture anyone will get of the creature. Also in the park, the **Fintry Queen**, a restored paddlewheeler that once saw service linking lake communities, now offers sightseeing and dinner cruises. Nearby, the beautifully serene **Kasugai Garden★** *(Queensway St. behind City Hall)*, is the most complete Japanese garden in the British Columbia interior.

Kelowna Centennial Museum – *470 Queensway Ave. Open year-round Tue–Sat 10am–5pm. Donation requested.* ⓑ ▣ ☎ *250-763-2417.* This store of community memories holds exhibits depicting the area's past, including the studio from the city's first radio station, an early trading post, and an extensive collection of Hudson's Bay Company artifacts and trade goods.

★**Father Pandosy Mission** – *Benvoulin and Casorso Rds. Open Easter-Thanksgiving Day daily 8am–8pm. $2.* ☎ *250-860-8369.* In 1860 Father Charles Pandosy established his mission here, amid the serene meadows leading down to the tall cottonwoods of nearby Mission Creek. The site's peaceful atmosphere suggests what the Oblate priests must have found attractive; the site was also chosen for its proximity to a large Salish fish camp along Mission Creek. Four of the buildings are original to the mission, including a chapel above which a cubbyhole room may have been Pandosy's residence. Pandosy died in 1891, and the property was sold 15 years later. Volunteers began to rescue it from decay in 1954; it is now owned by the Diocese of Nelson, and was designated a provincial heritage site in 1983. Made of hand-hewn cottonwood logs, the chapel, barn, brothers' house and root house evince the intricate **dovetail notching** that makes these buildings stand straight and true almost 150 years after they were erected.

★**Guisachan Heritage Site** – *1060 Cameron Ave. Open daily year-round.* ⚟ ⓑ ▣ ☎ *250-861-7188.* The handsome, low-slung estate house (pronounced GOO-see-kin) here was owned by Lord and Lady Aberdeen, part of the massive McDougall Ranch (1861) they bought in 1893. This last remnant of the original ranch is now a park surrounded by extensive perennial gardens. A gourmet restaurant operates in the estate house.

Father Pandosy Mission

■ Okanagan Wineries

One late fall night in 1991, a sudden cold snap froze a crop of grapes that an Okanagan Valley vineyard owner had not yet harvested. Taking advantage of the situation, she decided to attempt an ancient German wine-making technique for ice wine—pick the grapes (gingerly), press them frozen, then put them into tanks for slow fermentation. The resulting sweet dessert wine, replicated by several other Okanagan vineyards, has proved improbably popular in Asia and Hawaii, bringing attention to a district that struggled for more than a century to earn respect in the wine-making world.

The Okanagan's first vineyard was planted by Father Charles Pandosy, founder of the Kelowna mission, in 1860. But decades of confusing government policies and shifting market conditions kept the industry small and troubled until recently, when growers discovered that several varieties of vinifera grapes—including the popular Gewurztraminer, Chardonnay, Riesling, Pinot Gris, Merlot and Cabernet Sauvignon—can do well, especially in the south Okanagan. Not all varieties succeed every year, but some of the Okanagan's best wines have raised a few eyebrows in enthusiasts' circles. And the region's annual releases of ice wine cause a stir in Honolulu and Tokyo. The best way to tour the region's wineries is to use Kelowna or Penticton as a base and devote an autumn day to touring and tasting. (Summer tour buses sometimes overwhelm the major wineries.) The Wine Country Visitors Information Centre *(p 341)*, or tourism offices in Osoyoos, Penticton and Kelowna, can help sketch out a travel itinerary; although highway signs indicate major wineries, maps are essential for a deliberate tour. Almost all the wineries offer tastings and special-purchase bargains. Among the most notable Kelowna area wineries are Quail's Gate, Mission Hill, Summerhill, Gray Monk, St. Hubertus, Cedar Creek, Hainle Vineyards and Calona. In the Penticton area, highlights include Sumac Ridge, Stag's Hollow, Jackson Triggs, Tinhorn Creek, Gehringer Brothers, Hester Creek and Inniskillin. Of these, Quail's Gate, Summerhill, Cedar Creek, Tinhorn Creek, Gehringer Brothers and Hester Creek have especially scenic locations. As for the wines, most connoisseurs consider them interesting but so far not quite as complex and deep in character as California or European vintages. On the other hand, visitors won't have to endure the traffic jams that the northern California wine trails experience in autumn.

For information and maps, contact the Osoyoos Chamber of Commerce, Rtes. 3 and 97; ☎ 250-495-7142.

Kelowna Land & Orchard – *2930 Dunster Rd. Open Apr–Nov daily 9am–5pm.* ⚑ ☎ *250-763-1091.* Still a working farm, Kelowna Land & Orchard offers visitors tractor-drawn wagon tours of the orchards, explaining the sometimes tricky business of growing fruit, including Fuji apples that sell for $10 each in Asia. Visitors end their tour with a sample of hand-pressed cider.

Excursion

★**Kettle Valley Railway** – *1 hr. 13km (8.1mi) southeast of Kelowna at Myra Canyon Trestles. From Kelowna head east on Kelowna Land & Orchard. Rd. (KLO Rd.), then south (right) on McCulloch Rd. to Myra Forest Service Rd. Follow this south 8.5km (5.3mi) to parking lot. This site is difficult to find; obtain road map from Kelowna Chamber of Commerce (544 Harvey Ave. ☎ 250-861-1515).* For dizzying but spectacular **views**★★ of the Okanagan Valley, bike along this mountainside railbed. Converted into a bike (and foot) path by volunteers, the former rail route crosses 18 major trestles and passes through three tunnels. The Kettle Valley Railway was once one of the most amazing railroads in North America, winding almost 500km (310mi) from the Kootenays to Hope through a virtually impassable mountain landscape, though terrain constraints prevented the railroad from ever actually reaching Kelowna itself. Today the restored railbed is one of Kelowna's most popular recreation sites.

PENTICTON *1/2 day*

Trying to upgrade its image beyond the somewhat campy inferences of its old "beaches and peaches" slogan, Penticton is a busy commercial and retirement center splendidly situated on a neck of land between Okanagan and Skaha Lakes. That location provokes a profound transformation in early July, when the easygoing town turns into a frenzied tourist mecca and every hotel and motel room is filled. People flock to two main beaches, on the south end of Okanagan Lake and the north end of **Skaha Lake**★. The latter, a city park, is far prettier and better for swimming despite the nearby marina.

Borrowing an idea from Napa Valley, the **Wine Country Visitors Information Centre** *(888 Westminster Ave.; open Jul–Aug daily 8am–8pm; rest of the year Mon–Fri 9am–5pm, weekends 11am–5pm;* & ▯ ☎ *250-490-2005 or 800-663-5052; www.penticton.org)* not only offers a complete array of pamphlets, maps and local information, it maintains a comprehensive inventory of Okanagan wines for visitors to purchase.

Lining the main highway north and south of Penticton, abundant **fruit stands** offer a limitless array of produce. The most enjoyable way to experience the area's bounty is at U-pick facilities where you pay for what you take; whatever you can eat while picking (within reason) is free.

Art Gallery of the South Okanagan – *199 Front St. Open year-round Tue–Fri 10am–5pm, weekends 1pm–5pm. Closed major holidays. $2.* & ▯ ☎ *250-493-2928. www.galleries.bc.ca./aaso.* This spacious building along the lakeshore holds traveling exhibits by contemporary Canadian artists in a variety of mediums. The work of Okanagan Valley artists is also displayed.

Penticton Museum – *785 Main St. Open year-round Tue–Sat 10am–5pm. Closed major holidays.* & ▯ ☎ *250-490-2451.* Here you'll find a collection of local artifacts, including stuffed examples of the area's wildlife and a couple of full-wall dioramas of the valley before settlement.

Excursions

★**Vaseux Lake** – *1 hr. 30km (19mi) south of Penticton on Rte. 97.* Rating as one of Western Canada's most important waterfowl habitats, the shallow 3km– (1.9mi) long valley lake provides a stopping point at various times of the year for white swans, geese, ducks, grebes and dozens of other birds. The woods around the lake are home to the rare white-headed woodpecker, and the rocky desert hillside above it holds a healthy herd of native **bighorn sheep**. A wildlife preserve at the north end of the lake offers short hiking trails leading to the marshes and a viewing blind.

Keremeos – *1 hr. 45km (28mi) southwest of Penticton on Rtes. 97 and 3A to Keremeos.* The breathtaking **Similkameen River Valley**, in which Keremeos sits, is a cottonwood-lined vale between steep ridges—a Canadian Shangri-La. The lower end of the valley, a patchwork of pastures and hillside vineyards and orchards, leads up to Keremeos, a charming town with a dozen fruit stands, bracing views of the mountains, and a famously mild climate.

At the **Keremeos Grist Mill**★ *(1.4mi northeast of town, off 3A on Upper Bench Rd.; open mid-May–mid-Oct Tue–Mon 9:30am–5pm; $5;* ⅞ & ▯ ☎ *250-499-2888)*, a restored 1877 water-powered flour mill, visitors can watch the waterwheel drive the stone grinding machinery, and take home the flavorful, textured whole-wheat flour that results. An exhibit on North American wheat growing, gardens featuring heritage flowers and vegetables, and a wheat field with early native grain varieties round out the attractions. Set under cottonwoods along Keremeos Creek, the grounds make a fine site for a picnic; supplies are available in the museum cafe and bake shop.

★**Cathedral Provincial Park** – *2 hrs. 22km/14mi northwest of Keremeos along the Ashnola River Rd. Open May–Sept daily dawn–dusk.* △ ☎ *250-494-6500.* One of the premier high-country hiking areas in British Columbia, the park boasts five shimmering alpine basin lakes and an extensive network of timberline trails leading to unique rock formations. Thousands of hikers from across Canada and even Europe are drawn to this 33,400 ha (82,500-acre) wilderness. Hikers and campers can take a van to the top of the mountain *($65 round-trip)*. Van service is operated by **Cathedral Lake Lodge**, which provides rooms and cabins within the park *(open June–mid-Oct* ☎ *250-492-1606; www.cathedral-lake-lodge)*.

OSOYOOS *2 hrs*

Spread around **Osoyoos Lake**, this orchard center decided two decades ago to adopt a Southwestern motif replete with stucco, wrought iron and red-tile roofs to complement its climate and chief attraction—the lake. Although the lake's water fosters a Mediterranean clime (temperatures can reach the high 20sC/low 80sF), the accompanying man-made decor has been at best halfway successful. Garish hues color lakeside motels, and the town's rowdy peak-season crowds detract from the balmy atmosphere. Numerous motels and RV campgrounds line the lakeshore, and in July and August the waters become a froth of boat traffic. **Haynes Point Provincial Park** *(open May–Aug daily 8am–7pm; rest of the year Mon–Fri 9am–4pm;* & ▯ ☎ *250-495-7142)* which occupies a peninsula jutting out into the lake, is reputed to be Canada's most popular public campground, where reservations are necessary months ahead for a campsite. Highway 3 east of Osoyoos climbs steeply up 3km (1.9mi) to **Anarchist Mountain viewpoint**★★, a spectacular ledge affording one of the best vistas of the Okanagan Valley. According to popular legend, the mountain was named for a local 19C hermit who embraced anti-government views.

World Heritage List

UNESCO

In 1972, the United Nations Educational, Scientific and Cultural Organization (UNESCO) adopted a Convention for the preservation of cultural and natural sites. To date, more than 150 States Parties have signed this international agreement, which has listed over 500 sites «of outstanding universal value» on the World Heritage List. Each year, a committee of representatives from 21 countries, assisted by technical organizations (ICOMOS – International Council on Monuments and Sites; IUCN – International Union for Conservation of Nature and Natural Resources; ICCROM – International Centre for the Study of the Preservation and Restoration of Cultural Property, the Rome Centre), evaluates the proposals for new sites to be included on the list, which grows longer as new nominations are accepted and more countries sign the Convention. To be considered, a site must be nominated by the country in which it is located.

The protected cultural heritage may be monuments (buildings, sculptures, archaeological structures, etc.) with unique historical, artistic or scientific features, groups of buildings (such as religious communities, ancient cities); or sites (human settlements, examples of exceptional landscapes, cultural landscapes) which are the combined works of man and nature of exceptional beauty. Natural sites may be a testimony to the stages of the earth's geological history or to the development of human cultures and creative genius, or represent significant ongoing ecological processes, contain superlative natural phenomena or provide a habitat for threatened species.

Signatories of the Convention pledge to cooperate to preserve and protect these sites around the world as a common heritage to be shared by all humanity.

Some of the most well-known places which the World Heritage Committee has inscribed include: Australia's Great Barrier Reef (1981), the Canadian Rocky Mountain Parks (1984), The Great Wall of China (1987), the Statue of Liberty (1984), the Kremlin (1990), Mont-Saint-Michel and its Bay (France – 1979), Durham Castle and Cathedral (1986).

In the Pacific Northwest, UNESCO World Heritage sites are:

Alaska

Glacier Bay National Park and Preserve (1992)

Wrangell-St.Elias National Park and Preserve (1997)

Washington

Olympic National Park (1981)

Wrangell-St. Elias National Park and Preserve

© David Muench/Tony Stone Images

Alaska

Introduction to Alaska

Everything about Alaska seems larger than life, scaled to retain the state's mythic consciousness of itself as a last frontier. A land of superlatives, Alaska is huge—more than twice the size of Texas; it is tall, holding the 16 highest peaks in the country; and it claims by far more wildlife, more parkland, and more active volcanoes than any other state. The northernmost state, Alaska boasts 100,000 glaciers, 3 million lakes, and 33,000mi of shoreline. No wonder that in addition to "last frontier," the state goes by the moniker "the Great Land," translated from the Aleut word *Aleyska*.

Embracing 656,424sq mi, the state appears as a great knob on the northwestern corner of the continent, with its chain of Aleutian Islands arcing so far into the Pacific that from east to west it spans 2,350mi. A mere 51mi separate Alaska from Siberia, while some 500mi lie between Alaska and the contiguous US. Its eastern side borders the Yukon Territory and British Columbia. The Arctic Ocean lies to the north, the Chukchi and Bering Seas to the west, and the Pacific Ocean to the south. A total of 610,000 residents puts the state at third to last (behind Wyoming and Vermont) in population, but dead last in density.

Alaska State Facts

Capital: Juneau

Land Area: 570,374 square miles

Population: 614,010

Nickname: Land of the Midnight Sun

Motto: "North to the Future"

State Flower: Forget-Me-Not

Geographical Notes

Geologic Past – Alaska presents a living geology lab on a grand scale. Its broad landmass includes three major mountain chains—the Brooks, Alaska, and Coast ranges—and a vertical rise that varies from the 20,320ft summit of Mt. McKinley, the continent's highest mountain, to the Aleutian Trench, 25,000ft below sea level. With the Pacific tectonic plate continually grinding up against the North American plate along Alaska's southern coast, more than half the state is seismically active. Volcanoes regularly spew out smoke and ash, sometimes even across Cook Inlet onto Anchorage, and 10 percent of the world's earthquakes occur in Alaska. The Good Friday earthquake of 1964 destroyed the town of Valdez (on Prince William Sound) and caused serious damage to Anchorage and other southern ports.

Starting about two million years ago, the earth entered a series of four ice ages, with warm periods in between. The glaciers that blanket many of Alaska's southern mountains are recycled remnants of the last, or Wisconsin, Ice Age, which left glaciers up to 2,000ft thick—about half the thickness of much earlier glaciers. These periods of glaciation shaped the land by scouring out basins and fjords and whittling mountain ridges. With much of the globe's water locked up during the ice ages, sea levels dropped several hundred feet, exposing new features such as the Bering Land Bridge. Scientists believe it was during the most recent glacial period, some 15,000 to 30,000 years ago, that people found their way across this 900mi-wide bridge from Siberia to Alaska following the trails of animals that had gone before.

Regional Landscapes – The northernmost geographical region of the state, the **North Slope** is a broad plain falling gently from the Brooks Range to the Arctic seacoast, which stays frozen eight months of the year. Resting on a thick layer of permafrost (permanently frozen ground), the surface ground melts in summer and creates a network of channels, lakes and spongy terrain favored by caribou and hardy grasses and wildflowers. Mountains of the austere **Brooks Range** rise to more than 9,000ft near the Canadian border, then slope down to the western foothills above Kotzebue Sound; a few gaunt glaciers hold fast to the high, dry lees of these mountains. On the comparatively moist southern flanks, trees can grow.

Covering the greatest area of Alaska, the **Interior** spans the territory between the Brooks and Alaska Ranges and extends from Canada to the Seward Peninsula and southwest to the Yukon delta. Rolling hills and treeless tundra comprise much of the Interior, while other sections are forested and cut by streams and broad rivers such as the Yukon, Tanana, and Kuskokwim. Tremendous numbers of waterfowl and other migratory birds continue to nest here summer after summer. Girding the Interior on the south, the mighty **Alaska Range**, which bows up from the Aleutian Range on the southwest and the volcanic Wrangell Mountains on the southeast, tops out at snow-covered Mt. McKinley. The Talkeetna foothills, stepping down to the south, offer some of the state's finest hiking. The nearby **Interior Basins** include the wooded Copper River Basin and the low farmlands of the Matanuska and Susitna Valleys northeast of Anchorage.

The **Pacific Coast** region offers a diverging landscape of rocky islands, forested shores, and glacier-clad mountains. Starting with the rain forests of the southeastern panhandle, the region curves northwestward to the towering St. Elias Range and the Chugach Mountains, then across the Kenai Peninsula and down through the remote volcanoes and steam vents of the Alaska Peninsula. Coastal wildlife abounds here where the mountains flare up from the water, or, as the Aleuts put it—"where the sea breaks its back." A spine composed of thousands of islands and islets, the **Aleutian Range** stretches 1,100mi from the Alaska Peninsula out into the Pacific Ocean. Rough seas, fog and bone-chilling winds are common in this tempestuous region, the only part of North America invaded during World War II.

Aurora Borealis, Denali National Park

Climate – Alaska's great size and geographical variety result in a number of different climates. Blessed with warm winds from the Japan Current, southern Alaska enjoys relatively mild weather, with temperatures ranging from 40°F to 60°F degrees in summer and 20°F to 40°F in winter. Light but frequent precipitation falls throughout the region, with greatest accumulations in the Southeast. The same systems that bring rain to fishing villages unload snow on the coastal ranges just behind. Valdez and Baranof Island receive the most precipitation of any place in the state, with Valdez seeing up to 200 inches of snow a year. Interior temperatures average around 59°F in July and -9°F in January, though extremes in the high and dry areas are not uncommon: Fort Yukon recorded 100°F on June 27, 1915, and Prospect Creek, 100mi away, reached -80°F on January 23, 1971. A modest average precipitation of 11 inches falls here. The bitter Arctic averages -11°F in January and 47°F in July, with only four inches of annual precipitation. In all regions, conditions can change rapidly, making accurate weather prediction a difficult job.

Historical Notes

Across the Bering Strait – Though it may prove impossible to know exactly when the first people arrived in the Great Land, scholars generally think that sometime between 15,000 and 30,000 years ago nomadic bands crossed an exposed land bridge from Asia to America, with Alaska functioning as the gateway to the new world. Less understood is how that earliest stock spread out through North and South America and whether any groups stayed continuously in Alaska. Athabaskans have likely lived for about 8,000-9,000 years in Alaska, primarily in the Interior, with splinter groups traveling south to become the Apache and Navaho nations. Relative newcomers, the Eskimos have populated northwestern and southern shores for about 3,000 years, making a tough living hunting seals, polar bears and occasional whales, and ornamenting their bone and ivory weapons with delicate carvings for spiritual power. Tlingits and Aleuts arrived sometime between these two groups. In any event, when Europeans came in the 18C, the natives were long since established.

In 1741, Danish navigator **Vitus Bering**, commissioned by the Czar of Russia, set sail for southern Alaska. On a voyage 13 years earlier, he had determined that Siberia was not connected to North America, but fog had prevented him from sighting the American mainland. This time his expedition succeeded in actually landing—one party on Kayak Island and another on a nearby Southeast island. Though crew naturalist Georg Steller (for whom the Steller's jay and Steller's sea lion are named) advised Bering to hole up in Alaska through the winter, the captain was eager to return home. Enduring stormy seas, Bering's ship finally ran aground on an island off the Siberian coast, where Bering and 19 others died of scurvy. The remainder of the crew survived on fish until they could rebuild their wrecked vessel and sail home. Encouraged by sea otter pelts the survivors brought back, Russian fur traders developed a toehold

347

into a fur empire that in time stretched all the way from Siberia down to California. Taking Aleut slaves and reducing the sea otter population from four million to little more than 100,000, the Russians systematically plundered the natural resources that had easily sustained local seafarers for millennia. Astronomical prices paid by the Chinese for furs helped fuel the destructive trade. Headquartered in Sitka, the Russian-American Company faced fierce competition from British and American trade interests; treaties in 1824 and 1825 defined boundaries that settled these disputes. But the decline of the fur trade coupled with a crippling loss in the Crimean War (1853-56) spelled the end of Russia's tenure on Alaskan soil.

A Sucked Orange – Ambassador Baron Edouard de Stoeckl began meetings with US Secretary of State William Seward in 1866 to discuss selling off Alaska, and in October of 1867 the Russian flag over Sitka came down and the *Stars and Stripes* went up. Editorials immediately lambasted the deal, calling the area a worthless piece of real estate and tagging it Seward's Folly and Seward's Icebox. "Seward has sold us a sucked orange," griped the editor of the *New York World*. Some people, however, began to grow curious, for no one really knew what lay within that vast, forbidding tract.

For the next two decades, Congress ignored its new purchase, passing the responsibilities of management off to the War Department, then the Treasury Department and the Navy Department. Not until 1884 was the place provided with any judicial system; in that year federal district courts were set up and a school program begun. In the meantime, private companies had gone ahead and built canneries, initiating a salmon industry that would become the world's largest. Fish, as it turned out, were not the only riches awaiting in Seward's sucked orange. Discoveries of gold in Juneau in 1880, Nome in 1898, and the Fairbanks area in 1902 helped firmly entrench those towns and, along with the Klondike rush of 1897, swelled the population of Alaska in general.

Foreign Invasion – By the turn of the century Alaska was being taken seriously by the lower 48—so seriously that a delegation of US senators decided to come up in 1903 and have a look for themselves. They determined that if Alaska was to prosper— and the US to reap the benefits—the federal government should provide a transportation network. Trails, ferries, bridges and eventually railroads began connecting the less daunting outposts and even making incursions into the Interior. In 1906, Congress let Alaskans send a non-voting delegate to Washington, and by 1912 Alaska had mustered enough political clout to become an official US territory with a territorial legislature. Still, by the 1940s Alaska remained a quiet, almost unnoticed American backwater. That image would soon change.

With Alaska the last stop before Asia, the US during World War II began pouring money and military personnel to the region to build installations and a communications network. Despite the buildup, the territory was not fully prepared for the Japanese strike on the Aleutian Islands in early June 1942. As a diversion to their operations in the central Pacific, the Japanese bombed Dutch Harbor and landed on Attu and Kiska—undefended islands. The US responded with a series of air raids, losing more planes to dense fog and heavy winds than to enemy fire. Finally, the following May, 11,000 US troops swarmed onto Attu, which was held by 2,600 Japanese, and a fierce 18-day battle ensued. When the Japanese were down to a few hundred, their commander ordered a suicidal bayonet charge. Only 28 prisoners were taken.

By this time, more than 150,000 military personnel were stationed in Alaska, and the US Army Corps of Engineers had rammed its way through 1,500mi of rugged wilderness to complete the Alaska Highway. Linking Dawson City, British Columbia, to Fairbanks, the road would prove of vital importance in the future growth of the state. Alaska's potential and its strategic value during World War II, and the ensuing Cold War, led to greater recognition for its legitimate claims to statehood. Yet powerful lobbyists representing salmon canners, fearing restrictions on the industry, managed to stymie a 1950 Senate bill that would have made Alaska a state. But in 1958 the bill was approved 64 to 20, prompting a Nevada radio broadcaster to announce, "Texans, bow your heads. One hundred years of bragging have been pulled right out from under your feet." The following year Alaska became the 49th state of the union, the first new state since 1912.

The Last Frontier – Alaska's history in the latter part of the 20C has swirled primarily around two focal points—oil and land rights. Discoveries of oil and natural gas on the Kenai Peninsula and in Cook Inlet in the 1950s created a new economic boom and started an industry that would by the 1970s lead the state's mineral production. But it was the announcement of a major find by the Atlantic Richfield Company in 1968 that hurdled Alaska swiftly into the modern world, with its accompanying benefits and problems. The discovery of the Prudhoe Bay oil field ranks as one of the world's great oil strikes. Situated on the northern edge of the state, Prudhoe Bay holds the largest oil reserves in the continent. The difficulty, of course, was how to get the oil out in massive enough quantities to make it pay: The Arctic shore was frozen eight months of the year and there were no roads across the North Slope. The only practical solution, although it seemed a nearly Herculean task, was to construct a pipeline down to the nearest ice-free port, which happened to be at Valdez—800mi south, over two mountain ranges and across 350 rivers and streams. Native land claims and environmental studies held the project up for seven years until an Arab oil embargo forced Alaska's hand. Less than two years after work had begun, oil flowed south to Valdez. One of the modern world's most impressive feats of engineering, the pipeline is raised and insulated to keep its heat from melting the permafrost and causing sinkage; it furthermore allows for caribou migration and for shifting from earthquakes.

Money paid by oil companies to the state resulted in the Alaska Permanent Fund, the largest trust in the US, which pays every resident an annual dividend of about $1,000. The high revenues also allowed Alaska to do away with state income tax. But an early 1980s depression in the oil market and a steady depletion of the available reserves meant that Alaska could not stroll down easy street forever. Further complicating the North Slope picture were the age-old native claims that had never been settled. To pave the way for the pipeline, President Nixon signed the Alaska Native Claims Settlement Act in 1971, awarding 10 percent of Alaska's land (44 million acres) and nearly $1 billion to corporations set up by Native Americans; some of the claims have only recently been settled. Although North Slope Eskimos have been enriched by the oil boom, some side with environmentalists who report that caribou and other species in the fragile Arctic environment are being irreparably damaged by the invasion of modern technology. Natural gas has been discovered on the North Slope, but extraction was tabled by concerned citizens until recently. In August of 1998, US Secretary of the Interior Bruce Babbitt announced the opening of four million acres of northeastern tundra to oil and gas leases. Conservationists were displeased at the loss of protected habitats; oil companies were disappointed that the allowed acreage was not in the most oil-rich areas. Companies may drill, but expenses of transportation remain—one proposed solution is a second pipeline that would carry only gas.

In 1980 Congress passed the Alaska National Interest Lands Conservation Act, a key conservation measure that permanently set aside more than one-third of the state's total acreage as parks, national forests and wildlife refuges. Opponents of the controversial act charged (and still charge) that the federal government was trying to keep Alaska's land out of the hands of Alaskans. Before statehood, the government owned and managed nearly all of Alaska's land, acting as financial patron for many of its enterprises. While some residents are now ready to shake off the patronage system, others feel that within Alaska abides the last best hope for true wilderness, undisturbed by any work of man, and that without protection the land would be vulnerable to destruction. The 1989 spillage of 11 million gallons of crude oil by the tanker *Exxon Valdez* in Prince William Sound underscored for many the idea that the state's greatest resource is its wilderness, and that only by severely limiting development can Alaska keep its soul.

Economy

Natural Resources – Of Alaska's minerals, **oil** and **natural gas** rank as the leading economic mainstays. Rich petroleum reserves developed on the Arctic coast in the 1970s enabled the state to graduate from its dependence on federal government assistance for infrastructure growth. But complex land-use issues have forestalled further North Slope development. **Gold**, important in Alaska's frontier history, is still mined in the Yukon River Basin near Fairbanks. Mostly controlled by the federal government, the **land** continues to be a vital resource. Because of a short growing season and high labor costs, most of the fertile land has not been cleared and farmed. Nor has the state's tremendous waterpower potential yet been tapped. Local and outside investments remain, to a large extent, deterred by environmental constraints and the high costs of transportation over Alaska's vast area and challenging terrain—owing to limited ground transportation, airplanes provide the main links.

Industry – About a third of Alaska's gross state product is generated by the mining industry, heavily dominated by the production of **oil**. Only Texas produces more oil, and no state has a higher percentage of mineral income. Yet only about 10,000 people (four percent of the total work force) are employed in mining. **Fishing** dominates the economy in many areas, leading the country with a $1.5 billion annual harvest. In addition to salmon, fishermen bring in halibut, cod, pollock, and Dungeness and king crabs. Seafood processing plants provide an accessory boost to the economies of coastal towns. Playing a key role in Southeast and along the southern coast, **forestry** occurs mainly in the Tongass and Chugach national forests, the two largest in the United States. Pulp mills in Ketchikan and Sitka export to Japan, and timber goes to various Asian nations. **Agriculture** accounts for a small but significant wedge of the state's economic pie; milk, eggs and beef cattle are the major livestock products, while hay, barley, oats and potatoes round out the Alaskan farmer's offerings.

Though it still relies heavily on natural products, Alaska has developed its **service** industries to nearly 60 percent of the state's total economic output. The **tourism** industry, employing people from a variety of fields, has made strong gains in the last two decades. Cruises along the Inside Passage and inland excursions to Denali National

Park are perennial favorites of groups and individual travelers. Tourists spend about $1 billion every year in Alaska. Providing jobs for a full 28 percent of the labor pool, **government** maintains a strong presence in the economy. The combined activities of transportation, communication, and utilities generate about the same income as government, but employ only a third the number of people. Finance businesses also fire up the economy with relatively few numbers of workers, creating as much income as government with only four percent of the state's work force.

The State Today

If modern Alaska looks "north to the future," as its motto says, it also is looking within to determine how much it is willing to change to meet the demands of a swelling **population**. From 1980 to 1990, the state's population grew 37 percent and now contains a larger percentage of Alaskan-born citizens—about a third of the total. More people are coming and staying, and there is a growing diversity. Once a heavily male-populated pioneer state, Alaska now holds almost as many women as men. Approximately 16 percent of the populace is composed of Eskimo, the related Aleut, or Indian. The word "Eskimo," incidentally, derives from the Athabaskan for "raw meat eater," and many Eskimo prefer their own name, "Inuit." Of later immigrants, Russians still have a few descendants living in villages on the lower Kenai Peninsula, and places throughout the state bear Russian names, as well as names given by the later-arriving English, Spanish and French. Current minorities include blacks (4.1 percent), Asian and Pacific Islanders (3.6 percent), and Hispanics (3.2 percent). About two-thirds of the population lives in urban areas, primarily in Anchorage.

While Anchorage offers many of the cosmopolitan attractions of cities in the lower 48, it remains a small island in a sea of wilderness. And this is why people keep coming. The **recreational opportunities** are almost endless. With more than 100 million acres of protected park, refuge, and wilderness varying from spectacular coastal mountains and island-studded fjords to windswept tundras and bear-haunted boreal forests, visitors can choose to go kayaking one day, hiking the next, and then top the trip off with a flightseeing excursion. Rainy days (and there will be some) are good for exploring Alaska's colorful history and culture in a number of fine museums; totem poles and delicately carved bone and ivory objects are still being crafted by natives today. But rain does not stop anything in Alaska, especially in the busy summertime—cruises still go on schedule, as do most flights. Tours proceed rain or shine, and so should the independent traveler. It bears remarking that as far as tourism goes, Alaska can be as tame or as wild as you want to make it. The road system, though limited and sometimes slow, is perfectly adequate, as are roadside services. At the other end of the spectrum, those who have the money and outdoor expertise can charter planes to some of the most isolated countryside in the world.

Living in Alaska is another matter. Two things about the state that have not changed are the rigorous weather and formidable terrain. Winters in the Interior are not for the fainthearted, nor are the relentless days of wind that rip over the Aleutians and the highlands. Alaska tends to shake down its new arrivals in a hurry—they either adapt quickly or not at all. Long dark winters and torturing confinement to small, easily heated homes force many over the edge—depression and high alcohol consumption are but two side effects. Some choose to leave. The typical long-term Alaskan is resourceful, eccentric, and stubborn, and has faced the fact that Alaska ranks number one in the nation for deaths by accident. As poet Robert Service put it, "This is the law of the Yukon, and ever she makes it plain: Send not your foolish and feeble; send me your strong and your sane—Strong for the red rage of battle; sane for I harry them sore; Send me men girt for the combat, men who are grit to the core...."

© Galen Rowell

Horned Puffins

■ Alaska Safety Tips

Heeding the call of the wild, many visitors will make at least a short foray into the backcountry. You should be aware, though, that the designation "park"—state or national—often means miles and miles of trackless wilderness unlike anything in the lower 48 states. Along with the opportunity for surrounding yourself with that wilderness comes the responsibility of preparing for its hazards—particularly wild animals and cold.

Bears are common throughout the state. When hiking in bear country, wear bells or talk or sing to warn bears of your approach. If you are camping, check with a local ranger for information about keeping a clean, odor-free campsite—stringing food up at least 12ft from the ground is but one of many useful tips. If a bear does charge, hold your ground, wave your arms and talk in a loud voice. A running person could be mistaken for prey, and a bear can easily outrun a fast human. If the bear does not back down, drop to the fetal position and play dead; as a last resort, fight back with anything that comes to hand. Most bears will not even charge, but they are unpredictable. Remember that black bears, though smaller and generally less aggressive than grizzlies, can climb trees. Curiously, more people are injured by moose than bears. Do not venture close to a moose, especially one with calves. If charged by a moose, the best strategy is to run.

A more insidious danger, cold weather can quickly turn a carefree outing into a tragedy. Be aware of changing weather, and keep in mind that most hypothermia cases occur when the temperature is between 30-50°F. If you must ford rivers, wear sturdy shoes and undo your pack waist strap. Dress in layers that can be shed as you sweat and put back on when you start feeling cool; the best fabrics are wool or synthetics that "breathe." Goose down is warm but useless when wet. A warm hat is often the best way to prevent heat loss. Watch for these symptoms of hypothermia: slurred or incoherent speech, shivering and poor coordination. In very cold weather, look for white patches of skin that indicate the beginnings of frostbite—stop and warm these areas up immediately. Finally, if you plan to venture out in the winter, a class on survival skills might come in handy.

The Interior

Mount McKinley, Denali National Park/Art Wolfe/Tony Stone Images

A great rolling plain of tundra and taiga sandwiched between the Alaska and Brooks Ranges, the Interior has long been a haven for wildlife and a magnet for gold seekers. Largely undeveloped, the region is sliced by swift streams and dotted with bristly spruce and shimmery birch; wildflowers add dollops of color to the quilt of yellow-green mosses that record the shifting shadows of summer days. Much in the landscape has remained the same for millennia. The Pleistocene glaciers that covered the Brooks and Alaska mountains through the last Ice Age did not reach down onto the plains, thus leaving a refuge for plants and animals. Today the taiga, a boreal forest of spruce, alder, and willow, supports a great chain of mammalian life from bear, moose, wolf, and caribou to fox, snowshoe hare, and lynx. And shorebirds in the millions migrate through here across the tundra (a nearly treeless plain underlain by permafrost) as they have for tens of thousands of years, wings drumming the air, responding to the call of the north.

The Interior surged in population during the 1890s gold rush as thousands of prospectors made their way to the Klondike River in Canada. With the Yukon River serving as a western corridor, miners and traders and assorted profiteers came looking for pay dirt. The harsh climate and lonely surroundings forced many back; others stayed, eventually turning one town—FAIRBANKS—into a small city that is now home to the University of Alaska. The liquid gold rush of the 1970s, from the oil in Prudhoe Bay, resulted in a **pipeline** that cuts a narrow swath across the Interior, paralleling the Richardson Highway for much of its length.

Elsewhere, a few small towns and Athabaskan villages civilize the Interior, yet the region remains largely undeveloped and inaccessible by road. A paved highway and railroad do, however, lead to the place almost all Interior visitors come to see. Nearly three times the size of Yellowstone, Denali National Park is justly famous for its abundant wildlife and for views of its austere, snow-crowned monarch of the Alaska Range, Mt. McKinley.

DENALI NATIONAL PARK
AND PRESERVE★★★

Michelin map 930 Alaska inset and map pp 354-355
Tourist Information ☎ 907-683-2294 or www.nps.gov/dena

A must-see mecca for many visitors to Alaska, the six-million-acre Denali National Park and Preserve offers an incomparable cross section of the untamed Alaska Range, including the highest peak on the North American continent. Landscapes within Denali's boundaries vary from spruce forest to grassy tundra to forbidding granite spires mantled with snow and ice. Preserved in this northwestern haven is a vibrant and remarkably intact community of animals that ranges in size from grizzly bear and moose down to the arctic ground squirrel. Some 350,000 people a year, drawn by America's Everest, make pilgrimage here to catch a fleeting glimpse of **Mt. McKinley** and to immerse themselves in a pre-human world of grand design and dimension.

Geographical Notes

The High One – At 20,320ft, Mt. McKinley stands as the climactic feature of the park's—and the state's—varied landscape. Its vertical rise of 18,000ft above the low-lands around **Wonder Lake** makes it the highest exposed mountain in the world (Everest rises only 11,000ft from the Tibetan Plateau). McKinley's dizzying height is further accentuated by a lofty isolation among its peers: Most of the **Alaska Range** peaks top out at barely half McKinley's elevation—McKinley's pyramidal North Peak (19,470ft) and nearby Mt. Foraker (17,400ft) are the closest contenders.

The creation of the mountain began some 65 million years ago as the North American and the Pacific tectonic plates collided with each other; along the collision zone—the Denali Fault—the earth buckled into a tremendous mountain range that curves 600mi across the Alaskan interior. Where the Alaska Range joins the Aleutian Range, along the same fault line, volcanoes are still active, while up here in the park occasional moderate earthquakes attest to the ongoing forces of mountain building. McKinley's appearance today owes much to the last Ice Age. Though it ended about 10,000 years ago, the cold period left several glaciers that have scoured out cirques and chiseled razor-sharp ridges and precipitous valleys—a remote Olympian landscape that often floats in a world of its own above the clouds. With temperatures that dip below -50°F and winds that can exceed 150mph, the mountain lies blanketed in perennial snow and ice that start at about 6,000ft elevation and in places lie hundreds of feet thick.

Rival to Everest – Although early nomads likely wandered through the area on hunting and gathering forays, they left little evidence of permanent occupation. A later people, the Athabaskans, revered the mountain they called Denali ("the high one") as a central icon in their mythology. But very few outside people knew of the peak's existence until William A. Dickey, Princeton graduate and Alaska gold prospector, published an article in a New York paper in January of 1897, naming the mountain after soon-to-be-elected presidential candidate William McKinley and extolling it as "America's grandest rival to Mount Everest." Dickey's claims proved accurate when a US Geological Survey team measured the massif the following year. Their calculations, using 1890s instruments, were only 144ft above the official height recognized today. An abbreviated gold rush in the **Kantishna** area in the early 1900s gave way to an era of hunters and naturalists. Among these newcomers, Vermonter Charles Sheldon stands tall as the original spearhead of the movement for a national park. By 1917, 11 years after his arrival here, Sheldon saw his dream become a reality. Access to the park would follow with the advent of the railroad in 1923 and completion of a park road to Wonder Lake in 1938. The park was originally set aside as a wildlife refuge and did not include all of Mt. McKinley, but in 1980 the park's area was tripled to six million acres and Mount McKinley National Park became Denali National Park and Preserve. Within its borders is a designated wilderness that includes Mt. McKinley; in some contiguous "park" areas traditional subsistence uses are allowed, while the "pre-serve" areas allow for subsistence as well as some sport hunting, fishing and trapping. Several inholdings of private land within the park itself, including a handful of rustic lodges around Kantishna, further add to the complicated patchwork of Denali and testify to the statewide compromises between conservationists and developers as well as state politics and national interests.

Taking the Top – Along with the early exploration of the area came the inevitable attempts to scale the summit of McKinley. Among the notable early failures was a highly disputed claim by polar explorer Dr. Frederick Cook, whose so-called summit pictures turned out to have been snapped on a 5,300ft-high ridge 11mi south of McKinley. On another disputed climb, four veteran miners with homemade equipment were said to have made the final 10,000ft in a single day, fueled only by coffee and chocolate doughnuts. Three years later, in 1913, a party led by park superintendent Harry Karstens discovered a flagpole near the North Peak, proving that the miners' extraordinary feat was true after all. Of course, the North Peak stands 850ft lower than the rounded South Peak, so that the first successful summit bid actually belongs to Karstens' crew.

Since then, more than 10,000 people have climbed to the top of Mt. McKinley, their ages ranging from 12 to 72. Currently about 1,100 people a year test their mettle against the mountain. Climbers generally fly onto the Kahiltna Glacier situated at 7,200ft; they spend at least a month and between $3,000 and $5,000 on their attempts. About 50 percent are successful. Though not technically difficult, McKinley is a Himalayan-class climb, respected for its thin air, extremely low temperatures and gale-force winds. It has claimed the lives of some 88 climbers. Each year the park service must rescue about 10 climbers. The dramatic helicopter rescue of two British mountaineers in 1998, costing $280,000, prompted state officials to hold hearings on whether climbers should foot their own rescue bills. Still, for a $150 administrative fee (and 60-day advance registration), any visitor is welcome to have a crack at "the high one."

Taiga and Tundra – Leading up to the glaciated heights is a multihued subarctic wilderness braided with glacial streams and strewn with wildflowers. The lowlands ecosystem goes by the Russian name *taiga* (TIE-gah), which refers to the sparse evergreen forest—some of the smaller spruce, with trunks no thicker

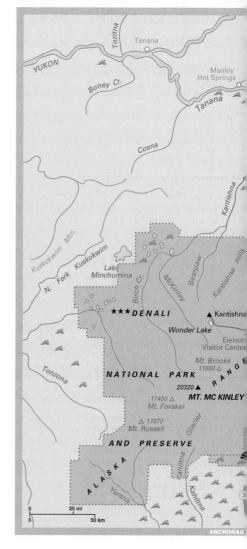

than a thumb, may be more than 200 years old, the harsh climate stunting their growth to bonsai proportions. Above the 2,700ft timberline on windswept slopes, the moist tundra begins, populated by willows, dwarf shrubs, sedges and mosses. Between 3,400ft and 7,500ft, the dry tundra spreads its lush carpet of low plants over thin, rocky soil.

The park's original raison d'être and the reason many people come here, Denali's abundant wildlife takes advantage of these varied niches. **Moose** favor the boggy, moist forest-tundra transition zone, while wolves and **grizzly bears** roam throughout. Small herds of caribou are often seen grazing the tundra, and plentiful Dall sheep dot the highlands. Altogether, 37 mammal species and 157 bird species reside in Denali.

VISIT *1 day*

Since the park entrance stands 75mi from Mt. McKinley, very few visitors will actually stand on the massif, nor get closer to it than about 30mi. Instead, the mountain serves as a stunning backdrop for those lucky enough to obtain a view. Because low-lying clouds often block views of the Alaska Range, only about 25 to 30 percent of visitors see McKinley. Those who stay a few days are more likely to get a view. Your chances of seeing moose and bears are better—80 and 95 percent respectively. Private vehicles are allowed only on the first 14.8mi of the park road. Beyond Savage River, unless you have a campground permit, access is only by foot, bicycle, or bus.

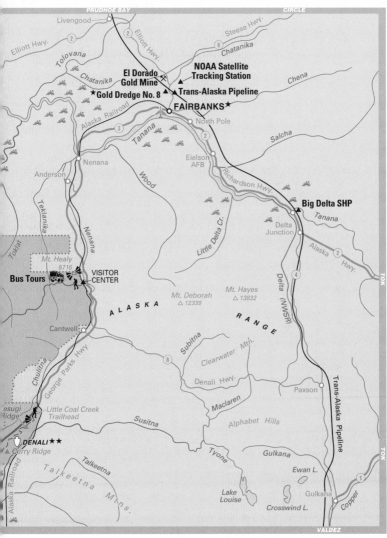

The **visitor center** *(just inside park entrance on right; open May–Sept daily 7am–8pm; rest of the year daily 8am–4:30pm; ☎ 907-683-1266)* offers a 12min slide program, a few exhibits, and a bookstore. Visitors may register here for shuttle tours and backcountry and camping permits. Pick up a copy of the *Denali Alpenglow* for information on ranger-led programs, sled-dog demonstrations, and other events. A larger visitor center, on the site of the former Denali Park Hotel, will be phased in over the next several years.

Hiking is a popular park activity, but it should be emphasized that, in keeping with a wilderness park, there are very few maintained trails. Trails near the hotel include a 1.5mi loop to Horseshoe Lake and a 5mi round-trip hike up Mt. Healy, which provides spectacular views of Mt. McKinley and the Nenana River valley. Further afield, ridge tops and river bars are good choices for walks; be sure to heed warnings about bears and hypothermia before setting out.

Bus tours – *Shuttle and tour buses operate mid-May–mid-Sept. Sixty-five percent of all shuttle-bus tickets are available by phone (starting in late Feb) ☎ 907-272-7275 or 800-622-7275; the remainder are available for walk-in purchase up to two days in advance. $12.50-$31. Because of high demand, there may be a two-day wait for choice times. The Tundra Wildlife Tour operates mid-May–mid-Sept daily 6am & 2pm; 6-8 hrs round-trip; $67, children $40; for reservations contact Denali Park Hotel ☎ 907-276-7234 or 800-276-7234. Both types of buses are operated by the park concessionaire and offer wildlife viewing. Bring binoculars. Also be aware that all are converted school buses and thus not plush; windows may fog during bad weather, restricting views.*

When to Go

The park road is open from Memorial Day to mid-September although weather conditions may close the road until early June. Private cars cannot go beyond Savage River (mile 14.8). Although the park road is closed in winter, the backcountry is accessible on foot, skis and by dogsled. Owing to the short season, early reservations for accommodations and camping sites are strongly recommended.

Getting There

By Air – Closest airports: **Anchorage International Airport** and **Fairbanks International Airport**.

By Bus and Train – There is no public bus transportation. **Mini-coach tours** leave from Anchorage *(June 1–Sept 10 daily; $59 one way)*; for schedules and reservations: Alaska Windsong Lodges, P.O. Box 22101, Anchorage AK 99522; ☎ 245-0200 or 800-208-0200; www.alaskalodges.com. The Alaska Railroad Corp. *(Box 107500, Anchorage AK 99510)* provides **train** service to Denali from Anchorage and Fairbanks *(mid-May–mid-Sept daily; in winter weekends only)*; schedules and reservations: ☎ 265-2494 or 800-544-0552. GrayLine of Alaska offers **Coach tours** and **overnight train trips** in private, glass-domed railcars *(mid-May–mid-Sept daily)*; schedules and reservations: ☎ 277-5581 or 800-544-2206.

By Car – The region is accessible year-round via Rte. 3; the main park entrance is 237mi north of Anchorage, 120mi south of Fairbanks. Gas is available on Rte. 3 north of park entrance (summer) and year-round in Healy and Cantwell.

General Information

Visitor Information – *The park is open year-round daily. $5/person, $10 family (valid for 7 days).* ⚠ ✗ ♿ ▣. Contact the superintendent, **Denali National Park & Preserve** *(P.O. Box 9, Denali National Park AK 99755-0009; ☎ 683-2294; www.nps.gov/dena)* to obtain maps and information on accommodations, recreation and seasonal events. For additional information contact **Alaska Division of Tourism**, P.O Box 110801, Juneau AK 99811 ☎ 465-2010, www.dced.state.ak.us/tourism.

Accommodations – Camp Denali and North Face Lodge *(open June–mid-Sept; $285/person all inclusive; ☎ 683-2290)*, Denali Backcountry Lodge *(open mid-May–Oct; $275/person all inclusive; ☎ 800-841-0692)* and Denali National Park Hotel *(open mid-May–Oct; $147/person; ☎ 683-2215)* are located inside park boundaries. Accommodations *(May–mid-Sept, ranging from $99-$177)* located close to park entrance are: Denali Cabins *(☎ 683-2643)*, Denali Princess Lodge *(☎ 683-2282)*, McKinley Chalet Resort *(☎ 276-7234)* and McKinley Village Lodge *(☎ 276-7234)*. A range of accommodations including lodges, bed-and-breakfast inns, resorts and cabins can be found year-round in Healy and Cantwell. **Denali Hotel Hotline:** ☎ 683-1422 or 800-354-6020.

Camping – There are seven **campgrounds** *($6-$40/night)*, some of which can be reserved in advance. Reserve in person or by phone at the visitor center up to 2 days in advance. Riley Creek Campground *(registration not required)* is open year-round. Overnight stays in the **backcountry** require a permit (free) available at the visitor center *(summer)* and from the park headquarters *(winter)*. *Observe park rules regarding wildlife-viewing safety and food storage-Bear Resistant Food Containers (BRFCs) are mandatory in the backcountry.*

Recreation

Sightseeing – Country Shuttle provides free service between Riley Creek Campground Visitor Center, Park Hotel and the Railroad Depot; the Savage River Shuttle offers service from the visitor center to the Savage River Bridge *(fee)*. **Scenic flights** including glacier landings, backpacking, skiing, as well as climbing transportation and expedition support, are offered by Talkeetna Air Taxi *(year-round daily; from $85; reservations: ☎ 733-2218)*.

Outdoor Activities – Among the many activities are ranger-led guided walks, wildlife viewing, photography, hiking, rafting the Nenana River, dog-sled rides and horseback riding. Biking is restricted to designated roadways. **Winter activities** inculde skiing, snowshoeing and dog-sledding. Be sure to check with park headquarters regarding weather conditions *(☎ 683-2294)*.
Mountain **climbing** on Mount McKinley and Mount Foraker requires registration and a climbing fee *(60 days in advance)*; for information, contact Talkeetna Ranger Station, Box 588, Talkeetna AK 99676, ☎ 733-2231.

Kim Heacox/Tony Stone Images

Shuttle Bus in Denali National Park

Shuttle-bus excursions★, like the tour-bus excursions, generally provide a running commentary by drivers who double as naturalists and are expert at spotting wildlife. These buses are a good option for those who want to get deep into the park. The park road gradually ascends from forested taiga to open tundra and, weather permitting, offers outstanding opportunities for photography and views of Mt. McKinley and the Alaska Range. Riders may get off buses at any point to hike or picnic, and take another bus back (on a space-available basis). Round-trip shuttle journeys last from 6-13 hrs, depending on your destination.

Those who prefer a briefer introduction to the park should opt for one of the **tour bus excursions★**. The 3 hr **Natural History Tour** takes visitors to Primrose Ridge *(mile 17)*, stopping along the way at a 1927 log cabin for an entertaining historical presentation by an interpretive naturalist. A snack is included. The 6-8 hr **Tundra Wildlife Tour** allows for a broader view of Denali's terrain and gives you a greater chance for spotting more wildlife. Box lunches are provided. On both tours, driver/guides outline the local geology, flora and fauna.

★★**Denali State Park** – *George Parks Hwy. (Rte. 3), Milepost 135-69. Open daily year-round; not plowed in winter.* △ ✗ 🅿 ☎ *907-745-3975*. Contiguous to Denali National Park, this gorgeous 325,240-acre piece of wilderness may offer visitors a better bet than the popular national park for spectacular views of Mt. McKinley. Straddling the Parks Highway, Denali State Park lies only 35mi from the summit— twice as close as the visitor center at the national park. There are fewer visitor facilities here, but more marked trails. The 35mi spines of Curry and Kesugi ridges runs right through the park, and hikers who start at Little Coal Creek Trailhead *(Mile 163.9, north end of park)*, heading up the Kesugi (Tanaina for "the ancient one"), can get above treeline in about 1.5mi and enjoy unimpeded views of the glaciers and mountains of the Alaska Range. A pullover at Mile 135.2 offers superlative views similar to those painted by noted artist Sydney Laurence in the early 1900s.

■ Alaskan Wildlife

With the vast majority of the state still undivided by highways, Alaska remains to a large extent an unaltered ecosystem of animals that have been here since the end of the last ice age, some 10,000 years ago. From the rain forests of the Southeast to the tundra of the Arctic, animals large and small roam freely across park and refuge boundaries. Opportunities for spotting and photographing wildlife—from casual sightings to organized expeditions—abound in all corners of the Great Land.

Alaska claims nearly 1,000 species of mammals, birds and fish, including 105 mammal species and over 400 kinds of birds. Reptiles and amphibians are few, snakes non-existent. Though the state harbors quite a variety of insect life, the good news is that the mosquito problem is mostly overstated. Boggy areas in the Interior sometimes breed mosquitoes, but coastal breezes tend to keep their numbers down in the Southeast and South Central regions.

Bald Eagle

Largest of the continent's land predators, **brown bears** symbolize the untamed country like no other animal. About 30,000 of these powerful creatures live throughout the state—the larger ones along coastal areas and the smaller (called grizzlies) in the Interior. The population of **black bears** in Alaska tops 50,000. They are likewise found in all parts of the state, though they favor the forested areas, particularly in the Kenai Peninsula, on Prince of Wales Island and along Prince William Sound. Since shades of fur vary widely, size makes for an easier distinction between species: Brown bears weigh from 500 to 1,400 pounds; the largest blacks are only about 200. Brown bears also have a rounder face and a muscular shoulder hump.

© Lynn M. Stone

The amazing and ungainly looking **moose**, which weighs up to 1,800 pounds and stands more than six feet tall at the shoulder, favors the Interior forest, especially where it gives way to wet tundra and muskeg (mossy bog). Among the stranger characteristics of moose is their ability to dive under water and stayed submerged for several minutes in search of aquatic plants.

Sure-footed **Dall sheep** inhabit the mountainous and dry tundra zones of the Interior and Arctic. Denali National Park and the Kenai Peninsula highlands are likely places to spot them grazing—from a distance herds often look like a group of unnaturally white boulders.

Coastal areas from the Kenai down to the Southeast make prime habitat for **bald eagles**, the majestic raptor that was until recently on the endangered species list. Eagle nests are readily visible in trees along the water's edge. With strong talons and wingspans of up to 8ft, they can carry a salmon equal to their own weight.

Of the great variety of Alaskan marine mammals, highest on the wish lists of most visitors are the **whales**. The sight of a humpback's tail flared as it dives or of orcas (killer whales) leaping in synchrony is sure to inspire awe. Boat excursions into Glacier Bay and other places on the Inside Passage are the best bets for sightings. Hundreds of whales summer in Alaskan waters, while spring and fall are reserved for migrations north and south.

FAIRBANKS★

Michelin map 930 Alaska inset and map p 360
Population 33,295
Tourist Information ☎ 907-456-5774 or www.explorefairbanks.com

Spread among low rolling hills along the banks of the sinuous Chena River, Fairbanks ranks as the second largest city in the state and serves as the commercial, military and transportation center for the Interior. Several major highways converge here; the Alaska Railroad terminates here; and airline flights to the Interior depart from here. Yet by most standards Fairbanks hardly qualifies for the label "city"—compared with Anchorage, its small population and low-lying architecture give this town a frontier feel. But visitors will find a full complement of worthy sites, as well as a friendly citizenry who pride themselves on their independent spirit and their adaptability to fierce winters.

Historical Notes

A Fortunate Mistake – When Ohio trader and ex-convict E.T. Barnette and his wife headed up the Tanana River on a steamer in 1901, they had no idea they would end up on a backwater called the Chena River. They had envisioned establishing a trading post to service the local gold miners far to the south in Tanacross. But after an already rigorous journey, they talked the captain into trying a shortcut up a tributary that turned out too shallow for the heavily-laden vessel. The captain dumped them and their provisions out on the banks, then headed off, leaving Barnette's wife in tears. Luckily, there were plenty of prospectors in the nearby hills; they soon struck gold, and the Barnettes stayed on to make a bundle themselves as traders and founders of the city's first bank.

With an eye on the main chance, Barnette named his growing outpost after US Senator Charles Fairbanks (later vice president under Theodore Roosevelt), the political patron of district court judge James Wickersham. He even named streets for Wickersham's cronies. With miners extracting an annual $6 million in gold from the local hills by 1905, the new town of Fairbanks was booming—services included a hospital, power plant, fire and police departments, and a busy red-light district. The gold business dried up within a few years, as did Barnette's bank, and when locals found out he had served time in Oregon for grand larceny, their founding father skipped town.

Boomtown Blues – A dwindling gold supply and numerous major fires were not enough to wipe Fairbanks out. The University of Alaska was established here in 1917, and a few years later the Alaska Railroad was completed, terminating in Fairbanks. Holding a population of only 3,500 by the time of World War II, the town surged forward with the building of two military installations nearby, Fort Wainwright and Eielson Air Force Base.

By the 1970s, Fairbanks was still a fairly quiet town of military personnel, students, and rugged individualists until the Trans-Alaska Pipeline project suddenly jolted it into the modern world. Key supply depot for the North Slope, the town became clogged with truckers, laborers, engineers and ancillary service providers. High prices, crowding and increased pollution were but a few of the problems, followed by an economic collapse once the pipeline was completed in 1977 and the workers and associated carpetbaggers had gone. Property values sank; unemployment soared; saloons proliferated. The lingering presence downtown of a few vagabonds and boarded buildings are reminders of that slump.

A Fresh Start – Having profited and learned from the mining and oil boom-and-bust cycles of the 20C, Fairbanks heads into a new century with a firmly entrenched survivor's attitude. Instead of aspiring to become more like Anchorage, the town aims to be more and more like itself—resourceful, educated, and more than a little strange. Known for its oddball characters, its motley gang of state legislators (libertarians, socialists, Democrats and Republicans), its short but wildly intense growing season that produces gargantuan vegetables, its midnight-sun baseball game, Indian Eskimo olympics, hairy legs contest, duct-tape boat regatta, international ice-sculpting competition, and tougher-than-the-Iditarod sled-dog race, Fairbanks opens its arms to those coming for a fresh start or just for a peek.

What usually sorts out long-termers from the merely curious is the winter. Brutal in its duration and strength, winter grips the town in snow and cold from September to May. In January temperatures of 60 below zero are not uncommon. Car batteries routinely fail; engines freeze up even with overnight heaters; water thrown out turns to ice before it hits the ground; furnaces die; and smog solidifies into a brown ice fog that seizes the city and turns people into a race of saturnine zombies. The saving grace of the long cold nights is the spectacle of the **northern lights**, or aurora borealis, a brilliant show of nature more than 200 nights a year. Still, while people in other climes may live for the weekend, Fairbanksans live for the nightless days of summer, when temperatures rise and the pulse of life quickens to make up for a long sleep.

SIGHTS *2 days*

Visitor Information Center – *550 1st Ave. Open May–Sept daily 8am–8pm. Rest of the year Mon–Fri 10am–5pm. Closed Jan 1, Thanksgiving Day, Dec 25.* ☎ *907-456-5774 or 800-327-5774. www.explorefairbanks.com.* a 1959 spruce log cabin with a sod roof offers information on attractions, tours, accommodations and restaurants. (Sod was used to provide insulation, as well as animal-free rooftop gardens.) Free courtesy phones are available for local calls. Pick up maps here for a self-guided walking tour of downtown. A pleasant if unspectacular stroll around the area takes you past the older homes and businesses. Adjacent to the visitor center is a monument to town founder E.T. Barnette at the approximate site of his landing, and the landscaped **Golden Heart Plaza**, noted for its clock tower and sculpture of the "Unknown First Family," dedicated to "all families past, present and future, and to the indomitable spirit of the people of Alaska's Interior."

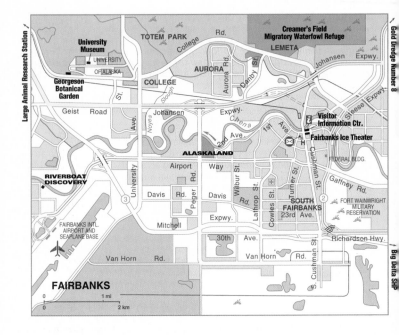

FAIRBANKS

Fairbanks Ice Theater – *500 2nd Ave. Open Jun–mid–Sept daily 10am–6pm. $6. Rest of the year operating as movie theater.* ♿ ☎ *907-451-8222.* Located in the 1939 Lacey Street Theater, this showcase of world ice art offers a vicarious look at one of Fairbanks' premier annual events. A 20min slide presentation takes viewers through the process of ice sculpting, from the harvesting of giant blocks of clear ice at a nearby pond to the carving of exquisitely detailed animals, ballerinas, warriors, and castles—some over 30ft tall—at the World Ice Art Championship in March. Visitors may then walk through a 20°F display case for a close-up look at 20 tons of ice art; a smaller 5°F freezer offers the feel of a typical March night in Fairbanks.

★**Alaskaland** – *Airport Way and Peger Rd. Grounds open year-round daily. Buildings are open Memorial Day–Labor Day daily 11am–9pm.* ♿ 🅿 ☎ *907-459-1087.* A number of state treasures are on exhibit at this 44-acre history theme park, built in 1967 in celebration of the Alaska Purchase centennial. The National Historic Landmark **S.S. Nenana**, a restored 237ft sternwheeler, transported passengers and supplies on the Yukon and its tributaries from 1933-52. Tours *($3)* take in the salon, pantry, dining room, engine room and smoking room; dioramas and photos depict Yukon and Nenana River villages of the 1930s. Another National Register property, the **"Denali"** was the plush railcar that carried President Warren Harding into the Interior in the early 1920s. On the trip he "drove in" the golden spike to complete the Alaska Railroad (after a ceremonial tap, an iron spike was substituted, which Harding missed on the first two tries before neatly polishing it off in two more blows).

The 1904 **Wickersham House** originally stood downtown; it was built and occupied by federal judge and Alaska politician James Wickersham, one of the most influential men of the early territorial days. The small frame house contains period and original furniture. Nearby **Gold Rush Town** harbors a number of turn-of-the-century wooden two-story buildings moved from downtown, which now operate as gift shops, snack stands, and the **Pioneer Museum** *($2)*, an old-fashioned collection of mining tools, whiskey stills, dog-sledding equipment, and other appurtenances of pioneer life. The big gold dome in the center of the park houses an **aviation museum**, a display of 14 aircraft and hundreds of photos and historical items. Elsewhere in the park are a native village, a miniature railroad, a playground, and a salmon-bake restaurant featuring salmon cooked over an open-fire and an all-you-can-eat buffet.

University Museum – *907 Yukon Dr. (west end of campus). Open Jun–Aug daily 9am–7pm, Sept & May daily 9am–5pm. Rest of the year Mon–Fri 9am–5pm, weekends noon–5pm. Closed Jan 1, Thanksgiving Day, Dec 25. $5.* ✗ ⚐ ▣ ☎ *907-474-7505. www.uaf.edu/museum.* Mounted animals, dioramas, hands-on objects, video programs and other items limn the history and culture of the state here. Divided into five regional displays, the museum contains totem poles, baskets and masks from the Southeast; seabirds and Russian icons from South Central; an exhibit on permafrost in the Interior section; a polar bear killed in 1971 and a gray whale skull from the Western Arctic Coast; and a display on the detention of Aleutians and Japanese Americans during World War II in the Southwest. Lording it over the gallery's entrance is an 8ft stuffed brown bear, "taken" in 1950. The museum offers two shows that play twice daily: Northern Inua highlights native games and songs with live demonstrations, and **Dynamic Aurora** is a technical but interesting slideshow and lecture about the northern lights. In the latter show, visitors learn that Fairbanks is perfectly situated in latitude and longitude for observation of the aurora borealis, a stream of shimmering light produced when electrons from the solar wind excite gases in the upper atmosphere (60-150mi up) to produce a colored ring around the magnetic pole. The thickest portion of that ring happens to be over the Fairbanks' night sky.

Other University of Alaska facilities of interest to visitors include the experimental farm's **Georgeson Botanical Garden** *(W. Tanana Loop.; open year-round daily dawn–dusk;* ▣ ☎ *907-474-1944 or 7627),* which sports vegetables and flowers that have grown into giants under the rays of the midnight sun. The **Large Animal Research Station** *(Yankovitch Rd.; open Jun–Aug Tue, Thu & Sat 11am–1:30pm; Sept Sat 11am–1:30pm; $3;* ▣ ☎ *907-474-7207)* holds musk oxen, caribou, bison and reindeer, and offers a viewing platform *(binoculars necessary)* just off the road.

Creamer's Field Migratory Waterfowl Refuge – *1300 College Rd. Visitor Center open Tue–Fri 10am–5pm, Sat 10am–4pm. Trails open daily year-round. For activity schedule:* ☎ *907-459-7307.* On the grounds of a former dairy, the peaceful 1,800-acre preserve hosts geese, ducks, swans, sandhill cranes, and other birds on their annual migrations. A nature center holds interpretive displays, and a 2mi trail loops the refuge. Moose are often spotted early mornings and late afternoons.

★Riverboat Discovery – *Discovery Rd. Departs Steamboat Landing mid-May–mid-Sept daily 8:45am, 12:30pm, 2pm, 5:30pm (Thu also 6:30pm). Round-trip 3.5 hrs. Commentary. Reservation required. $39.95.* ✗ ⚐ ▣ *Alaska Riverways, Inc.* ☎ *907-479-6673. www. riverboat discovery.com.* Although a 3.5 hr cruise down the meandering Chena and Tanana Rivers may not sound exciting, this tour garners high marks for its excellent commentary and non-stop sightseeing.

Riverboat *Discovery* on the Chena River

Vince Streano/Tony Stone Images

all in the comfort of a 900-passenger, four-decked sternwheeler outfitted with large picture windows and 16 viewing monitors. Along the way, you watch a bush pilot take off and land, see the winterized riverfront houses of prominent Fairbanksans, watch a bankside demonstration by Iditarod champion Susan Butcher's dogs, pass an Indian fish camp, and stop at a re-created Athabaskan village. The tour narrator conducts interviews via microphone with subjects along the riverbank, making you feel as if you are moving through a live documentary on the history and culture of Alaska. Son of Yukon steamboat pilot Charles Binkley, Jim Binkley opened the tour operation in 1950, and it has remained in the family ever since.

EXCURSIONS

Trans-Alaska Pipeline – *30min. 7.5mi northeast of Fairbanks on Steese Hwy. (Rte. 6). Parking on right. Open mid-May–mid-Sept daily 10am–6pm.* ⅋ ▣ ☎ *907-459-5871.* Snaking from Prudhoe Bay down to Valdez, the 800mi pipeline was built in the mid 1970s as a means of transporting crude oil from the North Slope to tankers at the closest ice-free port. It passes right along the highway here northeast of Fairbanks, and you can walk under the 4ft-diameter pipe and read information panels about it. Since the completion of the $8 billion project in 1977, the bay's oil reserves have declined significantly, but the pipeline still delivers more than 20 percent of the nation's domestically-produced oil.

Trans-Alaska Pipeline near Brooks Range

Paul Souders/Tony Stone Images

★**Gold Dredge Number 8** – *2 hrs. 8mi northeast of Fairbanks. Take Steese Hwy. (Rte. 6) to Goldstream Rd. Turn left and follow signs. Open mid-May–late Sept daily 9am–5:30pm. $20.* ▣ ☎ *907-457-6058.* From 1928 to 1959 this floating, riverbottom-devouring, gear-clanking monster churned out 500 ounces of gold a week on creeks near Fairbanks. Servicing the 99ft-long machine was a team of low-wage laborers who lived in drafty "dredge gray" wood-frame bunkhouses with corrugated iron roofs that amplified the drumming of the rain. The dredge was operated around the clock, its noise so loud that people in Fairbanks 12mi away complained. It now sits quietly in the creek where it last worked. Visits start with an introductory film and self-guided wandering through bunkhouses, bathhouse and a museum. Black-and-white photographs and informative panels give insight into Alaska gold– mining history and the hard life of a dredge worker. Items on exhibit include sagging beds, an antique radio, a giant hydraulic hose and a sewing machine. A 20min guided tour of the dank and dark dredge itself shows how the behemoth worked. Visitors are then given a poke sack of pay dirt and a panning demonstration; ten minutes of effort will yield about $4-$8, which you may take to the "assay office" for weighing.

El Dorado Gold Mine – *2 hrs. 11.3mi north of Fairbanks. Take Steese Hwy. (Rte. 6) to Fox, then go straight on Elliott Hwy. (Rte. 2) 1.3mi; turn left at gold mine. Guided tours (2 hrs) include train ride daily mid-May–mid-Sept $27.95 Call ahead for reservation.* ⅋ ▣ ☎ *907-479-7613. www.eldoradogoldmine.com.* Another Binkley family operation, El Dorado features a 2 hr tour that starts with a narrow-gauge train ride through a permafrost tunnel and a demonstration of placer mining techniques. Visitors pan for gold with sacks of dirt that have been salted with a few flecks of the precious metal; complimentary cookies and coffee are available in the gift shop.

■ The Arctic

If Alaska is a world unto itself, the Arctic embodies the essential spirit of oth-erworldly Alaska. With hardly a soul living in it, the region takes up nearly a third of the state, spreading from Canada 700mi to the Chukchi Sea; on its northern border lies the frigid Beaufort Sea; to the south, the Yukon River drops southwest and away into slightly warmer climes. An old saying has it that "There is no law above the Yukon, and no God above the Arctic Circle." But with fewer wild spaces existing today, many people would find in the purity of the Arctic proof of the perfection of nature's design.

An unforgiving land of extremes, the Arctic is perhaps the strangest, least understood of Alaska's many regions. Here the sun never sets in the sum-mer, never rises in the winter. Here, as Pulitzer-winner Barry Lopez wrote, "airplanes track icebergs the size of Cleveland, and polar bears fly down out of the stars." Here the **Brooks Range**, largely unexplored, arcs across the Arctic's midrift; frozen deserts dot the hinterlands; ice blisters up into hills called pingos; and shimmering streams etch sinuous patterns across the tun-dra. Snow falls any time of year (though it is the driest region in the state), and permafrost up to 2,000ft thick underlies nearly all the non-mountain-ous areas. Yet temperatures can reach the 90s in summer when life bursts forth—poppies and marsh marigolds bloom bravely in chill winds, herds of caribou thunder north to calving grounds, and the ground thaws into a com-plex network of tussocky islands and ribbons of water. Hikers find the land tough going; airplane passengers stay glued to the windows.

© Galen Rowell

Winter Sunset, Arctic Ocean, Barrow

The dominating feature of the Arctic landscape, the ancient Brooks Range, with its near-10,000ft peaks, runs east to west in seemingly endless bat-tlements and sharp spires. The Brooks and its many mountain systems define the Continental Divide in this region—north-flowing rivers channel across the desolate tundra to the Arctic Sea, those flowing south empty into the Bering Sea. Protecting a vast piece of this range, the 8.5-million-acre **Gates of the Arctic National Park and Preserve** is the second largest park in the system and probably the most remote. The tough 415mi Dalton Highway, an unpaved road running northwest of Fairbanks to the oil field at Prudhoe Bay, skirts the eastern edge of the park, but most visitors choose to fly from Fairbanks to Anaktuvuk Pass or Bettles, then charter a plane into the park. Bush pilots land on whatever flat piece of ground or water looks good, then agree on a pick-up date. There are no trails, no facilities, no visitor centers. Hikers and canoeists are on their own in an immense land of stark beauty.

Those not lucky enough to get out into the bush can savor some of the finest views by flying over it, perhaps on the way to the Eskimo commu-nities of **Barrow**, the northernmost town in the Western Hemisphere, or **Kotzebue**, where you can learn how the natives have lived in this harsh envi-ronment for thousands of years. Though now performed mainly for rituals and demonstrations, blanket tossing once helped natives scout the flat land-scape for prey.

NOOA Satellite Tracking Station – *1 hr. 13.5mi northeast of Fairbanks off Steese Hwy. (Rte. 6), on the right. Visit by guided tour (50min) only, Jun–Aug Mon–Fri 8am–4:30pm, Sat 9am–3pm. Rest of the year by appointment only.* & 🅿 ☏ *907-451-1200.* The northernmost civilian-operated tracking station, this 8,500-acre federal reservation has ten giant dishes that track polar-orbiting satellites for the National Oceanic and Atmospheric Administration. The data is received here, then sent to the Satellite Operations Control Center in Suitland, Maryland, for interpretation. The information can be used for predicting weather, finding missing ships, analyzing depletion of fisheries, studying holes in the ozone, monitoring volcanic activity and a host of other projects. Tours explain the impressive technology, including a Dr. No-like control room of transmitters, recorders and panels; outside, an 85ft-diameter antenna tilts when a satellite passes over (about every hour).

Big Delta State Historical Park – *1 hr. 87mi southeast of Fairbanks in Delta Junction. Take Rte. 2 south 87mi; turn left (mile 275 on Richardson Hwy.). Open mid-May–mid-Sept daily 9am–5pm.* △ 🍴 & 🅿 ☏ *907-895-4201.* In the early 1900s, weary prospectors traveling from Valdez north to the goldfields found accommodations and food at some 30 roadhouses along the way. This 10-acre site preserves one such establishment. Built on the broad and silty Tanana River, **Rika's Roadhouse** operated from 1909 until the late 1940s; the imposing log structure has been restored and the parlor, kitchen and one bedroom are open for guided or self-guided touring. Elsewhere on the property are a barn, garden, livestock and poultry pens and a cafeteria-style restaurant. A sod-roof museum displays home-made birch snowshoes, an old steel bear trap, huge one-man saws, and other pieces that illustrate the demanding work of clearing and living in the Alaskan Interior.

The Southeast

Johns Hopkins Glacier, Glacier Bay National Park/Bill Ross/Tony Stone Images

A complicated puzzle of land and water stretching 540mi from Misty Fiords National Monument up to Malaspina Glacier, Alaska's panhandle, known simply as the Southeast, lies closer to the lower 48 than does the rest of Alaska. Comprising only 6 percent of the state's land area, Southeast nevertheless totes up 30 percent of its shoreline with an irregular coast and the 1,000-island Alexander Archipelago. The landscape is also distinguished by a chain of coastal mountains that crests to more than 15,000ft, making it the highest such range in the world. Glaciers slip from the heights down to deep fjords, where seals bask on ice floes and seabirds nest on granite islands. The region receives some of the heaviest rainfall in the state, which, coupled with a sea-tempered climate, has created a lush covering of spruce-hemlock rain forest. The country's largest national forest, the **Tongass**, contains about 75 percent of the Southeast's land area.

For several thousand years, Tlingit (KLINK-it) Indians carved cedar canoes, harvested a good living from the sea, and traded with Indians in the Interior. Their fancifully carved totem poles told stories that would survive generations. When the Russians arrived here in the late 18C, continuing their southward expansion from Bering Island, they found millions of fur-bearing sea mammals whose pelts went for fabulous prices in Europe and China. A single sea-otter skin could return a 100 percent profit, the equivalent of three times a working man's yearly income. Sitka reigned as the Russian capital in the New World until the near extinction of sea otters and withdrawal of the Russians in the mid-19C.

Today ferries and cruise ships thread the island-sheltered **Inside Passage** on their way to such ports of call as Juneau, a charming state capital accessible only by air or water. Farther north, in Glacier Bay National Park, whales and bears hold dominion over sea and land, while bald eagles patrol the skies. An environment that can still support these animals in impressive numbers remains a rich breeding pool for other species as well. So rich, that fishing is still the main industry in most places, supplemented by tourism and timber.

Practical Information

Getting There – Alaska Airlines (☎ *800-426-0333)* provides service to Juneau, Gustavus (gateway to Glacier Bay National Park), Sitka, Ketchikan, Skagway, Petersburg and Wrangell airports. Access to the region for vehicles and passengers is via **ferry** only *(year-round; more frequent sailings May–Sept; reservations required)* except for roads that lead to Skagway, Haines and the northeast corner of Misty Fiords National Monument. For sailings in the summer, it is recommended to book months in advance. For schedules, contact Alaska Marine Highway System, Box 25535, Juneau 99802, ☎ 465-3941 or 800-642-0066. Ferry service from Vancouver Island to Prince Rupert is available through BC Ferries, 1112 Fort St., Victoria BC Canada V8V 4V2, ☎ 250-386-3431. Year-round **bus** service between Anchorage and Skagway is provided by Alaska Direct Bus Lines, ☎ 277-6652 or 800-770-6652. Access to the region by **car** is via Klondike Hwy. 2 to Skagway and Haines Hwy. 7.

Getting Around – Ferry access between islands is provided by the Alaska Marine Highway System *(above)*, local air-taxi services and boat charters. For a list of companies, contact local tourism agencies *(below)*. Few islands have public transportation. Independent car rental facilities can be found in most towns. Many lodging establishments offer transportation service to landing strips and ferry facilities.

Visitor Information – Contact the **Southeast Alaska Visitor Center** (50 Main St., Ketchikan AK 99901, ☎ 228-6214) for information and brochures on points of interest, accommodations, sightseeing, tour companies and seasonal events. For additional information: **Juneau Convention & Visitors Bureau**, 134 Third St., Juneau AK 99801, ☎ 586-2201; **Ketchikan Visitors Bureau**, 131 Front St., Ketchikan AK 99901, ☎ 225-6166; **Sitka Convention & Visitors Bureau**, P.O. Box 1226, Sitka AK 99835, ☎ 747-5940. **Skagway Chamber of Commerce**, P.O. Box 194, Skagway AK 99840, ☎ 983-1898.

Accommodations – Area visitors' guides from local tourism agencies *(above)* list a wide variety of lodgings including hotels, motels, bed-and-breakfast inns, cabins, fishing lodges and camps as well as campgrounds. **B&B Reservation Service**: Alaska B&B Association, 369 S. Franklin St., Suite 200, Juneau AK 99801 ☎ 586-2959. Because of the short tourist season *(mid-May–Sept)* and sparsely populated islands offering small lodging facilities, visitors should make reservations well in advance. **Youth Hostels**: Juneau (☎ *586-9559)*; Ketchikan (☎ *225-3319)*; Sitka (☎ *747-8611)*. The Forest Service maintains cabins *($25/night)* at remote lakes, rivers or on beaches; most are accessible by boat or floatplane only. For reservations, contact Reserve America ☎ 877-444-6777 or www.reserveusa.com.

Sightseeing – Visitors can enjoy spectacular scenery and abundant wildlife. Most sightseeing is done by the state-run ferry, custom boat charters, and flightseeing tours. Day-long trips include wildlife viewing, fishing and visits to native villages. Numerous cruise lines offer a variety of **cruises** that travel the Inside Passage: Holland America Line, Princess Cruises, Alaska Sightseeing/Cruise West (☎ *800-426-7702)*, Alaska/Glacier Bay Tours & Cruises (☎ *586-8687 or 800-451-5952)*. For a list of tour operators and outfitters, check with local tourism agencies *(above)*.

Recreation – Kayaking, hiking, bird-watching, backpacking, fishing and camping are some of the activities the summer season offers. Local outfitters provide equipment and offer guided activities throughout the region. Explore Misty Fiords National Monument on your own—access is via floatplane or boat; rustic cabins are available; contact Southeast Alaska Visitor Center *(above)*. Paddle with a naturalist in a **sea kayak** *(Aug; 12-day all-inclusive; $1,495);* Wilderness Inquiry, 1313 Fifth St., Minneapolis MN 55414, ☎ 612-379-3858 or 800-728-0719, www.wildernessinquiry.org; Journeys International, 4011 Jackson Rd., Ann Arbor MI 48103. Three-day *($695)* or 6-day *($1,625)* sea kayaking trips *(Jun–Sept)* focus on marine mammals and leave from Juneau. Another exciting adventure is a **bear watch** trip by floatplane from Juneau to Admiralty Island *(Jun–Aug; 9 hrs; $450)*. For reservations: Alaska Discovery, 5449 Shaune Dr., Suite 4, Juneau AK 99801, ☎ 780-6226 or 800-586-1911; www.akdiscovery.com. Kayak for 3 hrs *($50/person)* or up to 6 days *($950/person)* in Tongass National Forest and Misty Fiords National Monument *(May–Sept 15; all-inclusive guided trip)* with Southeast Exposure Sea Kayak Co., P.O. Box 9243, Ketchikan AK 99901, ☎ 225-8829 or www.southeastexposure.com. **Winter sports** include cross-country and glacier skiing, ice-fishing and sled-dog excursions.

GLACIER BAY NATIONAL PARK AND PRESERVE★★★

Michelin map 930 Alaska inset and map p 368
Tourist Information ☎ 907-697-2230

Encompassing nearly 3.3 million acres, Glacier Bay National Park and Preserve on the northern end of Southeast Alaska showcases the best that Alaska's wild lands have to offer—stunning views of ice-clad mountains, an incomparably rich constellation of marine and land animals, and seemingly limitless miles of unmarred wilderness to wrap yourself in. No roads traverse this watery sanctuary, and way up bay you have the distinct feeling that you are a privileged, if temporary, visitor to a natural kingdom by the sea, ruled only by whales and bears and the dramatic forces of nature. UNESCO recognized the unique value of this glacial landscape by dubbing it an International Biosphere Reserve in 1986 and a World Heritage Site in 1992.

Historical Notes

During the Little Ice Age, a cold period about 3,500 years ago, enough snow accumulated in the nearby mountains to push a 20mi-wide sheet of ice out in Icy Strait. But there, on meeting the ocean and its strong currents, the ice halted. By the late 18C it began retreating. When explorer George Vancouver sailed by here in 1794 he saw only an iced-in shoreline, with barely an indentation to suggest a retreating glacier. Glacier Bay had yet to form. Today the bay's frigid arms and fingers stretch back 65mi to where numerous tidewater glaciers still work to reshape the land, scooping out fjords and molding mountain valleys and peaks. Two glaciers on the bay's west side are advancing, but in the rest of the park they are in retreat, leaving behind a raw landscape of braided streams and gravel bars.

Though Tlingits occupied the area for perhaps 9,000 years, glacial action has obliterated almost all traces of their early lives. The first person to seriously study the area and bring it to the attention of the outside world, poet-naturalist **John Muir** (1838-1914) traveled to Glacier Bay in 1879 and inspired potential visitors with his bold descriptions: "Sunshine streamed through the luminous fringes of the clouds and fell on the green waters of the fjord, the glittering bergs, the crystal bluffs of the two vast glaciers, the intensely white, far-spreading fields of ice, and the ineffable chaste and spiritual heights of the Fairweather Range, which were now hidden, now partly revealed, the whole making a picture of icy wildness unspeakably pure and sublime." A San Francisco newspaper carried his stories, in which he urged his readers to go and see for themselves. Following his advice, Capt. James Carroll brought the first group of sightseers to Alaska aboard a steamer in 1883. An earthquake 16 years later caused Muir Glacier to calve so intensely that boats could not approach it for several years. Tours of Glacier Bay started up again in the 1950s but remained relatively light until the early 1970s, when cruises of the Inside Passage added the bay to their itineraries. With Muir Inlet growing long and narrow as its glacier rapidly retreated, the West Arm became the avenue for cruise ships and tour boats, leaving Muir Inlet to the quieter pursuits of kayakers.

As in much of Alaska, a tract of federally owned land the size of Glacier Bay National Park almost invariably invites dispute over proper use. Two bills recently submitted to Congress would allow commercial fishing to continue in the bay and along the park's outer coastline and would open parts of the park to subsistence hunting, fishing, mining and trapping. Conservationists consider such usage encroachment upon a protected marine ecosystem. The two sides continue to grapple with the question of how much can be sacrificed to meet the needs of a growing population and still maintain the integrity of the wilderness.

VISIT *2 days*

Most of the park is inaccessible to all but the most adventurous visitors, yet a daylong bay cruise can rank as a highlight of an Alaskan vacation. The small town of **Gustavus**, 10mi from the Glacier Bay boat dock, is the arrival and departure point for ferries and airplanes. Several inns and B&Bs are located in Gustavus; the Glacier Bay Lodge sits by the boat dock. *Most inns and B&Bs provide transportation to and from the ferry terminal, airport and boat dock.*

Only three short **hiking trails** cut through the park, including a 1mi nature loop that you can take with a ranger on a guided walk. Many visitors like to stroll the beach or walk the back roads of Gustavus and admire the trim houses and verdant summer gardens. Serious backcountry expeditions take some extra planning. While travel over glaciers requires special skills and equipment that few possess, **kayaking** excursions are more common. Outfitters in Gustavus offer rentals and guided half-day and full-day outings. The *Spirit of Adventure (p 369)* and other vessels will drop off and pick up kayakers who wish to camp in the wilderness. *All campers are issued bear-proof food containers and guidelines on clean, safe camping.*

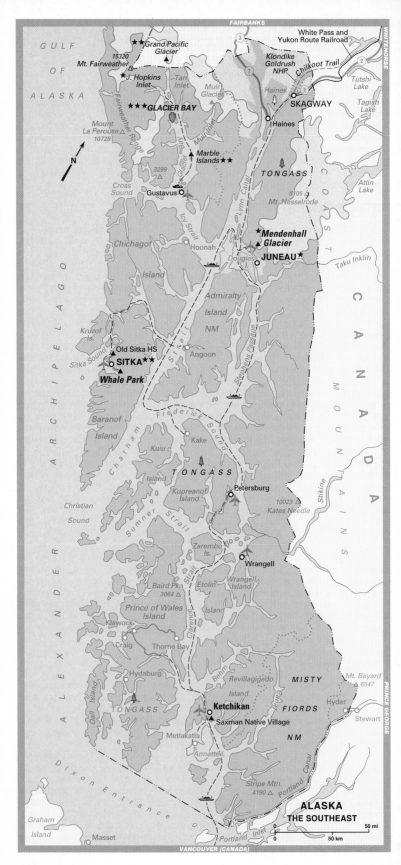

Alan Hicks/Tony Stone Images

Tourists near Margerie Glacier

★★ **Bay Tour** – *Departs from Barlett Cove May–mid-Sept daily 8am; bring rain gear and warm clothes; make reservations a month in advance; $156.50; children 12 & under $78.25;* ✗ ♿ 🅿 *Glacier Bay Tours & Cruises* ☎ *907-586-8687 or 800-451-5952.* For an unforgettable visit to the park take the nine-hour bay tour on the three-decker *Spirit of Adventure*. Smaller than the Inside Passage cruise ships, *Spirit* can maneuver close to islands and into small inlets, yet it is fully equipped with cushioned seats, tables, a galley, wildlife books, charts, binoculars, big viewing windows and outdoor decks. A park naturalist provides knowledgeable interpretation on wildlife and geology. Leaving from the boat dock on **Bartlett Cove**, tours head up into the lower bay where sea otters play and **humpbacks** breach, their tails fanning up as they dive. Those lucky enough may see a pod of **orcas** rolling in unison like black and white waves. The lower bay acts as a crossroads for maritime wildlife, making whale spotting more likely here.

Along the shores of islands and the mainland, look for **black bears** and **brown bears**; they often fish in the deltas of glacial streams. The tour pauses at **South Marble Island**★★ for photographs and long stares at the teeming birdlife and a noisy colony of sea lions. Thousands of kittiwakes, puffins, cormorants, murres and other birds fly and screech in their busy breeding and nesting activities. Looking around the bay and to the far shores, you may well be struck by what you *don't* see—there are no signs of civilization, nothing but the sounds of sea life and the waves lapping the boat.

The journey up bay is a journey into the past. Bartlett Cove sits just below a moraine, the only hill in Gustavus, with the surrounding woods covered in spruce. As you travel the 60mi up bay to the glaciers, vegetation thins to alders, mosses, and eventually great scarred areas left by recently retreated glaciers. **Johns Hopkins Inlet**★ boasts ten glaciers, while at the head of nearby Tarr Inlet, spectacular **Grand Pacific Glacier**★★ rears up 200ft and spreads 2mi from side to side. Because of the danger of falling ice, boats are not allowed closer than .25mi to the glacier—plenty close to hear the creak and groan of the ice and to witness magnificent splashes as building-size chunks calve into the water. This close the glacier looks veined and scored like the side of a huge slab of blue marble topped by a crystal city. The tour boat that appeared large back at Bartlett Cove here seems dwarfed by the glaciers' size. On clear days you can see the Fairweather Range, which supplies all the glaciers on the west side of the bay with ice. The crown prince, **Mt. Fairweather** rises to 15,320ft.

We welcome corrections and suggestions that may assist us in preparing the next edition. Please send us your comments:
Michelin Travel Publications
Editorial Department
P. O. Box 19001
Greenville, SC 29602-9001

■ Rivers of Ice

Curving down the sides of mountains like great white beasts, scaled with fissures and seracs (ice spires), glaciers evoke an image of a frozen, uninhabitable, far-north world. So why are all the glaciers in southern Alaska? In fact, cold alone does not a glacier make, and extreme cold can render glaciation nearly impossible. For a glacier to form, a delicate balance must exist between precipitation and temperature. There has to be enough snowfall and just enough year-round low temperature that the snow accumulates and compresses into ice quicker than it melts away. Furthermore, these snowfields have to form in high enough terrain that gravity will force them to flow downward—in other words, to glaciate. All these unique circumstances come together in Southeast Alaska and along the South Central coast, where warm, wet air rises from the water and falls as snow in the mountains.

The tremendous weight of a glacier creates friction on its base and, like a slow-motion skier, it begins to edge downslope on a thin film of water. As it moves, the glacier sculpts the land, scraping out valleys that may later fill in, during a melting stage, as fjords. The rocks and debris it carries and shoves aside, in addition to giving it a dirty-snow look, help do the scraping and end up forming moraines (piles of debris). When glaciers meet with very resistant rock formations, they simply flow around, leaving nunataks—visible as islands in the fjords, peaks in the snowfields.

Because of a warming trend over the last two centuries, most of Alaska's glaciers are now retreating, at about 20-30ft per year. But a slight shift in meteorological patterns could reverse that, and they could start advancing again. Imagine Glacier Bay totally iced-in, as it was when Captain Vancouver sailed by. On the other hand, if the present trend continues, picture the present glaciers as inlets teeming with sea life.

Among the popular drive-up glaciers, **Exit Glacier** *(p 390)* is the one you can get the closest to (on a short trail). **Portage Glacier** *(p 388)* and **Mendenhall Glacier** *(p 373)* have created such large outwash lakes that you must view them from a distance (from a boat in the case of Portage). Guided boat excursions in **Kenai Fjords National Park** *(p 389)* and **Glacier Bay National Park** *(p 367)* typically take in many glaciers, some of which calve into the water with booming splashes.

JUNEAU★

Michelin map 930 Alaska inset and map opposite
Population 30,191
Tourist Information ☎ 907-586-1737 or www.juneau.com

Tucked along the narrow strip of land between Gastineau Channel and the base of Mt. Roberts and Mt. Juneau, the state capital is accessible only by air or sea. Of Alaska's three largest cities, Juneau is the smallest and the most visually appealing, having the look and feel of a quaint European city with narrow streets that curve up from the waterfront to well-kept houses closely ranked on a steep hillside.

A tent city sprang into existence here when Joe Juneau and Richard Harris made a strike on Gold Creek in the Silverbow Basin in 1880. The two prospectors staked their claims and laid out a 160-acre townsite along the beach. What had been a seasonal fishing camp quickly grew into a center for a large hard-rock mining industry. The land in and around Mt. Roberts became honeycombed with so many mining tunnels that there are still more miles of tunnel than of road in Juneau. The Alaska Juneau Company, operating from 1897 to 1944, extracted more than $75 million worth of low-grade ore, and removed some 88 million tons of rock from Mt. Roberts—most of Juneau is built upon this rock fill. By World War II, lack of labor and supplies led to the end of the gold mining era. But Juneau had already become established as the seat of territorial government with the movement of the capital from Sitka in 1906. Built in 1912, the **Governor's Mansion** *(716 Calhoun St.; closed to the public)* is a white Neoclassical pile with a columned portico, the front lawn graced by a 1940 totem pole.

A move to relocate the capital closer to Anchorage was voted down in 1982. The presence of Alaska's power brokers thus continues to lend Juneau a solid place on the map, and its appealing setting on the Inside Passage keeps drawing boatloads of visitors. While state, federal and local government are the region's largest employers, in private industry tourism holds the lead. Some 600,000 cruise passengers a year generate about $65 million of commerce for Juneau. Though some locals decry the impact of so many visitors on their small community, most agree that the economic gain is worth the trouble. Some summer days several giant cruise ships carrying more than 1,000 passengers each disgorge a stream of visitors, who spend an average of $117 per person, primarily in the upscale gift shops on **Franklin Street** *(p 371)*.

SIGHTS *1 1/2 days*

Best covered on foot, the compact town of Juneau starts out level along the water-front, then rises to the north (as the street numbers ascend). The business and shopping district occupies the lower land, while Victorian-era homes hold the heights. Many residents now, however, live several miles north in Mendenhall Valley, near the airport. Juneau's boundaries encompass 3,100sq mi, making it one of the largest cities in the United States; its 60mi of roads stretch to Thane *(6mi southeast of town)*, out to Echo Cove *(40mi northwest)*, and across the Channel to Douglas Island. The area's Russian heritage is represented by the octagonal **St. Nicholas Russian Orthodox Church** *(326 5th St., call visitor center for tour times)*, built in 1894 and one of the oldest unaltered churches in Alaska. The **Forest Service Information Center** *(Centennial Hall Convention Center, Egan Dr. and Willoughby Ave.; open year-round Mon–Fri 8am–5pm; closed major holidays;* ♿ 🅿 ☎ *907-586-8751)* holds maps and infor-mation about Tongass National Forest and Glacier Bay National Park, and it has small displays on the Tlingit, the fur trade, fishing, logging and tourism.

★ **Mount Roberts Tramway** – *490 S. Franklin St. Operates May–Sept Mon–Sat 9am–9pm, Sun 9am–10pm. $19.75.* 🍴 ♿ 🅿 ☎ *907-463-3412 or 888-478-8726.* Located across from the cruise ship terminal, the 60-passenger tram rises 1,880 vertical feet, and provides the best views of Juneau for the least effort. On the way up, you can behold the harbor and its boats, and you can see how the town is clustered into a nook in the mountains with homes stacked as far up the hillside as possible. The complex at the top holds a restaurant and gift shop, outside of which an artisan is often at work carving a totem pole. A theater presents live performances and a 15min film on Tlingit culture. Out back a network of trails lead to more awesome views—the .5mi loop makes a good leg stretcher; the 4.2mi trek to 3,666ft Gastineau Peak and back is a serious workout. If the views are socked in, you can study the wonders of the surrounding rain forest, made lush by steady year-round moisture.

South Franklin and Front Streets – The historic heart of the commercial district, the four blocks of Franklin Street south of Fourth Street are lined by a parade of colorful two-story frame buildings from the turn of the century. Tourists just off cruise ships flock along here all summer, lured by high-priced galleries and gift shops that sell beads, native-carved ivory, fossilized whale bone sculpture, furs and baskets that fetch prices from $100 to $5,000. Though restaurants are few since cruises provide most meals, Franklin Street does have several saloons. The **Germania** *(162 S. Franklin)*, dating from 1895, was popular during the rowdy gold mining era, when some 30 bars operated here. Just up the street, the 1891 **Louvre Saloon** *(241 Front St., now called the Imperial)*, the town's oldest bar, boasts a pressed tin ceiling. A more refined atmosphere prevails at the 1913 **Alaskan Hotel and Bar** *(167 S. Franklin)*, with its dark paneling and Tiffany stained glass. The most well-known watering hole, the **Red Dog Saloon** *(278 S. Franklin)* is not as old as the others, but its authentic, clut-tered decor gives it an edge in the tourist trade. Other landmarks include the 1891 **Goldstein's Store** *(251 S. Franklin, now Filipino Hall)*; **Jorgenson's Hardware** *(225 Front St.)*, dating to 1897; and the 1901 **Alaska Steam Laundry** *(174 S. Franklin, now Emporium Mall)*, with its shingled turret and ornate parapet.

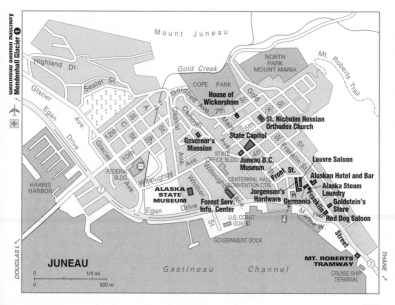

Red Dog Saloon

★★Alaska State Museum – *395 Whittier St. Open mid-May–mid-Sept daily 9am–6pm. Rest of the year Tue–Sat 10am–4pm. Closed major holidays.$4.* ᦞ 🅿 ☎ *907-465-2901. www.educ.state.ak.us/lam/museum.* The state's finest museum of history and culture harbors more than 23,000 artifacts and works of art in a 1967 concrete building. The core of the collection began as a territorial museum in 1900.

Visit – *1 hr.* The first floor opens with an orientation area that uses maps to illustrate Alaska's size, population centers, ecosystems, climatic zones and native language groups. Beyond lies the **Alaska Native Gallery★**, laid out in a way that makes sense of the often confusing array of native cultures. Sections of this display area are devoted to each of the four major groups—Northwest Coast (Tlingit and Haida), Athabaskan, Aleut, and Eskimo. Among the highlights are a Northwest Coast clan house, an 1870s totem of Abraham Lincoln, a case full of vivid Yupik Eskimo ceremonial spirit masks, a kayaker mannequin wearing a gutskin parka and sealskin pants, and a beautiful 38ft Inupiat Eskimo umiak (an open wooden boat). Occupying the ramp, the Natural History Gallery features a dramatic life-size diorama of an **eagle's nest** in a tree—as you ascend the circular ramp you see the nest and eagles from various points of view. An impressive mural around the ramp depicts a typically Alaskan panorama of mountains, sky, water and whales. The **State History Gallery**, on the second floor, covers the Russian-American period, the Alaskan Purchase, mining and early industry, maritime history and tourism. Exhibits include 19C Russian troika bells and mangles (laundry presses); brass samovars and icons; the cape of William Henry Seward, who negotiated the purchase of Alaska; and pull-out-drawer exhibits on such famous Alaskan characters as con man Soapy Smith and hostess Frances Muncaster. A hands-on children's area and temporary exhibits complete this excellent museum's offerings.

Juneau Douglas City Museum – *4th and Main Sts. Open May–Sept Mon–Fri 9am–5pm, weekends 10am–5pm. Rest of the year Fri–Sat noon–4pm. Closed major holidays. $3.* ᦞ ☎ *907-586-3572. www.juneau.lib.ak.us.parksrec/museum.* Worth a brief stop, this small repository of local history concentrates on Juneau's birth as a gold mining town. Other exhibits include a re-created pioneer kitchen and a re-created general merchandise store (1890-1930). Two of the most striking pieces here are the tall stained-glass windows created by contemporary local artists Rie Munoz and Bruce Elliot. Outside stands another fine piece of artwork: The *Four Story Totem Pole*, made by Haida master carver John Wallace in 1940, tells four different stories with such figures as Raven, Monster Frog and Bear Chief.

State Capitol – *4th and Main Sts. Open May–Aug Mon–Fri & Sun 8:30am–5pm. Rest of the year Mon–Fri 8:30am–5pm. Closed major holidays.* ᦞ ☎ *907-465-2479 (summer only) or 907-465-3800. www.legis.state.ak.us.* If this five-story brick– and limestone-faced edifice doesn't look like a capitol, that's because it wasn't intended as one. Built in 1931 as the Territorial and Federal Building, it became the capitol when Alaska attained statehood in 1959. While the main building material is reinforced concrete faced with brick, the lower facade and the four-columned portico boast handsome limestone and marble quarried on Prince of Wales Island in Southeast Alaska. Guided and self-guided tours cover senate and house chambers and various committee rooms.

House of Wickersham – *213 7th St. Call for hours:* ☎ *907-586-9001.* Situated at the top of a hill accessed by stairways or narrow roads, this rambling frame house and its wide sunporch command a fine view of the town and Gastineau Channel. The house was built by the superintendent of a local mining company in 1898, but is best known for being the final residence of pioneer statesman and explorer **James Wickersham** (1857-1939), one of the founding fathers of modern Alaska. Wickersham lived here the last 11 years of his life. One-hour tours of the recently restored home detail his accomplishments and, in the spirit of tours given by his niece in the early 1960s, include a cup of tea from the family's bone china and a hands-on examination of native artifacts that Wickersham collected in his travels throughout the territory.

★**Gastineau Salmon Hatchery** – *2697 Channel Dr. Open mid-May–mid-Sept Mon–Fri 10am–6pm, weekends 10am–5pm. Rest of the year open by appointment only. $3.* ♿ 🅿 ☎ *907-463-4810. www.alaska.net/~dipac.* To enhance the area's commercial and recreational fisheries, Douglas Island Pank and Chum, Inc. (DIPAC) built a facility that doubles as a visitor attraction and provides a fun way to learn about the life cycle of Alaska's most famous food. An underwater viewing window gives you an intimate look at salmon battling their way up a 450ft-long fish ladder—it takes from 2 hours to a week for a salmon to make the 24ft vertical ascent into the hatchery. Inside, the four species—king, pink, coho and sockeye—are zapped with electricity. The eggs and sperm are then collected, sloshed together in buckets, and stored in incubating tanks. This controlled care garners a 95 percent survival rate among developing salmon, as opposed to 5 percent in the wild. Up to 130 million fry are released annually for their 2,000mi journeys in the sea; about 2 percent of these will return to the hatchery as adults. An informative 10-minute commentary outlines the process, while inside are exhibits on the fishing industry and aquariums stocked with a variety of sea life from giant starfish to king crabs. You can rent a pole at the dock outside and have a go at the fish that teem the waters in late summer; the long migration reduces their tastiness, but locals smoke them or use them for bait, fertilizer or cat food.

EXCURSION *Map p 371*

★**Mendenhall Glacier** – *1 hr. 13mi northwest of Juneau via Egan Dr. and Mendenhall Loop Rd. Open May–Sept daily 8am–6pm. Rest of the year Wed–Sun 9am–4pm. Closed Jan 1, Thanksgiving Day, Dec 25. $3.* ♿ 🅿 ☎ *907-789-0097.* An easily accessible natural wonder, 1.5mi-wide Mendenhall Glacier stretches 12mi from the Juneau Icefield down to Mendenhall Lake, where it calves into the water. The glacier actually flows forward 2ft per day, but because of a warmer climate it has been in a retreat phase for the past 250 years—with the melt rate exceeding the flow rate, the glacier recedes about 50-70ft per year. A .3mi trail leads to the water's edge, while other trails explore forest succession and different views on the glacier. The 3mi East Glacier Loop gets hikers close to the glacier's edge. The newly renovated visitor center offers exhibits, an expanded theater, a three-dimensional model of the glacier and interactive video displays.

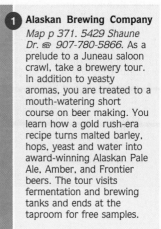

1 **Alaskan Brewing Company**
Map p 371. 5429 Shaune Dr. ☎ *907-780-5866.* As a prelude to a Juneau saloon crawl, take a brewery tour. In addition to yeasty aromas, you are treated to a mouth-watering short course on beer making. You learn how a gold rush-era recipe turns malted barley, hops, yeast and water into award-winning Alaskan Pale Ale, Amber, and Frontier beers. The tour visits fermentation and brewing tanks and ends at the taproom for free samples.

SITKA★★

Michelin map 930 Alaska inset and map p 368
Population 8,510
Tourist Information ☎ 907-747-5940

With mountains behind and a smattering of little islands out front, one of Alaska's loveliest and most historically important towns occupies a protected point on the west side of Baranof Island, facing Sitka Sound. Early Tlingits arrived here nearly 8,000 years ago and called the place Shee Atika, meaning "settlement on the seaward side of Shee island." Not until 1799 did a white set foot on the island. In that year, Russians under the management of Alexander Baranof established a fortress, gave it the bellicose name of Redoubt St. Archangel Michael, and proceeded to solicit native help for their fur-trade business. Although the outpost was intended to discourage English and American intervention in the area, ironically it was Indian suspicions that finally erupted in violence in 1802 when Tlingits attacked the redoubt and killed all the Aleut slaves and all but one of the Russian soldiers. The **Old Sitka Historical Site** *(7mi north on Halibut Point Rd.)* marks the event with an information panel in a quiet waterside park.

Not so easily dislodged, the Russians returned two years later, bombarded a new Indian fort (p 375) to the south and this time outfought the Tlingits. The victors moved in, renamed the settlement New Archangel, and began displacing Indian clan houses with fort-like dwellings. For a while the fur trade thrived, but with the depletion of sea otters by the mid-19C, Russian interests waned. The transfer of Alaska to the United States in 1867 took place in Sitka, and what had been the capital of Russian Alaska became the new territorial capital. After Juneau claimed that office in 1906, Sitka headed off into a becalmed period as a peaceful fishing village. Then, during World War II, more than 20,000 military personnel arrived to construct coastal fortifications and an air station. Now with a population of about 9,000, Sitka holds all the charms of an old seaside village. Its natural beauty and cultural attractions make it an obvious summer tourist destination, but, situated on the outside of the Inside Passage, it is often not on the itineraries of the larger ships. A music festival in June, performances by native dancers, a walkable town center and an easygoing attitude add to Sitka's multifaceted appeal.

View of Sitka from Japonski Island

SIGHTS *1 day*

Totem Square – *Lincoln and Katlian Sts.* A small but attractive harborside park makes a good place to begin a walking tour of Sitka. The imposing yellow stucco building facing the park is the 1934 **Pioneers' Home**, an improvement on Alaska's original retirement home, founded to provide for prospectors who had not struck it rich. A realistic bronze, *The Prospector* stands on the landscaped lawn, heading with loaded pack into the west. To the right downtown shops unfold along a three-block stretch of Lincoln Street, while up to the left stands a reconstructed **Russian blockhouse** on a little knoll. From up here you can, like the Russian soldiers, obtain good views of the town, the mountains and the island-sprinkled harbor.

St. Michael's Cathedral – *Lincoln and American Sts. Visit by guided tour (20min) only, mid-May–Sept Mon–Fri 9am–5pm, Sat 11:30am–3:30pm, Sun 2pm–4pm. Rest of the year no tours on weekends. $2.* & ☎ *907-747-8120.* Originally built by Russians in the 1840s, the highly visible town icon lasted about 120 years until a fire on January 2, 1966, brought it down. With temperatures below zero, there was little water to fight the fire, so townspeople formed a human chain to save the treasured religious objects treasured. They then raised enough funds to build an exact duplicate of the cathedral, this one with fireproof materials. Atop the domed sanctuary and the bell tower, the three bars of the crosses represent from top to bottom: the inscription bar on which was written "Jesus of Nazareth, King of the Jews"; the bar where Christ's hands were nailed; and a foot rest, slanted up to indicate the thief on the right side of Jesus (the one who repented). Inside the spacious sanctuary, walls are lined with paintings and cases holding icons and vestments dating back to the 17C. Services are held in English and Slavonic, with worshippers standing—hence the lack of chairs. The vast majority of the congregation is Tlingit, their ties to the Russian religion extending back more than 160 years.

Isabel Miller Museum – *Centennial Bldg., 330 Harbor Dr. Open mid-May–Sept daily 8am–5pm. Rest of the year Tue–Sat 10am–4pm. Closed major holidays.* ☞ ▣ ☎ *907-747-6455. www.sitka.org.* An informative if homespun collection of community ephemera features Tlingit spruce-root baskets, interesting then-and-now photos of a Tlingit summer fish camp (1900 to the present), and an exhibit on Russian culture. Other displays include a scale diorama of Sitka in 1867 at the time of the transfer of Alaska to the United States, and a maritime industries corner.

★**Sitka National Historical Park** – *Open mid-May–Sept daily 8am–5pm. Rest of the year Mon–Fri 8am–5pm. Closed major holidays.* ▣ ☎ *907-747-6281. www.nps.gov.* Commemorating the 1804 Battle of Sitka and the cultural clash created by Europeans in the New World, this 107-acre park consists of two units. The wooded fort site at the mouth of the Indian River focuses on the Tlingit history; the Bishop's House at the edge of town concentrates on the Russian-American period. A visitor center is located on the grounds of the fort site.

★★**Russian Bishop's House** – *Monastery and Lincoln Sts. Open mid-May–Sept daily 9am–1pm & 2pm–5pm. Rest of the year by appointment only. @Légende:f7$.* Bishop Innocent (Ivan Veniaminov) in 1843 declared this long, yellow ocher building a "mansion . . . one of the best, most solid and most beautiful structures in New Archangel." Built to last by Finnish shipwrights, the Bishop's House was first occupied by Innocent, then a long succession of bishops until it closed in 1969. An orphanage and a school for natives have also operated here. Impeccably restored to its former glory, the house retains more than 70 percent of its original structure. A tour gives you a feeling for the serious intentions of Russians to serve their God and Czar, even though, as they often lamented, "God is in His heaven, and the Czar is far away." The few exhibits on the first floor are well selected and displayed, with just enough text to keep you interested but not overwhelmed. Artifacts include kitchen implements, weapons, and one of several iron plates that were buried on Alaskan soil with the optimistic inscription, "This land belongs to Russia." One entire room is devoted to architecture—cutaways of ceiling, walls and wide-plank floors show off the building's masterful construction. Russian newspapers and wood chips were used for insulation. The guided tour of the upstairs moves through the bishop's private prayer nook, bedroom, dining room, servants' quarters, pantry and chapel. Most of the furnishings are original.

Fort Site – *Fort Site is 1mi east of Sitka on Lincoln St.* The park visitor center holds exhibits on Tlingits and the 1804 battle; in the building's cultural center Indian woodcarvers and silversmiths work and tell stories. Out back, you can take a 1mi loop through a spruce forest to the site of the Tlingit fort the Russians attacked. Along the way are several beautifully carved cedar totem poles, many of them copies of turn-of-the-century originals, which were beginning to deteriorate. Now merely a clearing in the trees, the fort site was the scene of a week-long battle in October 1804. A bombardment from the sea failing to damage the wooden fort, the Russians made an assault and were beaten back. For six days, they laid siege to the Indian garrison. On the seventh day they entered the fort, and heard only the cackling of ravens. The Indians had gone. You can still hear the maniacal calls of these birds as you walk the path. In the summer, step onto the Indian River Bridge and take a look at the swarm of salmon, finishing out their lives after long runs from the sea.

★**Sheldon Jackson Museum** – *104 College Dr. Open mid-May–mid-Sept daily 9am–5pm. Rest of the year Tue–Sat 10am–4pm. Closed major holidays. $3.* ☞ ▣ ☎ *907-747-8981. www.educ.state.ak.us/lam/museum.* The oldest museum and the best trove of native artifacts in the state is located on the campus of Sheldon Jackson College, where **James Michener** lived from 1984-86 while researching and writing his epic *Alaska*. Built in 1895 to house the 5,000-piece collection of Rev. Dr. Sheldon Jackson, the octagonal structure was the first concrete building in Alaska. Now, modern lighting, carpeting, and climate control add to the professionalism of this treasure-packed facility. The four major native groups are all represented, with the largest share devoted to Eskimos—exquisite ceremonial masks and ivory and bone tools are examples. From the Northwest Coast Indians come painted drums, black argillite carvings and a late 1800s mortuary pole with hollow cavities for cremated remains. An Aleut baidarka (skin-covered boat) and Athabaskan birch-bark baskets, along with many other art objects, tools and clothes, show the natives' remarkable adaptation to a demanding environment.

Whale Park – *6mi east on Sawmill Creek Rd. Open year-round daily 6am–10pm.* ♿ ▣ ☎ *907-747-1852.* Nearly 900ft of boardwalk and 5 gazebos outfitted with viewing scopes and information panels make this waterfront park a fine place to spot Silver Bay's multitude of marine life, including humpback whales (late fall to early spring), Steller's sea lions, sea otters, harbor seals and dolphins.

■ Ports of Call

Southeast Alaska, with its archipelago of large and small islands, was not made for automobiles—planes and boats are the rule here. Since visiting several towns in the region could become quite "spendy," as the locals say, a knowledge of what each has to offer can help narrow your selection. Planes connect the major towns, as does the Alaska Marine Highway (☎ *907-465-3941* or ☎ *800-642-0066)*, a ferry system. If you plan to take a ferry, book reservations in advance and bear in mind that distances can be great and travel times long; the 152mi trip from Juneau to Sitka, for example, takes over eight hours (overnight cabins are available). Cruise lines touring the famed **Inside Passage**, a 1,000mi waterway from Vancouver to Skagway, call at many ports, though itineraries vary from ship to ship. In addition to Glacier Bay, Juneau and Sitka, the following towns are well worth a visit.

The southernmost town in Alaska, and one of the wettest, **Ketchikan** bills itself the salmon capital of the world. Gateway to the granite-spired **Misty Fiords National Monument**, Ketchikan also offers several cultural attractions. Chief among them, the **Saxman Native Village** has a population of about 350 Tlingit Indians. Tours cover the tribal house, schoolhouse, carver's shed and a park punctuated with 28 totems. The **Totem Heritage Center** displays poles dating back nearly 200 years.

Situated on the north end of Wrangell Island, the community of **Wrangell** is the only Alaskan town to have flown the flags of Russia, Britain and the US. The beach contains boulders etched with petroglyphs by artists from an indeterminate period.

Founded by a Norwegian in 1897, **Petersburg** is inaccessible to all but the smallest of cruisers. This fishing village keeps its Scandinavian heritage alive with an annual festival and the hand-painted flowers that adorn many homes.

Haines, near the top of the Inside Passage, commands wonderful views of the Coastal Mountains and Portage Cove. Called Fort Seward, the south part of town was the site of an army post in the early 1900s but has since been converted into a residential and business area. Bald eagles by the thousands flock every winter to a reserve north of town, just off a road that connects Haines with Canada.

Northern terminus of the Inside Passage, historic **Skagway** was the rollicking, dangerous town through which tens of thousands of gold seekers passed on their arduous way up the Chilkoot Trail to the goldfields of the Yukon in 1898. The **Klondike Goldrush National Historical Park** preserves the famous trail and much of downtown, with its false-fronted buildings and wooden sidewalks. Brothels and gambling dens have been converted to gift shops and eateries. The **White Pass & Yukon Route** narrow-gauge railway takes passengers through the same breathtaking mountain scenery witnessed by the prospectors.

South Central Alaska

Kenai Fjords National Park/© David Muench/Tony Stone Images

South of the Alaska Range, the land gentles into fertile valleys and rolling forests, but instead of quietly falling away to the sea it suddenly buckles up again into another sky-scratching cordillera of glacier-clad mountains, like a fortress wall along the Gulf of Alaska. Land, sea and sky meet in grand proportions in South Central Alaska, a diverse region where goats clamber on precipitous cliffs in sight of spouting whales, and fishing villages reap the bounty of tens of millions of spawning salmon before the snows of winter close in. Transportation is the buzzword for understanding regional history. The ice-free ports of Valdez, Cordova, Seward, Homer and Kenai were staging points for early exploitation of copper, coal and gold. Then came the railroad in the 1910s, linking Seward with Anchorage and the Interior. A highway was built all the way down to Homer in the 1950s, but the coastline's daunting terrain means most of the region is still off limits to cars. As in most of Alaska, planes and boats ferry passengers from one destination to another.

The bulk of the state's population lives in Anchorage and the Matanuska farming belt just north. A cosmopolitan city with a rough-and-ready past, Anchorage is Alaska's only metropolitan area. Travelers here will find several worthwhile attractions to detain them before heading south to the Kenai Peninsula. A place where knife-ridged mountains appear to rise right from the sea, the Kenai holds a summer's worth of pleasures, from fresh seafood at dockside tables to wildlife cruises into Resurrection Bay. Weather here can vary from brilliant sun to chilly drizzle. Light rains saturate the coastline in summer; higher up the precipitation tends to fall as snow for most of the year, resulting in the icefields that push glaciers down to tidewater.

The region and its wildlife continue to recover from the massive *Exxon Valdez* oil spill of 1989, which dumped 258,000 barrels of oil and affected more than 1,500mi of shoreline from Prince William Sound to Kodiak Island. The spill, the worst in the US, initiated a $2.1 billion clean-up effort involving 10,000 workers.

ANCHORAGE★

Michelin map 930 Alaska inset and map p 382
Population 254,982
Tourist Information ☎ 907-276-4118 or www.anchorage.net

Sprawled over the one piece of flat ground between the arms of Cook Inlet and the sharp peaks of the Chugach Mountains, Alaska's largest city holds nearly half the state's population. The city's boundaries stretch from Eklutna on the north to Girdwood on the south—nearly 2,000sq mi, or about the size of Delaware. But 90 percent of this sizeable parcel of land is uninhabited, and beyond its borders is even more wilderness, making Anchorage a lantern shining in a tremendous forest, which sits farther north than St. Petersburg, Russia. Yet its proximity to the sea gives the city a more moderate climate than most of Alaska, and as the state's center of commerce and culture, Anchorage does a good job of welcoming business travelers and those heading out into the wilds.

Anchorage (c.1925)

Oregon Historical Society, ORHI70205

Historical Notes

Alaska City – Few settlers were living in the Anchorage area in 1914 when a tent city of several hundred pioneers mushroomed to life beneath the bluff on the north side of Ship Creek in anticipation of the federal railroad that would connect Seward with Fairbanks. By 1917, the railroad's middle and southern sections were joined at the Ship Creek construction camp, and the tent city had become railroad headquarters. Attendant with its rise in status, the burgeoning town had grown hazardous to its own health—garbage was being dumped in the river and sewage was leaking into the water supply. Drinkable water cost five cents a bucket.

Realizing the permanence, if not the ultimate importance of the city, planners platted a townsite on the tableland south of Ship Creek and auctioned off lots. Among proposed names for the town were Ship Creek Landing, Woodrow, Terminal, and Alaska City. The most votes went to Alaska City, but the US Post Office had already gone ahead with Anchorage. By the 1930s Anchorage was still a fledgling town of about 3,000, somewhat smaller than Fairbanks and Juneau. The young town flexed its muscles with both virtue and vice-social and civic organizations, sports teams and cultural activities flourished, as did prostitution, gambling and bootlegging. A frontier mentality prevailed until Anchorage received a shot in the arm in the form of World War II.

From the Ground Up – The construction of Fort Richardson and Elmendorf Air Force Base and the building of the Alaska Highway put Anchorage in the fast lane to growth. From 1939 to 1943 the city climbed from third largest to largest in the territory, nearly tripling in size to 12,000 residents. By the end of the decade, the population had swelled to more than 30,000. With the onset of the Cold War, the military continued to play a major role in town. Defense specialists determined that Alaska should be the first line of defense against Soviet air strikes. Russian military buildups in Siberia and their testing of an atom bomb on Wrangel Island in the Chukchi Sea in 1954 added incentive for military might in Alaska, headquartered in Anchorage. Again, with the sudden growth spurt came problems of all kinds—heavy traffic, poor sewage disposal, illicit activities and especially inadequate housing. To accommodate the booming population, trailer parks and cheap apartment buildings sprang up, as well as shacks and lean-tos. But the city kept growing, spurred on by the discovery of oil in the nearby Kenai Peninsula.

The 1960s are remembered in Anchorage for two events. On Good Friday of 1964, the most powerful earthquake in North America this century rocked Anchorage to its foundations. Though the city saw only 9 casualties of the 115 in south central Alaska, Anchorage was hit hard in property damage. But the re-building proved a kind of economic slingshot for downtown, invigorating the skyline with new life. To show his faith in the city's future, developer Walter Hickel (later governor) ignored the advice of geologists and built his Captain Cook Hotel practically on top of the slide zone. The second event, the announcement of a whopping oil strike in Prudhoe Bay in 1968, was earthshaking in a different way. The city was galvanized by the sudden arrival of oil executives, speculators, and journalists. Oilmen who came late slept in their corporate jets, or stayed awake calculating their offers for leases on North Slope oil fields. Bids totaled more than $900 million. Prudhoe Bay turned out to be one of the largest oil fields in the world, and the spillover profits engorged Anchorage's coffers.

Outward and Onward – The present-day appearance of Anchorage owes much to the Project 80s building boom, which funneled oil revenues into such projects as the new convention center, the Alaska Center for the Performing Arts, an expansion of the Anchorage Museum of History and Art, a sports arena, an ice arena, Town Square and the Tony Knowles Coastal Trail. The city was prospering as never before, resulting in a population growth of 1,000 a month. Then the bottom fell out. As oil prices went southward, so did the people, streaming out like migratory geese—by the thousands. Homeowners defaulted; banks closed; construction skidded to a stop. Ironically, it was the devastation caused by the *Exxon Valdez* oil spill in 1989 that helped pull Anchorage out; the cleanup spurred an economic boomlet, with so-called "spillionaires" taking tidy profits.

While oil is the leading money-maker for the state, only two percent of the city's work-force is employed in the oil and gas industry. More than 75 percent of Anchorage's jobs are in trade and government. The rest work in transportation businesses, finance, insurance, real estate, construction and manufacturing.

A city born in the 20C and forced to grow fast, Anchorage has bloated out in the only direction possible, southward, with neighborhoods, strip malls and discount stores, and it has its share of big-city crime and other woes. But with its relatively low population it also maintains a town atmosphere. Moose are often seen browsing the wetlands near the airport and other edges of town; brilliant bouquets of summertime flowers burst into bloom in 50 landscaped parks and countless private gardens; and except for a couple of 40-story skyscrapers on Seventh Avenue, the skyline has a gentle, almost tame aspect. In many ways Anchorage is the little brother of Seattle and other lower 48 sophisticates with whom it tries to keep pace. On tap for visitors year-round are a full range of fine restaurants, upscale galleries, sophisticated music and drama events, and scads of Seattle-style coffee shops.

Downtown Anchorage

Ken Graham/Tony Stone Images

Getting There

By Air – **Anchorage International Airport** (AIA): 6mi south of city; for information: ☎ 266-2525. Regional carriers operating scheduled flights, air-taxi and helicopter service: ERA Aviation (☎ 248-4422 or 800-866-8394); Penninsula Airways (☎ 800-448-4226); Yute Air Alaska (☎ 243-7090). Transportation to downtown via taxi ($12) and hotel courtesy shuttles. Rental car agencies (p 405) are located in the lower level of the domestic terminal.

By Train – The Alaska Railroad Corp. (Box 107500, Anchorage AK 99510) offers service between Anchorage and Fairbanks, via Denali National Park and south to Seward (mid-May–mid-Sept daily; in winter weekends only); for schedule and reservations, ☎ 265-2494 or 800-544-0552.

Getting Around

By Public Transportation – Local bus service "People Mover" (Mon–Sat 6am–10pm; limited schedule Sundays) provides free access to most attractions and activities in the downtown area; outside of downtown ($1 one-way; $2.50 Day Pass). Tickets, maps and brochures are available at People Mover Tansit Center, 6th Ave.& G St. Schedule and route information: ☎ 343-6543. Metered street and garage **parking** is available downtown.

By Taxi – **Alaska Cab** ☎ 563-5353; **Checker Cab** ☎ 276-1234; **Yellow Cab** ☎ 272-2422.

General Information

Visitor Information – For information on points of interest, seasonal events, accommodations, recreation and tour operators contact the **Log Cabin Visitor Information Center**, 4th Ave & F St., Anchorage AK 99501, ☎ 274-3531 or www.anchoragecvb.net (open daily June–Aug 7:30am–7pm; May & Sept daily 8am–6pm; rest of the year 9am–4pm; closed Jan 1, Thanksgiving Day, Dec 25).

Accommodations – Area visitor's guide including lodging directory available (free) from **Anchorage Convention & Visitors Bureau**, 524 W. Fourth Ave., Anchorage AK 99501-2212. Accommodations range from luxury hotels, guest houses, bed-and-breakfast inns, resort lodges, motels, camping and RV parks. **B&B reservation service**: Alaska Private Lodgings/Stay with A Friend, P.O. Box 200047 Anchorage AK 99520, ☎ 258-1717 or www.alaskabandb.com. Cabins, chalets and apartments are available through local rental property agencies. **Youth Hostels**: Anchorage Hostel ($19) ☎ 276-3635; International Backpackers Hostel ($15) ☎ 274-3870; Spenard Hostel International ($14) ☎ 248-5036.

DOWNTOWN 1 1/2 days

With its grid of numbered avenues (east-west) and lettered streets (north-south), downtown Anchorage is easy to navigate. Most of the gift shops and attractions, as well as a number of restaurants, are concentrated between C and G Streets and Fourth and Sixth Avenues. Here you will find a pleasant, strollable commercial district of Western-style two-story buildings, many of which date back to the town's early days. Public art graces many sidewalks and buildings, including the fabulous **whale mural** on the west wall of J.C. Penney (6th Ave. and E St.) and the sculptures around the convention center and adjacent Visitor Information Center (4th Ave. and F St.; open May & Sept daily 8am–6pm; Jun–Aug daily 7:30am–7pm; rest of the year daily 9am–4pm; ☞ ☎ 907-276-4118 or 800-478-1255; www.anchorage.net). A good place to begin your tour, the sod-roof log cabin visitor center—decked about with dahlia, fuchsia and other flowers—dispenses walking-tour maps, brochures and friendly advice.

Alaska Public Lands Information Center – 605 W. 4th Ave. Open Memorial Day-Labor Day daily 9am–5:30pm. Rest of the year Mon–Fri 10am–5:30pm. ☞ ☎ 907-271-2737. www.nps.gov/aplic/center. Serious hikers flip through topographical maps in one corner while a family screens videos on whales and bears in another. Planning an expedition or not, visitors will find much of interest at this walk-in website of information on Alaska's federal and state lands. Here you can check out a humorous diorama of good and bad camping techniques, study taxidermed animals, and view stereoscopic frontier scenes. Free films are shown on the hour on topics like Denali, grizzlies, earthquakes and the northern lights. Staff are on hand for questions.

Foreign Exchange Office – Thomas Cook Foreign Exchange, 311 F St. ☎ 278-2822.

Sightseeing – Guided walking tour of historic downtown *(Jun–early Sept Mon–Fri)* offered by Anchorage Historic Properties *(☎ 274-3600)*. Carriage rides in downtown range from 15min *($20)* to a one hour *($50)* scenic ride *(Jun–early Sept Mon–Sat 8pm–midnight)*; during the winter, sleigh rides and wagon rides leave from nearby Chugiak *(Mon–Sat; $50/half hour 4 persons)*. For schedules and reservations: Horse Drawn Carriage Co., 22012 Blair Ave. ☎ 688-6005. For a list of sightseeing companies, check with local tourism agencies *(above)*.

Shopping – For native arts and crafts: Alaska Ivory Exchange, 700 W. Fourth Ave.; Oomingmak Musk Ox Co-op, 604 H St.; Alaska Fur Exchange, 4417 Old Seward Hwy.

Entertainment – Consult the arts and entertainment section of the *Anchorage Daily News* (Friday) for schedule of cultural events and addresses of theaters and concert halls, such as the **Alaska Center for the Performing Arts** *(☎ 263-2900)*, and the **Anchorage Symphony Orchestra** *(Oct–May; ☎ 274-8668)*. Weekly Calendar of Events: ☎ 276-3200. Arts and sporting-events tickets: CARRS Tix ☎ 263-2787.

Sports and Recreation – **Golf:** Anchorage Golf Course *(mid-May–Sept)* ☎ 522-3363); Russian Jack Springs *(May–Sept)* ☎ 333-8338. **Horseback riding:** William Clarks Chamberlin Equestrian Center ☎ 522-1552. **Bike** the Coastal Trail; bike rentals *($20/day)* available at The Bicycle Shop, 1035 W. Northern Lights Blvd. ☎ 272-5219.

Winter sports: Ice-skating at Ben Boeke *(☎ 274-5715)*; or University of Alaska *(☎ 786-1231)*. Cross-country skiing at Girdwood Valley, Chugach State Park and area hiking trails; ski rentals from Recreational Equipment Inc. ☎ 272-4565. **Alyeska Ski Resort** at Girdwood offers alpine skiing, 6 chairlifts, a tram (also operates in summer), hotel and restaurants *(☎ 754-1111 or 800-880-3880)*.

Spectator Sports – **Hockey:** Anchorage Aces *(Oct–Apr)* Sullivan Arena ☎ 258-2237.

Useful Numbers.. ☎

Emergency fire, police, ambulance.. 911

Alaska State Division of Tourism 465-2010

Road Conditions Report.. 273-6037

Weather (recorded) 266-5145

Alaska Statehood Monument – *2nd Ave. and E St.* A bust of President Eisenhower pays tribute to the Alaska Statehood Act of 1959, which made Alaska the 49th state. Down the bluff from here you can see the handsomely renovated Alaska Railroad Depot (1942), historic headquarters for the railroad. Inside are original woodwork and a gift shop. Beyond are Ship Creek and the gritty waterfront area of cranes and storage tanks; trains blare and clank along here coming to and from the port. On the banks where Anchorage started as a tent city, anglers now cast for salmon during the seasonal runs.

The Imaginarium – ▥ *737 W. 5th Ave. Open year-round Mon–Sat 10am–6pm, Sun noon–5pm. Closed major holidays. $5.* ✗ ⅋ ▯ ☎ *907-276-3179. www.imaginarium.org.* Some 30 hands-on exhibits in 15,000sq ft of space make this decade-old science playland a hit with children. Of note are the big bubble lab, the galaxy room, the butterfly display and the wetlands exhibit-including a touch tank stocked with helmet crabs, sea stars and anemones.

① Cyrano's

Map p 382. 413 D St.. ☎ 907-274-2599. For an artsy evening downtown among Anchorage locals, try this cozy cafe/theater/bookstore. The Bistro Bergerac offers a tempting menu of French and Mediterranean specialties and a casual atmosphere for eavesdropping on the town's literati. Afterwards, choose a seat in an intimate 86-seat theater for an offbeat production of an old or new play. Between acts you can browse the bookstore's literary and Alaskana shelves-with 20,000 titles, you're likely to find something you'll want.

ANCHORAGE

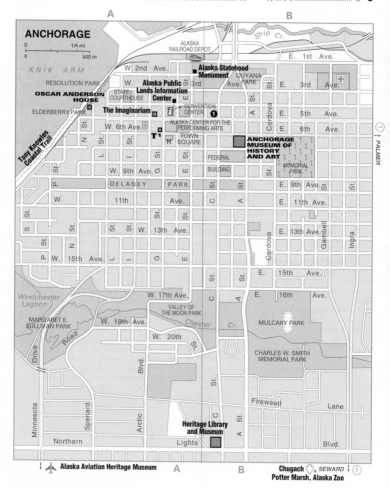

★ **Alaska Experience Theatre** – *705 W. 6th Ave. Open Memorial Day–Labor Day daily 9am–9pm. Rest of the year daily noon–6pm. Closed Jan 1, Thanksgiving Day, Dec 25. Film: $6.99; video $4.99; combination ticket $9.99.* ♿ 🅿 ☏ *907-276-3730.* A three-story-tall half-domed screen features *Alaska the Greatland*, a visually breath-taking film in 70mm format. Shot from airplanes, rafts and trains, the 40min film gives viewers the sensation of moving through spectacular scenery, pausing here and there to explore Alaska's wildlife and people. The print has been through the projector a few too many times—visuals are at times unfortunately grainy and the soundtrack wavers occasionally. In a separate room, a worthwhile earthquake exhibit details the devastating Alaska quake of 1964 and the state's continuing experience with earth-quakes. (Alaska comprises only 3 percent of the world's land area, yet accounts for 25 percent of its seismic energy.) Visitors can jump on a metal plate and watch a seis-mograph needle record the disturbance; photo and video displays round out the exhibit.

★ **Anchorage Museum of History and Art** – *121 W. 7th Ave. Open mid-May–mid-Sept daily 9am–9pm. Rest of the year Tue–Sat 10am–6pm, Sun 1pm–5pm. Closed Jan 1, Thanksgiving Day, Dec 25. $5.* ✗ ♿ 🅿 ☏ *907-343-4326. www.ci.anchorage.ak.us.* Taking up most of a city block, this handsome reposi-tory of Alaska's history, ethnography and art presents an in-depth walk through the state's culture. Six galleries on the first floor are devoted to the permanent art collection, which highlights far-northern people and landscapes drawn by artists from the early days of exploration to the present. One gallery contains several striking **landscapes★** executed in the luminist style by **Sydney Laurence** (1865-1940), Alaska's most famous painter. Other galleries on this floor house temporary and children's interactive exhibits. Upstairs, the Alaska Gallery holds more than 1,000 objects which illustrate the history of the state. Starting with people crossing the land bridge some 30,000 years ago, the gallery proceeds through Indian, Aleut and Eskimo lifestyles and then into the era of European contact. Though often heavy on text, the exhibits do offer memorable scenes: A life-size diorama of a late-18C Aleut house of whalebone, grass and sod has the feel of authenticity, and a 1910 miner's cabin with its chinked logs and tiny wood stove makes you appreciate modern comforts. Further along you'll find displays on fishing, the railroad, the pipeline and contemporary Anchorage.

★**Oscar Anderson House** – *420 M St. (Elderberry Park). Visit by guided tour (30min) only, Tue–Sat 11am–4pm. $3.* ☎ *907-274-2336.* The city's only house museum started out in 1915 as the home of meat packer Oscar Anderson, who lived here until 1969. One of the first houses in Anchorage, the gabled bungalow was moved from its original location across the street. Though at 800sq ft it is quite small by

■ The Iditarod

With great fanfare drummed up by thousands of spectators, mushers lead their teams of sled dogs through downtown Anchorage for the start of the Iditarod on the first Saturday of every March. Called the last great race on earth, the event spans an arduous 1,049mi of wind-raked tundra, frozen rivers, and icy mountain ranges, ending in the former gold-rush town of Nome, on the edge of the Bering Sea. At 25 checkpoints along the way, in Eskimo villages and abandoned gold towns, a host of volunteers stand ready to welcome tired dogs and racers, feed them, send home sick dogs if necessary, then see the survivors off. So that the same villages are not burdened every year, a southern route was added in 1977 and is used on alternating years.

Though the race dates from 1973, the original Iditarod Trail was blazed as a mail and gold-rush route in 1910 and ran all the way from Seward to Nome. It was along part of this trail that the legendary dogs Balto and Togo, among others, relayed serum to the diptheria-stricken town of Nome in 1925—the 674mi covered in a breathtaking

Musher Dee Dee Jonrowe, Iditarod 1993

Paul Souders /Tony Stone Images

five-and-a-half days. The modern race commemorates both the old trail and that heroic run. Improved equipment, trail conditions, and dog breeding and training have whittled the course time from 20 days in 1973 to just over 9. Sleds start out with 12 to 16 dogs and must finish with at least 5. Famous racers, Alaskan household names, include four-time winner Susan Butcher and five-time champion Rick Swenson. To first-place finishers today goes a purse of $52,500, a four-wheel-drive truck and the glory of the international sled-dog racing world.

today's standards, the house was considered luxurious for the frontier town. Informative 30min tours begin with a sketch of Anchorage history, then cover the parlor, dining room, kitchen and upstairs bedrooms. Among the original and period furniture are a player piano, phonograph and recessed china shelf.

Tony Knowles Coastal Trail – *West edge of city, accessible at 2nd, 5th, and 9th Aves.* Bikers, walkers, joggers, and skiers make good use of this 11mi paved trail along Cook Inlet. Named for the 1980s mayor of Anchorage and present governor of Alaska, the trail passes Westchester Lagoon and several parks before ending at Kincaid Park near the airport. Good

Hiker Overlooking Harriman Fjord, Chugach State Park

weather affords views of Mt. Susitna, Mt. McKinley, and the Chugach Mountains. The inlet boasts the second-largest tidal range (up to 38ft) in North America—bore tides with walls of water 6ft high sometimes form and shoot down Turnagain Arm. Avoid the temptation to walk out on the mud, which can act like quicksand.

Heritage Library and Museum – *Northern Lights Blvd. and C St. in the National Bank of Alaska Bldg. Open year-round Mon–Fri noon–4pm. Closed major holidays.* & 🅿 ☎ *907-265-2834.* A small but plush exhibit room holds several glass cases of elaborate walrus ivory carvings, baleen baskets, handmade parkas, harpoons, dolls and other native artifacts. Although dates for most of the items are unfortunately lacking, the displays provide an intimate look at the expert craftsmanship applied by Eskimos and other Alaska peoples to natural materials found in their environment. Also on display are a tremendous curving wooly mammoth tusk (about 30,000 years old) and several fine landscapes by Sydney Laurence.

★**Alaska Aviation Heritage Museum** – *4721 Aircraft Dr. at the seaplane base, south side of Lake Hood at Anchorage International Airport. Open mid-May–mid-Sept daily 9am–6pm. Rest of the year Tue–Sat 10am–4pm. Closed major holidays. $6.* 🅿 ☎ *907-248-5325.* The din of seaplanes taking off and landing on the lake outside adds realism to an impressive compendium of the state's aviation history. Indoor and outdoor displays include some 25 vintage bush planes, numerous photographs, a restoration room and a theater. Among highlights are a rare 1936 Stinson A Tri-Motor, a 1932 American Pilgrim and a 1928 **Stearman CZB**. The prize of the entire collection, the Stearman was restored in situ after a crash in the Brooks Range, then used as a mail carrier by the Arctic Prospecting and Development Company; during a deadly outbreak of diptheria in 1931, it carried serum to Point Barrow and other villages, and the next year made a daring rescue on Mt. McKinley. A bush pilot crashed it again in 1939—it was removed by helicopter in the 1960s and painstakingly restored by a couple in Montana over the next ten years. Other exhibits chronicle the Battle of Attu during World War II; the heroics of aviation pioneer Carl Ben Eielson (1897-1929), who died flying from Nome to North Cape; and the 1935 Alaskan odyssey of aviator Wiley Post and humorist Will Rogers, cut short by a crash that killed them both.

EXCURSIONS *Map p 382*

Alaska Zoo – 🚗 *1 hr. 7.5mi south of downtown Anchorage. Take Rte. 1 (Seward Hwy.) south to 4731 O'Malley Rd., then east 2mi. Open May–Oct daily 9am–6pm. Rest of the year daily 10am–5pm. Closed Thanksgiving Day. $7.* & 🅿 ☎ *907-346-3242.* Covering 30 acres and holding more than 50 species, this collection of mostly native birds and animals began in the mid 1960s when a local grocer won a promotional prize from the Crown Zellerbach paper company. The prize options were $3,000 or a baby

© Marc Muench/Tony Stone Images

elephant. "I'll take the elephant," the grocer told the sponsors. Surprised but true to their word, they located an 18-month-old elephant and flew her in. Since then, the zoo has grown to encompass 80 animals representing 38 species, including guaranteed sightings of caribou, Siberian tigers, wolverine, moose, Dall sheep, musk ox, wolves and the rare glacier bear. Children especially enjoy the above– and below-water seal viewing decks, the petting zoo, and an unusual enclosure housing both a polar bear and a brown bear.

Potter Marsh – *30min. 10.5mi south of downtown Anchorage via Rte. 1.* An easy place for spotting Canada geese, trumpeter swans, arctic terns, and many other seabirds lies just off the Seward Highway, along the gentle waters of Turnagain Arm. The 2,300-acre wetland, officially called the Anchorage Coastal Wildlife Refuge, acts as home base or migratory rest stop for more than 220 species of birds. A .25mi boardwalk equipped with information panels courses out into the marsh, where visitors with sharp eyes may see eagles and hawks as well as the usual waterfowl. Highway noise can add an unquieting note but does not seem to bother the birds.

★★**Chugach State Park** – *Various entrances, east of Anchorage. Headquarters, 12mi south on Rte. 1 (Seward Hwy.). Open daily year-round. Some areas closed in winter due to snow.* ⚠ ♿ 🅿 ☎ *907-345-5014.* Anchorage's playground, the third largest state park in the US comprises nearly a half-million acres of pristine forests, craggy mountains and shimmering lakes. A half-day excursion can get you into solid wilderness, perfect for such activities as hiking, cross-country skiing, berry-picking and wildlife-watching. With park elevations ranging from sea level to over 8,000ft, Chugach offers ample opportunities for inspiring views of peaks and watery expanses. In addition to providing information, park headquarters—located in a historic railroad section house—offers a look at life here in the 1910s. The foreman lived in the simple two-story section house; immigrant laborers contended with avalanches, rock slides, high tides and freezing temperatures to build a railroad along this rugged shoreline. South of here about 14mi is the **Bird Ridge** trailhead parking area *(free)*. A strenuous 1.5mi walk up an exposed and windy shoulder affords spectacular **vistas**★ of mountains and the Turnagain Arm. Two other easily accessible areas (🅿 *$5/day*) lie about 20min from town off O'Malley Road—**Prospect Heights** has a 2mi hike to Campbell Creek through a flowery spruce forest; and **Glen Alps** offers hikes and a .25mi paved loop to a panorama of Anchorage, Cook Inlet and the Alaska Range. About 45min northeast of town via the Glenn Highway brings you to **Eagle River Nature Center**, which offers wildlife exhibits and guided nature walks *(open May–Labor Day daily 10am–5pm; Labor Day–Oct Tue–Sat 10am–5pm; rest of the year Fri–Sun 10am–5pm;* ⚠ ♿ 🅿 *$5/day* ☎ *907-694-2108).*

★**Scenic Drive: Anchorage to Tok** *1 day. 320mi. Map p 10.*

An alternative route to Fairbanks, this daylong drive takes motorists along Route 1 (Glenn Highway and Tok Cutoff), north and then east from Anchorage through the broad, green Matanuska Valley that cleaves a path between the Chugach and Talkeetna Mountains. The route passes agricultural communities, a major glacier, and the mighty Wrangell Mountains before heading up the Copper River Basin to Tok. A worthwhile first stop, **Eklutna Historical Park** *(26mi northeast of Anchorage; open mid-May–mid-Sept daily 8am–6pm; $3.50;* ♿ 🅿 ☎ *907-688-6026; www.eklutna.com)* is located within an active Russian Orthodox-influenced Athabascan village. The Russian missionaries arrived in the early 19C, about

385

150 years after the natives had settled here, and got the Athabascans to build St. Nicholas Church. The reconstructed church and the multihued little spirit houses jumbled together in the cemetery are highlights. Farther up in the valley, **Palmer** is a quiet, clean farm town that started out with the arrival of 200 families from the depressed midwest in the 1930s; a **Musk Ox Farm** just east of town produces qiviut— a wool renowned for its softness, warmth and high price *(visit by 30min guided tour only, May–Sept daily 10am–6pm; rest of the year by appointment only; $8;* ❧ 🅿 ☎ *907-745-4151; www.muskoxfarm.org).* About 60mi east of Palmer, 4mi-wide **Matanuska Glacier** is clearly visible from a pull-off.

Continuing east, be prepared for rolling waves on the road surface; known as frost heaves, the waves occur on sections built over permafrost. Much of the summer road construction you see is an effort to flatten out these rises. Also be aware of moose and other wildlife wandering near the road. The highway soon provides excellent views of the snow-crowned peaks in **Wrangell-St. Elias National Park and Preserve★**, a magnificent wilderness of glaciers, streams and towering mountains; the park's 13.2 million acres make it the largest in the country. Park headquarters lies 10mi south of Glenallen, but along Route 1 there is not much easy access into this new and untamed sanctuary. The drive ends at the small town of **Tok** (pronounced TOKE), an Interior crossroads and sled-dog training center.

KENAI PENINSULA★★

Michelin map 930 Alaska inset and map p 389
Tourist Information ☎ 283-3850 or www.kenaipeninsula.org

Bulging into the Gulf of Alaska south of Anchorage, this muscular land of ice-blue glaciers, skyscraping ridges and saltwater bays lies separated from the mainland by an isthmus a mere 12mi wide that divides Cook Inlet from Prince William Sound. Before the giant glaciers that scoured out the peninsula could make an island of it, they retreated some 10,000 years ago, leaving the spine of the Chugach Mountains to connect the Kenai to the rest of Alaska. For more than 1,000 years, the Chugach Eskimo and the Tanana Indians lived and traveled through here, supported by the abundant game and fish. Russian fur hunters of the 1700s were followed by a succession of English explorers, sourdough gold seekers, railroad workers and homesteaders. The most noteworthy explorer, Capt. James Cook came looking for the elusive Northwest Passage in 1778; he sailed far into one inlet, but finding it another dead end, he had to "turn again." For modern travelers, the Turnagain Arm of Cook Inlet slices deep into the Kenai and provides a dramatic backdrop against the highway from Anchorage.

The discovery of oil on the Kenai Peninsula in 1957 brought a substantial infusion of wealth to Alaska and helped push it to statehood. Since then, more than 30 oil and gas fields on the peninsula and in Cook Inlet have fueled the area's economy, and today the extraction and processing of oil and gas, along with the associated service industries, account for up to 42 percent of all employment on the Kenai.

The tourist industry makes up an increasingly large share of the economic profile, with visitors from Anchorage dropping down for a day or a week of fishing, kayaking, hiking, skiing and general sightseeing. The **Kenai National Wildlife Refuge**, established in 1941, sprawls over nearly two million acres and helps maintain the area's fish and wildlife. Designated a national scenic byway, the **Seward Highway** takes motorists 127mi from Anchorage to Seward, skirting lovely Turnagain Arm, where beluga whales sometimes spout and breach, then running through the Chugach National Forest (second largest after the Tongass). Another well-paved road splits off from the Seward Highway about 90mi south of Anchorage and continues 130mi to Homer, on the southwestern end of the peninsula. In summer both roads can become quite busy with traffic, but are still manageable. *Though many sights advertise their location by mile marker (starting from Seward) on the Seward Highway, the markers are often not visible; use your odometer.*

GIRDWOOD *1/2 day.*

Crow Creek Mine – *Off Alyeska Hwy., 42mi south of Anchorage. Go 2mi west on Alyeska Hwy., then left on Crow Creek Rd. 3.5mi. Open year-round daily 9am–5pm. $5.* ⚠ ❧ 🅿 ☎ *907-278-8060.* Nestled among steeply shouldered mountains, a clutch of weathered turn-of-the-century buildings lends an authentic air of bygone days to this ski resort area. In its heyday, the mine yielded about 700 ounces of gold a month. The current owners still operate a 30ft sluice box in the off season and collect an average of an ounce a day. Visitors may poke through the blacksmith's shop, ice house, barn, mine owner's cabin and other buildings— each outfitted with some original tools and furnishings—or pan for gold in frothy Crow Creek.

Getting There

By Air – Closest airport: **Anchorage International Airport** (AIA). Scheduled airline service to regional airports in Homer and Kenai via ERA Aviation *(☎ 248-4422 or 800-866-8394)*.

By Bus and Train – Daily **bus** service between Anchorage and Seward: Seward Bus Line *(☎ 224-3608)* with connection to Homer. Alaska Railroad provides **rail** service from Anchorage to Seward *(mid-May–early Sept daily; schedules: ☎ 265-2494)*.

By Car – The region is accessible from Anchorage via Seward Hwy. 9 and Sterling Hwy. 1. Distance from Anchorage to Seward: 127mi; Anchorage to Homer: 226mi.

By Ferry – Scheduled service to Homer, Seward and Whittier as well as to Kodiak Island is offered by Alaska Marine Highway, Box 25535, Juneau AK 99802, ☎ 465-3941 or 800-642-0066 *(year-round; more frequent sailings May–Sept; reservations required)*.

General Information

Visitor Information – Contact the **Kenai Peninsula Tourism Marketing Council, Inc.** *(150 N. Willow, Suite 42, Kenai AK 99611, ☎ 283-3850 or 800-535-3624; www.kenaipeninsula.org)* for information and brochures on regional points of interest, accommodations, sightseeing, tour companies and seasonal events. For additional information: **Kenai Visitors & Convention Bureau, Inc.**, 11471 Kenai Spur Hwy., Kenai AK 99611 ☎ 283-1991; **Seward Chamber of Commerce & Visitors Bureau**, P.O. Box 749 KP, Seward AK 99664 ☎ 224-8051; **Soldotna Chamber of Commerce**, 44790 Sterling Hwy. KP, Soldotna AK 99669, ☎ 262-9814; **Homer Chamber of Commerce**, P.O. Box 541 KP, Homer AK 99603, ☎ 235-7740.

Accommodations – Area visitors' guides available from local tourism agencies *(above)* list a wide variety of lodgings including hotels, motels, bed-and-breakfast inns, cabins, fishing lodges and campgrounds as well as RV parks. **B&B Reservation Service**: Bed & Breakfast Assn., P.O. Box 2992, Kenai AK 99611, ☎ 262-6511 or 800-266-9091. **Youth Hostel**: Eagle Watch, P.O. Box 39083, Ninilchik AK 99639, ☎ 567-3905.

Sightseeing – The main tourist season for the Kenai Peninsula extends from mid-May through September. Day cruises and excursions combining wildlife-watching and glacier **cruises** of Prince William Sound can be arranged through Kenai Coastal Tours, 536 W. 3rd Ave., Anchorage AK 99501, ☎ 277-2131 or 800-770-9119; Kenai Fjords Tours, P.O. Box 1889, Seward AK 99664, ☎ 224-8068; Prince William Sound Cruises, P.O. Box 1297, Valdez AK 99686, ☎ 835-4731 or 800-992-1297. Gray Line of Alaska offers 2– and 3-day packages to Kenai Fjords National Park with stays in wilderness lodges; guided **fishing expeditions** are optional *(for schedules & reservations ☎ 277-5581 or 800-478-6388)*. Customized itineraries, sportfishing packages and **adventure tours** are offered by Alaska Statewide Tours & Travel, 1213 Ocean Dr., Suite 6, Homer AK 99603; for schedules & reservations, ☎ 235-7131 or 800-478-7131. For information regarding **ecotourism** and adventure travel, contact Alaska Wilderness Recreation & Tourism Assn., P.O. Box 22827, Juneau AK 99802, ☎ 463-3038 or www.alaska.net/~awrta. For a list of tour operators and outfitters, check with local tourism agencies *(above)*.
Flightseeing by floatplane, sportfishing, hiking, and canoe and kayak expeditions are also available. King Salmon offers jet service from Anchorage as well as accommodations.

Recreation – **Summer activities** feature hiking, camping, golf, salt– and freshwater fishing, canoeing, sea-kayaking, rafting and white-water rafting. **Winter activities** include wildlife-watching, skiing, snowmobiling, snowshoeing and sled-dog excursions.

★ **Alyeska Resort Tramway** – *Alyeska Resort, 3mi west of Seward Hwy. Operates mid-May–Sept daily 10:30am–9pm. Rest of the year daily 10:30am–5:30pm. $16.* ✗ & ☎ *907-754-1111. www.alyeskaresort.com*. Like flightseeing on the cheap, this enclosed cable car whisks visitors 2,300ft above the valley floor to the top of Alaska's premier skiing mountain for stunning views of Turnagain Arm and ice-bitten peaks. The 1mi ride lasts about 5min and offers the opportunity to study the landscape. Notice how areas clear-cut by avalanches wear a lighter shade of green than the surrounding hillsides. Two restaurants with views await visitors at the top, as does a network of walking trails. Signs warn hikers away from unexploded artillery shells that may have been left from winter avalanche-mitigation efforts.

Big Game Alaska – *Seward Hwy., Milepost 79. Open mid-May–Sept daily 8:30am–7pm. Rest of the year daily 10am–dusk. $5.* ✗ ⚹ 🅿 ☏ *907-783-202. www.biggameaslaska.com.* Set about by gorgeous snow-crowned peaks, a 150-acre site holds moose, bison, Sitka black-tailed deer, musk oxen and elk. Walk or drive the 1/3mi loop; also on display are bald eagles, hawks and owls.

★**Portage Glacier Recreation Area** – *5.5mi east of Seward Hwy., Milepost 79. Boggs Visitor Center open Memorial Day-Labor Day open daily 9am–6pm. Rest of the year weekends 10am–4pm.* △ ⚹ 🅿 ☏ *907-783-3242.* Although the visitor center boasts a wonderful picture window onto Portage Lake, the star attraction has not been seen here since 1994. Retreating 25ft a year, Portage Glacier has slipped around to the right and out of view. There is still good reason to visit: Two other glaciers, Byron and Burns, are visible in the distance; the lake is littered with chunks of ice that you can reach out and grab; and two easy trails offer a short course on glacial geography. The **Moraine Trail** *(.25mi)* provides a walk back in time along a moraine that has progressively filled in with lichens, alder shrubs, small spruce and finally a spruce forest. One hundred years ago the forest area was covered by ice. The **Byron Glacier Trail** *(2mi)* ends at an overlook of Byron Glacier. To see Portage Glacier itself, visitors must take a one-hour **boat tour** *(mid-May–mid-Sept daily at 10:30am, noon, 1:30pm, 3pm & 4:30pm; round-trip 1 hr; commentary; reservations suggested; $25, children $12.50;* ✗ ⚹ 🅿 *Gray Line of Alaska, Anchorage* ☏ *907-277-5581);* the 200-passenger vessels cruise close enough to see and hear the glacier calve into the lake.

★**SEWARD** *2 days.*

Named for William H. Seward, who engineered the purchase of Alaska from Russia, the Kenai's most popular destination presides at the head of mountain-rimmed Resurrection Bay. Seward began life in 1902 as the southern end of the Alaska Railroad into the Interior—surveyors were impressed with the location's possibilities as a deepwater, ice-free port. It soon became a key shipping link and was known as the "Gateway to Alaska." Severely damaged by tsunamis from the Good Friday earthquake of 1964, Seward regrouped and is now a spirited town of brightly painted stucco and clapboard bungalows with tidy gardens. Every July 4, the community turns out to cheer on the oldest footrace in the state—a run up and down 3,022ft Mt. Marathon. Begun in 1909 when one man bet that another could not run to the top of the mountain and back in under an hour, the grueling contest now attracts some 800 participants. Though the original runner lost the wager by 4 minutes, the record time currently stands at just over 43 minutes.

Still a railroad link, Seward also sits at the end of the Seward Highway and serves as a major port for cruise ships, thus welcoming thousands of visitors every summer who shop and eat at the picturesque Small Boat Harbor (at the north end of town) and take wildlife cruises into Resurrection Bay and the adjacent **Kenai Fjords National Park** *(p 389).* From restaurant windows in the Small Boat Harbor you can watch fishermen coming in with their catch, while kittiwakes wheel about with snow-capped mountains for a backdrop.

★★**Alaska SeaLife Center** – *301 Railway Ave. Open mid-May–mid-Sept daily 8am–8pm. Rest of the year daily 10am–5pm. Closed Jan 1, Thanksgiving Day, Dec 25. $12.50.* ✗ ⚹ 🅿 ☏ *907-224-6300 or 800-224-2525. www.alaska.sealife.org.* Not just an aquarium, this 115,000sq ft state-of-the-art facility, opened in 1998, has taken on a triple mission—research, rehabilitation and education. Visitors can gawk at marine mammals and watch scientists at work, leaving with the feeling that the animals are there for their own good, not just for entertainment. Two-thirds of the $56 million project was funded by a legal settlement from the 1989 *Exxon Valdez* oil spill, which severely damaged the area's marine ecosystem. One of the special features of the building is a rust-proof zinc exterior that is flexible enough to move with the steel structure should other earthquakes occur; another is the only escalator on the Kenai Peninsula.

Visit – *1 hr. Begin on the second level, arranging your visit around the scheduled demonstrations and programs.* After a few minutes in front of a non-narrated video of sea animals, move on to learn about the legacy of the *Valdez* oil spill, whose death toll included 250,000 seabirds, 2,000 sea otters and 300 harbor seals. An open-water exhibit displays Pacific halibut, sole and other sport fish.

A bit farther on, you'll find an intertidal tank stocked with beautiful vermilion stars, hermit crabs and pyncnopodia. A large viewing window *(west side of building)* gives onto a wet lab with pools and holding tanks for injured or homeless animals and big cranes for moving Steller's sea lions. Toward the east side, an exhibit on the homing habits of salmon speculates on how the sun and the earth's magnetic field may help guide these fish. From a porch, viewers may spot orcas, humpbacks and other creatures in Resurrection Bay.

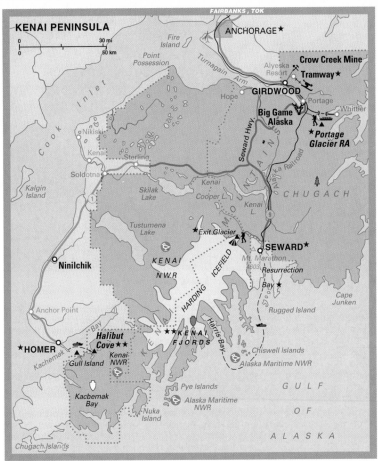

Highlights of the facility, the **harbor seals pool**★ and the adjacent **sea lions pool**★★ and **marine birds rock pool and cliffs**★ have above– and below-water viewing platforms. In this endlessly fascinating area, you can watch murres and puffins "flying" under-water; and learn that seals can dive an amazing 600ft under and stay down for 30 minutes. Downstairs, "Denizens of the Deep" features octopi, starry flounder, weathervane scallops and tremendous king crabs.

Seward Museum – *3rd Ave. and Jefferson St. (Community Center). Open May–Sept daily 9am–5pm. Rest of the year Mon–Fri 1pm–4pm; weekends noon–4pm. Closed major holidays. $2.* ⛔ 🅿 ☎ *907-224-3902.* A tile floor and 1920s music give this scrapbook of the community's life an old-fashioned feeling. In one corner is an exhibit on the Iditarod trail, which started from Seward, while over in another stands a wall clock that stopped during the 1964 earthquake. Other exhibits include native baskets, a display on Seward's role in World War II as the home of Fort Raymond, and random exhibits on unusual pioneers like Alaska Nellie, owner of numerous roadhouses.

★★**Kenai Fjords National Park** – *The park is open daily year-round. $5/car for Exit Glacier Area.* ⛺ 🅿 *In winter, the road is accessible by ski or snowshoes only. Headquarters and visitor center beside harbormaster's office, 4th Ave; open Memorial Day–Labor Day daily 8am–7pm. Rest of the year Mon–Fri 8am–5pm.* ☎ *907-224-2132. www.nps.gov/kefj.* Covering more than 600,000 acres of coastal fjords and glacier-clad mountains on the southeastern end of Kenai Peninsula, Kenai Fjords National Park preserves a rugged, untouched wilderness where thousands of marine mammals and seabirds find sanctuary. So large and inaccessible is the area covered by the park that many of its canyons, waterfalls and other natural features remain unnamed. The geologic forces set in motion eons ago continue to alter the landscape—glaciers carving out fjords and the land itself slowly sinking into the Gulf of Alaska. Feeding some 30 glaciers, the 700sq mi **Harding Icefield**, one of four remaining icefields in the United States, mantles the Kenai Mountains with a crust of ice that is perhaps several thousand

Sea Kayakers in Kenai Fjords National Park

feet thick. More than 30ft of snow a year replenish the icefield. Like creeping rivers of ice, eight of the glaciers descend all the way to the sea where they calve icebergs with such force the explosions can be heard up to 20mi away. The political boundaries also change: In 1998 more than 70,000 acres of park land were turned over to two Indian corporations under the Alaska Native Claims Settlement Act, thus converting the park map into a checkerboard of private and public holdings. Much of this acreage lies along the coast in prime fishing and camping areas *(if you plan to land on the coast, check with the park service regarding restrictions.*

Visit – *1 day.* The two main ways of visiting the park are by boat tours and by driving to Exit Glacier. In addition, flightseeing excursions operate out of the Seward airport and provide a privileged point of view for beholding the scenic wonders *(tours by plane are less expensive per hour than those by helicopter).* **Boat tours★** vary from 2 1/2-hour turns around **Resurrection Bay★** to 9 1/2-hour cruises to as far down as **Harris Bay** (about 50mi southwest) and Northwestern Glacier. They all have in common the spotting of numerous species of wildlife. High points include bird rookeries on the Chiswell Islands and Rugged Island— common murres, tufted and horned puffins, auklets, storm petrels and oystercatchers can be observed *(bring binoculars).* Along the way, you have a good chance of seeing several species of mammals, including humpback whales, orcas, sea lions, sea otters and Dall porpoises. These voyages also offer the opportunity of studying the drama of the landscape—how the mountains rise up sheer from the sea and how alpine glaciers have ground out steep valleys fit only for mountain goats and birds.

All charter boat operators are located in the Small Boat Harbor. Kenai Fjords Tours (☎ 800-478-8068) is the largest and offers a variety of packages; Major Marine Tours (☎ 800-764-7300) has a park service ranger on every tour; Renown Charters (☎ 800-655-3806), Mariah Tours (☎ 800-270-1238), and other smaller companies often have less crowded tours. The air on the bay, especially on a moving boat, is colder than on land—carry enough layers so that you can comfortably stand out on the observation decks.

At the north end of the park, the **Exit Glacier★** area *(9mi west of Seward Hwy. on Exit Glacier Rd.; first 4mi paved)* offers a series of trails to get visitors up close to the 3mi-long .5mi-wide glacier. The **Glacier Access Trail** *(.5mi; first .25mi paved)* is an easy stroll to a shelter with interpretive signs and then a view of Exit Glacier. A short ramble beyond takes you to the glacier's edge, where you can see 150ft-tall seracs (spires) and hear the ceaseless dripping inside blue ice caves. Like a scarred rock quarry, the land along here has been bulldozed by the glacier's motion. Take the .75mi **Nature Trail★** back along Exit Creek and the rippling outwash plain to observe how plant life changes from fireweed and moss to alders, cottonwoods and mature spruce as the glacier retreats. For a more strenuous walk, climb up the **Harding Icefield Trail★** *(7mi round-trip),* which ascends 3,000ft to spectacular **views** of the vast icefield from which jut sharp nunataks (Eskimo for "lonely peaks"), locked in a frozen sea. From the top, you can see in detail the folds and crevices of the glacier tonguing down the pass.

■ Berry-picking Time

Come summer, Alaskans young and old take to the hillsides, gathering nature's free gift of delicious wild berries. Some berries will go into muffins, pies or sourdough pancakes; others will be put away as jams and jellies. Many, of course, will be consumed on the spot. All you need to join in is a patch of public land (easy to come by in Alaska), a bucket and a little know-how. Most of the state's 50 species of berries are not edible, and a few, like the round red baneberry, are actually poisonous. But the common edible varieties are fairly easy to recognize. If in doubt, ask for help, or consult a good berrying handbook. Are you ready to begin?

Blueberries grow in abundance high, unforested areas in the Southeast and the Copper River Valley. You can even find them right along the Denali Highway and on roadsides on the Kenai Peninsula. A number of excellent varieties can be harvested, from the dwarf blueberry to the bright red huckleberry.

Another popular fruit, the tangy **salmonberry** is a harbinger of spring in Southeast Alaska. This large, seedy, berry grows on prickly canes up to 10ft high, in hues from dark red to pinkish orange. Bears find them irresistible.

Seek the tasty **lingonberry** on tundra and in wooded bogs. Sometimes called mountain or lowbush cranberries, they grow close to the ground and add flavor to relishes, sauces and liqueurs. The **highbush cranberry**, on the other hand, grows on tall shrubs and can be found along streams in the Interior. Though sour, the cranberries work well in both juice and jelly.

Raspberries and **red currants** are not uncommon in the South Central region. More scarce are gooseberries, crowberries, and the highly-prized nagoonberry, which hides in low meadows of the Southeast.

★HOMER *1 1/2 days.*

Guarding the entrance to Kachemak Bay in the lower Kenai Peninsula, the individualistic town of Homer sits at the end of the Sterling Highway, framed by lovely Cook Inlet and the jagged graph of the Kenai Mountains. Far across the inlet rise snowgirt Iliamna and Redoubt volcanoes, both topping 10,000ft; from more than 100mi away, they are only visible on a very clear day. Nearly surrounded by water, Homer has a gentler, less dramatic landscape than Seward. For decades it has served as a catchall for artists, retirees, fishermen and those who simply want to travel to the end of the road.

The area's first attraction for newcomers were the seams of coal on the north shore of Kachemak Bay. By the 1880s, a narrow-gauge railway was hauling coal down to a wharf on the Homer Spit, where it was loaded onto ships. But the town did not really dig in until Homer Pennock and his 50-man crew came and set up a gold mining business in 1896. Described by some as "the most talented confidence man who ever operated on this continent," Pennock stayed but a year—long enough anyway to give the town its name—before moving on with the Klondike gold rush. As the coal industry faded, fishing and canning became the community's lifeblood. A paved road linking the town with Anchorage in the early 1950s ensured that Homer, and not the fishing community of Seldovia across the bay, would grow into the area's major town.

Although the main part of the community today lies sprawled on the land bench above the west side of the bay, the 4.5mi **Spit** still acts as the nerve center of an extensive commercial and recreational fishing industry. The finger of land that is the focus of much activity resulted from either a terminal moraine left by a retreating glacier or from tidal deposits of gravel, sand and coal. Along here cluster numerous charter operations, restaurants, boardwalk shops, and beach campers known as "spit rats." Among popular hangouts, the landmark **Salty Dawg** saloon, with its cavelike interior and sawdust floor, originally housed offices of the coal company that operated on the Spit from 1889 to 1902. Some locals think development is turning the Spit into an unsightly mess; others favor the economic boon. Annual harvests of salmon, halibut, crab and shrimp inject nearly $30 million into the local economy, while the tourism industry continues to gain steam as visitors come to kayak the gentle coves of Kachemak Bay, sample the fresh seafood and browse the arts-and-crafts shops in town and in charming villages across the bay.

★Pratt Museum – *3779 Bartlett St. Open May–Sept daily 10am–6pm. Rest of the year Tue–Sun noon–5pm. $5.* & ☐ ☎ *907-235-8635. www.prattmuseum.org.* A first-rate collection of art and natural history, the Pratt welcomes visitors with a botanical garden of more than 150 native plant species. Inside, the lower floor offers a gut-wrenching and highly popular exhibit on the *Exxon Valdez* oil spill, complete with heartbreaking pictures and testimonials. One fisheries technician said of a rehab site: "It was like a war zone. We were getting 10 to 30 otters a day, all screaming...they were gouging their eyes out. There was so much pain." Among the shocking details highlighted here are expenses for saving otters—$30,000 a piece—and the total price tag on a cleanup that was widely considered more harmful than good—$2.1 billion. An adjacent exhibit outlines the ongoing spruce beetle epidemic that has already affected some 1.2 million acres of forest in the lower Kenai. Moving upstairs, you encounter a maritime gallery, equipped with an aquarium, a microscope for viewing plankton and a video monitor showing nesting birds on Gull Island out in Kachemak Bay, as well as grizzlies at McNeil River. Using touch-screen monitors, visitors manipulate camera angles to study particular birds and bears in greater detail. The next room up displays sea lion and whale skeletons, as well as fine examples of local art. Outside, you may walk through a furnished 1930s homesteader's cabin and take a short stroll along a spruce forest nature trail, decorated with whimsical sculpture.

Excursions

★★Halibut Cove – *4.5 hrs. Access by Danny J ferry from the Homer Spit Marina. Departs Memorial Day–Labor Day daily noon ($42) & 5pm ($21). Round-trip 5 hrs. Reservations suggested.* & ☐ *Central Charters* ☎ *907-235-7847 or 800-478-7847. www.central-charter.com.* In the early 1900s, more than 30 herring saltries operated on Halibut Cove. Today, the cove is a watery paradise, a tranquil curve of beach backed by a lagoon where houses on stilts are connected by boardwalks. The only way of getting around is by boat or foot. The daily 32-person ferry, part tourist operation and part resident transportation, makes a stop at the **Gull Island** rookery for close-ups of the thousands of seabirds that keep the barnacled rocks vibrant all summer. The 45min crossing also offers the opportunity for spotting whales and bald eagles. Halibut Cove itself is home to a few dozen families. You can eat at the restaurant, visit the galleries, buy locally made pottery, jewelry, or even watercolors made with octopus ink, and wander a trail to a bluff for exquisite bay views. Much of the land around Halibut Cove belongs to the 400,000-acre **Kachemak Bay State Park**, a primitive coastal wilderness of mountains, glaciers and rugged shoreline *(access by water taxi, private boat or airplane).*

Ninilchik – *1 hr. 37mi north of Homer on Rte. 1.* Settled in the 1820s by Russian fur traders, this tumbledown coastal village provides a no-frills excursion into Alaska's cultural past. Walk dirt lanes past late-19C log homes where ancient fishing boats sit amid overgrown yards. You can buy gifts and snacks at one small store and walk up the hill to the green-trimmed Russian Orthodox Church, with its onion dome and three-barred cross. Replacing a church that burned, the present structure dates from 1900. Though the church and churchyard are off-limits, **views** of the village and Cook Inlet from up here are well worth the stop. The town's small population swells in summer as fishermen take to the beaches and area creeks in quest of steelhead trout, salmon, halibut and clams.

Local Diner in Port Townsend, Washington

© Robert Holmes